Teaching Language and Literature in Elementary Classrooms

A RESOURCE BOOK FOR PROFESSIONAL DEVELOPMENT

Teaching Language and Literature in Elementary Classrooms

A RESOURCE BOOK FOR PROFESSIONAL DEVELOPMENT

Marcia S. Popp

Southern Illinois University at Edwardsville

LEA *Lawrence Erlbaum Associates, Publishers*
1996   Mahwah, New Jersey

For a free brochure on the first alphabet ever found in nature
and the 18″ × 24″ Butterfly Alphabet poster (© Kjell B. Sandved),
call 1-800-ABC-WING or write P.O. Box 39138, Washington, DC 20016.

Lawrence Erlbaum Associates, Inc., Publishers
10 Industrial Avenue
Mahwah, New Jersey 07430

Library of Congress Cataloging-in-Publication Data

Popp, Marcia.
    Teaching language and literature in elementary classrooms : a
resource book for professional development / Marcia Popp.
        p.   cm.
    Includes bibliographical references and index.
    ISBN 0-8058-2253-4 (pbk.)
    1. Language arts (Elementary)   2. Literature—Study and teaching
(Elementary)   I. Title.
    [LB1576.P656 1995]
    372.6′044—dc20   95-49925
                                                             CIP

Books published by Lawrence Erlbaum Associates are printed on acid-free
paper, and their bindings are chosen for strength and durability.

Printed in the United States of America
10 9 8 7 6 5 4 3 2 1

*For my mother, my first and best teacher;
and my husband, with whom I have an endless
conversation.*

Contents

CHAPTER THREE
Independent Reading   61

CHAPTER FOUR
Creating a Literature Base   91

CHAPTER FIVE
Shared and Guided Reading   129

CHAPTER SIX
Individual Reading Conferences   169

CHAPTER SEVEN
Listening and Speaking   213

CHAPTER EIGHT
Writing to Learn   261

CHAPTER NINE
Mini-Lessons   319

CHAPTER TWELVE
Language and Literature in Three Classrooms   **433**

To the Instructor

As an instructor in language arts methods, I wanted my students to have a textbook that could accompany them into the classroom, as a guide to practice. This is the kind of textbook I have tried to create: one that includes learning about literacy, but also outlines the specific planning and preparation steps necessary to implement a classroom program. *Teaching Language and Literature in Elementary Classrooms: A Resource Book for Professional Development* is designed to help the beginning or experienced teacher create a classroom environment that integrates literacy development with learning in all areas of the curriculum. The text identifies the major components of an integrated language program and describes how teachers can acquire the skills necessary to implement this kind of program in their own classrooms.

Pedagogically, the text assumes an interactive stance with readers, addressing them directly and reaching out to include their experiences, beliefs and knowledge in the text discussions. Chapters are presented in an approximate order of instructional complexity, beginning with the foundational practice of reading aloud and progressing to the more involved preparations for integrating language and literature throughout the curriculum. The discussions of each topic are consistent throughout the book and are designed to support the individual instructor's own presentation and interpretations.

Recurring sections of each chapter demonstrate teaching strategies that can be used with a variety of student groupings (individuals, pairs, small groups, entire class) at each elementary instructional level. Ways to prepare, present and evaluate instruction are described in a consistent manner from chapter to chapter, making it easy for readers to access the desired information for each topic. Each component of an integrated language arts program is comprehensively described, portrayed in classroom settings and carefully analyzed in terms of planning, preparation and presentation. The organization of information and ideas in a predictable chapter format is designed to build confidence and competence in the beginning teacher.

Extensive pedagogical devices are incorporated throughout the text to assist the reader, including preview/review questions, definition of terminology in context, annotated resources and step-by-step guidelines for implementing instruction. Extended observations in classrooms provide examples of teaching that can be analyzed and discussed, using additional criteria provided by individual instructors. Readers are encouraged to keep a journal of responses to the ideas they encounter in the text. Following the presentation of each section, questions ("What Do You Think?") reach out to readers, inviting them to connect the discussion with their own experience and to reflect on their responses to what they have just read. These open-ended questions, along with those in "Trying Out the Chapter Ideas" at the end of the chapter, are intended to help readers develop habits of reflective practice.

The classroom narratives were developed from my own experiences as an elementary classroom teacher and from thirteen years of observation in the public and parochial schools. In several instances, the dialogues and events are exactly as they occurred; in other cases, the narratives were constructed from field notes or adapted from classroom dialogues and teacher anecdotes. Each narrative is based on the teaching style and pedagogical approach of particular teachers who served as models for the interactions described. The narratives focus on the topic under discussion in each chapter and are intended to demonstrate how the individual elements of integrated language learning are used by practicing teachers at different levels of elementary school instruction.

To help readers observe these interactions in light of integrated language learning, each narrative is followed by an analysis of the conversations between teachers and students. These analyses create a context for the conversation by providing information about the teacher's goals and values and a description of the total classroom program, of which this interaction is a part. The teachers featured in Chapter 12 tell about their classroom programs in their own words and concur with the observational analyses that preceded these first-person narratives. They were provided with copies of the manuscript for this chapter and the sections entitled "From a Teacher's Journal" in each of the other chapters to review for accuracy of statement and interpretation of practice. The teachers and students featured in all the narratives represent a wide range of socioeconomic, racial, religious and ethnic backgrounds, in settings that included rural, urban and suburban communities.

As part of the discussion in each chapter, readers are introduced to relevant research associated with language learning. Annotated bibliographies at the end of each chapter indicate the variety of professional resources and references available to teachers. "Exploring Professional Literature" provides information on professional associations and suggests ways to examine and use professional journals and commercial materials. A section entitled "If This Is Your Situation" assists readers when they must adjust instruction to the expectations and restrictions of different educational settings. The contributions and perspectives of historical and contemporary educators are introduced in Chapter 1 and continue throughout the book in a section entitled "Perspectives." Observations in classrooms, interviews with practicing teachers and shared entries from teachers' journals provide models to complement and extend the experiences readers have with teachers in their fieldwork. Strategies to meet special learning needs in the classroom are integral to each chapter topic, and specific methods of working with differences and disabilities are addressed in a section entitled "Including Everyone."

Theoretically, the text is grounded in the ideas of the progressive tradition, cognitive learning theory, psycholinguistics and the constructivist approach to literature and English language learning. It assumes the interrelatedness of all language learning and emphasizes the use of children's trade literature as a resource for learning across the curriculum. Language is described as a tool for inquiry, communication, expression and problem solving. The teacher is portrayed as a reflective inquirer, facilitator, colearner, researcher and informed decision maker who helps create an environment that stimulates and supports learning. Students are seen as inquirers actively seeking meaning in their environment. The classroom is envisioned as a community of learners, where learning is social and collaborative and children engage in language activities that are authentic and productive. Practices in the professional community that are supported by this text include: the integrated language arts, the integrated curriculum, thematic teaching, the inquiry-based curriculum, whole language, writing-across-the-curriculum, reading–writing workshops, language experience and literature-based teaching.

Chapters 2 through 11 of the text describe classroom practices that create opportunities for integrated language learning: reading aloud; independent reading; constructing a literature base; guided reading; individual reading conferences; writing, listening and speaking activities; mini-lessons; using technology; and integrating the curriculum with language, literature and themes. The discussions for each topic are consistent throughout the text and are organized into the sections listed below:

Looking Ahead This section is prefaced with a quotation to set the tone of the chapter and is followed by a one-sentence summary definition of the practice under discussion. Key questions anticipate the chapter discussion and can be used to preview the topic or review major ideas at the completion of reading.

Section I. Focus This section examines a teaching practice that supports integrated language learning, relates it to those discussed in previous chapters and places it in the context of the broader curriculum.

Section II. Why It Is Important This section offers a rationale for the teaching practice, cites examples of relevant research and provides a framework for understanding the key elements of the classroom observations that follow.

Section III. Looking into Classrooms This section features classroom observations at the kindergarten, primary and intermediate levels to illustrate the particular element of language learning under discussion in the chapter. An analysis of the observation provides additional background information about the interaction, including the teacher's goals, student responses and events that preceded or followed this particular observation.

Section IV. Preparing for the Practice This section helps the reader plan for the language learning activity and includes suggestions for selecting and assembling materials, preparing the context and acquiring the necessary background knowledge or skill. Ways for both teachers and students to prepare for an activity are included.

Section V. Including Everyone This section is intended to alert the reader to ways that students might be excluded from full participation in classroom activities. It provides suggestions for facilitating full participation by students who face challenges of disability and suggests ways to foster respect for diversity. An annotated list of books offers readers the opportunity to explore differences and disability through the eyes of strong characters in children's literature.

Section VI. Step-by-Step This section provides suggestions for presentation, using guidelines that model the teacher in various roles, as colearner, mentor, facilitator and collaborator.

Section VII. If This Is Your Situation This section deals with the challenges that frequently confront teachers in terms of philosophical or economic restrictions and state or school district mandates that conflict with an integrated approach to language learning. Discussions identify the possible concerns of educators who impose mandates and practical ways to address the problems created.

Section VIII. Evaluating Progress This section contains context-responsive evaluation methods for assessing the learning progress of students. Emphasis is placed on: helping students to develop self-evaluation techniques; using evaluation to improve and guide teaching; measuring student achievement in terms of individual progress; and basing evaluation on multiple assessments.

Section IX. Creating Partners Readers are encouraged to reach out beyond the classroom to extend the learning environment for their students and tap the resources available. Throughout the text, this section describes ways to enlist the cooperative efforts of parents, students and teachers in other classes, special teachers and staff, principals, community members and resource persons at state, national and international levels for information and support.

Section X. Perspectives This section examines the philosophical and psychological foundations of integrated language arts instruction, including: the progressive education tradition, developmental psychology, cognitive science, psycholinguistic reading process theory and constructivist theory of reader response. In each chapter, the work of individual theorists is related to the language learning practice under discussion.

Section XI. Exploring Professional Literature Each chapter introduces a journal or other literature related to language or content area learning and describes the type of information a reader can expect to find in it. Readers are prompted to read articles that relate to the chapter topic and those of interest to them personally. Readers are also encouraged to consider student memberships in professional organizations.

Section XII. Resources for Teaching This section features an annotated bibliography of resources related to the topic of the chapter. The reader is directed to trade books and reference materials that can be ordered for a school library and those that are reasonably priced and recommended for personal purchase. The purpose of this section is to acquaint the reader with resources and references available to teachers.

Section XIII. Reflections This section includes personal journal entries of practicing teachers and is designed to model reflective practice. Readers are encouraged to respond to their reading in the chapter and reflect on their experience in their own journals. Other features of this section include suggestions for classroom observations and ideas for practicing the activities in the classroom.

To the Beginning Teacher

This text is intended to be a guide for your emerging progress as a beginning teacher. It provides information about integrating language learning into all areas of the curriculum and contains suggestions for creating learning environments. The descriptions and discussions included in the text are intended to anticipate your experience, but they are a record of my own or others' experiences. Your experiences will be similar, but unique. What you will add to this book is yourself—your own experiences, your particular talents and view of the world. In the end, you are the person who creates the meaning of this book. What you take away from your interaction with the text will be determined in large part by what you bring to it. Using your own style and experience, you will respond to the ideas, suggestions and information about planning and evaluating and make them yours. As you read and reflect, you will want to ask yourself: Do these ideas make sense to me? How do they relate to other things I have read? How do they relate to experiences I have had as a teacher or learner?

I encourage you to record your responses to the text in a personal journal. You will be invited to respond with your own ideas and experience following each section presentation throughout the text. In addition, you may want to note ideas about activities and projects for the classroom that draw your interest. Many educators who keep journals also include: ideas drawn from observing other teachers, articles about teaching, editorials, cartoons, relevant research, inspirational prose, poetry and quotes. A journal is more than a collection of ideas for your teaching. It will also be a record of your progress as a reflective practitioner.

Throughout the text, you will be encouraged to examine your own personal beliefs about teaching and learning. Your ideas about knowledge, learning and meaning are important because they will influence the decisions you make as a teacher. If, for example, you believe that knowledge is a thing, you may see your role as a teacher as one of giving facts and information to students. On the other hand, if you see knowledge as a process, you may see yourself as someone who helps students learn how to create meaning for themselves. As you reflect on these and other ideas about teaching and learning, you will be taking the first step toward the conscious creation of a learning environment in your classroom that will be an expression of your own values and beliefs.

You will also be encouraged to become a "kid-watcher" and "teacher-watcher," to observe how children learn and how teachers seem most productively to assist this process. The narratives in each chapter are designed to provide you with models of teaching that will complement your own observations in elementary school classrooms. Each narrative focuses on a particular practice of integrated language learning, and each is distilled from the practice of experienced teachers who support this kind of learning in their classrooms. As you listen to teachers and students talk to each other, imagine your own responses to what they say and do. Would you react differently, as a teacher? How is their experience similar to your own as a student? How is it different? What do you like about this person's teaching? What might you do differently?

As you begin your professional practice, you may have questions like: How do I introduce reading and writing activities to children? How do I integrate the curriculum with language and literature? What do I need to prepare in advance? What do I actually *say* and *do*? How will I know what students have learned? How do I help children who have difficulty learning? This text is designed to answer these kinds of questions—to help you know **what** to do, **how** to do it, and **why** these are theoretically sound instructional methods. The activities that are part of integrated language learning in the classroom are broken down into manageable parts so that you can observe them, practice them and have a chance to handle them successfully as you move from your methods course to student teaching and finally into a classroom of your own.

Classroom narratives are provided at the major instructional levels in elementary school: kindergarten, primary grades 1–3 and intermediate grades 4–6. It is helpful to know how language skills develop at every level, because students at any level will be at various stages of emerging literacy. For example, if you teach kindergarten, you will want to know how the experiences you provide for your students will positively influence their ability to develop as readers and writers at the primary and intermediate levels. Conversely, knowing how students develop literacy skills from the beginning will be beneficial to both primary- and intermediate-level teachers, as they seek to help students develop their skills at all levels of proficiency. This knowledge will be particularly useful as you assist students who have learning difficulties or those who speak little or no English.

To the Experienced Teacher

Many features of this material were developed in response to the concerns of practicing teachers who participated in a three-year whole language institute. These teachers had decided to move toward a more integrated approach to language learning for their students and wanted to know what this kind of teaching and learning looked like in the classroom. They asked why integrated practices were preferable to more traditional ones and how this kind of teaching affected children with special learning needs. They wanted to know how to introduce literature and language activities to their students and where they could look for help with problems and concerns. These teachers also faced challenges of state and local mandates and restrictions of physical space and availability of materials. These are problems shared by both beginning and experienced teachers, but seasoned practitioners are generally more acutely aware of how intensely these outside influences can affect classroom instruction.

If you are interested in moving toward a more integrated approach in your classroom, I invite you to read the narratives in this text. They record the experiences of other teachers like you who have met similar challenges and introduced these new methods to their students. I also encourage you to record your responses to the text in your own personal journal. The activity of writing is helpful for sorting out and organizing new ideas and creates a record of your experience. Some teachers chronicle the responses of their students to new methods in their journals and reread these entries for inspiration or direction for practice. Other teachers include magazine, journal and newspaper articles related to language learning and ideas they draw from observing other teachers.

You will already be using many of the activities presented in this text in some form in your classroom and may prefer to explore particular chapters for ideas to extend your current practice. The beginning sections of each chapter introduce a practice of integrated language learning and describe its importance to student learning. These sections will give you background information and provide you with a sound rationale for introducing a practice such as guided reading into your classroom. The information presented in these sections can also help you explain the reasons for changes in classroom activities to your students, colleagues and administrators.

The step-by-step planning and presentation sections provide guidelines for introducing new activities to your students, and special sections address inclusion issues, home–school partnerships and restrictions to practice. An annotated bibliography of resources includes handbooks that experienced teachers have found helpful as they move toward more integrated practices, and the "Teacher's Journal" records the experiences of several teachers as they introduce these practices into their classrooms. The classroom narratives are designed to give you a close-up look at how these practices are conducted at the major levels of elementary instruction.

Acknowledgments

I offer my sincere thanks to Naomi Silverman, Senior Editor at Lawrence Erlbaum Associates, who believed in this project and has contributed to its quality in immeasurable ways. I also deeply appreciate the comments and valuable suggestions provided by the reviewers of the text: Kathy Danielson, University of Nebraska at Omaha; Emily de la Cruz, Portland State University; Carol N. Dixon, University of California, Santa Barbara; Patricia J. Hagarty, University of Northern Colorado; Deborah A. Nieding, Gonzaga University; and Janet C. Richards, The University of Southern Mississippi.

The narratives in this text are modeled from the interactive styles of my friends and mentors in the public schools. It is with the deepest respect and admiration that I drew from the events and dialogues in their classrooms to create the narrative episodes. Students and fellow teachers at Haven Elementary School in Evanston, Illinois, where I first began teaching over thirty years ago, will recognize themselves in these narratives, as will my more recent colleagues: Charles Kamm, Gail Nave, Pat Sheahan, Jackie Hogue, Dick Koblitz, Kathy Burch and Cathy Woods.

I am particularly indebted to the students and teachers of Summerfield and Signal Hill grade schools, who welcomed me into their classrooms and shared their ideas about teaching and learning. Special thanks to: Christine Cook, Rebecca Culler, Ingrid Owens, Julie Parker, Christine Lanning, Kay Dunn, Deb Cryder, James Furkamp, Colleen West, Ruth Bush and Barbara Castello. I would also like to thank my students at McKendree College and Southern Illinois University for their support and inspiration.

I am especially grateful to my husband, Jerry, for his personal support and professional influence, and my son Tadd, for his encouragement and continuing interest in this project.

CHAPTER ONE

Integrating Language Learning in the Elementary Classroom

WHAT'S HAPPENING HERE? In schools where language learning is integrated throughout the curriculum, students have frequent opportunities to read and share books. Many teachers sponsor an activity called Book Buddies, where students from different grade levels meet to read and talk about their favorite books with each other.

"In our world," said Eustace, "a star is a huge ball of flaming gas."
"Even in your world, my son, [The Old Man replied] that is not
what a star is, but only what it is made of."
                              —C. S. Lewis, *The Voyage of the Dawn Treader*[1]

LOOKING AHEAD
1. How are language and literature used in the elementary classroom?
2. What is integrated language learning?
3. What is literature-based learning?
4. What activities characterize integrated language learning?
5. How do these activities compare with those in traditional classrooms?
6. What are the theoretical perspectives of traditional teaching?
7. What are the theoretical foundations of integrated language learning?

IN 25 WORDS OR LESS
In classrooms that integrate language learning into the curriculum, students use language, literature and their own experience to explore ideas and develop skills in the content areas.

I. Focus: Integrated Language Learning

Integrated language learning refers both to the natural way in which language skills develop and to the conscious effort made by educators to continue and extend this process within the school's curriculum. Language learning is an integral and continuous part of children's active efforts to make sense of what happens to them and to construct meaning from their experience. The question is not how to make children learn, but rather how to help them organize and direct their natural learning processes. This requires teachers to become careful observers of children and to know as much as possible about the experiences and knowledge students bring to school.

Teachers who integrate language learning into the curriculum create classroom environments that encourage students to expand their understanding of events and ideas and to be active in pursuing answers to their own real questions. Through the language arts, students examine, reflect on, organize and express their responses to ideas and information. They work together in cooperative, flexible groups, where they are encouraged to talk together, make decisions and solve their own learning problems. Many teachers integrate their classroom programs by organizing instruction around themes in literature or the content areas of science and social studies. Still others create theme cycles, which use the questions and interests of their classes as organizing ideas for the year's program. Theme cycles involve the concepts and skills that must be taught as part of school requirements, but include students in the selection, organization and sequencing of study topics.

When classroom programs feature integrated language learning throughout the curriculum, teachers have made decisions about the ways children best learn and their role in supporting and extending this learning. Teachers in more traditional programs make similar decisions, based on their beliefs about students, teaching and the purpose of the curriculum. In the **traditional** classroom, teachers believe it is their responsibility to minimize student talking and to create a quiet place for learning to occur. The curriculum is divided into subject areas, which are taught from **textbooks** that present information and provide questions designed to measure understanding. Language is seen as a set of separate skills to be taught and learned through drill practice. Traditional teachers see knowledge as a body of key facts and information that students need to know to be successful as students and later as citizens. It is the responsibility of traditional teachers to create meaning for students through their presentations of subject matter and follow-up assignments.

Teachers in both the traditional and more integrated kinds of classrooms want their students to learn the skills that will help them become lifelong learners. Both believe that the way their classrooms are organized will help students most effectively develop the abilities necessary to be well-educated adults. Differences in classroom activities result from different perspectives about the role of the teacher, ideas about how children learn, the purpose of the curriculum and beliefs about who creates meaning in the learning process. The theoretical foundations for these different beliefs will be explored further in the Perspectives section of this chapter.

WHAT DO YOU THINK? From the two kinds of classrooms described above, which most closely describes your experience in elementary school? What did you particularly like about the way you were helped to develop language skills? What did you dislike? Which approach seems more appealing to you at this time?

II. The Importance of Integrating Language Learning in the Classroom

Although children learn to speak and function in a language very well before they come to school, they do not accomplish this learning in a vacuum. From their parents, siblings and friends, they learn how to use language to express themselves, solve problems and obtain what they need from their environment. Integrating language learning into a school context provides additional opportunities to help children explore ideas and develop skills that will help them answer questions they have about the world. According to Jerome Bruner,[2] teachers assist this learning by activating, maintaining and directing a child's natural will to learn. This involves directing students' natural curiosity, providing assistance with difficult tasks, and modeling skills and strategies that will help them become more skillful and autonomous learners.

As children explore ideas across the curriculum, they use language to read, talk and write about what they are learning. James Britton[3] points out that language is the way we make sense of our experience, and Lev Vygotsky[4] observes that as we try to explain our thoughts to ourselves or someone else, we organize them and give them form. Janet Emig[5] says that in order to make sense of an experience, we must assimilate it in our own words, words that are familiar and comfortable to us.

When children write about their experience in journals, they come to a new understanding of themselves as persons and learners. As they talk in pairs or small groups, they come to a better understanding of their own ideas. In the process of reading or listening to the ideas of other students, they receive new insights and information that add directly to the meaning of their own experience. Bruner (op. cit.) and others have found that children understand and remember ideas when they have opportunities to talk and write about them. Vygotsky believes that language promotes thought and that this growth of thought, in turn, promotes language learning.[6] Language serves as a "deliberate structuring of meaning" (p. 100). It is through language that children create meaning from their experience, by examining it, reflecting on it and reconstructing it to achieve new understanding.

A report from the National Assessment of Educational Progress[7] indicates that using writing and talking to learn are necessary for students to develop full literary ability, which the authors define as: "the ability to reason effectively about what one reads and writes in order to extend one's understanding of the ideas expressed" (p. 9). To accomplish this literacy, there must be many opportunities for students to respond to what they read in literature and the content areas by talking and writing about these ideas.

Christopher Thaiss[8] believes that children understand and remember only what they have the opportunity to talk and write about or respond to in some meaningful way. In classrooms where language activities are interrelated and language learning occurs in the context of exploring ideas in the curriculum, children write and talk about what they read and hear. They make connections among all areas of knowledge and between the curriculum and their own experience. Language is integrated into all school learning, as children interact with many kinds of texts, with the teacher and with each other.

WHAT DO YOU THINK? Have you ever experienced learning something or increasing your understanding of it by writing or talking about it with someone else? How would you evaluate your own levels of reading and writing ability at this point in your schooling? What connections can you see between ideas in the sciences, humanities and arts in courses you have taken and your preparation as a teacher?

III. Looking into Classrooms

Kindergarten Level

Before school one morning, Mrs. Jamison shows the school principal a copy of Eric Carle's *The Very Quiet Cricket*,[9] a picture book with a surprise feature built into the last page.

"I just got this," she says. "Would you like to read it to my class?"

Mr. Wright reads the book, likes it and agrees to read it to the kindergarten.

At twelve-thirty, Mr. Wright arrives in the room, greets the students and sits down to read. Twenty interested children group around him on the floor, ready to listen.

He hands the book to Amy, who is partially sighted. She looks closely at the cover and hands it back.

"Is everyone comfortable?" he asks the class. He holds up the book and asks everyone if they can see. Some move around for a better view.

"What do you think this book will be about?" he begins.

"Bugs!" Jake guesses.

"Why do you say that?" the principal asks, and Jake points to the picture of the cricket on the cover.

"Any special kind of bug?" he asks.

"It's a cricket," says Kathy, who can read. "It says 'The Very Quiet Cricket.' "

"A quiet cricket?" He acts puzzled.

"Very quiet cricket," Kathy replies.

"Are crickets quiet?" he asks.

"No!" they chorus.

"Some are," Blake declares. "Some don't say anything."

"Do you know what kind?" the principal asks.

"Nope, just black ones."

"We'll have to find out about that," the principal says. "Maybe the book will tell us. Mrs. Jamison, are you planning to study about crickets that don't make any sounds?"

"We can certainly include that," she replies and makes a note on the question chart.

"What do crickets sound like?" he asks. "The ones that say something?" The children respond with cricket noises.

"Who do you think might have illustrated this book?" he asks. There is a pause as children study the cover.

"Eric Carle," Vicky guesses. "It looks like the pictures for *Rooster's Off To See the World*."[10]

"No, it's not," Michael disagrees. "It's more dark, like Ezra Jack Keats."

"Yeah," Jason agrees. "It's like the ones in the *Regards to the Man in the Moon*[11] book."

"Uh-uh," Tim says. "It's Eric Carle. He does more animals things."

"Crickets aren't animals," Will says.

"Uh-huh!" Tim retorts.

"Why do you think an insect is an animal, Tim?" Mr. Wright asks.

"Well . . . they move . . . and they got legs and . . . eyes and mouths," he replies.

"What do you think, Will?" the principal asks.

"They don't look like animals," Will says. "Animals got hair. Insects are too little to be animals."

"This sounds like another good question to put on the chart. What do you think?" he asks the children. They nod approval and Mrs. Jamison adds the question Are insects animals? to the question chart.

"Is it all right to wait until later to discuss this question?" he asks the boys. They nod approval. Later in the afternoon, Mrs. Jamison will return to the question as they explore a theme study on insects.

"You made some good guesses about the illustrator," Mr. Wright says. "It's Eric Carle. But you sure came up with good reasons for it being other artists, too," he adds. He begins to read, holding the book toward himself to read across the double open page and then turning it around for everyone to see the illustrations.

The story has a surprise ending and the students clap spontaneously. "Read it again," they chorus, and the principal reads the book again. By popular demand he reads it a third time and then reads the author's notes at the end of the book, where they discover the answer to the question about crickets that do not chirp. Then they take time to explore the pictures together.

"What do you see on this page that you didn't notice before?" the principal asks, showing the book to the class and then handing the book to Amy. Hands go up as children spot new details in the pictures. Mr. Wright talks about how crickets make their sound, and the children try rubbing their hands together to experiment with sounds made by friction. Before the principal leaves, several children volunteer to bring crickets to school. He gives them some pointers on how to catch crickets without harming them and suggests types of containers to keep them healthy and alive.

"My brother pulls the legs off of crickets," Davey says, as the principal gets up from his chair.

"Oooh!" the girls groan, making faces.

A few of the boys say, "Cool!"

"What do you think about that?" the principal asks him.

"I don't do it," he replies. The principal pats him on the shoulder. One of the boys who said "Cool!" catches Mr. Wright as he starts to leave the room. "I wouldn't do that either," he says.

"Good for you, Kevin. I didn't think you would," the principal replies. He stops a minute to greet Griswold, the teddy bear, who has just returned from an overnight stay at Teri's house. Every night and over the weekend Griswold goes home with someone in the classroom. He returns to school with an account of his visit written in his take-home journal, which parents and students help Griswold record. Every morning Mrs. Jamison reads Griswold's previous night's adventures aloud to the class. Today she reads about his overnight visit to Teri's house, where Griswold shared a pizza with Teri and her four brothers, watched a video and went for a ride in the car.

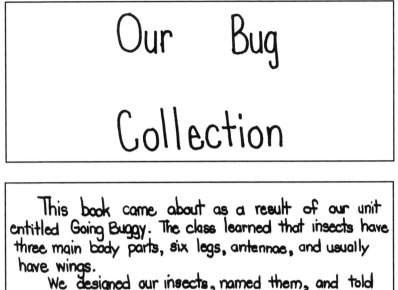

Our Bug Collection

This book came about as a result of our unit entitled Going Buggy. The class learned that insects have three main body parts, six legs, antennae, and usually have wings.

We designed our insects, named them, and told something special about them. We hope you enjoy our bug collection!

This is heart bug. He loves people.

Vincent

FIGURE 1.1
Students in this kindergarten created their own insects and collected them together in a class book. It was shared with the principal, other classes and parents and became a well-read part of the kindergarten library.

One of Teri's brothers cut his arm on a nail, so Griswold also visited the hospital emergency room. Tonight, he'll go home with Chelsea and attend a piano recital.

It is late fall and Griswold has visited every student's home at least once. He spent one weekend with the school principal and learned how to hunt mushrooms. He also visited Mrs. Jamison's home and helped her babysit her new granddaughter. The student teacher took Griswold to baseball and basketball games, where he talked to the cheerleaders and had his picture taken with the college mascot.

Other teachers send animal ambassadors like Griswold on trips around a school district, the country or the world. When someone leaves for a vacation at a distant spot, the class mascot goes along to visit another school. The mascot carries letters, pictures, photographs and a tape from the class in a backpack. Students at the school he visits write letters back to the class and may include pictures, photos and a tape in the package they return, before sending the mascot to another location. This journey continues until April, when the roving ambassador returns home at the request of an accompanying note.

WHAT HAPPENED HERE? ONE PERSPECTIVE

By asking the principal to read a particular book to her class, Mrs. Jamison offers him the opportunity to share his background in science in an informative and enjoyable way. Later in the day, she will refer to this experience several times, as students dictate the events of the day for her to record on a chart. "What did Mr. Wright tell us about how crickets make their sound?" she will ask, and "Why do you think an insect is an animal?"

As the principal reads aloud to the kindergarten, he offers children a model of adult reading, of someone who both values and enjoys reading as evidenced by his interest and enthusiasm. Reading aloud creates a comfortable context for discussing values with students, as illustrated in the interaction between the principal and several boys. The principal could tell that Davey was concerned about what his brother was doing and wanted to know how someone else viewed this behavior.

Griswold's visits to student homes involve parents in a reading/writing activity through which the ordinary becomes special, and children are recognized for the unique characteristics of their families. Visits to the most humble of homes never fail to be interesting because each visit is a story, and children enjoy hearing what happens in other children's lives. The process of recording Griswold's visits allows parents to be involved in their children's learning, and the response to this home/ school activity is most enthusiastic. Through the journal, Mrs. Jamison also learns about her students' families in a nonthreatening way, adding a new dimension to her understanding of each child. Several parents do not read or write, so the teacher provides a small tape recorder to record the visits. Many children choose to use the tape recorder so that no differences are perceived between families. An aide transcribes the visit into Griswold's journal when the tape is returned the next morning, and Mrs. Jamison reads the transcript of the story, or the class listens to the tape together, according to the child's wishes.

Primary Level

Lindsay pours over the entries in her learning log for a few minutes before she writes about her day. She glances up occasionally to refer to the class journal, which lists the day's activities on a large chart.

Wednesday, September 5

I learned how to write a poem in haiku today. I wonder if we could write to a Japanese class and exchange poems and stories.

I read two chapters of *The Lion, the Witch and the Wardrobe*. I'm going to start keeping a journal and pretend like I'm Lucy.

I picked the dodo bird to study, but I can't find too much to read about it. I'm going to try the CD ROM in the computer lab. We made a graph that shows how many animals are endangered.

We looked up the wildlife sanctuaries in our area. There is one for wolves and one for eagles. The zoo has some endangered animals, too.

We wrote Mrs. Ladd at the zoo and told her what we wanted to know about orangutans and gorillas, and she's going to talk to us when we visit.

Lindsay is writing in a learning journal, recording her daily goals, personal discoveries and classroom activities. Later this afternoon, she will use these entries to write a note home to her parents, telling them what she learned during the day and what she especially enjoyed doing.

"Lindsay," Megan taps her on the shoulder and motions for her to move her desk into the circle everyone is forming. "Come on, I'm going to show my dolls."

When everyone is ready, Megan begins. "These are my best Barbie dolls," she says. She has lined up six dolls on the low table in front of her. "I brought these because they're my best ones. Their clothes are nice and their hair looks good."

She picks up two of the dolls. "These are special edition dolls. You can't get them in most of the stores. They're more expensive and I just get one at Christmas or sometime like that. So I guess they're the best ones. This one," she holds up a doll dressed in a green formal, "is probably the very best because it cost the most . . . then this one . . . and then this one . . . and these three cost just the same," she says, holding up each doll in turn.

"Is there another way you value the dolls?" Miss McNulty asks.

She pauses and thinks for a minute.

"Well, . . . another way, I guess . . . this one would be the best," she says, holding up a doll in a space outfit. "I like this one best because I want to be an astronaut. Then this one because the hair is the best. Then this one because of the clothes. Then these three . . . I guess . . . this one's hair is better than the other two."

"So you can value the dolls in different ways?" the teacher asks.

"Yeah . . . their hair, and their clothes and how much they cost."

"And if you can't get 'em many places," Angie adds, and Lindsay nods her head.

Dane moves over to the low table with his box of small model cars. He carefully takes each model out and places them in a row. "These are my best cars," he says. "They're the best ones in my collection because I haven't played with them much and the paint and everything is still good on 'em. They're all GM cars too, and I like GM cars. This one's the best 'cause it's got all this chrome and it's a Cadillac. Then this Buick is next 'cause it's got lots of chrome too, but not as much as the Caddy. These are good too . . . these are my two Pontiacs and my Chevy. But they don't have as much chrome and they didn't cost as much."

Zach shows the group his six best pogs, Angelique has stamps and Justin shows coins from Germany where he lived with his family for a year. Carmen brings a scrapbook and shows pictures of her six favorite dream houses. Daren has postcards from his collection, and Marguite has photographs she has taken of her cat. Miss McNulty began this sharing session yesterday by showing the class six antique straw hats, from her larger collection. She showed them the condition of the straw, the ribbons and the flowers and talked a little about their age and value as antiques. She also told them that she really valued one of the smaller, less fancy hats the most because it had been worn by her great-grandmother.

Each child also interviewed a family member to find out about their collections and how they decide which items in these collections are the best. Later this week, Zach's father, who is an architect, will talk to the class about his portfolio and how he decides what to put in it. The art teacher from the high school will show her drawings and demonstrate how she includes work that shows new things she has tried and skills she has learned. When Miss McNulty introduces writing portfolios to the students the following week, they will have a beginning idea of how portfolios are used. The teacher will ask the children to store all their work (writing, artistic responses, charts, graphs, maps or other responses to literature and content area learning) in a folder during the week. Each Friday, they will decide what they want to put in the portfolio and will attach a note to any item explaining why it was included. They will be encouraged to put in examples of what they believe to be their best work, pieces that show something they have learned and something that indicates their range of interests and ability. Twice a month, they will take home examples from their portfolios to show their parents, and on alternate Fridays they will exchange their portfolios for peer review.

WHAT HAPPENED HERE? ONE PERSPECTIVE

The teacher in this classroom is providing opportunities for her students to develop skills of self-evaluation. She begins this process with an activity developed by Donald Graves,[12] an educator who studies children's writing. He suggests that teachers model a valuing activity, such as sharing a collection they bring from home. Children are invited to bring their own collections to school and talk about them. This activity prepares children to use portfolios to collect samples of their work that exemplify their learning. As children think about why they place something in their portfolios, they learn how to analyze and reflect on their own work and how to value both the processes and products of learning.

The learning journal described above helps children record and reflect on their ideas and learning experiences. It also provides reference material when students write notes home to their parents at the end of the day. This type of home–school communication helps increase involvement by parents. As they learn about what is happening at school, they frequently volunteer relevant materials or expertise that can enhance a particular study.

As children share the work in their portfolios with peers, they receive important feedback on their progress and learn about the interests and ideas of everyone else in the classroom. This activity makes it possible for every child to be known as a person, someone with special hopes and dreams, and to others, someone not so different than themselves.

Intermediate Level

"I'm ready to go," Kurt announces, as he wheels himself into the classroom.

"Go, Kurt!" Mark responds. "You've gotta do it for us, buddy," he says and gives the boy in the wheelchair a high five.

"Get ready to lose," Kurt says to Jennifer, his legal opponent in the courtroom case that is to be tried today in Mrs. Kelly's classroom.

"Some professional manner," Jennifer replies.

"That's what lawyers say to each other," Kurt replies.

"Well, then you're the one who's cruisin' for a bruisin'," Jennifer replies.

The exchange is good natured, and both retire to the table where their assistants sit ready to try the case of the explorer Christopher Columbus. Kurt and his team will try to convince an impartial jury (the fifth-grade class) that Columbus should be retained as an American hero. Jennifer and her team will argue that the behavior of this fifteenth-century explorer toward his crew and the Native peoples he encountered make him unfit for hero status.

"Ladies and gentlemen of the jury," Kurt begins. He peers over his glasses and affects courtroom dramatics. "My client is an upright man, a good man, an intelligent and forward-looking man. He did not set out to harm his crew. Indeed, we will show today that Columbus provided very well for his men and had their interests at heart for every journey made to the New World. In a special historical arrangement, we will interview some of these men today, who will tell you in their own words what it was like to sail on his ship. We will also hear from Mr. Columbus himself, who will tell you of his good and true intentions in sailing to the New World. This is a man who bravely sailed into a sea where others thought they would die. This is a man of courage, who is most deserving to be an American hero."

Jennifer consults in whispers with her team and then strides to the front of the courtroom.

"Did you hear that, ladies and gentlemen?" she begins. "This is the very attitude that is on trial here today. Mr. Wells refers to this continent, where people have lived for thousands of years, as the 'New World.' New World, indeed! This continent was the old world for many different cultures, all of which would be harmed in some way by the action of Mr. Columbus. We will call witnesses today who will testify to the damage done by the actions of this man and those who followed him. People who lost their land, their homes and their way of life. And all for what? Greed, that's what. All they wanted was gold to take back to Spain. I will ask you to consider if such a man should be regarded as an American hero."

After the opening statements, each side presents testimony from witnesses, with the defense promoting Columbus as a scholarly sailor who wanted only to find a new and shorter trade route to India. The prosecution calls witnesses who speak of mistreatment on ship and persecution of the Native populations. The defense produces witnesses among sailors and Natives who deny any bad treatment. They also point out that the Vikings actually explored the continent before Columbus and that Columbus did not treat Natives as badly as some who followed him. They portray him as a victim of poor press, created by sailors who held grudges.

Kurt finishes his witness examination by whirling around in his wheel-chair to face the jury.

"I ask you, ladies and gentlemen, if Columbus had not made these journeys, where would each of you be today? You might be hiding in fear in some terrible place in another country. You would not have the advantages you have as an American. Think about it!" he ends with a flourish.

"And at what cost to others are we here today?" Jennifer counters. "Nothing can excuse the terrible way he treated these people, giving orders to have them tortured and killed. One whole culture was destroyed by him in Hispaniola." The prosecution continues by saying that even if other explorers treated people poorly, that did not excuse Columbus. Throughout the trial, the lead lawyers consult for questioning points with their legal team, composed of four additional persons. The presiding judge listens carefully to testimony and objections by the lawyers, thinking carefully before overruling or sustaining the objections.

In her closing statement, Jennifer calls upon the jury to reconsider Columbus's stature as a hero, in light of the testimony of concerned witnesses, and to further consider what the world would be like if Columbus had not come to America. She concludes that Columbus should be remembered only for bringing smoking to Spain and overpopulation and pollution to America.

In his final statement, Kurt says that Columbus deserves recognition because the prosecution has been unable to produce any evidence showing that Columbus treated his sailors or the Natives any worse than did other explorers of his time and that it was not his intention to harm anyone with his exploration. If persons have to be perfect to be heroes, there would be few heroes in history, he observes. Kurt closes with the observation that Columbus showed determination and courage, traits that Americans typically honor.

The jury considers the case for one-half hour, during which time they ask to examine evidence in the form of maps, pictures and diaries that have been used in the trial. A student portraying a TV journalist reviews the case and evidence with the class while the jury is deliberating. When court reconvenes, the foreman reads the verdict. The jury finds Columbus guilty of mistreating sailors and harming Natives, but recommends that he still be recognized for his accomplishments as an explorer and navigator. Court reporters write up the basic arguments to include in a newsletter students prepare for distribution to other classes. At the end of the two-hour period, the fifth graders move on to science and math with another teacher and a new class enters the room.

In this print-rich classroom, students read, write, listen, think and talk about ideas in the curriculum, experiences that touch their lives and their personal responses to literature and life. Language is integrated into their interaction with each other, as they explore and exchange ideas. They have the opportunity to use expressive language frequently throughout the day in relaxed and informal situations. They also prepare for audiences in a more planned manner, and the content and style of these presentations reflect the value of the more informal practice.

The Columbus trial climaxes two weeks of preparation by the students. Half of the class was involved in the Columbus case, while the other half researched other explorers. Mrs. Kelly provided trade books and reference books on Columbus that featured historical diaries and current analyses of the exact routes of his journeys. Because only the prosecution and defense teams researched the specifics on Columbus, the jury had to depend for its decision on the information provided by witnesses and the arguments of the legal teams.

Each team had access to the same materials in the classroom, and each did a great deal of research from outside resources. The courtroom format encouraged students to examine each side of this issue carefully. They realized they would have to know the opposing arguments as well as their own in order to produce competing ideas. The entire class visited a courtroom to witness a trial and asked questions of a judge and several lawyers about the way cases were tried. They also investigated the rights of children in the legal system and learned the meaning of due process.

Mrs. Kelly receives the support of persons outside the classroom because she reaches out to involve parents, the school staff and the professional/ business members of her community. Although her class is officially designated as departmentalized language arts/social studies, she creates a learning environment that encourages students to practice language skills in the context of exploring ideas they are curious about, in any area. This teacher makes a great effort to talk to other teachers about the content, skills and strategies featured in their classes, so these can be integrated, as much as possible, into the language activities of her classroom.

IV. Preparing for Integrated Language Learning

Teachers who integrate language learning in their classroom programs prepare themselves in a variety of ways. They:

1. read widely in every kind of children's literature.
2. keep a brief record of what they read for future reference.
3. visit other classrooms, attend professional conferences, read professional literature and gather ideas for their own teaching from each of these sources.

4. use professional reference books, the suggestions of others and their own good judgment to carefully select a wide variety of trade books for their classrooms.
5. keep journals of their ideas, experiences and personal responses to literature.
6. practice their own skills of reading, writing, listening and speaking so that they can model language skills for their students.
7. organize resources and plan language experiences for the classroom.

You can begin many of these preparation activities while you are still a student. One of the most important of these is to read widely in all areas of children's literature: picture books, fantasy, contemporary and historical fiction, biography, poetry and informational nonfiction. You will want to explore every level of reading, from preschool through young adult. If you know the range of literature available for children, you will be able to provide satisfying reading experiences for all the children in your classroom at every ability level. You will also want to include good examples of multicultural books in each of the genres (kinds of books), particularly literature written by authors who represent the minority heritages of the students in your classroom, school and community.

You may want to begin keeping a log of children's books you read. If you briefly record some information about these books, you will create a resource you can use when you are planning a theme study or are looking for a good book to read aloud. A small spiral notebook with a pen attached to the binding makes a good log. It is a good idea to keep this book close to an area where you typically read and make notes similar to the following: title, author/illustrator, main theme and any ideas that strike you immediately about how it could be used. You may also want to develop your own entry codes to save writing time. Some teachers duplicate pages with spaces marked off for the categories listed above. They keep the entry pages handy and regularly insert completed records in a three-ring binder.

An important part of preparing the classroom environment for learning is establishing the social climate in which students will interact. Initially, this is the responsibility of the teacher, who sets a model for positive interaction, creates opportunities for classroom members to talk and learn together, and helps students develop acceptable standards of behavior. The values of respect and responsibility are stressed throughout the school day in such areas as the handling of books and materials, interactions with others, problem solving, patience, persistence, and generosity. As the parameters of social behavior are established and the norms are internalized by students, teacher intervention becomes less necessary.

Responsible social behavior, like any other skill, requires practice. Many teachers provide opportunities for students to develop responsibility as they read, write and discuss together. They also encourage them to take increased responsibility for their own learning by directing students to sources that can be used in the teacher's absence: Did you check in the dictionary? Where could you find out more about that? Who knows something about this subject? Which chart do you think that spelling might be on?

WHAT DO YOU THINK? Talking has traditionally been associated with misbehavior, from harmless whispering to talking out loud, out of turn or off the subject. How do you regard these types of talking? Of what value is it to students to have frequent opportunities to talk in school? Can you think of ways a teacher can model positive social interaction in the classroom? How do you think it will benefit your students if you are an active reader and writer?

V. Including Everyone

It might seem obvious that you would want to include all students in all activities of the classroom. This section is designed to help you reflect on ways students might inadvertently be excluded from full participation because of race, class, ethnicity, or physical or mental disability. Language learning is directly related to a child's ability to see, hear and attend to environmental stimuli. Communication also requires that children be able to speak in a manner that can be understood by listeners. To the extent that the function of any language receptors or producers is impaired, there will be a challenge to language learning and development. If a child is unusually distracted, impaired in seeing or hearing, or unable to write or speak understandably, the teacher must work with the child to accommodate these limitations and give full support to his or her efforts to participate fully in the classroom program.

Other children may encounter English as a second language or as an alternative dialect. These children can be brought into full participation when they have the opportunity to talk, write and read about their families, customs and cultural literature. Our experiences as human beings are similar enough to permit the sharing and understanding of common experience. The sharing of differences adds to the richness of our experience, and the sharing of common problems and challenges brings comfort and insight.

There will be other differences in children, depending on the literacy experiences they have had at home, their ages and developmental levels. In the midst of these differences, however, children and teachers can form communities of learners who share common classroom experiences and support each other's efforts to grow and learn. Teachers facilitate the building of these communities in their classrooms by creating a learning environment that will minimize differences of disability, celebrate the differences of culture, emphasize the common human experiences of everyone and develop new experiences that students can share together.

Books to Increase Understanding

Each of the following books illustrates the human hopes and fears that bind us together as citizens of the world. As you step inside the lives of the children portrayed in these books, you will experience a bond of familiarity with their hopes, fears and joys.

Light: Stories of a Small Kindness[13] by Nancy White Carlstrom includes seven stories about children from Mexico, Haiti, Guatemala and New York City, each of which features an act of kindness. Included are stories that tell how a bus filled with Down syndrome children escapes danger, how a young boy overcomes fear in a dark cave and how disabled children learn to overcome obstacles.

Face to Face: A Collection of Stories by Celebrated Soviet and American Writers[14] is edited by Thomas Pettepiece and Anatoly Aleksin. These stories by nine Russian and nine American authors provide insights into basic human values. They feature universal themes and issues, such as loyalty, responsibility and family. Familiar American authors include Robert Cormeir, Katherine Paterson, Jean Fritz and Walter Dean Myers.

The China Year[15] by Emily Cheney Neville describes the experience of a young girl who accompanies her family to China, where her father has a university appointment in Beijing. In the context of exploring the city with a young Chinese friend, she learns about differences of culture and deals with her homesickness for New York City.

Song of the Giraffe[16] by Shannon Jacobs explores ideas of growing up and family relationships in an African tribe. A young girl feels separated from those around her because she is smaller and has lighter skin and hair than the other girls in her tribe.

VI. Step-by-Step: Integrating Language Learning

The following are key activities to involve students in reading, writing, listening, speaking, thinking and inquiry in the classroom. Each of these activities is described and discussed in separate chapters throughout the text, but the following descriptions will help you see how these activities fit into the experience of a single day.

Reading Aloud

At every elementary grade level, teachers read aloud to their students, once or several times every day. These sessions help create a common experience for students and teachers to enjoy together and provide a pleasant contact with books and reading. Teachers use reading aloud to introduce students to different types of literature, to begin or enhance theme studies and to share their own enthusiasm for a particular book.

Independent Reading

Most teachers schedule at least one or more 10–30-minute independent reading sessions every day. This is a time when students select what they want to read for an uninterrupted period of time. Key to the success of this activity is the participation of teachers, who use this time to explore professional literature, extend their own acquaintance with children's literature or discover books that can be used throughout the curriculum. Independent reading periods are frequently scheduled during the first period in the morning or in the afternoon, after lunch.

Previewing Literature	Each day, teachers and students share books with the entire class by giving brief reviews of books they are reading. This activity most often occurs before or after independent reading and is used by the teacher to introduce students to the wide variety of books available for children and to acquaint them with books in the room that they might not examine for themselves. When orders are received from book clubs, these books are also highlighted, particularly those that have been ordered for the classroom library.
Shared and Guided Reading	Teachers help students learn how to search for meaning in texts by modeling strategies for reading with small groups of students or the entire class. At the kindergarten and early primary level, these common reading experiences might include reading together from Big Books or charts. Classes might also read poetry, plays, or songs aloud together. At the later primary and intermediate levels, students meet to read, study and discuss books together in **literature circles**. At all levels, students enjoy a reading experience, practice comprehension skills, develop vocabulary, and interact with each other to share their responses to literature. Guided reading sessions may be scheduled several times a day at the kindergarten and primary levels and in either the morning or afternoon at the later primary or intermediate levels.
Mini-lessons	Throughout the day, teachers observe students using language as they read, write, talk and listen to each other. They also observe students closely during individual reading and writing conferences. From these observations, teachers construct mini-lessons (little lessons), which are brief presentations to help students understand a concept or develop a specific skill to improve their language learning. Students use favorite books or their own writing to practice skills or strategies and record the content of the lesson in a writing log for future reference.
Individual Reading Conferences	Each day a number of students meet individually with the teacher to talk about a book they are reading. They read aloud from a passage they especially enjoy and share favorite illustrations. The teacher asks open-ended questions that assess vocabulary knowledge and comprehension and help students make connections between the story and their own experience. From these conferences, teachers can observe the skills and strategies children use to make meaning from print. Records of these conferences across the class indicate the need for specific instruction in an area, which can then be presented through mini-lessons.
Writing	At least once a week, all students meet with the teacher for an individual writing conference in order to share a piece they are working on or one they have finished. They write daily in journals, notebooks or logs, recording questions, ideas and information about literature, science, social studies and mathematics. Students also write daily in writing workshops, which feature time for independent writing on topics of their choice, mini-lessons to increase writing skill and the opportunity to share their writing with a small group or the entire class.
Listening and Speaking	There are many opportunities throughout the day for students to interact with each other in pairs, small groups and class discussion. They meet together to discuss their responses to books in literature groups, debate issues

in shared-pair groups, preview favorite books for the entire class and explore ideas in content area study groups. They practice both presentation and audience skills as they share personal responses to literature in Friday Afternoon Sharing Time.

Content Area Study   Students explore concepts in mathematics, science and the social studies using a variety of resources, including books from every genre of trade literature. Students work in pairs and small flexible groups to explore, discuss and share ideas. Language skills and strategies are learned, practiced and developed in the process of inquiry in these areas. Students are encouraged to make connections between their own experience and the topic of research and to find relationships among all the kinds of knowledge they explore.

Figure 1.2 demonstrates a few of the ways each of these elements of language learning are integrated into all activities in the classroom.

WHAT DO YOU   As you begin imagining yourself in a classroom like the one described
THINK?   above, what activities can you visualize most clearly? Which would you
like to observe further?

I.   **Reading aloud may include:**
Listening to high-quality, appealing books of every genre
Creating a common experience by discussing responses to a book together
Students reading the same book individually
Students reading other books: same genre, same topic, same author
Writing personal responses from listening to the book
Artistic responses
Introducing, illustrating, enhancing or extending a theme

II.   **Independent reading may include:**
Listening to previews and reviews of books
Talking about favorite books
Reading books of one's own choice or from the recommendations of others
Writing in response to favorite books
Artistic responses
Reading books on curriculum themes
Research in the content areas

III.   **Selecting literature may include:**
Exploring literature in every genre
Identifying the characteristics of each genre
Learning how to evaluate the quality of literature
Identifying award-winning literature
Learning how to select books for specific purposes
Learning how to identify books at one's reading level

FIGURE 1.2
(Continued on facing page)

IV. **Shared and guided reading may include:**
Reading literature in all genres
Talking and listening in small discussion groups
Exploring literary themes
Writing responses to share with others
Artistic responses
Connecting literature with content area inquiry
Previewing books for other students
Listening to previews by students and the teacher

V. **Individual conferences may include:**
Independent reading and writing on topics of interest
Teacher–student discussions
Artistic responses
Reading aloud to the teacher
Reading and writing to practice a skill or strategy

VI. **Writing activities may include:**
Writing in all genres
Reading to learn how to write in a genre
Reading aloud to share writing
Listening to other writing read aloud in small and large groups
Writing for a purpose and to explore ideas
Writing in response to books read
Writing to record, organize ideas, explain, report, persuade, express

VII. **Listening and speaking may include:**
Talking about books and writing
Talking in groups to express opinions and to share responses and information
Discussing themes and topics in literature and content area studies
Solving problems of classroom procedures, routines or social interaction
Talking to and listening to classroom visitors
Talking and reading aloud in pairs or larger groups to express opinions
Exploratory talk to clarify and organize ideas

VIII. **Mini-lessons may include:**
Using favorite books or student writing to practice skills
Practicing skills in all language areas
Practicing learning strategies
Learning inquiry skills
Practicing research strategies and reference skills
Practicing classroom procedures and routines

IX. **Using technology in the classroom may include:**
Support for special language, physical or learning disabilities
Word processing to create, store and publish writing
Exploration of ideas in CD ROM programs and encyclopedias
Exploration and communication on the Internet
Exploration of literature in other media

X. **Content area learning may include:**
Using language skills and strategies to explore science, math, and social studies
Making relationships among many kinds of knowledge
Using many kinds of literature to explore content area concepts
Talking and listening in pairs, small groups and the entire class
Sharing written and artistic responses with an audience
Sharing discoveries and the results of inquiry with an audience

FIGURE 1.2
Integrated language learning.

VII. If This Is Your Situation

Because well-intentioned educators view the learning process in differing ways, there will be times when you disagree about both the goals and methods of teaching with parents, other teachers and supervisors. How can this situation best be handled? When colleagues or supervisors have different beliefs about teaching and learning, complete agreement may not be possible. The goal for enlightened professionals is to see the situation as a whole and to understand other people's point of view. If others know that you share similar concerns, they will usually be more willing to hear your reasons for using methods that are different from theirs.

An alternative to this position is submission, but this option is extremely stressful to the peacemaker and creates resentment. Another option is to ignore the opposition of the other person and do it the way you want. Although this approach sometimes works, it is not effective in situations that call for cooperative effort. It does not resolve differences and often creates misunderstanding. Confrontation is another option, a direct approach, which may feel good, but is usually painful, exhausting and nonproductive.

An alternative way to deal with these conflicts is to enter the concerns of persons with whom you disagree and turn the conversation so that you are looking at a shared view. An example of a blending statement might be "We have different ideas about how to help students improve their spelling. Let's see if we can work out something that will be agreeable to both of us." When areas of agreement are discovered, alternative ways of reaching common goals can be discussed more rationally.

VIII. Evaluating Progress

The way learning is assessed in your school will determine, to a great extent, the goals, content and methodology for instruction. If these goals are meaningful and directed to authentic outcomes that are useful for children's language learning, assessment can be a valuable tool for directing instruction. On the other hand, when standardized tests are used to evaluate learning, these tests often become the goals of instruction. Teachers may conclude that if they will be evaluated on the basis of their students' performance on standardized tests, they may as well teach to the test.

The concern of traditional evaluators is that all children have access to the same instruction. Administrators and boards of education may want assurance that all fifth-grade children will receive grade-level-appropriate instruction in a standard curriculum. They believe that the best way to ensure that this instruction takes place is to test students for the content and skills deemed appropriate for this grade level. How well they are being taught is then assessed by comparing their achievement with that of other fifth-grade students who have completed the test, in their building, district, state or the nation.

The results of traditional evaluation are communicated to administrators, teachers and parents in the form of grade equivalents, age equivalents, percentile scores and standard scores. Unfortunately, this information does not provide any real direction for instruction, except in broad outlines. These scores are rarely understood by parents or students, and they provide little useful information to teachers and administrators. They do not test what is taught during class time, unless class time is used for learning strategies for taking multiple-choice tests.

Many educators believe that assessment methods should provide teachers with information that will direct and improve their teaching. They believe that the most helpful assessment occurs by observing students as they read, write, speak and listen. From these observations, they notice what is not being understood and create opportunities for information to be provided and skills and strategies to be introduced or practiced. When assessment is integrated into the teaching and learning process, time does not have to be taken away from teaching for testing.

Evaluation is most helpful for students when it shows them what they already know, what they need to learn and how to practice skills and strategies that will help them become better readers and writers. When students engage in self-evaluation, they learn to take control of their own learning. Many teachers use a portfolio system to help students develop self-evaluation skills. Portfolios also provide direction for instruction and contain examples of student work that demonstrate achievement and progress for parent conferences. In addition to portfolios, teachers may also use complementary assessment tools such as: performance checklists developed from local, state and national guidelines; anecdotes; developmental checklists; and parent–teacher conference guidelines.

Test-taking is considered to be a lifetime skill in our society, so most teachers use mini-lessons to share test-taking strategies with students. Some encourage students to construct their own multiple-choice questions for literature and the content areas, so that they are familiar with this common test format. Most teachers who integrate language learning in their classrooms discover that students do very well on standardized language learning tests, possibly because language study is much more intense when it is highlighted and practiced throughout the entire curriculum.

IX. Creating Partners–Parents

It is in the context of the home and family that children develop language and build the foundation for learning to read and write. Parents are a child's first teachers, and throughout the schooling years they can provide invaluable support for their child's developing literacy. It is important that parents be kept informed about the activities that support integrated language learning in your classroom. In most cases, this will not be the method by which they were taught, and they may have reservations about these methods being used in their child's classroom. How can you gain their trust and support for your classroom program? The following ideas have been used successfully by experienced teachers who face the same challenge.

1. **Inform** parents about your language learning program. You will want to establish communication with parents early in the school year. Some ways to do this are: send home a newsletter or bulletin describing your program and some of the activities you will be doing; demonstrate these activities during open house; make a videotape of children participating in language learning in the classroom and send it home by turns. Send home regular bulletins or newsletters that describe what is happening in the classroom.

2. **Involve** parents immediately and continuously throughout the year. Many teachers encourage parents to donate materials for classroom use and enlist their help in assembling instructional materials. They create opportunities for parents to be involved in the classroom by: helping with school book clubs and field trips; assisting with plays and costumes; reading aloud or practicing skills with individual children or small groups; assisting with student projects; participating in class activities; and attending class performances.

3. **Integrate** language learning into the home–school relationship. Send home materials that will involve parents in talking, listening, reading and writing activities with their child. Some popular projects include: books to read aloud or tapes to listen to; stuffed animals that visit and then tell their story to the class; class photo journals of activities or field trips; books, poems or stories written by the class that go home by turns.

Most schools schedule an open house for classrooms at the beginning of school in the fall. You might want to create a bulletin board for volunteers with lists of jobs and needed materials. Be sure to leave a space for parents to suggest their own ways of volunteering. Follow up with letters home to confirm dates and times for those who volunteer. For parents not in attendance, you can send letters home, including a list of jobs, a schedule and a sign-up sheet to be returned.

You will want to make a special effort to contact parents who speak little English to get them involved in the activities of the classroom as soon as possible. Enlist the aid of a family member, student, colleague or community member to help interpret. For all parents, be sure there is always something for them to do and encourage them to contact you when they will be unable to come. Some parents appreciate a reminder note, sent home with their children. You will also want to have a back-up plan, in the event a parent cannot come. Be sure to remind parents that they should make other arrangements for babies and toddlers in the family, as they will distract the attention of both the volunteer and students. When parents work directly with children in small groups, you will want to acquaint them with your approach to disruptive behavior and conflicts between students. Also let them know that you will handle any situation with which they feel uncomfortable.

WHAT DO YOU
THINK? How were your parents involved in your schooling? If you are a parent of a school-age child, how have you been involved with your child's classroom activities? Can you think of other ways of involving parents?

X. Perspectives

Where do teachers get their ideas about how children learn? As a student in a teacher education program, you have probably already explored ideas in the philosophy and history of education that emerge from systematic thinking about education. Possibly you have completed a course in educational psychology and are aware of several different theoretical viewpoints about learning. If you read professional journals and teacher's magazines, you will gain additional ideas about how learning occurs. All of this information and experience provide ways of seeing, thinking about and interpreting what happens in the classroom. Your own experiences as a learner and your natural intuition about children will combine with this background to assign importance and meaning to the events of learning.

As important as it is to know your own beliefs about teaching and learning, it is equally important to understand the beliefs that direct the practice of other teachers. A critic once commented to Cezanne, "That doesn't look anything like a sunset." Pondering his painting, Cezanne responded, "Then you don't see sunsets the way I do."[17] Educators, like artists, have different ways of seeing. They have different visions of what a classroom should look like, different beliefs about how children learn and different conceptions of the role of the teacher. For example, teachers may regard misspelled words in different ways. A first grader writes: "Dinosors are xteent, but arkeologsts dig up ther bons." One teacher may observe that the student is attaching symbols to sounds in a consistent manner and is using writing in a fluent way to express his ideas. Another may be concerned with misspelled words and be eager to correct them so that errors will not be repeated.

Educational theorists who develop systematic frameworks for looking at the way children learn differ in their explanations of the learning process. All theorists consider the genetic endowment of human beings (what they are born with) and the influence of the environment on their learning. But they differ in terms of the ways they see individuals interacting with their environments. Some theorists see the learner as the most important element. They regard persons as complete within themselves and learning as something that happens as **innate structures** unfold. The goal of teaching is to interfere as little as possible with the learner, allowing him or her to develop according to an internal plan. The main work of the innatist teacher is to create an environment that will be learner-friendly, nonimpositional and nurturing. Students follow their own interests and are given support as it is requested. The humanist theorists such as Jean Jacques Rousseau, Abraham Maslow and Erik Erickson represent this point of view.

Other theorists see children **developing through stages** as they interact with the environment. Jean Piaget believed that innate mental structures influence how experience is organized and interpreted and that meaning derives from the way an individual sees the world at each of these different stages. The goal of teaching is to be aware of these different ways of seeing and to plan and evaluate learning in a manner appropriate to the present stage of thinking.

Other theorists see the **environment** as the main determinant in learning. In its most extreme form, environmentalism holds that all behavior occurs because it is rewarded or reinforced in some way. B. F. Skinner, a behaviorist theorist, believed that student behavior is determined by the environment. According to Skinner, children are born with the capacity to be reinforced and that behavior that is reinforced (rewarded) is repeated. Teaching then becomes a process of reinforcing correct responses in the mastery of skills and information. The goal of the environmentalist teacher is to create a classroom where desirable behaviors are rewarded and undesirable behavior is ignored or punished. This requires a great deal of intervention by the teacher. It is also the role of the teacher to organize and present information and to supervise the practice of skills. Teachers create meaning and motivation for students by presenting lessons in an effective and interesting manner. Teachers who follow this model believe that children learn best by listening to the teacher explain ideas to them. It is also the role of the teacher to test for academic progress and to assign grades that indicate this progress. Teachers who follow the behaviorist model believe that students learn to read by mastering the individual sounds that make up words. Learning to read and write are academic tasks that can be divided into smaller parts and then mastered in sequence. This approach to instruction is sometimes called **part-to-whole**.

In "part-to-whole" learning, students begin with the smallest pieces of information. Reading instruction that proceeds in this manner begins with identification of the smallest part of the reading symbol system. Students learn letter sounds, move on to syllables and then to words, sentences and paragraphs. In traditional classrooms, this instruction is directed by a basal program, which features excerpts from literature or stories that have been rewritten with a controlled vocabulary. In the intermediate grades there may be a separate literature study, where students are given assignments to read in an anthology. They may also be encouraged to read books of their choice when all assigned work is completed. Instruction in science, mathematics and the social studies is based on content area textbooks.

Still other theorists, such as Jerome Bruner, believe that each of these approaches is incomplete. He sees the interaction of learners and their environments as the key element in explaining how learning occurs and assigns equal importance to genetic endowment and this interaction. Developmental theorists believe that children are born with cognitive structures that develop as they interact with the environment. Stage developmental theorists, such as Piaget, believe that cognitive structures are present at birth and unfold as children interact with the environment. Others, such as Bruner, see certain tendencies as inherent, but do not use the idea of stages to explain development. In Bruner's model of learning, children learn by creating meaning from what they hear, see, taste, feel, touch and smell. They are the active creators of their own meaning and are encouraged to read, listen to, talk about and write stories of interest to them. From stories and poems shared together with parents and later in the classroom, students gain familiarity with print and soon want to figure out words they do not know by applying sound/symbol rules (phonics) and context clues (gaining meaning from surrounding words or the main idea). This approach to language instruction is sometimes called **whole-to-part**, which emphasizes the processes of natural learning (the way people seem to learn in informal situations outside of the classroom).

WHAT DO YOU THINK?   Which of the theories described above seems to make the most sense to you? Ultimately, your own teaching will reflect two things: what seems reasonable from your own experience and what you really believe to be true about the nature of learning. Have you ever heard someone speak of teaching in one way, but act in another? Why do you think this happens?

XI.   Exploring Professional Literature

Throughout the text, you will be examining periodical literature that is published to share professional knowledge, information and inspiration with its readers. As you read in this literature, you will encounter terms such as whole language, immersion in print, developmental (or invented) spelling, community of learners, kid-watching, miscue analysis and emergent literacy. The following descriptions of these terms will help provide you with some background as you begin to explore the literature.

Whole language is a term used by educators such as Dorothy Watson, Jerome Harste,[18] Kenneth Goodman,[19] Frank Smith,[20] Andrea Butler[21] and others who see all of language and language learning as an interrelated process. These educators believe that language learning should involve children in using language functionally and for authentic purposes. Whole language teachers use literature throughout their curriculum for reading, writing about and exploring ideas in the content areas. This holistic approach to learning sees the student as a whole person, who brings relevant knowledge and experience to all new learning. Language and the curriculum are seen as an undivided entity, and there is an emphasis on learning from whole texts rather than excerpts, as in the basal system.

Immersion in print and **print-rich environments**.   Children learn to speak by being immersed in spoken language. Educators such as Altwerger, Edelsky and Flores[22] believe that children similarly learn to read and write by being immersed in environmental and storybook print. Yetta Goodman and others[23] describe how children build a print awareness in classroom environments where they are surrounded by many different kinds of books and reading materials, such as magazines, newspapers, brochures, posters, labels, menus, telephone books and maps. Charts and posters fill up the classroom with dictated stories, poems, songs, chants and lists of words and guidelines. Classroom libraries include a wide variety of fiction, nonfiction and high-quality picture book literature. The goal is to provide an environment where students have opportunities to explore and make sense of print.

Kid-watching[24] is another term you will encounter. It refers to systematic observation of students as they engage in speaking, listening, reading and writing activities. From these observations, teachers gain valuable information about the experience, skills and learning needs of their students. This "kid-watching" helps teachers evaluate the effectiveness of their instruction and the progress of their students. It also gives direction to their planning for future instruction.

Emergent literacy[25] or **emergent learners** are terms used to describe the developmental process by which students acquire language skills. Literacy begins in infancy when children learn how to speak. Reading and writing literacy emerge from these early beginnings as children encounter books and print in their environment. Traditionally, students have been evaluated as finished products who either did or did not develop skills at a certain level of performance by a set deadline. In contrast, **emergent learners** become readers and writers at a pace that develops their individual skills. For example, children in a typical kindergarten class will vary widely in their reading skills. Some recognize letters, others read words, and still others can read entire books. In classrooms that use a developmental approach, none is judged to be deficient, but rather as progressing at a particular level of literacy that is developing or emerging. Emphasis is placed on individual learners and their progress toward the goals of being able to read many different kinds of material to discover new ideas, explore new words, find information and solve problems that are real and interesting to them.

A **community of learners**[26] describes the full and interactive participation of both teachers and students as they explore and respond to ideas and experiences in the classroom. Teachers in these learning communities are not information givers, but colearners in the classroom, working to expand their own learning and that of their students.

Developmental spelling is sometimes referred to as **invented spelling**. Both terms refer to the developing ability of students to create symbols for what they want to say in writing. Emilia Ferreiro and Ana Teberosky,[27] educators who study the way children construct their writing system, believe that standard spelling proficiency develops over a period of time, as children discover that letters and sounds go together. Gradually, their efforts to communicate ideas in writing to others lead students to standardize their spelling.

Miscues and **miscue analysis** are terms developed by Kenneth Goodman.[28] Miscues, according to Goodman, are "deviations from expected responses to the print in oral reading." They involve inaccurate identification of words or the insertion of words or meanings not contained in the reading. Research in reading indicates that readers notice only enough of individual words to confirm their expectations in reading, and these "miscues" reflect the reader's attempt to make sense of what they are reading. Readers predict what is coming next, in terms of their own understanding and experience. They make inferences and merge them with what is already known, until what is gained from the text is a combination of what the reader brings to the text and the intention of the writer. A formal assessment of these miscues that uses developed guidelines and procedures is called a miscue analysis.

WHAT DO YOU
THINK? Have you encountered any of these terms in your reading? In what ways do you consider yourself an emergent learner? Can you see yourself as part of a community of learners? What do you do when you encounter unknown words in your own reading?

XII. Resources for Teaching

Many of the books annotated in this section were written by teachers and educators who have moved into more integrated methods of language learning in their own classrooms. These teachers share their ideas about classroom organization, learning strategies, materials, use of space, daily schedules and successful activities. You will want to explore a few chapters in each of these books to get an idea of the help you can receive from these colleagues in print. Other materials listed in this section are part of the current literature and will be referenced in many articles that you read. Each of these books is a favorite of many practicing teachers. Knowledge of these writings will help establish common grounds for discussions with your colleagues who are experienced teachers.

Thinking and Learning Together: Curriculum and Community in a Primary Classroom[29] by Bobbi Fisher describes ways to integrate language learning throughout a first-grade curriculum. The author explores different uses of literature, reading, writing, portfolio assessment, and ways to integrate language learning in math, science and social studies. There is also a chapter on communicating with parents and involving them actively in the classroom program. Bobbi Fisher is also the author of *Joyful Learning: A Whole Language Kindergarten*,[30] a practical guide used by many practicing teachers to integrate language learning at the kindergarten level.

Invitations: Changing as Teachers and Learners, K–12[31] by Regie Routman is full of mini-lessons for the beginning teacher or experienced teachers who want to move their classroom programs into a more integrated approach. There is information about: integrating language learning throughout the curriculum; guided reading; literature response logs; independent reading; journal writing; reading and writing strategies; and ways to help at-risk students. Most teachers are familiar with Regie Routman's *Transitions: From Literature to Literacy*,[32] which chronicles her decision to develop a literature-based program in her classroom.

In the Middle: Writing, Reading and Learning with Adolescents[33] by Nancie Atwell is a classic handbook of ideas for developing writer's workshops in the middle school. Her program can easily be adapted to late primary and intermediate grade levels and includes ideas for organizing and conducting independent writing sessions, mini-lessons and author's chair. Also included are suggestions for arranging classroom spaces and classroom management. Also by Nancie Atwell, *Coming to Know: Writing to Learn in the Intermediate Grades*[34] is a collection of articles by fourteen classroom teachers who describe strategies and materials for helping students use language and literature across the curriculum.

Awakening to Literacy,[35] edited by Hillel Goelman, Antoinette A. Oberg and Frank Smith, is a collection of essays by 14 internationally known researchers who have observed that children are powerful learners who grow into literacy as part of gaining mastery over their environments.

Ideas and Insights: Language Arts in the Elementary School,[36] edited by Dorothy Watson, contains ideas and strategies to use for language learning in grades K–6. Each idea has been successfully used by an experienced teacher and can easily be adapted to individual classroom programs. Activities include games such as "Language Detectives," "Literacy Olympics" and "Pasta Potpourri."

The Elements of the Whole Language Program by Andrea Butler (op. cit.) identifies ten elements of a whole language program, including: reading aloud from quality literature; shared reading of rhymes, songs, poems and stories; reading independently; reading and responding to literature in small groups; individual reading conferences; recording oral language; modeled writing; sharing with an audience; and content area work that uses reading and writing strategies to research and explore ideas.

What's Whole in Whole Language? by Kenneth Goodman (op. cit.) describes the essential features of a whole language approach to language learning in easy-to-understand terms. If you teach in a school that has adopted whole language methods or must explain this approach to parents, this is an excellent statement of the philosophy of holistic education.

Beginning in Whole Language: A Practical Guide[37] by Kristen Schlosser and Vicki Phillips is a good collection of classroom activities that will provide students opportunities to use language learning throughout the curriculum. The authors provide pictures, examples and instructions for creating centers, games, big books, journals, logs and a writing suitcase. There are helpful forms for evaluating progress in language development and sample letters, bulletins and newsletters to use as models in home–school communication.

WHAT DO YOU THINK?   When you have examined several of these books, reflect on the ones that seem to speak most directly to your present experience, concerns and professional values.

XIII. Reflections

From a Teacher's Journal—Dick Koblitz, Third Grade

The reflections of practicing teachers will be found in this section in each chapter of the text. Teachers who share their ideas and reflections in these journal entries see themselves as continually growing and changing, as they learn new ways to introduce language and literature into their classroom programs.

If someone had asked me what my philosophy of teaching and learning was when I started teaching twenty years ago, I would not have been able to articulate it. For the first ten years of my career I tried very hard to teach my students the prescribed curriculum, primarily by means of textbooks, lots of workbooks, skill sheets and a very didactic pedagogy. I worried about classroom management and discipline and did not realize there was any connection between behavior and instruction. I did not know or understand why I taught as I did, other than it was what everyone else was doing.

Today, I teach very differently. I have become a learner again, as well as a teacher. I question myself more and think about what I am doing and why I am doing it. I rarely use a textbook, except as a resource, or a workbook or skill sheet, unless it is a cloze exercise or an exercise the children themselves have created. Instruction is much more activity-based, with more modeling and student-to-student interaction.

It has been a tremendous change for my students and me, and one that has occurred slowly over the years. I moved to a schedule that included time for reading aloud each day, daily journal writing, guided and independent reading and larger blocks of time for work related to a theme unit of study. I stopped using the basal reader and accompanying workbooks and the individual texts for spelling, English, handwriting and phonics. I discontinued homogeneously-based reading groups as a means of organizing my reading program and began to set up literature study groups. It was the biggest risk I have ever taken. But the children loved it. The first year of this change, students did more real reading and writing than in any previous year and scored higher on the basal reader test I had to administer at the end of the year than any class I had ever had before.

TRYING OUT THE CHAPTER IDEAS

1. How do you use the **What Do You Think?** questions that follow each section of the chapter? Do you like to respond mentally or do you find it more helpful to write your responses? You might want to meet with other class members to discuss your responses. If you are keeping a journal to record and reflect on your responses to the text, you might want to note observations you make in the classroom that correspond to ideas presented in the text. You might also want to add articles, cartoons and photocopied excerpts from your professional reading about language learning.

2. College/university language arts methods classes sometimes adopt their own mascot to send home with a different person each class period. When the journal and mascot are returned, students read an account of the mascot's visit. Are there other students in your class who might like to join you in an activity like this? How might this kind of participation benefit you as a teacher?

3. Which of the learning theories described in the Perspectives section above seems to explain learning in a way that makes sense to you?

4. What kind of teacher do you imagine yourself becoming? How will you want to interact with your students? What will you want your classroom to look like?

5. When you recall your experiences as an elementary student, what do you remember about your own language arts instruction?

6. Do you enjoy reading? Why or why not?

7. What are your favorite kinds of reading? What was the last (non-textbook) book you read? Magazine? Newspaper?

8. Observe a classroom where language learning is integrated into the curriculum. If you are not currently enrolled in a field experience, your instructor will know teachers who welcome visitors. Record what you observe in your journal. What features described in this chapter do you notice?

Notes

1. C. S. Lewis, *The Voyage of the Dawn Treader* (New York: Macmillan, 1952), p. 175.
2. Jerome Bruner, *Toward a Theory of Instruction* (Cambridge, Mass.: Harvard University Press, 1966).
3. James Britton, *Language and Learning* (Montclair, N.J.: Boynton/Cook, 1970).
4. Lev Vygotsky, *Thought and Language* (Cambridge, Mass.: MIT Press, 1962).
5. Janet Emig, "Writing as a Model of Learning," in *College Composition and Communication* 28(1977):122–128.
6. Lev Vygotsky, *Thought and Language* (Cambridge, Mass.: MIT Press, 1962).
7. A. Applebee, J. Langer, and I. V. S. Mullis, *The Nation's Report Card: Learning to Be Literate in America* (Princeton, N.J.: National Assessment of Educational Progress, 1987).
8. Christopher Thaiss, *Language Across the Curriculum in the Elementary Grades* (Urbana, Ill.: National Council of Teachers of English, 1985).
9. Eric Carle, *The Very Quiet Cricket: A Multisensory Book* (New York: Philomel, 1990).
10. Eric Carle, *Rooster's Off To See the World* (New York: Picture Book Studio, 1991).
11. Ezra Jack Keats, *Regards to the Man in the Moon* (New York: Four Winds Press, 1981).
12. Donald Graves, "Building Portfolios: Keeping a Good Idea Growing," conference sponsored by Southern Illinois University at Edwardsville and Illini TAWL, Belleville, Ill., November 22, 1994.
13. Nancy White Carlstrom, *Light: Stories of a Small Kindness* (Waltham, Mass.: Little, Brown, 1990).
14. Thomas Pettepiece and Anatoly Aleksin, eds., *Face to Face: A Collection of Stories by Celebrated Soviet and American Writers* (East Rutherford, N.J.: Philomel, 1990).
15. Emily Cheney Neville, *The China Year* (Scranton, Penn.: HarperCollins, 1991).
16. Shannon K. Jacobs, *Song of the Giraffe* (Waltham, Mass.: Little, Brown, 1991).
17. L. P. Martinez, "Principal as Artist: A Model for Transforming a School Community," unpublished dissertation, December 1989.
18. Dorothy Watson, Carolyn Burke, and Jerome Harste, *Whole Language: Inquiring Voices* (New York: Scholastic, 1989).
19. Kenneth Goodman, *What's Whole in Whole Language?* (Portsmouth, N.H.: Heinemann, 1986).
20. Frank Smith, *Understanding Reading*, 2nd ed. (New York: Holt, Rinehart & Winston, 1978).
21. Andrea Butler, *The Elements of the Whole Language Program* (Crystal Lake, Ill.: Rigby, 1988).
22. Bess Altwerger, Carol Edelsky, and Barbara Flores, *Whole Language: What's the Difference?* (Portsmouth, N.H.: Heinemann, 1991).

23. Yetta Goodman, Bess Altwerger, and Ann Marek, *Print Awareness in Pre-school Children* (Tucson, Ariz.: University of Arizona, 1991).

24. Yetta Goodman, "Kidwatching: Observing Children in the Classroom," in *Observing the Language Learner*, edited by A. Jaggar and M. Trika Smith-Burke (Newark, Del.: International Reading Association, 1985).

25. Dorothy Strickland and Lesley Mandel Morrow, *Emerging Literacy: Young Children Learn to Read and Write* (Newark, Del.: International Reading Association, 1989).

26. Mary Kenner Glover, *A Community of Learners: An Insider's View of Whole Language* (Tempe, Ariz.: Awakening Seed Press, 1986).

27. Emilia Ferreiro and Ana Teberosky, *Literacy Before Schooling* (Portsmouth, N.H.: Heinemann, 1982).

28. Kenneth Goodman, *Miscue Analysis: Applications to Reading Instruction* (Urbana, Ill.: National Council of Teachers of English, 1973).

29. Bobbi Fisher, *Thinking and Learning Together: Curriculum and Community in a Primary Classroom* (Portsmouth, N.H.: Heinemann, 1995).

30. Bobbi Fisher, *Joyful Learning: A Whole Language Kindergarten* (Portsmouth, N.H.: Heinemann, 1991).

31. Regie Routman, *Invitations: Changing as Teachers and Learners, K–12* (Chicago, Ill.: Rigby, 1992).

32. Regie Routman, *Transitions: From Literature to Literacy* (Portsmouth, N.H.: Heinemann, 1988).

33. Nancie Atwell, *In the Middle: Writing, Reading and Learning with Adolescents* (Portsmouth, N.H.: Boynton/Cook, 1987).

34. Nancie Atwell, ed., *Coming to Know: Writing to Learn in the Intermediate Grades* (Portsmouth, N.H.: Heinemann, 1989).

35. Hillel Goelman, Antoinette A. Oberg, and Frank Smith, eds., *Awakening to Literacy* (Portsmouth, N.H.: Heinemann, 1984).

36. Dorothy Watson, ed., *Ideas and Insights: Language Arts in the Elementary School* (Urbana, Ill.: National Council of Teachers of English, 1987).

37. Kristen Schlosser and Vicki L. Phillips, *Beginning in Whole Language: A Practical Guide* (New York: Scholastic, 1991).

CHAPTER TWO

Reading Aloud

WHAT'S HAPPENING HERE? Children enjoy hearing books read aloud by classroom visitors. The school principal shares Eric Carle's *The Very Quiet Cricket* and helps introduce a study of insects in this kindergarten classroom.

"There is no frigate like a book to take us lands away . . ."
—Emily Dickinson[1]

LOOKING AHEAD   1. Why is it important to read aloud?
2. At what grade levels is reading aloud appropriate?
3. What kinds of literature can be read aloud?
4. How do you know if a book is a good one to read aloud?
5. What are some good resources for selecting books to read aloud?

IN 25 WORDS   Reading aloud to students aids language development, increases com-
OR LESS   prehension, enriches vocabulary, develops an interest in reading, and
creates a bond between reader and listeners.

I. Focus: Reading Aloud in the Classroom

Nearly everyone has had the experience of being read to, and perhaps you
have already had the experience of reading aloud to others. Reading aloud
is one of the most basic and important language-learning activities you can
provide for your students. Through this daily activity you can share the
language richness of prose and poetry and introduce study themes, authors
and the genres of literature. You can also share your own interests and
broaden the interests of your students. When you read aloud from a book
with enthusiasm and genuine interest, you model an adult response to
reading and demonstrate ways to make reading aloud appealing to listeners.

The activity of reading aloud is an intensely social activity. A unique
relationship is formed between reader and listener that crosses age and
gender differences to create a special bond between them. Many people
remember being read to as children, either by relatives or a favorite teacher.
Although you might not remember anything else about third grade, you can
probably still recall the book your teacher read every afternoon after lunch.

Reading aloud is truly the cornerstone of language learning in the classroom. It is not an optional activity to be included as time allows, but an
integral part of language arts instruction. It is through reading aloud that
children are drawn to books and begin to experience reading as a pleasurable
activity. When they have been exposed to the power and beauty of language
in well-written literature, students develop reading tastes that influence their
own reading selections. Books read aloud can increase student interest in

reading the same book, one by the same author, books in the same genre or other books on the same topic.

WHAT DO YOU THINK? What memories do you have of being read to at home or at school? Who read to you? What did you enjoy the most about being read to? What kinds of books were read to you? Do you remember a particular book being read at school?

II. The Importance of Reading Aloud

If you were read aloud to as a child at home or in school by your teacher, you will have some idea of the importance of reading aloud. Perhaps this is how you were introduced to the magical world of books—through rhymes, adventure, mystery, humor and information about interesting things. Through experiences with reading aloud, you have lived vicariously in other times and places, observed fantasy lands and explored the minds and hearts of ordinary people and the great heroes and heroines of literature. If this was your experience, you will be enthusiastic about reading aloud to your class because you are convinced of the pleasure it brings to listeners.

But reading aloud can provide other benefits for your students. At every grade level, it can enrich and expand their vocabulary, increase their skills in reading comprehension and improve the quality of their writing. Wigfield and Asher[2] found that the positive effects of reading aloud are extended by increasing the amount of time spent reading aloud and by improving the quality of materials selected for this purpose. Carol Chomsky[3] observed that reading aloud is most successful in promoting progress in learning when the levels of vocabulary and sentence structure are slightly above that used by students. Dorothy Cohen[4] found a high correlation between reading aloud and vocabulary development in children, and W. B. Elley[5] noted that children can sometimes learn the meaning of new words from a single exposure to a book read aloud. According to Cohen and Feitelson et al.,[6] reading stories aloud increases competency in reading comprehension. Feitelson also noted that frequent reading aloud in the classroom improves children's decoding (sounding out words) abilities.

Reading aloud increases the ability of children to predict when they read, a skill closely tied to competency in reading comprehension.[7] Research also indicates that reading literature aloud improves composition skills, including the increased use of complex phrases, clauses and sentences in writing. Children of all socioeconomic backgrounds seem to benefit equally. In their observation of natural readers (children who come to school already knowing how to read), researchers found that they were invariably those who were read to from an early age.[8] The national commission appointed to summarize the findings of research on reading concluded in *Becoming a Nation of Readers: The Report of the Commission on Reading*[9] that "the single most important activity for building the knowledge and skills eventually required for reading appears to be reading aloud to children."

What has been your experience of reading aloud to others? What do you most enjoy about reading aloud? Is there a particular type of book you like to read aloud? If you had to identify a single value for reading aloud, what would that be?

III. Looking into Classrooms

Kindergarten Level

After lunch, Mrs. Jamison pulls up a small chair in front of the room and children leave their tables to gather around her. Several students lie down or sprawl sideways at the back and sides of the group, so they do not touch or disturb anyone else.

"Is everyone comfortable?" Mrs. Jamison asks.

When the children nod their heads, Mrs. Jamison opens the book *Charlotte's Web*[10] and begins to read Chapter 11, "The Miracle." In this chapter, Wilbur the pig is spared being turned into bacon by the intervention of his friend, Charlotte the spider. Mrs. Jamison moves her audience into the story by taking time to describe the setting in a dramatic way. She looks down at the first sentence, puts it in her mind, and then looks up at the children sitting around her.

"The next day . . . (pause) . . . was foggy," she says, taking her time. She looks down at the book again. "Everything on the farm . . . (pause) . . . was dripping wet. The grass looked like a magic carpet . . . (pause) . . . The asparagus patch . . . (pause) . . ."

At this point, Mrs. Jamison looks up again at the children. ". . . looked like a silver forest."

Several children say, "Oooh . . ."

"What's asparagus?" Carrie asks.

"Green. It's a green vegetable," Michael says.

"You're right," Mrs. Jamison says. "Asparagus is a green vegetable that grows straight up in stalks. In the morning, with all the dew, asparagus plants look like little silver trees when the sun hits them. Who has seen asparagus?"

Only a few hands go up. "I'll bring some from my garden tomorrow, so you can see what it looks like."

Carrie is satisfied and Mrs. Jamison continues. In the paragraph that follows, she describes the web that Charlotte wove the night before and gestures with her hand as she pretends to read the message written in the web, "SOME PIG!"

When she reads that the hired man brushes his hand across his eyes in disbelief upon seeing the web, she uses the same gesture and stares into the corner. Most of the children, caught up in the story, turn around to look, expecting to see the miraculous web. "I'm seeing things," she whispers, reading the hired man's words, and the children lean toward her in anticipation.

When she finishes reading the chapter, Mrs. Jamison closes the book and waits for a minute, allowing the class some time to soak in the experience. Then she asks, "What do you think Charlotte's web looked like?"

"Silky," Hannah offers, "with little dewdrops on it, like the spider webs in our yard in the morning."

"I think it was HUMONGOUS!" Brian exclaims, gesturing the size with his outstretched arms. "It would have to be big for everyone to see it."

"And it has 'SOME PIG!' written on it," Jamie adds.

"Would you like to see how Garth Williams [the illustrator] saw the web?" Mrs. Jamison asks.

"Yes!" chorus the children, and she shows them the illustrations. Then she hands the open book to Amy, who has moderate sight loss and sees only shapes at more than five feet. Amy holds the book up to her face and smiles as the outline of the web comes into view.

"Does it look like you imagined, Amy?" the teacher asks.

"Just like I thought," she answers, "only smaller."

"How about the rest of you?" she asks.

"Not big enough," Brian agrees. "It needs to take up the whole page."

Mrs. Jamison asks if he would like to draw his own idea of the web and he is enthusiastic. In fact, everyone wants to draw a web, and the teacher is ready with paper and crayons. A large spider lives in a glass aquarium on the corner table, and groups of children crowd around to notice how she has spun her web. Amy picks up a magnifying glass to observe the spider and some of the others follow suit.

"Wow, look at all the hair on this spider!" Ashley exclaims.

On the front chalkboard the teacher writes the words "SOME PIG!" in response to the requests of several children. Others ask for the words "Wilbur," "Charlotte," "pig," "spider" and "web."

"If there are other words you want to write, just write the sounds you hear," Mrs. Jamison reminds them. She hands a sheet with the words written on it to Amy. Everyone is busy drawing and writing about the story, including Amy. She writes her story on paper with wide lines and fills up the art paper with a detailed picture of a spider. As they finish, students show their pictures and read aloud what they have written to Mrs. Jamison, the student teacher or the classroom aide.

WHAT HAPPENED HERE? ONE PERSPECTIVE

Mrs. Jamison introduced her class to a favorite children's story, one that was too difficult for them to read on their own, but very suitable for reading aloud in kindergarten. By reading them a chapter book in addition to the many picture books she shares with them daily, Mrs. Jamison is modeling the idea that wonderful stories are found in books with chapters and few pictures. At this point, most of the students are looking forward to the time when they can read chapter books on their own. This is a valuable attitude to begin building as soon as possible because many children begin to lose interest in reading when chapter books are introduced.

Mrs. Jamison asks the primary teachers in her school if the book she has chosen is one they plan to study in guided reading or for reading aloud. Although books can be examined at many levels at various ages, she is sensitive to the fact that many teachers have special books they like to introduce to their classes. Because Mrs. Jamison reads widely and feels comfortable choosing from a wide range of books, she extends this professional courtesy to other teachers who may wish to study the same book with their students from year to year.

This particular book was a favorite read-aloud of her own children, and from her college studies, she also knows that E. B. White's *Charlotte's Web* is a Newbery Award book and will offer her students exposure to a classic in children's literature. Each chapter moves forward in an interesting way, has well-defined characters with intriguing personalities and contains ideas that engage children of all ages: honor, friendship, loyalty, life and death. Primary and intermediate teachers often continue reading from E. B. White stories, such as *Stuart Little*[11] or *The Trumpet of the Swan*.[12]

Although Mrs. Jamison has read the book several times in the past, she reviews it before reading it aloud to get a renewed sense of the story. Each time she does this, she is surprised at how differently she relates to the story. She hopes that the book will become a favorite with her students as they grow older. Before each reading session, she plans how she will read the first few words, the first sentence, first paragraph and first page. The pace at which she began reading may have seemed slow and tedious in the retelling above, but the teacher knows that she must create a mood for something mysterious and wonderful to happen. She wants to draw her students into the story so that they can experience everything the author intended.

As part of her preparation, Mrs. Jamison also planned how she will share the few illustrations with her students. One of her goals for reading aloud is to help children develop their powers of imagination. She encourages them to form pictures in their own minds while she reads and then returns to the illustrations when she finishes the chapter. She has also established a routine for sharing illustrations with Amy, who is partially sighted. It is her practice to check often with Amy for suggestions about how best to support her participation in the classroom. At the beginning of the year she offered Amy a copy of any book she read aloud in class, so she could look closely at the illustrations. Because Amy wants to participate in the same way as everyone else, she soon asked to look at the pictures later. When Mrs. Jamison shared *The Snowman*,[13] a wordless book, with the children, Amy chose to stay with her decision and look at the pictures afterward. As a result of this experience, she changed her mind and decided to have her own copy of *Deep in the Forest*[14] when this book was shared with the class. "I could use my imagination for the snowman book," she said, "but when I looked at the pictures afterward, I wanted to talk about them with everyone else."

When Carrie asked about the asparagus, she was trying to make a picture in her mind. Many of the children in this kindergarten class have had limited experience with a wide variety of foods, and Mrs. Jamison was happy to see evidence of Carrie's curiosity. She allowed the students to make a response to Carrie before she added her own experience. She did not consider the question to be an interruption, nor did the rest of the class. The brief exchange did not seem to impair the flow of the story. The meanings of several words might have been discussed before reading began, but Mrs. Jamison believes that the reason for wanting to know the meaning of words comes from listening to a good story and wanting to understand everything about it. She also knows that her students will learn new words more quickly and permanently when they can attach their own meaning to them. In her teaching journal, she reminds herself to bring some fresh asparagus from her garden tomorrow and to cook a few spears to bring on Wednesday for tasting day.

From this core activity of reading aloud, every child in the class has participated in an activity that practices the skills of listening, speaking, reading and writing. In addition, their responses to listening to the story gave them a reason to observe the spider closely and to express themselves artistically. Although a magnifying glass was always part of the science center in years past, Amy's use of the glass has prompted more children to examine things closely, so now Mrs. Jamison has enough on hand for everyone to use.

Primary Level

When Mr. Hernandez laughed out loud during independent reading at the antics of Weeps and Wol in *Owls in the Family*,[15] his third-grade class demanded that he read the book to them. This was not the way he had planned to introduce a theme study on birds, but it could hardly have been more successful.

Before he begins to read, Mr. Hernandez checks to see that he is standing where Tony can see him easily. Although he wears two hearing aids, Tony also relies on lipreading to supplement what he does not hear. If Mr. Hernandez stands with the light behind him, Tony cannot see him without looking into the glare. Just as he has learned not to talk when he is writing on the blackboard, Mr. Hernandez remembers to keep the book down and away from his face, so that Tony's view of his speaking is not obstructed.

Today, Mr. Hernandez is reading Chapter 6 of *Owls in the Family*, which is a hilarious description of a pet parade that dissolves into chaos with the introduction of a surprise contestant. The class giggles and laughs out loud as they listen to Billy get his pets ready for the parade:

> I went back to putting the dolls' clothes on the owls, and it wasn't easy. Weeps just stood there and whimpered while I pulled a pink dress over his head and pinned a floppy hat on him. But Wol took one look at the sailor suit I had for him and then he rumpled himself up into a ball and began to clack his beak and hiss. (p. 46)

Mr. Hernandez finishes reading the chapter, closes the book and allows his listeners time to savor the experience. "Who's ready to work on bird books?" he asks, and class members pull out their notebooks to do individual and group research on the birds they have selected.

Mr. Hernandez found *Owls in the Family* as he was reviewing possible books to enhance a theme study about birds. The book drew interest as a stand-alone story, but it also prompted students to bring in owl pellets and feathers for the science table. Other books and magazines about owls have come from home, and one student brought a set of photographs of owls made by her father. Mr. Hernandez was amazed at the humorous bird stories students brought in from their families. These stories are being turned into books, which are popular choices to read during independent reading time.

If there is something that Tony misses in the story, he feels free to approach Mr. Hernandez after class to ask questions or read for himself. At the beginning of the year, Tony occasionally had outbursts of anger for no apparent reason. Now Mr. Hernandez realizes that Tony felt left out when he did not know why the class was laughing at something he missed or embarrassed when he did not understand instructions. He and the class have learned to support Tony's efforts to participate fully by making sure he hears and understands instructions and knows what is happening during playground games. Mr. Hernandez checks with Tony periodically for suggestions about how best to support his efforts to succeed.

Mr. Hernandez was delighted that his class asked him to share this particular book with them. Weeps and Wol are memorable characters, and he knows that *Owls in the Family* will be picked up and read this year and next as a favorite. This is especially important at the end of third grade, since students typically fall away from independent reading between the ages of eight and nine.

Intermediate Level

Sixth graders troop into Bill Chamberlain's classroom from P.E., hot, tired and cranky. Mr. Chamberlain used to hate this time of day, a period to suffer through together. He holds up a book for the class to see as they enter the door. He is not surprised to see the principal come in at the end of the line and take a seat in the back of the room. Students pick up the pace of getting to their desks, and as soon as everything is quiet he begins to read the next chapter in *Maniac Magee*[16] by Jerry Spinelli. If the class had trouble settling down, he would have moved into reading by asking where the story ended the day before. He alternates between standing in front of the class and sitting on the edge of his desk, remembering to stay above the heads of his students so his voice will carry to the back of the room.

Mr. Chamberlain picked up *Maniac Magee* to read one morning during independent reading time (Chapter 3). It was one of the bonus books he selected for the class library from the school book club (Chapter 4). He also knew it was a Newbery book, and one of his professional goals is to eventually read all of these award-winning books. When he finished the book, he could not wait to share it with his class. He tried it out on the special education teacher who works with his literature program, and she agreed that it was a good book to read aloud. Besides being a good story, *Maniac Magee* would touch the racial and poverty experiences of many of their students and provide insights into cultural differences and homelessness.

Mr. Chamberlain was fairly certain his class would like the book, but he was still amazed at the level of positive response the book received. Nearly every student in the room wanted to order the book in the next round of book club orders. Every chapter held their interest, and the discussions that sometimes followed the reading indicated a depth of identification with the characters. Today, Mr. Chamberlain is looking forward to their reactions to Grayson, the old man who takes the homeless Maniac under his wing. Yesterday, Maniac untied Cobble's Knot, a huge ball of tangled string that hangs in Cobble's Pizza Parlor. The special education teacher brought in a huge ball of tangled twine this morning and suspended it from the ceiling with a sign that said "Chamberlain's Knot." The class was delighted. When the principal asked about the knot, they invited him in to listen to the story.

Mr. Chamberlain looks over at Derek, who is getting out paper and pencil to draw during the story. At the beginning of the year, Derek was a wreck during this final period of the day. Overstimulated and distraught, he often resorted to throwing things and hitting other students when they returned from P.E. Mr. Grange, the physical education teacher, began to let him cool down early from physical activity by letting him round up the equipment or run an errand to the office. This helped some, but Derek still had problems staying in his desk during the read-aloud session, and the usual policy of letting him walk around the back of the room to drain off energy distracted other students.

It was also evident that he wanted to hear the stories read aloud, so he and Mr. Chamberlain brainstormed ideas about how he could release his extra energy and still listen to the story. They decided on drawing or squeezing the small rubber ball Derek kept in his desk. Mr. Chamberlain announced that anyone was free to draw while he read aloud and a few others joined Derek.

The class actually cheered yesterday when Maniac won a year's worth of pizza for untangling the knot, a response that was in stark contrast to the previous book he had tried out on them. There was no reaction at all for the first two chapters. "Too bad," he thought. "It was a great book and all the kids last year liked it." But that was one thing he learned early on about reading aloud to a class: If a book doesn't click in the first few chapters, go to something else. With all the thousands of good books in the world, he knew there was no point in wasting time with something they did not like. He left his copy in the library center for anyone who wanted to finish the book.

WHAT HAPPENED HERE? ONE PERSPECTIVE   Mr. Chamberlain discovered that not all good books appeal to every audience. And books selected for awards on the basis of excellence in writing are not always the best ones to read aloud. In the process of following his own reading goals, he discovered *Maniac Magee*, which he read and liked. Because his own experience with the book was positive, he was able to share it with interest and enthusiasm. He depended on the response of his students to continue, because the

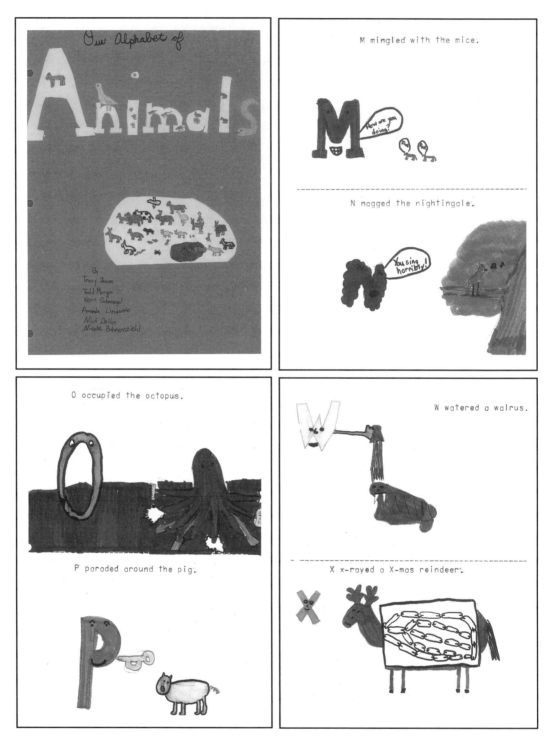

Figure 2.1
A fifth-grade class created this alphabet book for the kindergarten after studying alliteration.

whole point of reading aloud is to create a pleasant experience with books. The book he tried previously had worked with another class, but not with his current students. Differences in experiences, maturity and interests will influence different tastes in books, so he wisely moved on to another book.

Class response to *Maniac Magee* was rewarding and created a pleasant time of day for everyone. Maniac Magee was a strong character and the powerful story stood on its own. But the topics of racism, homelessness, aging and heroism were interesting enough to encourage reflection without being preachy and pedagogic. Indeed, it is through the reading of such compelling stories that some of the most meaningful and insightful discussions with young people are made possible.

Mr. Chamberlain worked with Derek to find ways for him to participate in the read-aloud session. They found a temporary solution, but will need to continue finding ways to help Derek realize full participation for this activity and others.

WHAT DO YOU THINK? Do you agree with the methods that these teachers used to include students with special challenges in the reading-aloud activity? Can you think of other methods they could use to include these children? What similarities do you notice among the teachers described? When you picture yourself reading aloud to a group of students, what age or grade level do you imagine? Can you think of several books you would enjoy reading aloud to this class? Why would you pick these particular books? How important do you think reading aloud is to the language arts programs in the classrooms described above?

IV. Preparing to Read Aloud

Selecting a book to read aloud will be guided by (1) your purpose for reading, (2) the experience and interests of your audience and (3) the books available to you from various resources.

Purpose for Reading Aloud

Teachers choose books to read aloud to:

Share enjoyment of a favorite book What kinds of stories and books do you enjoy? Reading aloud gives you the opportunity to share a good story from fictional favorites or interesting ideas and facts from nonfiction literature. As you increase your familiarity with children's literature through personal reading and class assignments, you will begin to build a list of books you want to share with your class. Talk with experienced teachers and ask them about books they have successfully read to their students. Look through the resource books mentioned at the end of this chapter and note the ones that attract your interest.

Introduce a topic or enhance a theme Topics in science, mathematics and social studies can be attractively presented through all types of literature, from poetry to historical fiction. Help students conceptualize large numbers by reading *How Much Is a Million?*[17] Try using the historical novel *April Morning*[18] by Howard Fast or the narrative poem "Paul Revere's Ride" by Henry Wadsworth Longfellow to introduce a study of the Revolutionary War. Ruth Heller's colorful books on nouns, verbs, adverbs and adjectives[19] feature creative verse and imaginative illustrations and are appropriate for use at all elementary grade levels. Investigate *The Random House Book of Poetry for Children*,[20] a collection of poems related to many topics. Read "Who Has Seen the Wind?" in this collection, written by Christina Rossetti, or *Thunder Cake*[21] by Patricia Polacco to begin a study of weather. The interaction of European settlers with Native Americans during colonial times is vividly portrayed in *The Courage of Sarah Noble*[22] for primary students and *Sign of the Beaver*[23] for intermediates.

Expose students to beautiful language and rich vocabulary Good literature provides students with a model for their own oral and written language. Books that generate laughter, stir the imagination or tap deep emotion usually contain language that is powerful and full of rhythmic pattern. Words that speak to the senses will enrich the vocabulary of your students and provide them with a quality listening experience.

Introduce a literary genre Reading aloud provides an excellent opportunity to introduce children to a wide variety of books. The resource books listed at the end of the chapter include annotations for picture books, folktales, myths, legends, poetry, contemporary fiction, historical fiction, biographies and modern fantasy. Included in the category of nonfiction are books on every topic imaginable: science, history, geography, the arts, sports, jokes and riddles, careers and hobbies. A more complete description and discussion of the various genres are found in Chapter 4.

Calm or restore positive interaction Never underestimate the power of a good book. There are difficult times in the average school day that can be improved by sharing a pleasurable experience with your class. Reading aloud offers everyone the opportunity to cool off, rest up and get interested in good stories and compelling ideas. Whenever possible, introduce humor into your interaction with students. Many practicing teachers keep copies of Shel Silverstein's *Where the Sidewalk Ends*[24] or Jack Prelutsky's *The New Kid on the Block: Poems*[25] on their desks. Reading a page or two from these popular collections of hilarious poetry is just what the doctor ordered for students and teachers who feel out-of-sorts with each other. Laughing together is good medicine, and it also models a positive way for students to make themselves feel better in stressful situations.

Never withdraw reading aloud as a punishment or threaten its withdrawal for undesirable behavior. In addition to the fact that reading aloud is the keystone of your language arts program, your goal as a teacher is to keep all associations with reading pleasant. Its restorative powers should be demonstrated whenever possible. The Resources for Teaching section at the end of this chapter lists other books you might want to have on hand for all occasions.

Experience and Interest of Your Audience

Matching up your particular class with just the right book is a skill to be practiced and learned. Begin by reading about books recommended for children of your students' age level. Ask your students and other children you know about the books they have read and enjoyed. Are there stories they would like to hear again? Do they have a favorite author? You might want to begin reading from the kind of book they already prefer. If they like animal adventure books like *Old Yeller*[26] and *The Incredible Journey*,[27] they will probably enjoy the antics of Weeps and Wol in *Owls in the Family* (op. cit.) or the escapades of the pet raccoon in *Rascal*.[28] Expand their awareness by choosing other types of books on favorite topics. Poetry about animals, non-fiction books that are packed with interesting animal facts, fantasy stories that feature animals with supernatural powers, biography and historical fiction that associate animals with historical characters, and animal picture book mysteries such as Graeme Base's *The Eleventh Hour*[29] are just a few of the possibilities.

Resources

You will want to choose from the very best books available when you read to your class. How will you know which books are the best? This important question is addressed more fully in the discussion of literature selection (Chapter 4), but there are ways to begin identifying high-quality books. If you have had a course in children's literature, you know about the Newbery and Caldecott Award books. These are books recognized for excellence in writing for children. You will remember from the discussion about Mr. Hernandez that well-written books do not always make satisfactory read-aloud books. Like Mr. Hernandez, you will discover that a certain book that is a favorite with one year's class may not be popular with the next. This is the trial and error part of reading aloud. On the other hand, certain books seem to find favor with a great number of listeners, and many of these are noted in resource books compiled by educators, librarians and parents. Several of these resources are annotated in the Resources for Teaching section at the end of this chapter and include examples of the books they recommend for reading aloud at various age levels.

You probably have noticed that many teachers have small libraries in their classrooms. Where do these books come from? In most cases, they have been collected by the individual teacher over a period of years. Sometimes you will inherit a book collection with your room, but this is the rare case. Parent groups will often help you begin or add to your library, but you will want to begin assembling a collection of books that you find personally appealing or which you believe might be helpful for your own teaching.

One of the best ways to begin a collection of read-aloud books is to borrow books from the public library or review the children's (PZ) collection in your college or university library. Knowing what you like will help you take advantage of special offerings at teacher's bookstores, library used-book sales and school book clubs. Building your own library will be a topic of discussion in Chapter 4. Before you begin teaching, you will want to explore the books available in your school and/or district media center. Talk to the librarian or browse on your own for titles listed as resource books at the end of this chapter.

When you have selected your book, it's time to **preview** the contents and **practice** reading it aloud.

Previewing

It is always a good idea to read any book you plan to read aloud all the way through before you share it with your class. Your own familiarity with the book will add to your ability to share its wealth to the fullest extent. Previewing a book before reading it aloud will allow you to spot any vocabulary or word pronunciations that might be unfamiliar. If there are parts of the story you think might lag or a great number of words that your listeners will not understand in the context of the story, you may omit them. It is not necessary to read every word just as it is printed. Just be sure that you keep the intention and spirit of the story. If too much must be omitted, it is better to choose something else.

Practicing

Reading aloud may look easy, but it is important to know how to do it in the best way possible in order to achieve the maximum results. One of the first things to consider is what the author wants to happen to readers or listeners as a result of reading his or her book. What can you do to help create the mood, so your listeners experience what was intended? You can begin by taking enough time to describe the setting in such a way that students can hear, see and feel what it would be like to be there. Remember that many students read around descriptive details in their own reading. This is a chance for them to experience the word pictures created by skillful writers. Speak the words of the characters so that they come alive for the listener. Use your voice to convey the mood—excitement, happiness, grief, anger, puzzlement—by varying the loudness, pitch and tone of your voice. Begin by reading slowly and:

Enjoy the book yourself. It is important to share something you are enthusiastic about. Your attitude toward what you are reading is impossible to conceal. It will be clearly communicated to your listeners, in both positive and negative terms.

Make a trial run. Practice reading parts of the book to someone else before you read it to your class. Friends, family members and other teachers are good possibilities. What is their response?

Record yourself. When you first begin to read aloud, try reading into a tape recorder or videotape yourself reading several pages. You can observe your pacing, style and voice qualities for areas that need improvement.

Stand still. Remember that students are trying to focus on what you are reading. If you pace or move around too much, this is distracting. An exception to this rule is the movement necessary to dramatize what you are reading. You may also want to recover the attention of a student by walking over to stand near him or her while you continue reading.

Let them wiggle. Do not be offended if younger students shift around while they are listening to you read. Just make sure that everyone has a comfortable space and is not being punched or poked because of crowding. Older children sometimes like to draw or doodle with a pencil while you read. People relax and enjoy being read to in a number of ways.

Draw them back. If there is slight but not major distraction, you may want to stop reading for a minute, look up at the class and wait. Say, "Is everyone ready?" or "Shall I go on?" Things will usually settle down. If not, it is time to stop anyway, with a comment like, "We'll get back to this later." If you suspect that the book may not hold interest for the class, you can take a straw poll by asking them to write "yes" or "no" on a slip of paper to put in a box on your desk. If the majority votes "yes," continue reading. If "no" votes predominate, choose something else. When this happens, be sure to offer the book to anyone who wants to continue reading it.

Almost any good reader can read aloud, but as most of us know from experience, the quality of this activity can vary widely. Reading is more than naming words and saying sentences aloud. Good reading creates a mood and catches listeners up into a feeling of being there. The story comes through you. Give it your best.

WHAT DO YOU THINK? With which of the preceding preparations do you feel most comfortable and confident? Which will you want to practice? Are there opportunities for you to begin practicing reading aloud to students or children now?

V. Including Everyone

Before you read aloud to your class, be sure you know about any special needs your students may have in terms of seeing, hearing and understanding you. Ordinarily, you will be briefed about any children who require additional supportive attention. It is always a good idea to schedule a conference with children who have any sight or hearing loss and those confined to wheelchairs because of physical challenges. Ask them what you can do to help them participate as fully as possible in the classroom. They not only have good ideas from their own experiences, but they also have preferences about how this support is offered.

You will want to stand or sit in a place where all students can see you. This is especially important for students who experience hearing loss because they may supplement the use of hearing aids with lipreading. Partially sighted students generally want to sit close during picture book reading so they can see illustrations more easily. You can also offer them their own copy to follow. You want everyone to have the chance to enjoy the beautiful, humorous or lively pictures in a good read-aloud book.

Children who are diagnosed with attention deficit disorder (ADD) can be planned for in a number of ways. (Note: A diagnosis of attention deficit disorder is made by a physician, who looks for symptoms of impulsive behavior, restlessness, and distraction that are disproportional to age or context.) It is important to remember that many children display this behavior to a greater or lesser degree in age- or context-appropriate ways. Our general expectations for student behavior are different for kindergartners than they are for sixth graders.

Although listening to stories is generally a favorite activity of all children, there are times when it is physically impossible for some children to sit still. Younger children may have to wander at the edges of the group if they are unable to sit still. Do not assume they aren't listening. Their bodies are making strenuous demands on them, but they usually follow the story and may surprise you with the extent to which they respond during subsequent discussions or artistic expression. Indicate to older students that you want them to enjoy the book you are reading aloud and brainstorm some ideas with them. Some possibilities include: sitting in the back of the room so they can get up and walk around (if it does not disturb the rest of the class); drawing or doodling; squeezing a small rubber ball; or tapping their feet on a sound-absorbent pad on the floor to drain off excess energy. Your goal is to help everyone enjoy these sessions as much as possible, providing the support necessary for each child to participate to the fullest extent.

What is the racial and cultural composition of your class? Use reference handbooks, such as those described at the end of this chapter, to find good read-aloud books that represent a wide range of cultures, particularly those that offer your students a chance to identify with the heroes and storytellers of their own cultural backgrounds. Read-aloud books can expand children's understanding of the values and ideals of other peoples of the world. By creating compelling characters for listeners to bond with, writers of these books help children feel a sense of kinship with children of other races and cultures as they face problems similar to theirs.

Books to Increase Understanding

The following books depict the variety of historical and contemporary experiences of Asian Americans. Students from Pacific Rim countries have histories, cultures and languages that are quite different from each other. The following books will help the reader begin to explore the experiences of children who have lived in these countries or been influenced by the cultures they contain.

Yang the Youngest and His Terrible Ear[30]   A young Chinese boy prefers playing baseball to playing the violin. This book explores the cultural values of two different families and examines stereotyping in an insightful and humorous manner.

Journey Home[31]   This is the story of Yuki and her family, who return from a World War II internment camp to continue their life as Japanese Americans on the West Coast of the United States. Although they were loyal Americans, they have lost everything because of their national origin. The first book in this story, *Journey to Topaz: A Story of the Japanese-American Evacuation,*[32] describes the tragic treatment of Japanese Americans after Pearl Harbor.

Year of Impossible Goodbyes[33]   This is a riveting story of a North Korean family during and after World War II. Sookan's family survives occupation by the

Japanese, only to be oppressed by the Communist Russian troops. An inspiring story of courage and family love awaits the reader.

A Boat to Nowhere[34] This book is a thrilling account of the tragic and courageous journey of Vietnamese boat people. It offers the reader insight into the reasons why they risked everything to seek a new life outside their country.

WHAT DO YOU THINK? Choose two books that represent two different Asian cultures. Compare the differences in culture that are described in each. How do the descriptions of childhood differ from your own? What experiences are similar to yours? How would you have reacted to the events in the story if you were the main character? What kinds of school experiences might have been valuable to you?

VI. Step-by-Step: Reading Aloud

The first sentence of a book is designed to catch your interest, so pay particular attention to the first sentence when you begin to read aloud. Open the book, look at your class, then look down at the book and read the first sentence slowly and with as much expression as possible. Beginning your reading this way will help you establish a manageable pace while you are getting used to reading. At first, most people tend to read too fast. Nervousness, involvement with the story and sheer momentum can propel you forward through a story in a blur. A slower pace will allow your listeners the opportunity to grasp any introductory information they will need to know to understand the story. It will also give you time to add expression for dramatic effect and draw your listeners into the book with you.

When you begin reading, remember to:

1. Take a deep breath.
2. Imagine the scene.
3. Create the story.
4. Slow down to add drama.
5. Read loud enough for everyone to hear.

You might want to make a sign that says **AYRTF** (Are You Reading Too Fast?) and put it somewhere in the room where you can see it while you are reading to help remind you to slow down. Remember also to read loud enough so that you can be heard easily in the back of the room. You do not want anyone to miss any part of what you are reading.

Imagine that you have decided to read *The Westing Game*.[35] On the first page, important elements of the mystery are established. How will you emphasize certain words or use a tone of voice to create questions in the minds of your listeners?

The sun sets in the west (just about everyone knows that), but Sunset Towers faced east. Strange!

Sunset Towers faced east and had no towers. This glittery, glassy apartment house stood alone on the Lake Michigan shore five stories high. Five empty stories high.

Then one day (it happened to be the Fourth of July), a most uncommon-looking delivery boy rode around town slipping letters under the doors of the chosen tenants-to-be. The letters were signed **Barney Northrup**.

The delivery boy was sixty-two years old, and there was no such person as Barney Northrup.

Contrast the ways you say "east" and "west," and alter your tone of voice when you say "Strange!" Then pause for a few seconds before you read the second piece of information, which culminates with the fact that Sunset Towers is currently empty. In the third paragraph, emphasize "uncommon-looking" and the name "Barney Northrup." And in the final sentence on the page, read slowly, emphasizing the age of the delivery boy and the word "was." Be sure to read this first page slowly and carefully so that the beginning of the puzzle is established firmly in the listeners' minds. When you look up at them at the end of this first page, you will see every eye on you. It is that kind of book.

WHAT DO YOU THINK? What has been your experience reading aloud? Is it a pleasant experience, or do you sometimes feel nervous? What kinds of preparation would help you feel less nervous?

VII. If This Is Your Situation

What will you do if the book you want to read contains questionable language or controversial topics? You might want to consider the following questions:

1. How comfortable are you with the language or topic? Reading a book aloud when there are things that make you feel uncomfortable or embarrassed will not work.
2. How distracting will the words or situations be to your audience? Your goal in reading aloud is to create a worthwhile experience for your listeners. Will certain words or events distract from the total effect of the story?
3. Can any words or sections of the story be deleted without seriously impairing the tone or purpose of the story?
4. What is the policy of your school or district school board with regard to questionable language or sensitive topics in literature? Check with your principal and other teachers in the school.

If you are uncomfortable with a book or have doubts about its appropriateness for your class, consider choosing another one. There are thousands of good books to read aloud.

WHAT DO YOU THINK?   When you read books aloud, what is your responsibility to your audience? What is the difference between reading a controversial book aloud and making it available for independent reading?

VIII. Evaluating Progress

When you read aloud, evaluation begins with your choice of a book to read and continues through your postreading assessment of the suitability of the book, the quality of your own performance and the response of your students. This information, in turn, is used to make future instructional decisions about what to read next.

Goals   What did you want to happen as a result of reading aloud to your students? An enjoyable experience? An introduction to new ideas, people or places? A vicarious experience? The degree to which you were successful can be evaluated directly or indirectly. Ask your students what they enjoyed about what you read or what interested them most. The response to these questions will measure the degree to which your students involved themselves in the reading. If you read aloud to introduce them to a new genre, do you notice them choosing to read this kind of literature with more frequency during independent reading or for reading conferences? Or do they attempt this kind of writing themselves?

You will also want to consider if your goals were realistic. Perhaps you planned to read aloud two chapters of the book. Your students were obviously interested during the first chapter, but grew restless as the second chapter progressed. With beginning listeners, five minutes of reading aloud may test their attention span, while other groups can listen for well over an hour. As you are reading, notice the response of your students. Are they leaning forward, eager to hear the next sentence? Are they listening in a relaxed fashion? Or is there constant movement and shuffling, whispering or a display of physical discomfort? You will want to stop reading as soon as inattention begins, so that only pleasant associations are made with reading aloud. As students become more experienced at listening, you can gradually lengthen this time. Between ten and twenty minutes per session is recommended, depending on the age and maturity of your students.

Students   Your selection of a book to read aloud was originally based on what you knew about the interests and maturity of your class. Did the story develop a new interest or expand an existing one? Did their responses indicate an understanding of what was read? Enjoyment? If there were problems, did they seem to be from physical discomfort or social distraction? Help your students learn how to make themselves comfortable during reading time by encouraging them to experiment with putting their heads down, closing their eyes, leaning back in their chairs or otherwise assuming a relaxed position. When students are assembled around you on the floor, preclude disruption from episodes of "He's touching me!" or "Stop crowding!" by waiting to read until everyone has a comfortable space to listen.

The Book Did you enjoy reading the book aloud to your students? Did they seem to enjoy listening to it? If students are inattentive from the beginning of a read-aloud session, it may be a matter of a good book that is unsuitable for reading aloud. Good writing does not always mean good reading aloud. Some books may not be interesting to your particular class. They may not be able to identify with the characters or action of the story, or you may have read past their ability to pay attention.

The Teacher Did you remember to read at a measured pace? Did you read with expression and create a sense of drama about the story you were reading? If you were reading facts and information, did you pause enough to allow students to take in a succession of interesting ideas? Did you draw them in at the beginning and stop before attention waned? Did you allow your students to be comfortable while they listened? Many teachers find it helpful to keep a read-aloud journal where they record the names of the books read aloud and a brief account of the response from their class. This enables them to find patterns in class and individual reactions to particular books and ideas. It also provides a record of progress that will give direction to future sessions of reading aloud.

WHAT DO YOU THINK? Do you remember being distracted when someone was reading aloud to you? What created the distraction? What could the reader have done to eliminate or reduce the distraction?

IX. Creating Partners

Nearly one hundred years ago, the educator Edmund Huey commented on the natural way of learning to read: "The secret of it all lies in parents' reading aloud to and with the child" (Edmund Huey, *The Psychology of Pedagogy*, 1908). Research has confirmed this belief, and teachers make every effort to involve parents in reading aloud to their children. They also invite the principal, parents and community members to read aloud to their students. This activity models adult interest in books and is usually quite popular with students. During National Book Week, there are often schoolwide programs that feature prominent readers, such as the mayor, police chief, newspaper editor, sports figures and town merchants. Some classrooms schedule a parent or community reader at least once a week. You can generate interest in this visiting reader program by writing to these persons and explaining the purpose of bringing in guest readers.

Book Buddies is a good way to provide students with additional read-aloud experience. Students can read in pairs or threes in the classroom or in an exchange program with another class, at grade level or between grades. Book Buddies that pair intermediate students with primary children are usually very successful. Even when there is a great difference between reading levels, children of all ages enjoy looking at picture books together. Younger children can tell older ones about their favorite books, point out favorite illustrations and receive help with reading books they want to read that are too difficult.

WHAT DO YOU THINK?   Did you ever read aloud to someone else when you were in elementary school? What do you think older children gain from reading aloud to younger students? What is the value of this experience for younger children?

X. Perspectives

Jim Trelease popularized the benefits of reading aloud to children in several editions of his *Read-Aloud Handbook*.[36] He believed that by reading aloud, teachers not only offer students the pleasure of reading, but they also provide them with a positive reading role model. Through listening to books read aloud, children gain new information about the world and are exposed to rich vocabulary and good grammar. He adds:

> At the same time, the child's imagination is stimulated, attention span stretched, listening comprehension improved, emotional development is nurtured, the reading–writing connection established, and where they exist negative attitudes reshaped to positive. (pp. 16–17)

Although most reading aloud is associated with stories, there is also a great storehouse of nonfiction literature that will enable you to share interesting concepts and facts in read-aloud form. Beverly Kobrin,[37] who has written an excellent guide to nonfictional literature, believes that children are naturally curious and are generally fascinated by good nonfiction writing. When you read aloud from books about history, science, math and the arts, you expand the experience of your listeners and give them new ideas to think about. These books otherwise might not be selected by students or they might be too difficult for them to read by themselves.

Both Trelease and Kobrin believe that reading aloud is a good advertisement for the entire reading process. Children who are not attracted to reading or who have difficulty with reading can often be sold on the activity when a teacher reads aloud from a good storybook or introduces them to the fascinating world of nonfiction literature. If negative associations have been made, reading aloud is one of the best ways to convince students that reading is a pleasurable experience. Those students who have not experienced the enjoyment of being read to at home or in previous grades can be drawn to reading by hearing good books read aloud at school.

Most teachers who read aloud believe that students at all grade levels should be read to on a daily basis and that this routine should begin on the first day of school. Trelease quotes a study[38] in which intermediate students were read to for twenty minutes a day, three times a week for twelve weeks.

At the end of this time, the researcher found statistically significant improvement in reading attitudes, independent reading and comprehension skills.

You might want to consider selecting one or more of the following handbooks for your professional library. They are inexpensive and full of good ideas and annotations.

> *The New Read-Aloud Handbook* (op. cit.) by Jim Trelease. This is a well-written and easy-to-read introduction to the benefits of reading aloud to children of all ages. He offers guidelines for reading aloud, discusses the benefits of independent reading, talks about the influence of television on reading and tells many read-aloud success stories. The last half of the book contains annotations of recommended books, which are arranged by type (wordless, picture, short novels, novels, anthologies) and recommended age level.

> *EyeOpeners! How to Choose and Use Children's Books About Real People, Places, and Things* (op. cit.) by Beverly Kobrin. This is one of the best available handbooks for using nonfiction literature in the classroom. It provides annotated lists of books arranged by popular study themes and features a "Quick Link" subject index that is helpful for locating books to include in a theme study. Individual annotations frequently include teaching tips for using a particular book in the classroom.

> *For Reading Out Loud! From Infancy to Teens*[39] by Margaret Mary Kimmel and Elizabeth Segel. This is an excellent source for choosing books to read aloud. Unlike many books of its type, this one provides enough description of each book to enable teachers to identify fiction and nonfiction that will be appropriate for their particular classrooms. Other features of this resource include: estimated reading time, good stopping points, cross-listings to find specific types of stories and a good discussion of reading aloud.

WHAT DO YOU THINK? Have you ever read aloud from informational literature? Why do you suppose students are interested in this kind of literature? What kinds of nonfiction do you enjoy?

XI. Exploring Professional Literature

Language Arts is a journal published by the National Council of Teachers of English (NCTE) and should be available to you through your college or university library. NCTE is a professional organization of educators concerned with the content and teaching of the language arts. Their publications include books, reference materials and journals for all levels of English teaching. Articles in *Language Arts* address issues affecting the teaching and learning of language arts of children, preschool through middle school.

What can you expect to find in this journal? Articles are solicited and published around general themes, such as "Technology and Language Arts Education" or "Language Arts for Special Populations." Regular features include reports on current research, book reviews of professional and children's books and profiles of language arts educators/authors. Also featured are reviews of NCTE publications for teachers. These books and materials are usually modestly priced and helpful. Members of NCTE can purchase these books at substantial savings. Look for annotations of these publications in the Resources for Teaching sections throughout this text.

How might this journal be helpful to you as a student? Each topic is examined from several perspectives by experienced educators, who have given extensive thought and reflection to the issues they address. As educator-colleagues, they offer you the opportunity to share their ideas and insights about teaching and learning. The "Bookalogue" section reviews picture books and chapter books for children that can be used in the classroom. "Reviews and Reflections" describes professional trade books and reference tools suitable for personal libraries.

The format of the articles in this journal can help you browse for ideas that interest you. When you have selected a theme issue, read the "Dear Reader" introduction, which describes each article and relates it to both the theme and other articles. At the beginning of each article is a brief summary that states the main idea, a research outcome and the instructional level involved. For instance, an article entitled "Fostering and Building Students' Intertextual Histories"[40] provides additional information in this summary by stating the following:

> Links—among children, among books, among children and books—are powerful factors in creating a community of readers in one first-grade classroom.

The key descriptors in this summary may draw your interest for a number of reasons. You might be specifically interested in first grade or you might want to know more about how to help students relate to each other and books. Key quotations from the article are highlighted to draw your interest and attention to the ideas being presented. Reading these may help you decide to read the article if you want more information on the topic.

Information about membership in the National Council of Teachers of English is available from: NCTE, 1111 Kenyon Road, Urbana, Illinois 61801-1096. Call 1-800-369-NCTE outside of Illinois and 217-328-3870 in state.

WHAT DO YOU THINK? The best way to measure the value of this journal to you personally is to examine several copies. Find one that addresses issues that interest you and read several articles. What did you like about this journal? What ideas did you find that were interesting or helpful?

XII. Resources for Teaching

The following books are favorites for the teacher's desk. When students are grumpy, tired or hungry, excerpts from these books are guaranteed to calm, entertain, amuse or amaze. Unless otherwise noted, all are appropriate to use throughout the elementary grades.

A Children's Almanac of Words at Play[41] by Willard Espy. This book is a collection of entries for every day of the year. It features riddles, jokes, limericks and word plays that will intrigue elementary students from kindergarten to sixth grade.

When Do Fish Sleep? And Other Imponderables of Everyday Life[42] by David Feldman. The title tells it all. Keep this book on your desk to answer the imponderable questions or read an entry aloud every day. Questions are addressed in an interesting and comprehensive way.

You Read to Me, I'll Read to You[43] by John Ciardi. Aimed at children in grades 1–4, this is a book of highly amusing and clever poems designed to be read aloud by both adults and children. Every other poem can be read by the average second-grade child, so put it on your desk and let your students entertain themselves, when you are not reading aloud from it. These are the kinds of poems students will request again and again, and they include the hilarious "Mummy Slept Late and Daddy Fixed Breakfast."

The Random House Book of Poetry for Children (op. cit.), Jack Prelutsky, editor. This is an excellent collection of 572 traditional and contemporary poems about everything from weather to animals. There are rhymes for all occasions, which makes it just right to have on the teacher's desk.

Classics to Read Aloud to Your Children[44] by William Russell. This is an excellent selection of poetry, short stories, myths and fairy tales to read aloud to your class, arranged in three listening levels, from early primary to upper intermediate grades. Each selection features an informational preface, estimated reading time and vocabulary notes.

The Random House Book of Humor for Children,[45] selected by Pamela Pollack. This is a collection of humorous tales from America's famous humorists, including Mark Twain, Garrison Keillor, T. H. White, Sid Fleischman and James Thurber. There are also excerpts from children's authors such as Judy Blume, Betsy Byars and Beverly Cleary. Selections are designed to draw the listener into the complete work from which excerpts are taken.

WHAT DO YOU THINK?   Which of these books look interesting to you? Why do you think they might be popular read-alouds for students of many ages?

XIII.   Reflections

From a Teacher's Journal—Charles Kamm, Retired Teacher and Principal

As a teacher and principal, I believe strongly in the importance of reading aloud to children. I do not read what I don't enjoy myself. I cannot fool children. When we share the joy of reading, the joy is mine *and* theirs. I see it as an opportunity, not an obligation. I want children to know that reading is a pleasurable activity, and I want to share that pleasure with them. More importantly, I believe that reading aloud provides continuity to our lives, as we pass along our ideas and ideals from parent to child, teacher to class, generation to generation, and age to age.

Lee had been in my class for several months, but peer acceptance of her was minimal. One day she arrived clutching a well-worn copy of Poe's writings. She had discovered "The Raven" and wanted to share it with me. I had not previously read this poem to my class—again I had underestimated their love of language. They were fascinated by Poe's musical, mystical melancholy. "Quoth the Raven: 'Nevermore' " became their spontaneous choral response as we read the poem several times. I needed no teacher's guide to lead us; the class's natural interest and curiosity served far better. Lee, and her book, through her book, became part of us.

The Pied Piper marched into our classroom much as he must have entered Hamelin Town hundreds of years ago, cloaked in language as foreign to our ears as his strange garb had been to the eyes of the Hamelin people. But through the lilting language of Browning, the Piper charmed us and led us as he had so many others before. True, we stumbled and hesitated along the way, but the pen of a powerful storyteller led us through the obstacles. And how, like the rats and the children, we raced through the lighter passages!

TRYING OUT THE CHAPTER IDEAS

1. What idea(s) in this chapter interested you?
2. Do you remember any experience of being read to by a relative, friend, librarian or teacher? What did you most enjoy?
3. Are there any books you would especially like to read aloud to a class?
4. What aspects of reading aloud will be the most challenging for you?
5. If possible, observe someone reading aloud (teacher, professor, librarian, media specialist). How does the reader introduce the book to the audience? How does he or she read to make the story interesting? Observe the audience: How do they respond? What was your response?
6. Practice reading aloud from a picture book and a short novel with a partner or a small group. Record your reading aloud and play it back. What kinds of feedback about your reading did you get from your partner or group? From the tape (or video) recorder?
7. Find an opportunity to read aloud to a child or a group of children in your cooperating school, a day-care center, recreational center, scout troop or nursery school. In your journal record your reasons for selecting your particular book and describe how you prepared to present it. Describe the response of your audience and anything you learned that will help you improve your reading aloud.
8. Interview a language arts teacher and/or a children's librarian. Ask them to name their five favorite children's books. What genres were most often mentioned? Compare your list with those of other classmates.

Notes

1. Emily Dickinson, *Poems by Emily Dickinson*, edited by her niece Martha Dickinson Bianchi and Alfred Leete Hampson (Boston: Little, Brown, 1957), p. 13.

2. A. Wigfield and S. R. Asher, "Social and Motivational Influences on Reading," in *Handbook of Research on Reading*, edited by P. D. Pearson, R. Barr, M. L. Kamil, and P. Mosenthal (New York: Longman, 1984), pp. 423–452.

3. Carol Chomsky, "Stages in Language Development and Reading Exposure," *Harvard Educational Review* 42(1972):1–33.

4. Dorothy Cohen, "The Effect of Literature on Vocabulary and Reading Achievement," *Elementary English* 45(1968):209–213.

5. W. B. Elley, "Vocabulary Acquisition from Listening to Stories," *Reading Research Quarterly* 24(1989):174–187.

6. D. Feitelson, B. Kita, and Z. Goldstein, "Effects of Listening to Series Stories on First Graders' Comprehension and Use of Language," *Research in the Teaching of English* 20(1986):339–356.

7. W. H. Teale, "Reading to Young Children: Its Significance in the Process of Literacy Development," in *Awakening To Literacy*, edited by H. Goelman, A. Oberg, and F. Smith (Exeter, N.H.: Heinemann, 1984), pp. 110–121.

8. Dolores Durkin, *Children Who Read Early* (New York: Teachers College Press, 1966).

9. R. Anderson, E. Hiebert, J. Scott, and I. Wilkinson, *Becoming a Nation of Readers: The Report of the Commission on Reading* (Washington, D.C.: National Institute of Education, 1985).

10. E. B. White, *Charlotte's Web* (New York: Harper & Row, 1952).

11. E. B. White, *Stuart Little* (New York: Harper & Row, 1973).

12. E. B. White, *The Trumpet of the Swan* (Harper & Row, 1970).

13. Raymond Briggs, *The Snowman* (New York: Random House, 1978).

14. Brinton Turkle, *Deep in the Forest* (New York: Dutton, 1976).

15. Farley Mowat, *Owls in the Family* (New York: Bantam Books, 1981).

16. Jerry Spinelli, *Maniac Magee* (Boston: Little, Brown, 1990).

17. David Schwartz, *How Much Is a Million?* (New York: Scholastic, 1985).

18. Howard Fast, *April Morning* (New York: Crown Publishers, 1987).

19. Ruth Heller, *Cache of Jewels and Other Collective Nouns* (New York: Putnam, 1987). Ruth Heller, *Kites Sail High: A Book About Verbs* (New York: Putnam, 1988). Ruth Heller, *Many Luscious Lollipops: A Book About Adjectives* (New York: Putnam, 1989). Ruth Heller, *Merry-Go-Round: A Book About Nouns* (New York: Putnam, 1990). Ruth Heller, *Up, Up, and Away: A Book About Adverbs* (New York: Putnam, 1991).

20. Jack Prelutsky, comp., *The Random House Book of Poetry for Children* (New York: Random House, 1983).

21. Patricia Polacco, *Thunder Cake* (New York: Philomel, 1990).

22. Alice Dalgliesh, *The Courage of Sarah Noble* (New York: Macmillan, 1987).

23. Elizabeth George Speare, *Sign of the Beaver* (New York: Houghton Mifflin, 1983).

24. Shel Silverstein, *Where the Sidewalk Ends* (New York: Harper & Row, 1974).

25. Jack Prelutsky, *The New Kid on the Block: Poems* (New York: Greenwillow, 1984).

26. Fred Gipson, *Old Yeller* (New York: HarperCollins Children's Books, 1990).

27. Sheila Burnford, *The Incredible Journey* (New York: Bantam, 1990).

28. Sterling North, *Rascal* (New York: Puffin Books, 1990).

29. Graeme Base, *The Eleventh Hour: A Curious Mystery* (New York: Abrams, 1989).

30. Lensey Namioka, *Yang the Youngest and His Terrible Ear* (Waltham, Mass.: Little, Brown, 1992).

31. Yoshiko Uchida, *Journey Home* (New York: Macmillan, 1978).

32. Yoshiko Uchida, *Journey to Topaz: A Story of the Japanese-American Evacuation* (New York: Creative Arts, 1985).

33. Sook Nyul Choi, *Year of Impossible Goodbyes* (Boston: Houghton Mifflin, 1991).

34. Maureen Crane Wartski, *A Boat to Nowhere* (Philadelphia: Westminster, 1980).

35. Ellen Raskin, *The Westing Game* (New York: Puffin, 1978). A Newbery book.

36. Jim Trelease, *The New Read-Aloud Handbook* (New York: Penguin, 1989).

37. Beverly Kobrin, *Eye Openers! How to Choose and Use Children's Books About Real People, Places, and Things* (New York: Penguin, 1988).

38. Maryellen Smith Cosgrove, "Reading Aloud to Children: The Effects of Listening on the Reading Comprehension and Attitudes of Sixth Graders in Six Communities in Connecticut," unpublished doctoral dissertation, University of Connecticut, 1987.

39. Margaret Mary Kimmel and Elizabeth Segel, *For Reading Out Loud! From Infancy to Teens* (New York: Dell, 1991).

40. Trevor H. Cairney, "Fostering and Building Students' Intertextual Histories," *Language Arts* 69(November 1992):502–514.

41. Willard Espy, *A Children's Almanac of Words at Play* (New York: Potter, 1982).

42. David Feldman, *When Do Fish Sleep? And Other Imponderables of Everyday Life* (New York: Harper & Row, 1989).

43. John Ciardi, *You Read to Me, I'll Read to You* (New York: Harper & Row, 1987).

44. William Russell, *Classics to Read Aloud to Your Children* (New York: Crown, 1984).

45. Pamela Pollack comp., *The Random House Book of Humor for Children* (New York: Random House, 1988).

Independent Reading

This student enjoys independent reading in a classroom that provides
him with a variety of books to explore. He looks forward to this time of
day, when he can investigate books that other children or the teacher
have talked about in book previews.

We may not always be able to look over his shoulder while a student is having a real literary experience, but we can do at least two things. First, we can be very careful to scrutinize all our procedures to be sure that we are not in actuality substituting other aims—things to do about literature—for the experience of literature. We can ask of every assignment or method or text, no matter what its short term effectiveness: Does it get in the way of the live sense of literature?

—Louise M. Rosenblatt, *Literature as Exploration*[1]

LOOKING AHEAD

1. What is the importance of independent reading to language learning?
2. Why is it important for teachers to read silently with their students?
3. Can students learn how to select books at their own reading level?
4. What reading strategies can students learn for independent reading?
5. What is the value of previewing books for students?
6. How can school book clubs help teachers build classroom libraries?
7. How will you select books for your classroom collection?

IN 25 WORDS OR LESS

Independent reading is the daily practice of teachers and students reading silently and autonomously for 10–30 minutes from materials they have self-selected.

I. Focus: Independent Reading

In many traditional classrooms, students spend most of the day doing things "about" reading and very little time actually reading. Teachers who integrate the language arts in their classrooms believe that students not only need to develop the ability to read, but also the desire to read that will help them become lifelong readers and learners. One way teachers can help students develop this desire is to provide daily opportunities for them to explore books of their own choosing, for the express purpose of enjoyment. Independent reading time in the classroom is referred to by a number of acronyms, but the practice is the same. Students and teachers read whatever they choose, uninterrupted, for a period of time ranging from ten to thirty minutes. Some of the terms used by teachers to designate independent reading include:

SSR	Silent Sustained Reading
DEAR	Drop Everything And Read
USSR	Uninterrupted Silent Sustained Reading
DIRT	Daily Individual Reading Time
SQUIRT	Sustained Quiet Uninterrupted Reading Time
RABBIT	Read A Book Because It's There

Although there may be slight variations from classroom to classroom, the important characteristics of independent reading programs are the following:

1. Both students and teacher are reading silently at the same time.
2. Nothing else happens during this time except reading.
3. Everyone is free to choose what he or she wishes to read from materials provided in the classroom.
4. A variety of reading materials is provided, representing a range of reading levels.
5. No assignments are associated with the reading.

Teachers who schedule independent reading time for their students believe that children learn to read by reading and that the more times children practice reading, the better readers they become. They also believe that frequent enjoyable experiences with reading develop pleasant associations that move students toward the disposition to be lifelong readers. Regular daily reading helps establish good reading habits and encourages children to consider reading as a leisure activity. Setting aside a period of time each day for independent reading gives status to this practice and communicates its importance to students. A time for sustained silent reading also provides an opportunity for all children to explore reading materials that might not be present in their own homes or that augment materials provided by their families.

A regular schedule for independent reading also offers children sufficient time to become involved with a book. Traditionally, independent reading was limited to students who finished assignments quickly. Reading was both a reward for fast work and a way to keep students busy until everyone finished assignments. It was often the case that students who already read well were rewarded with additional time to improve their reading ability, while those who did not read quickly or well were penalized by fewer opportunities to practice. Affording equal opportunity for all students to participate and enjoy a reading experience is critical to the success of independent reading times. That is why it is important to schedule this daily time for everyone to read and to provide reading materials for a wide range of reading levels and interests. Teachers help students participate successfully by teaching them techniques for selecting their own books and strategies for helping them understand what they read.

The benefits of independent reading are not limited to students. This time provides you, as a teacher, the opportunity to explore children's literature or articles of interest in professional journals and magazines. Your participation and modeling during this independent reading time is the key to successful participation by your students. Teachers who support independent reading in their classrooms and educational researchers who have observed the successful use of these programs agree on the two most important elements:

1. Teachers must read while their students are reading.
2. A wide variety of kinds and levels of reading material must be made available.

In almost every instance where independent reading time does not work well with a class, it can be traced to the teacher's lack of interest and modeling or the lack of suitable reading materials.

WHAT DO YOU THINK?   What kinds of literature do you enjoy the most? If you had the opportunity to read anything you wanted right now, what would it be? When was the last time you read something that was not required? What kind of material do you choose for leisure reading?

II. The Importance of Independent Reading

From its survey of the research literature, the National Commission on Reading[2] recommended that students should spend more time in independent reading—at least two hours per week. Educators who have reviewed the research in reading strongly recommend daily independent reading time and encourage teachers to plan activities that help create student interest in books. Providing a time each day for students to read self-selected material encourages students to practice their reading skills and develop increasingly positive attitudes toward reading. Students begin to see reading as an enjoyable activity and one that can help them discover new and interesting ideas.

Independent reading appears to benefit students of all ability and achievement levels, helping to increase comprehension skills and vocabulary development. In a notable study[3] that included the W. J. Maxey Boys' Training School in Michigan, significant gains were made by boys who had experienced reading failure, but who were provided books and time to read them. They self-selected the books and there were no book reports or tests on the material read. By the end of the school year, these boys showed significant gains in verbal proficiency, reading comprehension, literacy attitudes and self-esteem. Their scores were double those of the control group, another Midwestern training school for boys, that did not provide books.

In a review of research studies on literature-based reading instruction, Tunnell and Jacobs[4] found that in each of the successful programs examined, there was a specific time set aside for children at all grade levels to self-select and interact independently with books. Other researchers found that the amount of leisure reading and reading achievement are correlated[5] and that self-initiated reading produces more progress in reading because it helps make reading skills automatic.[6] They also concluded that the best predictor of comprehension test performance, size of vocabulary and gains in reading achievement between second and fifth grades was the average number of minutes students spent reading books per day.

Fielding et al.[7] found that children who have opportunities for independent reading at school do more reading at home than children from classrooms that do not promote independent reading. Teachers also play a critical role by providing reading materials to appeal to a wide range of interests and reading levels. By their own participation, they model reading as an activity important to adults. Their behavior during independent reading times is critical, because researchers have observed that students use the teacher as a role model[8] to shape their own responses.

WHAT DO YOU THINK? Were you surprised that research identified teacher modeling as critical to the success of independent reading sessions? Why might some teachers feel uncomfortable sitting and reading a book during this time? Can you imagine yourself doing this in the classroom?

III. Looking into Classrooms

Kindergarten Level

Mrs. Jamison puts up a sign on the door of the kindergarten room that says "Please Do Not Disturb—Reading in Progress." Several children playing near the door observe the sign and go immediately to the library corner to begin selecting their books. The teacher rings a small bell three times and the rest of the children begin putting away their blocks and toys to join the others in the library corner. One by one, they return to their tables with three or four books each and begin reading or looking at the pictures. Most have selected picture books with bright, attractive illustrations. Others choose books written by themselves or other students in the class. Still others choose books the class has made or easy reader books such as *The Cat in the Hat*,[9] *Frog and Toad Are Friends*,[10] or *Sammy the Seal*.[11] Mrs. Jamison reads from the stack of picture books on her desk.

As students finish looking at their books, many go through them again, having obviously enjoyed the first time through. Others put their books into a pile in the center of the table and take another book to read. Occasionally children chuckle at pictures or the stories they are reading, but for the most part the room is quiet, except for the sound of pages turning.

Mrs. Jamison rings the bell three times again, as a cue to put books away. Some children look up, obviously disappointed, while others stack their books and return them to the library center. Those who are still absorbed in their reading look at their books all the way back to the center, while others keep the books they have chosen and put them in their storage bins to check out later.

Everyone reads, including Mrs. Jamison, for the entire fifteen-minute period. "When we began independent reading," the teacher explains, "we read for five minutes, which was about the limit of most attention spans. Now, many would go on like this for half an hour or longer. There are other times during the day, such as during reading conferences, where children can do independent reading, but we also read silently as a group in the afternoon, right after rest period."

These opportunities for reading encourage kindergarten students to develop independent reading habits at their own level of emerging literacy (growing ability to read and write). Most of the children "read" the illustrations and follow the story by looking at the pictures. Others can read a few words and practice their decoding and context analysis skills. Once they select their books, children stay at their tables for the entire reading time. There are always plenty of books to read because other children at their table put the books they have completed reading in the middle for everyone to share. Children are usually interested in their classmates' selections and are thus exposed to books they might not otherwise choose for themselves.

Primary Level

"Does everyone have something to read?" Mrs. Scott asks her second-grade class. Jerry is still deciding between *The World Atlas for Children*[12] and *The Guinness Sports Record Book*.[13] Finally he chooses the atlas. "I'll take the other one home tonight," he says to himself, as he sits down on the floor to look at the book of maps. Rachel is still trying to find a book by Beverly Cleary. All the books by her favorite author have been taken and she looks downcast.

"There's a new book about snakes on my desk, Rachel," Mrs. Scott suggests. Rachel loves snakes and goes to pick up the book. "Tell me if you like it," she adds. Mrs. Scott has been waiting all morning to read the new Graeme Base book. She and her class both enjoyed *Animalia*,[14] a lavishly illustrated alphabet book, and *The Eleventh Hour*,[15] a mystery.

"What will you do about words you don't know?" she asks the class.

"Use our strategies," they reply, holding up laminated bookmarks.

Each student has decorated a personal bookmark with lists of strategies on both sides for figuring out words. One side is for independent reading time and the other is for "other times." The strategies were generated by the class at the beginning of the year to assist them during independent reading and include:

Go on
Read the pictures
Read the sentence again
Put in another word
Look for clues
Sound it out

The list on the other side of the bookmark includes all of these and adds:

Look it up
Ask someone

She reviews the strategies briefly with the class and they settle content-edly into their books. Soon quiet prevails, broken only by occasional sighs and giggles that do not seem to interrupt others' involvement with their own reading. Students read uninterrupted for nearly twenty minutes, until the low buzz of a timer tells them that they have two more minutes to bring their reading to a close.

"This is their favorite time of day," Mrs. Scott comments, as she puts her own book away in the desk. "I'm going to read this book aloud to them this afternoon," she adds. "It's great!"

WHAT HAPPENED HERE? ONE PERSPECTIVE

Like Mrs. Jamison, Mrs. Scott is a strong adult model for independent reading. She is highly involved in her own reading and makes a point of sharing good reading experiences with her students. Many classes, like Mrs. Scott's, become totally absorbed in their reading and would continue long past the time set aside for this independent activity. Timing helps keep the activity fresh and something to anticipate. Most children in this class continue their independent reading outside of school.

When Rachel could not find a book by her favorite author, she was disappointed. Mrs. Scott makes a note in her teaching journal to check the library for *Ramona Quimby, Age 8*.[16] She knows that Rachel does not have access to books in her home, and following a favorite author is a positive sign of developing reading tastes. She also knows that for other children who have many books available to them, not finding a favorite author prompts them to look at something new and helps them broaden the scope of their reading selection. In each case the teacher is looking for growth to encourage, and this is possible because she observes her students closely in order to learn about their experiences and interests.

Each week Mrs. Scott plans a mini-lesson that focuses on a compre-hension strategy to assist the independent reading skills of her students. She demonstrates how to use picture clues and how to figure out the word by rereading the sentence or looking at the words around it. She shows them how to substitute a word that makes sense, sound it out or skip it and keep going. These strategies encourage students to be prob-lem-solvers and permit them to become increasingly autonomous in their reading.

Intermediate Level

It is a typical morning outside Mr. Brown's fourth-grade classroom. Students are talking and laughing in the hallway, banging their lockers shut as they put away their coats and backpacks. It is 8:55 A.M. when Jill picks up a tally

· stick and puts it into the box under the lunch menu choice for soup and salad. She moves the index card with her name on it into the attendance display. Like everyone else in the class, she drew a picture about her favorite book on the other side. The colorful designs sit in paper pockets stapled onto the board. It is easy for the teacher to see whose name cards are left for attendance purposes, and the display of book cards is a source of interested browsing by all the students in the room.

This month, Jill drew a picture of Frightful, Sam Gribley's falcon in *My Side of the Mountain*.[17] She has read the book twice, once on her own and once with Carrie, her Book Buddy from third grade. Carrie saw the picture of the falcon one noon hour when the girls were reading together. Carrie's class was studying birds, and while they were reading the book, she chose the falcon for her research study. When she told Jill about *Owls in the Family*, which was being read aloud in her class, Jill found the book in the classroom library and read it at home.

She is working on her card for November and has decided to draw a picture of the locket given to Annemarie for safekeeping by her friend Ellen in *Number the Stars*,[18] the book she is reading now. Jill hurries to her desk and pulls out the book, eager to see if Annemarie will make it past the Nazi guards with the basket for her uncle. She has already told Carrie about the book and promises to loan it to her when she has finished it.

Nick decides on pizza for lunch and drops his tally stick in the labeled box. As he moves his attendance card with the drawing of a catapult into a pocket, he thinks about other drawings he has made from David Macaulay's *Castle*.[19] "That has to be the best book ever written," he thinks, and wonders if the book orders have arrived with his copy of Macaulay's *Pyramid*.[20] He checks with Mr. Brown, who thinks the order might come in today. Out of the corner of his eye, he sees that there is only a minute left until independent reading time, so he picks up a copy of *National Geographic*.[21] It initially draws his attention because there is a picture on the front cover of a boy making a face. He scans the contents on the front cover and finds an article on the Cambrian period. Near the back of the magazine he finds a long article about ancient sea creatures, complete with paintings and photographs of fossils.

Mark spends the entire five minutes looking for just the right book. He is looking for something about cars, preferably a book with lots of illustrations. He asks Mr. Brown if there are any books about cars on the table. "Keep looking, Mark," Mr. Brown says. "I think you'll find something you like." Mark looks more closely and finds *Monster Trucks and Other Giant Machines on Wheels*.[22] He opens the book to a picture of a tree crusher. It is just what he wants. After he studies the pictures for a few minutes, he will read about how the giant machines work.

All over the room, students take out books from their desks, find a book on the table or pick up one of several science, history or literary magazines and settle down to read. Mr. Brown pulls out a copy of *Louis Braille*[23] from his desk. Charles told him about the book in his last reading conference and made it sound so interesting that he decided to try it. At the end of the first chapter, Mr. Brown thinks it might be a good biography to read aloud to the entire class. When he finishes reading the book, he will read a little of the first chapter to his two sons, to test its read-aloud qualities. "No wonder

FIGURE 3.1
These are pages from a class almanac. Students illustrated and interpreted their favorite axiom as part of their study of Colonial America.

Charles liked this book," he thinks as he continues his reading. Louis Braille was a problem-solver and, just like Charles, was always thinking of ways to improve things. He makes a note in his teaching journal to tell Charles about *The Wright Brothers at Kitty Hawk,*[24] another biography about problem solving.

WHAT HAPPENED HERE? ONE PERSPECTIVE

Independent reading is part of the classroom management system for this teacher. Scheduling it as the first activity of the day establishes its importance and acts as a mechanism to draw the class immediately into academic involvement. Attendance and lunch count are accomplished by the students, freeing the teacher to be a resource as reading material is selected. Students in this room are encouraged to take responsibility for accomplishing routine tasks quickly and involving themselves academically as soon as they enter the classroom door.

Mr. Brown and Mr. Hernandez (Chapter 2—Looking into Classrooms: Primary Level) host a volunteer reading club called "Book Buddies" in their classrooms at noon. Interested third and fourth graders pair up to read books together. Jill and Carrie have developed a friendship, based on mutual reading interests, and have helped expand each other's involvement in books.

Mr. Brown sees himself as a colearner in the classroom and demonstrates this attitude by picking up on recommendations of good books to read from his students. He also learns a lot about his students from the kinds of books they choose to read. With this knowledge he can reinforce and broaden their reading habits, making available many different kinds of books on topics of their interest. He was happy to find the monster truck book in the public library because he knows that Mark looks for pictures of machinery and will likely make an effort to read the text to find out what he wants to know about trucks. Because Mr. Brown is aware of Charles's keen interest in science and problem solving from his individual reading conferences, he is able to recommend books, particularly biographies, that will expand this interest.

The parent/teacher organization in his school provides him with a subscription to a magazine of his choice, and he has chosen *National Geographic*. It is the most commonly read magazine in his class, and students often call his attention to articles in past issues that refer to topics they are studying in science and social studies. The school provides a magazine about current events, and he brings a children's literary magazine from home. It is important to Mr. Brown that his students have the opportunity to explore topics of interest from sources that are current and of high quality.

WHAT DO YOU THINK? What strategies do you use to figure out the pronunciation or meaning of unfamiliar words? Observe what you do when you encounter an unfamiliar word or a passage that is difficult to comprehend. Is this a strategy you might share with students?

IV. Preparing for Independent Reading

Planning for independent reading time involves preparation in three areas: establishing the physical setting; obtaining adequate reading materials; and introducing the idea to students.

Setting the Scene

You will want to make your collection of books as attractive as possible, displaying them in ways that make them readily accessible to your students. Where can books be displayed in your room? In addition to bookshelves, you can create space on tables, book carts and the tops of other classroom furniture. Discount stores sell colorful plastic crate holders that permit the stacking of books in classrooms short on space. Pieces of wood can be placed over unused features of the room, such as old radiators that are inoperative. Some older schools have deep windowsills where you can put boxes with the open end to the room to shield books from light.

Both hardback and paperback books must be protected from excessive light, heat and moisture. If there is much humidity in your climate, you may occasionally want to spray your room and its surfaces with a product that controls mold and mildew. Because paperbacks will gradually deteriorate from being crowded onto shelves and into desks and backpacks, you might want to consider having students keep books they are currently reading in a designated place in the room, to avoid the scrunch of desk storage. All paperbacks should be stored, if possible, in V-shaped holders that will allow the books to rest on two sides. Plastic storage bags with a piece of cardboard inside will allow books to be transported back and forth between school and home with a minimum of travel damage.

Just as it is easier to see what is available to eat when food is on the table rather than in the refrigerator, arranging books in an open display allows students greater access to what is available to read. They can see the covers easily, recognize familiar books and become interested in new ones. If lack of space is a problem, use the library method, setting up slightly opened books on every free surface of the room. For the brief selection time period of independent reading, books can be placed on chalkboard rails, desks, video stands and computer tables. In kindergarten, books are often placed on a rug on the floor for student selection.

When you have determined where to store and display books, you will want to plan the traffic pattern of the room to facilitate easy access to the books. Students must be able to move to and from the books with a minimum of chaos and disruption to others. Some teachers set up a centralized display where students can move easily around a table to make their choices. Older students will usually be reading longer books and may choose them well ahead of time as a part of a daily routine. Other classrooms feature small library areas where students visit by tables or rows to select their books. If books are chosen as part of the independent reading time, it is helpful to limit the time allotted for selection to no more than five minutes. Time to browse and explore the possibilities is important, but if the rest of the school day includes time for reading aloud and sharing books, most children will have a good idea of what they want to read when it is time for independent reading.

Selecting Books

When you begin to assemble your collection of books, you will want to make a connection with the books you are reading aloud to your class. Try to find books that have the same topic as your read-aloud books and also books by the same author, if this is possible. Chapter 4 of this book includes a description of the kinds of literature written for children and recommendations for selecting each type of book for your classroom collection. As you select books to be part of your classroom, you might want to consider the following:

Choose from the best reading material. Children will develop their reading tastes from what is made available to them. With thousands of books to choose from, it is important to provide the best. As part of the process of developing your own ability to find the best books, you might want to refer to resources such as *Best Books for Children*[25] or *Adventuring with Books: A Booklist for Pre-K–Grade 6*,[26] both of which provide helpful annotations and excellent indexes for book selection. These books are annotated in the Resources for Teaching section of this chapter. Criteria for judging the quality of each kind (genre) of literature will be introduced in Chapter 4.

Include a selection of good magazines that deal with science, history, the arts and literature. Descriptions of several high-quality magazines can be found in the endnotes of this chapter. They includes such favorites as *National Geographic, National Geographic World,*[27] *Ranger Rick,*[28] *Cricket, The Magazine for Children*[29] and *Highlights for Children.*[30] Other good magazines on a variety of themes are available from school book clubs.[31]

Choose materials from several reading levels, at least two levels below and three levels above the grade level of your students, to accommodate the range of reading levels you will have in your classroom. At the kindergarten and primary levels, include many picture books that will appeal to the age level and interests of emerging readers. Nonfiction picture books with limited text should be included at all levels, but especially for the intermediate grades where interest in a topic will often stimulate reading activity. Your personal class selection may vary if you have children who are exceptionally gifted readers or limited English speakers or who have serious reading disabilities.

Choose a wide variety of books, representing all the kinds of literature available for children: picture books, traditional folktales, modern fantasy, biography, historical and contemporary realistic fiction, poetry, plays and informational nonfiction in the areas of history, geography, math, science, the arts and social sciences.

Introducing Independent Reading

Tell your students that you plan to set aside a special time every day for them to read and enjoy books. Describe what you want to happen during this time and ask them to suggest guidelines that will help make these goals possible.

1. A daily time is provided for them to read a book or magazine of their choice.
2. Everyone, both teacher and students, is free from interruption during this time.
3. Everyone stays with a book long enough to find out what it is like.
4. Everyone is free to explore all kinds of books with no assignments attached.

Almost without exception, students of all ages come up with the necessary guidelines to accomplish these goals. You can, of course, simply tell students what the guidelines will be, which may be more comfortable for you. But when the parameters are established by students, they own the program and will take increased responsibility for its success. They will also often generate ideas about their particular situation that you might not have considered.

Student-generated guidelines usually include a variation of the following. If they fail to cover what is needed, ask them what guideline would help accomplish a particular goal.

1. Choose something you want to read.
2. Read when the timer starts and finish when the timer rings again.

3. Read at least the first chapter (one-half of a picture book) of any book you start.
4. Save talking until after independent reading.
5. Decide where you want to read and stay there.
6. Keep the room noise-free.

Notice that the list above is stated in positive terms. It describes behavior for students **to do**. Sometimes students will suggest these guidelines in negative terms, emphasizing what **not to do**, such as: No talking; No interrupting; No taking books back; No walking around the room; No drawing; No doing homework. If this happens, accept all contributions the first time through; then ask if they can state the guidelines in a way that tells them what they are **to do** during independent reading. Help them merge guidelines that are duplicated by asking, "Are there any guidelines that say the same thing?"

When everyone is satisfied with the guidelines, read them over together and make a poster of the guidelines to display for the first few weeks. If students talk, walk around the room or do not get involved in reading, you can gesture with your head toward the poster as a reminder. For prereaders, you can make a poster using drawings or pictures from a magazine to illustrate the guidelines. In the beginning, it helps to review the guidelines before each independent reading session.

Self-Selection Techniques

After you have selected the books for your classroom collection, your students will be making their choices from those you have assembled. Beyond being interested in a book, how will they know if it is written at a level they can read and enjoy? Of course, if students are not reading text yet, they will choose almost anything they like and enjoy looking at the pictures. When students are able to read text, they should be encouraged to try anything that draws their interest. Sometimes students will ask, "Is this too hard for me?" Perhaps the best answer is "Try it and see."

At the same time, it is important to help students find material that is possible to read and enjoy independently. Sometimes they will want to explore books that are clearly too difficult for them, but other times they would like to find something they can read and enjoy at their particular skill level. Is it possible for them to do this without the teacher's help? Believe it or not, as soon as they can read a few words, children can learn a technique that will allow them to select a book that they will enjoy, one that will provide practice for emerging skills and that will pose a minimum of reading frustration for them. They can even be taught how to identify books that contain just the right challenge to develop increased reading skill.

Systems for finding books for independent reading at both the primary and intermediate levels involve the use of fingers as markers. Students open the book they want to read to the middle. In picture books with a single line of text, students should read the text on both middle pages. In chapter books, students begin reading at the upper right-hand side. Demonstrate how to use the system and practice several times with the class after the initial demonstration. Students of all ages enjoy learning how to be more independent in their reading.

The Three Bears Guide (kindergarten/early primary) Rehearse the story of The Three Bears with your students: "Goldilocks tried all the bowls of porridge. One was too hot, one was too cold, and one was just right. When you want to read a book, you have to try it out just like porridge or a chair or a bed. You want one that is just right, so you can enjoy it. You can use your fingers to decide if a book is easy, hard or just right. It's fine for independent reading if the book is easy or just right, but you will want to know if it's too hard, so you can get some help learning to read it. You can check it out and take it home or ask your Book Buddy to read it with you." (You may want to emphasize that students should look at any book that interests them. They will often make great efforts to develop skill to read material they are highly motivated to read.)

Make a poster using cut-out bears and drawings or pictures of fingers on a hand to illustrate the system:

This one is easy—one or no fingers down
This one is hard—four or five fingers down
This one is just right—two or three fingers down

Explain the poster to your students: "Take a book and open it to the middle. Then put your hand down on the table next to it. Lift your fingers up just a little so that none of them is touching the table. Begin to read, and if you find a word you don't know, put one finger down. Read to the end of the page, and every time you find a word you don't know, put another finger down. When you reach the end of the page, count how many fingers you have down and remember The Three Bears. If you didn't put any fingers down or just one, that book is easy enough for you to read by yourself. If you put two or three fingers down, the book will be a little challenging. What if you put down four or five fingers?" (Students will usually chorus, "Too hard!") "Does this mean you shouldn't read this book? No, it just tells you this is a book you might enjoy reading with someone else at another time."

The Rule of Thumb (grades 3–6) Tell your students that you want to share a technique with them for locating a book that they can read independently. Your goal is to help them select a book that is below their frustration level (too many unknown words to understand or enjoy what they are reading). Explain that they can count the number of words that are unfamiliar to them on a page and tell whether the book will be comfortable to read. Remind students that they can try to read anything that interests them, but the Rule of Thumb will help them identify a comfortable level for independent reading. Tell them that when they are looking for a book to read independently, they can try it out on a typical page, putting down a finger on one hand for each word they do not know, starting with their little finger. When they reach their thumb (four fingers down), this means the book will be hard-going for independent reading. Two to three fingers mean they might want to have the dictionary handy. One or no fingers down usually indicates that the book can be read independently. Again, be sure to stress that books they really want to read that fail the Rule of Thumb test can be read with a Book Buddy or taken home.

Ask everyone to select a book and open it to the middle, where there is only text and no pictures. (Some nonfiction books and picture storybooks will have photographs or illustrations.) Encourage students to find a page near the middle that will be typical of what they find in the book. Ask them to begin reading silently at the top of the right-hand page and read to the end of the page. The number of fingers down will give them information they may want to have about the book. You might want to make a poster like the following for quick reference during the first week:

Good independent reading—one or no fingers down
Have a dictionary handy—two or three fingers down
Read with someone else—four or five fingers down

Students quickly gain proficiency with this technique and will not need the poster after the first few times. But most teachers keep the chart posted throughout the year to help new students entering the class or to explain the system to parents and visitors.

Generating Strategies

Ask your students what they can do about unfamiliar words when they are reading independently. Most classes will generate a list similar to the following:

Skip the word and keep reading, or read around the word.
Reread the sentence or paragraph for clues.
Use the pictures to figure out what is happening.
Substitute a word that makes sense.
Sound it out.

Also ask them to think about what they can do if they feel confused about what is happening in their stories. These are the kinds of suggestions students typically give:

Use the pictures (K–primary).
Go back and start the page (chapter, book) over.
Skip the confusing part and come back later.

These strategies can be transferred to a chart or poster for easy reference by students. You can also ask students to compress each idea into a key word or words to copy onto a personal bookmark. These can be decorated, laminated and used as a ready reference during independent reading time.

Previewing Books

When students read independently they will select books that have drawn their attention in some way. It may be an attractive cover, a recommendation from a friend, a book about something that has their current interest or a favorite book that was read aloud to the class. There are additional ways to interest students in exploring new books.

Best Bets Review

When a student enjoys a particular book, he or she writes a sentence or two on an index card, telling what was liked about the book. This card is posted on a bulletin board for review by class members and eventually filed in a Best

Bets index file for further reference by readers. Although this is a voluntary activity, most students choose to participate and almost all will use the index to get new ideas about good books to read. This review process is especially helpful in drawing students to books they otherwise might not consider. For example, *The House of Sixty Fathers*[32] by Meindert DeJong is an intriguing book about the courage of a young Chinese boy who is separated from his parents during wartime and is cared for by sixty American soldiers. Looking at the cover and glancing through the first few pages may not grab a student's interest, but seeing the book recommended by someone else will often draw attention to it. When students read and enjoy books recommended by another child, they may inquire about additional books the child has read. In this way, bonds are often established between students with similar reading tastes. Children who read great numbers of books will frequently explore various kinds of literature, and through the review process they draw others into similar explorations.

Book Talks

It takes only five minutes a day to give quick book talks to generate interest in the kinds of books available in the classroom. From the books you have read, choose two or three and ask a few questions about each that will draw student interest. For example, hold up a copy of *A Wrinkle in Time*[33] by Madeleine L'Engle and ask the class: "Do you know what a tesseract is? What if someone you knew was lost somewhere in time and space and couldn't get back? This book tells the story of Meg Murry and her brother Charles Wallace who try to rescue their father from the Dark Thing. Listen to the way the story begins . . ." Then read the first two pages. Hold up the book and ask, "Does anyone want to know more?" Usually many hands go up, but some students may want to see everything previewed before they commit themselves.

This is an excellent time to interest students in the wide variety of children's literature: picture books, historical fiction, biography, contemporary fiction, poetry, informational books, folktales, myths, legends and tall tales. It is also a good time to introduce students to the kinds of literature that will help them know more about and better understand their own and other cultures. You may also want to preview books that your students might someday want to know about, particularly those that deal sensitively with problems children face in growing up.

Friday Afternoon Sharing Time (FAST)

This activity is described more fully in Chapter 7. Students plan and make literature-related presentations to the entire class during the last hour on Friday afternoons. These presentations may be as simple as sharing a passage from a favorite book or as involved as creating dramatic presentations, pantomimes, puppet shows and character interviews.

Cover Enhancements

You can probably think of many occasions when you chose a book to read on the basis of its cover, only to be disappointed by what you found inside. By accident, you may also have discovered terrific books hidden away between unattractive covers. Students are drawn to colorful and intriguing book covers and will soon decide whether the book delivers on its promise. But many are put off from excellent reading when there is nothing on the outside to draw their attention. For convenience, book jackets are discarded in many school libraries, leaving only a plain cover binding with no clue as to what is inside. Books also become worn and are less appealing to new readers.

There are several things you can do to make books more attractive. On paperbacks where the covers are ragged but the text is still in good shape, you can tape a student-drawn picture, a picture from a publisher's catalog or a colorful magazine picture that captures some of the drama of the story or information inside. An adhesive that is not damaging to book covers or stick-up notes can be used to attach attractive pictures to the fronts of hardback books. Some teachers put special bookmarks in good books that lack distinctive covers. These bookmarks can be made by students and laminated or they may contain a sentence review of the book, such as the simple but effective one found in a weathered copy of *Rascal*: "This is the best and funniest animal book I ever read—Joey."

Obtaining Books for Independent Reading

You will probably be wondering where all these books, of whatever kinds and numbers, are going to come from. Assuming that you cannot fully stock a classroom library from your own financial resources during your first year of teaching, there are several options to consider. Remember that the first and most important thing is to **know what you want.** If you know that you want books illustrated by Eric Carle or Tomie dePaola or that specifically you want copies of *Blitzcat*[34] and *The Machine Gunners*[35] by Robert Westall for your study of Britain during World War II, you will have some direction for the books you seek from a variety of sources.

Visit your school library or media center as soon as possible and find out the number of books you can borrow for your room and how long you can keep them. Usually school libraries permit the loan of three to five books per student (in addition to the ones students can check out for themselves) for a two-week period. Your public library will also have a per-pupil check-out plan, as will your regional library. Books for special study that are not available from any of these sources can be ordered from the state library or a national network of libraries, depending on your particular system. Check with your school's media specialist or the public librarian for specific details on how to make use of these resources.

Contact your school parent support organization (PTO) for information on classroom projects and register your request for books. You may also want to make up a list to send home, asking for specific titles in used books. Some schools sponsor book club fairs that yield extensive paperback collections to participating teachers. Others have birthday clubs, where parents donate a paperback book of their child's choice to the classroom library on the child's birthday. Don't forget Saturday rummage sales and library used-book sales where very little money can buy many books. A word of caution about used books: Do not buy, or immediately discard, any books that have a mildew odor or brownish-edged pages. Mildew and paper parasites will spread to other books and quickly deteriorate the quality of your collection. Some of the best sources for high-quality, inexpensive books are school book clubs (described in Chapter 4). Classroom books can be ordered for free with bonus points earned from student book orders.

WHAT DO YOU THINK? People often select books by their covers. How do you choose the books you want to read? What things on a book cover attract your interest? Have you ever read a good book that had an uninteresting cover? A poorly written book that was attractively bound? Which one are you more apt to remember? Have you ever read a book that was so good that you wanted everyone to read it? Have you begun a collection of paperback books for your own classroom library? What books would you like to obtain?

V. Including Everyone

When you begin to select books for a particular class of students, you will want to provide materials for a wide range of reading levels and interests. You will also want to choose literature written by and about persons of different races, cultures and ethnic groups. The annotated reference books listed at the end of this chapter describe literature that involves the heritage and current lives of Native Americans, African Americans, Asian Americans and Latino/Latina Americans.

You will not want to force books that deal with life problems on your students, but you can make them available. There are excellent stories whose characters deal with death, divorce, disease, adoption, alcoholism, drug abuse, poverty, homelessness, disability and other family crises. These books are called, aptly enough, "problem novels," and they vary in quality, depending on the author. The best books of this type are good stories whose characters happen to be involved in stressful situations. The worst of this genre are heavily pedantic, with obvious points to make. Including some of the best in your collection will provide your students with insight, inspiration and comfort when it is most needed. How will your students know these books are available? You can tell them about one every other day during your book previews.

If you have students who have vision problems, you will want to check with your school's special education consultant to see if there are specific materials that should be made available for independent reading, such as large-print books or books on tape. It may be appropriate for some children to use earphones to listen to books read aloud, while they look at the print and pictures. Books are also available as computer programs, which can be accessed by children with severe learning problems or physical disabilities. Children with attention problems should be encouraged to do independent reading in a place where they will be comfortable and can observe the guideline about not interrupting the reading of others. Picture books on topics of interest are great reading motivators to children who are easily distracted, as are magazines with many photographs.

Occasionally, students in the upper-intermediate grades will be hesitant about participating in independent reading. Most often, this is because the practice of reading independently in school is new to them. Some may not be acquainted with their own reading interests; others may associate reading with unpleasant experiences at school. Regular independent reading time can help these students begin to have pleasant associations with reading, but it may take time to establish the trust that will permit full participation. You might want to have additional printed materials available, such as car and sports magazines and specialized topic magazines that deal with computers, history, mechanics, boats or science. Students of this age also enjoy the Guinness record books and interesting picture books of all kinds. Girls are attracted to books that feature romantic themes and nonfiction that addresses health concerns and personal appearance. Other printed materials such as travel brochures, driver's license manuals and informational pamphlets are often appealing to this age group. It is imperative to have reading material available for a wide range of reading levels, so that all students can have a selection from which to choose.

Perhaps the most important element of independent reading for the intermediate/middle-school levels is the active participation of the teacher. If the teacher grades papers or walks around the room to supervise compliance, students are more likely to regard this time as a challenge not to participate. It is also important to emphasize to students that this involvement with books is for enjoyment and that no further assignment will be associated with what they read. Students of this age often form cliques and closely monitor each other's behavior. While you will want to discover and respond to the reading interests of all your students, it will be helpful to begin with the leaders of these groups because the other students will carefully watch the response of this person and model his or her behavior accordingly.

Books to Increase Understanding

The characters in each of these books are so powerful that they will be remembered long after you finish reading about them. Written by African American authors, they represent a range of experience, both historical and contemporary.

To Be a Slave[36] by Julius Lester. This Newbery Honor book is a chronicle of the slavery experience, dictated by those who endured it to members of the American Anti-Slavery Society and other abolition groups in the first half of the nineteenth century, and later to persons in the Federal Writer's Project in the 1930s. The narratives cover the slave trade, slave auctions, plantation life and the perils of runaway slaves. It is impossible to read these tragic first-person accounts of slavery and be unmoved by them.

Undying Glory: The Story of the Massachusetts 54th Regiment[37] by Clinton Cox. This is the story of one of the first all-black regiments in the Civil War. Mustered in Massachusetts, the regiment drew volunteers from 22 states and included Lewis Douglass, the son of Frederick Douglass. Members of the regiment served gallantly at Fort Wagner, where they charged an impregnable fortress and lost many of their ranks. This compelling and historically accurate account of the "glory" regiment also includes pictures of recruiting posters and photographs of noted regimental members.

Roll of Thunder, Hear My Cry[38] by Mildred Taylor. This Newbery Award novel tells the story of a year in the life of Cassie Logan and her family in Depression-era Mississippi. During this year, Cassie becomes aware for the first time of threats to her home and family because of her race. The strength of family love and loyalty is vividly portrayed as they survive physical threats to themselves and their land by hostile landlords, night riders and burnings.

M.C. Higgins, the Great[39] by Virginia Hamilton. This tells the story of Mayo Cornelius, who sets up a forty-foot steel tower in front of his home in the mountains. From this perch he can see all of the valley and all of the strip mine rubble that threatens to bury his home. M.C. tries to think of ways to move his family away from the slag heap. His plans are tied to the stranger who tape records his mother's singing. The hopes, dreams and disappointments of this story are poignant, and M.C.'s interactions with his family are warm, real and unforgettable.

WHAT DO YOU THINK?   Why do you think it is important for children to find their culture reflected in the books they read? Which books have you read that you enjoyed because they portrayed family life that was familiar to you? What have you read that gave you insight into children's lives in other cultures?

VI. Step-by-Step: Independent Reading

It is important to be able to see your students during their independent reading and that they be able to see you. In the beginning you will want to monitor their level of involvement with reading to be able to adjust the types of books you make available and the length of time you provide for the activity. To begin the session, you might simply say, "It's time to read. Let's review the guidelines." After the program has been in progress for several weeks, students will begin to anticipate independent reading time and get their books out ready to read, from as small a gesture as a glance at the wall clock. Rehearsing the guidelines is usually necessary only at the beginning to help establish the routine.

It is helpful to put time limits on the book search process by saying something like: "You have until the timer rings to find your book and begin reading." Set the timer for three to five minutes and assist anyone who asks for help. If students are not accustomed to independent reading activity, they may need reassurance that they can really choose something they want to read.

When the timer rings, find a comfortable place to read. As everyone settles in, set the timer again for the length of time you have decided on, from five to thirty minutes depending on the age and maturity of your students. In schools that have adopted an all-school independent reading program, you may be asked to follow general school policy on a scheduled time for this activity. The length of time allotted for independent reading may also be determined by school policy or as a cooperative decision in team-teaching situations.

Students will be reading independently at other times throughout the day in content area and literature studies, but this particular time is specifically set aside for reading that is not associated with an assignment. Some children may try to use the time for homework, but it is important that the reading that occurs during this time is something that follows a personal interest, is not overly difficult and develops a habit of reading for pleasure. One teacher reported that a fifth grader who transferred into her class could not permit herself to read for enjoyment and would take notes from an encyclopedia during independent reading time. After several weeks of watching other students in the class read books of their own choice, she finally began to explore some on her own. A good way to monitor your students' use of this time is to ask them about it during their individual reading conferences. You might ask, "Tell me what you're reading for fun" to assess their use of this time.

WHAT DO YOU THINK? What books or magazines did you read independently when you were elementary school age? What kinds of books or magazines would you choose if you were participating as a teacher in independent reading today?

VII. If This Is Your Situation

Your school or district may have its own program for independent reading, which requires scheduling at the same time for the entire school or district. The staff in many schools, including the principal, librarian, special teachers, cafeteria workers and janitors, literally drop everything and read for a specified time each day. Although this reduces your flexibility in scheduling somewhat, it is often a matter of school spirit to participate and you will want to give your full cooperation. If the time allotted seems too brief, you might want to schedule an additional time right before or after lunch or during the last period of the day.

If the other teachers in your school do not schedule independent reading, you might want to work with a colleague to set up a program in both of your classrooms. When more than one person is experimenting with a classroom activity, there is less isolation. You will be able to support each other and exchange experiences. Choose a teacher who has extended friendship to you and try out the idea of planning independent reading time. This partner approach may expand into Book Buddy reading and presentation exchanges between your two rooms, practices that will extend your students' experiences with books and help create bonds between grade levels. You might also want to identify teachers at other schools who have successful independent reading programs. They can provide you with valuable tips from their own experience. If you teach in a departmentalized situation, you will want to include at least ten minutes of your teaching block for independent reading, regardless of the content area. Make available books of all kinds in your subject matter area. If you teach science, you can provide high-quality picture books, poetry, biographies, informational books and fantasy with science-fiction themes. In the social studies, there will be a wide variety of historical fiction, biographies, picture books and folk literature that will be both interesting and informative for your students. If you teach mathematics, you can choose from a wide range of appealing literature that deals with math concepts at every level of instruction.

WHAT DO YOU THINK? How might you encourage teachers in your team situation to adopt a period of independent reading? What children's trade books have you examined that would be good choices for independent reading in the content areas? How do you think the informational literature available for children has changed since you were in elementary school?

VIII. Evaluating Progress

How can you tell if your program of independent reading is beneficial to your students? Your goal is to help students increase their independent reading activity, so you will want to observe the following indications in your students that this goal is being reached:

1. Students read for longer periods of time.
2. They choose reading as an activity during free or unstructured time.
3. They take books home at night and on weekends.
4. Parents report an increased interest in books.
5. Students ask for books by particular authors.
6. Students request books in particular areas of interest.

You can tell by general restlessness, shuffling or whispering when most of your students have reached the limits of their attention span with reading. Try to conclude the reading session before there is widespread inattentiveness. Better to leave a good thing early than carry it past its maximum effect. It is a good idea to begin with short time periods (five minutes) with younger students and ten to fifteen minutes for older students. You can extend this time as your students gain experience and interest. If you begin with five minutes, add a two-minute increment. If this goes well, extend the time by two more minutes each day. With older children, use five-minute increments, up to a total of thirty minutes. You might also want to divide the time allotted to independent reading into two sessions, morning and afternoon.

If your students express regret when the independent reading time ends, this is a good sign that independent reading is working positively for your students. They are enjoying the activity, and the main goal of independent reading has been achieved. When students talk about what they are reading, this is another good indication of their involvement in books. You can assess this involvement by checking the Best Bets reviews and listening closely to comments made during guided reading (Chapter 5), individual reading conferences (Chapter 6) and Friday Afternoon Sharing Time (Chapter 7).

When independent reading is an important activity for students, they will ask for particular books or kinds of books to be included in the collection made available to them. To the best of your ability, try to respond to these requests, enlisting the help of your school librarian, the public library or a good resource handbook such as those listed in the Resources for Teaching section below.

Parents will often make comments such as, "What did you do to Nick? He's always got his nose in a book." Or they will ask where they can get a specific title or type of book in which the student shows interest. Take note when books are taken home at night because this indicates your student's interest in reading is extending into leisure time as a selected activity.

Do not forget to evaluate your own involvement with independent reading. Do you enjoy the reading time and do you look forward to it? Are you discovering books you want to share with your students or other teachers? Have you found new books or ideas that can be used in your teaching? If you can answer "yes" to one or more of these questions, you have established a positive involvement with independent reading yourself. Enjoy!

WHAT DO YOU THINK? When you were in elementary school, did you take library books home at night? Was time set aside for independent reading in any of your elementary grades? How often did you read real, whole books at school?

IX. Creating Partners

Many teachers encourage children to take books home for independent reading. Plastic zip-lock bags labeled with the classroom number provide protection and identification if the book is lost. (Safety officials discourage putting a child's name on any item that might be spotted by a stranger.) Some teachers send home their schedule of independent reading times during the week so parents or grandparents can join the class occasionally for these sessions. These visitors may stay in the class afterward to talk about their favorite books or help with other activities. Principals, special teachers, librarians, cafeteria workers, school secretaries, maintenance staff and community members can also be asked to join a class for independent reading. Some schools arrange occasional buddy days for independent reading, where classes at the same grade level visit and bring their favorite books to share.

These sessions might be scheduled immediately before a Friday Afternoon Sharing Time, so the visitors can remain as part of the audience.

WHAT DO YOU THINK?   What are the benefits to students when the teacher invites other people from the school and community to join them for independent reading? What do you think might be the benefits to the visitors?

X.   Perspectives

John Dewey, the great American educational philosopher of this century, believed that students will expend great efforts when they have a true interest in an idea or activity. He observed that many teachers try to motivate children in two equally unsuccessful ways: Some believe they have to create interest in learning tasks so that children will participate in activities that require effort; others believe it is in the students' best interests to require effort for learning tasks so they will develop the discipline necessary to master other tasks. Both of these approaches to learning assume that children's natural interests and efforts are foreign to school-related learning.

In classrooms where there are opportunities to engage in independent reading and there is a wide range of attractive reading materials to explore, students will display both interest and effort in their reading habits. Dewey believed that children are naturally curious and expend great effort to find out things they want to know. They spend hours developing skills that interest them and seek out information on projects or hobbies. Dewey believed that the school could harness this great natural enthusiasm for learning by providing opportunities for students to develop learning skills as they explored real interests. He spoke of this as giving direction to tendencies already present.

John Dewey wrote several books that are very accessible to teachers. The two annotated below examine ideas that are central to the ideas of integrated language learning.

> *Interest and Effort in Education*[40]   Dewey explores the ways teachers try to use either interest or effort to help students become successful learners. Each of these approaches makes an incorrect assumption about learning. A more effective approach considers the natural learning tendencies of children.

> *Experience and Education*[41]   Dewey believed that education should consider the experience of the student, building on this experience by helping children reorganize or reconstruct it. The goal of education for Dewey is to help children grow and become autonomous learners.

WHAT DO YOU THINK?   How true are Dewey's ideas about interest and effort to your own experience as a learner? What do you observe about your own efforts when you are truly interested in an activity?

XI. Exploring Professional Literature

The Children's Book Council (CBC) is a nonprofit association of children's and young adult trade book publishers. The council sponsors National Children's Book Week, which has been celebrated in schools and libraries since 1919, during the week before Thanksgiving. Materials to promote interest in books and celebrate National Book Week are available from CBC and include posters, bookmarks, informational pamphlets, banners, puzzles and games. The CBC has joint committees with various professional education associations, including the National Council of Teachers of English, the International Reading Association, the American Library Association, the National Council for the Social Studies and the National Science Teachers Association. These committees select outstanding books in literature, science and the social studies each year and print these lists annually in the respective content area journals. These lists are also available to anyone for the price of postage (see Resources for Teaching in Chapter 4 for more information).

Twice yearly, members receive the CBC Features Newsletter, which includes a materials brochure and CBC Features. There is a one-time lifetime fee that provides members with the newsletter, illustrated materials brochures and information on council activities. Each issue of the materials brochure includes lists of free materials that can be ordered from CBC member publishers. Teachers and librarians can request these materials by sending self-addressed, stamped envelopes to the marketing departments of various publishers. Publishers offer promotional materials for their books, including bookmarks, posters and author information. Some provide party and activity kits that come complete with posters, author biographies, invitations, party planners, puzzles and games.

CBC Features highlight a different topic of interest in each issue, with original articles written by trade book authors, illustrators, teachers, librarians and publishers. Many articles contain helpful ideas for using trade books to teach in the curriculum areas. Past issues have included suggestions for using literature to teach math concepts and ways to adapt books for reader's theater. Inquiries about membership or materials may be directed to: CBC Order Center, 350 Scotland Road, Orange, New Jersey 07050.

WHAT DO YOU THINK? Have you ever noticed the visual materials in public or school libraries? How do posters and banners draw interest to books? What interests do teachers, librarians and publishers have in common?

XII. Resources for Teaching

At some point in your preparation for teaching you will probably take a course in children's literature. Most of the texts used for these courses contain comprehensive discussions about books and constitute a valuable resource for your teaching later on. If a course in children's literature is not required, you may want to consider taking it as an elective or purchasing a text on your own. You will also want to be familiar with some of the reference books described below. Most can be found in your school library, but you may want to purchase one of your own, such as the relatively inexpensive *Adventuring with Books*, published by the National Council of Teachers of English.

> *Adventuring with Books: A Booklist for Pre-K–Grade 6* (op. cit.), 10th edition, Julie M. Jensen and Nancy L. Roser, editors. This volume contains brief plot synopses of children's books, information on illustrations and applications in the classroom. Also included are author, illustrator, subject and title indexes for use in locating titles or developing themes. There is a directory of publishers and a list of award-winning books. Included are books that feature holidays; humor; friendship; ethnic, racial and religious groups; human relationships; and disabilities.

> *Best Books for Children: Preschool through Grade 6* (op. cit.), 4th edition, by John Gillespie and Corinne Naden. There are title, author, illustrator and subject/grade-level indexes in this thousand-page hardbound volume. Major subjects are arranged alphabetically under broad categories that include all the genres of children's literature, books for younger and older readers, biographies, fairy tales, the arts, language, history, geography, science and recreation. There are books about mathematics, physics, mysteries, crafts, hobbies, jokes, puzzles, geology and chemistry. This reference book contains hundreds of subcategories, such as holidays, government, astronomy, sports figures and mythology. The index on ethnic groups includes stories about African Americans, Asian Americans (Vietnamese, Chinese, Japanese), Mexican Americans, Native Americans, the Inuit (Eskimo), and Jewish Americans. There is also a listing of historical fiction set in the United States and around the world.

> *The New York Times Parent's Guide to the Best Books for Children*[42] by Eden Ross Lipson, children's editor of *The New York Times*. This is an excellent guide to books, designed for parents but very helpful for teachers. Books are annotated and arranged by topic and age level. There are subject, author, and illustrator indexes, as well as those for selecting books that are age-appropriate and ones to read aloud.

XIII. Reflections

From a Teacher's Journal—Jackie Hogue, Fifth Grade

> The first day of school we talk about how we learn and discuss some strategies for good readers. I have signs all over the room, such as "Good Readers Take Chances—It's Okay to Make Mistakes." We talk about strategies for reading, such as: skipping words they don't know, as long as they understand what they are reading; reading for meaning; and rereading sentences that don't make sense. I encourage them to look for books written by favorite authors and to discuss their books with friends. I tell them that they can read anything they want during silent reading, and they can share what they've read with

a partner in a Buddy Journal. This is a great way to get kids writing about things they're interested in.

(Several months later . . .) I have a student in my class who was released from the LD reading program. This is the first year he has taken part in the regular classroom program. His mother and I were concerned about him keeping up with the rest of the class. Aaron has wonderful basic reading skills and a high level of concentration, but he reads very slowly. All he needs is practice. I had a conversation with Aaron's mother today. I told her how much I appreciate parents like her who follow through with suggestions. She always makes sure Aaron has quiet time to study and read, and she checks assignments to make sure they are completed. She told me Aaron has been reading lately just for the pleasure of reading. She has walked into his room several times and "caught" him reading! Aaron told his mom she could get rid of the baby books, because now he could read chapter books. He has even asked if he could go to the library to check out books I've read aloud to the class. Instead of asking to watch TV, he reads!

TRYING OUT THE CHAPTER IDEAS

1. What idea(s) interested you the most in this chapter?
2. When you have the opportunity to read, what kinds of books or reading material do you choose?
3. What was one of the best books you have ever read? Have you ever read a book more than once?
4. Find one of the three resource books listed above in your college/university or public library and research a topic of your interest. What kinds of books did you find on this topic?
5. Borrow a copy of the Children's Book Council Newsletter from the school librarian or the children's librarian at the public library. What topic is highlighted? Read several articles. Which interested you? Did you find anything helpful for teaching?
6. Select three picture books from a children's literature library. When you have read them, preview them for a small group of your classmates or the elementary class where you are observing.
7. Preview three picture books for a kindergarten class.
8. Preview two books suitable for primary students in a small group of your classmates or in an elementary classroom.
9. With your classmates, present a series of previews of intermediate-level books for an intermediate-level classroom.
10. Interview a school librarian or the children's librarian in a public library. What resources do they use to select new books? Where do they get materials for display?

Notes

1. Louise M. Rosenblatt, *Literature as Exploration*, 4th ed. (New York: Modern Language Association, 1983), p. 287.
2. R. Anderson, E. Hiebert, J. Scott, and I. Wilkinson, *Becoming a Nation of Readers* (Washington, D.C.: National Institute of Education, 1985), p. 119.

3. Daniel Fader, James Duggins, Tom Finn, and Elton McNeil, *The New Hooked on Books* (New York: Berkeley, 1976).

4. Michael O. Tunnell and James S. Jacobs, "Using 'Real' Books: Research Findings on Literature Based Reading Instruction," *The Reading Teacher* 42(March 1989):470–477.

5. D. V. Connor, "The Relationship between Reading Achievement and Voluntary Reading of Children," *Educational Review* 6:221–227. V. Greaney, "Factors Related to Amount and Type of Leisure Reading," *Reading Research Quarterly* 15:337–357.

6. Linda G. Fielding, Paul T. Wilson, and Richard Anderson, "A New Focus on Free Reading: The Role of Trade Books in Reading Instruction," in *The Contexts of School Based Literacy*, edited by Taffy E. Raphael (New York: Random House, 1984).

7. L. G. Fielding, P. T. Wilson, and R. C. Anderson, "Growth in Reading and How Children Spend Their Time Outside of School," *Reading Research Quarterly* 23(Summer 1988):285–303.

8. Robert A. McCracken and Marlene J. McCracken, "Modeling Is the Key to Sustained Silent Reading," *Reading Teacher* 31(January 1978):406–408.

9. Dr. Seuss, *The Cat in the Hat* (New York: Random House, 1987).

10. Arnold Lobel, *Frog and Toad Are Friends* (New York: HarperCollins Books for Children, 1970).

11. Sid Hoff, *Sammy the Seal* (New York: HarperCollins, 1980).

12. *The World Atlas for Children* (New York: Hammond, Inc., 1993).

13. David A. Boehm, ed., *The Guinness Sports Record Book* (New York: Sterling, 1992).

14. Graeme Base, *Animalia* (New York: Abrams, 1986).

15. Graeme Base, *The Eleventh Hour* (New York: Abrams, 1989).

16. Beverly Cleary, *Ramona Quimby, Age 8* (New York: William Morrow, 1981).

17. Jean George, *My Side of the Mountain* (New York: Dutton, 1975).

18. Lois Lowry, *Number the Stars* (New York: Houghton Mifflin, 1989).

19. David Macaulay, *Castle* (New York: Houghton Mifflin, 1982).

20. David Macaulay, *Pyramid* (New York: Houghton Mifflin, 1982).

21. *National Geographic*, the official journal of the National Geographic Society. This classic magazine is full of colorful photographs, paintings, drawings, charts, maps, people and animals from around the world. Topics include science, history, culture and the environment. Address: 1145 17th St. NW, Washington, DC 20036. Ph: 1-800-638-4077. This is a monthly journal sent to members of the society. Membership is $21/year.

22. Jerry Bushey, *Monster Trucks and Other Giant Machines on Wheels* (Minneapolis: Carolrhoda, 1985).

23. Stephen Keeler, *Louis Braille* (New York: Scholastic, 1988).

24. Donald Sobol, *The Wright Brothers at Kitty Hawk* (Jefferson City, Mo.: Scholastic Books, 1987).

25. John T. Gillespie and Corinne J. Naden, *Best Books for Children: Preschool through Grade 6*, 4th ed. (New York: Reed, 1990).

26. Julie M. Jensen and Nancy L. Roser, eds., *Adventuring with Books: A Booklist for Pre-K–Grade 6*, National Council of Teachers of English Bibliography Series (Urbana, Ill.: NCTE, 1993).

27. National Geographic Society, *National Geographic World*. This is a magazine for students ages 8–13 that features factual stories about outdoor adventures, natural history, sports, science and history. Subscriptions are $12.95/year for the monthly magazine. Address: 1145 17th St. NW, Washington, DC 20036.

28. National Wildlife Federation, *Ranger Rick*. This is a nature magazine featuring lots of animals. It is intended for students ages 6–12 and is $15/year for the monthly magazine. Address: Ranger Rick, National Wildlife Federation, 8925 Leesburg Pike, Vienna, VA 22184-0001.

29. *Cricket, The Magazine for Children*. This literary magazine for children ages 6–14 features stories and poems of generally high standards. It is issued monthly, and a year's subscription is $29.97. Address: Carus Publishing, 315 5th St., Peru, IL 61354.

30. *Highlights for Children*. A magazine for children ages 2–12 that features stories, poems, games and articles of interest to primary and intermediate children. A year's subscription is $21.95. Address: 803 Church Street, Honesdale, PA 18431.

31. Scholastic Books Magazines: *Early Childhood*; *Scholastic News* (graded editions, available also in Spanish, includes periodic news videos); *SuperScience* (primary, intermediate, middle school editions); *Language Arts* (grades 3–5, 6–8, and at-risk); *Math* (grades 3–4, 5–6, 7–10). Address: Scholastic Book Clubs, Inc., P.O. Box 3745, Jefferson City, MO 65102–9838.

32. Meindert DeJong, *The House of Sixty Fathers* (New York: HarperCollins, 1987).

33. Madeleine L'Engle, *A Wrinkle in Time* (New York: Farrar, 1962).

34. Robert Westall, *Blitzcat* (New York: Macmillan, 1989).

35. Robert Westall, *The Machine Gunners* (New York: William Morrow, 1975).

36. Julius Lester, *To Be a Slave* (New York: Scholastic, 1968).

37. Clinton Cox, *Undying Glory: The Story of the Massachusetts 54th Regiment* (New York: Scholastic, 1991).

38. Mildred D. Taylor, *Roll of Thunder, Hear My Cry* (New York: Dial, 1976).

39. Virginia Hamilton, *M.C. Higgins the Great* (New York: Macmillan, 1974).

40. John Dewey, *Interest and Effort in Education* (Carbondale, Ill.: Southern Illinois University Press, 1975).

41. John Dewey, *Experience and Education* (Carbondale, Ill.: Southern Illinois University Press, 1975).

42. Eden Ross Lipson, *The New York Times Parent's Guide to the Best Books for Children* (New York: Random House, 1988).

CHAPTER FOUR

Creating a Literature Base

WHAT'S HAPPENING HERE? This teacher reads aloud to her students and provides a wide variety of books for them to read independently and as a class. In a casual moment, she and her students share favorite passages from books they are currently reading.

Only the very rarest kind of best in anything can be good enough for the young.

—Walter de la Mare

A knowledge of different literatures is the best way to free one's self from the tyranny of any of them.

—Jose Marti

The man who does not read good books has no advantage over the man who can't read.

—Mark Twain

LOOKING AHEAD
1. What is literature-based learning?
2. What kinds of literature are available for children?
3. What does each type of literature offer children?
4. At what age levels can picture books be used?
5. What kinds of awards are given for books of quality?
6. What qualities characterize good examples of each genre?
7. Where can lists of good books be obtained?
8. What are the benefits of using school book clubs?
9. How can good literature assist multicultural understanding?

IN 25 WORDS OR LESS   To provide students with the best possible associations with literature, select a wide variety of books from the best examples of all the genres.

I. Focus: Selecting Literature for the Classroom

In traditional classrooms, **textbooks** are used for instruction in individual subject matter areas. Textbooks contain a broad range of information about a subject area, such as the language arts, science or the social studies. Students read assignments in these texts and complete exercises designed to help them retain knowledge or practice skills. In classrooms where literature and language are used to explore all areas of knowledge, teachers provide a wide variety of **trade books** to explore the content areas and for students to read independently.

Classrooms that integrate language and learning are **literature-based**, which means that high-quality trade books are used to support inquiry and learning in all areas of the curriculum. Teachers who develop a literature base for classroom learning incorporate all genres of children's literature into the curriculum. They select from each type of book to read aloud and to conduct guided reading, mini-lessons and writing workshops. A wide variety of fiction, nonfiction and poetry trade books are provided for students' independent reading and to introduce, expand and enrich content area studies. Students are encouraged to draw from all the genres for their individual reading conferences and to attempt each kind of writing on their own.

From the thousands of books published for children, how do teachers know which ones to choose for their classroom? This chapter describes the kinds of children's books, provides guidelines for selecting the best and suggests ways to build a classroom library. You will want to select books to support student learning from every **genre** of children's literature. A literary genre is a **specific kind** of literature, such as biography, poetry or historical fiction, and each genre has certain characteristics that distinguish it from the others. Biography, for example, is based on the known facts of a person's life, while historical fiction tells an imaginative story in an authentic historical setting. Like adult literature, children's literature can be broadly classified as fiction, nonfiction and poetry. **Fiction** is literature that is imaginative, an artistic creation of the writer, such as folktales, modern fantasy, historical fiction and modern realistic fiction. **Nonfiction**, on the other hand, is composed of those writings that tell about real persons, events or things. Biography and informational writing in the sciences, mathematics, social sciences and the arts are examples of this kind of writing. **Poetry** is characterized by the elements of rhyme, rhythm, repetition and imagery.

Classifying children's literature into genres is helpful for teachers and students alike because it encourages thinking and discussion about the purposes and significant elements of each type. In the chapters that follow, you will observe how teachers encourage children to read and write in the various genres and to use a wide range of literature to explore topics of interest to them. The following section provides a description of each kind of literature and lists reasons for including each type in the classroom.

Traditional Literature

A young girl is made to tend the fire by her cruel older sisters, causing her hands and face to become burned and scarred. But because she has a kind heart and is filled with courage, she alone can see the Invisible Being and is chosen to be his wife. *The Rough-Face Girl*[1] is a myth from the Algonquin Indians and is an example of traditional literature. This genre also includes folktales, fairy tales, fables, legends and tall tales that have been handed down in an oral tradition from generation to generation in a culture or society. Each of these kinds of stories are described below.

Folktales/fairy tales relate adventures of animals or humans and contain elements of the supernatural. There is usually a quest or task for the main character who is assisted by helpers with supernatural powers or opposed by magically endowed adversaries. A common theme for these tales is the reward of good and the punishment of evil. You probably recall many of these stories from your own childhood, such as The Three Bears, Little Red Riding Hood, Snow White, Sleeping Beauty, Puss-in-Boots, Rapunzel and Rumpelstiltskin.

Fables are stories that feature animals behaving like humans. Their purpose is to illustrate human foibles or to teach a lesson. The most famous of these is *Aesop's Fables*,[2] a collection of stories which show the folly of greed, impatience, vanity or ignorance. The hilarious *Fables*,[3] written and illustrated by Arnold Lobel, gives a contemporary flair to the old themes. Mitsumasa Anno's version[4] of the familiar tales is full of puzzles and contains a parallel story told by a fox.

Myths, such as the story of the Algonquin girl related above, are considered to be true in the societies in which they originate. These sacred accounts involve deities, humans and animals. Myths are accounts of events that happened in the earliest of times, with themes that deal with the origin of the world, human beings and natural phenomena, such as the seasons and weather.

Legends are also considered to be true by the storyteller and audience, but they are more contemporary than myths. They are set in the recent past rather than long ago and frequently exaggerate notable events, such as those which occur in times of war, plague and famine. Many, such as the Arthurian legends, feature royalty and brave deeds.

Tall tales are obviously exaggerated accounts of characters who exhibit superhuman strength or endurance. These stories feature larger-than-life persons, such as Paul Bunyan who could easily cut down an entire forest in a day. Other famous figures include the African American railroad builder John Henry and the infamous cowboy Pecos Bill. Steven Kellogg chronicles the lives of many tall tale figures, including a colorful retelling of the Mike Fink legend.[5]

Traditional literature provides experiences with time-honored values and ideals: the triumph of right over wrong, the rewards of hard work and perseverance, and the vindication of the persecuted, helpless or humble of society. These stories utilize fanciful beings, persons with exaggerated powers, talking animals and noble heros, all of which appeal to the imagination and provide a sense of adventure. Many of the stories contain predictable elements that create anticipation and allow listener participation. These stories in Big Book format are excellent for guided reading in kindergarten and early primary grades because they provide predictable and repetitive elements that can be easily assimilated by beginning readers.

Modern Fantasy

While they are hiding in an old wardrobe at their uncle's home, four children accidently enter the magical kingdom of Narnia, where they encounter an evil witch, talking animals, a deified lion and all manner of strange creatures. They are called on to fight the great evil that keeps the kingdom in continual winter. Eventually, the children become kings and queens of Narnia. When they return from their adventures they are surprised to discover that no time has elapsed, although their adventures lasted for years. *The Lion, the Witch and the Wardrobe*[6] typifies modern fantasy, with its strange creatures, mythical elements, magic, time warps and the forces of good and evil in great battle.

Modern fantasy shares themes with traditional literature and is created by altering one or more elements of reality. Because some elements of the story are based in reality, the reader is able to suspend disbelief and enter worlds that could not exist, in terms of current understanding. Fantasy is literature that is fantastic in some way—animals talk (*Further Tales of Uncle Remus*),[7] little people live in the walls (*The Borrowers*),[8] time travel is possible (*The Trolley to Yesterday*)[9] and entire worlds follow different rules of nature (*The White Mountains*).[10] Stories that feature the deep myths of a culture, such as the Arthurian legends, are featured in books such as *The Dark Is Rising* series.[11]

Fantasy helps develop a sense of imagination in children. It appeals to ideals of justice and confronts readers with issues of good and evil. Modern fantasy provides an escape from the burden of reality and helps children identify with characters who are strong and responsible. Most children enjoy reading about the clever and charming animals and persons who populate stories of fantasy. They like the exaggeration and preposterous situations, the great adventures and humor.

Modern fantasy also contains excellent examples of allegory, irony and figurative language. The "What if?" questions of fantasy writing (What if animals could talk? What if we could travel through time? What if man could fly? What if space were curved?) are characteristic of innovative thinkers through time, from Leonardo da Vinci to Einstein. As children read fantasy, they are encouraged to think creatively and to give credence to their own imaginings.

Science Fiction

This type of fantasy is based on scientific hypothesizing and includes tales of robots, spacecraft, mystery and civilizations from other times and places in the universe. Most stories are based on probable advances of science that have occurred on other planets or in a future time and appeal to children who are interested in space and "what if" story situations. *Outer Space and All That Junk*[12] is a good story to read aloud to introduce an ecology unit, while Madeleine L'Engle's classic trilogy that begins with *A Wrinkle in Time*[13] illustrates the best of this genre for intermediate students.

Modern Realistic Fiction

A young African American boy meets his long-absent father for the first time and accompanies him on a tragic but insightful trip across the country to his father's home. During the journey, the boy learns the character and history of his father and, in the process, learns a great deal about himself. *Somewhere in the Darkness*[14] is an example of modern realistic fiction, with its honest treatment of real problems that real children face. Although the most popular topics with elementary age children are animal stories, mysteries, sports stories and humor, they are also interested in reading about children who face challenges in their lives and families who have exciting adventures.

When children read realistic fiction, they identify with the characters in the story and discover that their hopes and fears are shared by others. They find insight into their own problems, broaden their interests, experience vicarious adventures and expand their understanding of persons of different backgrounds. This type of literature stimulates discussion, helps children share ideas and feelings and provides pleasure and escape. Everyone experiences fear and doubts about themselves, and realistic fiction provides children with models for dealing with these fears. In the context of a compelling story, they learn that children can be brave and intelligent, can solve difficult problems and can overcome obstacles of handicap, family disruption and challenges from nature.

Historical Fiction

A sixteen-year-old boy enters the Union army at the beginning of the Civil War and soon encounters exhaustion, starvation, and the death of his friends in battle. Like other soldiers in the conflict, he discovers that his sworn enemy, the Rebel soldier, is human and even admirable. *Rifles for Watie*[15] is an example of a story presented in a historically accurate setting. The major issues of the Civil War are seen by readers through the eyes of a young man with hopes and fears not unlike their own. When students read in this genre, they identify with a compelling main character and vicariously experience a period in history. They learn how people both affect and are affected by the times in which they live. Good historical fiction is painstakingly researched for authentic detail and is presented in a form that is attractive to student readers. Historical fiction helps people from the past come alive for students. They have the opportunity to live vicariously in another time, to discover what it was like to dress in period clothing, obtain and prepare the foods of that time, go to school, live in a log cabin, help build the pyramids, sail on a fishing boat, or live in a concentration camp.

From stories of historical fiction and their authentic details, students can gain a new understanding of their own and others' heritage. The values, beliefs, and customs included in the story provide insight into the significance of historical events and help develop an awareness and understanding of the past. This understanding often promotes an appreciation of the sacrifices and perseverance that created the benefits of the present. Vivid descriptions of history, presented in narrative form, are more interesting to students. They discover in this genre the human qualities that persist through time and connect us with the past.

Biography

Did you know that in the early days of trains the engineer had to stop the train every few miles so that it could be oiled? If you knew this, you probably also know about Elijah McCoy, an African American inventor who developed the self-lubricating oil cup for trains and later the graphite cup, variations of which are still in use today, even in spaceships. In fact, his invention was of such good quality that engineers always asked for "the real McCoy." The fascinating story of *The Real McCoy, The Life of an African-American Inventor*[16] is an example of biography. It is a factual presentation of the life of a famous or brave person, or someone who has made a significant contribution to society.

Subjects of biography include inventors, explorers, scientists, political and religious leaders, social reformers, artists, sports figures, doctors, teachers, writers, war heroes, people who have overcome obstacles of personal disability or environment to succeed and persons whose bravery or intelligence have changed or influenced our lives. Biographies help develop the idea that one person can make a difference in the lives of those around them. When children read biographies, they have the opportunity to learn from the lives of interesting people and to live vicariously through the challenges portrayed. They see that the most famous and brave were once children. They experience the joy and sadness of other persons and have the opportunity to read about the successes of those who are like them in gender, race, culture or disability. When students read about people they like or admire, they often continue to read more about them, the issues they faced, other persons mentioned in the biography and the particular time period.

Poetry

" 'Twas the night before Christmas, and all through the house, not a creature was stirring, not even a mouse" is familiar to most people. It is the beginning of the narrative poem *A Visit from St. Nicholas*[17] by Clement Moore and a time-honored part of the Santa Claus tradition. Indeed, Moore's description of St. Nicholas was a great influence in creating the American image of Santa Claus. This poem tells a story using patterns of rhyme and rhythm ("To the top of the porch! To the top of the wall! Now dash away! Dash away! Dash away all!") and frequent imagery ("His droll little mouth was drawn up like a bow. And the beard on his chin was as white as the snow").

Why is it important to include poetry in the literature you select for your classroom? Children enjoy listening to poetry, both classic and contemporary, rhymed and unrhymed. It helps them become more aware of sound patterns, expands their vocabulary and increases their appreciation of language. Poetry helps them see the value of carefully chosen words and encourages them to look at the world in new ways and with new appreciation. Well-written poetry models precision of thought and language and inspires wonder through the beauty of its words and the power of its images. Humorous poetry can lighten lives that are too serious and assist children's expression of feelings. Verse describes familiar moods and helps students identify with persons of other cultures, ages and gender. At its best, poetry gives them insight into themselves and others.

Plays and Reader's Theater

Plays written for children span a wide range of interests and subject matter. You can purchase commercially prepared dramas for the classroom from teacher's stores or borrow them from your school or public library. Commercially prepared play kits include instructions for presenting a performance and multiple copies of the script. Students also enjoy reading plays adapted from their favorite books in reader's theater. These scripts can be purchased commercially or can be adapted by your students from their favorite stories.

Multicultural Literature

A young Latina girl imagines that she and her grandmother are flying like birds, high above the city. They fly over the Statue of Liberty, where her grandmother arrived in the United States, and circle above the docks where workers are unloading fresh produce from the country where her grandmother grew up. They take a rest on the clouds and observe familiar surroundings of family and friends below them. This is the story of *Abuela*[18] (Grandmother) and it is an example of multicultural literature.

When children's literature in any genre is written from a cultural perspective, it is referred to as multicultural. In the United States, teachers pay particular attention to the literature by and about the racial and ethnic minorities who share the American culture, such as Native Americans, African Americans, Latino/Latina Americans, Asian Americans, Jewish Americans and the Amish. They also try to include books that represent additional cultures from around the world to help children develop an understanding and appreciation of their fellow citizens of the world.

Coming in contact with multicultural literature helps all children develop a sense of the richness of heritage shared as Americans. It sensitizes them to the difficulties faced by minority peoples in a society and helps them identify with minorities as real human beings, not as stereotypes. For minority children, literature that displays their heritage in a respectful manner helps them develop self-respect and a sense of identity. Multicultural literature includes writing in all the genres, with special emphasis on cultural holidays and celebrations. Other writing includes folktales and fairy tales, legends, informational nonfiction, historical fiction, contemporary realistic fiction, poetry, picture books and biography.

Informational Books

Where can you find out everything you wanted to know about polar wildlife? Of course you could look in the encyclopedia, but if you want to read about each animal in detail, while you look at pictures of caribou, wolves, penguins and whales and read interesting facts about them, then you would probably pick up and read *Polar Wildlife*[19] by Kamini Khanduri. Like most good informational books for children, this one features an index of terms, explanations, descriptions, definitions and colorful illustrations, designed to attract and hold a young reader's interest.

Informational books deal with real subjects, such as wildlife, history, geographical regions, culture, weather, the arts, science, math, health, recreation and crafts, to name a few. They satisfy children's curiosity, generate new interests, provide knowledge about the world and extend or enhance what they already know. Reading these books aloud to introduce or expand a theme study, previewing them for independent reading and including them in guided reading help students develop critical thinking skills. Informational literature stretches children's minds, expands their vocabularies and encourages them to look at the world creatively and with enjoyment. A good variety of informational books are the cornerstone of learning in all areas of the curriculum.

As Beverly Kobrin points out in her book *EyeOpeners! How to Choose and Use Children's Books About Real People, Places and Things* (annotated in Perspectives in Chapter 2), children are fascinated by the real world and frequently are not provided with enough high-quality nonfiction literature to satisfy their curiosity. When children learn that they can find answers to pressing questions in this type of literature, they are drawn to books as sources of information and inspiration. The experience of Charley, described in the book *Did You Carry the Flag Today, Charley?*,[20] is an excellent example. Charley is a kindergarten student whose first contact with books is puzzling. He has not been read to at home and is somewhat uncertain about the value of books. He does have a consuming interest in snakes, however, and when he discovers that he can find out about snakes in a book, his way of looking at books and reading changes.

Formats of Children's Literature

All of the kinds of children's literature described above are available in a variety of formats, including picture books, picture storybooks, Big Books, and anthologies. Novels and nonfiction chapter books are available in long (more than 100 pages) and short forms (fewer than 100 pages). Each of these is described below.

Picture books are characterized by their illustrations. They have little or no text because the illustrations tell the story. Picture books for children typically include Mother Goose and other nursery rhymes, alphabet and counting books, books that explain concepts, easy-to-read books, wordless books and toy books. In the past, picture books have been intended for preschool and primary age children, but increasingly there are many fine examples of these books that can be used for several purposes at other instructional levels. They can be studied for details during independent (Chapter 3) or guided reading (Chapter 5) or used to stimulate creative writing responses. These books represent every genre of children's literature, and their subject matter makes them valuable for introducing or supporting a wide range of studies in the content areas (Chapter 11). Multicultural themes are featured in a great many of these books, which make them especially useful for sharing the richness of customs and perspectives. The various kinds of picture books are listed below. Examples are provided, with suggested grade levels indicated by K: Kindergarten, P: Primary, and I: Intermediate.

Nursery rhymes   Traditionally known as Mother Goose rhymes, these picture book adaptations may feature collections of nursery rhymes or a single rhyme. K: *Tomie dePaola's Mother Goose*,[21] P: *Gregory Griggs and Other Nursery Rhyme People*,[22] I: *London Bridge Is Falling Down*[23]

Toy books   These are books that can be played with. Some are made with sturdy board covers and pages. Others have parts that pop up, open up, slide or flip. Some, such as *The Very Quiet Cricket*,[24] have small computer chips that provide animal sounds or other realistic sounds to accompany the story. K: *A Folding Alphabet Book*,[25] P: *Madeline*,[26] I: *Dinotopia*[27]

Alphabet books   There are many imaginative interpretations of the alphabet, the most popular of which feature animals. But other themes are frequently used, including seasons, holidays, other cultures, history and science. K: *Potluck*,[28] P: *Alef-Bet: A Hebrew Alphabet Book*,[29] I: *ABC Americana from the National Gallery of Art*[30]

Counting   These books help students learn to count sequentially and establish one-to-one correspondence. Popular counting books utilize animals, money, holidays and familiar objects. K: *What Comes in 2's, 3's and 4's?*,[31] P: *One Magic Box*,[32] I: *Under the Sun and Over the Moon*[33]

Concepts   Concept books develop an idea in a creative and clear manner. Most common are books about color, shapes, opposites, parts of speech, ideas and specialized vocabulary from the sciences and social sciences. K: *All About Where*,[34] P: *Color Dance*,[35] I: *The Inside-Outside Book of Paris*[36]

Easy-to-read   These books have limited vocabulary and are intended for beginning readers. The best have humorous or high interest themes, such as animals, sports or school. K: *Black Crow, Black Crow*,[37] P: *Fox Outfoxed*,[38] I: *Rats on the Roof*[39]

Wordless   In these books, the pictures tell the entire story. They are created to stimulate creative thinking and the ability to find clues for the action in the story. They allow students of widely different abilities and backgrounds to interact with a story. K: *Deep in the Forest*,[40] P: *The Snowman*,[41] I: *The Mysteries of Harris Burdick*[42]

In **picture storybooks** the text tells the story, complemented by pictures that enhance or extend the story in some way. These books are characterized by a creative approach to the subject matter and usually display great imagination and originality. All the genres of children's literature can be found in storybook format. Typical storybook characters, plots and settings are described below and include:

Animals as human beings (realistic fiction)   Although the characters in the illustrations are animals, these are stories about human life in human settings. Animals live in houses, wear human clothes and face the problems of human beings. If the story is heard without looking at the pictures, it is a human story. The comforting and homey *Bread and Jam for Frances*[43] and *Little Bear's Visit*[44] for primary readers are examples of this type of storybook.

Animals as human beings (fantasy)   In these stories, animals as human beings are involved in stories with a fantasy element, usually some form of magic. *Sylvester and the Magic Pebble*[45] is an example of this type of story.

Talking animals   These characters live in traditional animal settings, such as meadows, forests, jungles, barnyards or zoos. Although they live animal lives, they talk as humans and have human feelings and problems. Roger Duvoisin's *Petunia*[46] is an example of this type of book.

Personified objects   Inanimate objects, such as dolls and toys, have human feelings and characteristics. *The Steadfast Tin Soldier*[47] and *The Velveteen Rabbit*[48] are examples of these kinds of stories.

Realistic stories   These stories include the adventures, problems, concerns and pleasures of children in a wide range of settings. They portray the loving relationships in families and are intended to be reassuring to young readers. Books such as *Peter's Chair*[49] by Ezra Jack Keats and Lynd Ward's *The Biggest Bear*[50] are examples of this kind of story.

Humorous fantasy   These books are highly inventive and feature both humans and animals in unusual situations. Trinka Hakes Noble's series of books about a pet boa constrictor[51] illustrates this type of story.

Big Books are enlarged versions of picture books or picture storybooks. Designed for group reading activities, they permit everyone to see the pictures and follow the words. Because many of these books are intended for beginning readers, they often feature **predictable stories**, which are characterized by rhyming and repeated words, sentence patterns and refrains. These predictable features give emerging readers the sensation of reading and help them make associations between spoken and written words. All the genres of children's literature can be found in Big Book formats, including a Big Book magazine for the early primary grades, a Big Science library for grades 2–4 and multicultural folktales for the primary level.[52] Many Big Books are also available in Spanish.

Anthologies are collections of stories or poems. Often arranged by genre or topic, they encourage young readers to sample authors and types of literature. They are also excellent books for teachers to keep on their desks for frequent reading aloud. Examples of this type of book are: *South and North, East and West: The Oxfam Book of Children's Stories*[53] and *Thirteen Moons on Turtle's Back: A Native American Year of Moons.*[54]

Children's **novels** and **nonfiction literature** for older elementary students are typically bound in books of one hundred pages or more. Shorter novels and nonfiction for primary children feature a format of twenty to forty pages, fewer words per page, larger print and wider margins to make them more accessible to emerging readers.

WHAT DO YOU THINK? What books in each of the genres do you remember reading as a child? Do you remember having a favorite kind of book? Why do you think this genre appealed to you? With which genres of children's literature are you most familiar? Least familiar?

II. The Importance of Children's Literature

Researchers[55] have found that when children listen to and discuss different qualities of children's literature, those who are exposed to the higher-quality literature produce narrative writing that is significantly better. Eeds and Wells[56] found that the depth and complexity of literature discussion are influenced by the quality of literature. Books of exceptional quality offer students issues and questions to struggle with and promote exceptional discussions. Bissett[57] found that children in classrooms containing literature collections read fifty percent more books than children in classrooms without book collections.

How important is the appearance of your classroom to your students? Researchers have identified characteristics of classroom libraries that attract children to books.[58] One of the most important of these is having an area that is easily accessible and visually attractive. The area should have a feeling of privacy, provide comfortable seating (rocking chair, pillows, rug) and be large enough to accommodate five children at a time. There should be five to eight books per child in the room, a wide variety of children's books at different reading levels and a regular selection of new books (new to the room). They also suggest open-faced bookshelves to display particular books, attractive posters, literature-related bulletin boards and taped stories with headsets.

WHAT DO YOU THINK? Think of a classroom you have been in recently. Does it have a library? What features were attractive to you? Why do you think researchers found that listening to higher-quality literature read aloud improved the quality of children's writing?

III. Looking into Classrooms:
Developing Literature Selection Skills

As you begin to select books for your own classroom library, you have the opportunity to acquire more than just a collection of books. If you read widely from all the genres, consult respected reference books and elicit the ideas of teachers and students, you will develop book selection skills and valuable resources for your teaching in the process. Because your concerns for selecting literature will change and develop with classroom experience, this section describes key areas to explore as you move from pre-service methods courses, to student teaching and finally to a classroom of your own.

Pre-Service Preparation

Claudia is a second-semester junior, majoring in elementary education. She is beginning to think about the kinds of books she would like to have in her own classroom library, and although she hopes to teach kindergarten, she is exploring and collecting books for all elementary grade levels. In addition to a good picture book collection for kindergartners, she chooses several intermediate-level books that can be read aloud and primary-level books for those children who are already reading. She is also selecting a number of picture books with themes that can be used with older readers.

At this point in her teaching career, Claudia is trying to explore as many different kinds of children's literature as possible and is gaining familiarity with books that have become favorites with teachers and students. From her children's literature class, Claudia has learned about the classics in children's literature, and she has read many of the Newbery and Caldecott award-winning books. Her goal is to read and briefly note as many Newbery and Caldecott books as possible in her reading journal. She is making a special effort to explore more biographies and collections of children's poetry, where she is not as widely read.

As part of an assignment in children's literature, she interviewed several teachers and students at various grade levels to find out their favorite books. The teacher who supervised her first field experience recommended additional favorites, which she has since examined and listed in her journal. She orders several inexpensive paperback books a month from a school book club through this same teacher.

Although she was teased for requesting children's books for Christmas, she received *The Polar Express*[59] and *The Random House Book of Poetry for Children*[60] among her gifts. She noticed that the books drew the interest of other family members, who examined them closely after the gift exchange. On her birthday, her family gave her a gift certificate to the bookstore in the mall, which allowed her to add books by Tomi dePaola, Eric Carle and Ezra Jack Keats. Claudia plans to ask for the latest copy of *Best Books for Children: Preschool through Grade 6*[61] (annotated in Chapter 3) as a graduation gift.

Claudia spends at least one-half hour a week browsing children's books, either in the library at her cooperating school, the university library or the public library in town. This helps her gain familiarity with the collections and organization of different kinds of libraries. It also gives her good ideas for assembling and arranging her own classroom library. She records ideas about posters, book displays and room arrangements, and she asks librarians about the sources of display materials. Claudia also explores the periodicals for children, noting the types of literature available in each and the themes that are addressed.

Student Teaching

Tony is just beginning a semester of student teaching at Lincoln School. As he gradually assumes responsibility for his third-grade class, he is beginning to gather books for his part of a general theme study on "Meeting Challenges." His assignment is "Meeting the Challenges of Nature," and he will need books for reading aloud, guided reading and independent reading. He begins by finding out the titles of books available in multiple copies from the school or classroom libraries. Several sets are available, so he reviews his notes in the reading journal he began during his junior year in college. From these sources, he selects *Call It Courage*,[62] *Sarah Bishop*,[63] *The Legend of the Bluebonnet*[64] and *The Cay*[65] as possibilities. He decides to use *The Cay* as a book to read aloud and chooses both *Call It Courage* and *Sarah Bishop* for guided literature study. He plans to check out a Big Book edition of *The Legend of the Bluebonnet* from his university library to use as an introduction to the theme of the study.

Tony volunteers to manage the book club orders during the semester he is student teaching. He previews the selections for the class, places the orders and coordinates the distribution of the books when they arrive. When he begins teaching on his own, he will feel familiar with the entire process. As his cooperating teacher discusses the use of bonus book points, Tony begins to see how classroom libraries can benefit from book club participation. His teacher suggests keeping in mind the curriculum study areas for the entire year, so that books can be selected that will support themes or individual subjects.

Tony observes that his cooperating teacher reads aloud from books in all genres. He tells Tony that children build strong attachments to books at this age, and he wants them to know how many different kinds there are to enjoy. From years of experience, he knows that informational books are just as appealing to children as storybooks because they satisfy children's curiosity and often draw in the reluctant readers, when they discover that books contain answers to the questions they have. Tony's teacher also points out the wide range of books he stocks for the classroom library, to accommodate a wide range of interests and reading abilities. He encourages Tony to present brief book talks to the class in order to stimulate student interest in books for independent reading time and draw their attention to books they otherwise might not select.

With his cooperating teacher, Tony attends several sessions of the area TAWL (Teachers Applying Whole Language) group, which provides support for teachers who integrate the language arts in their classrooms, and a workshop sponsored by the regional reading council. When he completes his student teaching, Tony will visit the classrooms of several teachers who welcome visitors into their classrooms. His teacher has also encouraged him to join a professional group, such as the National Council of Teachers of English or the International Reading Association, so he can receive their journals at a modest student rate. These journals deal with issues in language arts teaching and contain book reviews and helpful ideas for practicing teachers.

Beginning Teaching

Maria will begin teaching fifth grade in a large urban elementary school in the fall. She has visited the school several times during the summer and has had the opportunity to meet with several other fifth-grade teachers. They have included her in their team meetings to plan the curriculum for the year and have loaned her copies of several journals, including *Social Education*[66] and *MSJ: Middle School Journal*.[67] Maria used both journals as resources for projects in methods courses and is aware of the teaching helps contained in both.

She also schedules an appointment with the school librarian to review the school's collection of books and other materials. Although this review will be part of a new-teacher orientation in the fall, Maria can begin planning much sooner if she knows what will be available to her. She learns that three books per child can be borrowed for the classroom library for three weeks at a time. Individual students can borrow three books for two weeks, and this number can be increased for special research projects. The librarian encourages students to come to the media center to do research, where parents, high school student aides and community volunteers are available to help students locate information. She tells Maria to notify her when students might be requesting certain topics or types of information and tells her she will be asking for input on library purchases sometime during October. From this interview, Maria discovers that computers can be checked out for a week at a time to individual classrooms and that programs on CD-ROM are available to support science, social studies and literature studies in the curriculum. She learns how to use the computer search program and how to order books from the regional and state libraries.

Maria also visits the city library and learns about the services available to her and her students from this source. She is pleased to discover that she can borrow two books per child for three weeks from the public library and that they have a pickup and delivery service to the school. The librarian gives her a copy of the videotapes and computer programs available for loan, and Maria is happy to see that this includes the PBS programs on the Civil War.

One of Maria's colleagues at school tells her about the lending library available from the area TAWL group, and another promises to share intermediate book club order forms when they arrive in late August. Parent volunteers manage the book club ordering and distribution, and her colleagues explain how this system works. These teachers have also told her about the titles available in multiple copies in the fifth-grade paperback library.

Maria will teach United States history in a departmentalized fifth grade. She knows that her classes will have two hours of time in the media center each week, so she plans for this time to be used with reference books related to this study. She begins exploring her school and community resources for both nonfiction and fictional literature to support these studies during guided reading and independent reading. As she gets to know her class better, she will select additional books designed to support individual interests and reading levels.

WHAT HAPPENED HERE? ONE PERSPECTIVE   At each level of experience, these pre-service and beginning teachers are preparing themselves to be informed users of literature. They read constantly, note books that might be relevant to their teaching, participate in book clubs and professional groups, interview persons who manage resources and visit the places where materials are available for loan to classrooms. As they interact with persons who work with children and books, they will continue to gain new ideas. Librarians, media specialists, colleagues and family will share their own discoveries of new books as they learn the areas in which each is especially interested. When funds become available to them, from sources such as parent organizations, civic groups, school allotments or library budgets, they will know exactly what they want for their classroom libraries.

WHAT DO YOU THINK?   In what ways are you getting ready to teach? Did the experiences of the students described above give you any ideas about different ways to prepare?

IV. Preparing a Classroom Library

When you begin building your classroom collection, you will want to include award-winning books—literature that has been recognized and honored for its excellence. There are many awards given each year for outstanding contributions to children's literature in the United States and in other countries throughout the world. Why is it important to consider award-winning books? From your own reading, you are probably aware that all books are not of equal quality. You will want to make the finest literature available to your students, and one of the best ways to do this is to include books that have been recognized for excellence in writing and illustration. The best of these books are characterized by insight into the human condition, noble thoughts, memorable characters and vivid examples of the best and worst that persons can be. These books come from all cultures and countries of the world and deal with the common experiences of human beings everywhere: loneliness, courage, grief, aspiration, humor and joy. The best illustrations portray truly great art: color, line, shape and characterization that draws the eye and enhances or enlarges storytelling or nonfiction description.

The best written and illustrated books have something for everyone. Children who have been to the zoo are excited by the beautiful depictions of the tiger and other jungle animals in *Who Is the Beast?*,[68] a picture storybook that examines the concept of "beast" from various perspectives. Children who have never been to the zoo are drawn to the warm colors and exotic pictures. Adult readers are captivated by the theme of the book and the lavish paintings.

Generations of children have entered the everyday world of Winnie-the-Pooh, the imaginary kingdom of Narnia and the exotic locales of the Hobbit. When they reread the same books as adults, they are always amazed at how their life experiences bring new meaning to the familiar stories. A classic is not only a standard of excellence for a certain age of readers, but also a book that can be enjoyed over a lifetime, gaining and giving meaning as it is read and reread.

Who gives book awards and what are their qualifications to make these evaluations? Awards are presented by publishers, organizations and groups who are interested in the quality of children's books. Books are recommended to these groups by committees of persons who read widely from all the new books published in children's literature each year, such as book editors, librarians and teachers. Some awards are for literature about specific groups or topics, while others honor the works of specific authors in particular countries. Most readers are familiar with the Newbery and Caldecott Awards. When you find books that have been given these awards in bookstores, they are distinguished from other books by the gold and silver seals affixed to hardback editions and printed on paperbacks. The gold seal indicates the primary award, and honor books are designated with silver seals.

The **Newbery Award** is presented annually for the most distinguished contribution to children's literature published in the United States. The Newbery Medal has been awarded since 1922, when it honored *The Story of Mankind*[69] by Hendrik Willem Van Loon. This informational book traced the development of man from prehistoric times to the early twentieth century and was a benchmark in children's nonfiction literature because it presented historical ideas in an exciting and comprehensive manner. The award is named for John Newbery, the first English publisher of books for children, and is presented by the Children's Services Division of the American Library Association.

As you examine books that have been honored with this award, you will notice how they reflect the national problems and concerns of their times. Broad universal themes such as the quest for tolerance, a desire for peace and concern with the effects of racism, war and environmental damage can be found in many of these books. Amazingly, very few are dated and can be read with interest and enjoyment by contemporary readers.

The **Caldecott Award** was first presented in 1938 to Dorothy Lathrop for her illustrations in *Animals of the Bible*.[70] The award is named for Randolph Caldecott, a British illustrator of children's books, and is presented annually by the Children's Services Division of the American Library Association. A great variety of artistic styles and media are represented in these beautifully illustrated books, including woodcuts, watercolor, oil painting, acrylics, pastels, stencil and collage. Like the Newbery winners, the Caldecott Awards have reflected the broad concerns of readers and a genuine effort to include illustrations and illustrators who represent the many cultures of the world community.

School Book Clubs

If possible, you will want to observe the operation of a school book club before you begin teaching. Most elementary teachers participate in one or more of these clubs, as do many college and university instructors. Some book clubs feature regular selections from award-winning books and sets of books to support curriculum themes. Others have teacher support materials that are helpful. You may want to ask your instructor or teachers at your cooperating school about the kinds of service they receive from the individual clubs.

Each month during the school year, teachers receive a package of flyers from the book club to distribute to students. These papers describe the books offered and provide a form for ordering. Teachers set a time, usually a week, for the forms to be returned. There are a number of tasks involved with ordering from book clubs, which can be shared by classroom aides, school secretaries, volunteer parents and older students. In some schools, teachers submit orders to parent organization volunteers or the school secretary for processing. In others, teachers handle all orders independently. When you begin teaching, check with other teachers in your school to see how orders are handled. If teachers are not using book clubs in the school where you teach, you can always call or write the book clubs[71] for order forms.

The following guidelines will help you set up and conduct a school book club in your classroom. If you will be handling the entire procedure, you may want to delegate some of the work to students or other volunteers:

1. **Review the teacher's packet** that comes with the book order materials. These usually include a brief annotation of each book and a list of awards or favorable reviews. Sometimes there are suggestions for using specific books in the curriculum.

2. **Distribute order forms to students**. Talk about the books that are offered, using information provided in the teacher's packet. Point out the books that have won awards, including those that have received Children's Choice awards or starred reviews from *Kirkus Reviews*, *School Library Journal* and publications of the American Library Association. (See the endnotes for descriptions of these review sources.)

3. **Ask for recommendations from students** if they have read any of the books offered. Some teachers play a prediction game with book club offerings that no one has read. The entire class or study teams discuss and record what they think the books are about. When the bonus books arrive, they are read and reviewed for comparison with the predictions. Teachers frequently ask for student input for using the bonus points. When a book is already known to students, it may draw enough interest to warrant ordering several copies.

4. **Set a date** for all orders to be received, allowing about a week. **Provide envelopes** for money and order forms. Students should write their

names on their own envelopes and use them throughout the year for bringing orders to school.

5. **Decide which books will be ordered with bonus points**. Which books are reviewed by reliable sources? Are there any Newbery, Caldecott, Coretta Scott King or other award winners? Will any of the books offered support content area study or a theme cycle in your classroom?

6. **Receive** the orders and **validate** the correct amount of money submitted for each order.

7. **Tally** each order on a copy made from the teacher's order form. **Total** the order and **check** for a correct total of money.

8. **Select** the books to be ordered using bonus points.

9. **Transfer** all information to the original order form. Place the copy in your file folder with the individual student order forms.

10. **Obtain a money order** for the total amount or write a personal check. Sometimes the school secretary will handle this.

11. **Check the invoice** when the book order arrives. It will list the individual titles and the total number of each book sent. Compare these numbers with the copy of your original order form.

12. **Count** the books sent and **check** these numbers with the amounts on the invoice.

13. On a large surface, **assemble the student orders** and **distribute** any bonus gifts, such as posters, stickers or bookmarks. Keep orders together with large rubber bands or place books in large manilla envelopes with the students' names on them. These can be reused throughout the year.

14. **Distribute** book orders to students and provide time for reading and sharing books informally in literature circles. Make bonus books available so that everyone can look at the new selections.

Are school book clubs worth the teacher time and effort invested in them? You will have to decide this for yourself. Teachers who use children's literature as part of an integrated language learning program see book clubs as integral to their classroom programs. Ordering from book clubs creates student interest and excitement about books. Book clubs provide opportunities for students to obtain sturdy and inexpensive books of high quality, many of which are priced considerably less than the regular paperback versions. Because order forms are sent home with students, parents have an opportunity to review the books offered. Most parents are eager to help their children succeed in school and will support the purchase of one or two books a month. Even if they do not order anything, they will have noticed the names and topics of good children's literature.

What about children who want books, but cannot afford them? All students can be involved in deciding the use of some of the bonus points. Ask them to submit requests on a piece of paper and try to include the preferences of those who typically do not order books. In lieu of this, you might decide to use bonus points to order a copy of every high-quality book offered for the class library.

WHAT DO YOU THINK? Did you order books from a school book club when you were in elementary school? What kinds of books did you like best? Did anyone help you choose books to order? Examine flyers from several book clubs. Which clubs do experienced teachers recommend? Which ones seem to offer the best selection? Which books interest you?

V. Including Everyone in the Literature Base

Literature selection provides the foundation for building upon individual interests, abilities and backgrounds in your classroom. Browse through any of the resources on book selection mentioned in previous chapters and you will find many categories of children's interests, from cars and spaceships to dinosaurs and dolls. Remember to select books for all reading abilities in your classroom and include good picture books at all levels.

It is vital to provide your students with good examples of literature from all the cultures represented in your classroom. With a thoughtful selection of books, you can help create an environment in which students who are in the minority learn and grow from their experiences with literature. All children like to read about experiences to which they can relate in some way. This is how they gain meaning from what they read or listen to, by relating it to what they already know. They identify with illustrations and text that reflect familiar persons and settings. When you provide a variety of books for minority students, you maximize their efforts to make sense out of print by building on their experience.

Children who represent the majority culture in the community can gain a new view of the world from exposure to these literatures. When students read books that feature family and community life in other cultures, they observe events, activities and behavior that are common to all peoples: birth, death, celebrations, work, play, hope, fear, joy and grief. They see that people have more similarities than differences and begin to see that everyone has a unique perception of the world, shaped by individual experience.

Research the cultural composition of the community where you will be teaching. Remember that many cultures compose all communities and you will want to have them all represented in your classroom library. In addition to any ethnic or racial cultures, try to include books that portray all ages of persons, people with disabilities, books that represent families of varied composition and income levels and those that accurately depict life in both urban and rural areas.

When you are selecting books from other cultures, look for authors who are members of these minority communities or those who have demonstrated sensitivity to the cultures they are writing about or illustrating. The Multicultural Publisher's Exchange, listed in the Resources for Teaching section, identifies books and other materials judged noteworthy by specific minorities in our country. The section on Children's Book Awards lists awards presented by ethnic and racial groups to honor high-quality books that depict these cultures.

As you select books for intermediate students, you will want to choose those that will help children see the world as an interdependent human community, faced with common problems of food, health, ecology, conflict and education. From books that describe holidays and celebrations, children get a taste of the joy and solemnity of special days in many cultures. The best of multicultural literature stresses the integrity and worth of the individual and communicates the idea that diversity is a part of life, making it rich and interesting.

You will also want to consider the reading needs and interests of children in your room who face physical, social or emotional challenges. Schedule a meeting with any special teachers or counselors your students will meet with during the year and ask their assistance in finding suitable literature. They will be able to direct you to central libraries of large-print books, talking books, tapes, computer programs and other materials specifically designed to meet the reading needs of children with special challenges.

Books to Increase Understanding

Each of these books chronicles a journey of self-discovery for young people in several of the many Eskimo cultures. All search for an identity within their culture by interacting with natural forces.

Water Sky[72] by Jean Craighead George lets the reader explore Eskimo culture through the eyes of Lincoln Noah Stonewright, who goes to Alaska to search for his uncle and explore his Ologak ancestry. In the process he joins a whaling crew and must deal with conflicting issues of culture and conservation.

Dogsong[73] by Gary Paulsen. Like many of Paulsen's books, *Dogsong* is filled with adventure, personal insight and a confrontation with natural elements. Russell Suskitt is inspired to find his own "song" and escape the modern ways of his village by Oogruk, an Eskimo shaman. This mystical journey takes him into the tundra and mountains, paralleling a dream he has of another self from long ago. From what he learns in the dream he is able to save a young pregnant Eskimo girl and kill a polar bear, using the ancient ways.

Julie of the Wolves[74] by Jean Craighead George. This is an intense and thrilling adventure story of a young girl who runs away from home and becomes lost in the Alaskan wilderness. A pack of Arctic wolves accepts her and helps keep her alive through the winter. From this experience, she becomes more aware of her heritage and develops a deep bond with the wolves.

WHAT DO YOU THINK? There are many tribal cultures in Alaska that you will want to find out about, especially if you live in this state or your students will be studying this area. When you were in elementary school, did the writing and illustrations of books you read reflect life as you experienced it? What kinds of books would you liked to have seen more of? Do you remember reading books that helped you understand or appreciate another culture?

VI. Step-by-Step: Creating a Literature Base for Learning

When you have learned how to select the best children's literature and have discovered the resources of your school and community, you will be ready to begin using all the genres of children's literature in your classroom. Here are a few of the ways you can use these different kinds of books to support language and content area learning.

Reading Aloud

Choose books from the different genres to introduce every kind of literature to children throughout the year. Children are attracted to books that are read aloud by the teacher and will read that particular book or others like it on their own. Illuminate the characters and events of a historical period by reading from historical fiction. Introduce a literary theme or a content area study with poetry, a biography or a well-written informational book on the topic. Interest students in books by good authors by reading a compelling example of their work aloud. You can find ideas for good reading-aloud books in all the genres from the reference books listed at the end of Chapter 2.

Independent Reading

Provide examples of each kind of children's literature in a wide range of reading levels. When you read from a particular genre, such as biography or modern fantasy, try to borrow as many different biographies or examples of modern fantasy as you can find from your school and public libraries. You will also want to have on hand as many books as possible that relate to your content area studies.

Guided Reading

In Chapter 5, you will learn how to conduct shared and guided reading sessions for your students. These are opportunities for students to enjoy reading poetry, chants, songs and plays aloud together or to practice reading skills and strategies through group interaction. Through the reading of Big Books at the kindergarten or primary level and the discussions of literature study groups, teachers help students explore the characteristics of all the genres of literature.

Individual Reading Conferences

At least once a week, all students in the class meet individually with the teacher to share ideas and responses to books they are currently reading. Children usually have a checklist of all the genres and will try to bring a different kind of book to each conference. During these conferences, teachers learn the kinds of books that children enjoy and can often recommend books that would interest them. For example, if a student loves dinosaurs, the teacher might show them Jack Prelutsky's *Tyrannosaurus Was a Beast: Dinosaur Poems*.[75] These verses, although extremely funny, are also scientifically correct and will catch the fancy of true enthusiasts. Who could ever forget "Clankety clankety, clankety clank, Ankelosaurus was built like a tank"?

Writing

Throughout the day, you will be providing many opportunities for your students to practice their writing skills. Students enjoy trying their hand at writing in the various genres in response to their own experience, content areas studies and topics in literature. Through writing, they develop an appreciation for the characteristics of each kind of literature and the skill of authors who write in these genres.

Speaking and Listening

Throughout the day, children talk about books they enjoy—to the teacher and to each other in small groups and pairs. In preview sessions and Friday Afternoon presentations (Chapter 7), each kind of literature can be shared with an audience. In addition to play kits that can be purchased commercially or checked out from the library, you will want to explore ways to use reader's theater in your classroom, thus providing a means of adapting literature to drama.

Content Area Learning and Themes

Your knowledge of many different kinds of literature will help you establish a literature base for your students' learning in all areas of the curriculum. Students can use the genres of literature to expand and enrich their understanding and appreciation of specific subject matter. If your school district mandates the use of curriculum texts, you can supplement this material with trade books in these areas from all the genres.

As children develop competency in reading, they are frequently drawn to favorite topics or genres. Some may want to read only books about dinosaurs or cars. Others prefer reading only modern fantasy, while still others select all their books from nonfiction. The best way to help children from being stuck in one genre is to introduce them to compelling examples of other types of literature. What books about the same topic can be found in other genres? Check the topics index in one of the reference books described in this and previous chapters. These are specifically designed to include both school themes and student interests. If a student reads exclusively in fiction about horses, you can provide informational books about horses to show the value of nonfiction reading. Try finding poetry, traditional tales, historical fiction or biography that involve horses as significant players. Biographies of Robert E. Lee will include extensive discussions of his faithful horse Traveler. Encourage them to read the memorable tall tale of Pecos Bill, which features the jealous horse Widowmaker, who flings Pecos Bill's beloved into outer space. Direct them toward modern fantasy, whose stories celebrate the heroism of noble horses. Avid science-fiction readers can be introduced to biographies of famous scientists, such as Einstein, or informational books that treat the subjects typically found in science fiction, such as quantum mechanics and genetic engineering.

Many young readers get hooked on formula series books, which feature thin plots, little character development and easy resolution to contrived conflict. Because many of these popular books are based on family interactions, you might want to introduce your students to family series books that feature dynamic characters and authentic adventures, such as those of the Ingalls family,[76] the Murrys,[77] the Austins,[78] the Blossoms[79] or the Tillermans.[80] The books in these series exemplify the strength and pride of family ties and the courage of young persons as they face life's problems.

WHAT DO YOU THINK?

Can you think of other ways to use literature in the classroom? Were trade books used for learning when you were an elementary student? Have you ever read formula books? What was their most appealing characteristic? What are your preferences for reading topics and genre? Have you ever been drawn to a particular genre of books because you read one that really interested you? Have you ever read intensely on a topic in many genres because you were interested in that topic?

VII.   If This Is Your Situation

Many school districts mandate the use of textbooks for science and social studies. Teachers in this situation frequently use the textbook to demonstrate how knowledge about a topic can be organized. Students explore the types of information contained in the text and examine headings, indexes, glossaries and special features. Some teachers begin a topic of study by asking students what questions they have about it. Then everyone reads in the text to find answers to the questions that have been posed. As a class, they discuss other things they want to know about the topic and the teacher provides relevant trade books for them to examine. In these situations, reading aloud from high-quality trade books and providing a wide variety of books for students to explore on the study topic will help students expand their learning and enrich the concepts presented in the texts.

Textbooks provide students with a broad survey of a content area. Through textbook reading, students can begin to identify the concepts and issues believed to be important by educators in the field. When textbook reading is combined with reading in high-quality trade books, students can begin to examine how authors select important ideas and communicate them to a reader. This provides students with experience in evaluating the expertise and authority of different types of writing and encourages them to regard texts as a resource, rather than as a final or complete authority. They can compare the purposes and styles of writing in textbooks and trade books and become increasingly proficient in utilizing the distinct qualities of each for their own learning.

WHAT DO YOU THINK? Can you think of additional ways to use a textbook as a learning resource? Have you examined recent trade books for children in the areas of history, geography or science? How are they different from those available to you as a child?

VIII.   Evaluating Children's Literature: Choosing the Best

There are many reference books that will help you select high-quality literature for your classroom. But as you expand your reading in children's literature, you will want to know how to judge these books on your own. What criteria can you use to determine if the book is a good example of its genre?

Picture Books   Look for attractive or compelling illustrations that accurately portray the story events, extend the text and give information about the setting, plot or characters. Is the language and style of the book appropriate for the children in your class? Do the text and illustrations avoid stereotypes of gender or race? Do the pictures help establish the mood of the story by increasing the sense of adventure or encouraging aesthetic appreciation?

Traditional Stories   Traditional stories are retold by contemporary authors. It is their interpretations of these folktales, fables, myths, legends and tall tales that you will be evaluating. Their illustrations, selection of words and re-creation of the story are individual interpretations whose quality can vary widely. Look for illustrations that reflect the tone of the story and that are true to the events described. Read a little of the book aloud. Does the writer create a picture of the events or the characters? Is the tone of the retelling appropriate to its type? Are myths and legends retold with respect and dignity? Is the humor successful? Does it hold your interest?

Modern Fantasy   It is vital that the setting, plot, characters and point of view are believable in this type of literature. There should be a logical framework to the story, so that disbelief is suspended. From your interaction with the story, can you really believe that animals can talk, that tiny people live inside an old shoe or that it is possible to travel through time? Good modern fantasy should deal with universal themes, such as the struggle between good and evil, perseverance in the face of obstacles, social responsibility, love and friendship. It should create a sense of wonder, inspiration or delight.

Realistic Fiction   These stories should be honest and not preachy. The language used should accurately reflect the background of the characters and lend credibility to the story. Strong characters in authentic settings will help students identify with the deeper meanings of the plot. The story should help the reader develop a hopeful perspective about the topics addressed and should provide them with some insight into their own lives or the lives of others.

Historical Fiction   This literature must be both good history and good fiction. The story should be the main focus and should not overwhelm the reader with historical details. The values and beliefs expressed by the characters should be true to what is known about the time period, as should all elements of the story (characters, plot, setting). When possible, the dialogue between characters should be authentic for the time without being too difficult to understand. Readers should come away from reading the book feeling like they were really there.

Biography   The key elements to well-written biographies are factual accuracy, good characterization, a worthy subject and a balance between story and facts. The subject of the biography should be presented as a real person, with sufficient details of the person's life included to help create a sense of the time and place in which he or she lived. Persons who influenced the subject's life should be portrayed believably. If the biography is simplified for younger readers, this should not create inaccurate impressions about the subject.

Another important factor to consider in biographies is the worthiness of the subject. Is the person really worth reading about? Has he or she made an impact on society that children should know about (good or bad)? Watch for the way the author infers what the subject is thinking. Some biographies for children are partially fictionalized. Does the author acknowledge this? Does the author tell about the sources used to write the biography, including any primary sources, such as letters, diaries, newspapers, manuscripts or documents?

Poetry

You may have heard that elementary children prefer poetry that is humorous and based on familiar experiences. This is true, but they also enjoy all other kinds of poetry. Some poems that might not draw student interest when read aloud may attract them when accompanied by illustrations. Visual impact or arrangement on the page often draws older students into poetry. Beautiful or creative illustrations attract younger students. When you examine collections of poetry, read a number of the poems. Will they appeal to various children in your class by topic and style? Are the poems arranged helpfully by topic for use in content area study or to illustrate themes?

Plays and Reader's Theater

These kits should contain information that will help students participate successfully in these performances. If the play is adapted from a well-known book, all of the elements of the drama should be true to the original story. You will want to read the play aloud to see if the dialogue is realistic and convincing. Many children's plays have stilted dialogue that calls attention to itself and not the story. Multiple copies of the play or story should be available, as well as tips for interpretation of characters, costuming, rehearsals and publicity. Material to use for reader's theater should follow the original dialogue of the book from which it is adapted, retaining the purpose and tone of the original work.

Multicultural Literature

Found in all the genres, multicultural literature consists of material written by, for and about the various cultures that compose our country and world. All the criteria used to evaluate the best in each of the genres described above are appropriate for evaluating multicultural literature. In addition, look for characters who are free from stereotyping in appearance and behavior, who are portrayed as individuals and not clichéd representatives of a race or ethnic group. Find books that treat the history and culture of various groups with honesty, respect and dignity, neither depreciating nor glorifying individuals and situations. Look for authentic settings and accurate depiction of the values and customs of cultural groups. Check the Resources for Teaching section at the end of this chapter for references that can help you evaluate multicultural literature from the perspective of various groups in our culture.

Informational Books

High-quality books of this genre should be characterized by accuracy, a lack of stereotyping and illustrations that clarify or extend the text. Information should be logically organized and interestingly presented. Graphs and charts should be easy to read and interpret. Somewhere in the book (preface, afterword, notes) the qualifications of the author should be detailed, with a listing of sources that were consulted for this writing, such as experts, books, references, journals, diaries, letters, documents, photographs, charts or graphs. If you are acquainted with the content, be alert to omissions of significant information. When appropriate, differing views on the topic should be presented.

You will also want to assess the enthusiasm of the writer for the subject. Does the author just report the facts or are you drawn to the subject matter because of its presentation? When books involve experiments or cooking, notice if proper precautions are stated. Adequate warnings should also be included for books that involve dangerous interactions with animals or performing stunts. Notice if the book is helpfully arranged, with an index for easy location of information.

WHAT DO YOU THINK?   An easy way to begin evaluating books is to begin with picture books. They are attractive, fairly brief, and represent all of the genres of children's literature. Select a few that draw your interest and evaluate them according to the criteria described above. Compare your first impression of quality or lack of quality with your more intensive evaluation. How good was your first impression? Did you learn anything useful from this experience?

IX.   Creating Partners

Professional librarians and media specialists can provide you and your students with invaluable assistance as you assemble materials for your classroom. It is a good idea to introduce yourself immediately to these persons in the schools where you assist, student teach or have obtained a position. In addition to giving you information about the holdings of the school library and policies for using books and materials, they can also assist you with ideas about resources for content area theme studies. If you plan to study ecology in your third-grade class, the librarian can direct you to good fiction and nonfiction books, magazines that highlight wildlife or conservation, videotapes from the National Geographic Society and a CD-ROM encyclopedia that allows children to explore the characteristics of their favorite animals. They will also know about community resources and speakers who will visit the classroom for special presentations.

Media specialists and librarians can assist you and your students with information about how to access the resources of the library, including where to find information on a topic or a particular book, how to use audio and video equipment and how to search for information using the computer. In addition, they will frequently make special presentations for your class, such as how to use the resources of the genealogy library to research ancestors. Many will schedule times to read books aloud to your class, tell stories or put on a puppet play.

How can you help librarians support your learning program? One of the best ways is to keep them informed about what you are teaching and what you are looking for in terms of grade-level reading, theme literature or artistic connections with content area studies. Librarians read many reviews of new books and will be alert to the type of literature you are looking for. You will also want to ask questions: What equipment should you know how to operate? Are students taught how to computer search, or is this something you will be responsible for? What are the guidelines for bringing a class to the media center? If you are in an open classroom situation, the media center may be part of your learning area. You will want to know any regulations that apply to the use of materials and space. How should students be prepared? You might want to ask a public librarian if there are any programs planned for the year that will relate to your curriculum.

It is important to keep this relationship cooperative and strong by returning books, tapes, printed materials and equipment on time and in good condition and by reviewing guidelines with students for respectful use of the media center and its resources.

WHAT DO YOU THINK? What has been your experience with public and school librarians or media specialists? Do you use any library frequently? How much do you know about the resources of school or public libraries? What will you want to know more about?

X. Perspectives

John Dewey often talked about the purposes of education. He was interested in how our goals for education are related to the ways we try to realize them and spoke of this as the "means–ends" relationship. He believed that our goals in teaching are the best direction for selecting the proper ways of reaching them. When teachers have a clear idea of what they want children to achieve in terms of language learning, they can better choose activities that will create an environment to support this learning.

In turn, Dewey also believed that the means teachers use to achieve their goals can affect the goals themselves.

> A goal cannot be intelligently set forth apart from the path which leads to it. Ends cannot be conceived as operative ends, as directors of action, apart from consideration of conditions which obstruct and means which promote them.[81]

Indeed, he believed that the means and ends of education are essentially the same because each participates in the other. For example, researchers suggest that one of the best ways to interest children in reading is to provide an attractive display of many kinds of books in the classroom. But if students' access to these books is limited or restricted throughout the day, the original goal will be defeated. If a school reading program is dominated by trying to get students to read large numbers of books for contests or other extrinsic rewards, children may miss the deeply personal rewards that come from reading and savoring a single book. Educators agree that reading aloud is an excellent way to help children develop an enjoyable association with books. But if books are read aloud in a distracting manner, or if read-aloud sessions are taken away as punishment, the goal will not be realized. The way you go about doing things in the classroom is very important because it directly affects the goals you hope to achieve.

WHAT DO YOU THINK? Can you think of examples in your own life where having goals helped direct you to ways of realizing them? What examples can you think of where the means you used to get something you wanted actually interfered with realizing your goal?

XI. Exploring Professional Literature

As you create a literature base for learning in your classroom, you will want to know about new books that will provide high-quality reading experiences for your students. College and university libraries and most school and public libraries include *The Horn Book Magazine*[82] in their holdings for this purpose. This magazine is published six times a year and contains reviews of children's books, articles by children's writers and book recommendations. Reviews helpfully tell enough about the content and quality of the book to enable the reader to make informed choices on book selection. Most of the books reviewed are recommended, but any reservations are clearly stated. The reviews are grouped in approximate age-level sections and include publisher information, number of pages, cost and ISBN number. They include picture books, novels for intermediate (9–12) and older readers (12 through young adult), folklore, poetry, nonfiction and books of interest to adults. There are also sections of briefer reviews, recommended paperbacks in all the categories listed above and noteworthy children's books in Spanish. The magazine also publishes the acceptance speeches of the Newbery and Caldecott Award winners each year, providing insight into the artistic minds that create these notable books.

You might also like to examine *The Lion and the Unicorn*,[83] a journal that explores issues in children's literature within themes and genres, such as minority literature, fairy tales, child heroes and popular culture. Another journal that provides helpful and insightful information on children's literature is *The New Advocate*,[84] a publication of the Advocates of Literature for Young People. This journal is published quarterly and features book reviews and articles written by editors, educators and librarians.

Sometimes favorable reviews are quoted on the back covers of children's books. Knowing the source of these reviews will help you evaluate the credibility of comments made about the book. Some of the more respected and frequently quoted reviews are from *Kirkus Reviews*[85] (Kirkus), the American Library Association[86] (ALA) and the *School Library Journal*[87] (SLJ). High-quality children's books are also reviewed in professional journals, such as *The Reading Teacher* and *Language Arts*; in weekly newsmagazines and newspapers, such as *The New York Times Review of Books*; and in teacher's magazines, such as *Learning* and *Instructor*.

WHAT DO YOU THINK?   Which of the periodicals described above most interests you? When you have examined a copy of the *Horn Book* in your college/university library, consider what features of this periodical might be most helpful to you as a teacher.

XII.   Resources for Teaching

In previous chapters you have explored resources for children's book selection, including reference materials that suggest books to read aloud (Chapter 2) and those that appeal to children's independent reading interests (Chapter 3). These resources describe titles that can enhance or extend learning in every area of the curriculum and those that have been honored for excellence in writing or illustration. As you develop your classroom collection, you might want to refer to additional resources, such as *Adventuring with Books: A Booklist for Pre-K–Grade 6* and *Best Books for Children: Preschool through Grade 6*, both of which are annotated in Chapter 3. The former reference tool is inexpensive, and you might want to consider purchasing it for your own professional library. The latter book is more expensive, but many school libraries have a copy or may be willing to purchase it at your request.

The following books and reference materials focus on award-winning books. Some of these are either free or relatively inexpensive, while others will usually be available in your school or public library:

Children's Books: Awards and Prizes[88]   This reference book is published and updated periodically by the Children's Book Council. It contains historical lists of the major awards in children's literature in the United States and internationally. State awards are also included, including those determined by children's balloting. This paperback is probably too expensive for a personal library, but you will probably find it in the reference section of your school or public children's library.

The Newbery and Caldecott Awards: A Guide to the Medal and Honor Books[89] This affordable paperback is available from the American Library Association and is updated annually.

Multicultural Publisher's Exchange, *Catalog of Books By and About People of Color*[90]   The Multicultural Publisher's Exchange is a professional organization of African, Hispanic, Asian/Pacific Islander, Native and White American small-press publishers of multicultural books. Their listings include: children's books in all the genres, young adult fiction and biography, drama and literature, history, games and puzzles, posters, music, art, audio books, curriculum materials, journals and newsletters, self-help books, Kwanzaa materials and reference books.

Notable Children's Trade Books in the Field of Social Studies These books are selected by a joint committee of the National Council for the Social Studies and the Children's Book Council. Written primarily for elementary age children, they emphasize human relations, present an original theme, are highly readable and, where appropriate, contain maps and illustrations. The complete list appears yearly in the April/May issue of *Social Education*, a journal of the National Council for the Social Studies. You can obtain a free copy of the list by sending a stamped (3 oz.), 6″ × 9″ self-addressed envelope to: Children's Book Council, 568 Broadway, Suite 404, New York, NY 10012.

Outstanding Science Trade Books for Children A joint committee of the National Science Teacher's Association and the Children's Book Council selects books that are readable, contain information consistent with current scientific knowledge, are pleasing in format and illustrations, and are non-sexist, nonracist and nonviolent. The complete list of these books can be found in the March issue of *Science and Children*, a journal of the National Science Teacher's Association. A free copy of this list can be obtained by sending a stamped (3 oz.), 6″ × 9″ self-addressed envelope to: Children's Book Council, 568 Broadway, Suite 404, New York, NY 10012.

American Library Association Notable Children's Books This is a list of books that are notable for their literary quality, originality of text or illustration, design, format, subject matter, or interest and value to children and likelihood of acceptance by children. The Notable Children's Books appear yearly in the March 15 issue of *Booklist*, a journal published by the American Library Association.

Children's Choices Awards Each year a joint committee from the International Reading Association and the Children's Book Council selects a group of books to be made available to children for their consideration and vote. The list contains those books that received the most votes. A complete list of Children's Choices can be found each year in the November issue of *The Reading Teacher*. You can get a free copy of this list by sending a stamped (4 oz.), 9″ × 15″ self-addressed envelope to: The International Reading Association, 800 Barksdale Road, P.O. Box 8139, Newark, DE 19714-8139.

Children's Book Awards

The following awards include those presented by organizations or media, those that recognize lifetime contributions to children's literature and awards that reflect religious, racial or ethical concerns.

Boston Globe/Horn Book Awards are awarded annually in three categories: outstanding fiction or poetry, outstanding nonfiction and outstanding illustration. Books honored by these awards have included Newbery winners such as *M.C. Higgins the Great*, *The Westing Game* and *Maniac Magee*, and Caldecott winners such as *Lon Po Po*.

The **Children's Book Award** is presented annually by the International Reading Association to authors from any country whose first or second book shows unusual promise. It was first presented in 1975 to T. Degens for *Transport 7-41* and more recently for *Letter from Rifka*, which is described more fully in Chapter 5.

The **Laura Ingalls Wilder Medal** is presented every five years by the Children's Book Division of the American Library Association to an author or illustrator whose books have made a lasting contribution to children's literature. Awarded in 1954 to Laura Ingalls Wilder, its honorees have included E. B. White, Beverly Cleary, Dr. Seuss, Maurice Sendak and Jean Fritz.

The **Scott O'Dell Award for Historical Fiction** is given annually by the Advisory Committee of the Bulletin of the Center for Children's Books to honor distinguished historical fiction for children. The setting for the book must be in North, South or Central America. Scott O'Dell's own books include such favorites as *Sing Down the Moon*[91] and *Island of the Blue Dolphins*.[92] O'Dell is also a winner of the Hans Christian Anderson Award.

The **Hans Christian Anderson International Medal** In 1956, Eleanor Farjeon of Great Britain (who also won a Carnegie Medal for *The Little Bookworm* that year) received the first award by the International Board on Books for Young People. Since that time, this award has honored authors and illustrators from a dozen countries around the world. It is presented every two years to a living author and illustrator whose total works have made an outstanding contribution to children's literature. Each of the five members of the award committee represents a different country.

The **Coretta Scott King Award** has been awarded annually since 1970 to black authors and illustrators for outstanding inspirational and educational contributions to children's literature. These awards are presented by the Social Responsibilities Round Table of the American Library Association. The first award was given to Mildred Taylor for her book *The Friendship*[93] and John Steptoe for *Mufaro's Beautiful Daughters*,[94] which he wrote and illustrated and which was also a Caldecott Honor book for that year.

National Jewish Book Awards are sponsored by the Jewish Book Council and designed to promote American Jewish literary creativity and an appreciation of Jewish literature. Awards are given for a specific book or a cumulative contribution to Jewish juvenile literature. An award is also given to recognize excellence in illustration. The first award was presented in 1952 to Sydney Taylor for the wonderful stories of the *All-of-a-Kind Family*. The first award for illustration honored Michael Deraney in 1985 for his illustrations of *Yussel's Prayer: A Yom Kippur Story* by Barbara Cohen.

The **Jane Adams Children's Book Award** is awarded annually by the Jane Addams Peace Association and the Women's International League for Peace and Freedom. First presented in 1953, it honors books that most effectively promote peace, world community and social justice or equality of sexes and of all races. The first award honored *People Are Important* by Eva Knox Evans.

Additional awards you may want to watch for include: The Canadian Library Awards (Canada), The Carnegie Medal (United Kingdom), Amelia Frances Howard-Gibbon Medal (Canada), Kate Greenaway Medal (United Kingdom) and the Mildred L. Batchelder Award (United States). Many states honor favorite son or daughter authors with awards such as the William Allen White Children's Book Award in Kansas and the Rebecca Caudill Award in Illinois.

From the annotations of books listed in the endnotes, which would you like to read? How do you decide which books you want to explore or examine more closely? When you were a child, which of these books might you have chosen to read? What author does your state honor with an award? Have you ever read any of this person's writing?

XIII.   Reflections

From a Teacher's Journal—Gail Nave, Kindergarten

I can remember a time when I smiled as my students went to first grade, knowing they knew all their letters and sounds. However, these children didn't have a clue as to what to do with those sounds. They needed to see these sounds in the context of whole words and as parts of whole stories. I remember working with a child who was having trouble identifying sounds in words. As he struggled, I pointed out to him that the word had a long "a" in it. "Mrs. Nave," he said, "that 'a' don't look any longer than any other!"

I always include chapter books among the books I read aloud to my class, and on several occasions I've seen the benefits of this practice. One year, I read *Sarah, Plain and Tall* to my class in the fall. The following spring, we attended an outdoor education day at the YMCA in a nearby city. Close by, there was a large man-made lake, whose waters were green and shining. As we walked beside it, one of my most deprived students tugged at my sleeve and asked, "Mrs. Nave, I wonder if this is the color of Sarah's sea?"

TRYING OUT THE
CHAPTER IDEAS

1. What idea(s) in this chapter interested you?
2. What is your favorite genre for personal reading?
3. Can you remember any children's books you read in any of the genres described? Did you have a favorite genre or reading topic when you were a child?
4. Did you order books from a book club when you were an elementary student? What do you remember about your experience?
5. In the classroom where you observe, review the books available for students. Is there a balance of selections for each genre? Varied Interests? Levels of reading ability?
6. Using one of the resource books annotated in this or other chapters, choose one book from each genre of children's literature that interests you.
7. Choose a grade level and select a book from each genre that would be appropriate to include in your classroom collection for this level.
8. Become a "teacher-watcher," a collector of good ideas that can be adapted to your own classroom. Keep a notebook with you whenever you visit a school. Notice the kinds of displays in the hallways and any schoolwide projects that look interesting. Ask teachers or the principal about any displays. They will be pleased to be asked and you will get more information about how the project began and its success.

9. Interview a teacher who uses school book clubs. What club do they prefer? What advantages do they see in using book clubs for children?

Notes

1. Rafe Martin, *The Rough-Face Girl* (New York: Putnam, 1992). Doing menial work over a fire scars the face of a young girl. Abused by other members of her tribe, she still sees beauty in all things. She alone is able to see the face of the Invisible Being and becomes his wife.

2. Anne Gatti, reteller, *Aesop's Fables* (Orlando, Fla.: Harcourt, 1992). Retellings of 58 familiar and less well known fables by the Greek writer Aesop.

3. Arnold Lobel, *Fables* (Chicago: Harper, 1980). Outrageous illustrations and witty stories with a modern flavor. This Caldecott book is Lobel at his best.

4. Mitsumasa Anno, *Anno's Aesop: A Book of Fables by Aesop and Mr. Fox* (New York: Orchard Press, 1989). Mr. Fox pretends to read a copy of *Aesop's Fables* that his son finds. This interesting book contains the original Aesop's fables, as well as the stories Freddy's father tells him.

5. Steven Kellogg, reteller, *Mike Fink: A Tall Tale* (New York: Morrow Junior Books, 1992). Humorous, detailed illustrations tell the story of the legendary keelboat hero. Others in this series recall the exploits of Pecos Bill, Johnny Appleseed and Paul Bunyan.

6. C. S. Lewis, *The Lion, the Witch and the Wardrobe* (New York: Macmillan, 1950).

7. Julius Lester, *Further Tales of Uncle Remus: The Misadventures of Brer Rabbit, Brer Fox, Brer Wolf, the Doodang, and Other Creatures* (Bergenfield, N.J.: Dial, 1990). ‹

8. Mary Norton, *The Borrowers* (Orlando, Fla.: Harcourt Brace, 1953).

9. John Bellairs, *The Trolley to Yesterday* (New York: Dial, 1989).

10. John Christopher, *The White Mountains* (New York: Macmillan, 1990).

11. Susan Cooper, *The Dark Is Rising* (New York: Macmillan, 1976). The third book in a five-volume series that pits the powers of goodness against the vast powers of Darkness. An intriguing story involving a young boy who discovers he is one of the "old ones" who must fight the forces of evil. The final books in the series are based on Arthurian legends.

12. Mel Gilden, *Outer Space and All That Junk* (New York: Lippincott, 1989). A science-fiction mystery based on the idea that junk sitting around the planet is really alien life waiting to go home.

13. Madeleine L'Engle, *A Wrinkle in Time* (New York: Farrar, Strauss and Giroux, 1976). A young girl learns patience as she works to free her scientist father from the dark forces of the universe. Other books in this trilogy include *A Wind in the Door* and *A Swiftly Tilting Planet*.

14. Walter Dean Myers, *Somewhere in the Darkness* (New York: Scholastic, 1992).

15. Harold Keith, *Rifles for Watie* (New York: HarperCollins, 1957).

16. Wendy Towle, *The Real McCoy, the Life of an African-American Inventor* (New York: Scholastic, 1993).

17. Clement C. Moore, *The Night Before Christmas* (New York: Scholastic, 1985).

18. Arthur Dorros, *Abuela* (New York: The Trumpet Club, 1993).

19. Kamini Khanduri, *Usborne World Wildlife: Polar Wildlife* (New York: Scholastic, 1992).

20. Rebecca Caudill, *Did You Carry the Flag Today, Charley?* (New York: Holt, 1966).

21. Tomie dePaola, *Tomie dePaola's Mother Goose* (New York: Putnam, 1985). The large, bright pictures and traditional rhymes are a perfect match for kindergarten listeners.

22. Arnold Lobel, *Gregory Griggs and Other Nursery Rhyme People* (New York: Greenwillow, 1978). Funny rhymes that are less well known. The verse and pictures appeal to primary age students.

23. Peter Spier, *London Bridge Is Falling Down* (New York: Doubleday, 1969). Intermediates studying British history will be fascinated with the detail of times and customs in the illustrations for this famous nursery rhyme song.

24. Eric Carle, *The Very Quiet Cricket* (New York: Philomel, 1990).

25. Monika Beisner, *A Folding Alphabet Book* (New York: Farrar, Strauss & Giroux, 1981). A folded book that features animals and objects that form letters.

26. Ludwig Bemelmans, *Madeline: A Pop-up Book Based on the Original* (New York: Viking Kestral, 1987). This adaptation features pop-ups and pull tabs of the familiar Paris landmarks and the twelve little girls under Miss Clavel's charge.

27. James Gurney, *Dinotopia* (Atlanta: Turner Publishing, 1993). A fascinating and detailed pop-up version of the lavish original conception of a utopian country where dinosaurs and humans live peacefully and productively.

28. Anne Shelby, *Potluck* (New York: Orchard Books, 1991). Foods from around the world are brought alphabetically to the table. Features cultural variety as friends bring asparagus soup, bagels, yogurt and zucchini casserole to share.

29. Michelle Edwards, *Alef-Bet: A Hebrew Alphabet Book* (New York: Lothrop, Lee and Shephard Books, 1992). The Hebrew alphabet (alef-bet) is presented, with household words, translations and pronunciations. A wonderfully warm book that features the children in a family.

30. Cynthia Elyce Rubin, *ABC Americana from the National Gallery of Art* (Orlando, Fla.: Harcourt Brace Jovanovich, 1989). Watercolor paintings of representative objects of American design and folk art. A final page identifies the original objects and artists.

31. Suzanne Aker, *What Comes in 2's, 3's and 4's?* (New York: Simon and Schuster, 1990). A multi-use book that presents objects that come in 2's (hands, eyes, feet), 3's (tricycle wheels, meals in a day, poison ivy leaves) and 4's (legs on tables and chairs, seasons of the year).

32. Roger Chouinard and Mariko Chouinard, *One Magic Box* (New York: Doubleday, 1989). A rhyming tale that begins with one magic box, locked with two locks, and ends with fifteen magic stars. Brilliant colors and unusual perspectives intrigue students.

33. Kevin Crossley-Holland, *Under the Sun and Over the Moon* (New York: G. P. Putnam's Sons, 1989). In a stroll through ten gardens a boy sees one of every object in the first garden, pairs of objects in the second garden, and so on. Intriguing illustrations accompanied by verses that give clues for finding items in the pictures.

34. Tana Hoban, *All About Where* (New York: Greenwillow, 1991). Photographs that show how objects relate to each other. Readers choose from a list of prepositions to describe the action.

35. Ann Jonas, *Color Dance* (New York: Greenwillow, 1989). Three dancers with red, yellow and blue scarves demonstrate the combination of colors to create other colors. A fourth dancer introduces white, gray and black. Also included are a color wheel and a description of the relationships among the colors.

36. Roxie Munro, *The Inside-Outside Book of Paris* (New York: E. P. Dutton, 1992). A tour of Paris, with a panorama of the Tuileries and a view from the observation deck of L'Arc de Triomphe.

37. Ginger Foglesong Guy, *Black Crow, Black Crow* (New York: Greenwillow, 1991). The story of a busy mother crow related in rhythmic language and repetitive text.

38. James Marshall, *Fox Outfoxed* (New York: Dial, 1992). Three funny stories about a fox who is outfoxed by his own tricks.

39. James Marshall, *Rats on the Roof* (New York: Dial, 1991). Seven fables that feature animals that cleverly escape disastrous situations, such as two sheep who almost end up as a meal for a wolf, but manage to bore the wolf to sleep with their conversation!

40. Brinton Turkle, *Deep in the Forest* (New York: Dutton, 1976). In this reversal of the Goldilocks story, a bear cub visits the forest home of humans, tasting food, upsetting chairs and finally going to sleep in one of the beds.

41. Raymond Briggs, *The Snowman* (New York: Random House, 1978). The beautifully illustrated adventures of a boy and the snowman he has made. This book prompts thoughtful responses from all ages of readers.

42. Chris Van Allsburg, *The Mysteries of Harris Burdick* (New York: Houghton Mifflin, 1984). A series of intriguing pictures that encourage readers to create their own stories.

43. Russell Hoban, *Bread and Jam for Frances* (New York: Scholastic, 1964). One of a number of engaging stories about a little badger. Frances prefers bread and jam to all other food, until her mother serves it to her for dinner. This book actually makes the most finicky eater hungry! Other titles include *A Baby Sister for Frances* (Harper & Row, 1964), *A Bargain for Frances* (Harper & Row, 1970) and *Best Friends for Frances* (Harper & Row, 1969).

44. Esle Holmelund Minarik, *Little Bear's Visit* (New York, Harper & Row, 1961). This is one of a series of "I Can Read" books that features stories told to a little bear by his grandparents while he is waiting for his parents to return home. Other titles include *Little Bear, Father Bear Comes Home, Little Bear's Friend* and *No Fighting, No Biting*, all published by Harper & Row.

45. William Steig, *Sylvester and the Magic Pebble* (New York: Simon and Schuster, 1969). Sylvester the donkey finds a magic pebble that grants wishes. When he needs to hide from an enemy, he wishes he were a rock and his wish is granted. Now, he can't hold the pebble to wish himself to be a donkey again. His family finds him and wishes him back to himself.

46. Roger Duvoisin, *Petunia* (New York: Knopf, 1950). With nearly tragic results, a barnyard goose is convinced that she is wise because she is carrying a book around.

47. Hans Christian Anderson, *The Steadfast Tin Soldier* (New York: Prentice Hall, 1981). The story of a brave tin soldier and his love for a paper-doll ballerina.

48. Margery Williams, *The Velveteen Rabbit: Or How Toys Became Real* (New York: Doubleday, 1958). The story of a much-beloved toy rabbit that must be destroyed after a young boy's illness. Spared by the intercession of a fairy, the toy becomes a real rabbit.

49. Ezra Jack Keats, *Peter's Chair* (New York: Harper & Row, 1967). Describes how a young boy deals with his jealousy of a new baby sister.

50. Lynd Ward, *The Biggest Bear* (New York: Houghton Mifflin, 1952). A pet bear cub becomes a community nuisance, and the young owner must face a difficult decision.

51. Trinka Hakes Noble, *Jimmy's Boa and the Big Splash Birthday Bash* (New York: Trumpet Club, 1989). The improbable but hilarious account of a birthday visit to Sealand, which involves children and a boa constrictor diving in among sharks and whales.

52. Scholastic Big Books, *Big Multicultural Tales, Big Science, Big Book Magazine*. Available from: Scholastic Book Clubs, Inc., 2931 East McCarty St., P.O. Box 7503, Jefferson City, MO 65102-9966.

53. Michael Rosen, ed., *South and North, East and West: The Oxfam Book of Children's Stories* (Bergenfield, N.J.: Candlewick Press, 1992).

54. Joseph Bruchac and Jonathan London, *Thirteen Moons on Turtle's Back: A Native American Year of Moons* (East Rutherford, N.J.: Philomel Books, 1992).

55. Janice Hartwick Dressel, "The Effects of Listening to and Discussing Different Qualities of Children's Literature on the Narrative Writing of Fifth Graders," *Research in the Teaching of English* 24(1990):397–414.

56. M. Eeds and D. Wells, "Grand Conversations: An Exploration of Meaning Construction in Literature Study Groups," *Research in the Teaching of English* 23(1989):4–29.

57. Donald Bissett, "The Amount and Effect of Recreational Reading in Selected Fifth Grade Classes," unpublished doctoral dissertation, Syracuse University, 1969.

58. R. C. Anderson, P. T. Wilson, and L. G. Fielding, "A New Focus on Free-Reading: The Role of Trade Books in Reading Instruction," in *Contexts of School Based Literacy*, T. E. Raphael (ed.) (New York: Random House, 1986).

    J. L. Ingham, *Books and Reading Development: The Bradford Book Flood Experiment* (Exeter, N.H.: Heinemann Educational Books, 1981).

    L. M. Morrow, "Relationships between Literature Programs, Library Corner Designs and Children's Use of Literature," *Journal of Educational Research* 75(1982):339–344.

    L. M. Morrow and C. S. Weinstein, "Increasing Children's Use of Literature Through Program and Physical Design Changes," *Elementary School Journal* 83:131–137.

59. Chris Van Allsburg, *The Polar Express* (New York: Houghton Mifflin, 1984). This Caldecott winner describes a Christmas Eve journey via the Polar Express to the North Pole, where a young boy receives the first gift of Christmas from Santa Claus. This beautifully illustrated modern classic captures the essence of what it means to believe in Santa Claus.

60. Jack Prelutsky, compiler, *The Random House Book of Poetry for Children: A Treasury of 572 Poems for Today's Child* (New York: Random House, 1983).

61. John T. Gillespie and Corinne J. Naden, *Best Books for Children: Preschool through Grade 6*, 4th ed. (New York: Bowker, 1990).

62. Armstrong Sperry, *Call It Courage* (New York: Macmillan, 1940). The story of a young Polynesian boy who battles his fear of the sea to survive shipwreck and cannibals.

63. Scott O'Dell, *Sarah Bishop* (New York: Houghton Mifflin, 1980). An inspiring survival story for girls that portrays the trials of a young girl at the time of the American Revolution.

64. Tomie dePaola, reteller, *The Legend of the Bluebonnet: An Old Tale of Texas* (New York: Putnam, 1983). Beautifully illustrated picture storybook that retells the legend of a young Comanche girl's sacrifice, which was the legendary origin of the Texas bluebonnet flower.

65. Theodore Taylor, *The Cay* (New York: Doubleday, 1969). This is a story of physical survival in the West Indies, but also survival of the spirit as a young blind American boy and a West Indian native struggle to understand and support each other in the face of overwhelming environmental challenges.

66. *Social Education* is the official journal of the National Council for the Social Studies. Information on membership is available from NCSS, 3501 Newark Street, NW, Washington, DC 20016. Each issue features a collection of articles on a theme, treated from various perspectives in the social sciences. For example, an issue may feature the Pacific Rim countries and explore them in terms of history, geography, economics, sociology and political concerns. Departments and features address additional issues, demonstrate teaching methods and review books of interest to teachers of social studies.

67. *MSJ: Middle School Journal* is the journal of the National Middle School Association. Articles in this journal are organized around a theme, such as alternative

assessment and interdisciplinary instruction. While designed specifically for middle school teachers, many of the ideas will be helpful to self-contained and departmentalized intermediate-level instructors. Articles explain and illustrate theory and provide practical assistance to classroom teachers. Information on membership is available from the National Middle School Association, 4807 Evanswood Drive, Columbus, OH 43229-6292.

68. Keith Baker, *Who Is the Beast?* (New York: Trumpet Club, 1990). Animals flee from a tiger, whom they call the beast, when they see his stripes, tail, whiskers and other features. When the tiger hears them talking about a beast, he wonders who the beast is. He spots bees with stripes, a monkey with a tail and a catfish with whiskers and concludes that if these features describe a beast, they all are beasts. Large, colorful illustrations.

69. Hendrik Willem Van Loon, *The Story of Mankind* (Liverwright, 1984).

70. Helen Dean Fish, *Animals of the Bible*, illustrated by Dorothy Lathrop (New York: Lippincott, 1938).

71. Scholastic Book Clubs, Inc., 2931 East McCarty Street, P.O. Box 7503, Jefferson City, MO 65102-7503. Or call 1-800-724-2424 to have information sent to you. Scholastic clubs are available in both Spanish and English. The grade-level clubs are: Firefly (preschool–K), SeeSaw (1–2), Lucky (3–4), Arrow (5–6), and Tab (7–8). Depending on your particular class, you may wish to order from more than one club.

    The Trumpet Club, P.O. Box 604, Holmes, PA 19043. You can call the club for information at 1-800-826-0110. Clubs are available at the following instructional levels: Early Years (preschool, K), Primary Grades (1, 2, 3), and Middle Grades (4, 5, 6).

    Weekly Reader Paperback Clubs, 2981 East McCarty Street, P.O. Box 3750, Jefferson City, MO 65102-9840. Clubs are available for primary and intermediate grade levels. The toll-free number is 1-800-828-1696.

72. Jean Craighead George, *Water Sky* (Scranton, Penn.: HarperCollins, 1987).

73. Gary Paulsen, *Dogsong* (New York: Scholastic, 1985).

74. Jean Craighead George, *Julie of the Wolves* (New York: Harper & Row, 1972).

75. Jack Prelutsky, *Tyrannosaurus Was a Beast: Dinosaur Poems* (New York: Greenwillow, 1988).

76. Laura Ingalls Wilder, *Little House in the Big Woods, Little House on the Prairie, Farmer Boy* and *On the Banks of Plum Creek* for primary students and *By the Shores of Silver Lake, Little House on the Prairie, The Long Winter*, and *These Happy Golden Years* for intermediates. Many intermediate students also enjoy the earlier books in the series (Scranton, Penn.: Harper, 1953).

77. Madeleine L'Engle, *A Wrinkle in Time* (New York: Dell, 1973). First in a series of modern fantasy trips through time for the Murry family, which includes Meg, twin brothers Sandy and Dennys, a precocious younger brother, Charles Wallace and their parents who are both renowned scientists. Excellent adventure for children who like fantasy and science fiction.

78. Madeleine L'Engle, *Meet the Austins* (New York: Dell, 1981). First in a series of family adventures, featuring Vicky Austin, Suzy, her sister and brothers John and Rob. Various challenges face the family, which are portrayed in warm and believable scenes.

79. Betsy Byars, *The Not-Just-Anybody-Family* (New York: Delacorte, 1986). This is the first in a series of books about the Blossom family, featuring the unforgettable characters and adventures of Junior Blossom, his grandfather, mother, brothers and sister.

80. Cynthia Voigt, *Homecoming* (New York: Ballantine, 1991). This is the first in a series of books about Dicey Tillerman and her brothers and sisters, James,

Maybeth and Sammy. First their father, then their mother abandons them. This story tells of the trip they make, seeking a new home with their grandmother who lives several states away.

81. John Dewey, "The Underlying Philosophy of Education," in *The Educational Frontier*, edited by William Kilpatrick (New York: Century Company, 1933), pp. 287–319.

82. *The Horn Book Magazine*, The Horn Book, Inc. Information on current subscription rates can be obtained from The Horn Book, Inc., 14 Beacon Street, Boston, MA 02108-9765, or by calling 1-800-325-1170 outside of Massachusetts and 617-277-1555 within state.

83. *The Lion and the Unicorn* is published semiannually by Johns Hopkins University Press. Information on current subscription rates is available from The Johns Hopkins University Press, Journals Division, 701 W. 40th Street, Suite 275, Baltimore, MD 21211.

84. *The New Advocate*, Christopher-Gordon Publishers, Inc. Information on current subscription rates is available from The New Advocate, 480 Washington Street, Norwood, MA 02062.

85. *Kirkus Reviews*, 200 Park Avenue South, New York, NY 10003. This periodical reviews books before publication and identifies books of special merit published for children and young people.

86. American Library Association, 50 East Huron Street, Chicago, IL 60611. This association publishes *Booklist*, which reviews children's and young adult books and special interest publications. It gives "star" reviews to books of special merit and publishes an annual "Editor's Choices" list. The association also publishes the quarterly *Book Links*, which describes ways to use literature across the curriculum. It sponsors annual lists, such as "Notable Children's Books," "Best Books for Young Adults" and "Recommended Books for the Reluctant Young Reader."

87. *School Library Journal*, 249 West 17th Street, New York, NY 10011. This monthly periodical reviews all new children's and young adult books. Reviews award stars and identify "Best Books."

88. Children's Book Council, *Children's Books: Awards & Prizes* (New York: Children's Book Council, Inc., 1992).

89. American Library Association, *The Newbery and Caldecott Awards: A Guide to the Medal and Honor Books*. To order, contact Order Department, American Library Association, 50 Huron Street, Chicago, IL 60611.

90. Multicultural Publisher's Exchange, *Catalog of Books By and About People of Color* (Fort Atkinson, Wisc.: The Highsmith Company). A free catalog is available from The Highsmith Company, Inc., W5527 Highway 106, P. O. Box 800, Fort Atkinson, WI 53538-0800 or by phone at 1-800-558-2110.

91. Scott O'Dell, *Sing Down the Moon* (New York: Dell, 1970).

92. Scott O'Dell, *Island of the Blue Dolphins* (New York: Dell, 1960).

93. Mildred Taylor, *The Friendship* (New York: Dial Books for Young Readers, 1988).

94. John Steptoe, *Mufaro's Beautiful Daughters* (New York: Lothrop, Lee & Shepard Books, 1988).

Shared and Guided Reading

WHAT'S HAPPENING HERE? This third-grade class enjoys reading a favorite book together. The teacher invites members of the group to share their responses to what they have read and to analyze the characters and plot of the story. He asks them what they like about the book and encourages them to find connections between the story and their own experience.

*All good books are alike in that they are truer than if they had really
happened and after you are finished reading one you will feel that all
that happened to you and afterwards it all belongs to you: the good
and the bad, the ecstasy, the remorse and sorrow, the people and the
places and how the weather was.*

—Ernest Hemingway[1]

LOOKING AHEAD   1. What are the benefits of shared reading experiences?
2. What kinds of literature are appropriate for shared reading?
3. What is guided reading? What is its value?
4. What do students gain from discussing literature in groups?
5. How do teachers affect children's responses to literature?
6. What kinds of questions help children explore literature for meaning?

IN 25 WORDS   Reading and discussing real books in small groups help students interact
OR LESS   with literature, share ideas and develop language and thinking skills.

I. Focus: Shared and Guided Reading

When teachers and students read aloud together from Big Book stories,
poetry and plays or sing from lyrics printed on a chart, they are participating
in a **shared reading** experience. These sessions promote the sheer pleasure
of reading and provide emerging readers with a sense of how it feels to read.
Predictable stories with repetitive, rhythmic or rhyming elements support
these readers' efforts to identify and learn familiar words and match sounds
with their symbols. Sharing favorite books by reading them aloud together
also helps create a sense of community in a classroom, giving students
common experiences to refer to and natural extensions into guided reading.

Guided reading activities often emerge from shared reading experiences,
but have an added feature. These conversations about books involve a more
intensive examination of literature and encourage students to give deliberate
thought to what they read. Peterson and Eeds[2] refer to this conscious
reflection on literature as "intensive reading," a sharing of the intelligence
and imagination of each member of a literature study group. During these
"grand conversations," students share ideas and experiences that increase
their understanding of what has been read or listened to.

Just as teachers share enthusiasm for books by reading aloud and model adult interest in reading by participating in silent sustained reading, they similarly demonstrate the activities of a mature reader in guided reading sessions. Teachers model strategies for successful reading and help students make connections with their own experiences that will increase their understanding of what they read. Through their comments and questions, teachers encourage children to search for meaning in what they read. They model ways to analyze, interpret and evaluate stories and illustrations and show students how to examine literary devices, characterization, plot, setting, illustrations and accuracy in the books they read. In these sessions, teachers encourage students to make personal connections with their own experience and to compare their interpretations and understanding with others. Through open-ended questions they prompt children to examine what they read for interesting details and to relate the content to their knowledge or experience in other contexts.

At the kindergarten or beginning reading levels, Big Books are frequently used for guided reading. These oversized texts with large print feature predictable stories, folktales and poems that allow children to experience a sense of reading and to establish sound/symbol associations. Conversations with beginning readers usually involve open-ended questions that stimulate interaction with print and stories. In the process of examining the story, students become acquainted with the conventions of grammar, punctuation and capitalization. In the context of a favorite or familiar story, students practice identifying and reading familiar words, use context and decoding strategies to figure out unfamiliar words, analyze illustrations, practice reading with expression and learn to identify literary genres. They relate their own experiences to the books they are reading, discuss the purposes of the author or illustrator, compare books and authors and connect the theme of the story to other areas of the curriculum.

Older students read and discuss books together in small **literature groups** or as an entire class. In these groups they share their personal responses to literature, talk about ideas that interest them and examine relationships between what they read and their own experience. Together, they explore the meaning of the story, interpret the behavior of characters, examine the plot and identify the themes and values portrayed. When questions arise, teachers act as a resource or refer students to resources that will help them find the answer on their own.

Guided literature study is an ideal medium for including all students in the classroom. Students read at their own rate, respond in a preferred mode and interact with others on the basis of common interests. Open-ended questions permit participation at many levels, and small-group dynamics provide helpful support for the physically or academically challenged. Students with limited English speaking proficiency have increased opportunities to practice language skills in small groups. Academically challenged readers particularly seem to profit from small-group interaction, which encourages them to organize their thoughts and practice expressing them, as they explore and discuss ideas with other students.

As students develop skill in exploring books in small groups, teachers may introduce multiple titles on a common theme. They may also use these sessions to introduce different genres of books or titles related to a study in the content areas. Teachers often provide different books by the same author or a variety of books in a literary genre to encourage students to group themselves by common interests. During these small-group interactions, teachers may join different groups to observe, share ideas, monitor group dynamics or make suggestions that will improve the quality of discussions.

WHAT DO YOU THINK? Did your teachers use Big Books for reading aloud when you were in elementary school? If not, did you ever wish that a read-aloud book was big enough so you could see the pictures more easily? Have you ever read books and shared ideas in a literature group? What did you like or dislike about the experience? What do you think children might especially enjoy about these sessions?

II. The Importance of Guided Reading

Guided reading experiences are highly social interactions that help create common experiences for students. The goal of these sessions is to increase the meaning of reading for the individual, but this search for meaning involves understanding the purposes of the author and is enhanced by the responses of others. As students make an effort to share their understanding of literature, they better organize their ideas, and their understanding is often enhanced or enriched by the thoughts of others.

Louise Rosenblatt[3] describes reading as a **transaction** between literature and an individual reader. She believes that readers re-create the intended meaning of an author in light of their own experience:

> We would not forget, of course, that the text was an event in the life of an author, that he produced it at a particular moment in his life and in the history of his world. But we would not forget, either, that the poem becomes an event in the life of each reader as he re-creates it from the text. (*Literature As Exploration*, p. 282)

If the experience of literature is an individual creation, what is the value of discussing it in groups? Rosenblatt says,

> The uniqueness of the transaction between reader and text is not inconsistent with the fact that both elements in this relationship have social origins and social effects. If each author were completely different from every other human being, and if each reader were totally unique, there could, of course, be no communication. There are many experiences that we all have in common—birth, growth, love, death. We can communicate because of a common core of experience, even though there may be infinite personal variations. (*Literature As Exploration*, pp. 27–28)

This common core of experiences is what makes the sharing of responses in literature groups possible. The deepening and broadening of ideas and insight that result from this sharing support the value of using guided reading as part of an integrated language learning program.

Research indicates that students who have the opportunity to ask questions and make comments about what they read show increased comprehension and vocabulary development. They learn the strategies of good readers, practice skills of analysis, have the opportunity to express themselves orally and are challenged to defend their points of view. Through study questions, they learn to look for important features of a literary genre and are challenged into a deeper and more complex understanding of reading material.

McClure[4] found that peers support each other in literary response in a variety of ways. They help to refine and clarify meanings, serve as an audience for each other and share their collective memory. She also found that complexity of responses to literature in group situations depends more on the cooperative nature of the discussion context than the students' developmental characteristics.

Eeds and Wells[5] found that children engage in what they call "grand conversations" when they meet together in literature groups. Their studies show that students help one another respond more fully to stories by collaborating in the construction of simple meaning, sharing personal stories inspired by the books and actively questioning what they have read to uncover meaning. They also found that the kind and quality of the text being discussed influence the quality of these discussions.

Hepler and Hickman[6] observed that informal talk about books occurs among peers. This talking about a book helps them rehearse or organize the content of the book. This point is underscored for challenged readers, for whom the sharing of information in which the student is intensely interested may be the key factor, both for motivating students to read and for providing the optimal vehicle for students to be evaluated.[7]

Hickman[8] recorded children's responses to literature in a natural setting, looking for behavior that revealed some connection between children and literature. She found that children responded to literature by applauding after a book was read, joining in refrains, browsing among books or keeping books close to them. They often read together with other children, shared discoveries in books and commented on them without stimulus. They also participated in dramatic play, made pictures or games and wrote about the stories they had read.

Martinez and Roser[9] described several changes that indicate a difference in children's responses as they listen to stories repeatedly: (1) they talk more frequently about familiar stories; (2) they make more comments when listening to familiar stories; (3) they ask more questions about unfamiliar stories; (4) they gain control over particular aspects of the story so they are able to attend to other dimensions; and (5) they make more complex responses. Lehr[10] found that children who receive increased exposure to literature are more able to identify story themes and that greater experience with literature enabled them to respond in more sophisticated ways to books.

Morrow[11] found that students who are encouraged to ask questions and make comments about stories read to them show an increase in comprehension and in the number and complexity of their comments and questions. She also noted that repeated readings of the same book increased the quantity and complexity of student responses.[12] Repeated experiences with stories produced a wider variety of responses and more interpretive comments than single readings of a book. Hickman (op. cit.) noticed that successful teachers planned for cumulative experiences with literature, allowing children to consider selections and genre in depth and in a variety of ways over time. She also found that children's responses to particular books change over time. The length of time involved with a book increases the quality of response because it provides opportunities for repetition and reflection.

Kiefer[13] observed that in naturally occurring responses to picture books in the classroom, the teacher plays a key role in influencing response. When teachers read and re-read books, children's responses deepen and broaden because of repeated opportunities to interact with a book. He also found that open-ended discussion encourages a variety of responses and that language used by the teacher to describe books is adopted into the conversation of students when they talk about books. Roser and Martinez[14] found that adult reading-aloud style influences children's responses to literature. Teachers model for children the process of the mature reader in interaction with the text, showing the importance of making sense from print and modeling strategies for doing this.

WHAT DO YOU THINK?   What interested you about the research described above? Were any of the findings surprising? Did you have a favorite book that you read or wanted read to you as a child? What do you think was the drawing power of this particular book?

III. Looking into Classrooms

Kindergarten Level

Mrs. Jamison uses a pointer to touch the words on the large Big Book pages as seventeen kindergarten children chant the lively story verse of *Chicka Chicka Boom Boom*.[15] "**A** told **B**, and **B** told **C**, I'll meet you at the top of the coconut tree!" they sing together.

When they reach the end of the story, Mrs. Jamison returns to the beginning of the book. "Let's read it again," she says. "Who wants to read with me?"

"Me! Me!" comes the response.

She begins the story again, first leaving out selected letters, which the children read easily. Then she begins to leave out parts of the refrain, beginning with "boom boom!" She continues through the book, stopping at words that she knows are familiar for most of her students. Several are able to read fairly well with the teacher, and all join in on the refrain.

"What do you think of the pictures in this book?" she begins, and many hands go up.

"I like 'em," Brian replies.

"Any particular reason?" Mrs. Jamison asks.

"I like the colors. . . ."

"Anything else?"

"The way they climb up the tree."

"Yeah," Jason agrees, "and they all fall down!"

"They're all jumbly under the tree," Jessica adds.

"Does this story have a main character?" the teacher asks.

The children look puzzled. They look at each other and shake their heads.

"The letters?" Amy questions.

"Which ones?" Mrs. Jamison asks.

"All of 'em."

"That's too many main characters," Jessica says.

"Let's look through the book and see if it gives us any more ideas," Mrs. Jamison suggests, and she begins to turn the large pages one by one.

The children lean forward to look closely. Amy, who is partially sighted, has her own copy. She pages through quickly, and about halfway through the book she exclaims, "The tree! It's the tree. It's on every page!"

"What do you think?" Mrs. Jamison asks the other children as she continues to turn the pages.

By now, everyone has noticed that the coconut tree is on every page and they are nodding their assent.

"It's the tree **and** the alphabet," Peter says.

"Go on," Mrs. Jamison says.

"There's letters on every page, too."

"Uh-uh!" A few children disagree.

"Let's look again," the teacher suggests, and she begins to turn the pages again. Near the end of the book, the tree stands alone against the moon and the night sky.

"See?" Marty says to Peter.

"Well . . . one page. But there's letters on all the others." Peter pauses a few seconds. It is obvious that he is still gathering his evidence. "And the first page and the last one have letters . . . two whole pages," he adds.

Jennifer wants to see the tree-only page. "The tree's on two pages, too," she announces, "and so's the one at the front of the book."

"Before you decide this," Mrs. Jamison says, "why don't you think about the setting for the story. Where does it all happen?"

The children look at each other. Amy scrambles through the pages. "Could be Hawaii. It's a palm tree."

"Florida, too," Peter ventures. "It could be Florida."

Amy turns the last page in the book, looks up and says, "I've got an idea. Is it the tree?"

"What do you think?" Mrs. Jamison asks back. The other children hum with the question. Mrs. Jamison waits.

"It's where everything happens," Danny says. It's his first contribution.

"Then maybe the **letters** are the main characters," Amy ventures.

"What does everyone else think?" the teacher asks.

The other children nod assent.

"Yep, that's it," Peter agrees, "and the tree's the setting."

"What about the verse?" Mrs. Jamison asks. "What do you like about it?"

"It jiggles!" Dane replies, illustrating its rhythm by nodding his head.

"Yeah . . . jiggles!" the others agree, bobbing back and forth as they remember the reading. "Jiggle jiggle boom boom!" someone says.

"Hey, I like that," Mrs. Jamison says.

"Wiggle wiggle boom boom!" someone else says.

"Good for you!" Mrs. Jamison responds. "What else can you think of?"

Someone says, "Clicka clicka zoom zoom" and everyone laughs. They are starting to play with the words.

"Keep going," Mrs. Jamison says. More rhymes emerge, including varoom, broom and room.

"Can you make up a verse to rhyme with 'boom'? she asks. "Chicka chicka boom boom. . . ." She waits.

"Sweep 'em with a broom broom," suggests Amy.

"Push 'em out the room room," Peter says.

"Make 'em speed, v'room v'room," Dane adds.

"Faster faster zoom zoom," Brian says. Mrs. Jamison writes the new verses on the board and everyone reads them together.

They read the book again, this time all together. Mrs. Jamison distributes standard-sized individual copies of the book to each student to give them the opportunity to examine details in the illustrations, such as "e's" stubbed toe and the bandage on the letter "f." Finding such delightful features in illustrations encourages children to look for similar details in books they read on their own. The teacher also has several other books illustrated by Lois Ehlert on display in the library corner, including the colorful *Eating the Alphabet: Fruits and Vegetables from A to Z*[16] and *Color Farm*,[17] so that children can observe other examples of her illustrative style (watercolor collage and cut-paper shapes).

Individual copies of *Chicka Chicka Boom Boom* will go home with students, protected from in-transit damage by plastic freezer bags labeled with the kindergarten room number, so lost books can be easily returned. (Note: Safety experts caution against students wearing or carrying clothes or items that display their names.) Students read the books aloud at home with their parents, talking about features of the story and illustrations. Suggestions for these discussions are printed on a sheet of paper, folded inside the book. Mrs. Jamison explained her policy of sending books home at the beginning of the year, and parents have been enthusiastic participants since that time.

Students have daily opportunities to respond in writing, drama and art to the book. They take turns reenacting the story, with children pantomiming the letters climbing up the tree, while the teacher reads the verse. They fall down and are picked up and dusted off by students who portray the parent letters.

Each day students write a sentence or more about their response to the book, which provides the teacher with information about how well students understand the interaction of the guided reading sessions. When Mrs. Jamison first introduced guided reading, she encouraged children to draw pictures about the stories and write captions (descriptive titles) for them. Soon her students wanted to write more about their pictures, and this led to using separate sheets of paper for writing. (Captioning and picture stories will be discussed further in Chapter 8.)

As her students write, Mrs. Jamison looks for individual uses of words from the story, improved sound–symbol relationships (spelling accuracy) and the use of correct punctuation. She observes the length of sentences, which she encourages by allowing students to use developmental spelling (using letters or a combination of letters to represent the sounds of the words they want to write), described more fully in Chapter 8. Mrs. Jamison also observes her students while they are writing, watching to see how they hold their pencils and slant their paper. She helps students adjust awkward pencil grips and monitors student behavior that might indicate vision problems, such as putting their faces too close to the paper. She notices and records the resources students use to spell their words. Most use a combination of developmental spelling and reference to the Big Book or other charts around the room. Some ask each other for help in spelling the words they want to use.

Students respond artistically to the book in several ways. They draw and decorate letters to show the various bumps and bruises sustained from falling out of the coconut tree. They cut out leaves, trunks and coconuts that they have drawn freehand and construct their own trees, choosing the color for the background and creating frames from construction paper and colored markers. The teacher provides stickers of upper- and lowercase letters for them to use in their pictures, but some choose to draw their own and cut them out.

The variety of finished pictures is striking. There are fat trunks and skinny trunks, trees that stand straight, lean sideways and bend over, imitating the positions of the tree throughout the story. Students have cut out leaves in every imaginable shape and size, and some have drawn veins on the leaves, hair on the coconuts and bark on the trunks. Frames add a festive touch to the palm trees and reflect each artist's favorite colors and designs. Obviously, no two are alike. For the next two weeks, these creations will provide a festive look across the back of the room. After that time, they will go home or be filed in student portfolio collections (Chapter 8).

WHAT HAPPENED HERE? ONE PERSPECTIVE

This experience of shared and guided reading encourages active participation by every child in the classroom. Regardless of reading proficiency, each can join the repeated chorus of the story, and everyone can participate in the discussions and observations. As they look more closely at the elements of the book, students learn the conventions of print and practice skills of analysis and reflection that will enhance their understanding and appreciation of literature. The spontaneous word play that produces rhymes is appreciated and encouraged by the teacher. Notice that the majority of the teacher's contributions are prompts such as "What do you like?," "What do you think?" and "Go on." She waits for students to express themselves and encourages them to finish or expand their thoughts. She asks for personal responses to the book to encourage students to make a personal connection with what they read and to underscore the value of each person's contribution. Because children of this age may focus their attention on single events or features of a book, the teacher sees this sharing of responses in a group as a good way to review the variety of appealing elements to be found in a story.

She also allows the debate about main characters and setting to continue, limiting her participation to questions that will help students direct their own inquiry. They test their hypotheses by searching for evidence and resolve the debate in a manner that is satisfying to the participants.

Chicka Chicka Boom Boom, like all good picture books, contains illustrations and text that will provide days of interaction. When children bond with the attractive features of a book, repetition is pleasant and exciting. The predictable elements of this book, like those of many fairy tales, folktales, poems, chants and songs, permit all children to join in the reading. Mrs. Jamison helps them make connections between what they are saying and hearing and the symbols that represent this expression.

When Mrs. Jamison calls attention to details of illustration or text and talks about various features of the story, she is modeling reading strategies to her students. She is showing them what good readers do to make sense of print and helping them gain increased appreciation for the aesthetic content and information conveyed in illustrations.

WHAT DO YOU THINK? Using your own knowledge and experience, review the observation again. What do **you** see happening? What do you think was most rewarding about this interaction for the teacher? What do you think you

FIGURE 5.1
Students in a kindergarten class wrote a story together after listening to a book read aloud by a visitor. Each child selected part of the story to illustrate, and the pages were bound into a class book.

would most enjoy about working with children of this age? What would be the greatest challenge?

Primary Level

While Mrs. Scott's students are putting away their books from silent sustained reading, she places a stack of books on her desk. Students begin to pull their desks together into groups of four. One member of each group goes to the teacher's desk to get copies of the book. It is time for guided reading.

When all the books are passed out, Mrs. Scott begins to read *Tommy at the Grocery Store*,[18] a humorous picture storybook with lively illustrations. Members of the class giggle as they listen to the story. A little pig is left at the grocery store by his absent-minded mother. He is subsequently taken home and then returned by a series of shoppers who mistake him for something else. The grocer puts him in the deli because he thinks he's a salami. A shopper buys him, takes him home and decides he's a potato because he has eyes. He's returned to the store and soon mistaken for corn because he has ears. And so the story continues until his mother comes to rescue him.

Some children follow along in their books; others listen to the teacher. When she finishes, Mrs. Scott asks, "What do you think?" and the students respond enthusiastically.

"We'll study the book in groups for about twenty minutes," she says. "If you have problems, try to work them out with each other. If you still have a problem, you can ask me."

From their previous work in guided reading, the students in each group know how to begin exploring the book on their own. They begin by reading it again together as a group. In some groups, each person reads a page aloud, while in other groups students read several pages. In one group, they decide to read aloud all together. Occasionally there is an unfamiliar word and the groups use their decoding and context clues to figure it out. If they still have difficulty, Mrs. Scott gives them clues for words they already know but cannot identify, or she refers them to a chart in the room or the dictionary.

In the group nearest the teacher's desk, Zachary, a new transfer student, offers his turn at reading to Angela. "You read it," he says. "I like how you read."

Angela looks at the teacher, who nods her head to approve, and Angela reads an extra page. When all groups finish reading, they address the questions on their discussion sheets.

"What was your favorite part of this book?" Angela reads.

"When the teacher took Tommy home," Zachary says. "Read it again," he asks. "It's my favorite part." When Angela finishes, he recites the verse from memory: "Next a teacher bought him and took him home to eat, and very nearly fainted when she noticed he had feet." He continues reciting the entire page.

Everyone in the group laughs. "How'd you do that?" Blain asks Zachary.

"Cinchy," he replies. "Just do it."

"That's pretty fast. You're good," Blain says.

Zachary looks pleased. Angela continues reading the questions and each person in the group responds.

"What are these purple things on the front cover?" Blain asks.

"Eggplant," Caitlin says. "You cut it up and fry it."

"Yuck, eggplant," Zachary says. "I hate it. It's all rubbery."

"Not when my mom fixes it," Caitlin says. "It's crunchy, with cheese and spaghetti sauce all over it."

"What are these?" Amber asks. "They look like fat onions."

"Leeks," Zachary says. "My mom makes leek soup."

"Like onions?" Amber asks.

"Kinda like onions," he answers, "only better."

They decide that the grocery items that create a frame for the main characters make a good cover for the story. Blain thinks it would have been more interesting if the artist had used the same grocery items that were part of the story. Everyone likes the illustrations. Caitlin says they remind her of Rosemary Wells's characters, and the others agree. No one has read anything else by written by Bill Grossman, so they decide to ask the librarian if there are any other books written by him in the library.

"What do you like best about the story?" Amber reads.

"The pictures," Caitlin says.

"I liked the rhyme," Zachary adds. "It makes me want to dance!"

The others laugh and nod their heads.

The group agrees that the book is make-believe. "Nobody would think a little pig was an ear of corn," Zachary says. "That's stupid."

"Or a ruler." "Or a pie." "Or a bottle," the others join in.

"But it's funny," Zachary adds, and the others giggle.

"What kind of story is it?" Amber reads.

"Is it modern fantasy?" Caitlin asks, looking at the choices on their literature response sheet.

"It has to be," Amber says. "It's not long ago, 'cause the pictures are like now. So it's not a folktale."

"It couldn't happen, either," Caitlin says. "Pigs don't wear clothes and go to the store." They all agree.

"It rhymes," Blain adds. "It's poetry."

"And a picture book," Amber adds.

"A picture STORY book," Blain corrects. "It has to have words. You can't tell what's going on without the words."

When they have decided that the book fits all three categories, they individually record their responses to the book in their response journals and answer the remaining questions that ask for written responses.

Zachary watches as they write. "Do you want help?" Amber inquires.

"Can you write what I say?" he asks.

Amber looks up at Mrs. Scott, who nods approval. She reads the response questions and records what Zachary says. "Now read what I said," he asks and she does. "Yeah, that's it," he says. "That's what I said."

Later, when students are drawing their responses to the book, Zachary will make up a new verse for the story and illustrate it with strikingly sophisticated artwork.

WHAT HAPPENED HERE? ONE PERSPECTIVE

Three things are apparent in this observation: The children enjoyed reading and examining the book together; the teacher supported this interaction by providing a good book and encouraging them to prob-lem-solve; everyone was involved in responding to the book, including Zachary, who has great difficulty with reading and writing.

The students were drawn to the book because of its lively illustrations and humorous verse. They will spend time with it in their groups and individually because they enjoy it and want to share this pleasure with others. With subsequent re-reading they will notice more detail in the illustrations and pick up more subtle bits of humor from the verse. Students have also been introduced to figurative language in a colorful and pleasant way. During the next session of guided reading, Mrs. Scott will write the term "figurative language" on the board and they will copy it in their writing journals. Throughout the year, they will add examples of figurative language to their list in this book, which they will use as a resource for their own writing.

In the case of Zachary, who is a new transfer student, Mrs. Scott encourages interaction in his team to provide him the assistance he needs. With initial help from Amber, he is able to function in ways that would not be possible in traditional language arts instruction. He re-ceives praise for his good memory from other group members and is rewarded with laughter for his witty contributions to the discussions. Through Zachary's artistic and poetic responses, the teacher is able to see that he not only understands the content and form of the book, but is able to create new extensions for it. In a traditional classroom, other students (and the teacher) would probably be unaware of his talents. The developmental nature of reading experiences in this classroom will encourage Zachary to use these strengths to improve his reading and writing skills. Although he will receive individual help with his reading from the Chapter I teacher and from Mrs. Scott during individual reading conferences (see Chapter 6), he will be highly motivated in his efforts by the interaction that occurs within his study group.

Interaction in all the teams permits students to share each other's varied experiences. The questions they discuss are designed to enhance awareness of genre, authors, illustrators, story content and organization. When the groups meet together the following day, they will read the story again and compose an additional verse. They will also practice reading the verses aloud to share with the kindergarten and their Book Buddies in the sixth grade. Most take their books home to continue practicing and to share the book with their parents.

WHAT DO YOU THINK?

What else did you observe in this second-grade classroom? Were any of these reading activities familiar to you? How do they compare to the way you were taught to read? What do you think these children enjoyed most about their literature groups? Second and third grades are most often selected as the grades undergraduates would like to teach. Why do you think this is so?

> 10/4/93 Stone Fox   Erin Gillam
>   By John Reynolds Gardiner
>
>   Willy was smart to think of
> what to do to get money, but he didn't
> know alot. He kept asking all these
> questions that I knew the answers to
> and I thought that what he came
> up with was a good idea. His idea
> was to win a race. I liked that he had
> confidence in himself. He knew he could
> win. The thing I really liked about this book
> is that it made you feel like it was really
> happening. I thought that it was really sad
> at the end. If I hadn't been at school
> I probably would have started crying
> I did get tears in my eyes. Though the
> whole book I thought Stone Fox was
> really mean. But when I read the last
> page my mind totally changed.

FIGURE 5.2

Entry from a third-grade student's literature log, expressing a response to reading John Reynolds Gardiner's Stone Fox. *The story tells about Little Willy, who competes against the Indian, Stone Fox, in the National Dogsled Races. [John Reynolds Gardiner,* Stone Fox *(Scranton, Penn.: Harper and Row, 1980).]*

Intermediate Level

Mr. Robinson has just finished reading *North to Freedom*[19] to his sixth-grade class. The story traces the journey of a twelve-year-old boy who escapes from an East European prison camp. When the book is finished, the teacher asks the class if they would like to read more books like it for literature study. There is an enthusiastic response. He asks the class to make recommendations that might fit a theme, such as courage, survival or war.

During the next week, students submit ideas for themes and books. The class decides on the theme of courage. Several books are suggested in the category, and the teacher adds these to other titles he has collected, including: *Hatchet*,[20] which describes how a young boy survives in the Canadian wilderness with only a hatchet to provide for his needs and defend him from a hostile environment; *Island of the Blue Dolphins*,[21] the story of a Native American girl left to survive alone for eighteen years on an abandoned island off the coast of California; *The Cay*,[22] a survival story of a West Indian native and a blind American boy; *Sign of the Beaver*,[23] a story of survival and interdependence featuring a colonial boy and his Native American counterpart in the pre-Revolutionary Maine wilderness; *Sarah Bishop*,[24] a first-person narrative of a courageous girl who escapes her tormentors at the beginning of the Revolutionary War by living alone in a cave; *Call It Courage*,[25] the story of a young boy in the South Sea Islands who faces extraordinary peril to prove his courage; *Julie of the Wolves*,[26] the story of a young Inuit girl who survives a winter on the tundra with the help of a pack of wolves; and *Incident at Hawk's Hill*,[27] the unusual story of a badger that protects and nourishes a six-year-old boy who becomes lost on the prairie.

"There are eight books to choose from this time," the teacher says, as he introduces the study. "Each group will be reading a different book, and you can discuss and write about the one you choose."

Mr. Robinson passes out a list of the books so students can jot down pertinent notes beside each one as he previews it. He describes each book briefly and reads a paragraph or two from the beginning or from an exciting passage. As Mr. Robinson talks about the books, students make notes and put checkmarks beside the ones that interest them. When the previews are finished, students put their names on their individual lists and circle the books they would like to read, numbered in order of preference. From this list, Mr. Robinson will form groups of four students who have expressed interest in the same book.

While his students read and prepare for individual reading conferences (see Chapter 6), the teacher decides on the groups, writing student names under the appropriate book titles. At the beginning of the year, students tried to find out what their friends had chosen so they could be in the same group. But eventually, reading interests won out, and membership in groups varied from theme to theme.

When the teacher reads their names, students pick up the book they have selected and pull their desks together to begin reading. Mr. Robinson reminds them to bring a bookmark with them to their groups. Students have collections of bookmarks, made to celebrate favorite books or themes.

Some groups take turns reading aloud quietly, while others read silently as individuals. If the group reads silently, students lay out their bookmark when they have finished reading the first chapter and are ready for discussion. If others are still completing their reading, an individual can continue into the next chapter. When everyone's bookmark is out, one member of the study team gets a copy of the discussion questions from the teacher's desk and they begin talking about the book.

Amanda, Vickie, Lindsay and Margo form a group to study Scott O'Dell's *Sarah Bishop*, the story of a girl caught up in the turmoil of the Revolutionary War.

"What do you like about the book so far?" Amanda reads from the study questions.

"Well, it's different," Lindsay says.

"Different how?" Amanda asks.

"Well, . . . usually in Revolutionary War books it's all one side . . . you know, George Washington and Jefferson. I never thought about how the Tories had it, like Sarah's dad."

"I like it that it's her telling the story," Vickie adds. "It makes it more real."

"I like the details," Margo says. "I always like a book that talks about the everyday stuff in the old days."

Amanda is leading the discussion, so she adds her comments last. "I like it because it was interesting right away. I don't like books that take a long time to get going."

"Sometimes the slow ones turn out the best," Vickie comments. "I almost gave up reading *The Hobbit*[28] 'cause it was so slow. Lots of description and stuff."

"That's what I **liked** about it," Margo says with surprise. "Didn't you like the way he told about Bilbo's house and everything? I could just see it."

"Well, . . . yeah, I guess," Vickie says, "but I liked it better when there was more action, with the Gollum and the dragon and all."

"Yeah, me too," Amanda agrees. "Anyway, it looks like we might all like this one." She looks down at the study questions and reads the next question. "Did anything about this first chapter connect to other things you know or your own experience?"

"You know the Skinners they were talking about?" Lindsay asks. The others nod. "The way Sarah talked about them reminds me of the border ruffians we read about when we studied the Civil War last year. Remember? Some of them went around Kansas and Missouri burning houses and shooting people they thought were rebels."

"Yeah, and on the other side, they tried to scare off settlers that were against slavery," Vickie adds. "It wasn't safe to live there at all."

"I read about that in a book at my other school last year," Margo adds. "Did you ever read *Across Five Aprils*[29]? They did terrible things to people they thought were Southern sympathizers during the Civil War."

"Wait a minute," Vickie says, "Skinners . . . that reminds me of the skinheads. You know, the guys that shave their heads and cruise around beating people up and trashing their property just 'cause they're different?"

"That part where the guy is shooting at their house reminds me of what happened when my dad was on the school board and they were trying to pass the bond issue for the new high school," Amanda says. "People called us up at all times of day or night and called him names and threatened to wreck our store."

"Yeah, that was terrible," Vickie sympathizes.

The next question asks them to predict something that might happen in the story.

"Well, . . . Sarah probably learns to use a gun," Lindsay says. "She's standing there with one in her hand, right here on the front cover."

"You get the idea that things aren't going to get better right away, with them being shot at and all," Vickie adds.

"Well, we already know there's going to be a war, but we don't know how these characters will be involved," Margo says.

"I think Sarah's brother will go off to be a soldier," Amanda guesses.

"No fair," Vickie protests. "You probably read ahead."

"I read the next chapter, but it doesn't say anything one way or the other. But I can tell you that Jim Quarme gets nastier."

They proceed to the next question. "Were there any words you didn't understand?"

"I wrote down one," Lindsay says. "In that excerpt at the beginning, Sarah talks about 'Whitehall slip.' I don't know what a 'slip' is, the way they use it. Maybe I'll understand it when it comes to that part."

"A slip? Where does it say anything about a slip?" Amanda asks.

"You know . . . in that excerpt they have here in the front of the book. Didn't you read it?" Lindsay asks, showing her the place.

"I guess not," Amanda says. "I didn't even see it."

"I don't read those things," Vickie says. "It's like watching those previews for movies or TV. Sometimes they tell you the best part, and I want to be surprised."

The girls read through the excerpt and find the part of the book it was taken from. They read the section and decide that "slip" is a nautical term.

"There's still a whole bunch of things it could mean," Amanda says.

"When we read *The True Confessions of Charlotte Doyle*,[30] Teri was in my group and she knew a whole lot about boats and things," Vickie says.

"Ask her then, at the break," Amanda says. "If she doesn't know, we'll look in the library. Research . . . right?"

Others have written down the words "mahogany," "russet," "fishcake," "muslin," "firelock" and "trestle." One by one they share what they already know about the words and check the dictionary for information they still need.

Amanda reads the next question, which asks for a one-sentence description of three main characters. The girls write individually, then share their sentences, comparing notes on the features they included. They talk about how they might share the story with others and decide they will either create a television interview with Sarah or a period newspaper with articles about her adventures. They will decide on a final project when all have completed reading the book. When their discussion is finished, each continues reading independently.

WHAT HAPPENED HERE? ONE PERSPECTIVE

Mr. Robinson introduces a guided literature study by responding to his students' enthusiasm for a book read aloud. He involves them in selecting books that are similar in theme and accepts suggestions for specific titles to include. Previews of each title give students some background for following their own interests in content, characters or writing style. Students indicate their interest in particular books in response, and the teacher tries to assign them to groups that reflect their first or second choices.

He selects eight novels that portray young people in situations that require extraordinary courage to survive. Ranges of reading levels are included, which are helpfully referenced in his copy of *Adventuring with Books: A Booklist for Pre-K–Grade 6*.[31] When he first began teaching, Mr. Robinson used the grade-level indications on the backs of the paperback books as a guide. But the literature reference book provides him with additional information about each book and gives him ideas about new books and themes for guided reading.

The teacher purposely chooses both historical and contemporary fiction that represents a variety of cultures. He also selects books that feature both girls and boys as heroes. His goal is to introduce students to an exciting and rewarding type of literature that will provide opportunities for discussion and material to extend their understanding of other people. He knows that choosing the best examples of literature will ensure the presence of intriguing characters and well-conceived plots. Drawn by the power of these books, students will quickly bond with the characters.

The interaction in the study group reveals the personal nature of responses to literature. The types of questions asked begin with the experience of each individual, to help him or her make a meaningful transaction with the book chosen to be read. The knowledge, background and skill of each team member are expanded by the group interaction. Students work together to construct their own meaning from the book, guided by the open-ended questions provided by the teacher. Exercises that ask them to describe the story, setting or characters in a single sentence help them organize their thoughts and develop precision in written responses.

In another group, four boys who are friends have decided to read *Sign of the Beaver* (op. cit.). One of their members, Justin, has great difficulty with reading, but is highly motivated and makes a great effort. The teacher has found, in Justin's case, that struggling to read and understand something interesting has worked better than assigning him to simplified versions of the books read by the rest of the class. He still chooses easy material to read during independent reading, but is motivated to tackle difficult material with the support of other members in his group. He also regularly takes his book home, reading ahead with the help of his father or brother. Then he re-reads in class with the rest of his team and is better prepared to join the discussion.

WHAT DO YOU THINK? Did you observe other things that happened in Mr. Robinson's sixth-grade classroom? Were any of the books chosen for the literature theme familiar to you? From their brief descriptions, which one might you have chosen to read with a group? What do you see as the greatest challenge for teachers working with intermediate age children? What do you think is the greatest reward? Are you planning to teach a certain grade level? Why do you think you chose this particular age group?

IV. Preparing for Guided Reading

Planning for guided reading at all levels requires similar preparation: selecting high-quality books for your students; choosing a reading level or levels appropriate for the students in your class; and determining the type of interaction you want to happen between your students and literature.

You already know that there are thousands of books to choose from in high-quality children's literature, and from previous chapters of this text you know where to find examples of the best. As you will remember from the discussion in previous sections of this chapter, research indicates that quality literature attracts and keeps children's interest. It encourages them to analyze and evaluate stories, illustrations, characters, plot and meaning.

The reference books *Adventuring with Books: A Booklist for Pre-K–Grade 6* (op. cit.) or *Best Books for Children: Preschool through Grade 6*[32] (annotated in Resources for Teaching in Chapter 3) can be used to find books on a multitude of literary themes or content area topics in all the genres of children's literature. These resources also identify books that are appropriate for the age, interest and reading ability levels in your classroom. You will also discover books on your own as you continue to explore children's literature, and other teachers will tell you about books they have used successfully in their own classrooms. The program *Reading Rainbow*, shown on public television stations, is another good source of ideas for using high-quality books organized around a theme.

You know how important it is to read carefully any book you plan to read aloud. The same rule holds true with books you introduce to your students for guided literature study. Whether you read a Big Book aloud, provide copies of a book that your class reads together or coordinate the reading of several books on a theme, you will want to read and explore these books carefully before presenting them to your students.

Read first as you wish your students to read, straight through for enjoyment. Jot down any ideas that occur to you as you read or when you finish. Then return to the book, looking for passages that contain particularly powerful descriptions, tension, conflict or resolution.

1. Do the illustrations tell something not found in the text? Are there examples of foreshadowing, figurative language or metaphor?
2. What difficulties might students have with understanding the vocabulary and concepts or with locating the story in time?
3. Is the story such that students can work successfully in groups to read it aloud and explore its meaning?
4. Will you need to find alternative books for students with special learning needs?
5. Might there be strong objections to particular books among the parents of your students?

Make the books you plan to use available for parents to read. If they have reservations about any of them, they can communicate this to their children, who can make their choices accordingly without affecting the rest of the class. This is, of course, a type of censorship. But your goal is to have children read and explore books, not to engage in ideological conflicts. There are thousands of high-quality books available, most of which will not be objected to.

As you examine the books you plan to use, you will begin to think of ways to help your students explore them. You may have school or district curriculum requirements that must be met in language arts. As you will notice below, most of these objectives can be easily met within any literature study.

Remember that if you know what you want to share with your students in terms of reading strategies, you can introduce these naturally within the discussion of literature, without making it a structured "lesson."

Kindergarten Level

At the beginning level, you will be reading aloud to your students and initiating conversations to help them explore the meaning, form and content of the story. What questions will you ask? What conventions of punctuation or grammar will you call attention to? What strategies for reading will you model? The following strategies and questions are designed to help students increase their understanding of content and develop reading skills in the context of a favorite story.

1. **Finding meaning in the story**   What do you think this story is about? What do you think the author/illustrator was trying to say?
2. **Learning the meaning of new words**   Can you tell what this word means by reading (or listening to) the words around it? Does this word look like another word you know? Do you recognize any part of this word?
3. **Decoding unfamiliar words**   How could you figure out this word? Decoding refers to figuring out the sounds of a word by looking at: initial letters and final letters; medial vowels (in the middle of a word); letter blends (bl, cl, gr, dr, for instance); diphthongs (au, ou, oo, oi); digraphs (sh, ph, ch, th); and small words contained in larger ones (all, and, or, old). Students also figure out unfamiliar words by considering them in the context of the sentence.
4. **Practicing familiar words**   Research has shown that even the process of passing one's eyes over print increases its familiarity. For readers of all ages, practice does indeed make perfect. As the words in a story become familiar to students, they develop a sense of competency with their reading that is vital to the learning process. Good practice is accomplished by reading a Big Book or parts of it together as a group. Another practice activity popular with many teachers is reading the story and leaving out words for students to fill in. This is called the **cloze** procedure. You might want to begin by leaving out an often-repeated word or a rhyming word from the end of a refrain. As students build skill in reading, you can challenge them with more difficult omissions. Other interesting cloze activities can be found in *Literacy Through Literature* (described in Resources for Teaching in this chapter) and in Chapter 7.
5. **Learning from illustrations**   As you talk with students about details in illustrations, you help them become more analytical in their comments. Questions such as: What do you think of this picture? What do you think the artist was trying to say about the bear? or How do these colors make you feel about the story? model a mature reader responding to illustrations and help students see themselves as an important part of the literature/reader transaction.

6. **Reading with expression** Guided reading with Big Books provides an excellent opportunity to model and reinforce the use of intonation to communicate meaning in reading. As you raise your voice to indicate the bravado of a character or lower it to a hush when someone is telling a secret, you show children that reading is more than saying words; it is interpreting what the story means. When children read aloud, encourage them to show you what the characters are feeling or how the setting looks by using their voices. If a volcano erupts or an ocean roars, how can they read those words to show the action? How does the emphasis on different words in a sentence change its meaning? For example, the sentence "Mother is here" can be read "**Mother** is here" to indicate that a certain person is present; "Mother **is** here" confirms her presence; "Mother is **here**" gives her location.

7. **Conventions of capitalization and punctuation** From Mrs. Jamison's interaction with her kindergarten you can probably see how learning about basic forms of capitalization and punctuation helps readers better understand literature. Capitals tell us when a new idea begins, and punctuation communicates the sense or tone of that idea. Using the same sentence "Mother is here" as an example, you can contrast the different meanings obtained by ending the sentence with a period, question mark or exclamation point.

8. **Understanding genre, characterization, setting, plot** Each of these terms will become familiar and helpful to your students if you regularly ask them about the characters, setting and action of the stories you read together with questions such as: Does this character remind you of anyone you know? Where do you think this story takes place? What clues do you have? What do you think will happen next in the story? Does this story remind you of any other story you've read? Have we read any other stories that begin this way? Could this story really happen? What clues tell us when this story happened?

9. **Relating experience to books** The more a reader's interests, background and experience are initially activated in a reading experience, the better. After all, it is this very core of experience that enables the reader to draw into the story, bond with its characters and gain new experience from the interaction. Questions that help develop these connections include: How are you like the main character? What things are different about the way we live today? Has anything like this ever happened to you?

10. **Synonyms, antonyms, homonyms** Guided reading of a favorite text provides many opportunities to talk about words that mean the same or opposite or that sound the same but mean different things according to context. Comparing and contrasting words that create characters, plot or setting help beginning readers look for these elements in other books they read.

11. **Rhyming words** Many Big Books feature nursery rhymes or other verse with rhyming elements. As children respond to words that sound alike, you can point out the ways these words look alike, modeling a decoding strategy in the context of an enjoyable reading experience.

12. **Relating a story or its theme to other areas** Informational Big Books provide artistic presentations of subjects such as animals, plants, the rain forest, farms, dinosaurs, parts of speech, the stars, counting, seasons, history and geography. Still others lend themselves to integrating mathematical, scientific and social science concepts. Take advantage of every opportunity to call attention to these naturally occurring relationships. Big Books are also available in Spanish. If you have students who speak Spanish at home or if you teach in a school that integrates foreign language instruction into the curriculum, Big Books provide a wide range of literature, both fiction and nonfiction, for group enjoyment and exploration. Catalogs of Big Books are available to teachers from school book clubs.[33]

Primary Level

At the early primary level, you will probably use short books or picture story books for literature study that involves the entire group. When students read different books by interest in small groups, they may choose to read the longer chapter books. The questions you prepare for primary students should include those that will help create a conversation about the book they are reading. These questions can be shared orally with the class by the teacher or prepared as a set of printed questions for students to respond to in groups.

What kinds of questions are appropriate for primary age students? The same categories used at the kindergarten level can be used to help primary students explore literature. At every level of instruction, your goal in creating response questions is not to quiz or create a pseudo book report, but rather to model the way a mature reader interacts with books for pleasure, learning and problem solving. With these criteria in mind, ask questions that probe your students' personal responses to the book, such as: What did you like about this book? Is this like any other book you've read? Which character did you like best?

Questions that will help students stretch their comprehension of the story include: What kind of story is this? What is this story about? How does the time or place affect this story? Ask questions that develop skills of interpretation, of looking beyond the obvious elements of the story: Why do you think Fran Ellen liked school, in spite of the way she was treated? Why do you think she was afraid to tell her teacher that her mother was ill? You can help students develop a sense of plot sequence by asking them to tell you what happened in the story and to identify the beginning, middle and end of the story: How did the story begin? What happened next? Then what happened? How did the story end?

Mechanical skills (word analysis, definitions, finding details) can be developed through questions that highlight the meaning of words and provide strategies for analyzing unknown words, such as: What do you think this word means? Can you tell me another word that means the same thing? Are there words you don't know? How can you figure out what they say? What can you find in this word that is familiar (for example, letters, sounds, blends, digraphs, diphthongs, small words)? Where does the story tell how Fran Ellen took care of her baby sister?

Exploring the format of a book together helps students practice good study strategies. As part of your discussion, ask such questions as: Where can we find the list of chapters in this book? What part of the book lists important words or topics? How do the pictures help you understand or enjoy the story? How does the map help explain why it took so long for the boat to reach shore? Where else could you find out something about the topic in this story?

You will also want to provide questions that students can respond to on an individual basis and then share with a small group. Some possibilities might include the following:

1. What do you like about this book?
2. What character would you like to be in this story? Why?
3. How do the pictures make you feel? Do they help tell the story?
4. What do you think this book is about?
5. Did anything like this ever happen to you? (Protecting the confidential nature of these kinds of responses is a topic of discussion in Chapter 8.)
6. What really interested you about this book?
7. Can you find examples of synonyms, antonyms, homonyms, figures of speech, parts of speech (verbs, nouns, adjectives, adverbs)? (On handouts, students can circle the item to be identified.)

Intermediate Level

At the intermediate level, students are able to read independently and discuss in small groups. You might select a single book for students to read and respond to as a class. You might also select several books by the same author or on the same theme. If you use combinations of books, you will want to prepare the class by presenting previews. Be sure to obtain enough multiple copies if you plan to allow students to choose from an assortment of books. You will need to decide on response questions and select those that will be used for whole-class dialogue, personal journal entries and group discussion. If possible, provide a printed copy of the questions for each student. In Chapter 6 you will learn how to create open-ended questions that can be used by students to respond to the elements of almost every book, but for guided reading you will also want to provide questions that are specific to the book(s) being read.

Types of questions appropriate for intermediate age students include those mentioned for other instructional levels, with additional emphasis on interpretation, inference, prediction and values. Suggestions for questions in each category are listed below. Remember that you will choose only a few questions each time for students to respond to. They are classified to help you identify the kinds of questions that assess student ability to respond to certain elements of the story. The purpose of each question is included in parentheses.

1. **Personal response** What about this story interested you? Would you read another book: of this type; by this author; on this theme? (How positively or negatively did this book affect the student?)

2. **Personal experience**   Have you read other books of this type, or on this theme, or by the same author? Did you ever have to solve a problem like this? (What experiences do students bring to the book in terms of previous reading or real-life experience?)

3. **Comprehension**   What do you think this story is about? Briefly tell the story. (How well does the student grasp the main ideas of the book?)

4. **Meaning**   What do you think is the theme of this story? What was the author trying to say? (How well do students understand the broad theme(s) of the story? Can they go outside the story and look at it as a story about deprivation, courage, loneliness?)

5. **Interpretation/Inference**   What important decisions did the main character have to make? Why do you think he/she chose these particular ways to solve his/her problems? What evidence can you find to support your ideas about the character or plot? (How well can the student think about the story, adding personal experience, insight and analysis?)

6. **Word analysis**   How is this word pronounced? Can you find a sound you know? Can you find a smaller word in this word? How does the word start? How does it end? Do you know the sound in the middle? This word sounds like (car, star, far), but it begins in a different way. Can you figure it out now? (Models ways to decode unfamiliar words using preexisting knowledge of initial, medial and ending sounds, blends, digraphs, diphthongs.)

7. **Word meaning**   What do you think this word means? Does it look like any other word you know? Can you tell what the word means from the rest of the sentence? Can you discover what it means from other sentences around this one? (Models ways for students to analyze unknown words.)

8. **Character, plot, setting, genre**   What ways did the author use to tell you about this character? Would it have made any difference if the main character were a boy instead of a girl? Have you read any other books that were similar to this one? How did this particular setting influence the story? What kind of story is this? (Helps students begin to analyze and think critically about the elements of a story.)

9. **Theme, values**   What do you think is the meaning of this story? What is it really about (in one word or a short sentence)? What values do you think were important to the main character? Other characters? Do you share or disagree with these values? (Helps students begin to look for layers of meaning in a story.)

WHAT DO YOU THINK?   What aspects of preparation for guided reading would you most enjoy? Which would be the greatest challenge? Choose a question from each of the categories and respond to them using a children's book of your choice. Did the consideration of these questions help increase the meaning of the story for you? Try this exercise with one or more classmates. In what ways do other responses to these questions add to your own understanding?

V. Including Everyone in Literature Study

Your goal as a teacher is to make literature available to every student in your classroom. How will you support everyone's full participation? Large-type trade books are available for students with visual difficulties, usually through your special education coordinator or consultant, who can order titles you request from a central library. Books on tape are also available, but you can make your own or enlist the help of parent volunteers, classroom aides or students.

If a student experiences difficulty with hearing, be sure to involve other members of the study group to make certain the student can hear the conversation and is able to see everyone's face for visual cues. Regardless of any sensory challenge, it is a good idea to prepare all students to check each other's understanding as part of the procedure of working in groups.

Students with learning difficulties are drawn to the discussion format of guided reading because they can participate fully, sharing their ideas in ways not restricted by traditional methods. You can maximize the benefits of involving these students with literature by providing opportunities for alternative responses, such as artistic expression. Students can listen to books on tape, take books home to preread with their families or listen to another student read the book aloud. As shown in the classroom observations, peer group members will also support each other's efforts on their own. The goal in guided reading for these students is to alert them to their learning strengths, while providing opportunities for them to develop their emerging literacy skills. Literature study is the ideal medium to include everyone. It provides the opportunity to become highly involved in books, offers the chance for students to respond in a preferred mode and gives all students the experience of interacting with others in a positive and constructive way.

Books to Increase Understanding

The following titles in children's literature will help you (and your students) gain a better understanding of children whose backgrounds may be different than yours or alert you to disabilities that might interfere with their full participation in the classroom.

> From Anna[34] is the account of a partially sighted German girl who faces ridicule in her family and torment at school because of an undiagnosed vision problem. When her family migrates to Canada to escape Nazi persecution, Anna's condition is finally discovered. The sequel to this book, Listen for the Singing,[35] is a stirring account of Anna's venture back into public school after successfully adjusting to a special school for the partially sighted. In addition to the visual challenges she faces, there is prejudice against her nationality, as she tries to make friends and adjust to the new school.

> Have you ever wondered what it is like to be the child in class who no one likes and no one understands? Meet Bradley Chalkers in There's a Boy in the Girl's Bathroom[36] and Fran Ellen in The Bear's House.[37] Bradley has difficulty making sense out of anything in the classroom, and Fran Ellen is distracted

by secrets at home. It is unlikely that you will ever forget either of these two children.

WHAT DO YOU   Choose one or more of these books to read and record your reactions
THINK?   in your journal. How did the story make you feel? How would you feel
                    if you were the main character in this story? If you were the main
                    character, how might you want your teacher to relate to you? The
                    teachers in these stories have widely differing assumptions about chil-
                    dren and how they learn. With which one would you most agree?

VI. Step-by-Step: Introducing Guided Literature Study

In your preparation for guided literature study, you have selected your book(s), decided on the kind of interaction that will occur and constructed the questions for small- and whole-group dialogue. Now you are ready to introduce guided reading to your class. This introduction will set the tone for the interaction with literature to follow. Whether you are reading aloud from a Big Book to kindergarten children or creating an environment for written, verbal and artistic responses to several books at the intermediate level, you will want to establish a context that places high value on student response.

What can you do to show students that you value their responses to literature? Be receptive to diverse responses from students, with sincere remarks such as, "I never thought of that" or "That's a new way of looking at the story." Value experimentation and divergence ("I can tell that you've thought about this"). Nod appreciatively at comments. This will not be an act on your part if you listen closely during discussions. Children's comments about books are quite insightful and represent a point of view sometimes lost as we mature. We also show that we value a child's contributions by saying, "Tell me more," "Go on," or "That sounds interesting." Ask students to **tell you about** their pictures, dance, sculpture, model or chart that they have created in response to their reading. Avoid asking, "What's this?" or "What's this supposed to be?" You will learn a great deal about students' understanding of what they have read if you encourage them to talk about their response. This approach to evaluation is discussed further in Chapter 11.

In the following paragraphs you will find suggestions for introducing guided literature study to students at the kindergarten, primary and intermediate levels. Keep in mind that techniques used at one level can be successfully adapted to other levels.

Kindergarten Level

Gather your class around you at an easel that supports the Big Book you will be using for guided reading. After everyone is settled comfortably, hold the book in your hands and introduce it.

"We're going to read a book together today. I'll read it to you first and then we'll look at it more closely and talk together about what you liked. Let's look at the cover for a minute. What do you see?" Children will respond to illustrations and some will be able to read the words. If they cannot read the title, read it aloud and point to the words. Also read the name of the author and illustrator. Put the book back on the easel and begin reading the story aloud. On the first reading, concentrate on making the book as interesting as possible. When you finish reading, ask your students what they think about the book. As they respond, turn to the pages they mention.

Remember that the order of discussion is not as important as the types of questions asked. When you first begin guided discussion, you might want to put a copy of possible response questions on your lap or on the floor where you can glance at them from time to time. It is not necessary to ask every question or be locked into asking them in a particular way. As you gain experience, you will see opportunities to direct exploration of a book in many ways that are impossible to plan in advance. You will also find better questions in the context of your interaction with your students than you had previously anticipated.

The most important thing to remember about these discussions is to **listen to your students** and respond to what they say. What do they understand? What confuses them? What do they like or dislike? As it was noted above, the questions you prepare in advance are guideposts for exploration. The exciting part of guided reading is what you discover about a story together with your students.

Monitor your students' attention and involvement carefully. It is better to explore a few ideas intensely and leave the guided reading session with the enthusiasm of your students still intact than to "cover" everything and create a weariness with the book and the exploration process. Avoid turning "grand conversations" into "gentle inquisitions"! (Eeds & Wells, op. cit.).

Primary Level

Big Books can also be used successfully at the primary level. There are many that deal with science, math or social studies concepts, and the large format is ideal for group discussion. If you are using a standard-sized paperback, present the book you have selected as a read-aloud. Talk together briefly about the cover and what the book might be about. After you finish reading the book, tell your students that you have copies of the book for everyone to read and that they can take turns reading it aloud to each other. When they finish reading, they will talk about what they liked and write their responses to the story. Ask students to sit with their study groups and send one member to get enough books (with the response questions folded inside) for everyone in their group.

Before they begin reading, review the response questions with the entire class to make sure they understand what is expected of them. Explain to your students that the questions will help them explore the story and pictures. Some of the questions will be talked about, while responses to others will be written down. Review with them what they should do if they encounter words they cannot pronounce or do not understand (confer with each other; use the dictionary; ask the teacher). Some teachers have children create and laminate bookmarks that list these strategies, for easy reference. Others post the strategies on a prominent poster in the room.

As groups finish their individual written work, those who finish more quickly may reread the book for additional practice. A special response to this rereading might be recorded in their literature journals: "What new thing did you discover about the book when you read it this time?" This question encourages children who read quickly to look more closely at what they have read. They take great pride in finding details in text or illustrations that might have missed their notice the first time through.

Intermediate Level

At this level, there are several options for literature discussion groups. Depending on the age and maturity level of your students, you can adjust the ways the groups are formed, the number of book choices and the types of responses you suggest. The method described below is probably the most structured model. You will want to adapt it to your own situation and comfort level.

"What would you do if you found yourself lost in the middle of the Canadian wilderness, with no communication to the outside world? What if all you had to keep yourself alive was (hold up the book *Hatchet*, op. cit.) a hatchet? That's what happened to the boy in this book. We're going to read about him today in groups. Everyone will have a copy of the book to read and should read the book at a rate each finds comfortable."

Have books distributed with colored bookmarks enclosed. "Look at your bookmark and find the colored marker in the room that shows where you'll meet with your group to talk about the book. In a few minutes I'll have you move a group at a time to your place in the room. But first we need to talk about how these groups will work. After you've read a chapter of the book, you'll discuss four response questions about the chapter together. Some responses will involve talking about the book and others will be written in your individual literature journals. Decide on someone to ask the questions you will all be discussing today. Tomorrow, someone else should read the questions to the group until everyone has taken a turn. When the bell rings, we'll talk about some of your responses together as a class.

"You're probably wondering what you should do if you finish reading before others in your group. This is the procedure: Put your bookmark out on your desk to show that you've finished the chapter and continue to read. When everyone's bookmark is out, send someone to the front desk to get the response questions and begin working on them together, as directed on the sheet. Are there any questions?" Move individuals to their groups one color at a time until everyone is situated.

Before or after this initial experience, you will also want to talk to your class about the goals of shared reading in groups and let them contribute ideas for participation guidelines, in the same way they were involved in creating guidelines for independent reading. As students interact with literature and share responses, they will become increasingly aware of problems that must be solved to help the groups work successfully. When this happens, encourage your students to create the necessary guidelines on their own. Additional experiences with speaking and listening, such as those described in Chapter 7, will also assist full participation by all group members.

As students gain experience working in literature response groups, you will be able to introduce multiple titles that involve reading on a particular theme, different books by the same author and a variety of books that represent a literary genre. This will encourage the grouping of students with common interests, as described earlier in this chapter.

WHAT DO YOU THINK? In what ways might it be fun to read the same book that everyone else in the class reads? How would this experience vary if everyone read a different book on the same theme or different books by the same author? Have you ever helped create guidelines for group activity? Were they successful?

VII. If This Is Your Situation

Your school may require that you follow a commercial reading program that includes reading skills workbooks and copies of children's trade books. This system is perhaps the easiest to adapt to integrated language learning because the skills to be learned are clearly identified and can be incorporated into guided learning that involves any text. Frequently, high-quality, award-winning books are also provided in sets, and these can be used in a variety of ways, including guided reading and individual reading conferences.

From your reading in previous chapters, you know there are many reasons why school districts choose to adopt a basal reading system for their students. You also know how important it is to understand the educational concerns of the decision makers involved. Traditionally, basal programs have been chosen for one or more of the following reasons:

1. **Familiarity** Basal programs have been around long enough that most people regard the basal approach as the accepted way to teach reading.
2. **Budget** Basal programs are big business for commercial publishers. They have large advertising budgets that put the names of their programs in all the periodical literature of persons in decision-making positions, including teachers, administrators and school board members.
3. **Standardization** Decision makers who choose basal programs believe that this approach will provide every child with the benefit of everything the program has to offer. They believe that these programs decrease variability among teaching styles and abilities.
4. **State mandates** Increasingly, schools are evaluated on the basis of standardized measures of achievement. Many states require school

district scores to increase every year. Formalized programs that emphasize the teaching of individual skills in a sequenced manner may
seem to offer the best support for this kind of evaluation.

The standardization argument is perhaps the one most frequently used
because it is an attempt to provide equal education for all students. Unfortunately, most of these programs create great inequality since every student
gets the same instruction, regardless of the fact that some may not need it at
all and it is not enough for others. The challenge to teachers who want to
integrate language learning in their classrooms is to demonstrate that their
students can acquire the necessary skills to score well on standardized tests.

If you are required to use a basal program for reading instruction, your
level of involvement with these materials will vary, depending on the
involvement of other persons concerned. At every level, however, there are
ways to integrate language learning into the curriculum and still meet the
curriculum objectives of your school district.

Level One

At this level, your class will be self-contained (you are responsible for all
instruction in the language arts and content areas). This situation is most
common at the kindergarten and primary levels and in many parochial
schools in the intermediate and junior high grades. You decide how and
when to use basal materials and the amount of time you will spend on reading
instruction. In this situation, you can use the best of the trade books provided
for guided reading sessions, supplement them by reading aloud from good
books and provide time and additional books for independent reading. To
meet the skills requirement, simply make a list of the skills to be developed
and present them as mini-lessons throughout the year, using methods described in this chapter and the mini-lessons chapter (Chapter 9) to identify
student needs.

Level Two

At this level, you share instructional responsibility with other teachers.
Students of an identified ability level will come to your classroom for
instruction and students of other ability levels will leave your classroom for
instruction by other teachers. If you must accommodate the teaching schedules of other teachers, you can still create a common experience for all the
students in your grouping by reading aloud to them and using common
experiences of the class to develop the required skills.

Level Three

This is perhaps the most challenging level of involvement with a basal
program. At this level, all materials must be used, as presented, by state,
district or local administrator mandate. Examine the material for reading,
writing, listening and speaking activities that are commensurate with integrated language learning. Under the strictest scrutiny, there will still be
opportunities to share good literature and build on student experience. Read
the curriculum objectives for reading at your grade level and examine the
teacher's manual for the basal program carefully. At what points do these
objectives agree with those of an integrated program? Write them down and
use them as a guideline and rationale for the way you conduct your instruction.

If you want to provide for integrated language learning within a basal system, your work will be more challenging, but not impossible. Experienced teachers have discovered that skill instruction that is based on the experiences of individual students and particular groups of students is more effective, because students are willing to practice the skills they need to read what they want to read. They will also be able to demonstrate their comprehension and vocabulary skills on standardized tests because they have learned and practiced these skills in meaningful situations.

WHAT DO YOU THINK? Do you remember any language arts instruction from your elementary school days? How would you describe it? How might your teacher have used this instruction to provide more integration of language learning into the curriculum?

VIII. Evaluating Progress

After you discuss a book with a kindergarten class, jot down a few notes about the dialogue. What did they like about the book? At what points did they experience difficulties? At the primary and intermediate levels, briefly visit each literature group during guided reading and take notes, where appropriate. When students read aloud to each other, listen for problems. As they talk about books with each other, monitor their responses to gauge the depth of their understanding. Observe how well they interact together as a group.

During these observations, you will have good opportunities to evaluate how well students use their reading, speaking and listening skills in an authentic context. (Writing progress can be noted when individual written responses are reviewed.) Does everyone participate? Is there a lack of interest in the book? Note any difficulties that might signal the need for a mini-lesson for a particular individual, the group or the entire class.

When your students respond to a story in writing or artistically, be a careful observer. Take notes on what you see as students work on their writing or drawing.

1. Do they prefer responding in a particular way? Is writing more comfortable than drawing, or vice versa?
2. Are they able to communicate their understanding more clearly using an artistic medium?
3. When there is a choice, what media do they choose for expression?
4. Are they involved with responding to literature or discussion, or are they easily distracted?
5. Do they attempt new ways of responding to literature?

As students react to what they have read in creative ways, you will have increased indications of the extent of their involvement by their written and artistic responses.

Does written work:

1. Indicate an understanding of the genre? the main idea of the book?
2. Show evidence of bringing their own experience to bear on what they read?
3. Reveal the use of new terms or phrases found in the book?

Does artistic response:

1. Indicate an understanding of the story?
2. Show relevant details?
3. Show evidence that the story inspired creativity or insight?

It is important to decide what you want students to demonstrate in terms of learning as you plan the response questions and activities for guided reading. For example, the question "In what ways is Madeleine L'Engle's *Meet the Austins*[38] different from her book *A Wrinkle in Time*[39]?" is designed to help students sort out the differences between realistic fiction and fantasy. If you plan for children to respond to a book by drawing pictures, you will want to observe the details they include that indicate their level of response to the story. Remember that it is important to consider a wide range of responses when evaluating a student's growth.

Careful observation of student responses to literature can supply you with information to provide direction for future guided reading sessions or for mini-lesson presentations if more direct teaching is required.

WHAT DO YOU THINK?   Have you ever discussed literature with a small group of people? What did you like and dislike about this experience? What kinds of problems did the group encounter? How did it solve them? If you could choose a favorite way of responding to a book, what would it be? If you were to be evaluated on your understanding of a book, how would you choose to demonstrate this?

IX. Creating Partners

The effectiveness of guided reading activities in your classroom can be enhanced and extended by creating opportunities for students to interact with books and persons in their wider social communities. Here are some possibilities:

1. **Cross-grade Book Buddies** Many teachers plan in 20-minute daily segments or several times a week for children in different grades to read to each other. Others schedule part of the noon hour for this activity once or twice a week, with teachers taking turns monitoring the classroom. Reading proficiency improves with this activity, but there are other bonuses. Friendships develop between older and younger students that help improve intergrade relations on the

playground. The attention of older children is highly motivating to most students. Assisting younger students helps create self-confidence in the older ones.

2. **Same-grade Book Buddies** This activity permits a sharing of reading interests among students who may be looking for someone to explore similar topics.

3. **Parents** Send copies of books home that are being used in guided reading. Involve your parents at the beginning of the year by enlisting their help in this activity. Provide guidelines and suggestions for reading aloud to a family member or friend.

4. **School staff** Who might be available to read to students occasionally in school or listen to children read aloud? Parents, aides, special education teachers, librarians, other teachers and principals frequently take turns with this activity.

5. **Community members** Senior citizens and retired teachers often express interest in assisting in the classroom. These are resourceful persons to contact for assistance.

WHAT DO YOU THINK? Have you ever shared a book with someone by taking turns reading it aloud? Did you listen to books read aloud by a family member or someone else when you were a child? What did you like about these experiences? What do you think children enjoy about sharing books with cross-age peers?

X. Perspectives on Guided Reading

For many years, educational theorists have described the benefits of students interacting in groups. In previous chapters, the ideas of the philosopher John Dewey and those of educational psychologists such as Jean Piaget and Jerome Bruner have been examined. In what ways do their ideas support the practice of students discussing literature in groups? Dewey believed that intelligence, while unique to each individual, is also a social construction and that persons who interact in purposeful groups are exposed to ideas, experience and connections that otherwise would not be available to them as individuals.

> Not only is social life identical with communication, but all communication (and hence all genuine social life) is educative. To be a recipient of a communication is to have an enlarged and changed experience. One shares in what another has thought and felt and in so far, meagerly or amply, has his own attitude modified. Nor is the one who communicates left unaffected. . . . The experience has to be formulated in order to be communicated. To formulate requires getting outside of it, seeing it as another would see it, considering what points of contact it has with the life of another so that it may be got into such form that he can appreciate its meaning. (*Democracy and Education,*[40] p. 5)

Dewey believed that democratic values are promoted in classrooms where individual voices are heard and valued and where students gain respect for diversity by comparing ideas and experience. Guided reading incorporates these ideals of progressive education by providing opportunities for students to share ideas and experience and to pursue common goals of inquiry.

Jean Piaget[41] was concerned with the processes by which children develop increased understanding of their environments. He believed that a child's ideas about how the world works are constantly challenged (disequilibrated) and revised (accommodated) by new experience. In guided reading, when students discuss their experience and ideas in groups, they are faced with conceptions of the world that will challenge their own personal understandings. Ideas that are apparent to some will create disequilibration in others. In small groups, students begin to accommodate new ideas and new ways of thinking with the support they receive from their peers. Students clarify ideas for each other, present alternative points of view and create new perspectives as they share their responses with each other. Teachers who respect the developmental nature of learning know that students will differ in the levels and kinds of understanding they have of literature. Some will interpret language and literature in a literal manner (concrete thinking), while others will function easily within the symbolic (formal thinking) aspects of literacy experiences. These teachers anticipate and respect these differences as qualities of emerging literacy.

Jerome Bruner[42] observed that students display a "will to learn" characterized by intrinsic motivators, such as **curiosity** about one's environment, a desire to communicate with others (**reciprocity**) and a drive for **competence**. His theory explains the enthusiasm students show for discussing literature in small groups. Students are **curious** about books and each other and are able to interact creatively with both in literature groups. These conversations also satisfy children's great desire for **reciprocity** as they talk together, solve problems and generate bonds of common interest. As children pursue individual interests in reading and make an effort to interact with others, they are also **striving for competence**: to have something interesting to say, to make connections with their own experience and to understand and explain what is happening in the literature.

Recommended Reading

Each of these books is referenced in the endnotes. Other recommended books by these theorists are annotated in other chapters.

Democracy and Education by John Dewey. The first four chapters of this book describe the major tenets of progressive education and outline the interrelationship of society and the individual.

A Piaget Primer: How a Child Thinks by Dorothy G. Singer and Tracey A. Revenson. This interesting little book describes Piaget's theory using characters in children's literature, including Winnie-the-Pooh and Alice in Wonderland.

Toward a Theory of Instruction by Jerome Bruner. This classic has an excellent chapter, entitled "The Will to Learn," that describes the natural sources of children's motivation to learn.

Literature As Exploration by Louise Rosenblatt. Explore the first few chapters of this book for ideas about how readers interact with what they read. Although they are written about secondary English teaching, the same principles apply to elementary teaching.

WHAT DO YOU THINK? What do you see as the main benefits for students reading and responding to literature in groups? Do you perceive any difficulties with shared literature study that were not addressed in this chapter? Can you think of examples in your own experience of your "will to learn"? Do you observe the features of curiosity, reciprocity and drive for competence in your own life?

XI. Exploring Professional Literature

The Reading Teacher is the journal published by the International Reading Association for elementary teachers. Articles in this journal deal with a variety of literacy issues and include descriptions of exemplary programs in reading and the language arts. Each article is prefaced with a brief summary statement, and many include charts, graphs and other figures to assist the reader's understanding of concepts presented. Both theoretical and practical applications of theory are included in the journal, and all articles include bibliographies to guide further reading on a topic. When classroom programs are described, the author usually includes tips for planning, checklists or examples of student work.

Regular features include reviews of children's books within a theme, such as Living in Harmony or The Humanities in Children's Literature, and a department that explores issues and trends in language learning. Other sections review current research, discuss assessment procedures and share ideas for professional resources and classroom teaching. This journal, which is published eight times a year, is a favorite of elementary classroom teachers because it allows them to keep up with new developments in reading and language arts instruction and provides them with helpful ideas for their own teaching. Information on student membership is available from the International Reading Association, 800 Barksdale Road, P.O. Box 8139, Newark, DE 19714-8139.

WHAT DO YOU THINK? Examine a copy of *The Reading Teacher*, noting any articles or features that draw your interest in your journal. Read several articles and note their helpfulness to you. Do any of the articles relate to ideas discussed in this chapter?

XII. Resources for Teaching

The following books contain ideas and activities for shared reading experiences at the K–primary levels and literature study groups at the primary–intermediate levels. Kindergarten teachers will appreciate the practical suggestions in Bobbi Fisher's and Betty Coody's books. *Literacy Through Literature* and *Grand Conversations* are excellent teaching companions for primary and intermediate teachers. The final recommended title is a collection of good ideas for sharing appreciation of literature with students. Many can be incorporated at all levels in shared reading experiences or within literature groups.

Literacy Through Literature[43] by Terry Johnson and Daphne Louis. This compact handbook contains an excellent collection of ideas to use with both younger and older students. The authors present activities that can be used for individual study or whole-group guided reading, including variations of the cloze procedure, story ladders, story maps, literary passports, posters, literary interviews, drama and reader's theater.

Grand Conversations: Literature Groups in Action[44] by Ralph Peterson and Maryann Eeds. This popular book describes a literature-based reading program and tells how to organize literature groups. The authors stress the importance of using high-quality literature that will provide layers of meaning for students to explore. The reader can "listen in" to real student conversations about books and observe how teachers help students discover the elements of story. Also included are checklists and evaluation forms for use by students and teachers.

Joyful Learning: A Whole Language Kindergarten[45] by Bobbi Fisher. The author, a public school teacher, describes typical shared reading sessions, the goals and benefits of shared reading and ways to help children develop skills and strategies for reading. She also includes suggested schedules and activities, ways to integrate other curriculum areas into shared reading and ideas for using songs, poetry, Big Books and drama. Chapters 5 and 6, which describe the theory and practice of shared reading, are especially helpful.

Multicultural Voices in Contemporary Literature[46] by Francis Ann Day. This handbook, designed for teachers of intermediate and middle school students, describes the lives and work of 39 authors and illustrators. It includes bibliographies, author birthdays and activities. This is a good reference for expanding understanding of writing styles, language subtleties and world views.

The Blue Pages: Resources for Teachers from "Invitations."[47] This is an updated and expanded version of the blue pages in *Invitations* by Regie Routman. Lists of children's literature are indexed by author and title. Also included are multicultural listings, journals, articles and literacy extension resources.

Using Literature with Young Children[48] by Betty Coody. Chapters 3 through 9 include literature response ideas, with descriptions of books that stimulate drama, creative writing, art and cooking projects. Chapters 8 and 9 feature responses to holidays and children's special needs. This is an easy-to-use handbook for kindergarten teachers, but many ideas can be used also in early primary classes.

Using Literature in the Elementary Classroom,[49] edited by John Stewig and Sam Sebesta. This is a collection of seven articles written by teachers describing the use of children's books in the classroom. Topics include using picture books, the reading–writing connection, creative drama and literature across the curriculum. Authors share ideas about promoting discussion in literature groups and assessing student progress.

WHAT DO YOU THINK? From the descriptions of the books listed above, which one most appeals to you? Explore one, noting any helpful aspects or interesting ideas in your journal.

XIII. Reflections

From a Teacher's Journal—Pat Sheahan, Second Grade

I was moved to integrate language learning in my classroom from several experiences: My students were not showing progress using the basal text and the endless worksheets, and they were experiencing success when they used trade books to learn about all areas of the curriculum. After giving much thought to the curriculum appropriate to my grade level, I realized that children could acquire these skills in more meaningful, positive and hands-on ways than they could by using the traditional methods.

For several years, my children had been immersed in literature: reading the newspaper, enjoying poetry and chart readings, and corresponding with award-winning authors. These activities allowed me to integrate the language processes—reading, writing, speaking and listening—into all subject areas. This foundation helped me move toward even more integration of language learning throughout the curriculum.

One of my students' favorite activities is the author study. I introduce an author by giving a biographical sketch and showing his or her picture. For some authors, I read one to two books a day, depending on the length of the books. I always write the title(s) on a chart, and each day we review the titles we've already enjoyed. I have often used the book in a content area and then reintroduced it in this shared book experience. For example, I use *When I Was Young in the Mountains* by Cynthia Rylant as part of an author study and also as part of a social studies unit on families.

Once a book has been shared in a class session, it is available to children on a daily basis. Books are divided into crates, which are labeled with the author's name. Books for the content areas are on shelves or on chalkboard ledges for display. There will be a bulletin board for any topic we are studying, with books on that topic displayed in the same area. Books are also grouped in crates or on the display racks into independent reading, chapter books, poetry, holiday books and those that are favorites for Book Buddy reading.

1. Explore several of the books described in this chapter. Which ones do you especially like?

2. Choose a picture book to read and respond to it in several ways: writing, drawing, composing a poem, making a craft, sculpting in clay, making up a song or creating your own version.

3. Borrow a copy of a Big Book from your curriculum library or cooperating school. **If You Can** With the permission of a classroom teacher, prepare a guided reading lesson for a small group of kindergarten or primary students.

4. Observe guided reading sessions at the kindergarten, primary and intermediate levels. Identify the skills being practiced by the students. Observe one student more closely and describe his or her responses in your journal.

5. Choose a picture book and develop guided reading questions to share with a small group of your classmates. Record your questions in your journal. **If You Can** With the permission of a classroom teacher, present the book to a group of students.

6. Using your own knowledge of books or one of the literature reference books annotated in Chapters 2 or 3, select several books on a theme appropriate for an intermediate study. Be sure to include books for a variety of reading levels.

7. Interview teachers at the kindergarten, primary or intermediate level who use guided reading. How do they decide which questions to ask about literature? How do they know which reading skills to practice or reinforce with their students? Which books do they especially like for guided reading? How do they plan for students with special learning needs?

8. Interview teachers who use a basal reading program. How do they decide which activities to use from the ones described? What do they like best about using a basal system?

9. Examine the teacher's copy of a basal reading program. What kinds of activities are suggested? Could any be used as part of an integrated language program?

Notes

1. Ernest Hemingway, "Old Newsman Writes," *Esquire*, December 1934.

2. Ralph Peterson and Maryann Eeds, *Grand Conversations: Literature Groups in Action* (New York: Scholastic, 1990).

3. Louise Rosenblatt, *Literature As Exploration*, 4th ed. (New York: Modern Language Association, 1991).

4. A. A. McClure, "Children's Responses to Poetry in a Supportive Context," unpublished doctoral dissertation, The Ohio State University, 1985.

5. M. Eeds and D. Wells, "Grand Conversations: An Exploration of Meaning Construction in Literature Study Groups," *Research in the Teaching of English* 23(1989):4–29.

6. S. Hepler and J. Hickman, " 'The Book Was Okay. I Love You'—Social Aspects of Response to Literature," *Theory Into Practice* 21(1982):278–283.

7. Peter Afflerbach, "STAIR: A System for Recording and Using What We Observe and Know About Our Students," *The Reading Teacher* 47(1993):260–263.

8. J. Hickman, "A New Perspective on Response to Literature: Research in an Elementary School Setting," *Research in the Teaching of English* 15(1981):343–354.

9. M. Martinez and N. Roser, "Read It Again: The Value of Repeated Readings during Storytime," *The Reading Teacher* 38:782–786.

10. S. Lehr, "The Child's Developing Sense of Theme as a Response to Literature," *Reading Research Quarterly* 23(1988):337–357.

11. Lesley Mandel Morrow, "Small Group Story Readings: The Effects on Children's Comprehension and Responses to Literature," *Reading Research and Instruction* 29(Summer 1990):1–17.

12. L. M. Morrow, "Young Children's Responses to One-to-One Story Readings in School Settings," *Reading Research Quarterly* 23(1988):89–107.

13. B. Keifer, "The Responses of Children in a Combination First/Second Grade Classroom to Picture Books in a Variety of Artistic Styles," *Journal of Research and Development in Education* 16(1983):14–20.

14. N. Roser and M. Martinez, "Roles Adults Play in Preschoolers' Response to Literature," *Language Arts* 62(1985):485–490.

15. Bill Martin, Jr. and John Archambault, *Chicka Chicka Boom Boom* (New York: Simon and Schuster, 1989).

16. Lois Ehlert, *Eating the Alphabet: Fruits and Vegetables from A to Z* (Orlando, Fla.: Harcourt, 1989). Features watercolor collages of familiar and exotic fruits and vegetables. A glossary contains histories of each one.

17. Lois Ehlert, *Color Farm* (Philadelphia: Lippincott, 1990). Layered cutout shapes form familiar farm animals as pages are turned.

18. Bill Grossman, *Tommy at the Grocery Store* (New York: HarperCollins, 1989).

19. Anne Holm, *North to Freedom* (New York: Harcourt, 1974).

20. Gary Paulsen, *Hatchet* (New York: Bradbury, 1987).

21. Scott O'Dell, *Island of the Blue Dolphins* (Burlington, Mass.: Houghton Mifflin, 1960).

22. Theodore Taylor, *The Cay* (New York: Doubleday, 1969).

23. Elizabeth George Speare, *Sign of the Beaver* (Burlington, Mass.: Houghton Mifflin, 1983).

24. Scott O'Dell, *Sarah Bishop* (Burlington, Mass.: Houghton Mifflin, 1980).

25. Armstrong Sperry, *Call It Courage* (New York: Macmillan, 1940).

26. Jean Craighead George, *Julie of the Wolves* (Scranton, Penn.: Harper, 1972).

27. Allan W. Eckert, *Incident at Hawk's Hill* (Waltham, Mass.: Little, Brown, 1971).

28. J. R. R. Tolkien, *The Hobbit* (New York: Random House, 1974).

29. Irene Hunt, *Across Five Aprils* (New York: Berkley, 1964).

30. Avi, *The True Confessions of Charlotte Doyle* (New York: Orchard Books, 1990).

31. Julie M. Jensen and Nancy L. Roser, eds., *Adventuring with Books: A Booklist for Pre-K–Grade 6*, 10th ed. (Urbana, Ill.: National Council of Teachers of English, 1993). NCTE Bibliography Series.

32. John T. Gillespie and Corinne J. Naden, eds., *Best Books for Children: Preschool through Grade 6* (New York: R. R. Bowker, 1990).

33. Big Book hotline, Scholastic Inc., Box 7502, Jefferson City, MO 65102. 1-800-325-6149. In Missouri: 1-800-392-2179.

34. Jean Little, *From Anna* (New York: Harper, 1972).

35. Jean Little, *Listen for the Singing* (New York: HarperCollins, 1991).

36. Louis Sachar, *There's a Boy in the Girl's Bathroom* (Westminster, Md.: Knopf, 1987).

37. Marilyn Sachs, *The Bear's House* (Bergenfield, N.J.: Dutton, 1987).

38. Madeleine L'Engle, *Meet the Austins* (New York: Vanguard, 1961).

39. Madeleine L'Engle, *A Wrinkle in Time* (New York: Farrar, 1962).

40. John Dewey, *Democracy and Education* (New York: Macmillan, 1964).

41. Dorothy G. Singer and Tracey A. Revenson, *A Piaget Primer: How a Child Thinks* (New York: Signet, 1978).

42. Jerome Bruner, *Toward a Theory of Instruction* (Cambridge, Mass.: Harvard University Press, 1966).

43. Terry D. Johnson and Daphne R. Louis, *Literacy Through Literature* (Portsmouth, N.H.: Heinemann, 1987).

44. Ralph Peterson and Maryann Eeds, *Grand Conversations: Literature Groups in Action* (New York: Scholastic, 1990).

45. Bobbi Fisher, *Joyful Learning: A Whole Language Kindergarten* (Portsmouth, N.H.: Heinemann, 1991).

46. Francis Ann Day, *Multicultural Voices in Contemporary Literature* (New York: Scholastic, 1994).

47. Regie Routman, *The Blue Pages: Resources for Teachers from "Invitations"* (New York: Scholastic, 1994).

48. Betty Coody, *Using Literature with Young Children*, 4th ed. (Dubuque, Iowa: William C. Brown, 1992).

49. John Warren Stewig and Sam Leaton Sebesta, eds., *Using Literature in the Elementary Classroom* (Urbana, Ill.: NCTE, 1989).

CHAPTER SIX

Individual Reading Conferences

WHAT'S
HAPPENING
HERE?
This student is showing the teacher her favorite pictures in a book about horses. Some of the book is above her reading level, but she is able to read most of the text and the captions under pictures. She practices all her reading skills to find information that interests her and enjoys sharing this new information with her teacher.

'Tis the good reader that makes the good book; in every book he finds passages which seem confidences or asides hidden from all else and unmistakably meant for his ear; the profit of books is according to the sensibility of the reader; the profoundest thought or passion sleeps as in a mine, until it is discovered by an equal mind and heart.
—Ralph Waldo Emerson, *Success*

LOOKING AHEAD
1. What can teachers learn from reading conferences?
2. What benefits do students gain from reading conferences?
3. How do reading conferences provide direction for instruction?
4. How do conferences provide information for parent conferences?
5. What kinds of questions should be asked in reading conferences?
6. How do you prepare for a reading conference?
7. How can you help students prepare for a reading conference?
8. How do you set up an independent work period?
9. What are the relationships among individual conferences, mini-lessons and guided reading?

IN 25 WORDS OR LESS   Individual reading conferences provide teachers with information about both the progress of individual students and patterns of learning needs in the classroom.

I. Focus: The Individual Reading Conference

An individual reading conference is a planned meeting between a student and teacher to discuss a book the student has selected. Students prepare for these sessions by reading a book and preparing a short selection to read aloud to the teacher. They also research unfamiliar vocabulary words, analyze literary elements and connect the story to their own experience. Most teachers encourage students to read in a different genre for each of these conferences and provide students with guidelines for analyzing and interpreting what they read. Students may bring questions and problems related to their reading to the conference, and the teacher will also note any difficulties observed as they discuss various elements of the book.

In traditional reading programs, students usually meet in ability groups for instruction. In these groups, students take turns reading aloud from a basal text, listen to instruction and begin workbook or skillsheet assignments.

When teachers are satisfied that students can complete these assignments independently, they dismiss the students to work on their own. Another group joins the teacher for a similar kind of instruction at another level.

In contrast, students who meet with teachers for individual reading conferences choose their own book to read and prepare their read-aloud selections carefully in advance in order to demonstrate their best reading to the teacher. From the teacher's own model of reading aloud, they will put great thought and effort into both the selection of this passage and their interpretative performance. They know that they are not just reading words, but sharing ideas and creating interest in the book they have read. The challenges they encounter in this reading will be their own, allowing the teacher's assistance to be both specific and helpful. Because students will be developing skill to read what they want to read, they are highly motivated to identify and practice the skills that will help them achieve this goal. Teachers who use individual conferences are better able to assess the reading proficiency of individual students and can better judge their progress over a period of time.

Because students bring their favorite books to these conferences, teachers learn about the individual reading likes and dislikes of their students, which gives them information for selecting literature to meet individual interests. Teachers also gain information about what students believe is important from these conversations and can more accurately identify areas of thinking that need encouragement or support. If they discover that a student needs to know a specific skill, they might teach it immediately and assign appropriate practice as a follow-up activity. If the skill or strategy requires additional time to explain or demonstrate, or if several children could benefit from the instruction, the teacher will make a note to add the skill to guided reading or create a mini-lesson for a small group or the entire class.

Individual conferences allow students to choose what they want to read, to explore a variety of interests and to read at their own levels. Independent work periods give them time to browse through many kinds of books to find one that interests them. And, unlike their counterparts in traditional classrooms, students can read as quickly or slowly as they are capable, with no penalty. As they prepare for conferences, students respond to guidelines that help direct their attention to details and encourage them to analyze the literary elements of a text. These individual interactions with books help students develop responsibility for their own learning and increase their autonomy as learners.

What do other students do while individual students meet with the teacher for these conferences? They choose books they want to read, using one of the self-selection techniques described in Chapter 3. When they have read the book for pleasure, they begin to study it more closely, using guidelines similar to those they have used in guided reading sessions. Indeed, these group sessions provide a model for students to find meaning in literature on their own. During independent work periods, students also practice reading aloud the passage they will share with the teacher and record any questions they have about their reading. If they have just completed an individual conference, they may practice a particular skill or strategy that will help develop their reading proficiency.

Teachers create the independent worktime environment in several different ways. Most provide a schedule of activities, some of which are completed by all students and others which are self-selected, according to need or interest. When all students participate in the same activities, the length of time spent on each task is determined by individual students. If an hour and a half is scheduled for reading conferences, students may be expected to read something of their own choosing for at least 20 minutes, spend approximately 15 minutes responding in writing to their reading and devote 15 minutes to some form of practice to improve their reading skills. In the time remaining, students may choose to draw, paint, or create a drama or other response project. They might also begin reading a new book, practice a reading skill or prepare for an individual conference.

II. The Importance of Individual Reading Conferences

One of the most valuable benefits of individual reading conferences is the bond that develops between teacher and student as they talk about books together. This is one occasion when individual students have the teacher's full attention to talk about something that interests them. The teacher, in turn, has the opportunity to get acquainted with individual students in a way not possible in the context of the entire class. As teachers talk together with students about the meaning of stories and share what is important about life with them, a relationship develops that carries over into other parts of the school day. New understandings are created between persons of any age when they share a funny poem or talk about how a powerful book affected them.

Karen Gallas[1] suggests that teachers play a key role in helping students respond to literature by providing opportunities for them to respond, through talking, writing, drawing and dramatizing. Cochran-Smith[2] observed that teachers also assist students in developing their levels and proficiency of responses by modeling the response of a mature reader. Heath[3] found that teachers help children develop their reading skill by discussing the meaning of words in stories and by helping expand the ideas of the text. By conjecturing, making connections between elements of the story and experience, asking questions aloud and demonstrating appreciation for literature, teachers encourage their students' active participation in the reading process. Teachers further support student responses by encouraging experimentation and by valuing the diversity of student contributions.

James Britton[4] believes that the goal of teaching should be "to refine and develop responses the children are already making" rather than to instruct those responses. Cochran-Smith (op. cit.) observed that teachers help children respond to literature by acting as mediators, helping them learn to take the knowledge they have to make sense of the books they read. Teachers also help children apply meanings gained from books to their own lives and add to their knowledge of how to respond as a listener by modeling their own responses and asking questions that signal appropriate feelings. Kiefer[5] found that language used by teachers to talk about books is adopted by students and that open-ended discussion strategies encourage a wide variety of listener responses.

Hickman,[6] who pioneered the study of children's responses to literature in naturally occurring contexts, found that teachers who discuss books with children often use critical terminology to help support children who have an idea, but need words to express that idea. Hickman also found that children more readily expressed their responses when they had the book in hand. More reflective thinking (artwork, writing, discussion) emerged when children had direct access to the books they were responding to.

III. Looking into Classrooms

Kindergarten Level

"Does everyone have some books to read about insects?" Mrs. Jamison asks the class. Each student holds up one to three books selected in the previous five minutes. The class is studying insects as part of a theme study.

"Good," she says. "While I talk to Cameron, what will you do?"

"Read," they reply.

"What will you do when you've looked at your books?" she asks.

"Practice," they reply and point to a chart on the wall that has pictures of choices for practicing reading skills. They can read aloud with a partner, look for particular letters or words in favorite books or work in various centers around the room.

"How will you read and work together?" she asks.

"Quietly," they whisper, putting fingers to lips.

"And how many people at a center?" she inquires.

"Four," they reply.

"What happens if the center is full?" she asks.

"Go to another one," they respond.

"Good work," the teacher says and turns her attention to Cameron, who has brought his book to the desk. The rest of the class settles into looking at books in pairs and small groups in their favorite reading places around the room.

"Tell me about this book," Mrs. Jamison says, as Cameron presents her with a paperback edition of In the Tall, Tall Grass.[7]

"It's about things in the grass," Cameron responds, turning through the pages and pointing out caterpillars, bees, ants and rabbits.

"What do you want to show me about this book?" the teacher asks.

"I can read some of it," Cameron declares, and he demonstrates by pointing to the words in the title and saying, "In the tall, tall grass."

Mrs. Jamison knows that Cameron is reading the title from memory, but she recognizes this as developmentally positive. Cameron increasingly associates printed and spoken words, one of the first steps toward literacy.

"Can you point to just one word in the title and read it for me?" the teacher asks.

Cameron confidently indicates the word "tall."

"Tall," he says. Then he points to the next word. " 'Tall' again. 'Tall, tall.' " Cameron took this book home several times during the week, and it has been read aloud to him often enough for this word to have been learned by sight.

"Good for you," the teacher says. "Can you find that word anywhere else in your book?" Cameron proceeds through the book and shows her where "tall" is found in four other places. "How does 'tall' begin?" she asks.

"T," he replies, pointing to the letter.

"What if I cover up the *t*?" the teacher asks. "Is this a word you know?"

"All!" he replies.

"Do you remember seeing this word anyplace?" she asks.

"In *Chicka Chicka Boom Boom*," he says. "All, fall, call, hall, ball . . ."

"Good for you!" the teacher says. "What's your favorite picture?"

Cameron turns to the middle of the book and shows her a picture of frogs catching flies with their tongues.

"What do you like about this picture?" the teacher asks.

"Their tongues," he says. "I drew a picture of a frog catching a fly."

"I'd like to see it," the teacher says.

"It's home. I'll bring it tomorrow."

"How do you think the artist made these pictures?" she asks.

Cameron studies the watercolor stencils carefully. "It looks like paint," he says finally. "It's kind of smeared here." He points to the color differences on one of the frogs. "I think it's a stencil."

"You looked at that very carefully," the teacher says. "Does this book remind you of any other books you've read?" she asks.

"Eric Carle books," he says immediately. "I thought this one was going to be like *The Very Hungry Caterpillar*," he adds, as he turns to the first page. "See . . . 'crunch, munch, caterpillars lunch,' and look . . ." He turns the pages carefully. "The caterpillar is on every page! You have to look for him sometimes though, like down here at the bottom on this page."

"I bet you can't find him here," Cameron says, showing the teacher a page with a picture of large ants. Mrs. Jamison looks at the page closely. The caterpillar isn't evident.

"Ha!" Cameron says, triumphantly. "He's here! This big thing in back of the anthill is the caterpillar. See, he's great big, compared to ants."

"You're right, Cameron," the teacher says. "That's an ant's-eye view of a caterpillar."

"I didn't think he was on the page either, 'til I looked at it a lot of times," Cameron says comfortingly to the teacher.

"You really observe very well," she remarks, and he looks pleased.

"Do these words tell what's happening?" she asks, pointing to the words on the page.

"Zip, zap, tongues snap," Cameron reads from memory. "Wait. I practiced," he says. Then he reads the words again, this time emphasizing the final letters and creating a dramatic effect with his voice.

"Wow!" Mrs. Jamison says. "That really got my attention."

"Good," Cameron replies. His assignment this week was to practice reading to get his listener's attention.

"How come this frog's tongue is short and these others reach clear out here?" he asks, pointing to the frogs' tongues that are in various stages of extension and retrieval.

"Their tongues are all the same length," the teacher explains. "See, this first frog zips [she points to the word "zip"] out his tongue to catch the fly and this one is getting ready to zap [she points to the word "zap"] the fly. You can see this one beginning to snap [she points to the word "snap"] his tongue back to his mouth so he can eat the fly."

"Zip, zap, snap," Cameron says, pointing to each of the frogs. "Zip, his tongue goes out. Zap, he catches the fly. Snap, he pulls it back. Zip, zap, snap," he says, pointing to each of the frogs.

"Can you find the words that begin with z?" the teacher asks.

Cameron points to "zip" and "zap," and the teacher writes each word on a separate card for them to study together.

"What letter is at the end of 'zip' and 'zap'?" she asks.

"P," he replies.

"Are these two words just the same?" she asks.

Cameron studies the words carefully. "No, here's an a and here's an i," he says.

"Show me the sounds," the teacher asks.

"Zzz," he begins, pointing to the z in "zip." "No e on the end, so i doesn't say his name." He looks up at the alphabet card on the wall to find a picture for i. There are two pictures: a bib and a bike.

"Is the middle sound like 'bib' or 'bike'?" the teacher asks.

"Bib," Cameron says. "Zzzz . . . i . . . p. Zip. Zip, zip, zip."

"Good for you," the teacher says. "Now how about this one?"

Cameron looks at the word "zap." "Zzzz . . ." He looks at the alphabet card for A.

"Is that a like 'map' or 'tape'?" the teacher asks.

"Map," he says. "No e on the end. Zzzz . . . a . . . p. Zap. Zap, zap . . . goes the map!"

"You made a rhyme," the teacher says. Cameron looks pleased.

"Zip and zap. What other words sound like these words?" she asks.

"Tip and tap," he says and rolls his eyes up to think harder. "Rip, rap, skip, skap, lip, lap, trip, trap . . . the Three Billy Goats Gruff!"

"Good for you," the teacher says. "Look, I've written down the words you said. I'm not sure if 'skap' is a word, but maybe you invented it. Let's read your list together."

When they have read the list together several times, Mrs. Jamison asks Cameron to read the list on his own, which he does easily.

"This week, will you look in the books you read for words that look like 'zip' and 'zap'?" she asks. "Here, I'll write them down for you in your Word Book. Where else can you look for them?"

"On the charts," he says, "and at home."

"You had a good conference today," Mrs. Jamison says. "Thanks for showing me where to look for the caterpillar."

Cameron grins and gets up to leave.

To be able to give Cameron her full attention, Mrs. Jamison must know that the other children in the room are productively engaged and will not interrupt the conference. During the first month of school, conferences were more informal. While children established routines of playing and working in the various centers in the classroom, Mrs. Jamison spoke briefly with individuals about books they were reading. As students developed their skills in independent activities, she introduced the idea of individual conferences and used role-playing to demonstrate what everyone would be doing. She began by meeting with one student for a few minutes several times during the day and moved gradually to four students, so that she now meets individually with each of her twenty students at least once a week. In the beginning, students needed reminding about not interrupting the conferences, but now a review of the rules at the beginning of the session helps them remember. Her students value their time alone with the teacher's full attention and have learned how everyone's behavior makes a difference when it is their turn. If noise in the room becomes disruptive, Mrs. Jamison rings a small bell and students lower their voices. Most of the time, this is not necessary because children are highly involved in independent work.

What did Mrs. Jamison learn from her conference with Cameron? In addition to specific reading mechanics, she observed the following:

1. Cameron knows the purpose of illustrations in a picture book. He observes details carefully and is aware that this observation will add to his enjoyment of the book.
2. He uses illustrations to derive context clues to help with his reading and is aware that illustrations expand his understanding of text.
3. He is able to use the alphabet as a tool to find the sounds in words.
4. He asks questions to better understand what he is reading.
5. He has read or listened to the book many times. He is at ease in getting around the book.
6. He is developing the idea that reading aloud is an opportunity to share interesting ideas with others. He is also developing a sense of audience when he prepares for the conference with his teacher and shows heightened awareness of story interpretation by emphasizing key sounds and adding a tone of mystery to his oral reading.

Children enjoy talking about things that interest them. That is why the teacher asks Cameron to share his favorite picture. As he talks about what he likes, the conversation can easily extend to the characteristics of letters and words. From their discussion, the teacher sees that Cameron is puzzled by the varying lengths of the frogs' tongues in the pictures. She helps him understand how their tongues work and makes a note to ask the principal if he will bring a frog to school for the children to observe. The principal is an avid naturalist, who regularly supplies the terrarium with interesting specimens. She will also call up frogs out of the animal program on interactive video on Wednesday, when the kindergarten has access to the CD-ROM equipment during the morning.

At several points in the conference, Cameron breaks into a spontaneous rhyme. Mrs. Jamison is delighted with this activity and encourages him to continue. In daily guided reading children increasingly become aware of sounds and are encouraged to make up rhymes as a group. When Cameron says "Skip, skap," the teacher suggests that "skap" may be a word he has invented. At a later time, she might ask him to check the word in the dictionary. If it cannot be found, she might suggest that he think about what it could mean and add it to the class dictionary of invented words.

Beginning teachers often wonder how to handle the contribution of inappropriate words (curses or scatology) during individual or group sessions. The simplest response is to accept the word, but not write it down. Sometimes children will not be aware of an inappropriate meaning, while other times the word may be forwarded for its shock value. In any case you can say, "That's not a word we use at school. Can you think of another one?"

The assignment for Cameron encourages him to notice words that are similar to the ones he has worked with during the conference and helps him continue practicing on his own. This week he will point out similar words in books, on the charts and in a newspaper he brings from home. He will also bring in a copy of *TV Guide* to show the teacher "rip" and "rap." He is now alert to the way these letter combinations sound and will use this knowledge to unlock hundreds of words.

Three years ago, Mrs. Jamison asked the art teacher to create examples of the types of illustrations found in children's picture books, including watercolors, stencils, collages, acrylics and woodcuts. On a table beneath this display, Mrs. Jamison has an assortment of books for children to browse through and match to the examples. This exhibit stays up all year to help children identify the kinds of artwork to be found in the books they are reading. Since she began using the display, Mrs. Jamison notices that her students are more creative in their own artistic responses, choosing from a wider variety of materials and styles to illustrate their writing.

Early Primary Level

"What book did you bring to read to me today?" Mrs. Gardiner asks Jamil.

"This one," he says, handing the first-grade teacher a bright red, black and white paperback copy of *Anansi the Spider*.[8]

"Tell me about the cover," Mrs. Gardiner begins.

"That's Anansi. He's a spider," Jamil says, pointing to the large, stylized spider on the front cover. He counts the spider's legs out loud.

"Is this a special spider?" the teacher asks.

"Uh-huh," Jamil replies. The teacher waits.

"Tell me about him," she asks.

"He gets in trouble," Jamil replies.

"That sounds serious," the teacher says.

"He fall in a river," he says, showing her the picture.

"Oh, oh," the teacher responds. "What's happening here?"

"A fish be swallowin' him up."

"Wow," the teacher says, and waits.

"He gets saved," Jamil continues, savoring his role as a narrator.

"That's a relief," the teacher says. "How does he get rescued?"

"He got six sons. They help him."

Mrs. Gardiner continues to ask Jamil to tell her about the story. Next to oral response, she checks the "developing" category because Jamil is replying in short sentences. This is quite an improvement from no response or the one-word responses characteristic of his earlier conferences.

"What are your favorite pictures in this whole book?" the teacher asks.

Jamil turns without hesitation to a two-page spread. "These," he says, looking with interest at the pictures.

"Can you read the pages to me?" Mrs. Gardiner asks.

Jamil hesitates.

"Why don't you tell me what happens on this page?" she asks.

Jamil looks relieved. "This here is Cushion. He's one of the sons. And he be real soft like a pillow. And here's his father fallin' down, 'cause a bird drop him . . . and he land here on top of Cushion and don't get hurt. He land soft."

In his excitement about the pictures, Jamil forgets his reticence and reveals his interest in the story with an accurate portrayal of the events. He also begins to express himself in longer sentences.

The teacher tries again with oral reading. From the interaction so far, she is satisfied that Jamil understands the story events. "Why don't I read this page and you read that one?" she suggests. "You can help me if I get stuck." She begins to read, "Now Cushion ran to help . . ." and she points to the last word in the sentence.

"Father," Jamil says.

The teacher continues. "Very soft, Anansi . . ." She points to the last two words.

". . . came down," Jamil finishes.

"Now you read and point to words for me to say," the teacher suggests.

Jamil shows some interest. He turns the page and begins reading. "They were very . . ." He pauses and the teacher reads, "Happy." Jamil grins and continues. ". . . that spider family." He turns the page again and continues reading. "All home again that . . ."

". . . night," the teacher says. Jamil nods his head in teacherlike fashion to indicate that she is to continue. She reads, "Kwaku Anansi found a thing in the . . ." Jamil fills in the word "forest."

"Now," says Mrs. Gardiner. "Let's try something else. What's happening here on this page?" she asks.

"Anansi found the moon," he replies.

"How does he feel about this?" the teacher asks.

"Surprised. He want to give it to his sons."

"Can you read this sentence to show me he was surprised?" she asks.

Jamil studies the three-word sentence. He takes a deep breath. "What is **this**?" he booms out. Several nearby children are startled. The teacher smiles at them and they return to their own reading.

"Go on," the teacher says. Jamil reads the sentence again, for effect. He is pleased with the way his voice sounds. "What is this? A great glob of light?"

"Wonderful," the teacher says. "I could tell you were surprised. Look at this word again. It doesn't say 'glob,' but that's very close. It says 'globe.' Can you tell me why?"

Jamil studies the word. "I **like** 'glob,' " he says.

"It's a good word," the teacher agrees. "But 'globe' means something special about the moon. It means it's round . . . all around, like a basketball. Remember how we looked at the United States on the globe?" She points out the globe in the library area.

"Hmmm. Can I say 'glob' when I read it to myself?" he asks.

"Certainly. That's your privilege," the teacher replies. "Can you show me the letter that makes this word say 'globe'?"

Jamil studies the word again. "*E*," he says, pointing. "This *e*."

"Good for you!" the teacher says. "Let's look at the front cover for a few minutes. Do you notice anything unusual about Anansi?" the teacher asks.

Jamil studies the spider. "Shapes," he observes.

"Tell me about the shapes," the teacher asks.

"Well, . . .," he pauses, tracing around the features of the spider. "Circles," he says, pointing to the eyes.

"Can you tell me a little more about the circles?" the teacher asks.

"His eyes are circles . . . and these here on his nose. And these . . . are his eyebrows . . . they're triangles . . . and his mouth has two triangles and these things on his chest . . ."

"His markings?"

"Yeah, his markings are triangles. . . ." Suddenly he notices that the spider's body is a triangle too and points this out to the teacher.

"What did you think about this book?" Mrs. Gardiner asks.

"It was good."

"You know, some other people agree with you. How can you tell?"

Jamil points to the silver Caldecott Honor symbol in the upper right-hand corner of the cover.

"This gives you three Caldecott books on your list," the teacher notes. "Do you remember the others?"

Jamil leafs back through his notebook and indicates *Shadow*[9] and *Ten, Nine, Eight*.[10] His preference for bold shapes and color is evident.

"What would you like to share about your book on Friday?" Mrs. Gardiner asks.

Jamil hesitates. "Can I do something with Ahmed?" he asks.

"Certainly," she replies. "Be sure to tell me by Wednesday, so we know how much time to save for you. What do you plan to read next?"

Jamil answers immediately, "Ahmed's book."

"The one about the dinosaur?" she asks.

"Yeah, all about a boy who wants a dinosaur,"[11] he replies.

"It sounds like you're looking forward to reading it," the teacher says.

"Ahmed's already read parts of it to me. I want to read it myself."

When Jamil returns to his table, Mrs. Gardiner makes a few notes on Jamil's progress sheet in her three-ring notebook, in addition to the items she checked during the conference.

What did Mrs. Gardiner learn from her conference with Jamil?

1. Jamil pays close attention to the details in illustrations, which helps him better understand the content of what he reads.
2. Jamil's oral reading difficulties are a matter of confidence, not lack of ability.
3. Jamil's verbal proficiency in standard English is improving.
4. His comprehension of the story is good, and he is able to analyze words using rules.
5. He is very creative and likes bold, bright colors.

If Jamil had participated in a traditional reading group, the teacher may have assumed that Jamil could not read aloud or express himself verbally. Jamil's hesitancy to commit himself by speaking would also prevent a teacher from knowing Jamil's skill in word analysis or his ability to interpret illustrations. Because Jamil went to a preschool where his English was constantly corrected, he subsequently reduced his schooltime speech to a minimum of words and short sentences to avoid this unpleasant experience. Mrs. Gardiner understands his reaction and tries to provide a model for standard English, while encouraging his fluency. She knows that Jamil needs to feel that he can express himself without penalty. When he listens to books read aloud, listens to recorded books and immerses himself in the guided reading sessions with the teacher and other students, he has the opportunity to see and hear models of standard English that he can adopt as the school language. His teacher respects the language of Jamil's home and community. A member of the community herself, she sees her responsibility to Jamil as one of helping him master an additional form of English that will allow him to succeed in situations beyond his community.

Mrs. Gardiner is delighted when Jamil prefers the word "glob" to "globe." It represents a highly personal transaction with the language in the story. He has publicly expressed a preference, something new to him and a sizeable risk. From their conversation, she is certain Jamil knows what the word says and can tell the difference between "glob" and "globe."

Jamil is hesitant to read aloud to the teacher. She moves him into the activity in gradual steps by reading his favorite part of the book together. First she encourages him to read words she leaves out. Then Jamil directs the reading, indicating the words the teacher should read. This activity allows the teacher to evaluate Jamil's performance in a nonthreatening way.

Mrs. Gardiner helps Jamil explore the illustrations by asking him to describe the action and look more closely at details. He is drawn to the bright colors and geometric shapes and will look for the Ashanti designs in other books of African American stories. Although Jamil has strong preferences for the books he selects, he is also drawn to the books his friend Ahmed reads. This relationship is positive for both boys. Ahmed likes Jamil's creativity and Jamil explores books he otherwise might not select. The dinosaur book is somewhat above his reading level, but he will get enough help on the dinosaur terminology from Ahmed.

Late Primary Level

Four third graders sign their names on the board under a picture of an open book, indicating that they are ready to talk about books they have read. If there is additional time, Mrs. Parks will ask for other volunteers. Most children are prepared for conferences on a daily basis. She rings a small bell and Susan brings her book to the table.

"I liked this book," she begins, holding up *Latkes and Applesauce: A Hanukkah Story.*[12] "It's about latkes and it made me hungry to read it."

"This sounds like a good book," the teacher agrees. "What's it about?"

"Well, . . . it's about a family . . . they don't have much food. They don't even have applesauce and latkes for Hanukkah."

"That would be disappointing," Mrs. Parks says.

"But the name of the book . . . it's a surprise. I bet you can't guess."

"Well, I know that latkes and applesauce are special foods for Hanukkah," the teacher ventures.

Susan covers her mouth to keep the secret and giggles. "That's not the surprise," she says.

"Now you've really got me interested," the teacher says. "When will I know about this surprise title?"

"When I read you my favorite part," she replies.

"I can't wait!" the teacher says. "Why don't you tell me a little about the story and why this family doesn't have latkes and applesauce."

"Well, . . . they're poor . . . but they aren't sad. They have a little food and they play dreidel and sing."

"They go ahead with the celebration anyway?" the teacher asks.

"Yes, and they even share their little food with a dog and cat who come to the door."

"They sound like a kind family."

"And then the dog digs up potatoes in the snow and they find apples in the tree for applesauce."

"How wonderful! Then what happens?"

"The mother makes latkes and applesauce for everybody."

"How does the story end?"

"That's the surprise part, the part I'm going to read," she says and begins to read aloud. She is excited about what she is reading and reads very quickly. Then she stops, looks up at the teacher and says, "Oops!" She starts over, this time reading more slowly and with dramatic emphasis the part of the story that tells how the lost animals are named.

"The dog is called Latke because he found the potatoes and the cat Applesauce because she found the apples."

"That **is** a surprise!" the teacher says. "Now when I look at the title of the book, it has a new meaning." Susan beams.

"Do you have some favorite pictures in this book?" the teacher asks.

Susan opens the book to a marker. "These," she says. The drawings portray the family and the kitten playing with a dreidel. "They look happy here."

"Is there any special reason you like this picture?" the teacher asks.

"It looks like they're all having fun. It's how I feel when I play dreidel."

"Tell me some more about the picture."

"It's kind of soft. It looks warm and cozy."

"What else do you like?"

"It's funny, too. Listen . . .," and she reads, "The little kitten spun the dreidel so well, she won two nuts and a raisin!"

Mrs. Parks and Susan laugh together.

"This looks like a special candleholder," the teacher says, pointing to the picture.

"It's a menorah," Susan explains. "We light the candles every night in Hanukkah."

"There's a place for nine candles. Is there a special reason for nine candles?" the teacher asks.

"There's eight for the days the oil lasted in the Temple a long time ago," Susan replies. "The one in the middle is the shammes, the servant candle. It lights all the rest."

"Did you have any problems with particular words?" Mrs. Parks asks.

Susan opens her Word Book. "These I didn't know how to say," she says, pointing to furious and whistling, "and these I didn't know what they meant," she adds, indicating flickered, dwindling, sagely and gazed.

"How did you figure them out?"

"Well, this one says 'furious,' " Susan explains. "I thought it said 'fur-e-us.' " She points out "furious blizzard" in the book. "I thought it must mean really windy 'cause that's what the picture shows. I looked it up in the dictionary and it means stormy, but you say it different than I thought. It's 'fyoo-re-us.' "

"Good for you," the teacher says. "Can it mean anything else?"

"My mom told me it means really angry."

"Can you use it that way?"

"When we track mud into the kitchen, my mom gets furious," she replies, grinning.

"How did you find out what the other words meant?" the teacher asks.

"I looked in the dictionary for whistling and then I knew what it meant. And I asked my sister about dwindling. I figured out what gazed meant by the sentence, 'Let us go out and gaze at the stars,' " she reads. "I thought it meant to look at the stars, and I was just about right. But it means to look at something for a while, to study it. My sister didn't know what sagely meant, so I asked my Dad. He said it meant wise."

"Did you write any sentences with the new words you discovered?" the teacher asks.

"Here they are." Susan hands her the Word Book and Mrs. Parks looks at the sentences.

"These look great," she says. "Do you think you'll be able to remember them if you want to use them sometime?"

"I think so. I like dwindling the best. It makes you smile."

Mrs. Parks looks puzzled.

"Watch," she says. "When you say it, it makes your mouth go in a smile," and she says the word to demonstrate.

Mrs. Parks laughs. "That's an interesting observation," she says. "I never thought about words creating facial expressions."

"The others do, too," she points out. "Whistling makes you show your teeth."

Mrs. Parks laughs again. "This is a great discovery," she says. "There's another book over in the library you might like," she adds. "It's about Hanukkah too, and it's funny."

Susan looks interested.

"A grandmother can't see too well and she mistakes a big bear for the rabbi," the teacher says. "It's called *The Chanukkah Guest*,[13] and it has a picture of a bear with a red scarf on the cover."

"I'll try it," Susan says. "I like funny books."

"You were going to practice reading aloud to your family this week," the teacher notes. "How did that go?"

"We're all reading *My Side of the Mountain*[14] together," she explains. "And I've read two whole chapters."

"Good," Mrs. Parks says. "Are you practicing your audience skills?"

"Yes," she replies. "I'm trying to read slower, so everyone can understand better."

"What do you plan to read next?" the teacher asks.

"I've got a book in my desk about bats," she replies. "It's going to be my science information book."

WHAT HAPPENED HERE? ONE PERSPECTIVE What did the teacher learn about Susan's reading progress in this ten-minute conference? As she listens to Susan talk about the book and interacts with her about her reading, she observes:

1. Susan's ability to choose a book at an instructional level.
2. Her approximate reading instruction level.
3. Her word analysis skills and resources for finding word meanings.
4. Some of Susan's interests, experiences, values and sense of humor.
5. Her oral reading proficiency.
6. Her reading comprehension skill.

Susan tends to read aloud as quickly as she reads silently. By asking her to read aloud to her family, the teacher is helping her develop a sense of audience. With this awareness, she will learn how to share her enjoyment of reading with others. Mrs. Parks has already noticed a difference when Susan reads aloud to her kindergarten Book Buddy and was pleased to see that she self-corrected when she read aloud during the conference.

Intermediate Level

Karla brings a copy of *Letters from Rifka*[15] to the reading conference with her sixth-grade teacher, Ms. Ho. "This was a good book," she begins. "It was kind of different . . ."

"Different in what way?" Ms. Ho asks.

"Well, . . . all the things she goes through . . . Rifka . . . the main character. You'd think the book would be pretty depressing. And it is, in parts. Terrible things happen to her. But in other ways, it seemed optimistic. She . . . Rifka . . . was really strong and you don't feel sorry for her, even though she went through a lot."

"This sounds like a good story," Ms. Ho comments. "Why don't you tell me about it?"

"Well, like the title says, the book is all the letters that Rifka wrote to her cousin Tovah after her family left Russia in 1919 to go to the United States. They're Jewish and everyone persecutes them because someone told the peasants they were responsible for bad times. They have a terrible time getting out of Europe. The whole family gets typhus, and Rifka finally has to stay in Belgium by herself for a year because she has ringworm and they won't let her into the United States. And the reason she got ringworm is because she helped a poor girl on a train fix her hair to look nice for her sister."

"It sounds like she had a difficult time," Ms. Ho says.

"Really bad," Karla agrees. "See, she writes these letters to her cousin, but she doesn't send them. They kind of comfort her because she can pretend she's talking to her cousin. She doesn't have any paper, so she writes on the blank pages and in the margins of this book of poetry her cousin gave her before she left."

Karla opens the book and indicates some lines at the beginning of the chapter. "This is the poet . . . Pushkin. I looked him up. He was a great Russian poet. His poems are sad though. There are parts of them at the beginning of each chapter."

"Why do you think the author used Pushkin's poetry that way?" the teacher asks.

"Well, it sort of makes you think a certain way before you read the chapter. It gets you in the mood."

"Did you find out anything else about the poet?" Ms. Ho asks.

"I looked him up in *Benet's Reader's Encyclopedia*,"[16] Karla replies. "It said he was like Shakespeare to the Russian people. And I also found out that he wrote a novel in verse called *Eugene Onegin*. I know that Tchaikovsky made an opera out of the story because we listened to it on the radio a few weeks ago. And I found another one of his poems in an anthology." She reads the poem aloud and then comments, "He must have been a sad person . . . everything he writes is sad . . . some of the music in the opera seemed sad," she observes. She tells the teacher about Pushkin's early death as the result of a duel and then lapses into silence. Both teacher and student sit quietly for a moment. The teacher nods her head to acknowledge Karla's feelings.

"Everyone is looking for examples of similes in their reading this week," the teacher says. "What did you find?"

"Lots," she says. "Here's the first one I found. It's when she's trying to distract some soldiers away from a train where her family is hiding: 'Inside I twisted like a wrung rag, but on the outside I held still.' Then here's another one. She's telling about the guard at the train station as they were trying to escape from Berdichev where they lived: 'His eyes were like the Teterev in the spring when the snow melts, churning with green ice.' "

"Those are both very powerful," the teacher agrees.

"And listen to this one," Karla says. "This is the best. It's when Rifka is talking to the boy she takes care of on Ellis Island. She's trying to get him to read."

> I looked down at Ilya. "Read to them," I ordered in Russian. "Show them that you are smart enough to live in America. I know how clever you are, Ilya. But Mr. Fargate needs to know. Your uncle needs to know too."
>
> I looked back to where the uncle sat with his hat in his lap. The man's eyes never left Ilya. He drank in the sight of his nephew the way a thirsty man pulls at a dipper of water. (p. 133)

"The last line I read . . . that's the simile."

"Excellent," the teacher says. "The examples you chose make me want to read the book."

Karla looks pleased.

"We'll be looking for metaphors next week," Ms. Ho says. "Do you remember what they are?"

Karla consults her Word Book. "It's when you say something is something else, to make it more interesting or vivid."

"Can you give an example?" Ms. Ho asks.

Karla thinks for a minute. "The class is a sleeping dragon."

"I hope not!" the teacher exclaims. They both laugh.

"Let's get back to your book," the teacher continues. "What did you most like about Rifka as a person?"

"I liked that she was so strong. Things she went through . . . really scary things . . . and depressing. I would have just given up. But she kept going."

"Does she ever get to the United States?" the teacher asks.

"Yes, finally," Karla replies. "She has to stay in Belgium for a year until the ringworm is cured and then . . ." Karla laughs. "It really isn't funny, but it's like nothing can go right for her. She gets herself together and all these terrible things keep happening. The boat she's on is caught in a storm and a boy who really likes her is drowned. Then the immigration officials won't let her in because her hair hasn't grown back in from the ringworm."

"Why is that important?" the teacher asks.

"They're afraid no one will want to marry her if she's bald. Then the state will have to take care of her. Is that really true, Ms. Ho?" Karla asks. "Did they really keep people out of America for reasons like that?"

"Yes, it's true," Ms. Ho replies. "There were so many people who wanted to come to America that it was necessary to make sure they could take care of themselves once they were here. Remember that this was the early part of the century, and most women were economically dependent on their husbands."

"Well, the story gets better, anyway," Karla says. "Rifka has to stay in a special hospital on Ellis Island while they decide what to do with her. She takes care of a little Russian peasant boy who has been sent to live with an uncle. The uncle never comes to visit him, and everyone thinks he's retarded because he never speaks. She reads her poetry book to Ilya and also some poetry that she's written herself. You know that part I read to you before, about the uncle listening to Ilya read?"

Ms. Ho nods her head.

"Well, that's how Rifka helps Ilya get his admission papers. She shows he's not retarded by making him read from her poetry book. He's only seven years old, so it shows he's really smart and can take care of himself. Then Ilya shows the examiners how smart Rifka is by reading her poetry to them. They're impressed because she's so good in English and can speak other languages, too. And she took care of everyone who was sick in her ward, so that shows she has other talents and can maybe even become a doctor. There's a really good surprise at the end, too. Her hair finally grows back!"

"It sounds like a lot goes on in this book," the teacher says.

"There's a lot more, too," Karla says. "I didn't even tell you about her brothers or how her mother treats her or what she did in Belgium."

"I'm just going to have to read the book myself," Ms. Ho says. "Did you find any words that were new to you?"

"Lots," Karla says. "But they were all interesting." She reads her list and the definitions she found for each one: fumigate, typhus, Berdichev, Teterev, peruke, tallis, rucksack, Yiddish.

"Did Rifka change in this story?" Ms. Ho asks.

"She learns to understand other people better as she goes along," Karla says. "And she understands herself better, too. At the beginning, people were either good or bad, but at the end she could see reasons for the way people acted. And she's more sure of herself, too. Even if they won't let her into the United States, she's going to work out a plan for her life."

"Did any of the characters in the book remind you of anyone you know?" the teacher asks.

"My older brother Mark reminds me of Rifka's brother, Saul," Karla says. "He teases me all the time and I think he really can't stand me. But once somebody chased me at school and I fell down and got a bloody knee. Mark took me to the nurse's office and was really nice to me the whole time, like Saul was when Rifka had typhus."

"What do you think is the main idea of this book?" Ms. Ho asks.

"Well, I think it's probably about prejudice. People were really bad to Rifka and her family because they were Jews, and they blamed them for things that weren't their fault. But Rifka saw that she had prejudice too, when she was afraid of people in other countries because some foreigners had treated her badly. When she went to Belgium and the people were kind, she had to change her mind. And she was angry at all Russian peasants because of what happened to her family. But she learned to love Ilya, even though Ilya was a peasant and the peasants drove her family out of Russia."

"Was there a message in this book?" the teacher asks.

"To not make up your mind ahead of time how things are going to be. Get to know people and not judge them one way or the other because they belong to some group or another."

"Did the author give you any background on this story?"

"Yes. In the beginning she tells how she got the story, from her great-aunt. Then in the back, it tells about how the Jewish people were driven out of Russia. The government made the peasants prejudiced against the Jews to take away their anger at the government. Then the peasants beat the Jews and burned their houses or even murdered them."

"Has the book been recognized in any way?" the teacher asks.

"Lots!" Karla replies and she shows her the list on the back of the book that includes a Christopher Medal, an International Reading Association Award and recognition as an American Library Association Notable Book, Best Book for Young Adults and a School Library Journal Best Book.

"Very impressive," Ms. Ho agrees. "Would **you** give this book an award?"

"A definite thumbs up," she replies. "It's one of the best books I ever read. Are there any more books like this one?"

"Alike in what way?" the teacher asks.

"About how people react to war and hardship. Ones where girls are the heroes."

"I can think of several in our library that you might like," Ms. Ho says. "Would you like to write them down?"

Karla takes out her notebook.

"*Year of Impossible Goodbyes*[17] is about a young girl trying to escape from Korea after the Chinese Communists take over the country in 1945," the teacher says, "and *The Road from Home*[18] tells about how the Armenians were driven from their homes in Turkey in 1915. *The Devil's Arithmetic*[19] tells about a young Jewish girl who goes back in time to a Nazi concentration camp during World War II. I think you'd like any of these."

"Did any of them win any awards?" she asks.

"All of them did," Ms. Ho replies.

"I liked *Number the Stars*.[20] Are these as good?" Karla asks.

"I think so," said Mrs. Ho. "But don't take my word for it."

Karla laughs. This is the line on the television show *Reading Rainbow*. "I know," she says. "I can find out myself."

"Have you decided what you're going to share on Friday?" Ms. Ho asks.

"I'm going to try something different," she confides. "I hope everyone doesn't laugh. Josh read the book already and he's going to play the immigration official who questions Rifka. I'll play Rifka and I'm going to get my little Book Buddy James to play Ilya. We're doing the scene in the book where Ilya shows he can read. We're going to practice at noon."

"That sounds great," the teacher says. "I don't think anyone will laugh. Be sure to give the class enough background so they understand where this interview fits in the story." The teacher hesitates. "Why do you think the class might laugh?"

"Well, Rifka is bald, and I'll have to tie a scarf over my head and all."

"What will you do if they laugh?"

"Just go on," Karla says. "That's what Rifka would do."

WHAT HAPPENED HERE? ONE PERSPECTIVE

In this conference, the student does most of the talking. To help Karla reflect on both the content and style of the book, Ms. Ho asks open-ended questions, such as: Why is that important? What do you think the author was trying to say? Was there a message in this book? Why do you think the author did this? As Karla talks about her interaction with the book, Ms. Ho responds, inquires and observes. Conferencing provides Karla the opportunity to ask Ms. Ho questions to check the credibility of what she has read. When she wants to know about the immigration rules, she is asking for confirmation from a previous generation: Did this happen? Why did it happen?

The teacher asks questions to assess Karla's understanding of character development and her personal identification with the story: Did any of the characters remind you of anyone you know? Did Rifka change in any way?

These are some of the things she learns from her conference with Karla.

1. Karla has clearly grasped the main idea of the book and is able to make inferences, based on her knowledge of the story.
2. She understands the meaning of what she has read and is interested in exploring other books that deal with persecution and prejudice.
3. She is able to analyze the character in the story in some detail and is able to recognize character growth.
4. She is alert to the use of figurative language and identifies excellent examples.
5. She is able to identify with the characters in the story and their motivations.
6. Her family background helps her make rich connections with her reading. Because they listen to opera as a family, she recognizes Pushkin as the author of the text on which the opera *Eugene Onegin* is based.

It is obvious to Ms. Ho that Karla has learned a great deal from this book. The poet Pushkin was introduced in a manner so integral to this exciting story that Karla was compelled to find out more about him and read some of his poetry. She gained new ideas about a time period and events in history and increased her knowledge about a geographical area. She added new words to her vocabulary and learned something about prejudice, the problems of immigration and the causes and consequences of war. The book also provided her with a glimpse of medical knowledge and practice in the early part of the century.

Most of all, Karla was attracted to the courage and persistence of the main character and to a story that took her beyond herself and her own experience. Karla's experience with this book will add meaning to her future reading, increase her understanding of the human condition and help develop the skills she needs to encounter gradually more difficult reading. It also helps establish the idea that difficult books are worth the effort. She will continue to explore award-winning books because they might have ideas worth knowing.

Karla has prepared for this conference with the expectation of certain types of questions from the teacher. She has a copy of the general questions and knows that the teacher will inquire not only for assessment purposes, but also because she is interested in what Karla has read. Students will often extend their exploration and research so that they can share more interesting background about their book. They have an appreciative audience who will be just as excited as they are with their findings.

At this level of reading, the teacher emphasizes literary elements and devices. Similes and metaphors were introduced in mini-lessons and literature study. Each week, students look for examples of one or more elements in their own reading, record them in their Word Books and use them in their own writing.

WHAT DO YOU THINK? How did the teachers described above make the conferences specific to the individual student? Did you have the feeling that these teachers enjoyed their conversations with these students? Have you ever talked one-on-one with someone about a book you especially liked? What was your experience?

IV. Preparing for Individual Reading Conferences

An individual reading conference is a meeting that involves preparation by both the teacher and the student. Teachers review their notes and checklists from previous conferences and select questions to ask that will allow them to observe skill and progress in reading. Students also use a set of guidelines to help them prepare for the conference. In addition to the opportunity to talk about a book that interests them, they also want to demonstrate their understanding and skill development to the teacher.

Guidelines for independent work should be posted in the classroom, and all activities must be self-directed. This means that directions and materials necessary for participation must be in place before conferences begin, to avoid any unnecessary interruptions. You will want to rehearse this independent study time with your students, so that you can observe possible problems and help students gain experience in working in a self-directed fashion. If all students will be completing the same kinds of activities, such as reading silently, practicing skills, writing in journals or working in groups, this schedule should also be rehearsed for at least a week, or until everyone feels comfortable with it and is able to function independently.

When problems arise, talk about it together. If a group is talking too loud in the back of the room and others cannot concentrate on their reading, how can the problem be solved? What constitutes a problem serious enough to warrant interrupting a conference? What happens if someone comes to the door during a conference? What if someone feels ill or there is an accident? What if someone is bothering others when they are trying to work? Role-play situations and ask for ideas. This kind of discussion involves students in solving their own problems.

It is a good idea to involve students in creating guidelines for the independent work period. One way to begin this discussion is to tell the students about the benefits of individual conferencing and independent study, which include:

1. Uninterrupted time with the teacher. (You might want to role-play this so students can experience how it feels to be interrupted.)

2. Time to read books of their own choosing; opportunities to practice skills that will improve their ability to read whatever they want.

3. Opportunities to respond to books in ways that they choose: art, drama, music, crafts.

When students are asked to brainstorm ways to support these benefits for everyone, they usually generate rules similar to the following:

1. Have a plan.
2. Do not disturb anyone else.
3. Finish independent work first.
4. Consult others when their plans involve yours.

When you are confident that your class can work independently for a period of time, you are ready to begin preparing for individual conferences. One of the most basic and important ways you can prepare for all your reading conferences is to read as widely as possible. The more books you have read, the more you will be able to interact thoughtfully with the materials your students bring to conferences. When students express an interest in a topic or author, you will know other books to suggest. Of course, you can also look up these topics and authors in your reference books, but a wide acquaintance with books allows you to recommend them out of your own experience.

In many classrooms, teachers ask students to record the names of the books they want to bring to conference a day in advance, so there will be time to preview them. When they know the book beforehand, they can often ask more interesting and specific questions. Familiarity with the book allows them to better share the student's delight in the book and relate to his or her responses more easily. If it is not possible to read the book in advance, you can still ask questions that will advance a conversation about the book and show an interest in what the students are reading. General questions, like those asked by the teachers in the narratives above, can help students indicate their understanding of the story and demonstrate their reading skills and study strategies.

There are four major activities associated with conferences and many ways to practice the skills necessary to conduct them. These activities include: **sharing** ideas about the book, **observing** student performance, **assisting** student skill development and **recording** notes on student performance. An easy mnemonic is **SOAR**: share, observe, assist and record. Each of these processes can be practiced, one at a time, until you feel comfortable with them individually. Here are some ways you might want to practice your conferencing skills:

Share Have a simple conversation with a student about a book. Extend your practice by talking with students of different age levels, using these same questions:

1. What did you like about this book?
2. Show me your favorite picture or
   Tell me something about your favorite part of the book.
3. What is this book about? (nonfiction) or
   What is this story about? (fiction)

Observe Have the same discussion with another student, using the questions above. But this time, when you ask the questions, observe the student's responses.

1. Is he excited about the book?
2. Does he have definite ideas about what he likes?
3. Can he tell you what the book is about?

Assist-questions The following questions provide opportunities to assist students with reading strategies or to offer direct help and information:

1. Were there any words in this book that were hard to pronounce? Were there words whose meaning you weren't sure of? How did you figure them out?
2. Why do you think the artist made these pictures this way? What do you think the writer was trying to say?
3. Does this book remind you of any other book you have read? or Do these pictures remind you of any other pictures you have looked at?
4. Read me something from your favorite part of the book.

Assist-strategies The following are examples of ways to assist students during a conference:

1. **Word pronunciation** Help students use sound clues; divide the word into syllables; find small parts of words in the more difficult one.
2. **Word meaning** Are there any clues to the meaning in the spelling? Is the word similar to another one that the student might know?
3. **Picture or text interpretation** Encourage the student to look for details that expand the meaning of the picture or text. How does the artwork (or story) make them feel? What does the artist (or writer) do to make the reader feel this way?
4. **Relationships** Ask students to connect their experiences with books or pictures to help them begin to see patterns in writing and illustration.
5. **Oral reading** Prompt students on difficult words or help them figure them out. Encourage them to read a sentence so that you can really feel how happy (or sad, or puzzled or angry) the character is, or how exciting the story is, or how interesting the nonfiction excerpt is.

Record Conduct the same type of interview, but this time use an interview similar to the one below to evaluate the student's performance. Make notes when they will help you remember an observation.

1. **Personal response to the book**: What did you like about this book?
2. **Main idea**: What was this story about?
3. **Critical reading**: What kind of book was this?
4. **Plot sequence**: What was the best part of this story? What happened before that? After that?
5. **Vocabulary**: Do you know what this word means?
6. **Study skills**: Ask a question about finding things in the index or table of contents, details in pictures, locations on maps.

7. **Word analysis**: Were there any words you did not recognize in this story? How did you figure them out?
8. **Oral reading**: Read your favorite part to me.
9. **Retelling**: Tell me the story in just a few sentences.

As often as you have an opportunity, talk to students about books they have read until you feel comfortable asking questions and making notes about student responses. Additional questions in each category can be found in Section VI.

Finding a Place

It is important to find an area in your classroom where you will have some privacy with each student during individual conferences. A small table and two chairs located in one corner of the room is a preferable arrangement. This will allow you to sit next to the student and share the book. It also provides a surface for your conference notebook. You should be able to hear what is going on in the classroom and students should be able to see you, but not hear the conversation of the conference. Avoid sitting near an area where students must go regularly for any reason, such as any of the centers, the restroom, the door or the pencil sharpener.

Student Preparation for Conferences

Guidelines for the student's preparation for a conference complement those used by the teacher. Their purpose is to provide direction to students preparing for conferences during independent worktime. As children gain experience with conferences, these guidelines will help them interact with their books in an analytical and reflective manner. Samples of primary- and intermediate-level student preparation guidelines can be found at the end of the chapter. There are also sample forms to help students identify the various genres in their reading.

In the beginning, you may want to indicate certain items that will be asked of every student. Later you will know from past conferences the types of questions that will provide the most information for individual students. Many teachers encourage students to include a question they would like to be asked on their conference memo form (see the conference memo at the end of the chapter). After you have seen every student the first time, each should sign up for subsequent conferences on a weekly basis. Some teachers have a weekly or monthly calendar on their desk or the bulletin board where students can enter their names on a preferred date. Others ask children to move an index card with their name on it to a special place in a file box, while still others have children write their names under a conference title on the blackboard or on a piece of paper that is placed in a special box.

Reading conferences represent a sample of a student's reading interests and skills. Students read all week in order to pursue individual interests during independent reading and study times and to research ideas of interest in theme or content area studies. From this broad range of reading, they select something they especially like, to share with the teacher. For five to ten minutes, they have the teacher's undivided attention, and most students give this time their full effort, in terms of preparation. They examine the literary elements of what they are reading and practice strategies that develop their ability to interact with literature. When analysis and skill building are based on material chosen by the student, the reading process becomes more meaningful.

WHAT DO YOU THINK? What do you think motivates children to stay involved with reading and responses to literature during an independent work period? If you were a student in one of the classrooms described above, what interests in reading would you have pursued? How would you have responded to your reading? Art? Dance? Drama? Music? Crafts?

V. Including Everyone

At whatever level you teach, you will find that some students are distracted during these independent work sessions. In previous chapters, the problems of children with ADD (attention deficit disorder) were discussed. But many children who do not pay attention to reading activities may simply lack experience with books. Those who have been read to at home usually become immediate and attentive listeners when the teacher opens a book to read aloud. They look forward to independent reading because it gives them time to enjoy the books they want to read. From personal experience, they associate pleasure with reading and know how to respond to these familiar activities.

If these activities have not been part of children's experience, they may resist reading or ignore it. Individual conferences allow teachers to begin at the beginning with these students by providing them individual time and attention with books. These conversations can help students see books and reading in a new light, as the teacher becomes better acquainted with their needs and interests. It is especially important for beginning readers to supplement these conferences with Book Buddy paired reading and the individual attention of an aide or parent volunteer who can read aloud to them and talk with them about their books.

If you have children who must always be in your line of sight, such as the students with chronic illness, severe disability or attention deficit disorder, you can place them somewhere close to you, so that they are in your peripheral (side) vision at all times and you can be aware of any emergencies or problems. Some teachers supply these students with a small bell to ring if they should experience a physical difficulty during conferencing.

A positive benefit of individual conferences is the opportunity to identify vision problems. When children hold the book too close to their faces, squint to make out words, have difficulty tracking words across a page or blink repeatedly, you will want to record the particular difficulty and report the symptoms to the school or district nurse. You can also contrast the attentiveness and interactive levels of children between conference times during whole-class activities, when you suspect someone might have a speech or hearing problem.

Individual conferences will also help you better evaluate students who are reticent to speak in groups, who have difficulties expressing themselves, or who are just beginning to learn English. If your school has an inclusion program, you may have students with more severe physical, emotional or mental challenges. But you will also have a special education teacher or aide who will help attend to these special needs. The purpose of inclusion is to allow all students to participate as fully as possible in a classroom with age-level peers. Providing equal access to the curriculum requires team planning, and many teachers find that this program offers them new ideas and extra help in planning activities for the entire classroom.

Books to Increase Understanding

The following books provide insight into the lives of children who must struggle to survive each day, in the absence of a secure or safe home. They put a face on homelessness and poverty in ways that are not possible with news stories. There will be students in your classes who need special care and understanding to overcome these challenges to their childhood. Although you may be unable to change the condition of their lives, your sensitivity and caring can help create a secure and comforting environment for them in your classroom.

Monkey Island[21] This Social Studies Notable Book provides a view into the terrifying and tragic situation of homelessness through the eyes of eleven-year-old Clay Garrity. His father disappears and then his mother, leaving him to search for food and shelter in the city streets.

Slake's Limbo[22] Honored as an ALA Notable Book and a Best Book for Young Adults, this is the story of Aremis Slake, a young boy constantly under attack from his environment. Driven into the subway tunnels of New York City to protect himself, he decides to stay there and survives for 121 days.

Blue Willow[23] This Newbery Honor book tells the touching story of Janey Larkin, whose father works in the cotton fields. The family must move constantly so that her father can find work, and Janey longs for a home of her own. When illness strikes, there is no money to pay the rent, and Janey must make a decision about her only treasure, a blue willow plate. This story was written in 1940, but the conditions of life for rural children who live in poverty are tragically timeless.

WHAT DO YOU THINK? If you were the teacher of one of these children, how might you reach out to him or her in the classroom? How can teachers provide a sense of security for students? Are there experiences in your own life that will help you better understand the challenges they face?

VI. Step-by-Step: Conducting an Individual Conference

A week before you plan to begin conferences, distribute a list of conference preparations to each student. Give each child a reading notebook of one color (or include the purchase of all notebooks on the school supplies list at the beginning of the year). Explain that you want to meet individually with all students at least once a week during the school year to hear about one of the books they are reading. Tell them that you will want them to share interesting features of the book and talk about some of the topics listed on the student conference preparation sheet (sample at the end of the chapter). Go over all the questions and ask them if they can respond to them from a book they have read. Make certain that they understand each question.

Explain that you will occasionally mark on a form or write brief notes during the conference, but that these are not grading marks. These notations will help you remember the skills they have achieved and remind you about areas where you can offer assistance. Tell students that at the close of the conference, you will discuss areas for practice, which they will write down in their reading notebooks and use for reference during independent study time. Ask them to complete a conference memo at least a day before the conference so that you can preview the book they will be talking about (sample at the end of the chapter). Be sure to ask if there are any questions.

There is usually a great deal of curiosity about these conferences at the primary level, and students can be engaged at the beginning on a voluntary basis. A simple invitation such as "Who would like to go first?" usually garners at least five or six volunteers. Later you can ask, "Who is ready for a conference?" and get the same results. At the intermediate level, students may be more cautious initially because of peer expectations—it isn't cool to be too eager. In this event, you could take the class alphabetically or have students draw numbers to establish the sequence for the first conferences. As students experience the positive effects of conferences, they line up to volunteer.

When everyone understands the purpose of the conferences, review the independent study time procedures with the entire class. Does everyone know what to do? Does everyone understand that the conferences are not to be interrupted, except for emergencies? Some teachers check in with all students, asking them to announce their plans for the independent work period. Others ask students to submit their plan in writing, believing that this helps them organize their thinking about the worktime. If centers are used, this is the time to give any information that will be necessary to use them. Go over the rules for independent work and ask if everyone is ready to work. Then you are ready for your first conference.

Place the chairs for the conference side by side, not facing each other. This arrangement permits you to share the book with a student, looking at illustrations or calling attention to words or text features. You can also monitor oral reading this way and identify skipped or substituted words. Perhaps the best feature of this arrangement is the intimacy it creates for talking about books, resembling a child's first experience with being read to by family members. If this is not part of a child's experience, it is all the more necessary to create the pleasant benefits of having a person's full attention. If this arrangement is not comfortable for you, sit at a desk or table at right angles, so that you can still share a single book.

Open your conference book on the table, desk or your lap so that you can see the questions easily and enter data as needed. Call the first conferee and you have begun. Be sure to welcome the student and indicate where he or she is to sit. Begin by saying, "Tell me about this book," "What did you like best about this book?" or "This looks like an interesting book. I'd like to hear about it." You may be a little nervous about conferences in the beginning, but you will feel more relaxed as students begin talking about their books, and you will become less self-conscious as the conversation progresses.

It is important to set a time limit on the conference since it is possible to spend at least half an hour with each student once discussion has begun. Begin with a ten-minute limit, but try not to hurry. If you do not ask every question during each conference, you can make a note to ask it the next time. Listen carefully to student responses. This is where you will get information about understanding and skill progress. Remember that eye contact will show the student you are interested in what he or she is saying. Nod appreciatively when appropriate and respond to what each has to say.

The first conference is essentially a "get acquainted" meeting to establish a pattern of expectations. If students have not prepared well, tell them what they might do for the next time. They might need to practice their oral reading selection at home, into the tape recorder or with a reading partner. Perhaps they did not understand the questions. Be clear about what you expect from them and recheck their understanding before they leave the conference.

When you ask questions during the conference, your first purpose will be to assess the student's involvement with the book. The second purpose is to help students expand their understanding by encouraging them to reflect on their experience. Certain types of questions accomplish these purposes better than others, and these are described below.

1. **Open-ended** These are questions that begin with why, what or how and require students to organize their thinking: Why do you think Caddie Woodlawn disliked her cousin? What kinds of problems did the early settlers have with raising crops? How did the spiders rescue their father? Questions that can be answered either "yes" or "no" provide little information about what students have understood or learned.

2. **Experience-related** These questions help children relate what they have read to their own experience: Can you connect this book to anything in your own experience? Do you know anyone who had an experience like this? Do you know anyone like this character? Have you ever been anyplace like this?

3. **Expanding** These questions help students extend their ideas about what they have read and stretch their ability to answer: What kinds of problems would you have today if you wanted to sell an invention? Why do you think immigrants want to come to the United States? If this fantasy were true, how would it affect space travel?

4. **Point of view** These questions encourage students to consider other points of view in the story: Why do you think the principal was so strict? Can you think of any reason why the bully acted this way? How would this situation look if you were the dog?

The way you ask questions and respond to student answers will also influence the quality of your discussion. Be alert to the following:

1. **Give time for the student to answer.** Avoid rapid-fire questions and encourage thoughtful and reflective answers.
2. **Encourage original answers.** Comment positively on creative responses or responses new to you, such as: "I never thought of it that way" or "That's really a new way of looking at the whole problem."
3. **Be genuine.** Ask questions because you really want to know the student's ideas, not ones to help him or her guess what you have in mind: "What did you think about Chibi?" "What impressed you the most about Sam's experience in the woods?"
4. **Encourage** students as they talk to you by saying such things as: "Go on." "And then what happened?" "How do you think he/she felt?" "Why do you think that happened?"

There are four major categories of questions that will help you evaluate student involvement with a book. You will want to know something about their personal response to the story or presentation; how well they understood the major ideas of what they read; their proficiency in observing details and decoding unfamiliar words; and their oral reading ability. You may want to add other categories to fit your particular situation, but the following explore some of the basic areas of reading skill development.

Personal Response   These questions help assess the reader's identification with the characters, situation or values and help students gain insight into the behavior of the characters in the story:

What did you like about this book?
Who was your favorite character?
Who did you most admire in this story?
Did any of the characters remind you of anyone you know?
Have you ever had to face a similar challenge?
Why do you think this character did this?
Why do you think this character changed beliefs? behavior?
What do you think of this character's behavior?
Could this character have done this differently?

Comprehension   This type of question helps students look for the main idea of a story, make inferences, read critically and assess the purpose of the author:

What was this story about?
Tell me the story.
Did this story have a message?
What do you think the main character learned?
What happened first, next?

What happened in the beginning of the story, the middle, the end?
Why do you think this character did this?
What would have happened if this character did this instead of that?
How would this story change in a different setting? (geographical, historical)
What do you think the author wanted you to feel when you read this book?
Why do you think the author wrote this story?

Mechanics

These kinds of questions help you observe students' skill in word analysis, pronunciation, vocabulary, study skills and attention to details:

What does this word say?
Does it look like any other word you know?
Can you tell what this word is by reading other words around it?
Can you figure out this word by looking at the pictures?
How did you figure out the pronunciation of this word?
How did you figure out what this word means?
What sound does this word start with? end with?
What is the sound in the middle? How do you know?
Show me how you use the index, table of contents, glossary.
Can you show me where this is on the map?
How did you find out more about this place, time, author, book?
Where in the story did it tell about . . . ?
Did that happen in the beginning? middle? end?
What do these pictures (photographs, drawings, paintings) tell you about the story? characters? setting? mood?

Sense of Audience

These questions involve a demonstration of skill in oral reading, interpretation and retelling a story briefly:

Read me your favorite part, page, paragraph, scene.
Read something about your favorite character, setting.
What have you decided to read to me?
What are you going to share with me today?
Can you show me how the author might hear this character talking?
Can you show me how the author might want this scene read?
Would this character talk in a special way?
Can you show me with your voice how scared, happy, angry, hurt this character was?
Can you show me with your voice how windy, cold, hot, stormy the weather was?
Very quickly, tell me the main parts of the story.
Tell me the story in your own words.

How to End a Conference

This is a critical time for the conference. Some children will have a lot to share with you, and you do not want to dampen their spirits or enthusiasm. On the other hand, having time limits makes the entire process work. The main goal is to bring the conference to a conclusion in a satisfying way. Some teachers set a small timer, which is an impersonal reminder. This lets both parties know that there is still one minute to wrap up the conversation.

During this time, you can summarize what has happened in the conference, show personal interest in the student and assign any necessary practice. Here are some examples:

Summarizing the Conference

"You shared a lot of information with me about whales. You've learned about where they live, how they communicate and why they're endangered. You also showed me how you figured out many technical terms. I really enjoyed the part you read to me about whales singing."

"Thanks for sharing your book about the daughter of Chief Joseph. You told me a lot about Native American life and why you're so interested in it. You also did good background research about the Nez Perce. I enjoyed it all."

"You put a lot of work into this conference. It was a difficult book to read, and you had to look up many words to understand it. You also figured out some complex maps and charts to show me where the ship sailed."

Showing Personal Interest

"You really chose a challenging book. I can tell you learned a lot of information from it."
"This was really an interesting conference."
"You got me so interested in this book, I want to read it myself."
"Our conversation about this book makes me want to read it again."
"I can tell that you really liked this book."
"It's obvious that you did a lot of preparation for this conference."
"You really like stories about space, don't you? What do you plan to read next?"
"Our time is up for now, but I'll look forward to hearing about your next book."

Making Assignments

Immediate "We worked today on finding the number of syllables in a word. When you go back to your desk, write a list of your ten favorite words from your book and put the number of syllables in each word next to it. Put the paper on my desk for checking."

Weekly "While you're reading this week, see if you can find some examples of onomatopoeia. Write down anything you find in your notebook and bring it to your next conference."

For review "You were really enthusiastic about your story today, but you're having trouble remembering how the plot progresses and the order of events. Go back and review the important parts of the story, so that you know what happens after the shots are fired at Lexington, where the boy spends the rest of the day and how he finally finds his way home."

Lack of preparation "There are some things you need to practice to improve your reading. Would you like to read this book again to practice these things or choose a new one?" (Offer a choice.)

The book chosen is too difficult "This book may be too difficult for right now. Choose a new one you'd like to read and we'll do the Rule of Thumb on it together." (Review self-selection techniques.)

Repeated difficulty in choosing books "Here are ten books about dinosaurs (cars, space, pioneers). Choose one or two that you like." (Provide books at an appropriate reading level in the student's interest area.)

WHAT DO YOU Do you like to talk to other people about books? What kinds of things
THINK? do you share about the books you are reading? Do you ever ask other
people about what they are reading? What do you enjoy most about
these conversations? From the questions asked above, which do you
like the best? Which would you enjoy responding to about a favorite
book? Choose a few questions in each category and use them to think
about a book you have recently read.

VII.   If This Is Your Situation

Some schools or districts require the use of basal reading materials for
instruction. It is possible to use these materials and still retain the individual
reading conferences for your students. Instead of meeting in small ability
groups, students can choose stories in the reader for their conferences. Many
basal programs currently draw their excerpts from high-quality children's
trade books, and you can encourage children to explore the books from
which the excerpts are taken. Other programs feature collections of paperback books, which can be used both for individual and guided reading. As
they are needed by individual students, duplicated materials and workbooks
can be used for practicing specific skills.

If you modify a school reading program, it is important to reassure
supervisors or parents that students will be learning the same skills as
effectively as they would under the standard program. You can do this by
putting your plan in writing, describing what you will be doing and how you
will be utilizing the materials provided by the district. If you use a checklist
of the curriculum objectives for each student in your class, you will also be
able to document student progress and achievement in an impressive way.

It is important to maintain good communication with parents by involving them in practice and enrichment activities with their children's reading.
Principals and supervisors appreciate hearing success stories and will usually
support alternative approaches to using materials if they are kept informed.
The Creating Partners section of this chapter provides suggestions for
developing this involvement.

VIII.   Evaluating Progress

Individual conferences allow you to observe each student interact with
books. From these observations you discover the skills already mastered and
those needed to be taught or practiced. Sample observation lists and evaluation guidelines are included at the end of this chapter (Figures 6.1, 6.2, 6.3),
but they are intended only as a guide. You will want to modify these or create
your own in terms of your own teaching situation.

Begin by carefully reviewing the curriculum objectives for your grade
level. Create a checklist from these objectives and duplicate the checklist

for every student in your classroom. Place the name of each student at the top of a separate page and place these forms in a three-ring notebook. To track skill development across the class, record skills across the top of a page in a standard grade book. At the end of the week, patterns will emerge to inform the content of guided reading and mini-lessons.

You will also want to provide your students with guidelines to help them prepare for their individual conferences. Sample guidelines can be found at the end of the chapter to help students identify the genres they are reading (Figures 6.4, 6.5, 6.6, 6.7) and assist them as they prepare for the conference (Figures 6.8, 6.9, 6.10). Assemble a list of questions to ask your students about their reading and duplicate enough of these lists to have at least a month's supply on hand. For each conference, place the question form and the skills checklist so that they open in the notebook facing each other. This allows you to move back and forth easily between questions and the checklist. From the information gained in these individual conferences, you will discover the particular skills students need to learn.

When a number of students indicate that they need instruction in a particular area, you can create a mini-lesson. Mini-lessons are brief presentations on a single topic that are drawn from students' need to understand a particular concept or practice a particular skill. In reading conferences, you may simply give the information to a child directly. If many children in the class need assistance in a particular area, you can plan a mini-lesson for the entire class. In each case, however, the instruction should be related directly to favorite literature, and students should have sufficient time to practice the new skill or strategy. Further information about planning and preparing for mini-lessons is included in Chapter 9.

WHAT DO YOU THINK? Do you think it is possible to know a child's reading ability without individual conferences? How were you grouped for reading instruction when you were in elementary school? Did you feel either pride or humiliation because of the ability group you were in? Did you ever experience individual reading conferences in elementary school? Do you think it will be difficult to plan for learning experiences you have not had yourself? How might you address this problem?

IX. Creating Partners

Many parents, especially those at the kindergarten and primary levels, will approach you to ask how they can help their child succeed in school. Using the information you gain from individual reading conferences, you can provide direction for parents who want to assist their children's reading development.

At the beginning of the year when you meet with parents, or in a letter sent home, you can tell them you will be assigning homework that will help develop the reading skills of each child in the classroom. Explain that homework assignments will rotate among such activities as reading aloud to someone in the family, recording oral reading, reading independently, writing for a purpose, and practicing skills and strategies that will help them become better readers and writers.

You will be giving each child an assignment for a skill or strategy to practice at the close of each conference period. Intermediate-level students will record these assignments in notebooks, but at the kindergarten and early primary levels, you might write the assignment on an index card to be placed inside a favorite book to take home. Tell parents they can help their children develop their reading skill by asking them to discuss what they need to practice and then observing this practice for a few minutes each day. You might also ask parents to encourage their child to read aloud to them from a chapter book each night. For busy parents, this reading can accompany preparing a meal, washing dishes or folding clothes. Children enjoy reading to their parents, and parents will find these sessions equally rewarding.

WHAT DO YOU THINK? How did your parents involve themselves in your schooling? Did you ever read aloud to anyone at home? If not, is this an activity you would have enjoyed? What are the benefits to children when parents play an active role in their learning?

X. Perspectives

Jerome Bruner, who was introduced in Chapters 1 and 5 of this text, believes that teachers play an important part in students' learning by encouraging them to explore alternatives and discover new relationships. According to Bruner, children are intrinsically motivated to learn. They learn constantly because they are curious, possess an innate drive for competence and are eager to interact with others. Bruner believes that teachers can take advantage of this intrinsic will to learn by:

Activating children's curiosity. An example of this is reading aloud from interesting books, asking questions to create interest in an idea, and providing stimulating print materials for children to explore.

Maintaining exploration. Once children become involved in exploring an idea or looking for a solution, they must be convinced that the classroom setting is the best place to do this exploration, because learning with the direction of a teacher, in this case, is physically safer, more effective or more rewarding than learning on their own.

Directing exploration. To be meaningful, exploration must have direction. Teachers assist children by helping them visualize goals and determine if the activities they participate in are relevant to the achievement of these goals.

In addition to this first principle of instruction, which is motivation, Bruner also describes three other principles—structure, sequence and reinforcement—that help teachers create effective learning environments for students. You may want to explore these ideas further in his book *Toward a Theory of Instruction*.[24]

WHAT DO YOU THINK? From your own elementary school days, can you remember an instance when your curiosity was activated by an experience in the classroom? Can you think of any experiences where someone helped you explore an idea or suggested ways to help you reach a goal?

XI. Exploring Professional Literature

Primary Voices K–6[25] is a journal for language arts educators who teach elementary children and is designed for teachers who want to explore the relationship between theory and practice in the classroom. Each issue is produced by a different literacy group, such as a school, instructional team, TAWL group or NCTE affiliate, which addresses a particular topic in the curriculum, such as writing to learn or inquiry-based instruction.

Each issue is introduced by an article that establishes the theoretical framework for the discussion and is written by a key professional in the field, such as Donald Graves, Dorothy Strickland or Jerome Harste. This statement is followed by three articles that provide classroom portraits of the topic. Each article demonstrates how the particular practice looks in a specific classroom and includes descriptions and examples of student activities. Writers talk about the problems they faced and list questions they still have about their classroom progress. Each article usually includes helpful bibliographies and outlines of the classroom program.

Primary Voices K–6 is published four times a year by the National Council of Teachers of English. It can be ordered separately for a modest price or be included as an option in NCTE membership. Information about subscriptions is available from the National Council of Teachers of English, 1111 W. Kenyon Road, Urbana, IL 61801-1096, or by calling 217-328-3870.

WHAT DO YOU THINK? Examine a copy of *Primary Voices K–6*. What interested you about the way the journal was structured? Did you learn anything helpful from any of the articles? How might it be helpful to read about teachers who are exploring the applications of theory in their classrooms?

XII. Resources for Teaching

Students enjoy hearing stories about their favorite authors and illustrators. The following books are excellent sources of information and anecdotes about authors and illustrators of children's literature:

The Sixth Book of Junior Authors and Illustrators,[26] edited by Sally Holm Holtze, is a collection of personal autobiographical statements by children's authors and illustrators. Entries include artists and writers who have come to prominence since the previous publication in 1983. Most libraries have copies of the entire set, beginning with *The Junior Book of Authors* published in 1935. Entries are arranged in alphabetical order. There is an helpful index and a cross reference for pen names.

Meet the Authors and Illustrators[27] by Deborah Kovacs and James Preller is part of the Scholastic Reference Library collection. It contains biographies of sixty award-winning authors and illustrators and is presented in a highly readable manner that makes the information accessible to both teachers and students. Each entry includes a picture, selected titles, descriptions of the author's or illustrator's life and challenges each faced in writing or illustrating. There are also suggestions for young artists or writers to try on their own, an excellent feature that provides an artist's perspective on the creative process.

XIII. Reflections

From a Teacher's Journal—Pat Sheahan, Second Grade

Many children in my class receive help from Chapter and LD resource programs. I involve these children in hands-on activities for immediate success. Paper and pencil tasks often defeat and discourage these children. Learning centers allow active children to be out of their seats, participating in a variety of activities in a cooperative context. I also observe the attraction between these children and particular authors, and then make sure that many of these authors' books are available.

I believe that students learn best when they are involved in activities that are both purposeful and functional in their daily lives. The classroom needs to be full of print: books, magazines, dictionaries, encyclopedias, newspapers, telephone books, menus, maps, posters and labels. All kinds of bulletin boards, charts and signs should provide interesting information to read, and there should be as many opportunities as possible for children to interact with computers, audiotapes, and hands-on science activities.

I keep a notebook divided into sections for each child. I date and write comments on various skills: writing sentences; spelling; newspaper activities; creating story maps; math skills; grammar skills; understanding in content areas. I observe children closely when they are working at the centers or are engaged in reading or writing activities and then use this information to create mini-lessons that one or more of the children may need.

The first year that I moved toward a more integrated language approach in my classroom, I occasionally wondered if all the skills were being presented as thoroughly as they had previously been. In early March, our school district administered the Iowa Test of Basic Skills. As I gave the directions, one of my students excitedly announced, "Mrs. Sheahan, we did this in a mini-lesson!"

TRYING OUT THE CHAPTER IDEAS Although it is helpful to observe other teachers conducting conferences, it is important to begin getting this first-hand experience yourself. Practice your conferencing skills with any child who is willing to talk about a book; practice interviewing cooperative friends or family members. Conferencing is a skill that will improve with practice. Don't worry if these first attempts stretch out beyond the time limits. You will gradually develop a sense of what is important and how to move the conference along. The following exercises are designed to help you develop confidence and competence in conferencing.

Warm-up Exercise #1
Read a favorite picture book, a short novel and a longer novel. Choose both fiction and nonfiction examples.

Respond to a question from each category on the skills checklist: comprehension, vocabulary, word analysis, study skill, interpretation.

What questions were most interesting to you? Which ones made you think about what you had read?

Warm-up Exercise #2
Observe someone else conducting a conference, either a teacher or a classmate.

Conduct a conference with a classmate. Take turns asking questions and taking notes on your observations.

Warm-up Exercise #3
From one of the books you read above, practice making connections between the story and your own experience. What kinds of ideas or memories did the book create for you? What did you already know or what experiences did you bring to this book that made it meaningful? What connections did you notice in the book between characters? the plot and setting? the illustrations and story?

Notes

1. Karen Gallas, *The Languages of Learning: How Children Talk, Write, Dance, Draw, and Sing Their Understanding of the World* (New York: Teachers College Press, 1994).
2. M. Cochran-Smith, *The Making of a Reader* (Norwood, N.J.: Ablex, 1984).
3. S. B. Heath, *Ways with Words: Language, Life, and Work in Communities and Classrooms* (Cambridge, Mass.: Harvard University Press, 1983).
4. James Britton, "Response to Literature," in *Response to Literature*, edited by J. R. Squire (Champaign, Ill.: National Council of Teachers of English, 1968), pp. 3–9.
5. B. Keifer, "The Child and the Picture Book: Creating Live Circuits," *Children's Literature Association Quarterly* 11(1986):63–68.
6. J. Hickman, "A New Perspective on Response to Literature: Research in an Elementary School Setting," *Research in the Teaching of English* 15(1981):343–354.
7. Denise Fleming, *In the Tall, Tall Grass* (New York: Henry Holt, 1991).
8. Gerald McDermott, *Anansi the Spider: A Tale from the Ashanti* (New York: Holt, Rinehart & Winston, 1972).
9. Blaise Cendrars, *Shadow* (New York: Macmillan, 1982). An exploration of the world of shadows, featuring cut-paper shapes in an African setting.
10. Molly Bang, *Ten, Nine, Eight* (New York: Penguin, 1983). A counting book that features the bedtime of an African American child.
11. Hiawyn Oram, *A Boy Wants a Dinosaur* (New York: Farrar, Straus & Giroux, 1990).
12. Fran Manushkin, *Latkes and Applesauce: A Hanukkah Story* (New York: Scholastic, Inc., 1990).

13. Eric A. Kimmel, *The Chanukkah Guest* (New York: Holiday House, 1988).

14. Jean Craighead George, *My Side of the Mountain* (New York: Trumpet Club, 1988).

15. Karen Hesse, *Letters from Rifka* (New York: Henry Holt, 1992; Trumpet Club, 1993).

16. William Rose Benet, *Benet's Reader's Encyclopedia*, 3d ed. (New York: HarperCollins, 1987), p. 801.

17. Sook Nyul Choi, *Year of Impossible Goodbyes* (New York: Houghton Mifflin, 1991).

18. David Kherdian, *The Road from Home: The Story of an Armenian Girl* (New York: Scholastic, 1992).

19. Jane Yolen, *The Devil's Arithmetic* (New York: Viking, 1988).

20. Lois Lowry, *Number the Stars* (Boston: Houghton Mifflin, 1989).

21. Paula Fox, *Monkey Island* (New York: Orchard Books, 1991).

22. Felice Holman, *Slake's Limbo* (New York: Scholastic, 1974).

23. Doris Gates, *Blue Willow* (New York: Scholastic, 1968).

24. Jerome Bruner, *Toward a Theory of Instruction* (Cambridge, Mass.: Harvard University Press, 1966).

25. *Primary Voices K–6*, National Council of Teachers of English (Urbana, Ill.: NCTE, published quarterly).

26. Sally Holm Holtze, ed., *The Sixth Book of Junior Authors and Illustrators* (New York: H. W. Wilson, 1989).

27. Deborah Kovacs and James Preller, *Meet the Authors and Illustrators* (New York: Scholastic, 1991).

SKILLS CHECKLIST: KINDERGARTEN

Key: + = Achieved

1. **Recognizes these words:**

2. **Letter recognition:**
   Capitals
   Lower case

3. **Initial sounds**

4. **Ending sounds**

5. **Rhymes**

6. **Vowels: long, short**

7. **Blends**

8. **Punctuation:**
   Period
   Question mark
   Exclamation point

9. **Student understands:**
   Main idea
   Characters
   Author
   Fiction/Nonfiction
   Illustrations

10. **Student has read these books:**

FIGURE 6.1
Skills checklist for kindergarten level.

SKILLS CHECKLIST: PRIMARY

Key: + = Acceptable   / = Needs work   ? = Check again

Oral reading:
Smooth
Unhesitant
Pleasant tone
Good rate
Accurate

Uses:
Context
Index
Table of contents
Maps
Graphs
Illustrations
Endings—rhymes

Can recognize or apply:
Two-vowel rule
Vowels + R
Silent E
Vowels: long, short
Vowel diphthongs: long and short oo, au, oi
Syllables
Compound words
Consonant digraphs: sh, ch, ph, th
Soft C
Soft G

FIGURE 6.2
Skills checklist for primary level.

SKILLS CHECKLIST: INTERMEDIATE

Key: + = identifies   / = unsure

1. **Figurative language**
   Simile
   Metaphor
   Personification
   Irony
2. **Onomatopoeia**
3. **Synonyms**
4. **Antonyms**
5. **Homonyms**
6. **Homographs**
7. **Foreshadowing**
8. **Plot**
9. **Character development**
10. **Main idea**
11. **Genres**

FIGURE 6.3
Skills checklist for intermediate level.

```
IDENTIFYING THE GENRE: KINDERGARTEN

Symbols for individual portfolios and chart display:
    Toy books—picture of a toy
    Easy-to-read—book with words
    Wordless—book with pictures
    Counting—numbers
    Alphabet—letters
    Nursery rhymes—Mother Goose
    Concept—time, length, opposites
```

FIGURE 6.4
Identifying genre for kindergarten level.

```
IDENTIFYING THE GENRE: PRIMARY
```

I. Is this book about real persons, places or things? Then it is **nonfiction**. Write the name of the book in the space below.

   What kind of nonfiction book is it? Underline the one that best describes your book.

   > Biography—tells the story of a famous person's life.
   > Informational—gives information about such things as science, health, math, history, geography, art, people, weather, animals, plants, space.
   > Entertainment—puzzles, jokes, riddles, puns, cartoons.

   What kinds of things help you enjoy and understand this book? Underline all that apply.

index	charts
table of contents	maps
illustrations	glossary
drawings	preface
pictures	afterword

II. Does this book tell a story that was made up by the author? If it does, then it is **fiction**. Write the name of the book in the space below.

   What kind of fiction book is it? Read the descriptions and underline the one that best describes your book.

   > Traditional stories—myths, legends, folktales, fairy tales or tall tales. They sometimes begin with the words "Once upon a time . . ." or "A long time ago . . ." There may be strange creatures, great powers, magic and great bravery.

   > Modern fantasy—stories about things that couldn't happen, such as animals talking, time travel, tiny people who live in clocks. They are similar to traditional stories, but they take place in more recent time.

   > Historical fiction—stories from history that might have real persons, places or events, but the story is imagined.

   > Contemporary fiction—stories that are about everyday life.

III. Does your book have verses that rhyme or have rhythm or repetition?
   Then your book is a **poetry** book. Write the name of the book in the space below.

   What kind of poetry book is it? Underline the ones that apply.

   > Narrative poem—tells a story
   > Lyrical poetry—verses that sing
   > Poetry collections—a number of verses about one thing
   > Anthology—a collection of many kinds of poems

FIGURE 6.5
Identifying genre for primary level.

```
┌──────────────────────────────────────────────────────────────┐
│            IDENTIFYING THE GENRE: INTERMEDIATE                 │
│                                                                │
│  How to use this form:                                         │
│        First ask the question: Is this book fiction (a story), │
│        nonfiction (facts or information) or poetry (written in │
│        verse)?                                                 │
│        When you have answered question #1, then ask: What kind │
│        of fiction (nonfiction or poetry) is this? Check the    │
│        categories for the characteristics of your book:        │
│                                                                │
│  Fiction—A book that tells a story created by the author.      │
│        Traditional stories—myths, legends, folktales, fairy    │
│        tales, or tall tales. They sometimes begin with the     │
│        words "Once upon a time . . ." or "A long time ago . . ."│
│        There are strange creatures, great powers, magic and    │
│        great bravery.                                          │
│        Modern fantasy—stories about things that couldn't       │
│        happen, such as animals talking, time travel, tiny      │
│        people who live in clocks. These stories may be similar │
│        to traditional stories, but they take place in more     │
│        recent time.                                            │
│        Historical fiction—stories from history that might have │
│        real persons, places or events, but the story is        │
│        imagined.                                               │
│        Contemporary fiction—stories about everyday life,       │
│        created by an author.                                   │
│                                                                │
│  Nonfiction—A book that is a true story or gives true          │
│  information.                                                  │
│        Biography—the story of a real person's life, usually    │
│        someone whose achievements or courage have made a       │
│        significant contribution to others.                     │
│        Informational books—books that describe or explain      │
│        words or ideas about history, science, geography, math, │
│        science, music, art, or sports.                         │
│        Entertainment books—collections of jokes, riddles,      │
│        tongue-twisters, palindromes, puzzles and cartoons.     │
│        They add humor or challenge your mind.                  │
│                                                                │
│  Special features of this informational book:                 │
│                                                                │
│        index                  table of contents                │
│        maps                   glossary of terms                │
│        charts                 photographs                      │
│        pictures               afterword                        │
│        drawings               notes                            │
│                                                                │
└──────────────────────────────────────────────────────────────┘
```

FIGURE 6.6
Identifying genre for intermediate level.

READING EVERY KIND OF LITERATURE: INTERMEDIATE

A Genre Checklist

Underline each kind of book as you read it. Beside each type of book, write the country or culture of its origin. Where provided, underline the appropriate category. Write the title of the book in the space below the category.

Legend	Country/Culture:
Myth	Country/Culture:
Folktale	Country/Culture:
Fairy tale	Country/Culture:
Tall tale	Country/Culture:
Fable	Country/Culture:
Modern fantasy	Country/Culture:
Historical fiction	U.S.: Colonial Revolutionary War Pioneer Civil War Twentieth century: WWI WWII Korean War Vietnam War Other
Historical fiction	Asia Europe Africa South America Canada Middle East Other
Contemporary fiction	U.S.
Contemporary fiction	Asia Europe Africa South America Canada Middle East Other
Poetry	U.S. European African Asian Hispanic Native American Lyric Narrative Ballad Concrete Free verse Haiku Other
Biography	U.S. European African Asian Hispanic Native American Other
Informational	Science History Geography Art Math Health Space Sports Other
Environment	
Multicultural	Genre:
Picture books	Genre:
Entertainment	Puzzles Jokes Riddles Cartoons Other

FIGURE 6.7
Genre checklist for intermediate level.

STUDENT CONFERENCE PREPARATION: PRIMARY

1. **Pages to read aloud**
2. **Pictures to show**
3. **Problems**
   How I solved them
4. **Difficult words**
   How I figured them out
5. **What the story was about**
6. **My favorite part**
7. **Why I liked or didn't like the book**
8. **Kind of book**

FIGURE 6.8
Student conference preparation for primary level.

STUDENT CONFERENCE PREPARATION: INTERMEDIATE

1. Prepare a short passage to read aloud (one or two paragraphs) from your book. Write the page number beside #1 in your reading notebook.
2. When you read aloud to the teacher, tell what happened before the part where you read. After you read, tell what happened afterward.
3. These are some things you might talk about during conferences. Make notes or record page numbers to help you remember your responses.

What words were difficult? How did you solve the difficulty?
What ideas or situations were hard to understand?
What was the story about?
Can you briefly tell what happened?
What did you like most about this book?
What was your favorite part of the book? your favorite character? your favorite picture(s)? (if applicable)
What kind of book is this? (Use the genre identification form.)
Have you read any books like this one before? same genre or same topic?
Did this story have a message?
How did the author make the characters real?
How did the author establish the mood of the story?
If this book is informational, what kind of special features helped you understand the material? (indexes, maps, pictures, photographs)
Note anything else you'd like to talk about.

FIGURE 6.9
Student conference preparation for intermediate level.

CONFERENCE MEMO

Name _____

Book _____

A question I'd like to answer:

_____

_____

_____

_____

_____

_____

_____

Plans for sharing the book:

_____

_____

_____

_____

_____

_____

_____

_____

_____

_____

FIGURE 6.10
Sample conference memo.

CHAPTER SEVEN

Listening and Speaking

WHAT'S HAPPENING HERE? Griswold, the class mascot, has just returned from an overnight visit to this student's home. She and her parents wrote an account of Griswold's visit in his journal, which the teacher will read aloud to the class. The student will also talk about the picture she has drawn of Griswold and answer questions from other students about the visit.

One ought, every day at least, to hear a little song, read a good poem, see a fine picture, and, if it were possible, to speak a few reasonable words.

—Johann Wolfgang von Goethe

LOOKING AHEAD
1. How do listening and speaking help children learn to read and write?
2. Why is it important for children to read aloud well?
3. What are some guidelines for class conversations?
4. What is exploratory talk?
5. What is the importance of sharing responses to literature?
6. How do "shared-pair" discussions work?
7. What is reader's theater?
8. How can puppetry help develop speaking and listening skills?
9. How do you prepare for Friday Afternoon Sharing Time?

IN 25 WORDS OR LESS   Students' speaking and listening skills improve with increased opportunities to speak and listen in a variety of contexts for a variety of purposes.

I. Focus: Speaking and Listening in the Classroom

Although most teachers would agree that speaking and listening are important language skills, it has not always been evident how to provide for their practice in the classroom. In traditional classrooms, student talk is frequently discouraged because it is believed to be distracting to the academic environment. Desks are arranged in straight rows, and students are encouraged to keep their eyes straight ahead or on their own paper. Exchange of ideas between students typically occurs in whole-class discussions, which necessarily limits the number of participants.

Teachers who integrate language learning into the curriculum believe that speaking and listening are developed through practice. They also believe that students can practice thinking skills by participating in **exploratory talk** about all areas of the curriculum. This informal speech allows students to explore ideas and increase their understanding of concepts in science, mathematics and the social studies. Teachers who integrate language learning into the content areas provide many opportunities throughout the day for students to interact by talking and listening to each other. In pairs, small groups and whole-class situations, students share their thoughts, persuade, explain, problem solve and respond to each other's ideas. Students usually self-select membership in these flexible groups and are drawn to individual discussions by interest in the topic or compatibility with other group members. This interaction is planned and monitored by the teacher, who helps the groups develop productive guidelines for their discussions. In contrast to the straight rows of the traditional classroom, furniture is flexibly arranged to promote interaction or privacy, according to the purpose of individual activities.

Opportunities to speak and listen in the classroom build on one of the most powerful motivations children bring to school: the desire to share their ideas and experiences with others. They are eager to talk about what they have seen, heard or thought about and want to know what someone else thinks about what they have to say. They are also interested in the activities and stories of other students. Jerome Bruner refers to these elements of natural learning as reciprocity[1] (the desire to interact with others) and narration[2] (the telling of stories about our experiences). Providing opportunities for both spontaneous and formal sharing of ideas and experiences through talking and listening encourages the practice and refinement of these critical skills.

What kinds of activities provide this practice? In classrooms that integrate language learning, students are sharing constantly, in formal and spontaneous situations. They talk together about topics of mutual interest, read to each other and share their writing aloud to a variety of listeners. With some modifications, students at all grade levels recite poems, sing songs, create charts, talk about content area learning and discuss books they have read. Students are encouraged to reflect on the experiences they talk about and are given opportunities to relate these experiences to others they have had. Before they write, they share ideas with other students in prewriting activities. First drafts are brought to writing workshops to read aloud and discuss. During independent study time, students meet in small groups to discuss content area projects and plan oral reports.

In these classrooms there are also activities that are specifically planned to provide practice for speaking and listening skills. They include opportunities for students to read aloud, preview books for an audience, interact in small groups to discuss and persuade, create puppet shows, participate in reader's theater or creative drama and make presentations for regular weekly sharing sessions.

Oral Reading   In the traditional classroom, oral reading was usually confined to round-robin reading in ability groups or taking turns reading aloud with the whole class from science or social studies textbooks. More recently, teachers who integrate language learning into the curriculum are providing increased opportunities for students to read aloud because they believe that it is important for every child to read well for an audience. This skill helps students see how their own interpretation of a writer's ideas adds to someone else's understanding and appreciation. From oral reading, students learn to assume the minds of their audience and to adjust their expression to achieve maximum audience response. Reading aloud for a purpose provides practice in analyzing the tone of literature and sensing the creative relationship between text and reader. Students learn how to vary their expression according to the material being read and how to use their voice to achieve different reading purposes. With practice they develop the ability to adjust the volume, tone and pitch of their voices to produce a variety of effects.

Book Previews

In a regular cycle that includes everyone in the class, students are given the opportunity to talk to their classmates on a daily basis about books that interest them. These are informal presentations that provide practice for speaking skills in a relaxed context. This activity also assists literature study groups because it identifies persons who might have the same interests. Previews are usually scheduled immediately before or after independent reading sessions in order to provide students the opportunity to interest others in the books they are reading.

Shared-Pair Discussion

This activity provides opportunities for students to combine critical thinking with listening. Pairs of students discuss both sides of an issue until they arrive at a consensus. Then this pair switches partners with another pair of students to continue the debate and compare notes. Both pairs form a small group to further discuss the issue; this group in turn elects a spokesperson to discuss its ideas in a whole-class setting. This activity provides talking, thinking and listening practice for every student in the classroom. Those who are shy or hesitant benefit from these increased opportunities to express their ideas in one-to-one and small-group discussions. It also benefits the more verbal students who have additional opportunities to express their ideas in a group.

Creative Drama

This is a process-oriented activity that helps students draw on their own thoughts and feelings to examine human experience. Through creative drama, students explore movement, sound, speech, character, sequence, story and their environment. Through the power of imagination, students enter the setting of a story and become its characters. They consider and dramatize the answer to questions such as: How does the wind feel on top of a mountain? What does a lonely Irish immigrant think about as she huddles in the dark hold of a ship? What does Narnia really look like?

Groupings for this activity may involve the entire class or a small group of students who create dialogue for characters in a favorite story and act out the parts. Pairs of students or individuals might create a soliloquy or act multiple parts in a drama. These exercises help develop an appreciation for the methods and literature of the theater and are appropriate to use at all elementary instructional levels.

Reader's Theater

Students enjoy reading plays together or making stories into plays. This activity provides excellent opportunities to practice and improve oral reading expression. It can involve the entire class in a production or small groups of four to six persons, who read a play based on a book that they have read. When these dramas are purchased commercially, they usually consist of a set of six books and a guide, with a model script that can be duplicated and distributed to students. It is also possible, and less expensive, for students to create these dramas themselves from books that feature dialogue between characters. Reading plays is an excellent activity for literature study groups. It helps students "try on" the experience and mind-set of other persons. Participants in drama learn to better understand the motives of others and to experiment with ways to behave in a setting that allows the consequences to educate or inform rather than penalize.

Puppet Shows

Puppets allow students to express themselves imaginatively and with ease. These wonderful speaking props permit even the most hesitant children to have magical powers as they create characters and action for an audience. Puppets can be as simple as moving a sock on one hand or as involved as a drama, with props, sound effects and costumes. Creating puppet shows can help stimulate critical thinking, develop planning skills and encourage children to assess the effects of sound and movement. This is another speaking and listening activity that is appropriate and effective throughout all elementary grade levels.

Friday Afternoon Sharing Time (FAST)[3]

In many classrooms additional time is set aside for sharing responses to literature with the entire class or visitors such as parents, the principal and other classes. These presentations encourage students to practice their skills of organizing information, preparing material for an audience and public speaking. Each student also participates as an active audience member, learning both critical and appreciative listening skills.

At every age, students are interested in what other students are doing. They like to see what others have written, researched and created. Because there are endless ways to respond creatively to literature, all students have the opportunity to demonstrate individual strengths in their responses. These sharing times help develop a sense of competence and self-worth in the presenters and provide a pleasant experience for members of the audience.

Sharing times are generally scheduled for Friday afternoons from 2:00 to 3:00, the traditional time for cleaning desks, drill practice, worksheets, puzzles and games. Teachers have sometimes regarded this final period of the week as throwaway time because students are worn out or too distracted to give academic matters their full attention. But in classrooms where students read and write about topics that interest them and have many opportunities to express their responses, they are energized by the chance to share what they have experienced with others. Once students have experienced the pleasure of these presentations, they approach them with anticipation and give them their full attention.

Through the week, students respond to books they have read with writing, drawing, research or creative projects. During FAST, they share these responses with the entire class or in small interest groups. This sharing may involve **displays** of writing—book covers, bookmarks, cartoons, magazines, newspapers and artistic creations. Students may also create **presentations**, such as puppet shows, pantomimes, game shows, interviews, news broadcasts or five-minute dramas. Sometimes they just want to read aloud from a book that is particularly interesting to them or share poetry that is beautiful or humorous.

WHAT DO YOU
THINK? What do you remember about opportunities to practice speaking when
you were in elementary school? How do you feel about speaking before
an audience today? Are you a good listener? Who in your life has been
a good listener? What kinds of behavior does a good listener exhibit?

II. The Importance of Listening and Speaking

For many years, language arts educators have agreed on the importance of
being able to listen and speak effectively. In a joint statement more than
thirty years ago by the National Council of Teachers of English, the International Reading Association, the Association for Childhood Education
International and the Association for Supervision and Curriculum Development, the authors of *Children and Oral Language*[4] said:

> We share with all educators the concern about written communication and
> the recognition that reading skills are basic to all learning. But we have voiced
> the need for equal concern about educating all children to be effective
> speakers and listeners. . . . The ability to speak and listen effectively is
> probably the most important asset that [they] can acquire and maintain
> throughout a lifetime. (p. 36)

More recently, in a report of *The English Coalition Conference: Democracy
Through Language*,[5] listening and speaking were recognized as central to both
communication and learning. Communication skills permit effective social
interaction, assist students as they seek knowledge and help them display
what they know.

> Students not only must know the content of academic subjects, they must
> learn the appropriate form in which to cast their knowledge. That is,
> competent membership in the classroom community involves employing
> interactional skills and abilities in the display of academic knowledge. They
> must know with whom, when, and where they can speak and act, and they
> must provide the speech and behavior that are appropriate for a given
> classroom situation.[6] (p. 133)

Although there is agreement that these skills are essential, there is
disagreement about how they should be developed. Should there be specific
instruction in these areas, or are they rather to be regarded as tools for
learning and integrated throughout the curriculum? A more traditional
approach favors specific instruction, with exercises and activities designed
to accomplish certain objectives in listening and speaking, such as the ability
to follow directions correctly or present a persuasive argument. In this view,
listening and speaking are regarded as separate subject areas to be taught and
learned.

Teachers who regard listening and speaking as tools for learning integrate
the learning and practice of these skills into the rest of the curriculum,
because they believe that the ability to speak and listen effectively assists all
learning. As students speak and listen, they attend to important features of
information, bring past knowledge to bear on a present situation, relate

personal experience to what is being heard and engage in the process of conversation. Speaking and listening interrelate, as people interact with each other to converse, debate, discuss, persuade and express themselves.

Dunkin and Biddle[7] found that in order for students to develop competence in oral communication, they must be given many opportunities to talk. Wells[8] observed that students learn language and its function by using it in social situations for realistic purposes in a variety of contexts. According to Delamont,[9] students use oral language to seek and derive meaning from other students and the teacher. They receive feedback on their communicative effectiveness from peers, as they attempt to display their knowledge of classroom learning. Siks[10] reported a close link between imagination and both the expression and control of emotion. Children who are encouraged to participate in dramatic activities and show early interest in make-believe play display more self-control in other situations, persist longer at tasks, sit quietly when it is necessary to wait, evidence leadership with other children and develop certain cognitive skills more rapidly than those deprived of these experiences.

WHAT DO YOU THINK? Be alert as you participate in conversations today: What do you know that helps you understand the conversation? What do you assume the other person knows when you converse? Why do you think that there might be a close link between opportunities for dramatic play and a capacity for self-discipline? Were there other ideas from research that interested you in the paragraph above?

III. Looking into Classrooms

Kindergarten Level

Blake and Jordan come into the kindergarten room arguing.

"Is so, is so!" Jordan claims.

"No, it's not!" Blake retorts, banging the back of his chair with his hand for emphasis.

"I know it's going to rain . . . my mom made me bring an umbrella 'cause she can't come get me after school," Jordan says with authority. Blake is disappointed because he is looking forward to a joint recess with the sixth graders to practice for the buddy baseball game.

"Can you solve it with words?" Mrs. Jamison asks.

Blake scowls.

"You really feel disappointed, don't you?" she sympathizes.

Blake nods. "I don't want it to rain," he declares. "It's not going to rain."

"Is too, is too," Jordan chants at him from behind the teacher.

"Can you say something else if you disagree?" she asks, turning around to Jordan.

He pauses. "Excuse me, I have a different idea?"

"That sounds pretty good. What will you say to support your different idea?"

Jordan thinks a minute. "Tell why I have that idea. Give some evidence."

"Try it," the teacher says.

"Excuse me," Jordan says to Blake. "I have a different idea. It's going to rain. I think it's going to rain because my mom told me."

"Your mom's wrong," Blake mumbles. "It's not going to rain."

"How else could you say that?" the teacher asks.

"I have a different idea. It's not going to rain."

"And your evidence?"

"I just don't want it to."

"Could you find out?"

He rolls his eyes up to think. "We could ask Mr. Wright to listen to the radio," he says finally.

"What do you think, Jordan?"

"Yeah, Mr. Wright. He can prove it."

"What will you say to him?" the teacher asks.

"Mr. Wright, we want to find out if it's going to rain this afternoon," Jordan says.

"He will want to know why you're interested," the teacher says. "What will you say?"

"I want us to play buddy baseball," Blake replies.

"What part will you say to Mr. Wright, Jordan?"

"The part about will he listen to the radio," he replies.

"And I'll tell the reason part," Blake answers.

"Good enough," the teacher says. "Take the hall key and come back as soon as possible. We're going to have Discussion in a few minutes."

The boys return from the office with news that satisfies them both. Mr. Wright has heard the weather prediction for rain, but has promised Blake that he will supervise twenty minutes in the gym for the two classes to practice playing catch if rain spoils their other plans.

Mrs. Jamison moves to the Discussion Chair and sits down. Twenty children gather around her, sitting on the rug.

"How can we make visitors feel welcome in our room?" the teacher asks the group.

"Give 'em a hug," Nicole suggests. The others giggle.

"I'm sure that would make them feel **very** welcome," Mrs. Jamison agrees, and she writes "hug" on the blackboard behind her. "What else can you think of?"

"You could give 'em a chair," Blake says.

"That's sounds good," the teacher replies, adding "chair" to the list. "Why do visitors come to our room?" she asks.

"To see us read and do things," Courtney volunteers.

"Because they're learning to be teachers," Jordan says, "like my mom."

"And Mr. Wright comes to see us," Jennifer says, "and our parents."

"What helps them have a good time in our room?"

"They just do," Blake replies.

"When we go down to the sixth-grade room for poetry reading, what do you like best about going into their room?" Mrs. Jamison asks.

A number of hands go up.

"They're friends for us. They're big, but they're not mean."

"Would you say that they're friendly?" the teacher asks. The students nod their heads in agreement and Mrs. Jamison adds "friendly" to the list.

"And my Book Buddy comes for me and we go to our special place in the room," Julie says.

"And Mark asks me what I want to read. He lets me decide," Justin adds.

Several children volunteer their ideas at once. "First Jordan, then Connor and then Taylor," the teacher says. "One at a time now, so I can hear your ideas," Mrs. Wright says, and she adds the words "choices" and "special place" to the list on the blackboard.

"They show us around the room every time and we see stuff they make," Jordan says, "like the rain forest."

"And they wrote books for us," Connor says.

"And they give us crackers and raisins and peanuts," Taylor adds.

"Wait a minute," the teacher says. "Let me catch up," and she writes the words "displays," "books" and "refreshments."

When Mrs. Jamison has recorded a key word for each contribution, she asks the children to read the list with her.

"Which of these things could you do for visitors to **our** classroom?" she asks.

All hands go up and there is a scramble to talk.

"Who will go first?" she asks. The children look at each other.

"Megan first, then Connor and then me," Blake says.

"Good work," Mrs. Jamison says.

"We can be friendly," Megan begins. "And we can give them a special place where it's nice, like the beanbag chair."

"Justin said he liked it when Mark asked him what he wanted to read or do. Can we do something like that for our visitors?" Mrs. Jamison asks.

"We could ask them what they want to look at," Blair suggests.

"You should have another chair," Cassie adds. "My Grandma couldn't sit in a beanbag."

"Very thoughtful," the teacher says. "Are there other places that visitors could sit?" The class identifies chairs at the listening center, the rocker in the story area and a chair at the piano.

"Can they see what is happening from each of those places?" she asks. A volunteer goes to each area and reports that the visitor's view would be blocked if they sat at the piano.

"What could be done?" the teacher asks.

"We could move the chair for just when a visitor comes," Jordan suggests.

"What about food?" Taylor says. "We should give them some food."

"What do you have in mind?" Mrs. Jamison asks.

Children suggest peanuts, raisins, juice and crackers. Jordan says, "A cake!"

"That costs too much money," Amy says.

"My mother could bake one," Kristen suggests.

"We could all have some," Taylor says.

"What kind of food do we already have in the classroom?" Mrs. Jamison asks.

"Crackers and juice," Jeremy says, "and raisins and peanuts."

"Do you think a visitor would enjoy sharing those with us?" she asks. The children look at each other and nod their heads.

"They'd like cake better," Taylor grumbles.

"You know, a cake does sound like a good idea for a special occasion," Mrs. Jamison agrees. "What about having cake when we give our play?"

"Yeah, a big cake so everyone can have some," Taylor agrees. It is obvious that he is hungry.

"Taylor, all this talk about food is making me hungry," the teacher says. "Why don't you bring the peanut and raisin boxes over so we can have a snack and perk up our brains."

As the children munch, Mrs. Jamison asks, "If you want to be friendly to someone, what do you say? And what do you do?"

Responses, given with examples from their own experience, include smiling, saying something nice, taking their hand to lead them to a special place, showing them interesting things in the classroom and reading a book to them.

"Let's practice," the teacher says. "Who would like to be the greeter, the person who makes the visitor feel welcome?" Courtney volunteers. "And the visitor?" Megan raises her hand.

Megan goes outside and then comes in to pick up a large purse from the dress-up box. She returns to the hall, closes the door and knocks. The children giggle. Courtney stands where she is.

"Who should answer the door?" she asks.

"Me," Courtney replies, and she hesitates.

"Go on," Blake says. "She wants to come in."

Courtney goes to the door and opens it. Megan begins to giggle and the class joins in. The teacher waits. The two girls look at her.

"Why have you come to visit the class?" Mrs. Jamison asks Megan.

Megan thinks for a minute. "I want to see this class read their charts again," she replies. "They are just amazing."

The class gets still. The dialogue has captured their interest.

"What will you say when Courtney opens the door?" she prompts.

"Good morning, I'm from the college. Can I come in?"

Courtney looks puzzled.

"Say somethin' back!" Blake coaches.

She pauses a minute and then replies. "Yes, come in. We like visitors. Come in, 'cause we're going to be amazing today," she says.

"Thank you," Megan says, and comes into the room dragging her make-believe briefcase.

"Good job," Mrs. Jamison says, and the girls sit down.

"How did Courtney make the visitor feel welcome?" she asks the group.

"She was friendly," Justin says.

"She told something interesting," Blair adds. "We're going to be amazing, so she'll probably want to stay and watch us." The others agree.

"What could the greeter do next to make the visitor feel welcome?" the teacher asks. There are many suggestions: read a favorite book, show her a place to put her coat, escort her to a place to sit down, invite her to look around the room, show her the centers, explain about the reading/writing charts and artwork around the room.

"When it's time to leave the sixth-grade room, what do your Book Buddies say?" the teacher asks.

"See you later, alligator!" "Bye!" "Thanks for coming!" "Come back again." "We'll see you next week," they volunteer.

"Could you say any of those things to a visitor?" she asks.

"Not the alligator thing," Amy says, "unless it's the sixth graders."

"We could say, 'Thanks for coming,' " Amy says.

"And 'Come back again,' " Blair adds.

"And smile," Blake says, "so they know we're friendly."

"Excellent ideas," Mrs. Jamison says. She reviews the role of greeter with the students and then lets them group in pairs to practice conducting a tour of the room. When everyone has had a turn, she draws the group back together and asks them what they liked best about what their greeter said or did.

"She smiled a lot," Justin says of Courtney.

"Jordan told me all about the stuff on the science table," Megan says.

"Amy showed me the computer station and told how we make Big Books," Julie says.

When all students have shared their experience, Mrs. Jamison tells the class that they will have the opportunity to practice being greeters during the afternoon. A class of students from the college will be coming to help with artwork for the Insects study, so there will be enough visitors for everyone to be a greeter. The children look interested.

"What if we forget what we're supposed to say?" Blake worries.

"Just be friendly," Amy suggests.

"Good advice," Mrs. Jamison says. "I'll move your suggestions for making visitors feel welcome to the chart and you can look at it for ideas."

"What if we can't remember what the words say?" Blake asks.

"What do you suggest?" she asks.

He thinks a minute. "You could put up some picture clues," he says.

"Good idea," she replies. "How about helping me draw some?"

WHAT HAPPENED HERE? ONE PERSPECTIVE

Mrs. Jamison's first purpose in the above conversation is to give students practice in thinking, talking and problem solving. The second purpose is to help children develop social interaction skills that can be practiced and reinforced on a daily basis. In each interaction, the teacher asks open-ended questions to encourage the students to think about their options, solve problems and reflect on their experience.

When Blake enters the room upset about possible rain, Mrs. Jamison immediately moves to acknowledge his unhappiness so that he does not have to demonstrate it further. She encourages both boys to use language to solve their conflict. Because the dispute was created with language, she wants them to experience the power of language to resolve it. Because Blake could identify the cause of his distress, the principal was able to respond to this disappointment with the indoor recess. On other occasions when a schedule adjustment has not been possible, the principal acknowledges the disappointment and asks students what they can do to make the afternoon successful without recess.

At the beginning of the group session, students respond rather perfunctorily to Mrs. Jamison's question about how to make visitors feel welcome in the classroom. When it is apparent that this question has not tapped into their own experience, she encourages them to report their own feelings about being a classroom visitor. At various times in the discussion, several children talk at the same time, a common occurrence when they are interested or excited about the topic. When this happens the first time, the teacher sorts out the confusion and reminds them that taking turns will assure a good audience for their ideas. In the second instance, she allows a student to guide the discussion, encouraging students to take increased responsibility for the process.

Each time the class talks together, Mrs. Jamison introduces or practices a principle of good discussion. At the beginning of the year she encouraged students to add ideas to what they say, helping them move from one word or condensed responses. Through modeling and role-playing she demonstrates the value of being understood and the responsibility of speakers to speak clearly, loud enough to be heard and in a voice that is pleasant to listen to. She has focused on speaking with a volume and tone appropriate to the occasion and models ways to disagree politely. She suggests alternate ways to express disagreement and encourages students to provide evidence for their opinions. This activity builds the foundation for successful group participation and helps children practice the fundamental processes of social interaction.

During the visit in the afternoon, her students will experience warm responses for their efforts as greeters. As they practice this skill, they will develop increased self-confidence in their speaking and a feeling of competence in their ability to interact socially. A rotating chart for greeters ensures everyone practice, and frequent role-playing allows Mrs. Jamison to observe skills that might need additional practice.

In this kindergarten there are many opportunities for children to practice speaking and listening skills. They dictate stories individually and as a group to the teacher or into a tape recorder. They create and act out their own plays, based on predictable stories. Poems, songs and chants related to the current curriculum theme are a daily routine. Throughout the day students practice talking and listening to each other critically and appreciatively. They talk about things that interest them—personal experiences; school, community and world events; and books they have read. They create puppet shows and plays for visitors and engage the visitors in lively discussions. Music is an integral part of classroom activities, and students listen closely to favorites to learn the melody and words.

All of these events arise from things that are immediate and interesting to students. By creating an environment full of opportunities to actively practice listening and speaking, the teacher helps students develop these skills. Each student learns to share a variety of information for a variety of purposes with a variety of listeners. As members of an audience, they develop skills of appreciation, encouragement and support.

Primary Level

"Mrs. Logan! My great-grandma loaned me the pictures!" Haley announces, as she deposits a plastic bag on the teacher's desk.

"How exciting," Mrs. Logan responds. "Let's take a look," and she carefully slides the cardboard-backed photographs from the protective plastic cover.

"See, here's her friend Esther," Haley points to a class picture, taken early in the century. "This is when they were in first grade. They've been friends for eighty years! And here's a picture of them now." She shows the teacher a smaller photograph of the two friends sitting at the piano.

"They played duets together when they were young and they still do sometimes. Esther's mother was my great-grandma's piano teacher."

"This looks like a very interesting presentation," Mrs. Logan says.

Haley looks pleased. "I worked really hard on it," she says.

"Do you have all the equipment you need?" the teacher asks.

"I tested my tape in the listening center recorder. It works all right."

"Have you practiced the volume and starting and stopping at the right places?" the teacher asks.

"Yes," Haley replies. "I practiced at home."

"Well, good luck," the teacher adds. "I'm really looking forward to your presentation." Haley thanks Mrs. Logan, collects her pictures and goes to the art center for materials to make signs for her display.

At 2:00 students put away books from independent reading and begin to set up displays and pictures. Kevin has requested blackboard space to put up pictures of submarines, and he lines up submarine models along the chalk ledge. He will be showing the class his current book on submarines[11] and reading a letter from his uncle, who is stationed on a nuclear submarine somewhere in the Atlantic Ocean.

"Is everyone ready?" Molly asks the class, as the presenters put the finishing touches on their displays. "We can start when everyone is quiet," she tells the class, and the talking stops.

"Our first presenters today are Claire, Susan, Sarah, Jill, Mark and Corey. They are going to give a play they made from Jan Brett's *The Mitten: A Ukrainian Folktale*."[12] The class applauds as Claire carries a white sheet to the front of the room. It has been basted together at the sides to make a large sack, and a pillowcase has been stitched on to make the thumb for the mitten. The students have used watercolor black markers to create the effect of a knitted mitten.

"We're going to give this play to the kindergarten class," Claire explains. "And we wanted to practice it on another audience first."

Each performer has a mask of the animal to be portrayed. As Claire reads about each animal that seeks refuge in the mitten, the performers climb into the sheet sack that represents the ever-enlarging mitten. At the climax of the story, the bear sneezes and the sack explodes. The performers tumble out on cue, drawing the applause and laughter of the audience.

"Do you have any comments?" Claire asks, when the performance is completed.

"Do it again," Kevin says. "I liked it!"

"You did a good job making the mitten," Haley says.

"That was my favorite story when I was in kindergarten," Karen remarks.

"How could we make it better?" Claire asks.

"Did you ever think about doing the masks a different way?" Samantha asks.

"Like how?"

"Well, I like the masks you made and everything, but . . ."

"But what?"

"What if you put them onto some kind of sack, so you didn't have to hold them up to your face? It would make getting in and out of the sack easier and look more like animals."

"We were trying to do the masks like Japanese plays," Sarah responds for the group. "But it would be easier if we didn't have to hold them up."

"Maybe we'll think about it," Claire concludes. "It wouldn't be too hard to put them on something like a sack. Any questions?"

"How did you make the masks?" someone asks.

"Miss Krueger [the art teacher] set up the overhead projector and we traced the pictures we wanted," Corey answers. "Then we cut out the pictures and glued them to cardboard. Miss Krueger helped us staple the masks to the sticks," Claire replies.

"Why did you choose this story for a play?" Brian asks.

"We found it in the library when we were looking for folktales from eastern Europe. Mark read it to Jordan down in kindergarten during Book Buddies and he really liked it. We asked Mrs. Jamison if she'd like to have us make a play about it, and she told us to go ahead," Jill replies.

"Did you know there are other versions of this story?" Mrs. Logan asks. "I had one of them when I was in elementary school. It was also called *The Mitten*,[13] and it told a similar story."

Claire looks at her group and they shake their heads.

"It's not in the library," Susan says, "because we looked at every single book about Russian and Ukrainian folktales. I'd like to see what it looks like, though. Do you still have your copy?"

Mrs. Logan laughs. "I'll have to call my mother," she replies. "That was a long time ago. If she can't find it, you might ask the librarian if she could order a copy from the regional library. I'm sure there are versions from other countries, also. Let us know what you find."

Molly has allowed three minutes for questions and raises her hand to indicate the end of question time. Next she introduces Kevin, who draws a great deal of interest in his eight-minute presentation with the letter from his uncle, complete with anecdotes about life on a submarine. Because there are many questions, Molly allows extra time for Kevin to answer inquiries about how a submarine works.

Haley is next, with the oral biography of her great-grandmother, a project she became interested in after reading a book about how to collect oral biographies.[14] She begins by telling the group about the book. "When you collect an oral biography, you try to ask good questions and then record the answers people give. I didn't know what questions to ask at first, but the book gives you ideas. They must be pretty good questions because my great-grandma said she liked them. She said they made her think about interesting things. I recommend this book if you would like to know more about your relatives. I never thought about my great-grandma ever being my age. When she was little, people didn't have radios or telephones or TV. Here are some of the other things we talked about."

As students listen to the taped conversation between Haley and her great-grandmother, she shows them pictures of the people who are being talked about. The class listens attentively to stories about a springtime flood, an Easter blizzard and a runaway horse, all vividly recalled by Haley's great-grandmother. Enthusiastic applause follows. Students ask her if she is going to interview anyone else. Someone asks to borrow the book.

"Would anyone else like to do a project like this?" Mrs. Logan asks.

There is immediate and enthusiastic approval. Haley's project has provided a highly motivating introduction to an interview technique that will enhance the next theme study on communities.

Nathaniel is introduced next. "I made a game," he says, holding up a bundle of large cards made from cardboard separators he got from the janitor. "It's about the Borrowers.[15] How many of you have read this book?" he asks, holding up the book. Three hands go up.

"Well, I like this book because it shows how little people make things they need by borrowing them from humans. They live right inside the same houses and get their names from the places they live, like the Mantlepieces. I'm going to hold up a picture and you pretend like you're about three inches high and decide what you can do with it. I also made some Borrower furniture that's over on the table," he concludes.

He holds up a picture of a spool of thread. The class guesses a table, wheels for a cart and a yard hose holder. Nathaniel tells how the spool is used in the story and moves to the next pictures, which include scissors, a matchbox, a postage stamp and a teacup. This creative presentation earns ardent applause. Someone in the class who has read the book asks if Mary Norton wrote any other books about the Borrowers.

"My mom said she read a whole bunch of Borrower books when she was my age," Nathaniel says. "And there are some new ones . . . well, kind of newer ones," he adds. "I'm going to read *Poor Stainless*[16] next."

Robert and Daniel give the final presentation, reading *Knots on a Counting Rope*[17] aloud together. This conversation between a blind Native American boy and his grandfather is somewhat of a struggle for the two boys, but they persevere and are obviously very much caught up in the meaning of the story. They have made their own Native American costumes and sit around a fire made from fireplace logs, colored tissue paper and a flashlight. This is a touching performance, and when it is finished there is thoughtful silence, broken in a few seconds by warm applause. There is great interest in how the boys made their outfits. Some want to see the pictures in the book and they pass it around.

While some students look at artwork and various projects related to literature displayed on a table at the front of the room, others pick up evaluation forms and fill them out. The forms are used to provide audience feedback to the presenters. When completed, they are returned to trays on the teacher's desk, marked with each presenter's name. After the teacher reviews the forms, they are distributed to the presenters. Students are encouraged to list what they liked about each presentation and to give any suggestions that would help them understand or appreciate the presentation better the next time.

In this third-grade classroom, students also participate in creative drama. They plan and present puppet shows and plays based on books they have read. Each day, one-third of the students talk briefly to the entire class about a book they are reading. Another discussion session allows students to talk about events in their own lives, the community or the world that interest them. Like the students in Mrs. Jamison's class, these children are learning to be critical and appreciative listeners.

WHAT HAPPENED HERE? ONE PERSPECTIVE

At the beginning of the year, Mrs. Logan models respectful applause as each presenter is introduced. She explains that this initial audience response shows appreciation for the work that students have already done in preparing for the presentation. The effect of the applause on the presenters is noticeable, providing encouragement and support for their efforts.

At the beginning of the school year, students contribute positive comments after each presentation, telling what they especially like about each one. They may also provide helpful feedback—such as speaking louder or slower, using charts and pictures or providing more explanation—if they think it will make the presentation better. In January, the class began recording evaluations in writing, and students are encouraged to ask questions after each presentation.

The written evaluations are responses to the questions: "What did you like?" and "Do you have any suggestions?" Mrs. Logan models appropriate responses to these questions by giving examples such as: "I liked hearing what it was like to go to school a long time ago," or "The poem you read was beautiful." If it was difficult to hear a presentation, the evaluator might say: "I couldn't hear too well." If the presentation needed more visual cues, they might say: "I couldn't remember the parts of the submarine." When presenters review their evaluations, they note any suggestions and respond to them. This summary is then shared with the teacher during individual writing conferences. Students can accept or reject the suggestions, but must tell why they are doing so.

Allowing students to share their responses to literature increases and enriches the experience of everyone in the classroom. Levels of student maturity and achievement can be easily accommodated because presentations are a reflection of individual interests and talents. Students work from FAST guidelines that encourage them to explore different kinds of books and new ways of sharing them. Mrs. Logan uses a rotating schedule to assign turns for introducing the presentations and making sure that everyone who signs up to present is ready when the time comes. Other students set up tables, create spaces for displays and assist each other in finding needed materials.

Intermediate Level

"What's the big debate about today?" Harrison asks Mr. Robinson.

"I think you'll like this one," the sixth-grade teacher replies, but gives no other clue.

Students check the schedule for their discussion partner and shared pair, then move into groups of four.

"What about an idea from *The Giver*[18]?" he asks, holding up the Newbery Award winner he has just finished reading aloud to the class.

"All right!" Joshua says. The others look equally enthusiastic. Students submit ideas for shared-pair discussion, and there have been several requests to talk about the book.

The Giver tells the story of Jonas, a young boy in a utopian community who is chosen to be the Receiver of Memories. The utopia exists in a protected environment that has eliminated the necessity of personal decisions. All citizens are treated the same and all are regarded the same. All are clothed, housed, fed and cared for from birth to death. All have an occupation that is suited to their talents. Those whose problems disrupt the community, such as infants with sleeping difficulties, the elderly or persons who repeatedly disobey rules, are released—a euphemism for euthanasia. Young Jonas receives the memories of the Giver and becomes the only person in the community able to see color. He also is able to feel other forbidden experiences, such as pain, joy, the warmth of family, the joy of celebrations, the knowledge of death and the sensations of snow, rain and sun. His new knowledge separates him from his family, and he escapes the community with an infant designated to be "released."

Mr. Robinson writes the topic on the board: "In spite of its flaws, the utopian community described in *The Giver* was essentially a good one."

Students hurriedly copy down the topic and begin to take notes on their thoughts. After five minutes, the teacher rings a bell and students turn to talk with their partners.

"Can I be 'For' to start with?" Mallory asks Samantha.

"Okay," Samantha assents. "Go ahead with yours first. Most of my ideas are 'Against' anyway."

"Well, first of all, nobody ever went hungry," Mallory begins.

The two girls enter their own shorthand for this idea on a duplicated tree chart. Mallory writes "No one hungry" and Samantha writes "Enough food."

"And everyone got a good education for what they were suited for," Mallory continues. "There was no pain and no one had to worry about anything, not even fixing meals or buying clothes. Everything was given to them. Everyone was nice to each other, and people were trained to be whatever they were good at."

The girls record this list in the "For" column. "Did you have any ideas for the 'Against' side?" Samantha asks.

"A couple," Mallory replies. "They didn't have any Christmas or any real holidays. And I hated the part about 'releasing' people."

"Me, too," Samantha agrees. "I sort of thought that's what they did, but Jonas's parents were so nice, I couldn't imagine them really hurting anyone."

"That's what I thought, too," Mallory says. "What did you have on your list?"

"I had the two you said and also that they couldn't see color or hear music. There weren't any birds or trees or snow or sunshine. That would be terrible. I can't even imagine not being able to see color. It'd be like living in the old black and white movies. Kind of scary," Samantha says. "And they all kind of acted nice and pretended there weren't any differences, but everyone knew there were, like Jonas's eyes were different from everybody else's. And then his assignment to be the Keeper of Memories . . . that was **way** different. He really didn't have any friends after that."

The two girls record Samantha's ideas in the "Against" column.

"Did you have any reasons 'For'?" Mallory asks.

"The same as the ones you already said," she replies. "About having enough food and clothes . . . oh, and everyone had a nice place to live." The girls add this idea to their lists. A warning bell rings, indicating two minutes to write a conclusion.

"So what's our consensus?" Mallory asks.

"We liked the good things and hated the bad things," Samantha says.

"We have to have reasons," Mallory reminds her.

"I think they paid too big a price for all those things," Samantha says. "No one was allowed to be different. They lost their freedom."

"Why is that important?" Mallory asks, using one of the discussion guidelines.

"Because, without any freedom, you can't make choices."

"Why is that bad?"

Samantha thinks. "You have to answer some of this, too," she complains.

"Well, there were just so many rules, no one really did anything because they really felt it . . . like Jonas's parents," Mallory explains. "They did things to follow the rules, but like his dad didn't really care about the babies he took care of, except as failures or successes."

"Yeah," Samantha agrees.

"So what do we want to say for a concluding statement?" Mallory asks.

"What about: 'This wasn't a good community, because there wasn't any freedom or change or love,' " Samantha suggests.

"But that wouldn't matter if you didn't think those things were important, like if you thought everybody being the same and having enough food and everything was more important, then you'd think that was good," Mallory answers.

"Well, . . . what about saying: 'If you wanted to always live the same, with no freedom or change or love, then this community would be good,' " Samantha suggests.

"That's good," Mallory agrees, "or we could say: 'This community would be good if freedom and change and love were not important to you.' "

"Yeah, that's good," Samantha says. "Let's write it that way."

Another bell rings and each girl turns to continue the discussion with a member of the other pair of discussants in their group. First each pair compares notes, sharing the ideas of the previous pairings. Then they work to create a consensus statement.

"Read your other statement again," Mallory asks.

Diedre reads: "This wasn't a good community because they just killed people that were old or had a problem or were different."

"Can we just add our statement in there, like: 'This would be a good community if you didn't think killing people was wrong and if freedom and change and love weren't important to you.' "

"It's kind of long," Diedre hesitates. "Can we say it shorter . . . I mean with fewer words?" She laughs.

"What's the matter?" Mallory asks.

"I was just thinking like Jonas. Trying to be precise, like it was wrong to use a word if there was a better one."

Mallory reflects on this. "I've thought about that a few times, too," she said. "It's good to use the best words, but it's not such a crime like it was for Jonas."

"Why can't we just say: 'This was not a good community because there were too many flaws. They didn't have any freedom or love and they got rid of problem people by killing them,' " Diedre suggests.

"What about the good parts, then?" Mallory asks. "How do we show that?"

The girls are thinking as the two-minute bell rings.

"What about just saying what we think?" Diedre suggests: " 'We believe the flaws in this community were more important than the good parts, because we value freedom and love.' "

"That's good," Mallory says. "It tells our opinion and why we have it."

The girls are satisfied with their consensus and pull together with the other pair to decide on a final statement and a spokesperson for the group.

"What are we going to say?" Samantha asks.

"Read us what you and Brittany wrote," Diedre asks.

"This community had too many flaws to be called 'good,' " she reads, "because there wasn't any freedom or love."

"Here's ours," Mallory says, and she reads their statement.

"We all agree that the community had so many bad parts that we can't say it's good," Brittany says. The others nod their heads.

"So that's our consensus. It wasn't a good community."

"Not if freedom and love are important," Samantha adds.

"So that's our position," Diedre says.

"But the other things are important, too," Mallory adds. "Having enough food and clothes and education for everybody."

"Right, but not more important," Brittany says. "They made too many sacrifices to get those things, and they ended up solving their problems by killing people."

"So could we say that those things are important . . . like food and clothes and everything for everyone, but not if it means getting rid of freedom and love?"

"Yeah, that's good," Samantha says. "That sounds like our position."

"Who wants to be spokesperson?" Mallory asks.

"Who hasn't been for a while?" Diedre replies. "I spoke in my group yesterday."

"So did I," Samantha says. "What about you, Brittany? Have you had a turn this week?"

"No, but I don't want one . . . yet."

"But you said all the things we were talking about. You can tell what we said."

"Well, . . . all right. But I don't like to."

"You'll do all right," Diedre says. "Just talk to them like you talk to us." Brittany looks doubtful.

"I'll do it if you don't want to," Mallory says.

"No . . . I'll do it . . . I think."

"Look, if you get scared at the last minute, just look at me and I'll do it," Mallory promises. Brittany looks relieved. When the time comes, however, she stands and gives the consensus of the group. When she sits down, her group gives her a pantomimed cheer, and she looks happy with her performance.

There are similar consensus statements from other groups. Some focus on the value of diversity versus sameness. Others concentrate on what was lost to the community to achieve freedom from physical needs. The consensus reached by the class as a whole is that the utopian society described in *The Giver* requires too many sacrifices for its benefits.

WHAT HAPPENED HERE? ONE PERSPECTIVE

At all ages, students enjoy talking to each other. But at the intermediate level, students are intensely interested in what their peers think about. Language learning is promoted when teachers provide many opportunities for students to exchange ideas: about events and people that affect their lives, books they have read, themes and content area subject matter. Shared-pair discussions help students develop their skills of critical thinking and positive interaction. In these sessions, students learn how to express their opinions, state and defend a position and respect the ideas of their classmates.

In the discussion above, each girl takes turns being the discussion leader. At the beginning of the year, they refer frequently to key questions, but have assimilated them into their interactions at this point, three months into the school year. Questions such as: What did you have? Did you have anything else? Why is that good (or bad)? What reasons do we have for saying this? help focus the discussion. Focus is also encouraged by having time limits for each stage of the shared-pair discussion. Students know they have to stay on task to arrive at consensus within the designated time.

This arrangement of pairs allows all students to participate in a discussion at three levels: in pairs, in shared pairs and in a small group. One out of four students participates in the final all-class discussion. Shy or hesitant students build confidence in their speaking within the dyads and small groups, and they receive group encouragement to contribute in the larger forum.

WHAT DO YOU THINK?

In your imagination, place the students described above in traditional classrooms. How would the conflict between the two kindergarten boys typically be resolved? What learning opportunities would be missed in

Mrs. Logan's room if there were no sharing sessions? What opportunities would be present for the shy or hesitant students in Mr. Robinson's room to develop speaking skills?

IV. Preparing for Listening and Speaking Activities

Oral Reading

In traditional classrooms, oral reading is usually limited to round-robin reading in ability groups. Teachers who integrate speaking and listening practice into the curriculum encourage their students to read aloud to share interesting ideas or to stimulate others to read something they have enjoyed. With this purpose in mind, students are encouraged to practice reading aloud as often as possible: in pairs, in small groups, to family members and friends. Most children also enjoy reading into a tape recorder and monitoring their progress. You will want to model the elements of successful oral reading on many occasions, demonstrating ways to adjust expression to match the tone and purpose of the literature. The following exercises can be demonstrated in a mini-lesson (Chapter 9) and practiced by individuals or small groups of students:

1. Practice reading the following sentences using the volume and expression of your voice to communicate the content:

   The snow fell from the darkened sky in quiet heaps around the barn. Rain began with a steady 'plink, plink, plink' on the tin roof of the lean-to.

   Great streaks of lightening brightened the sky, while thunder rolled on and on and on, pounding the air like a giant hammer.

2. When you read the following sentences, use your voice to create a picture of each one:

   Slowly, the lion arched himself to his feet, baring his teeth. "What do you mean, disturbing my sleep?" he roared.

   "What do you want?" I asked the kitten. She responded with a tiny but brave "meow."

   As the pterodactyl flashed over my head, its deafening cry flattened me to the ground.

   "Where are you going?" the cobra hissed. "I would be happy to show you the ruins, if you have the time," he added, as he coiled up into a ring.

3. Use your voice to describe the sad, fearful, angry, happy, or excited emotions in the following:

   Panic rose in my chest and my teeth began to chatter uncontrollably. Fear was in every cell of my body, shaking me apart.

I took the hated skates and flung them to the ground. Then I picked them up and threw them down again and again, until I no longer had strength to show how angry I still felt.

I held the owl in my arms, joyous with relief. I stroked his wet feathers and whispered over and over again, "Thank you, thank you, thank you for coming home!"

What could it mean? Were we to enter our new homeland after all? After all the years of waiting, I could not believe it could be so. In a moment we would know if all our hopes and dreams were finally to come true.

I looked at the small ball of fur lying beneath the tree and felt as if my heart would break. It had no chance against the elements and I was too late to make any difference in its survival.

4. Practice reading the exercises above or anything of your choice into the tape recorder. Look for the following:

> Can you easily understand the words?
> Does your voice show emotion?
> Does your reading have variety in volume and expression?
> Do you read slowly and with enough volume to be understood?

5. Practice reading aloud with a partner in different settings: your room at home, outdoors, on the playground. How must your voice change in these different settings to be heard and understood by listeners?

Book Previews

You will want to prepare students for previewing books by providing practice so that the activity of standing up and talking about a book gradually becomes one that is comfortable and familiar. During these warm-up exercises, every student participates by responding to a single question about his or her book. Begin the first week by asking everyone to respond to the same question. For example, on Monday students will stand and tell the title and author of the book they are reading. On Tuesday they will tell briefly what their book is about. Other questions for an entire week might include:

1. What do you like most about the book you are reading?
2. Why might someone else like this book?
3. What is something you have learned from reading this book?

During the second week, put up a poster of response questions for reference, and each day ask a group of four or five students to respond to all of the questions about their books. At the beginning of the third week, distribute Book Preview Guidelines (see Step-by-Step later in this chapter for suggested guidelines) to the class and establish a rotating schedule that permits every student to give a book preview at least once a week. Encourage students to add their own questions and comments to their previews.

Shared-Pair Discussions

These discussions can center around an idea in literature, science or the social studies. Classroom, school, community, national and international events can also be debated in this format. Individual brainstorming, paired discussions and group consensus should be allotted approximately five minutes each. Whole-class sharing should last about ten minutes. This provides fifteen minutes of intense talking and listening for each student and moderate interaction for the remaining fifteen.

These discussions promote listening and speaking, but they also help develop critical thinking skills. Your most important contribution to this activity will be identifying topics for discussion from student interests and from issues connected with study themes. You will also want to prepare students to participate successfully in these meetings by describing what is to happen and providing guidelines for their future reference. Create a schedule that alternates pairs and provides the opportunity during a month's time for students to interact as a pair with every other student in the classroom.

Creative Drama

The best way to learn how to use creative drama in the classroom is to participate in these exercises under the direction of a trained professional. Some school districts include creative drama in the intermediate language arts curriculum. When drama specialists are not available, contact amateur thespians in the local little theater group or professors in the theater department of your area university or college. Students majoring in speech communication or theater are often interested in working with school children for the experience it provides them. If there are no resources of this kind available to you, consider taking creative drama as part of your coursework. You might want to explore the possibility of taking a class of this kind from the area community college or the continuing education program at a local high school. There are also several excellent "how-to-do-it" books listed in the Resources for Teaching section at the end of the chapter that describe methods for helping students explore ideas through creative drama.

Puppet Theater

One of the best possible introductions to puppet theater is attending a well-presented live puppet show. Many school districts sponsor a fine arts series that includes puppetry or marionettes. It may also be possible to plan field trips to provide your students with this experience. If these resources are not available to you, consult your media specialist or public librarian. They often have training in puppetry and will visit your class to present a story. If you are a primary or kindergarten teacher, check with the intermediate teachers in your building. They may be planning puppetry for their classes and you can sign up your class as a possible audience.

Like live theater, professionally presented live puppet shows give students the experience of interacting as an audience with skilled performers. There really is nothing like the real thing. But much can be learned and enjoyed from watching videotapes of good puppets. Most children have grown up with the puppets on public television, such as *Sesame Street, Eureeka's Castle, The Shari Lewis Show* or Mr. *Roger's Neighborhood*. They have some idea about what puppets can do and the kinds of stories puppets best portray. Make use of this experience to talk with your students about the elements of successful scripts, costuming and sets. Ask them to watch one of these shows closely, to study the scenery or props. What special effects are used? How is a puppet's personality created? What kinds of puppets do they most enjoy?

In kindergarten and the early primary grades, many teachers use hand puppets to help tell a story. Extend this experience to your students by letting them create their own hand puppets from a sock or paper sack. Let students choose a partner to talk back and forth with, using puppets. You can also encourage peer and cross-grade Book Buddies to use puppets when they read aloud to each other.

Reader's Theater

You can obtain commercially prepared materials for reader's theater[19] from your curriculum library, teacher's stores and school book clubs. But you and your students can also prepare excellent dramas from favorite literature. The following guidelines are designed to help you adapt books into the reader's theater format.

1. Choose a scene from a book that is mostly dialogue. The story should be straightforward and action-oriented, and the characters' motivation should be evident within the scene selected.
2. Decide who the main characters are. Talk about how they relate to each other. Have students draw from their own experience to imagine how each character feels and responds to the events in the story.
3. Underline the dialogue parts in the story. Paperback copies can be used for this purpose, or dialogue can be written or typed out.
4. Decide what the narrator will read as descriptive material between the dialogue.
5. Read through the play several times for practice and enjoyment.
6. If the play is to be presented for an audience, write down ideas about possible scenery, props and costumes.
7. A publicity committee can design flyers and programs for the play. Pictures taken during rehearsal can be used for promoting the play, and refreshments related to the theme of the play can be arranged by this committee.

Friday Afternoon Sharing Time (FAST)

The first goal for this sharing time is to provide an opportunity for students to talk about books and experiences that are interesting to them. The second goal is to create an ongoing activity that is planned and executed by the students themselves. Most of the teacher's planning for FAST will involve constructing guidelines for these interactions and modeling appropriate responses to presentations. At the kindergarten and early primary levels you will probably want to put up posters with guidelines for audience participation and presenter preparation, which can be reviewed before the activities take place. Late primary and intermediate students can keep copies of the guidelines, evaluation sheets and recordkeeping forms in their reading or writing notebooks for easy reference. Sample forms are shown in Figures 7.1–7.3.

It is helpful to establish a rotating schedule for all tasks that can be easily assumed by students, including arranging furniture, setting up displays, greeting guests, introducing presentations and distributing audience evaluation forms. You might want to create a calendar that features a schedule of student assistants for the different tasks.

When you begin Friday Afternoon Sharing Time, review the entire process with your students, role-playing where necessary. Distribute guidelines for presenters and audiences and go over each item, asking students why they think each might be important. You will also want to talk about the different ways students could choose to share their responses to books during these sessions. Ask for their ideas and encourage them to write down the suggestions that interest them. Emphasize the idea that as they gain experience with preparing and presenting their responses, they will be adding their own creative touches.

Guidelines for Presenters

As part of the preparation for FAST, students will need to know how much time will be available to them, what constitutes appropriate content, possible ways to share their books and the deadline for signing up for presentations or displays. Encourage students to try different kinds of presentations each week, to work with new partners and to share their experiences with a variety of literature genres.

The guidelines in the remainder of this section are intended as suggestions to be adapted for use in your particular classroom. You will want to discuss them and any additional expectations you might have for students in terms of appropriate responses before, during and after these presentations.

Ideas for Presentations

1. Talk about a book you have read this week.
2. Read aloud a passage you especially enjoyed.
3. Read something you have written in response to something read.
4. Display writing, drawings, paintings or murals created in response to a book.
5. Pantomime a scene from a book you have read.
6. Create a puppet show from an event in a book.
7. Display bookmarks, book covers, paper or clay sculpture created in response to a book read.
8. Present a five-minute drama based on an event in your book.
9. Share additional research about an author, illustrator or book topic that will help readers enjoy or appreciate a book more.
10. Share responses to letters written to authors.
11. Host a game show based on information in a book.
12. Interview the main character in a story.

13. Present a newscast based on the story.
14. Create a magazine with pictures, based on the story.
15. Share research on the geography or history of the setting in a book.
16. When many students have read the book, act out scenes and ask the class to guess the character.
17. Host a TV talk show based on the characters, events or topic of your book.
18. Create a cartoon, an editorial or a feature for a newspaper based on the events, topic or characters in your book.
19. Create a conversation between characters of different books you have read, such as Maniac Magee and M.C. Higgins or Laura Ingalls and Caddie Woodlawn.
20. Create a newspaper or magazine from a time period.
21. Talk about food from a particular place or time in your book. Bring samples.
22. Talk about clothes from a particular place or time in your book. Try to create an outfit similar to that in the book.
23. Play or sing music from the time or place of your book.
24. Perform and/or teach a dance from a time or place in your book.
25. Make and display/talk about artifacts you have made that tell something about your book, such as a lunch box burglar alarm from *Dear Mr. Henshaw* or Cobble's Knot from *Maniac Magee*.

FAST Proposal
(Please submit by Thursday of each week)

Name(s) of presenter(s):
Title(s) of book(s):
Brief description of presentation:
Time required (limit—10 minutes):

Guidelines for Preparing Your Presentations

1. What part of this book do I want to share?
2. What are some ways that it could be shared?
3. Is this a new genre?
4. Is this a new kind of presentation?
5. Will this presentation be displayed or talked about?
6. Will what I have planned fit into 10 minutes? Should I ask for more time?
7. Have I practiced the presentation at least 3 times? (More, if needed.)
8. From past presentations, is there something I want to improve?
9. Will I need props?
10. What kind of space will I need?

FIGURE 7.1
Sample of a FAST proposal.

Physical Space Arrangements   When students have submitted their ideas for displays and presentations, help them assess the kind and amount of space they will need. Where should the hornet's nest and the honeycomb go? What is the best place to display a Japanese kimono and a Boys Day Kite? Can the displays be touched or are they fragile? Will sunlight be harmful to fabric or paper? Should objects be shown by the presenter or placed in a central area for students to observe?

One group may need space for a colonial dance demonstration. Can desks be moved to one end of the room or would it be better to go to the gym? How many guests will be invited? Can students sit on the floor? How many chairs will be needed for adult guests? Where should these chairs be placed?

As much as possible, students should be responsible for estimating the space they will require, moving desks, setting up tables and displays and greeting guests. They should also take turns introducing their classmates and the presentations. Suggested introduction guidelines are included below; distribute copies to all students and role-play introductions well in advance of the first sharing session.

Introduction Guidelines

The following are suggestions for introducing a presentation.

1. Interview the person ahead of time and agree on the information you will use in your introduction.
2. Use your own words and ideas, but be sure to include the person's name and tell something about the presentation.
3. Encourage the presenter by leading an introductory applause and final applause at the end of the presentation.

Example:

"I would like to introduce Mary Klein. She read *Shabanu* during SSR and became especially interested in the camels. She's going to read her favorite part and tell us about some research she did on how camels dance. Let's give Mary some encouragement." (Lead applause)

At the end of the presentation, say "Let's show Mary our appreciation." (Lead applause)

Audience Preparation   Learning to be a good audience takes practice. You will want to brainstorm some guidelines for audience participation before your first sharing session. Tell your students what you hope will happen during FAST: that people will share books and ideas they have enjoyed during the week. How can they help the presenter feel comfortable? How can they show interest, respect and appreciation? How can they help the presenter give his or her best performance? Most classes generate guidelines similar to the following:

Guidelines for Audience Participation

1. Listen carefully. Look at the presenter. Give your full attention.
2. Show appreciation: smile, nod, applaud.
3. Be patient if something goes wrong. It happens to everyone.
4. Think about the presentation: What did you like? What would improve it?

Presentation Review Form

Name _____

1. What did you like?

   _____

   _____

   _____

2. What did you learn?

   _____

   _____

   _____

3. How about . . . ?
   (Make suggestions that might help improve this presentation.
   Be specific and positive.)

   _____

   _____

   _____

   _____

FIGURE 7.2
Sample of presentation review form.

To help students develop their critical listening and audience appreciation skills, encourage brief, positive oral responses at the conclusion of all presentations. As students gain confidence as presenters you will also want them to practice writing evaluations. Besides providing practice for thoughtful audience participation, these forms also give helpful information and encouragement to presenters.

Response examples from presentation review form (Figure 7.2):

A student displays a student newspaper based on the book *Ralph Mouse.*

I liked: the cartoons and the sports. It was neat.
I learned: how to make a newspaper from a book.
How about: putting all the articles that are alike together, like sports, and
                 have sections like they do in real newspapers.

A student reads a page aloud from *Dragonwings*.

I liked: hearing about the San Francisco earthquake.
I learned: that people lived in the parks when their homes were destroyed.
How about: reading a little slower next time.

Three students create a dramatic scene from *Pippi Longstocking*.

I liked: how funny the play was and the props that showed how strong Pippi was.
I learned: that I'd really like to read this book.
How about: not changing anything. It was great!

Two students present a research project about wolves (based on the book *Julie of the Wolves*).

I liked: all the information about the social habits of wolves.
I learned: that wolves ordinarily do not attack humans.
How about: writing technical terms on the board.

FAST Presentation Record

Name:

Names of students you have worked with on presentations:

Dates when you have introduced presentations (use this format: January 3, 1996, as 1/3/96):

Put a check mark beside each kind of presentation you have made:
___ display of writing
___ display of art
___ display of artifacts
___ book sharing
___ reading aloud
___ drama
___ puppets
___ TV show
___ interview
___ newspaper

Put a check mark beside each type of literature you have shared:
___ traditional literature
___ modern fantasy
___ modern fiction
___ historical fiction
___ poetry
___ biography
___ multicultural books
___ nonfiction: science, social science, art, other

FIGURE 7.3
Sample of FAST presentation record.

Recordkeeping   It will be helpful if both you and each of your students keep a record of the types of books they respond to and the kinds of presentations they make. The sample form in Figure 7.3 helps students review their past efforts and plan for future presentations.

WHAT DO YOU   Which of the activities described above are most appealing to you? Why
THINK?   do you think some activities appeal to some students and not to others? Do you think it is important to offer a choice of ways to interact and respond?

V. Including Everyone

In addition to Friday Afternoon Sharing Times, all occasions for student listening and speaking can assist students who have language difficulties. These interactions provide both opportunity to practice and support from peers. By asking questions like: "What did you like about the way Jonah read his poem?" or "What can you say to encourage Jonah about his reading?" you will model support for students who are struggling to gain competency. The shared-pair activities described in the sections above provide excellent one-on-one and small-group opportunities for shy or language-deficient students to express themselves.

As non- or limited-English-speaking children listen to classroom discussions, they hear the cadences and inflections of the language. When a topic is discussed, they hear some words repeatedly, as well as words commonly used with this topic. At the kindergarten level, discussions about a new dog will involve not only the word "dog," but other words such as fur, ears, nose, tail, dog food, bark and pet. When the object under discussion is not present, teachers can hold up a picture or draw an outline on the board, so that students can see what is being talked about. Student presenters for FAST should also be encouraged to provide visual aids as often as possible. In later grades, teachers can write a word or words that title the discussion on the board while students are talking during discussion or FAST presentations. ESL students can record these words in their reading or writing notebooks, with any descriptions or drawings they find helpful. During individual conferences, teachers can check on these words and their descriptions for accuracy and to use for instruction.

Remember that appropriate codes for speaking and listening may differ among the cultures of children you have in a classroom. Research this area most carefully. It is important to recognize and respect the communication mores of the community in which you teach. If these customs are at odds with the successful functioning of your students in the larger society, you will want to explain this variance to them. For example, African American children may turn their heads or avert their eyes from the teacher or principal to show respect for authority.[20] If you insist that a child look you in the eye when you are talking to him, you may be creating a conflict in his effort to respond appropriately to you. Learn how minority children begin and continue conversations. How does the physical context of interaction and body movement influence what is said and what is considered appropriate audience response?

It is also important to remember that dialectical varieties of nonstandard English, such as African American, Native American, Puerto Rican, Appalachian, Chinese and Vietnamese, follow different but complex and regularly patterned linguistic rules. As the teacher of children who use these dialects, you will not seek to eradicate or replace them or to label them as deficient. Your goal will be to expand these children's experience with the mainstream dialect, in the context of respect for dialectical variation. When you want to encourage children to speak or write in standard English, you can differentiate between the two dialects by asking children to express themselves in "school talk," as opposed to "home talk."

When there are children from different racial, cultural and religious groups in your classroom, you may want to involve them in sharing ideas and experiences from their cultural backgrounds. But remember that this is an activity they must feel comfortable with, and all requests should be private. Each child in your class is an individual and not a representative for his or her particular race or ethnic group. Individual children may not have the necessary information to talk about holidays or celebrations in their cultures, and many older children feel uncomfortable drawing attention to themselves, particularly if this activity sets them apart from the majority culture.

Often, parents and community members indicate their willingness to share information and experiences from their respective cultures. You can send home letters asking for parents to volunteer to talk to the class about their cultural heritage. Of course, some children will be eager to share their experiences with customs that are unfamiliar to the rest of the class, and many will volunteer their parents or other relatives as well. Always call or write to parents to explain these situations. If you ask the parents to call, they may feel embarrassed and forced to do something they would not feel comfortable doing. Tell them what the class was discussing when their child volunteered their time or talent and explain that this type of contribution would be welcome, if it is something they wish to do.

Books to Increase Understanding

Children's books often contain vivid first-hand descriptions of how it feels to struggle with a mainstream language or survive within a majority culture. The following books help the reader imagine what it must be like to try to make sense of people and events in a culture, when the language and values are very different from one's own.

In the Year of the Boar and Jackie Robinson.[21] Bette Bao Lord tells the story of Shirley Temple Wong, who moves to America from China after World War II. Her struggles to learn English and fit in at school reflect courage, good humor and persistence. An especially inspiring part of this story deals with

Shirley's identification with Jackie Robinson and the Brooklyn Dodgers baseball team.

Plain Girl[22] by Virginia Sorenson is the story of Esther, an Amish girl who is forced to attend public school in Pennsylvania against her father's wishes. Esther is fascinated by the world at school, but is alienated from it by her strongly held religious beliefs. This is a view from the inside that helps the reader imagine how it must feel to struggle with contradicting values and to be "one black bird against the sky,"

WHAT DO YOU THINK?   What kind of response do you notice in yourself when you hear people speak in a different dialect? How important do you think it is for teachers to be aware of these responses? What dialects are represented in the schools where you observe or are student teaching? What information about these dialects would be helpful for you to know? What are some ways you could learn more about these dialects?

VI. Step-by-Step: Listening and Speaking Activities

Oral Reading   Walk around the classroom while students are reading aloud to each other. Alternate listening with making supportive comments when appropriate. Tell students what you like about their reading, such as "I really liked the way you hissed out those words! It sounded just like how a snake might talk," or "You've been practicing . . . you knew all the words." This is also a good time to make observations and take notes on students' speaking and listening skills. A suggested list for observation is included as part of the next section on evaluation.

Book Previews   Provide at least ten minutes each day for several students to give a brief preview of a book they are currently reading. As students gain confidence with the warm-up exercises described in the previous section, establish a weekly schedule for these presentations that will include every student in the classroom. In most classrooms this can be accomplished by scheduling four, five or six students per day. You can adapt the following form for your grade level to help students prepare for their presentations.

Book Preview Guidelines

1. Introduce the book by showing it to the class and naming the author and/or illustrator. Tell about any awards it has won and other books the author or illustrator has written or illustrated.

    Example: I'm going to tell you about *The Planet of Junior Brown.*[23] It was written by Virginia Hamilton, and it was a Newbery Honor Book in 1972. Virginia Hamilton wrote *The House of Dies Drear,*[24] which we read for our study of the Civil War, and M.C. *Higgins the Great,*[25] which some of us read for our Living in America theme in literature study.

2. Tell briefly what the book is about.

    Example: This is a story about two boys who are friends with a janitor in their high school. The janitor used to be a teacher, and he tries to help the boys with their problems. Junior Brown is a really big kid who is a musical genius, but no one understands him. The other boy, Buddy, is homeless, but no one knows it. The story tells about thousands of homeless boys in New York City. Buddy is one of the older boys who takes care of a group of younger children in abandoned buildings to keep them out of foster homes.

3. Tell why you like the book.

    Example: Reading this book was like entering a whole different world. I'd never even thought what it might be like not to have parents or a place to live. It reminded me of *Maniac Magee* and *Slake's Limbo*. I like reading about really good guys who try to make a difference where they live, even if it's rough.

4. Tell why you think someone else might like it.

    Example: If you like to solve problems, you'll probably like this book because the main character has to solve a lot of major problems for himself and the boys he takes care of.

5. Read a short passage to show what the writing is like.

    Example: This is a conversation between two boys who are trying to take care of other boys, getting them food and clothing and sending them to school. Each of these boys has the name "Tomorrow Billy," and each has a "planet" which is their assigned area to take care of. This passage shows how they think about their responsibilities. Remember that they're both just kids themselves, and they're really trying to be parents to other kids like them.

    Buddy was glad that the night before this one, there had been nobody but himself on his planet in the abandoned building. He had gone to bed about ten and had slept until it was time to go to work. Tonight he would get no sleep.

    Between 59th Street and 102nd Street Buddy dropped his clothing off at an all-night laundry and stopped at two more planets. Each of the planets had a full house but both Tomorrow Billys were broke. Buddy listened to the story of the second Tomorrow Billy, alert to the Billy's calm sincerity.

    "The work is drying up," the young man was saying. "I can't even pick up a busboy job anymore. Students are moving in on us, man. I got to feed these kids so I guess I'm going to have to lift more food than I usually do."

    There was danger in stealing too much, Buddy knew. "How are you for sweaters and stuff?" Buddy asked the Billy.

    "I got nothing left, man, but some long-sleeved polo shirts," the Billy said. "They not going to keep nobody warm, either. I been thinking about making capes out of the sleeping bags but then I figure the kids would stand out wearing something like that."

If students show an interest in the book, they can sign up to read it by entering their name on an index card with the name of the book on it. These "Next in Line" cards can be kept in a file box in the library area of the classroom.

Shared-Pair Discussions

During these discussions, you will want to move around the room to observe pairs and groups. Stay a few minutes with each group, and before you leave, comment on anything positive you have observed. If there are difficulties, ask the group a question that will help them reflect on their discussion, such as: "Are you being careful about not interrupting other people before they are done speaking?" or "How can you show others you are hearing what they say?"

Shared-Pair Discussion Guidelines

1. Read the issue carefully. What are your thoughts about this issue? What do you agree with? Disagree with? What evidence do you have for your opinion?
2. Make some notes about your thoughts.
3. Find your partner for the day and share your ideas, taking turns speaking and listening. Record what you agree with and disagree with.
4. Find your shared-pair partner and repeat the process above.
5. Meet together as a group of four and construct a position on the issue. Appoint a spokesperson from your group to tell your ideas to the entire class.
6. Listen carefully to what other people say. Did you learn something new? Do you see the issue in a different way than when you started thinking about it?

Puppet Theater

When students have had experience seeing puppet shows and have created and used their own puppets, explore the idea of writing or adapting a story for puppets to act out.

1. Choose a story or write one together. Popular choices in the primary grades include folktales and predictable stories. Older students enjoy tinkering with stories and creating modernized versions of traditional literature. All ages like to make up "origin" tales, such as how the horse got its tail or why potatoes grow underground. Good questions to ask are: What would happen if . . . ? Why would the characters do that?
2. When you have decided on a story, list and describe the major scenes, telling where and when they take place. Make an outline that briefly describes the setting, scenery and mood of the characters. Think about how to leave a scene in an interesting way and how to generate interest in the next one. What will be the conflict in the story and how will it be resolved?
3. If you are using a prepared puppet script, decide who will play the individual parts. If you are writing an original story or making an adaptation, encourage students to create lively dialogue and to include lots of action. Suggest varying the kinds of sentences and the length of individual speeches for contrast.

4. What background scenery should be made? How will scenery be moved? Will someone describe the setting and time ("This is Cinderella's room in the attic"), or will this information be placed on a poster beside the stage at the appropriate moment (Cinderella's Room—Before the Ball)? Some of these decisions must be made with the audience in mind. Musical or sound cues can indicate the passage of time, or posters can display a sun and moon.

5. What kinds of props will be required? Which can be found in the classroom or at home? Which will have to be made? What materials for constructing props and scenery are available in the classroom? What sound effects will be needed? Would music help the story? What special effects would make the play more interesting?

6. How many characters will be involved? What will they look like? What kinds of puppets will be made? Should they be talking mouth or action style? What kinds of materials will be needed? Who will make each puppet? How will the puppet's personality be revealed in its appearance or in the way it is made or moves?

7. It helps to practice the actions first, with someone reading them from the script. Students should concentrate on the movement of characters until they feel comfortable. The script can also be practiced on several read-throughs before putting the actions and dialogue together. Practice the play. Bring in ideas from oral reading to emphasize expression and encourage lots of action. How can performers use movement instead of dialogue to move the plot along? What moves look mysterious? Scary? Funny? Create a final script with simple directions for action and description of the scenes.

8. Decide who will be invited to the play. Generate interest by making posters and flyers to distribute to other classes that are invited. Decorate theme bookmarks to hand out to guests after the show.

9. Before the show, warm up the audience and relax the performers with a sing-a-long led by a puppet (student, teacher, music teacher). Afterward, have a question and answer period between the guests and the puppets. Tape the show to send home with students or to share with nursing homes.

Creative Drama

Exercises in creative drama are designed to stimulate imagination and enhance appreciation of sensory experience. When used in conjunction with literature study, students re-create a story by examining the context and exploring the feelings and motivations of characters. These exercises benefit skill development in speaking and listening, but they also enrich the reading and writing experience with their emphasis on imagery.

These are simple exercises to use before reading a story or as preparation for writing:

1. Begin with a relaxation exercise. Ask students to take two deep breaths and close their eyes.

2. Read the setting of a story. Ask students to imagine they are in the setting of the story: the hold of a ship, hiding in the dark near a pyramid, bouncing over ruts in a covered wagon.

3. Imagine that you are the main character in this story. How do you feel? What do you see?
4. What might happen in this story?

Examples:

You have just read the story of *The Three Billy Goats Gruff* to your class of kindergarten students. Taking each part of the story, the setting and the characters, ask questions that will help children imagine they are hungry goats, standing on one side of the bridge looking over to the other side. What does it feel like to be a goat? What do they look like? How does it feel to have horns on their heads and sharp hooves? Are they really, really hungry? As you ask the questions or provide students with prompts, let them act out what the goats are thinking and doing. How do they feel about crossing the bridge where a troll might come up and eat them? Explore what they are thinking and feeling during each part of the story.

Your sixth graders have just finished reading *The Giver* (op. cit.). In the final chapter, the main character, Jonas, uses his memory of snow to feel cold and transfer this experience to the baby he has fled with into the countryside. He is doing this to escape notice by heat-seeking planes that have been dispatched to capture him. Ask students to work in pairs, taking turns being Jonas and trying to transfer the memory of snow to their partner. Ask them to imagine the other feelings that Jonas is feeling, such as fear, desperation and hope.

Friday Afternoon Sharing Time

Because the goal of these sessions is to involve students as much as possible in their planning and presentation, your main responsibility will be in the early weeks of developing guidelines and modeling appropriate participation. As students gain experience and assume increasing responsibility for this sharing time, you will have more opportunities to observe their developing listening and speaking skills. Use this time to note the following, using a simple code such as: 0 (not observed); + (developing); and + + (well developed).

Student Name:

1. Interacts positively with others to plan.
2. Assumes responsibility for presentation details.
3. Responds positively to presentations.
4. Critical comments are diplomatic.
5. Critical comments show careful listening.

In the beginning, you will want to make a final-day check with everyone who has signed up for a presentation and be certain that all necessary physical arrangements have been made for displays and dramas. You will also want to meet with the person who is introducing the presenters or guests to make certain he or she has all necessary information. Place any forms that are to be distributed in a convenient place.

After a month or so, establish a rotating schedule for students to attend to each of these responsibilities. At first, you might want this group of students to report their work to you sometime before the session is to begin, so that you can be informed about their progress. Greet any guests who may arrive, then sit back and enjoy what your students have to share. Resist intruding if there are difficulties and allow students to solve their own problems.

WHAT DO YOU THINK? Can you imagine yourself as the teacher in the classrooms described above? With which of the activities described above are you most familiar? Which most appeal to you? Did you have any experience with these activities in elementary school? Later? Which ones would you like to have more experience with before you introduce them to your students? Which would you have enjoyed when you were in elementary school?

VII. If This Is Your Situation

If language arts teaching is departmentalized in your school or you must create a teamed program with other teachers, you can still provide many opportunities for your students to engage in speaking and listening activities. Begin by looking at the curriculum objectives. Most likely, there will be several that relate to listening and speaking skills. Which can be accomplished by scheduling book preview sessions? FAST presentations? Shared-pair discussions? Even in tightly scheduled classrooms, book previews can fill up spare minutes in the time before a noon bell or afternoon dismissal.

If you can demonstrate to a supervisor or a team colleague that students are learning and practicing the skills required by the curriculum objectives, you will probably be given the latitude to meet these objectives in any manner that you choose. It will be helpful to describe the activities you plan to do in writing to submit to the appropriate supervisor. Be sure to include explanations of how these activities will help students achieve the curriculum goals.

If a required schedule for team teaching seems to minimize opportunities for activities like the ones described above, approach the teachers on your team about the possibility of allowing students to work in small groups for projects and presentations in content area studies. Would they be interested in a joint FAST session to share projects in literature, science or social studies? Often, your colleagues will be happy to add these new experiences for students if you can gain the necessary approval from supervisors and volunteer to organize the project. Do not be discouraged if more experienced teachers are hesitant about trying something different. This is an understandable response and should not be taken personally. Remember that they have seen many educational innovations come and go and may be more cautious about trying new things. Most are very protective of new teachers and may want to spare them the disappointment that sometimes accompanies experimenting with new methods. Their experience and wisdom are invaluable in many instances, but as a beginning teacher, you will want to

experiment with new ideas in order to discover your own teaching style and
the methods that will work best for you and your students.

WHAT DO YOU   Why might more traditional teachers hesitate to add activities that
THINK?   encourage students to talk to each other? What difficulties might you
experience when you work together on these activities with other
teachers? Can you think of reasons why teachers might have experienced disappointment or discouragement with educational innovations?

VIII. Evaluating Speaking and Listening Activities

All during the day, students talk and listen to you and to each other. During
some of these times, you will be highly involved in the discussions and less
able to observe individual expression and response. You will want to target
specific times to observe your students speaking and listening when you are
able to record what is happening. These observations in turn can provide
direction for mini-lessons and future speaking and listening sessions. Try to
observe students when they are talking informally to each other in pairs or
small groups. Note how well they listen to each other in conversation. In
what speaking and listening situations are they most comfortable?

In addition to the guidelines for evaluating FAST presentations, you
might want to use a checklist similar to the following to observe speaking
and listening behaviors in students when they interact in groups. When you
are looking for development in these areas, it might be helpful to indicate a
baseline observation for each, marked by a code of: O—Often; R—Rarely;
and N—Never. Then you can record M—Maintained; D—Developing; or
ND—Not Developing in subsequent observations. Remember that your goal
for these evaluations is to help individual students increase these behaviors,
and this may mean providing additional opportunities for them to practice
these skills in pairs or small groups.

Listening and Speaking Assessment

Makes eye contact when talking
Makes eye contact when listening (see Section V for cultural variance)
Listens without interrupting
Is confident about talking
Takes turns talking
Includes others by asking questions
Assumes role of leader
Keeps group on task

It is always a good idea to hold a discussion time immediately after
presentations on health or safety to evaluate how well children understand
what was presented. Can they talk about it accurately? Are there any

misconceptions? Ask each child to respond to the prompt: "This is what I heard . . . ," or "This is what I learned . . ." Other children should be encouraged to respond to these statements with: "I heard that, too," or "I heard something different."

In these discussions you can also create a discussion chain to practice and clarify ideas. An example from a presentation on relating to strangers might involve the first student saying: "I learned . . . not to walk close to cars on the street." A second child would then say: "I learned not to walk close to cars on the street and to run away if someone bothers me." Depending on the age of students, these chains can build from two to six statements, with each child using the previous rule and adding one of his or her own.

At the intermediate level, you can encourage students to summarize what they have learned in response to prompts like: "The most important thing I learned was . . . ," or "The two most important things I learned were . . ." These summaries can be generated by individual students or created in small groups, written down and then shared with the rest of the group in the shared-pair format. Chaining and summarizing help you see immediately what students have learned from presentations critical to their health or safety.

WHAT DO YOU THINK? Can you think of other behaviors to observe in children that indicate they are developing skill in listening and speaking? Can you think of other situations where it is important to know what children understand from what they have heard?

IX. Creating Partners

Help your students share what they learned at school and build connections with their families' experiences by asking them to draw or write down something they learned at the end of the school day. Encourage them to talk with family members about what they drew or wrote. Children will discover that parents and other family members know something about many of the things they are learning. There may be an uncle who was in the Vietnam War or a picture of a great-great grandfather who fought in the Civil War. Relatives may live in urban areas, in the country or in countries being studied. Parents may remember their own parents telling them about the Depression or a World's Fair. Someone may have a small bag of ash and vivid memories of the Mount St. Helen's eruption. These home–school conversations help children see a connection between what they study at school and the experience of their own families. They also help you tap knowledge and expertise in the families of your students.

Many teachers extend opportunities for students to practice reading aloud by providing small portable tape recorders for use at home. Children can check out the tape recorders or use their own, if available, to record their oral reading. At every grade level, children can evaluate their progress by keeping a portfolio of several tapes. On their own, with friends or with members of their family, students can practice reading aloud favorite stories and plays; they can also record music and sound effects for classroom presentations, such as puppet plays. These activities allow children to be involved in their own oral language skill assessment.

If your students prepare FAST presentations, be sure to invite different kinds of audiences to participate. Students can create the publicity and invitations for these weekly events in the form of flyers, posters and individual notes. You might want to begin with other classes, school staff, the principal and special teachers. At other times, parents might be the best audience, or you can extend the invitation to other members of the community. Some schools sponsor activities such as Adopt-a-Grandparent or School Friends, which pair their students with nursing-home residents or children in day-care facilities for shared literacy events, such as choral readings, plays, puppet shows, Book Buddy reading and songfests.

X. Perspectives

Theorists who study the ways people acquire and use language are called **linguists**. All linguists agree that the structure of the English language includes **phonemes** (sounds), **syntax** (sentence order), **semantics** (word meanings) and **pragmatics** (the way language functions in a context), but they have differing beliefs about the importance each of these elements assumes in language acquisition. You already know that there are differing theories about the way people learn; because linguistics deals with the way people learn language, there are correspondingly different theories about language acquisition.

Descriptive linguists study language as it exists in human society and look for a system of rules within language itself. This is an **environmental** model, which sees speech development as a product of reinforcement and language itself as the product of an individual culture. When a baby begins to make random sounds, some of these sounds are reinforced by the environment when they are heard as words, such as "da-da" and "ma-ma." According to behaviorist theory, behavior that is reinforced becomes more frequent: The more a child is rewarded with smiles and exclamations for saying certain words, the more he or she repeats them. As a child makes other sounds, these in turn are reinforced or ignored. Teachers who follow a behaviorist model in their language arts teaching will try to help students imitate correct sounds, memorize vocabulary and learn rules of grammar, with the goal of helping them develop appropriate language.

In contrast, the **transformational-generative** linguists study the processes by which language is produced, the deep structures that explain the meaning of speech. They follow the **nativist** or **innatist** model, which describes speech as a process of unfolding thought. Language is generated by the child as he or she develops hypotheses about linguistic rules. The environment does not impose language; it supports it by providing opportunities for it to develop and grow, through modification and enrichment.

Piaget and Inhelder[26] see speech as arising from within children and developing in stages as they interact with the environment. Language is a developing process that is modified through experience and by an increased knowledge of how to use the structures of language. They believe that adults should not interfere with this naturally developing process by imposing adult models or standards for language use.

Cognitive psychologists and **semiotic** theorists such as Lev Vygotsky[27] believe that language has a social origin and is a system in a complex interrelationship with the culture itself. This is an **interactive** model of language acquisition and development, one that emphasizes the importance of social interaction. Unlike the innatist model that describes speech as coming from self, Vygotsky sees speech as moving from the social to self, from social speech to inner speech. Vygotsky and others see a more active role for parents and teachers in the development of language. According to this theory, children will acquire and develop language skills more readily when they are encouraged to communicate for authentic reasons.

Teachers who adopt this point of view integrate language learning into the curriculum and relate writing to their students' real-life experiences. They challenge students to more sophisticated language use by encouraging them to talk about the functions of language and to experiment with their language expression in speaking and writing.

Michael Halliday[28] identified seven social functions for language that develop before a child enters school. They include: an **instrumental** function to satisfy basic needs; a **regulatory** function to influence the behavior of others; an **interactional** function to mediate relationships with others; a **personal** function to express the self; a **heuristic** function to explore the environment; an **imaginative** function to explore an imaginative world; and an **informative** function to communicate information to others. These functions gradually merge into three more general functions[29] that are used simultaneously in adult language: the **interpersonal** function for maintaining social relationships; the **ideational** function for reflecting on personal relationships and exploring the environment; and the **textual** function, which uses language resources to speak coherently within the context of a situation.

Linguists who see language as either a product or a process study the **sentence** as the unit of meaning, while the semiotic linguist looks at a **text** (a unit of meaningful exchange, such as a conversation, a story or a poem) in its relationship to the context in which it is produced and the meaning it expresses. They see the text as the minimal unit of language and believe that the context of conversations guides the language and is the key to its understanding. These contexts usually involve the physical environment, the people involved, their background knowledge and the event or topic at hand.

Kenneth Goodman et al.[30] believe that these alternative explanations of the ways language develops are complementary, useful for different purposes and applications. Examination of language as a product may help explain why communication breaks down with dialect differences, while a process description of language may be helpful in trying to identify comprehension problems in reading. The more functional interactive explanation is helpful to understand the use and development of language as it occurs in a social context.

As a teacher of language arts, you will continue to be interested in the ways children acquire and develop language skills. You may want to explore the work of Vygotsky and Halliday, whose theories are important resources for the integrated approach to language learning.

> Lev Vygotsky, *Mind in Society* (op. cit.) The Russian psychologist believes that children learn language in a social context, with support from adults and peers. Teachers and classmates can help individuals construct meaning from new experience by sharing ideas, strategies and techniques for language learning.

> Michael Halliday, *Learning How to Mean: Explorations in the Development of Language* (op. cit.) Halliday sees language learning as an active process that involves experimentation and approximations of standard language. Usage errors are to be expected because language is developmental, and children gradually perfect their usage through experience. Halliday believes that children learn language holistically, in a social context. He identifies seven functions of children's language, which he believes are important for children to experience in the classroom.

> James Britton, *Language and Learning: The Importance of Speech in Children's Development*[31] This classic book explores the relationships among language, experience and thought. Britton describes the way children use speech to interact with people and things to create experience and develop thinking skills. He sees children as meaning makers who construct knowledge in terms of their own experience.

WHAT DO YOU THINK? Which of the linguistic theories best supports the way you were taught language arts in elementary school? Which theory most closely supports what you currently believe about language learning?

XI. Exploring Professional Literature

In addition to professional journals that can inform and inspire your teaching, you will want to examine the major research reference guide for language arts teaching, the *Handbook of Research on Teaching the English Language Arts*.[32] This volume, which you can find in the reference section of your curriculum library, is designed to provide teachers with information about basic research findings in language arts teaching and to indicate directions the field might be taking in the future. Articles are written by prominent scholars and educational leaders, who summarize and interpret research findings that can provide a foundation for classroom decision making.

What kinds of articles will you find in this handbook? You might want to begin with the article "Understanding Research on Teaching the English

Language Arts: An Introduction for Teachers"[33] in the section that describes methods of research in language arts teaching. If you want to learn more about linguistics, you will find an article entitled "Linguistics and Teaching the Language Arts"[34] in the section that discusses the theoretical bases for language arts teaching. If you want to learn more about how to teach children whose dialects differ from the mainstream, you would be interested in "Dialects, Culture, and Teaching the English Language Arts"[35] in the section that deals with research on language learners. As you reach out to parents and other community members, you might want to refer to "The Community and Language Arts"[36] in the section that describes environments for language arts teaching. If you want to convince yourself and others that integrating the language arts is a sound practice, you might want to examine research on specific aspects of language arts, such as "Language Across the Curriculum,"[37] which examines the theoretical bases for integrated language learning.

You can examine the ideas in this book by consulting the subject index, or you might want to see what certain educators have to say about language arts by using the name index. Because this handbook summarizes a great many research studies, it can direct you toward relevant studies on almost any topic and provide a broader context for current reading in professional journals.

WHAT DO YOU THINK? As you read an article of your choice in the *Handbook,* jot down ideas that draw your interest or provide you with information you think might be helpful. Remember that this book is intended for a wide range of professional educators. What part of the article do you think was intended for you? Which of your own experiences helped you connect with the ideas presented in the article?

XII. Resources for Teaching

The books listed in this section will provide you with additional ideas for integrating listening and speaking activities into your classroom program.

Cycles of Meaning: Exploring the Potential of Talk in Learning Communities[38] This is a collection of essays written by practicing classroom teachers. It provides ideas for involving students in discussions through literature and helps them discover new meaning in what they read by talking together in small groups. The essays include ways to involve students in special education, those who are bilingual or who are part of an ESL program.

Dramatizing Literature in Whole Language Classrooms[39] This is a good book for beginners that describes improvised drama and shows how to connect this activity with other areas of the curriculum. It contains ideas and examples for all levels of elementary instruction and includes suggestions for poems and stories to use as prompts.

Drama with Children by Geraldine Siks (op. cit.) reflects thirty years of research in the field of creative drama. Dr. Siks sees drama as integral to developing skill in the language arts. Listening, speaking, reading and writing are the core of students' dramatic experience as creative players, critical audience, script performers and playwrights. She regards drama as a process for problem solving, one that involves the development and exercise of cognitive skills.

How to Tape Instant Oral Biographies: Recording Your Family's Life Story in Sound and Sight by Bill Zimmerman (op. cit.) is an easy-to-read, large-type book is filled with ideas for helping children become better acquainted with the older generations in their families. It includes ideas and questions for interviews, video and home movie ideas and tips for taking notes. This is an excellent student resource, with easy-to-understand guidelines that competently direct both individual and group research activity.

The Creative Classroom: A Guide for Using Creative Drama in the Classroom, PreK–6[40] This is an excellent book to help you begin exploring creative drama in the classroom. It is especially designed for teachers who have no previous experience with creative drama, with step-by-step instructions for implementing each activity. Techniques described can be used to reinforce concepts in all curriculum areas and to promote language, comprehension and thinking skills. The book includes sample lessons and modifications for different curriculum areas and grade levels. All activities have been developed from direct work with students and have been used successfully by a wide range of teachers.

Storymaking and Drama: An Approach to Teaching Language and Literature[41] Good ideas for using creative drama to explore literature are presented. The author uses stories from many different cultures to illustrate strategies and includes a section on using drama with students who have limited English proficiency.

Talking to Learn[42] This is a collection of teaching ideas to help develop listening and speaking skills. The individual essays describe activities at all levels of instruction, but many of the ideas for secondary classrooms can be adapted for use in the intermediate grades.

Creative Drama and Imagination: Transforming Ideas into Action[43] This is an excellent introduction to using dramatic activities in the classroom. More than half the book is devoted to descriptions of these activities, which tell the reader how to set them up and conduct them. They also identify the perspective the activity is intended to inform or enrich (director, actor, critic, designer, playwright) and offer information about the dramatic stimulus, suggested props, ways to evaluate and possible extensions. Case studies from the world of theater and examples from school settings make this book an excellent resource for teachers interested in using drama in the classroom.

Playbuilding: A Guide for Group Creation of Plays with Young People[44] This helpful manual provides instructions for creating plays from prompts. The author illustrates method by showing examples from plays he has created with students, beginning with initial discussions and ending with final performances. The book is richly illustrated with photographs of student performances.

On Stage: The Trumpet Club's Classroom Play Kit[45] This kit includes twenty-six pages of general instructions for putting on a classroom play, a glossary of theatrical terms and a glossary of production responsibilities. Also included is a script for *How to Eat Fried Worms*,[46] adapted from the book by Thomas Rockwell. A boy makes a bet that he can eat fifteen worms a day. The story tells how his family and friends help him keep his bet. There are general and specific acting exercises and tip sheets with ideas for tryouts, rehearsals, props, publicity, scenery, costumes, staging, improvisation and blocking. This is a good basic kit to help students see what is involved in putting on a play. From these general directions, they can adapt other favorite books on their own.

Tomie dePaola's *Little Grunt and the Big Egg*[47] This play, an adaptation of a favorite primary book, has parts for as many as twenty players and a narrator, although the play can be presented with as few as eight children.

Puppet Shows Made Easy! by Nancy Renfro is an excellent "how-to-do-it" guide for preparing and presenting puppet shows, including how to adapt stories, make scripts and build scenery and puppets. Props, songs, stages, sound effects and special effects and illusions are also described. The author permits reproduction of all patterns, drawings and scripts in the book for use in the classroom. Other books in the *Puppetry in Education Series*[48] by the same author include: *Puppet Corner in Every Library*, *Puppetry and the Art of Story Creation*, *Puppetry and Creative Dramatics in Storytelling*, *Make Amazing Puppets* and *Pocketful of Puppets*.

WHAT DO YOU THINK? Which of the resources described above draw your interest? Is there an activity like puppetry or creative drama that you would like to learn more about?

XIII. Reflections

From a Teacher's Journal—Jackie Hogue, Fifth Grade

We read two stories for enjoyment and discussed them. The discussions were not as lively as I would have liked. We talked about participation. . . . We began reading *Island of the Blue Dolphins*. Discussions are going better. I've encouraged students to discuss the book as they read with a partner or small group. This seems to help class discussions because it brings to mind what they've discussed with their partners.

We're going to begin a study of Native Americans, and we need a way to let parents know what we're doing. I suggested the idea of a newspaper, and they were so excited about choosing what they wanted to write that they wanted to start immediately. I gave them an author's checklist to help with revising and editing. They were definitely ON TASK! After the kids completed the articles, I made copies of the newspaper. They kicked off their shoes, relaxed and read their very own newspaper. Kurt said it was the most interesting writing he'd ever read! He said it was so cool! I had a lot of positive feedback from the parents, too. They want us to publish more, because they want to know what is going on in class. Good PR.

Another neat experience—The kids had mentioned in their journals that they'd like a visitor with Native American expertise to come to the classroom.

I know a lady who was married to a Native American at one time. The whole class wanted to call her and were ready to do so without putting any thought into it. When I asked what they would say to her, they thought we better discuss it. We brainstormed all the details and picked two boys who would make the call. The class quizzed them to see if they could remember everything, so they decided to make notes. To get the phone number, they wanted to ask the secretary, but we encouraged them to look it up themselves. We reviewed telephone manners, they went down to the office to make the call, and she's coming Thursday!

I noticed that many kids were using dependent clauses at the beginning of their sentences. We talked about what makes a clause dependent and discussed how to use a comma correctly. I told them that they would learn about dependent clauses in high school, but since they were writing like high schoolers, we would discuss it now. They were all ears. Adam drew a cartoon of Santa Claus standing under water in the deep end of a swimming pool and labeled it "A Deep-ended Claus!"

TRYING OUT THE CHAPTER IDEAS

1. If you are able to observe a classroom, notice the opportunities students have to develop their speaking ability. Notice particularly how often they speak to ask questions of concern to themselves or to express their ideas.

2. Observe one child in the classroom for at least an hour. Tally the times this particular child has opportunities to speak. What kinds of groups is she/he a part of? How often does he/she participate in discussions, compared to others in the group?

3. Use the assessment list for group participation in the evaluation section of this chapter. Walk around the room and practice noticing these behaviors in the students you observe. Do you see a wide variation?

4. Offer to sponsor a FAST presentation for your classroom. Be sure to tell your cooperating teacher exactly what is involved for preparation and presentation. Record your experience, noting what went well and what might be helpful to plan for the next time.

5. Observe how teachers handle disputes between children in their classrooms. Do they help students use language in a constructive manner to settle their differences? Did you see anything you would like to remember for your own use?

6. Find a play designed for reader's theater and read it aloud with a group of classmates.

7. Plan a reader's theater session with the students in your field-experience classroom.

8. Explore an area of language expression that you are least familiar with. Try making different kinds of puppets or responding to literature in one of the ways described in the FAST section. You might want to experiment with your new knowledge by helping your students make puppets or by showing them how to develop a play from a favorite story.

Notes

1. Jerome Bruner, *Toward a Theory of Instruction* (Cambridge, Mass.: Harvard University Press, 1966).

2. Jerome Bruner, *Acts of Meaning* (Cambridge, Mass.: Harvard University Press, 1990).

3. Developed by the author for use in the elementary classroom.

4. H. K. Mackintosh, *Children and Oral Language* (Urbana, Ill.: National Council of Teachers of English, 1964). A joint statement of the Association for Childhood Education International, Association for Supervision and Curriculum Development, International Reading Association, National Council of Teachers of English.

5. R. Lloyd-Jones and A. A. Lunsford, eds., *The English Coalition Conference: Democracy Through Language* (Urbana, Ill.: National Council of Teachers of English, 1989).

6. H. Mehan, *Learning Lessons: Social Organization in the Classroom* (Cambridge, Mass.: Harvard University Press, 1979).

7. M. J. Dunkin and B. J. Biddle, *The Study of Teaching* (New York: Holt, Rinehart & Winston, 1974).

8. G. Wells, *Learning Through Interaction: The Study of Language Development* (Cambridge: Cambridge University Press, 1981).

9. S. Delamont, *Interaction in the Classroom: Contemporary Sociology of the School*, 2d ed. (London: Methuen, 1983).

10. Geraldine Siks, *Drama with Children*, 2d ed. (New York: Harper & Row, 1983).

11. Jonathan Rutland, *See Inside a Submarine* (New York: Watts, 1988).

12. Jan Brett, adapter, *The Mitten: A Ukrainian Folktale* (East Rutherford, N.J.: G. P. Putnam's Sons, 1989).

13. Alvin Tresselt, *The Mitten* (Fairfield, N.J.: Lothrop, 1964).

14. Bill Zimmerman, *How to Tape Instant Oral Biographies: Recording Your Family's Life Story in Sound and Sight* (New York: Bantam, 1992).

15. Mary Norton, *The Borrowers* (New York: Harcourt, 1953). Sequels include: *The Borrowers Afield* (1955), *The Borrowers Afloat* (1959), *The Borrowers Aloft* (1961), *The Borrowers Avenged* (1982), *Poor Stainless* (1985).

16. Mary Norton, *Poor Stainless: A New Story About the Borrowers* (New York: Harcourt, 1985).

17. Bill Martin, Jr. and John Archambault, *Knots on a Counting Rope* (New York: Trumpet Club, 1987). This beautifully illustrated book is a chanted conversation between a blind Native American boy and his grandfather.

18. Lois Lowry, *The Giver* (New York: Houghton Mifflin, 1993).

19. Caroline Feller Bauer, *Presenting Reader's Theater* (New York: H. W. Wilson, 1987).

20. Janice Hale Benson, *Black Children: Their Roots, Culture, and Learning* (Baltimore, Md.: The Johns Hopkins University Press, 1986), p. 16.

21. Bette Bao Lord, *In the Year of the Boar and Jackie Robinson* (New York: Trumpet Club, 1984).

22. Virginia Sorenson, *Plain Girl* (New York: Scholastic, 1983).

23. Virginia Hamilton, *The Planet of Junior Brown* (New York: Macmillan, 1971).

24. Virginia Hamilton, *The House of Dies Drear* (New York: Macmillan, 1968).

25. Virginia Hamilton, M.C. *Higgins the Great* (New York: MacMillan, 1974). The story of a young African American boy growing up in Appalachia. Warm family setting; deals with prejudice, fear and problem solving.

26. J. Piaget and B. Inhelder, *The Psychology of the Child* (New York: Basic Books, 1969).

27. Lev Vygotsky, *Mind in Society* (Cambridge, Mass.: Harvard University Press, 1978).

28. Michael Halliday, *Explorations in the Functions of Language* (London: Edward Arnold, 1973).

29. Michael Halliday, *Learning How to Mean: Explorations in the Development of Language* (London: Edward Arnold, 1975).

30. Kenneth S. Goodman, E. Brooks Smith, Robert Meredith, and Yetta Goodman, *Language and Thinking in School: A Whole-Language Curriculum*, 3d ed. (New York: Richard C. Owen Publishers, Inc., 1987).

31. James Britton, *Language and Learning: The Importance of Speech in Children's Development*, 2d ed. (New York: Boynton/Cook, 1993).

32. James Flood, Julie M. Jensen, Diane Lapp, and James R. Squire, eds., *Handbook of Research on Teaching the English Language Arts* (New York: Macmillan, 1991).

33. Sandra Stotsky with V. Cindy Mall, "Understanding Research on Teaching the English Language Arts: An Introduction for Teachers," in *Handbook of Research on Teaching the English Language Arts* (New York: Macmillan, 1991).

34. Paula Menyuk, "Linguistics and Teaching the Language Arts," in *Handbook of Research on Teaching the English Language Arts* (New York: Macmillan, 1991).

35. Marcia Farr, "Dialects, Culture, and Teaching the English Language Arts," in *Handbook of Research on Teaching the English Language Arts* (New York: Macmillan, 1991).

36. Walt Wolfram, "The Community and Language Arts," in *Handbook of Research on Teaching the English Language Arts* (New York: Macmillan, 1991).

37. Mary K. Healy and Mary A. Barr, "Language Across the Curriculum," in *Handbook of Research on Teaching the English Language Arts* (New York: Macmillan, 1991).

38. Kathryn Mitchell Pierce, *Cycles of Meaning: Exploring the Potential of Talk in Learning Communities* (Portsmouth, N.H.: Heinemann, 1993).

39. John Warren Stewig, *Dramatizing Literature in Whole Language Classrooms* (New York: Teachers College Press, 1994).

40. Lenore Blank Kelner, *The Creative Classroom: A Guide for Using Creative Drama in the Classroom, PreK–6* (Portsmouth, N.H.: Heinemann, 1993).

41. Nancy King, *Storymaking and Drama: An Approach to Teaching Language and Literature* (Portsmouth, N.H.: Heinemann, 1993).

42. Patricia Phelan, Chair, and the Committee on Classroom Practices, *Talking to Learn: Classroom Practices in Teaching English, Vol. 24* (Urbana, Ill.: National Council of Teachers of English, 1989).

43. Helane S. Rosenberg, *Creative Drama and Imagination: Transforming Ideas into Action* (New York: CBS College Publishing, 1987).

44. Errol Bray, *Playbuilding: A Guide for Group Creation of Plays with Young People* (Portsmouth, N.H.: Heinemann, 1994).

45. The Trumpet Club, *On Stage: The Trumpet Club's Classroom Play Kit.* Can be obtained from the Trumpet Club, P.O. Box 604, Holmes, PA 19043.

46. Thomas Rockwell, *How to Eat Fried Worms* (New York: Dell, 1973).

47. *Little Grunt and the Big Egg: A Play* is a script adapted by William Morton from Tomie dePaola's *Little Grunt and the Big Egg: A Prehistoric Fairy Tale.*

48. Nancy Renfro, *Puppetry in Education Series* (Austin, Texas: Nancy Renfro, 1984). Each of these books can be obtained from: Nancy Renfro Studios, 1117 W. 9th Street, Austin, Texas 78703. A free catalog is available on request.

CHAPTER EIGHT

Writing to Learn

WHAT'S HAPPENING HERE? What do you notice about this child's concentration? This young author is writing and illustrating her own book, which will be laminated, bound and placed in the classroom library. Student-authored books are well-worn from repeated use by the end of the school year. Why do you think students enjoy reading each other's writing?

Whatever sentence will bear to be read twice, we may be sure was thought twice.

—Henry David Thoreau

Learn as much by writing as by reading.

—Lord Acton

Reading maketh a full man, conference a ready man, and writing an exact man.

—Sir Francis Bacon

LOOKING AHEAD
1. What is the relationship of writing to reading?
2. Why is an audience important to a writer?
3. What happens during an individual writing conference?
4. How does a student prepare for a writing conference?
5. What can teachers learn during a writing conference?
6. How are portfolios used?
7. What is developmental spelling?
8. How does student self-evaluation improve the quality of writing?

IN 25 WORDS OR LESS Writing activities help students organize their ideas and express their feelings, in contexts designed to help them expand their experience and improve their writing.

I. Focus: A Closer Look at Writing

In classrooms where language learning is an integral part of the curriculum, students have many opportunities to write throughout the day. At the kindergarten level, children write captions for pictures they draw, participate in group writing activities, write words and sentences in response to theme studies and search for words they want to use in writing from a variety of sources. At the primary and intermediate levels, students record books they have read, write responses to literature, keep notes in a research journal, write reports, explore the various writing genres, participate in prewriting exercises and publish their writing efforts for others to read.

Writing is a reciprocal and complementary part of language learning. When teachers read an exciting or humorous story to children, they are sharing someone's writing efforts. When beginning writers talk about their experiences or responses to literature and the teacher records these words, they see how what they hear and say turns into something that can be written down and read. Educators who study young children observe that pre-schoolers' first attempts to read are tied to their efforts to write. They scribble circles and lines that resemble their impressions of writing and then "read" the words or stories they have created.

In traditional classrooms, teachers frequently teach **about** writing and provide exercises for constructing sentences and paragraphs. Most writing, in terms of completed projects, is completed outside of class. Students write papers, poems or themes as homework assignments, which are then graded and handed back for corrections. The purpose of writing, in topic and form, is to meet a certain set of grading criteria.

In classrooms that integrate language learning into the curriculum, students write to express their ideas and communicate with others for real purposes. Teachers in these classrooms see writing as a **process** and believe that students need to experience the entire writing process with each project. They provide students the opportunity to engage in prewriting activities that will help them develop ideas and explore possibilities. They model the ideas of rhetorical stance, assisting students as they define the purpose of their writing, establish a voice, anticipate an audience and decide on the best form to communicate their ideas. Teachers also provide opportunities for post-writing activities, such as revising, editing, proofreading, sharing and publishing. They plan for students to experience and practice all elements of writing during class time so that they are available to coach and monitor progress.

In these classrooms literature often provides models for writing. Story or content area themes stimulate research and encourage children to write about similar topics. Students attempt their own writing in the various literary genres and refer back to favorite authors as models for their writing. Teachers provide many opportunities for children to write because they know that writing, like reading, improves with practice and is a valuable tool for learning. They model different approaches to writing and help students organize their thoughts, reflect on their experience, make relationships and compare and contrast ideas they are exploring.

Students are encouraged to communicate with others in letters, essays and newspaper articles. They compose songs, create posters and write reviews of books, films and television programs. Students work together to write radio and TV news broadcasts, conduct interviews and write advertisements and editorials. They write letters to the editors of community newspapers and correspond with pen pals and favorite authors. They record their thoughts in personal journals or diaries and respond to literature, individually or in small groups. As a class, they create dictionaries and content area theme books. As individuals, students write and publish their own books. They write to explore and learn about concepts in all areas of the curriculum.

Each of these activities is based on the premise that students create meaning through their writing and communicate this meaning to themselves and others. Writing is an excellent way to express joy, sadness, anger or loneliness. Through writing, students can discover what they understand and what they need to know. The process of writing helps children clarify their ideas and gives them new insights into their own thoughts and feelings. When writing is shared with others, the listener's response usually provides an immediate and satisfying reward to the writer.

Teachers in these classrooms support the use of **developmental spelling** in student writing. When students are eager to express their ideas, they write the sounds they hear in words, without worrying at this stage about correct spelling. Standard spelling gradually emerges, but it is considered an editing procedure, separate from the creative process. Students pay increased attention to standardized spelling as they increase their desire to communicate and share ideas with others. With many opportunities to examine words in print and with experience in writing their own ideas, they become aware of spelling conventions. If a word does not look right, they leave spaces for missing letters or circle it. When they are finished writing, they look up the words in the dictionary or ask someone for assistance. The spellings of words they use frequently are recorded in personal dictionaries for future reference.

Although **handwriting** is a mechanical skill that students develop throughout the elementary grades, many teachers regard handwriting as a tool that allows children to express their ideas for themselves and communicate them to others. They provide models to form manuscript or cursive letters, but the emphasis is on helping individual students write in a style that is legible, consistent and comfortable for them personally. Teachers provide opportunities for beginning students to trace letters in the air, on each other's backs and on paper, as they write about things and ideas that interest them.

Students at all elementary levels can assume responsibility for dating and filing examples of their work in individual folders. In a continuing process of self-evaluation, they select examples of their work to include in their **portfolios**, which are collections of work that represent the best efforts of a student and demonstrate progress over a period of time.

This chapter contains descriptions of writing activities that can be found in classrooms that integrate language learning into the entire curriculum. Some, such as writing workshops and the composition of language experience charts, feature group interaction. Others, like key word dictation and individual writing conferences, feature one-on-one interaction between the teacher and individual students. Prewriting activities, such as brainstorming, mapping and data charts, which help students generate, organize and explore ideas, are described in Chapter 11. Other prewriting exercises, such as timed writing, webbing and word banks, and the postwriting activities of revision, editing, proofreading and book publishing are described in Chapter 9.

Key word dictation is one of the most basic and successful writing activities for beginning writers. On a daily basis, teachers ask individual students for their favorite word, writing it down on a piece of tagboard or in a student notebook. The teacher helps the student trace the word with his or her finger, talks about the sounds the letters make and provides materials and time for the student to practice writing the word. When key words are used for beginning reading, they give children or ESL students an immediate sense of being able to read and write about things that are important to them.

Captioning is also an excellent beginning activity to establish the reading–writing connection with students. A **caption** is a word or several words written at the top of a page to describe a picture, a discussion or a story. This is one of the first types of writing that children attempt when they scribble something next to pictures they have drawn to name them. In kindergarten, children may begin the year by asking teachers to title their drawings, but with encouragement, they soon write their own captions. Eventually, these captions expand to sentences and then paragraphs as students develop confidence in their ability to record experiences that are meaningful to them.

Teachers also use captions to help students develop the idea of topics in writing. When students dictate stories, as individuals or in a group, they are encouraged to think about the main ideas of their discussion. These ideas are then distilled into single words or phrases and moved around as part of an outline for writing. Captions are also used to help students generate titles that express the main idea of completed writing.

Language experience charts fill up the classrooms of teachers who integrate language learning into the entire curriculum. These charts are posters or large pieces of paper with oversized writing, displayed on easels and walls or hung from wire or string across the room, for easy reference by students. Charts are constructed daily from group conversations about personal and school experiences and include accounts of group experiences, lists of things to do, stories, poems, recipes, observations, schedules, cafeteria menus, instructions and lists of words in specific categories.

At the beginning level, students learn that what they say can be written down and that this writing is something that can be read to reconstruct what they say. When students write independently, they find many of the words they want to use on these charts, from words about winter to the correct spelling for a favorite dinosaur. At the intermediate level, charts display content area terminology, definitions, and guidelines for discussions, writing and research. ESL students use the story charts as models for spelling and sentence construction.

Recording activities vary from classroom to classroom, but most teachers encourage students to use combinations of the following: writing and literature logs; personal dictionaries; diaries; literature response journals; research journals. The purpose of these activities is to create references for writing by keeping a record of ideas, words and resources. Each time students read a book, they record an entry in their **literature log**, along with a brief description or notes on what they liked about it. **Writing logs** contain ideas for writing, guidelines for individual conferences, skill practice assignments and a list of writing projects completed. When students want to know how to spell a word, they look it up in the dictionary or ask the teacher. The teacher helps the student use decoding and context skills to find the correct spelling, which is then entered into their **personal dictionary**. Information and examples from mini-lessons are also recorded in these books, which become reference tools for writing.

Literature journals, which were described in Chapter 5, are loose-leaf or spiral notebooks used independently by students to record ideas and questions about books they have read. They are also used in small groups for sharing and discussing ideas about literature. When teachers respond in writing to their entries, these books are called literature response journals. Diaries are more personal journals of ideas and responses to everyday experiences and events in a student's life. Essentially private conversations with themselves, these diaries are sometimes shared on a voluntary basis with the teacher, as part of a continuing conversation about things the student believes to be important. Students submit individual entries or mark the pages in a spiral notebook when they want the teacher to read and respond to what they have written. Students use research or learning journals to record information about topics or themes in science, mathematics or the social studies.

In writing workshops everyone (including the teacher) writes independently and without interruption for a set period of time. Mini-lessons may precede these sessions, and time is usually provided for several students to read their writing aloud to the rest of the class. Students volunteer to read a completed work or a work-in-progress for comment by their peers. As students take turns sitting in the author's chair to share their writing, they provide an audience for each other and help each other improve the quality of their writing. These sessions, which may last from twenty minutes to an hour, usually provide time to evaluate and discuss four to six examples of writing. Members of the audience contribute positive comments and suggestions aloud or submit written evaluations to the presenter. Because audience participation is regarded as an emerging skill, each student learns to develop ways to respond positively and critically to the presentations with the help of teacher modeling, student-developed guidelines and lots of practice.

Individual writing conferences are scheduled with students on a weekly basis. More informal interactions between individual students and the teacher occur daily in brief walk-around conferences that will be described later in this chapter. Students prepare for conferences by writing daily in response to literature, personal experience and content area study, recording their thoughts and ideas in creative ways. They bring an example of their writing to share with the teacher, either something they believe to be their best work or a piece that is giving them difficulty. They may read it aloud to the teacher during the conference or submit it in advance for prereading. During the conference, the teacher comments on the positive aspects of the writing and asks pertinent questions that will help students improve the quality of their expression.

WHAT DO YOU THINK? In what ways have you used writing today? When was the last time you wrote something to express your own ideas? As a student in elementary school, which of the above writing activities were included in your curriculum? Do you think writing proficiency is more or less important now than in the past?

II. The Importance of Writing

Donald Graves[1] describes the importance of writing in his book *Build a Literate Classroom*. He believes that when children write about ideas and experiences that have meaning for them and share these ideas with others, they become increasingly aware of the "durable power" of writing as a permanent record of things they have experienced or thought about (p. 48). As they practice taking notes about things they have read about or seen, children begin to understand that information can be stored through writing. Sharing their writing by reading it aloud in a friendly group helps children share the unique way they see the world. The responses of others to their writing also help them discover new things about the people, places, things or ideas they have written about.

Lucy Calkins[2] believes that children learn to think on paper. In the process of writing down their thoughts and memories, they often discover ideas to write about and find direction for their writing. Marilyn Boutwell[3] describes students' behavior during writing as a continuous process of alternating between writing and reading. A child writes, then reads what has been written, and returns to writing as part of a strategy of making sense in his or her communication. Lucy Calkins[4] observes that students read continually as they write in order to enjoy what they have written, to edit and rehearse their ideas and to create momentum for further writing. Students read their writing aloud to others and study others' writing for inspiration and direction for their own. Calkins also observes that the skills used in writing are useful skills for reading, such as finding the main idea, identifying cause and effect, supplying supporting details and developing conclusions.

Tierney and Pearson[5] see reading and writing as essentially similar processes. Writers create for readers, and readers must re-create the ideas of the writers to gain the intended message or experience. Both reader and writer are trying to make sense of what is happening on the page. Goodman et al.[6] observe, however, that reading and writing are not reverse processes. Readers are free to pick and choose many of their clues for meaning. Depending on their own knowledge and background, they can move toward comprehension in a personal way. Writers, on the other hand, must engage in a more complete and systematic process that considers the knowledge and experience of the intended readers.

Is there a relationship between writing and reading proficiency? A review of reading/writing research by Sandra Stotsky[7] concluded that good writers are also good readers. Correlational studies indicated that better writers tend to read more, and better readers tend to produce better writing.

How important is your involvement as a teacher to your students' writing development? Very important, according to researchers such as McClure,[8] who found that time, space, materials and teacher conviction are directly tied to the success of a writing program in the classroom. Other teacher factors that support student interaction with literature include the support of experimentation and divergent thinking, praise and feedback, acknowledgment of writing as a challenging process, clear-cut expectations within which children can work comfortably and the encouragement of self-determination.

WHAT DO YOU THINK?   Can you think of an experience in your own schooling where you were encouraged to take risks with your writing by trying something new in content or form or expression? What happened? Why do you think that good writers are also good readers?

III. Looking into Classrooms

Kindergarten Level—Captions and Key Words

"Did you bring some writing to show me?" Mrs. Morning Light asks.

Bright Feather hands her a detailed picture of warriors on horseback hunting buffalo.

"Tell me about your picture," she says, and Bright Feather tells her an extended story that reaches beyond the picture into preparation for the hunt, the participants and the eventual conclusion.

"And what do you call your picture?" she asks when he has finished describing it.

"Buffalo Hunt," he says proudly, indicating the words at the top of the page. "My sister showed me the letters for 'buffalo' and I spelled 'hunt' myself, except she said to make the *h* a big letter," he adds.

"I like your picture," Mrs. Morning Light says. "It has much life in it."

Bright Feather nods modestly.

"Your letters are easy to read," the teacher says. She pulls a paper from Bright Feather's portfolio. "Look at this paper you wrote last month and tell me the ways you have improved," she says, handing him the paper.

Bright Feather examines the two papers carefully. "This *B*," he says, pointing to the first letter in his title. "It's better."

"How is it better?" the teacher asks.

"It's bigger than the other letters." He points to the capital *B*'s he wrote to caption a picture called "Bright Feather's Brothers," where the capital letters were the same size as the lowercase letters.

"I can tell that you've been working hard on that," the teacher says. "Why is it important for readers to see capitals?" she asks.

"They're signals," Bright Feather replies.

"What kind of signals are these?" the teacher asks, pointing to the title "Bright Feather's Brothers."

"Title signals," he replies, "and names, too."

"And these?" she asks, pointing to "Buffalo Hunt."

"It's a title signal," he replies.

"What else has improved?" the teacher asks.

Bright Feather looks closely at the two papers. "This *a* is better," he concludes. "It's closed on top so it doesn't look like a *u*."

"You observe very well," the teacher says. "Did you bring some sentences to show me?"

Bright Feather hands her a piece of lined paper with two sentences written on it. The letters are nicely formed, but spacing is somewhat uneven.

"Show me your best word," she asks.

Bright Feather considers this and points to "hunter."

"What would you like to improve?" she asks.

"I can't make the words stay on the line too good," he says, indicating two words that float above the line.

"Why is that important?" Mrs. Morning Light asks.

"It's harder to read," he answers.

"What can you do?" the teacher asks.

"Practice," he responds.

"Sometimes it helps to think about the line when you write the first letter in the word," the teacher suggests. "Try writing one of your sentences or a new one when you go back to your table and see if that helps."

WHAT HAPPENED HERE?
Daily monitoring of individual student writing gives Mrs. Morning Light a good idea of her students' developing writing skills. As she assists them in their writing, she is also helping students develop skills of evaluation. She models the use of portfolios by asking Bright Feather to compare previous work with his current skill, so that he is aware of the progress he is making. She helps him assess his work in terms of how well it communicates his ideas, and it is in this context that Mrs. Morning Light discusses capital letters in reading and writing with her student, stressing their use as signals to give information to the reader. Since the beginning of the year, students have discovered capital letters in their own and others' names, in the titles of stories, and in the names of events, places and specific things. This activity seems to heighten student awareness of capital letter use, both in their reading and their own writing.

From this conference, it is evident that this teacher encourages her students to consult a variety of resources for assistance in writing. Students are given many opportunities to read their writing aloud to each other and to consult each other about the spelling of words. Picture dictionaries, Big Books and language experience charts of all kinds can be found in the reading and writing centers and other places throughout the room. A poster in the writing center reminds students of these resources, with pictures of family members, friends, reference books, charts and books that students can refer to as they compose their ideas.

WHAT DO YOU THINK?
When you were Bright Feather's age, what might you have written about in a classroom environment that encouraged you to write about your own experience or things important to you?

FIGURE 8.1

Kindergarten Level—Key Words

"What word do you want this morning, Eric?" Mrs. Jamison asks. Eric is jumping up and down with excitement. It is obvious that he has been ready for this question since he arrived at school.

"James!" he says. "James that starts with a *J*."

"Is this a special name?" Mrs. Jamison asks.

"My new baby brother!" he announces. "His name is James and I'm going to write him a letter."

"A good idea," Mrs. Jamison agrees.

"Everybody in our family is writing a letter for his baby book and I want to write my own."

"Good for you!" Mrs. Jamison says. "You've already told me how 'James' begins . . . with a *J*. I wonder if you can hear any other sounds?" She prints a capital *J* on a 3 × 8″ strip of tagboard.

"J . . . a . . . m . . . e . . . s." Eric says the name slowly. "There's an *a*. I can hear an *a*."

"Good for you," Mrs. Jamison says, and she prints an *a*. "An *a* is next. What else?"

"Mmmm," he replies, thinking.

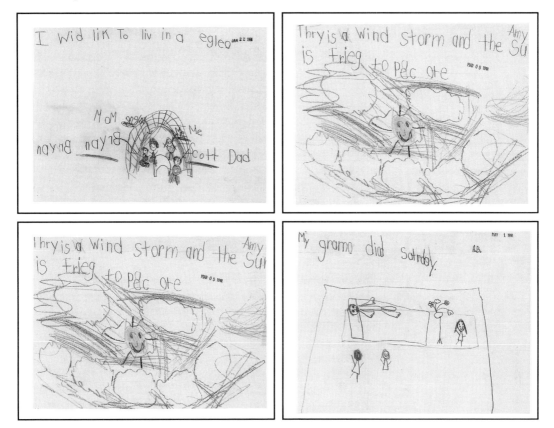

FIGURE 8.1

(Continued)

These are writing samples that a kindergarten child dated and filed in her portfolio throughout the year. At the beginning of the year she uses a collection of letters to describe her picture. At the end of the year she is able to use writing to express deep feelings of fear and sadness.

(1) She begins in August by drawing a picture and writing a story about it, using all the letters she knows.

(2) By September she is writing a caption for her picture, drawn after studying Donald Crew's Freight Train *illustrations in guided reading.*

(3) In October she finds words she wants to use from charts in the room.

(4) At Christmas she writes a sentence: "I love Christmas 'cause Santa brings me Christmas presents."

(5) In January she writes: "I would like to live in a igloo" and labels the people in her picture. Notice that she purposely reverses the order of letters in the names to the left, perhaps to indicate the perspective of the people in the picture or to allow them to see their own names.

(6) In March she writes from observation: "There is a wind storm and the sun is trying to peek out."

(7) In April she draws in black crayon and writes about a traumatic experience: "I had surgery and I got stitches."

(8) In May she writes and draws in pencil to express sadness: "My grandma died Saturday."

"Did you check the alphabet?" the teacher asks. "Get your mouth ready to make the *m* sound."

Eric looks at the large, colorful picture and letter cards that ring the room. He nods his head in the rhythm established by the daily review of letter sounds. "A . . . apple, angel too; B . . . bear, bat and boo!; C . . . caterpillar, circus, clown; D . . . dinosaur, digging, down . . ." He reaches M and rehearses, "M . . . mountain . . . it's *m*. M is next," he says.

"Wonderful!" Mrs. Jamison comments, adding an *m* to the word. She waits. "Anything else?"

"That's all I hear," he replies.

"Can you hear any other sound at the end of 'James'?" she asks.

He repeats the word to himself and nods. "Jamessss. There's an s."

"Great!" Mrs. Jamison replies. "There certainly is an s." She writes the s, leaving room for another letter to precede it.

"Let's look at your word," Mrs. Jamison says, and she points to each letter, saying the sound. "These are all the sounds you can hear. But right now the word says 'jams.' How can you make this a say its name?"

Eric looks puzzled. "There's a letter missing," he observes.

"Yes," the teacher agrees, and she waits.

"Does it say a sound?" he asks.

"No," she answers, "you're on the right track."

"It doesn't say a sound," Eric thinks out loud.

"Why don't you look through some of your other words for a clue?" she suggests. "Or on one of the charts in the room," and she gestures toward the winter weather words.

Eric reaches down to his belt to retrieve his other key words, which are fastened together with a metal ring to the belt loop on his pants. He looks through the words, stopping at one that says "game."

"Maybe this one," he says.

"What about this one?" Mrs. Jamison asks.

"Well, a says its name," he replies.

"Who helps a say its name?" she asks.

A grin breaks out on Eric's face. "It's e!" he says. "Silent e, the enforcer. It makes a say its name!"

The teacher prints an e in the space and says, "James," running her finger beneath the word as she says it.

Eric takes the word. "James," he says proudly and traces each letter with his finger.

Mrs. Jamison watches him form the letters. "If you start here on the a," she says, demonstrating the formation of the letter, "it's easier to write."

Eric traces the word two more times. Each time he says each letter as he is tracing. Then he runs his finger underneath the word, imitating the action of the teacher. "I'm going to use it now," he says and returns with all his words to a table to write the letter to his new brother. As he writes, he asks for additional words from other students and the classroom aide. He also consults several of the many charts around the room that contain words he wants to use.

Amy is next up to the writing center. She asks for a four-syllable dinosaur name that she heard on a science program. She hears most of the sounds, but Mrs. Jamison shows her the silent p in "pterodactyl" and the y that sounds like short i. Amy's other words, which she keeps in a wide, dark-lined primary tablet, include the names of other dinosaurs: Tyrannosaurus rex, Triceratops and Stegosaurus. On the back of each sheet, she has asked the teacher to write what each name means: king of the terrible lizards, three-horned face and so on. Amy is partially sighted, but she has read since she was four years old. She can find most of the words she wants to use in her writing by searching for them in books or on the charts, but interacting with the teacher for special words helps her build her word analysis skills.

While he waits his turn, Diem works with the classroom aide, practicing words for the objects he has pointed out in the room on previous days. He has accumulated twenty words in addition to his stack of "at home" cards, which he takes home every night to share with his family, who have recently arrived from Vietnam. The cards he has added this week have the names of household furniture and appliances, such as bed, table, chair, sofa, refrigerator, stove.

The aide hands Diem a word, printed with black marking pen on an index card. He looks at the word carefully, then places it appropriately in the room. This is an exercise they do every morning. When he is finished, he will have distributed cards that say: book, bookcase, library, bathroom, coatroom, floor, wall, paper, pencils, crayons, door, window, blocks, train, car and playhouse.

Another activity that both he and his classmates like to play is the Name Game, which will follow the key word exercise. Each child has a sign to wear for the game that has his or her name on it. Someone collects the signs and puts them in the middle of a circle. One by one they pick a sign and try to figure out who it belongs to. Students also practice the Picture Matching Game during free time, a favorite activity of small groups of children. On a bulletin board there is a picture of each student glued to a pocket made by stapling an index card to the surface. Each pocket holds another card placed vertically and labeled with the name of a student in the classroom. Players remove all the cards and try to match the names with the faces.

As Diem approaches the table, he pulls out a picture from his pocket and smooths it flat. It is an advertisement for Disney World and he points to the figure of Mickey Mouse.

"Who is this, Diem?" the teacher asks.

"Mouse. His name . . . Mickey. His word, please."

"Wonderful!" Mrs. Jamison says. "This is Mickey Mouse. Is that what you want, Diem? Mickey Mouse?"

"Yes, yes!" he replies. "Mickey Mouse, please."

Mrs. Jamison begins writing the name, saying each letter as she prints it. When she finishes the word "Mickey," she runs her finger beneath it and says, "Mickey." Then Diem says each letter after the teacher and runs his finger beneath the word, saying "Mickey." She repeats this procedure with the word "Mouse," and Diem says the letters and the word after her.

"Mickey Mouse," the teacher says, running her finger under the words as she says them.

"Mickey Mouse," Diem says proudly. "My family like this!" he says. "We like . . . ," he pauses and points to Mickey, . . . "Mickey Mouse."

"Good work, Diem," Mrs. Jamison says, smiling. She points to herself. "I like Mickey Mouse, too." She asks the aide, "Do you like Mickey Mouse?" The aide responds enthusiastically. Diem returns to his table to cut out the picture of Mickey Mouse, which he will paste on the back of the word card and take home to show his family.

| **WHAT HAPPENED HERE? ONE PERSPECTIVE** | Mrs. Jamison provides an opportunity for her students to turn words they are using into print. These key words are already invested with students' interests, experience and emotion and are usually instant additions to a child's reading vocabulary. They provide occasions for students to |

examine a word that is meaningful to them and to find clues for spelling and writing. There is a certain intimacy that develops when children share these words with the teacher because they are sharing their experiences, their interests and, sometimes, their deepest feelings about life. When a pet dies or something frightens children, they are apt to request words associated with these occasions, giving the teacher opportunities to show understanding and provide comfort when it is most needed.

You will notice that Mrs. Jamison waits for Eric to figure out the sounds in the word he wants to write. She encourages him to consult his resources: the charts, alphabet cards and his other key words. She also gives him time to remember how to use silent *e*. This waiting encourages Eric to see himself as someone who can analyze words and use them for his own purposes. It is possible to show all children in this classroom how to make the symbols for words that are significant to them, regardless of their level of reading proficiency. These words, because they arise out of interest and experience, already belong to the students; the teacher simply demonstrates the configuration that will help them express their ideas to others.

Amy displays proficiency in reading and writing that is beyond what is usually seen at the kindergarten level. She shares this talent generously with her classmates when they need the spelling or meaning of a word. Because Amy is visually challenged, her teacher provides her

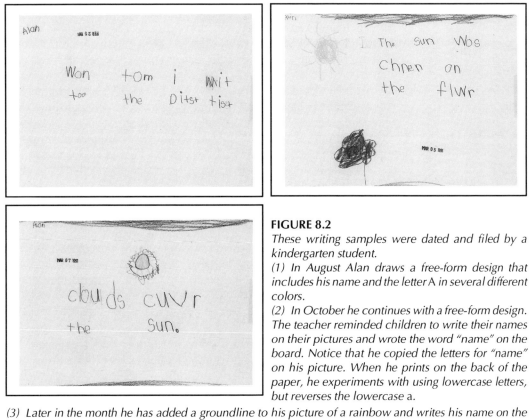

FIGURE 8.2

These writing samples were dated and filed by a kindergarten student.

(1) In August Alan draws a free-form design that includes his name and the letter A in several different colors.

(2) In October he continues with a free-form design. The teacher reminded children to write their names on their pictures and wrote the word "name" on the board. Notice that he copied the letters for "name" on his picture. When he prints on the back of the paper, he experiments with using lowercase letters, but reverses the lowercase a.

(3) Later in the month he has added a groundline to his picture of a rainbow and writes his name on the back. The letters are well formed, but the lowercase a is still reversed.

(4) In December he wrote "I see presents" and underlined "presents" for emphasis.

(5) The a in his name is no longer reversed, and Alan writes: "One time I went to the dentist." He is writing what he wants to say and using the sounds he hears in the words.

(6) In March he writes from observation: "The sun was shining on the flower." In addition to a groundline, he adds sky and a sun.

(7) Later that week he writes and illustrates another observation: "Clouds cover the sun." His letters are well formed, and he has added a period at the end of the sentence.

with black marking pens and paper with darker lines than the ordinary primary lined paper. She also provides her with many opportunities to use the magnified computer monitor screen for word processing. Amy's classmates are delighted with the stories she writes and shares with them. She has written and illustrated several books that are laminated and available for student reading in the classroom library. Because Amy is so aware of words and is interested in their meaning, Mrs. Jamison writes additional information about each word on the back side of the word sheets in her primary tablet.

The teacher encourages Diem to complement his word learning with pictures pasted on the back of his cards. This allows him to practice with the cards by looking at the picture and trying to remember the word or by looking at the word and trying to remember what it represents. High-interest words, such as "Mickey Mouse," will be used later on to help Diem unlock the sounds of English. He rehearses the special alphabet several times a day with the aide and with other children who are practicing sound/symbol relationships. As Diem becomes more fluent in his speaking, the aide will take additional dictation from him to demonstrate that what he says creates writing that he can read.

The teacher also establishes a helpful home–school relationship with Diem's family by sending home the word cards for Diem to practice. This encourages parents and children to assist each other as they learn a new language. As Diem begins to read, storybooks will go home each night for him to read aloud. She has obtained several picture books of folktales from Vietnam that will be especially helpful to Diem's family, enabling them to develop their English proficiency in the context of familiar and respected stories.

As the students in this classroom label their drawings, write sentences about their pictures or experiences and finally create books, they will discover that writing is a way of expressing themselves in a deeply satisfying way. It is also a way to share their ideas with others. As they work to express the meaning in their own lives, they become increasingly aware of the effort required to create the literature they enjoy reading or listening to themselves. They are learning to be authors.

WHAT DO YOU THINK? Do you remember sitting in a science, math or foreign language class where the meaning of symbols was not readily apparent? What was your initial response as the teacher used these symbols or when you first began to read text that contained them?

Kindergarten Level—Language Experience

"What would you like to write about today?" Mrs. Jamison asks her class, who are gathered on the floor around her.

"The star chamber!" some chorus.

"No, the flood," others say.

"Basketball," someone offers.

"Which one first?" the teacher asks, writing the suggestions on the board. "Raise your hands for the star chamber." Most hands go up. They have just come from a presentation by a volunteer from the planetarium in a nearby city.

"How about the flood?" she asks, and a few hands go up. "Basketball?" One eager hand defends this choice.

"It's the star chamber first and the flood second," she announces. "Brian, how about getting a group together later to write about basketball?"

A few boys nod to Brian, and he is satisfied.

"What do you want to say about the star chamber?" the teacher asks, and everyone's hand goes up.

"We could see stars the same as in the sky," Ashley says.

"So what is the first word you want me to write?" the teacher asks.

"We," the group responds.

"Let me see how your mouths look when you start to say 'we,' " she asks. The children pucker their mouths.

"Put your hands in your lap when you find what begins with that sound on the alphabet cards," she says. One by one, children find the walrus on the *W* card and put their hands in their laps.

"What letter will start the sentence?" she asks.

They answer *W* and she asks, "What kind of *W?*"

"A capital," they reply.

"Who can show me where to start writing?" she asks. Jessica comes up to the easel and taps the upper left-hand corner.

The teacher writes the word "We" on the board in large print and then the rest of the sentence, saying each word as she writes it.

Then she passes her hand under the complete sentence and says it at a speaking rate. "Who can read the sentence?" she asks. Several hands go up. Tim reads, "We could see the stars in the sky."

"Very close," the teacher says, and reads the sentence correctly. "Let's all read it together."

"What else do you want to say?" she asks, when they have read the sentence.

"We had to crawl into the star chamber," Zachary suggests, and the teacher repeats the same writing and reading procedure.

"Do you want to say what happened first, next and last?" Mrs. Jamison asks.

There is a chorus of agreement. "What happened first?" she asks.

"First we went to the gym," Amy says, and Mrs. Jamison records the sentence.

Keith raises his hand. "Then the lady told us how to act in the star chamber," he says.

"Is it all right to say, 'Ms. May told us how to act in the star chamber'?" she asks.

"Yep," he replies. "I forgot her name."

The children take turns contributing sentences, with the teacher asking, "What happened next?" To activate their memories if events are out of sequence, she asks, "Did anything important happen before that?"

"Can you tell the rest of what happened in two sentences?" Mrs. Jamison asks. "You might like to use one sentence to tell how you felt about the presentation."

Damien suggests, "Then we came back to our room," and Amy says, "We liked it so much that we wrote a story about it." The sentences are written on the chart and practiced, and the story is complete.

"Let's read the whole story together," Mrs. Jamison says, "and then you can decide on a title for it."

The class reads the story aloud and decides to call it "A Visit to the Star Chamber." Then Mrs. Jamison asks who can find the words "star chamber," giving several children the opportunity to frame the word with their hands, the cardboard window or the rectangular magnifier. She reads a sentence and asks whose it is. Can they read it? What word does it begin with? Who can find a question mark? How do you read a sentence that ends that way? Can someone draw a circle around the "little words"? Mark finds "the" ten times and Josh finds "a" and "an" nine times.

They read the story again all together, and Mrs. Jamison asks for volunteers to read individual sentences. She calls on children to show their favorite words and read their favorite sentences. "Who would like to draw a picture of the star chamber?" she asks. All hands go up. "What are some words you could use in your caption?" she inquires.

"Star chamber," Elise volunteers.

"Can you show me that word?" Mrs. Jamison asks, and Elise frames the correct word.

"What else could you use for a caption?" she asks, and Tim suggests using the title of the story the group has composed. Others contribute words that tell about going to the gym, listening to the teacher, experiencing the dark inside of the chamber, or watching the constellations.

"Some of you might like to write your own story," Mrs. Jamison adds. "If you write more than a sentence, use the lined paper." She briefly reviews the rules for independent writing with the group, and everyone leaves to draw and write. During this time, she will observe students as they write, watching for the ways they use resources to figure out the words they want to spell and noting how they form their letters and hold their pencils.

WHAT HAPPENED HERE? ONE PERSPECTIVE

Mrs. Jamison schedules a writing workshop soon after a particularly enjoyable experience. She asks them to reconstruct their experience in the star chamber, giving them the opportunity to organize their thoughts and reflect on what happened. This process also encourages additional learning because each child notices certain things more closely. Comments such as: "I didn't see that." "When did she say that?" or "Where did she say you could see those stars?" illustrate different experiences that can be shared or expanded through this rehearsal of events. This guided interaction helps children share their impressions and remember what they have seen.

As she creates the chart, Mrs. Jamison says the words as she writes them and then reads the entire sentence at a normal rate. She asks students to tell her where to begin writing and passes her hand under each sentence when it is completed, reinforcing the up to down and left to right progression of English reading, helpful both to beginning readers and ESL students who may have learned to read in languages that progress from right to left and from the lower right-hand corner of the page.

Mrs. Jamison models ways to use the alphabet as a tool in spelling, showing them how the shape of their mouths, sounds and symbols relate to each other. She asks children to find individual words and favorite words, which gives everyone at every ability level the chance to participate. If a child simply points to any word, the teacher can say, "Good, you chose 'gym.' Everyone say Paul's word with him." Likewise, she can say, "Who would like to read Paul's sentence?" giving status to the sentence generator. She also encourages risk-taking among nonreaders, validating Tim's memory reading of the first sentence by saying, "Very close," and then reading it correctly. The class rehearses the concept of main idea by creating a title for its story. Students also practice punctuation rules, capitalization and sight words "a," "an," and "the," which Mrs. Jamison now calls "little words," but will soon begin to label as articles.

Students practice sequencing events as the teacher asks, "What happened first? Next? Then what happened?" She asks permission to rephrase a contribution and might ask students to say something a different way, if a sentence is constructed awkwardly. At other times, the teacher might ask if a student can make a longer sentence or a shorter one, depending on the situation. She might also ask if they can think of a different word to substitute for a repeated word.

WHAT DO YOU THINK? Think of an exciting experience you have had recently that you shared with someone else—a trip, concert, adventure, wedding, new baby. How did you communicate your excitement to others who were also present? How would you have written about it in a letter to someone not there? On a postcard?

Primary Level—Journals

The snowfall and cold temperatures of mid-January have captured the attention of many students in Mrs. Logan's third-grade class. When it is time to make journal entries, several decide to write about the weather.

"Let's write poems," Jennifer suggests to the other girls in her group and they agree. Two of the girls pull out their journals to record their efforts, while Jennifer and Marcy take out notebook paper to write and illustrate their poems. "If this is good, I want to put it in my portfolio," Jennifer says.

"I need a word to rhyme with snow," Jennifer says to herself. She pulls out a small notebook where she has recorded lists of rhyming words for just this occasion. "Snow . . . blow? stow? crow? below? to and fro?" She gets an idea and returns to her writing. "It's going to snow. Look out below! Old leaves [rusel] to and fro," she writes. She reads her poem again, decides that "rusel" doesn't look quite right and draws a circle around it.

When the girls finish their poems, they read them aloud to each other. No one is certain how to spell "rustle," so they look in the dictionary. They fail to find the spelling in this source, so Jennifer consults the teacher. Mrs. Logan shows her the correct spelling, which Jennifer records in her personal dictionary. The teacher also encourages her to think of other words that might have a similar spelling, and she discovers and records "hustle" and "bustle." "Muscle" is entered as a rhyming word that is spelled differently. At this point, she thinks of another verse for her poem. She revises her poem, copies it into her journal and then makes a final copy to date and file.

Others around the classroom consult their word lists and look around at the charts for additional ideas. Martin turns the seasons chart to winter and finds what he is looking for, the spelling for "January." "January brings the snow. Today it must be 10 below!" he writes. Pleased with the rhyme, he sits back and grins at what he has written.

There are words everywhere in the classroom. Charts of seasonal and holiday words stand in one corner of the room, as do several charts of stories written by students to describe field trips and responses to books read aloud. Other charts are fastened by clothespins to lines strung across the room. These include words that rhyme, words that change with different endings and words associated with current studies in science, math and social studies, such as parts of the body, names of geometric shapes, names of the planets, names of continents and countries in South America. In the library corner,

there are ten books written and illustrated by the class and several others
written by individuals. Some of these books are creative adaptations of other
books they have read, and others are original stories or nonfiction accounts
of ideas they have studied in science or social studies.

Primary Level—The Individual Writing Conference

"I brought my biography, but it's not very good," Haley says to the teacher
as she sits down at the conference table in one corner of the classroom.

"Tell me what you're trying to do," Mrs. Logan responds.

"It's about my great-grandmother but it's not very interesting."

"Why don't you start at the beginning and read it to me," the teacher
suggests.

> My great-grandma was born in 1909. Her mother was very pretty and her
> father was a [bucher]. Once she got a red [umbrela] from a [travling] salesman
> and once she almost got run over by a horse. She called her grandma
> [grosmuter] and her father [grosfater]. Her [grosfater] gave her a gold dollar
> and when she grew up she paid for [collage] with it.
>
> When she was ten years old her mother took her and her little brothers
> and sisters to the circus and when she was older there was a big flood and a
> big snowstorm. My grandma went to [collage] and then she was a teacher.
> She taught children about art. When those children grew up, she taught their
> children. She gave piano lessons to children and some of her students won
> prizes.
>
> She got married, then she had two children and one of them is my
> grandma. Then my grandma had two children and one of them is my Dad.
> My Aunt Debbie called my great-grandma Nonnie when she was a little girl.
> That's how she got her name.

Haley stops reading. "See? I've got all the parts in, but it's not how I want
it to be." She looks discouraged.

"Can you tell me a little more about how you'd like it to be?" the teacher
asks.

"I don't know," Haley replies. "I guess I wanted it to be like *Caddie
Woodlawn* or *Little House on the Prairie*," she adds. "More exciting."

"Do you want it to sound more like a story?" Mrs. Logan asks.

Haley thinks for a minute and then nods her head.

"Then I think you might have everything here to make your writing what
you want it to be," the teacher says.

Haley looks puzzled.

"At the beginning of your biography you talk about all these exciting
things that happened to your great-grandmother when she was little. Do you
know something more about any of these stories?"

"Yes, I know all of the stories."

"Do you have your outline for biographies?" the teacher asks.

Haley takes out her outline for biographical writing. The form provides
space for notes on the subject's life: early life facts; early life anecdote; adult
life facts; adult life anecdote; contributions to society facts; contribution
anecdote; later life; end of life. There is also a place to list sources: books,
magazines, encyclopedias, interviews, newspapers, diaries, journals.

"In your first sentence you have some early life facts. You tell where and when your great-grandma was born. Then you list some of the things that happened to her, and these look like pretty interesting events. Do you remember how Helen Keller's biography began?" the teacher asks.

Haley shakes her head.

"Why don't you go get a copy from my desk," the teacher says. Mrs. Logan keeps a copy of each genre of writing that she reads aloud on her desk. Haley returns with the book, opens it to the first page and begins to read to herself.

"It just starts right in with a story," she observes. "I could do that. I could tell one of the stories first to make it interesting."

"Why don't you make a note about that," the teacher suggests, and Haley writes "Start with story" under the planning section on the outline.

"Can I borrow this book for a while?" Haley asks. "I want to look at some more things."

"There are several copies in the library corner," the teacher says, "and several others you might like to look at. If you can't find any, you are welcome to use this one," she adds. All copies of the read-aloud books have orange covers so they can be easily located from borrowers if they are needed for conferences. "Which story do you think you might use to start your biography?" she asks.

"The one about the horse running away," she says immediately. "That's the most exciting one and if the neighbor boy hadn't rescued her, she might have died." She thinks a minute, and then says, "I wouldn't be me."

"Well, I'm glad you're you and that you have a great-grandmother with such interesting stories," the teacher says.

Haley looks pleased.

"Are there any words in your biography that readers might want to know more about?" Mrs. Logan asks.

"Hmmm," Haley says, as she reads over her writing. "Well, they might not know what a butcher did in those days. It's different than now. They even had to go cut out ice from the rivers in the winter to keep the meat cold."

She continues looking while the teacher waits. "Traveling salesmen . . . they sold everything when Nonnie was a little girl. And 'grossfatter' and 'grossmutter' . . . most people wouldn't know what that meant," she adds.

"Can you explain them as part of your story?" the teacher asks. "You might want to look at the Helen Keller book to see how the writer explains things about her time period that readers might not understand."

Haley nods her head enthusiastically. It is evident that she wants to return to her writing, so Mrs. Logan finishes up her questions quickly.

"Shall we do your circled words?" she asks. Haley has five words whose spelling she did not know. "I can ask my great-grandma to spell 'grossfatter' and 'grossmutter' to me on the phone when I talk to her tonight," she says.

The teacher helps Haley use phonetic clues and similar words to figure out the spellings of butcher, traveling, college and umbrella. Haley enters the correct spellings in her personal dictionary.

WHAT HAPPENED HERE? ONE PERSPECTIVE

This classroom provides children with a rich print environment. When they want to express themselves in writing, they can consult their own resources, standard reference books, a wide range of fiction and non-

```
                        CREATIVE WRITING

        The Tyrannosaurus Rex was big And had big big big teeth.
    And what ever got in his way was dinner to him.  Brontosaurus
    was a plant eater.  Brontosaurus means '''thunder liserd.'''
    And he wade more '''then 3000''' pownds.  Now Brakryosaurus was
    veary simler to Brontosaurus.  But Brakyosaurus had a dome on
    his hed.  And he was in the water almoqst all of the time.  And
    stegosares was my farvert.  He was put together rong.  His frunt
    legs where little.  And his bakc legs where big.  On his back
    where bony plaets.  On his taill there where more.  But the meat
    eaters would never pick a fight with him!  Boacause he had '''
    three spikes on hi taill!'''  Trysuerstops had three horns.  And
    ealsy could cill meat eaters.  And would walk like an armerd tangk.
    And had a shelld head.
                                                Sean
```

FIGURE 8.3

Students are able to write with more fluency when they are encouraged to use sounds to indicate words they are unable to spell. This second grader's description of his favorite dinosaurs would be significantly less passionate if he was required to use only words he knew how to spell or was forced to look up or ask for every word he wanted to use in his writing. Notice his attempt to use writing conventions in his definitions and when he wants to create emphasis. Sean writes:

The Tyrannosaurus Rex was big and had big, big, big teeth. And whatever got in his way was dinner to him. Brontosaurus was a plant eater. Brontosaurus means "thunder lizard." And he weighed more than 3000 pounds. Now Brachiosaurus was very similar to Brontosaurus. But Brachiosaurus had a dome on his head. And he was in the water almost all of the time. And stegosaurus was my favorite. He was put together wrong. His front legs were little. And his back legs were big. On his back were boney plates. On his tail there were more. But the meat eaters would never pick a fight with him! Because he had three spikes on his tail! Triceratops had three horns. And easily could kill meat eaters. And would walk like an armored tank. And had a shielded head.

fiction books or one of the many student-created charts available around the room. All students are provided with time to record their thoughts in a daily journal and to engage in writing that is meaningful to them. They write letters, essays, poems, books, newspaper and magazine articles, editorials, lists of things they enjoy and lists of things to do. They take notes as they research topics in science and the social studies and create written reports of information in a variety of formats. Few children sit around chewing on their pencils, wondering what to write. Everyone writes because everyone has ideas to express and share.

As students work on various writing projects, they do not interrupt the creative process by looking up the correct spelling of each word they want to use. They write the sounds they hear and circle the word, which reminds them to edit later. This is an example of **developmental spelling**, where children approximate the words they want to use as they write. They are motivated to find the correct spelling for words that will be part of something they prepare for an audience because they are eager for their readers to understand what they have to say. Students have personal dictionaries to record words they want to know and use these references frequently in their writing. At the end of the year, all children will have a notebook full of the words they have learned to spell, as part of their desire to communicate in writing.

In the writing conference, Mrs. Logan encourages Haley to read her writing aloud and to express her feelings about what she has written. Even when students are pleased with their writing, this practice helps create an awareness of problems missed with silent reading. The teacher comments sincerely about positive elements of Haley's biography and helps her address structural problems that concern her. Mrs. Logan knows that students have a storehouse of wonderful stories in them, but may experience frustration in trying to state them to their own satisfaction. She tries to help Haley identify her writing purposes and encourages her to use a familiar piece of biographical writing as a model.

Haley enters words she wants to use in her writing in her personal dictionary. There are two pages for each letter of the alphabet for easy reference when she wants to use the words again. She copies each one carefully and will practice these words during independent study time as part of her personal spelling list for the week.

In traditional classrooms, teachers often believe it is necessary to correct every error in a child's writing. One child who was handed back a paper decorated in the teacher's red ink commented to her neighbor, "Look, my paper is bleeding!" It was an apt metaphor. Mrs. Logan does not try to correct everything at once in Haley's writing, but focuses on an aspect that most concerns her as a writer. Over the period of a year, through these individual conferences, writing workshops, guided reading and mini-lessons, other writing skills will be introduced, practiced and evaluated on countless occasions. Awkward wording, such as Haley's repeated use of "then," will be picked up by listeners when she reads her work aloud to a partner or to a larger group in writing workshop. She may also hear this problem discussed by other writers during the workshop. Mrs. Logan encourages Haley to take notes about things she plans to work on, as a reminder of their discussion when she returns to her work. This teacher never writes on a student composition because she believes that as children make their own corrections and create notes to make improvements, both the ownership of the work and responsibility for improving it stay with the author.

Haley will work with her biographical writing for several weeks. She plans to enlarge one of her great-grandmother's stories and put it at the beginning of her writing. She will later explore dialogue as a way to add interest to this kind of writing and will interview her great-grandmother to see if she can remember things she said or things that might have been said during events in her childhood. She will also ask her great-grandmother for stories from the time she was a teacher and for more information about her successful students. In the process of learning to write a biography, she is developing writing skills and facing the challenges of all writers. When she is finished, she will know the key elements of biography and more deeply appreciate the efforts and skills of biographical writers.

Although Haley will eventually work with topic, theme, characters, sentence structure and dialogue, her most immediate concern at this point is trying to make what she writes appealing to her readers. She

```
        The penguins started pecking at the
polar bear like pigeons pecking at
popcorn. Finally the polar bear leaped
back out the window. Mr.Popper was
astonished by what the penguins did.
Then everyone went back to bed. In the
morning when Mr.Popper looked out the
broken window he saw that the rope that
tied up the boat had broken.

        Mr.Popper ran to Admiral Drake's
room and yelled, "Admiral! Admiral! Get
up! The rope broke that held the
boat!"" What?" said Admiral Drake." The
rope broke!" yelled Mr.Popper. The
Admiral shot up like a bullit. I have
an idea, Admiral Drake went into the
penguin's room and was back in two
minutes. Then he told Mr.Popper his
idea.

        They both walked outside with the
penguins. Then Mr.Popper took the
penguins out to where the rope had
broken. Then he let the penguins go.
They swam out to the boat. All 12 bit
the other end of the  boat and started
pulling. The penguins pulled the boat
back to the ice. And they all got in
and sailed back to Stillwater.

                    THE END
```

FIGURE 8.4
This third-grade student wrote his own addition to the book Mr. Popper's Penguins, *using similes as part of his narration.*

already has a sense of audience because she wants what she writes to be interesting, not just for herself but for others who will read what she has written. This desire to communicate is typical of most elementary age students. "Did you get it?" they'll ask, or "Do you understand what I was trying to say?"

WHAT DO YOU THINK? Have you ever had a negative experience with grading marks written on a composition you submitted in a class? How did this experience affect your future writing? Have you ever been encouraged by someone who made positive comments about your writing?

Intermediate Level—Author's Chair

Mr. Schupak's sixth-grade class has just completed forty-five minutes of independent writing. Although most students write the entire time on their own, several pairs exchange work and share comments with each other in one corner of the room. As he always does, Mr. Schupak works for fifteen minutes on his own writing, a book review he is preparing for a local TAWL group newsletter. During the rest of the writing period he has individual writing conferences with students.

At the end of the forty-five-minute period, Mr. Schupak asks, "Who has something they want to read today?" Students pull their desks into a great circle and most bring something they are writing. There's a moment's hesitation, then several hands go up. Mr. Schupak checks his list and sees that Herschel brought something for the author's chair yesterday that he did not get a chance to read.

"Herschel?"

"I'm still working on my science-fiction story," he says. "I want to read the third chapter . . . the one I rewrote." He begins reading a fairly complex account of space travelers entering a new universe. Everyone around the room listens closely. They have heard the story develop week by week and are interested in what happens. When he finishes, Mr. Schupak asks for class response.

"I liked what you did with the Junio character," Karen begins. "I couldn't tell before how Junio felt about risking the lives of his crew to change the mission."

"I still like the action part the best," Paul says. "That's what I like the best about the whole story."

"The part about the flight path was good," Isaac says. "And I liked where Junio loaded the sky geography into his own mind and then put it on automatic pilot."

"I think it helped to tell about the spaceship that Junio lost before," Sarah volunteers. "I didn't really understand about how much risk he was taking, in terms of what had happened to him already. The way you changed it makes the story more exciting."

"Any suggestions?" Herschel asks.

"More information about the other crew members," Elizabeth suggests. "Like Sarah said about knowing more about the people . . . it makes it more exciting. Also, I didn't know right away what the trans-accelerator was. I know you tell about it a few pages later, but I kept wondering what it was and lost track of the story for a while."

Herschel makes some notes on his paper while the others are talking.

"I think you ought to have more alien crew members," Danielle suggests. "It would make it more interesting to have people from different backgrounds, like they do on *Star Trek*."

Herschel nods. "I thought about that, but I don't think I can do it in this story," he concludes. "I want to work on describing events, so I kept the number of characters down this time." The class laughs. Herschel's last story had twenty-seven characters and it was difficult to keep track of everyone.

"What if they could do something with mind control, like opening and shutting hatches?" Beth asks. "It could be like a computer chip that would operate everything with the remote control built in."

"Yeah," Herschel says, and he writes down several sentences quickly. "That's how they could operate most of the systems. What if everyone was specialized and then someone was knocked unconscious or got sick? They couldn't operate that particular system."

"What about a fail-safe system?" Paul asks. "If they're that sophisticated, they'd have a fail-safe system."

"You're right," Herschel agrees, "but what happens when the fail-safe system malfunctions? It could happen."

"What do you think about the responses from the group, Herschel?" Mr. Schupak asks.

"Well, some of it is pretty helpful," he replies. "I'm glad they liked what I did with Captain Junio . . . I'll think about adding more information about the other crew members. But I don't think I'll add any more characters because I want to pay more attention to the story this time. I liked the idea about using your mind to operate systems on the spacecraft. That might add something interesting to the story. I'll wait and see."

The class members applaud Herschel's efforts and move on to consider a narrative poem about time travel that Sarah has written. The topic for writing workshop in this three-week period is science, and class members have experimented with a wide range of genres. Paul will present an informational piece written for the school newspaper on genetic engineering, and Winfield will entertain everyone with a satiric essay entitled "May the Force Be with You: The Trip of an Historic Apple, by I. Zak Newton." Several have written historical fiction based on inventions occurring at an earlier time, such as the development of a working airplane by Leonardo da Vinci. Isaac has developed several modern fables based on ecological problems, and Elizabeth has written a biography of Stephen Hawking.

The audience is attentive and involved, which represents progress from the first few weeks when writers were so eager to read their own work that they were inattentive during presentations and perfunctory about their comments to the presenters. They have learned to be diplomatic in their suggestions, which are directed toward clarification or enrichment of ideas presented. Presenters are free to accept or reject suggestions, and most, as Herschel demonstrated above, make notations of ideas to think about later.

WHAT HAPPENED HERE? ONE PERSPECTIVE

When author's chair was first introduced in this classroom, students were initially hesitant to contribute. But this timidity soon wore off and everyone wanted to read what he or she had written, sometimes to the point of not being able to give attention to the writing of others. Attentiveness improved with time and experience. After the first month, students began to develop a balance between wanting to share what they had written and providing a supportive audience for someone else.

When the sessions first began, Mr. Schupak modeled appropriate responses by telling the writer what he particularly enjoyed. Criticism was framed in terms of: "Have you ever thought about . . ?" or "I wondered what happened to this particular character," or "I wondered what the inside of the spaceship looked like." These comments helped the writer see what needed to be clarified or expanded to make the writing clear and understandable. One of the goals of writing in this classroom is to help young writers communicate effectively to their listeners and readers, and the author's chair activity supports this goal with opportunities for frequent feedback on the clarity of expression.

Because all students in class are writing on a similar theme, they can contribute ideas to each other. In previous sessions, students experimented with a single genre and any topic of their choosing. At this point

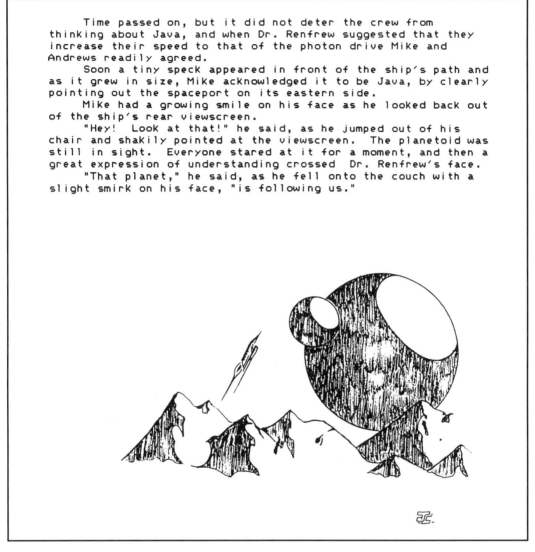

Time passed on, but it did not deter the crew from
thinking about Java, and when Dr. Renfrew suggested that they
increase their speed to that of the photon drive Mike and
Andrews readily agreed.
    Soon a tiny speck appeared in front of the ship's path and
as it grew in size, Mike acknowledged it to be Java, by clearly
pointing out the spaceport on its eastern side.
    Mike had a growing smile on his face as he looked back out
of the ship's rear viewscreen.
    "Hey! Look at that!" he said, as he jumped out of his
chair and shakily pointed at the viewscreen. The planetoid was
still in sight. Everyone stared at it for a moment, and then a
great expression of understanding crossed Dr. Renfrew's face.
    "That planet," he said, as he fell onto the couch with a
slight smirk on his face, "is following us."

FIGURE 8.5
This excerpt and illustration are from an eighty-page novel written by a sixth grader. His vocabulary use, dialogue and plot development are unusually sophisticated for his age and indicate the influence of extensive reading in science fiction. Other students enjoy reading or listening to his writing and provide valuable feedback to him about the clarity of his expression.

in their writing development, they are exploring broad topics by selecting the genre of their choice.

WHAT DO YOU THINK? If you were the teacher in this class, what kinds of literature would you try to have on hand for your students? What kind of read-aloud literature might you select? Who else in the school might enjoy their writing? If you were a student in this class, what writing genre might you choose to write about a topic in science?

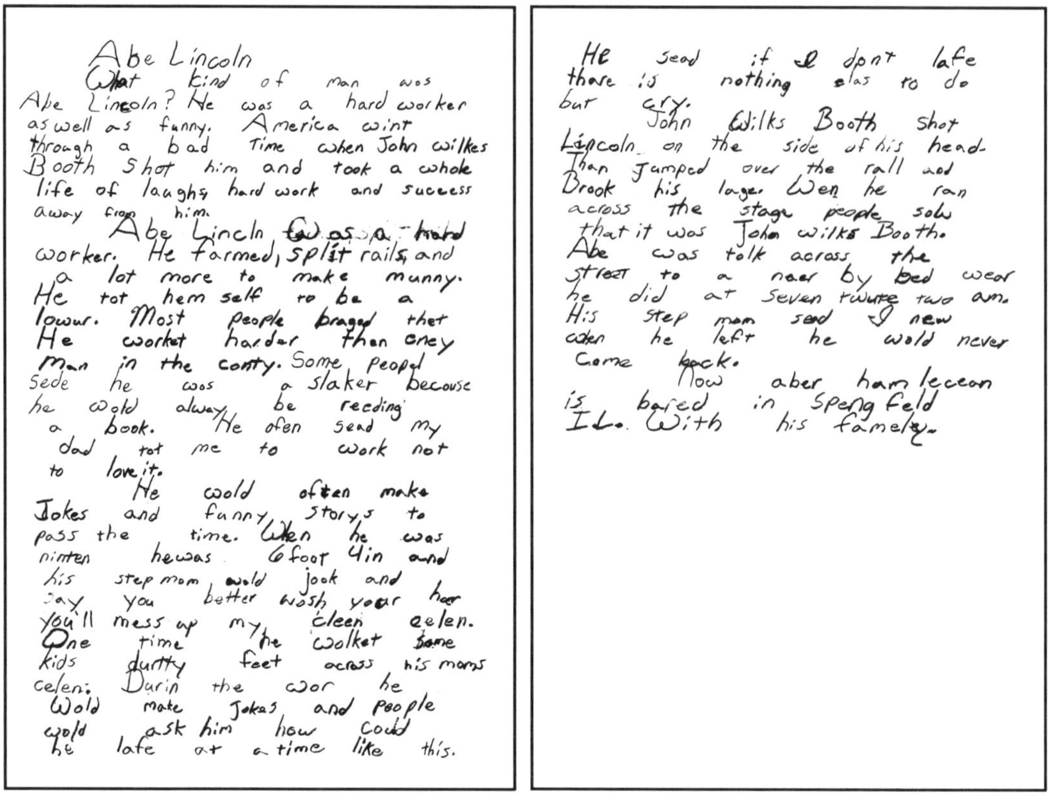

Abe Lincoln

What kind of man was Abe Lincoln? He was a hard worker as well as funny. America wint through a bad time when John wilkes Booth Shot him and took a whole life of laughs hard work and success away from him.

Abe Lincln was a hard worker. He farmed, split rails, and a lot more to make munny. He tot hem self to be a lowur. Most people braged thet He workt harder then eney man in the conty. Some peopel sede he was a slaker becouse he wold alway be reeding a book. He ofen sead my dad tot me to work not to love it.

He wold often make Jokes and funny storys to pass the time. When he was ninten he was 6 foot 4in and his step mom wold jook and say you better wosh your heer you'll mess up my cleen celen. One time he wolket some kids durty feet across his moms celen. Durin the wor he Wold make Jokes and People wold ask him how cold he lafe at a time like this. He sead if I dont lafe there is nothing elas to do but cry.

John Wilks Booth shot Lincoln on the side of his head. Than Jumped over the rall and Brook his lage. Wen he ran across the stage people sow that it was John wilks Booth. Abe was tolk across the street to a near by bed wear he did at seven twenty two a.m. His step mom sead I new when he left he wold never Come back.

Now aber ham lecean is bered in Speng feld IL. With his famely.

FIGURE 8.6

This fifth-grade student shows proficiency as a storyteller, as he describes Abraham Lincoln's life. Although his spelling and handwriting proficiency are still developing, he writes in an engaging manner about his subject.

IV. Preparing for Writing Activities

The sections below list specific suggestions for preparing to use key words, captions, language experience charts, recording activities, individual writing conferences and writing workshops. You will want to provide a file folder for each student that can be easily accessed in a writing center or on a small table. When finished work is not contained in notebooks, it should be filed immediately. Provide a dated stamp and ink pad next to the file box, so that students can record the date on their writing. Students of all ages easily learn to check for the correct date and move it accordingly. When students sit at tables instead of desks, teachers may provide cartons or shelf space for writing notebooks and journals, in addition to general storage areas for individual student supplies and books.

Preparing for Key Words

To prepare to use key words with your students, you will need to decide how they will be recorded and stored. Here are two possibilities:

1. Write each word on a separate strip of tagboard ($8 \times 3''$). Use a paper punch to cut a hole in the end of each strip and fasten the strips together with colored yarn, string or a metal ring. As noted above, definitions or descriptions of words can be written on the opposite sides or pictures can be drawn or pasted on the reverse side for children's independent practice during the school day or at home. Many teachers prefer the tagboard strips because they are attractive to children, and their format encourages students to play with the words, to practice saying them and to use them for writing during the day.

2. Write each word in a small notebook that children can refer to easily. Children can decorate the front cover with drawings and their name. These books can be taken home for additional practice. Teachers sometimes prefer the notebooks because they are easier to use and can be stored more easily than the tagboard word cards. Some teachers begin with the tagboard strips, then move to the individual notebooks a month or two later.

If you choose the tagboard strips, you will need to assemble these weekly. Older students or a classroom aide may be able to help you with this preparation. Some teachers use lightweight tag in $8\frac{1}{2}$-by-11-inch pages and enlist the help of their students in cutting apart the sheets for their own week's use.

If you decide to use small notebooks, you will need to add them to the student supply list, requisition them in advance from your school's stores, request them from a classroom fund established by a parent group, or buy them yourself. At office supply stores they can sometimes be purchased in bulk quite inexpensively.

You will also need a water-based black marking pen to write on the tagboard or a black ball-point pen if you use the notebooks. Some markers will bleed onto the reverse side of tagboard or subsequent pages in notebooks, so you will want to experiment with various types of felt-tip pens before you begin.

You can fasten strips of tagboard together in several ways by using adjustable metal rings, key holders, colored string or yarn. Choose the method that seems easiest for you and one that will hold up to heavy student use. Teachers will have different preferences according to their own experience.

When you have your materials prepared, decide when you will meet with your students for key word time and the kinds of activities other children will do while you spend this time with individual students. Some teachers work with key words during playtime or while the majority of children are involved in work at centers. Others conduct these mini-conferences while all children are participating in a writing or drawing activity.

Preparing for Captions

For captioning activities you will need:

1. Paper of various sizes and kinds, including primary lined paper and drawing, painting and construction paper. If any of these are in short supply in your school, use whatever is available. Parents, churches or businesses can sometimes supply you with computer paper from end

runs or print drafts. You may be able to get out-of-date wallpaper samples from stores; these samples are great for making collages and they can receive paint on the back.

2. Materials for painting, drawing and writing, including primary pencils, crayons, chalk, colored pencils, watercolors and tempera. Some tempera paints come in dry bulk and must be mixed with water in advance. *Note*: Some children find it more comfortable to write with standard-size pencils. Encourage your students to try out various pencil sizes and use the one that helps them write easily. If children do not provide their own crayons, be sure you have enough for every child in the classroom. One teacher worried about the emotional state of a child who drew an entire picture in black. When asked why, the student replied, "It was the only one left!"

After students have learned to use art and writing materials responsibly, make them available at centers for independent worktime. If possible, provide places for displays of drawing and writing near the center or at an established location in the classroom.

Preparing for Language Experience Charts

Both students and teachers can suggest topics for charts, such as a list of winter words or words about a theme study. Other times you will draw on the shared experience of a book, videotape, visitor, weather event or field trip. Whatever the topic, you may want to prepare a list of skills to practice during the session, similar to your preparation for guided reading. These can be derived from the curriculum objectives for writing at your level of instruction. Generally, at the kindergarten level there is an emphasis on letter and word recognition, capitalization, simple punctuation, initial sounds, ending rhymes, and left to right and top to bottom progression on the page. Each of these objectives can be easily accommodated in most writing sessions.

In addition to questions, you will also need these materials for recording language experience and providing for follow-up activities:

Large-size newsprint tablets
Easels for dictation and display
Loose newsprint
Large paper clamps, clip clothespins, string or wire
Drawing paper and crayons
Writing paper and pencils

Preparing for Recording Activities

For each type of recording activity (writing log, literature log, response journal, research notebook, personal dictionary, diary), students will need a separate spiral notebook or a three-ring binder with labeled dividers. When guidelines are part of the writing activity, you can staple, clip, tape or glue these to the inside covers of notebooks for easy reference. If students use three-ring binders, these guidelines can be punched and placed appropriately. Some teachers ask students to tie a pen or pencil to the spiral with string, so that a writing instrument is readily available. Notebooks may be provided as part of your classroom materials or requested from home, as part of a school supplies list.

To help organize these books or dividers, you can distribute white self-stick labels to put on the front covers, which can be filled in by students with the appropriate titles. Some teachers also distribute self-stick colored dots to place in the upper right-hand corner of the notebooks. "Bring the red-dot books to your conference" is a quick instruction that is easy to follow.

Preparing for Individual Writing Conferences

Teacher Preparation   Your preparation for writing conferences includes finding a place to meet with students, establishing an independent writing period for the entire class, developing questions to ask about the student's writing and assembling a skills checklist. You will want to create a sense of privacy as you listen to students read their writing aloud or when you both discuss the features of a particular piece of writing. Sitting next to each other at a table is the ideal situation because it allows you to look at the writing together. This arrangement also permits you to make notes in a conference book and mark off skills on a checklist. You will need a three-ring conference notebook and a conference record for each student in the classroom. You will want to select several items to evaluate and promote in each conference. A sample conference record (Figure 8.7) and a skills checklist (Figure 8.8) are shown below.

Student Preparation   Students prepare for individual writing conferences by reviewing their completed writing projects or works-in-progress. If they have completed a number of writing projects and filed them in their portfolios, they will try to choose work that illustrates their best efforts. If they have questions about writing or problems with a particular piece of writing, they may also bring these to a conference. Students use conference guidelines, similar to the ones shown below, to help them prepare for the discussion and as a checklist for self-correction.

Writing Conference Guidelines

1. Read what you have written aloud. Be sure to practice.
2. If the work is long, read your favorite part.
3. What do you like best about what you wrote?
4. What do you think is most successful about this work?
5. What are you trying to say?
6. What is the main idea?
7. Are you having any problems?
8. What would you like to improve?
9. Refer to the genre guidelines. Tell how you tried to address them.
10. Did you check to see how another author solved this problem?
11. Did you read your story aloud to anyone else? What did they have to say?
12. What are your writing plans for the next day? (week, two weeks)
13. What is the purpose of this writing? Who is the audience? What voice is used? Why is this a good form for this writing?

Conference Record

Name _____

Date _____

Work Title _____

Type of Writing _____

Comments _____

Questions for Writing Conference

1. Read me what you have written.
2. Read your favorite part.
3. What do you like best about what you have written?
4. What do you think is most successful about this work?
5. What are you trying to say?
6. What is the main idea?
7. Are you having any problems?
8. What would you like to improve?
9. Let's look at the genre guidelines. Tell me how you have tried to address them.
10. Did you check to see how another author solved this problem?
11. Did you read your story aloud to anyone else? What did they have to say?
12. What are your writing plans for the next week? (day, two weeks)

Comments:

FIGURE 8.7
Sample of conference record.

At the primary level and above, students should be provided with guidelines for writing in the various genres. These can be adapted for a range of grade levels from the genre descriptions in Chapter 4. An example for biographies is given below.

Guidelines for Biographical Writing

Early life facts:
Early life anecdote:
Adult life facts:
Adult life anecdote:
Contributions to society facts:
Contribution to society anecdote:
Later life:
End of life:
Sources: book, magazine, encyclopedia, newspaper, diary, journal, interview, other

	Exceptional	Adequate	Developing
Handwriting			
Appearance of work			
Sentence formation			
Paragraphs			
Vocabulary			
Word use			
Decoding skills			
Idea			
Spelling			
Clarity			
Consistency			
Sequence			
Genre accuracy			
Characterization			
Authenticity			
Accurate use of terms			

FIGURE 8.8
Sample of writing skills checklist.

Students anticipate that the teacher will be interested in hearing what they have written and will be able to help them sort out writing difficulties. The teacher will also work with them to identify writing skills for practice during independent writing time.

Preparing for Writer's Workshops

Teacher Preparation   Where will students do their independent writing? Nancie Atwell[9] suggests designating separate areas of the room that communicate the type of writing students are doing. If they are seated at their desks, it is permissible for others to ask for help or schedule a peer review session. If a student moves to a reserved table, this is a sign that serious writing is happening and the author does not want to be disturbed. Other set-apart areas should include a place for peer review conferences and for individual conferences with the teacher.

When students finish this period of independent writing, you will need to decide on the best place to gather them together for a mini-lesson or an author's chair session. If you plan to include the entire class, you might want to have students draw their desks together into a semicircle. If there is enough space in the room, students can sit together on a rug around the author's chair, which is the place of honor for students sharing their written work. If you plan to include a mini-lesson in the writer's workshop, you will need to prepare for a presentation that demonstrates a writing skill, describes a genre or introduces a literary technique (see Chapter 9).

Student Preparation   The best way to prepare students for writing workshops is to role-play what will happen. Rehearse what everyone does during independent writing and the purpose for each writing area in the room. Describe the author's chair format for taking turns to share their work and explain how this activity will help them with their writing. Share something with your students that you have written. Let them practice responding by reacting to your writing. What do they like? What else would they like to know? What would help them understand the writing better?

During the initial practice session, ask students to look at something they have written. What feedback about their work would they like to receive from an audience? Model the types of information that an audience can provide: Does the work seem finished? Do listeners understand what was read? Are the characters developed enough? Can they visualize the setting? Are the descriptions adequate? Does the story hold listeners' interest? Do they want to know more about it?

Distribute audience guidelines (see Figure 8.9, page 301) and discuss them with your class, or tell them what you want to happen during the workshop and ask your students what guidelines will help achieve these goals.

WHAT DO YOU THINK?   For what reasons have you written today? What kinds of writing do you enjoy? How might it be helpful to attempt the same writing assignments as your students? Do you think you might feel hesitant about sharing something you have written? Why?

V. Including Everyone

When students with limited English proficiency are placed in a regular classroom, they enter a world of total immersion in a foreign language. For most children, this is an extremely intimidating experience. If you can imagine yourself in a similar situation, you can see how frightening it would be not to understand what is being said around you or to be able to make yourself clearly understood. Even persons who try to help often talk louder in their effort to be more clear, creating a situation where everyone is shouting at the person who already faces difficulty with the language. It is, of course, important to speak clearly. But keep your voice at a normal level and maximize opportunities for students to work individually with you, an aide and other students.

At the primary and kindergarten levels, label everything in the classroom at a time when the student can watch you. Make a game of going around the room with the student to let him or her distribute labels for familiar objects and activity areas. Play this game on a daily basis and try to involve others as helpers, including peers, Book Buddies from other classes and classroom aides. You can also print the names of objects on index cards and ask the student for the one that says "book," "library," "piano" and so on. Gradually add pictures of actions, such as "The boy runs," or descriptions like "purple flower." It is helpful to beginning readers to write the parts of speech in different colors to provide prompts for identification, such as red for nouns, purple for adjectives and green for verbs. When you create a language experience chart, be sure to use illustrations to help students identify words and provide additional clues to their meaning.

You can help new students acclimate to your classroom by providing a volunteer mentor. Some schools assign these mentors, or you can ask for volunteers. When students volunteer their efforts to involve a new student in language activities, they work hard to help the student be successful. As the student experiences success, this is personally rewarding to the mentors, and bonds of friendship often result. Other students begin to volunteer their help and see each success of the new student as their own. Students will show enormous patience and ingenuity in their peer tutoring, approaching the new student in ways not possible for the teacher.

Enlist the help of your school or public librarian to obtain English-language versions of stories, poems and folktales of your students' countries of origin. In many areas, English-language issues of newspapers and magazines from other countries are also available. Contact travel agencies for copies of travel brochures in English and write the embassy or consulate of the particular countries to obtain free illustrated materials in English. Display a map of the student's country that includes the countries around it to allow the student to explore the geography and talk about it with other students. All students in the class will be interested in folktales from other countries and will enjoy finding elements in common between these new stories and those with which they are already familiar. Enlist the help of a librarian or consult one of the reference books described in Chapters 3 and 4 to locate folktales from countries around the world. If you live near a military base, these kinds of books may be available from the base library or from parents of children in your school who have lived in different countries.

Children who experience hearing loss can participate in the author's chair activity with minimal assistance. Teachers and students can help by making sure they face the student when they talk, and teachers can monitor the light to avoid glare that might interfere with the student being able to see the speaker's face. Encourage children with hearing difficulties to practice reading aloud what they want to share before the session. They may also want to tape record the mini-lesson portions of writing workshops to review at a later time at a higher sound volume. In some hearing support programs, students wear special hearing aids that amplify the teacher's speech. Teachers wear a special microphone and monitor that permits them to speak normally, but allows students to adjust the volume to their own individual needs. It is important to model simple courtesies for all students such as: "Can you speak louder, please?" and "Can you say it again, please?"

If you have students who are physically challenged, they may be eligible for special equipment to assist their writing. Computer keyboards with large keys that can be tapped with a pointer attached to a head strap have been particularly effective with students who must deal with the challenges presented by cerebral palsy or muscular dystrophy. Some computer programs have speaker systems that can read aloud any text entered into it, enabling students who have speech difficulties to participate in writing and discussion activities. This configuration is also useful to students whose vision prohibits great amounts of reading. Stories and entire books can be loaded for reading aloud. If students routinely enter their stories on the word processor, they can be listened to for enjoyment by all classmates, including those with physical challenges.

The most important goal for teachers is to provide all students with the **opportunity** to write, as often as possible, in response to ideas and experiences that are meaningful to each individual. Stay alert to all the ways this goal can be realized for each student in your classroom, making adjustments as necessary for special needs and adding the support of technology when appropriate and available (see Chapter 10).

Books to Increase Understanding

The books recommended below chronicle attempts by children from different cultures to adapt to life in America. For many, there are multiple challenges of dealing with prejudice, learning a new language and responding to new cultural expectations.

I Hate English![10] Mei Mei resists learning English because she fears she will lose her identity in the new language. This is the story of a teacher who helps Mei Mei learn to be comfortable in both of her languages.

Journey Home[11] This touching story by Yoshiko Uchida describes the hardships faced by Japanese Americans interned in concentration camps during World War II. Most children are not aware of this tragic time in U.S. history and will be interested in this first-hand account.

Dragonwings[12] This exciting Newbery Award winner by Lawrence Yep describes the experiences of Chinese immigrants in San Francisco at the turn of the century. Students will be interested in the description of living conditions and the way characters of several cultures resolve their prejudices. There is also a vivid account of the great San Francisco earthquake. *Dragon's Gate*,[13] also by Yep, describes the harrowing experiences of Chinese workers who helped to build the intercontinental railway.

Journey of the Sparrows[14] This unusual story chronicles the journey of four children who are nailed into a crate and sent to Chicago from El Salvador. They struggle to find work, eat and survive in a culture where they must remain invisible or risk being returned to their country to face certain death. This story of courage and hope realistically portrays the fears and challenges that are part of the daily life of many immigrant children in the United States. Other stories about the Latino/Latina American experience include *Felita*[15] by Nicolasa Mohr, an account of a Puerto Rican family living where no Spanish is spoken, and *I Speak English for My Mom*[16] by Muriel Stanek, the story of a young Mexican American girl who must translate for her mother, who cannot read English.

WHAT DO YOU If you read one of the books listed above, what impressed you about
THINK? the experience of the child you read about? How would you have dealt
with similar challenges? How would you have responded to this child
as a teacher?

VI. Step-by-Step: Guidelines for Writing Activities

Each of the writing activities described below can be used appropriately at
any level of elementary instruction. Even the captioning and language
experience charts, observed in a kindergarten classroom, can be adapted for
use with older students who have limited English proficiency. At each level,
portfolios are created and maintained as a shared responsibility of the teacher
and students.

Captions

You can begin this activity with kindergarten and early primary students by
asking them to tell you about pictures they have drawn or painted. Avoid
asking "What's this?" or guessing about the contents of the picture. If you
say "Tell me about your picture," students will respond by telling the
meaning of the pictures and symbols. You might then ask if they would like
to have some words at the top of their picture to tell others about what they
have told you. When they have decided on a caption, help them identify the
sounds in the word(s). Write the completed caption on an index card for
them to copy onto their paper.

Key Words

When you introduce key words to your students, you might show them
several of your favorite words, written on tagboard and fastened together. If
you are comfortable doing it, you could model several ways they could carry
the cards around during the day—by fastening them to a belt loop or
attaching them to a yarn bracelet. Tell your students that the cards have
some of your favorite words written on them. Show them each card and read
them aloud. Tell them that beginning today, they will have a chance to get
a new card every day with one of their favorite words written on it. It is theirs
to keep and practice, and they can choose a new one each day. It can be any
word they choose, but they should think about it carefully to make sure it is
the best one they can think of. Ask them to think about a word they would
like to be able to read and write. In the next half-hour, you will give everyone
his or her own special word.

*Language
Experience Charts*

Meet for conversations with groups of five to seven children. Plan separate
groups that will support contributions by reluctant speakers and allow highly
verbal children frequent opportunities to express themselves. This arrangement will permit contributions by children who are hesitant or who process
information at a slower rate. They will be less likely to be intimidated or
excluded by conversations that are fast-paced. Children who are highly
verbal will have increased opportunities to practice developing skills and be
challenged by the ideas of others of similar abilities.

During the school day, children interact frequently in homogeneous groups to talk, listen, read and write with each other. Occasional grouping by language proficiency allows students the chance to participate more fully. It also creates a more positive experience for the teacher, who is not forced to juggle competing forces by suppressing the activity of those who are more fluent and trying to pull contributions out of children who are not eager to participate, for whatever reason. You can also use the guidelines in the remainder of this section for taking dictation from an individual child. This activity is especially important for children who have limited English proficiency because it gives them increased opportunities to create writing from their own speaking and to read what they have written.

Any discussion can be used to create language experience charts. You might want to begin a sharing session by commenting on the weather or a shared experience, such as a school assembly, a class visitor, a film, theme study or a book that has just been read. You can make a statement or ask a question: "There's snow all over the daffodils," or "What do you think about the snowstorm?" will usually start the conversation. You can begin as simply as "What would you like to talk about today?"

As your students add their own ideas, record words that serve as one-word captions. For example, one group of children commented on the way the unseasonal snowstorm covered all the flowers. Others mentioned the slippery roads during the bus ride to school, the snow that fell out of the trees on their heads as they walked to school and sledding possibilities on a local hill. The teacher wrote the words "snow," "flowers," "roads," "trees," and "sleds" on the board.

When everyone has had a chance to contribute to the discussion, ask the students if they would like to write a story about their discussion. If they are interested in the topic, they will be excited about recording their talk. If not, continue talking about other things of interest until a topic engages them. Some teachers discuss a wide range of ideas and then ask students to decide which one will be made into a story.

Ask your students how they want to begin the story or inquire: "Who has a sentence?" Before you write the sentence, ask them where you should begin writing. In the beginning, you will want individual students to come up and point to the correct section of the chart. Ask them what kind of letter should be used to begin the sentence, and as you record the sentence, say each word aloud as you write it. When you finish the sentence, ask your students what punctuation mark should be placed at the end. Read the entire sentence as you run your hand underneath it to draw attention to the words creating the sentence and model the left to right progression.

Ask your students: "What do you want to say next?" or "What happened next?" depending on the type of story. If the story requires sequence, such as the events of a trip or the retelling of literature, help children sort out the order by asking: "Did anything important happen before this?" or "What happened while we were on the way to the zoo?" As you write, leave spaces that will allow you to insert an additional sentence in a sequence of ideas. If the story is descriptive, such as the snowstorm mentioned above, it may not require a sequence. Encourage children to group ideas by asking: "Is there anything else you want to say about the slippery roads?" or "Shall we save that sentence for when we write about the flowers?"

As you record children's ideas for sentences, model the writer's mind by asking such questions as: "How can we show that this word starts a sentence?" or "What kind of punctuation mark should we use?" You can also ask them to identify parts of the composition by asking: "Can anyone read this sentence?" "Can you find a word in here that you know?" "Whose sentence was this?" When the story is complete, ask your students to read it aloud together and then decide what caption or title to use at the top. When several suggestions have been generated, let the group vote on the one to use. Encourage students to interact with the dictated story in the same manner used for guided reading (Chapter 5). Students also enjoy retelling stories, which provides practice in recalling details and ordering events.

Group-generated lists are helpful visual aids for writing. You might want to take dictation for these on the blackboard and transfer them in more orderly fashion to charts at another time. These lists of words should be displayed where students can see or access them easily for their writing throughout the day in order to help generate ideas and relationships and provide spelling assistance. Popular charts include holiday words and words about space, dinosaurs, animals and plants. Include brainstorming sessions to develop lists of synonyms, antonyms and paired words, such as girl–boy, knife–fork, cat–dog. Record the names of things at home or school and things they see on the playground, in the classroom, media center, hallway, cafeteria and gym. Lists can be made of things that are certain shapes, textures or colors. Generate words that accompany seasons, the weather or months of the year. Create words or sentences related to a literary theme or topics in science, the social studies or fine arts. Record the daily weather. Make lists of instructions for using the centers.

Students can create a mural, drawing pictures of things they can do, and these can be labeled (James can take care of his baby brother; Amy can draw dinosaurs). They can name as many things as they can remember on the way to school or on the bus and record all the things they can know through their senses. What can different animals do? What can machines do? Have children list names of things that are sweet, sour, hard, soft, salty or bitter. What things can they name that are made of cotton, wool, metal or stone?

Teachers in the late primary and intermediate grades can create lists of content area terminology and their definitions and provide examples of language constructions, such as metaphors and similes. Instructions, rules and guidelines can also be generated by students for easy reference. Some teachers begin lists that promote research and can be added to by students throughout a particular study.

Recording Activities Introduce these activities gradually, as part of a mini-lesson that precedes the activity itself. Distribute notebooks to students or describe how to assemble them. Explain the purpose of each activity, review the guidelines and supervise their placement into a permanent location by stapling, clipping or gluing. Demonstrate an entry by writing on the board or using an overhead projector. To introduce each activity, you might say something like the following:

Literature journal These notebooks will be used to record your ideas and questions about what you read. You will want to create a section to list the books you read, another section to write your ideas about what you read and still another to record responses to literature discussion questions. For each entry, write the date, the title of the book and the author and/or illustrator.

Diary This book is to record your ideas about anything you are thinking about. It is private and for your eyes only. If you want to share any of these ideas with me, I will be happy to read them and write back to you. The guidelines list some things you might like to write about, but you should feel free to write about anything you choose.

Personal dictionary This is a place to record words you use in your writing. You will want to save at least two pages for words beginning with each letter of the alphabet. Each time you learn the correct spelling of a word you want to use in your writing, record it on the appropriate page. When you are writing and do not know how to spell a word, write the sounds you hear and then circle the word if you think it is incorrect. Later, you can look it up in the dictionary or ask someone for help.

Writing journal This notebook will be used as reference for your writing. Make a section for prewriting exercises, one for entering research on your topics and another for recording ideas you have for writing. At the front of your notebook, insert the guidelines for conferences, writing genres and audience participation.

Learning journal or **academic research notebook** This is a notebook for you to use when you are finding out facts and information about a topic in science or social studies. You can write questions you have about a topic in this book and any questions we generate as a group. As you find the answers to these questions, you can record them in this notebook. You might also want to add other material, such as newspaper clippings, cartoons, pictures, and your own drawings that are related to a topic.

Writer's Workshop— The Author's Chair

When students begin meeting together to share their writing at the author's chair, you will want to review the purpose of the group and create guidelines for participation as both a presenter and a listener. The following are suggestions for introducing the first session:

Purposes of group sharing Tell your students that the entire class (or smaller groups) will meet daily to share their writing. They may bring anything they want from their literature journals for the first workshop, but after that students will be asked to write in response to particular broad topics or to write in a particular genre. They may volunteer to share their work, but everyone will have a turn. The purpose of the workshop is to gain experience with reading and talking about their writing, to get new ideas from the group about making their writing communicate effectively and to participate as involved listeners.

Creating the guidelines Ask your students to develop guidelines that will help achieve the purposes of the writer's workshop. Most students will come up with guidelines similar to the ones in Figure 8.9 and generally respond more favorably to them because of their involvement in creating them. Encourage them to keep the number of guidelines to no more than three or four.

Talk with your students about the kinds of questions that are helpful for both the writer and listener, such as: Where did they get the idea for their

---

Author's Chair—Audience Guidelines

1. Give the author your full attention by maintaining eye contact and provide encouragement with your responses.

2. Be positive when you talk about another person's writing. Tell what you especially liked about the story—the characters, descriptions, humor or language use, for example.

3. When you have suggestions, begin your comments positively, such as: "Did you ever think about . . . ?" or "I liked this part, but I had difficulty understanding . . ."

FIGURE 8.9
Audience guidelines for author's chair.

writing? How did they find out about the topic? Is the work finished? What else do they plan to add?

Students should be encouraged to evaluate writing in terms of how well it drew and held their interest. Was it understandable? Would it help to read it again? Is it the kind of writing that might be better understood if it were read silently? Were there parts where the listener felt confused? How might this be addressed?

If the writing is fiction, listeners might want to consider if the writer tells enough about the setting so that it can be visualized. Are the characters described fully enough? If the writing was in a particular genre, such as historical fiction or modern fantasy, does it have the necessary features? Is terminology used in nonfiction explained clearly?

Keep in mind that writer's workshops will be most effective if they are coordinated with guided reading. When you are studying literature in a genre or for a particular theme, this is the best time to practice writing in that context. The more experience students have with genres or themes, the more proficient they will become in expressing themselves, analyzing the relevant components and synthesizing this experience in new and creative ways. Themes and genre writing are also helpful for writing clubs because they tend to create a focus for student writing.

Writing Clubs Groups of students may elect to meet together across grade levels to share their writing and produce magazines, books or newspapers. Some clubs encourage members to submit their writing for publication by outside sources. Check a current copy of the *Children's Writer's and Illustrator's Market* (annotated in the Resources for Teaching section) for children's writing contests and the names and addresses of magazines that publish children's writing. In many schools, students initiate these clubs and meet during the noon hour or after school with a faculty sponsor. Classroom teachers, language arts teachers, music teachers, librarians, special education teachers, interested community members or parents may volunteer to supervise these meetings. The main requirement is an interest in student writing and the ability to help students of different age levels interact productively.

Students who show an interest in this type of club should be encouraged to do as much of the organizational work as possible. Writing groups will succeed to the extent that most of the members are involved in all planning from the beginning. The following questions should be addressed by student organizers, with the understanding that modifications to responses may be necessary after meeting together as a group. For example, one group initially wanted everyone to share his or her writing at every session, but soon discovered that this would not work because of the large numbers of students involved. The guidelines were changed accordingly.

1. Where will the group meet? When will the group meet and how often?
2. Who will be invited? How many people should be asked?
3. How will writing be shared? Will members provide multiple copies to be read in small groups, or will they read aloud to the entire group?
4. What kinds of responses will be helpful from listeners?
5. What kinds of suggestions are appropriate to make?
6. What does the group expect of the faculty sponsor? What does the faculty sponsor expect of the group?
7. What is the purpose of the group? Will they produce a magazine or newspaper? A collection of stories?

A copy of the organizational plan should be submitted for suggestions and approval to an appropriate person, which might be the faculty sponsor, the principal or officers of the student council, depending on the school situation. If you have volunteered to be a sponsor, be sure that all necessary persons have been notified, including the principal and any other teachers whose students may be invited. Request permission to use any meeting area that is outside your own classroom.

Individual Writing Conferences

When you meet with students to discuss their writing, you will be using guidelines similar to those described in the preparation section. These questions are designed to help students identify the purpose of their writing and to consider the effectiveness of their communication to an audience. Students will prepare for these conferences using similar guidelines. You will want to help them consider how their content and writing mechanics add to or detract from their writing purposes. Review your discussion at the end of the conference to help students establish a direction for additional writing, revision or the start of a new project.

In addition to the standard conference questions, you may want to add additional comments to help students clarify their writing or to encourage them to reflect on what they have written. The following questions are examples of questions you may want to add to your list:

1. Did you have any difficulties with your writing? What would you like to work on today?
2. You circled this word. How can you find out how to spell it? Does it look like another word you already know how to spell?
3. Can you explain what you mean here? I'm not familiar with this term. Can you tell me what it means?

4. Is this part as clear as you can make it? Read it to me again and then we'll think about it some more.

5. Why don't you bring this chapter to the author's chair for some suggestions? How about reading it to others to see what they think?

6. I'm not sure I understand this part. Tell me about it in your own words. Do you think you said all that in your writing? I would understand it better if you told me more about. . . .

7. If I were reading this sentence, I wouldn't be sure how the character felt. Could you add some of his/her thoughts here? Could you help me understand it better with a different punctuation mark?

8. Could you compare this to something else that would help me understand how cold (surprised, frightened, angry) your character was?

9. Do you have some evidence that this really happened? Where could you look or who could you interview to find out the facts about this?

10. Could you add more information here? Would it add interest to interview someone who was there (knows about this)? Can you call on your own experience to add some background here? What could you add to the description of this scene to help the reader see it more clearly?

For each conference, students should take notes on the ideas discussed. What do they need to know more about to make their writing clearer or more interesting? What needs additional practice to create clear communication? Some teachers provide students with a simple memo form for note-taking. The following is an example:

Student Self-Evaluation Guide

I need more information about: (how polliwogs change into frogs; how to write a biography)

I need more practice: (writing the cursive capital Q; writing topic sentences; describing characters)

Establish a time limit for these conferences and try to follow it. It is better to aim for weekly rather than daily conferences so that you will have sufficient time to listen and interact for five to ten minutes, depending on the age and ability level of your students. Schedule three to five conferences per day or enough to create time for each student during the week. Students will have their most important questions established before the conference, and you will have decided what you most want to know about a student's writing in advance. Greet students pleasantly, listen to them read and then ask your most important questions.

WHAT DO YOU THINK? What strengths do you see in yourself as a writer? What would you like to improve? How can thinking about these questions help you assist students with their writing?

VII. If This Is Your Situation

Your school district or state may have mandates about how writing is taught. If language skills are taught as separate subject areas, you may also have specific directives for teaching composition, handwriting, spelling and English grammar. The concern of the educators or governing bodies who create these mandates is that the level of writing performance has decreased among students. They believe that assigned projects and frequent assessments will improve student writing and help ensure that all students will receive at least minimal instruction.

Teachers who have established successful writing programs on their own may feel unfairly penalized by these restrictions, which they see as obstructing achievement in their students. They have, however, worked successfully with administrators who are under pressure to show improvement in writing skills. These teachers initiate contact with their principals by sharing their concerns about several children in their class early in the school year. These may be students who frequently reverse letters or who write very little. During the year they keep principals informed of these students' progress, telling success stories and showing them samples of improvement.

As an individual teacher, you can respond to mandates in several ways, depending on the level of restrictions imposed on your decision making:

Level One—The school district lists curriculum objectives. Make a list of the skills required or word lists that must be mastered. Word lists can be administered at the beginning of the year during a week's time. At the kindergarten level, required word identification lists can be checked off as individual children learn these words throughout the year. At the primary and intermediate levels, individual students can copy words they need to learn to spell or define and create their own word lists to study and master throughout the year. As words are spelled or used correctly, they can be checked off on the teacher's master list. Instructional audiotapes or videotapes for handwriting can be used, as needed, by students who require assistance with handwriting skills. English grammar objectives can be easily adapted into mini-lessons.

Level Two—A specific writing program is mandated. Sometimes districts have specific writing programs, with activities that must be completed by all grade levels. States may also assign writing topics or projects as part of an assessment program. All of the writing activities described in this chapter can be used as warm-up exercises or informal practice for the more formal assigned topics or projects. The concern here is that students will be able to perform well on writing tests. The additional practice helps achieve this goal.

Level Three—Writing instruction is a team effort or another teacher's responsibility. Occasionally at the primary level, but more often at the intermediate-grade levels, language arts instruction is **departmentalized**. This means that one teacher is responsible for teaching language arts to all classes at a grade level or, in smaller schools, to all intermediate grades. If this is your situation and you are the language arts teacher, you may be able to create an integrated program with each group of students you teach, subject to the restrictions noted above. If you must correlate your teaching with a team, you can still use these guidelines. If you are not the language arts teacher and your assignment is social studies, science or math, you can use all the language arts as tools for learning, expression and communication. Ideas for integrating language arts into the content areas are discussed in detail in Chapter 11.

WHAT DO YOU THINK?   How do you think educators develop their ideas about the most effective way to teaching writing? Do you see yourself as a problem-solver? What do you think will be your greatest challenge as you attempt to integrate writing into the curriculum?

VIII.   Evaluating Progress

For students to progress in their writing, it is important for them to be involved in self-evaluation. From the time they first begin to write, students can be encouraged to look at their writing in light of their personal goals for expression. They can identify elements that indicate progress and those that require attention. The teacher's role in this process is to model ways for students to evaluate themselves. Questions such as the following direct attention to their best expression:

1. Show me your best letter.
2. Which sentence do you like the best?
3. What part of your story is your favorite?
4. What kind of writing do you do best?
5. Read me your best description.

Teachers can also help students spot areas of difficulty in their writing:

1. What was the hardest letter to make?
2. Are there any sentences that do not sound right to you?
3. What do you think about this part? Does it satisfy you? What do you think it needs?
4. Did you have any problems with this sentence?
5. Read this paragraph again. Does it say what you want it to?
6. I'm not sure I understand this idea (or what happened). Can you give me some more information?

From teacher modeling and interaction with a variety of audiences, students begin to ask these questions of themselves, gradually internalizing standards of clear, comprehensive expression that will help them evaluate their own progress.

It is also important for students to monitor their progress. Student files and portfolio collections are an invaluable asset for this activity. Because all work is dated when it is filed, students can easily compare their previous and present skills to observe progress in such areas as letter formation, sentence construction or character development.

Evaluation by teachers is complementary to student self-evaluation. It models the kinds of questions students can learn to ask themselves: How well does this writing express my ideas? and How have I progressed toward this goal? Teachers collect information about their students' writing throughout the day as students write about their ideas and share them with a variety of audiences. They observe students as they participate in writer's workshop or share their writing in individual conferences. Using checklists and brief written comments, they note the progress and difficulties of individual students and use this information to direct their teaching. Portfolios and two-minute conferences provide additional information on the development of student writing skills.

Portfolios   One of the most helpful ways that teachers assemble information about student writing is by helping students create a portfolio of their work. A **portfolio** is a collection of an individual student's writing that is representative of the work that particular student has produced. Most teachers provide folders and files for students to contribute to these portfolios. When students complete a piece of writing, they stamp it with the date and put it in their file. They may bring samples of their best writing from this file to writing conferences or writer's workshop. Teachers review these files when they assemble material for required evaluations, such as parent conferences, report cards and reviews by supervisors.

Not all writing that students complete is evaluated by the teacher. There are two reasons for this. When students are encouraged to write throughout the day for many purposes, they generate more writing than could possibly be read and evaluated. Second, some of this writing is, by its very nature, private. Recording activities such as diaries are intended to help students explore their thoughts and feelings and to organize their thinking through written expression. This writing provides practice for writing skills and creates habits of thinking through writing, but it is not intended to be part of a portfolio evaluation.

According to Donald Graves,[17] a good way to introduce portfolios to students is to invite parents or professionals who maintain portfolios in their workplace to share their collections with the class. These persons might include antique collectors, salespersons, artists, clothing designers, interior decorators, landscape engineers or architects. As part of the invitation, he suggests asking them to share the following:

The way they select their best work
How they choose something that indicates learning
An example that shows growth
A skill they are trying to develop

Graves also suggests inviting students to bring in six to eight items from any collection they have at home. These collections might be dolls, toys, cars, baseball cards, caps, pictures, photographs, drawings, dishes, stamps, letters, coins, rocks or plants. Most children are collectors and have no difficulty with this assignment. They could also bring in a dream collection—pictures of houses, boats, cars, sports figures, animals, food or clothes—to demonstrate their interests. In turn, each student is asked to tell: why they choose these items; how they should be ranked in order of quality; and why one is better than the other. This exercise helps children begin to develop a language of valuing and demonstrates the key principles of evaluating. He also recommends that teachers show students their own portfolios or collections and explain why these things are significant to them.

When writing portfolios are introduced to students, they should be told to include not only their best efforts at writing, but also examples of things that show their growth or indicate something they have learned from a mistake. Work from all areas of the curriculum can be added to indicate their depth and range as learners. They should also include work that portrays them as persons and indicates what is important in their lives, their interests and things they can do. These items give them a sense of identity and history, a sense of the future and a sense of values. This part of the collection might include past papers, quotes, ideas, content area projects, drawings, poems and newspaper clippings.

Before any item is added to the portfolio, however, it must be justified in writing. Students must respond to the questions: Why is this item in here? What does it show? Is it my best work? Did I learn something from this? Does it show that I really know a lot about this subject? Does it show my ability to do other things? Does it show something I think is important? The appropriate justification can be numbered to the item on a single explanation sheet or attached to the individual item with a self-stick note.

Two-Minute Conferences Donald Graves (op. cit.) suggests that teachers conduct brief, walk-around writing conferences with students on a daily basis to keep in touch with their writing progress. This contact, approximately two minutes in length, should include questions that encourage students to consider the past, present and future of the piece they are working on (this is what I have tried to do; this is what I am currently working on; and this is what I plan to do).

In a two-minute version of the interaction between Haley and Mrs. Logan, recorded in Section 4 of this chapter, the teacher might stop briefly at Haley's desk and ask her how the biography is coming along. Haley would tell the teacher what she was trying to do and relate her dissatisfaction with her progress. Mrs. Logan might ask Haley if she had consulted other biographies as models, and as the teacher moved on, Haley would consider this possibility for future action.

Questions to assess writing in this way can be considered in advance. Donald Graves suggests questions like "Have you run into any difficulties?" or "What did you hope would happen with this writing?" as ways to set the writing in a historical perspective. To assess the current status of the piece, ask "What are you working on now?" or "How is it going?" Students can be encouraged to consider future plans with questions like "What do you think will happen next?" or "What are you going to work on next?" Notice that the questions are brief and to the point. Your goal is to encourage the student to do all the talking, while you listen carefully. This process of talking out loud about a project helps students focus on their writing in terms of their purposes and progress and encourages autonomy in solving problems that arise.

For these two-minute conferences, you can prepare a simple checklist with the names of all students in the classroom. As you move from student to student, progress or difficulty can be noted with plus or minus signs. Brief notations about specific difficulties can provide information for planning mini-lessons or writing workshops.

WHAT DO YOU THINK? Why do you think it is important to develop skills of self-evaluation? Do you feel confident evaluating your own writing? Are you ever surprised at either negative or positive evaluations of your writing?

IX.   Creating Partners

A good way to communicate with parents and enlist their help in writing activities is to extend the activity of writing notes home, described in this section in Chapter 7. At the end of the day, review all of the day's activities and list them on the board. Some classrooms have a rotating secretary who records the day's activities on a large chart at the front of the room. With these prompts, students can write their own notes home, commenting on what they enjoyed or are looking forward to. They might also describe activities that individual family members would be interested in.

Haley writes a note to her father, describing her efforts at writing during the school day.

> Dear Daddy, Today I worked on my story about Nonnie. I couldn't get it to be the way I wanted, so I looked at the Helen Keller story. I decided to start with a story about Nonnie, the one about the runaway horse. Can I call Nonnie tonight so she can tell me how to spell some words?

Herschel, who has added part of a new chapter to his science-fiction story, writes:

> Mom: I think this space odyssey piece is going somewhere (no pun intended). I read it out loud for the workshop and got some good ideas. What do you think about this? Each crew member has a computer chip that controls certain features of the ship. What would happen if there were a single malfunction or someone dies? Guess what? Somebody actually thought there should be more characters! Can you believe that, after the unmanageable crowd in *Zander's Quest?* Our research group set up an appointment to talk on the Internet to a professor at Stanford who's part of a team monitoring radio waves for signs of life in outer space.

Bright Feather takes home his captioned picture of the buffalo hunt to share with his family. He has also drawn pictures to remind himself to ask his uncle about some words he needs to write about the buffalo hunt. Diem takes home picture word cards he has made to show his day's activities.

These letters home can be addressed to anyone and are intended to provide information about a child's interests and activities at school. They help students organize their thoughts about their work during the day and provide daily practice in the lost art of letter writing. This activity promotes conversation at home about what children are learning at school and is an antidote for the typical response of "Nothing" to the question "What did you learn at school today?" Students may vary the type of written communication they take home by writing brief descriptions of the day's activities or more detailed descriptions of a single activity that especially drew their interest.

Most teachers also write home to parents. They describe current learning activities and talk about how parents can provide assistance. At the beginning of the year they may ask for volunteer help with writing activities, such as taking dictation, typing up stories or helping students learn to use the word processor. They may also send home a list of ideas for families to support writing at home, such as providing opportunities for children to write for a purpose. Students can help make grocery lists, leave messages for family members, take phone messages, write up catalog orders, write letters to family and friends who live far away, order free materials, write about trips or things that interest them and keep a journal or diary during a family trip or visit.

Reach out to the broader community of your school and area to expand your students' concepts of writing as a career. Invite local writers, newspaper editors and feature writers for sports, food, business and education to share what they do. How did they get interested in writing? What problems do they encounter with their writing? How do they solve them? You might also encourage students to interview school personnel, family members and community workers to ask how they use writing in their work.

WHAT DO YOU THINK? What would you enjoy most about receiving a letter from your child about his or her schoolwork? Can you think of other persons from the community who might be invited into the classroom to share ideas about writing? What other benefits from projects like these can you identify?

X. Perspectives

Our ideas about children and writing have been given a new perspective by the work of educators who are interested in children's writing. Among these are Sylvia Ashton-Warner and Donald Graves. In *Teacher*,[18] Sylvia Ashton-Warner says:

> A child's writing is his own affair and is an exercise in integration which makes for better work. The more it means to him the more value it is to him. And it means everything to him. It is part of him as an arranged subject could never be. It is not a page of sentences written round set words, resulting in a jumble of disconnected facts as you so often see. It is the unbroken line of thought that we cultivate so carefully in our own writing and conversation. (p. 54)

This view of children's writing was developed by Ms. Warner from her experience teaching the Maori, the native peoples of New Zealand. Key words, discussed earlier in this chapter, were first described by Ashton-Warner, and later used by Jeanette Veatch,[19] as the basis for beginning reading instruction. Both educators reported that children easily learned words that were part of their experience. Ashton-Warner asked beginning students to tell her the words they wanted to know and recorded them on cards that she gave to the children to keep. Words from these cards were copied and used in stories or as captions for pictures. She observed that children requested words that had strong feelings attached to them—powerful words of love, fear, anger and important events in their lives. Usually students needed to see these words only once to remember them because of their strong personal meaning.

Donald Graves[20] believes that the root of evaluation is **self-evaluation** and that it is important for students to develop a language of valuing. Self-evaluation requires that students have an awareness of themselves and their own values and a sense of excellence about things and ideas. In the classroom, children will have different things that they value, and by sharing they learn to value diversity. He believes that the goal for classroom teachers is to help students learn how to express values and to become aware of what they value and why they value it. From this evaluation base, they are better able to assess their own writing, in terms of criteria for excellence, growth, and a sense of their history and future as learners.

Graves sees portfolios as a useful tool for students to learn self-evaluation. He differentiates between writing folders and portfolios. All written work goes into the writing folder, but the portfolio is reserved for work selected according to criteria. He believes it is important to a student's developing ability to self-evaluate that anything put into the portfolio must be justified. The key idea, according to Graves, is selection: applying values to find significance.

He compares standardized evaluation techniques to snapshots, which are frozen in time. This kind of assessment cannot indicate what a child can do with what he knows. Portfolios, on the other hand, are fluid and more like a videotape that tells a story over time. Work included in portfolios indicates more accurately how a child can use knowledge or skill to learn, explore or discover in an authentic setting.

Recommended Reading

Teacher (op. cit.) by Sylvia Ashton-Warner is an account of the author's experiences teaching Maori children in New Zealand. In anecdotal form, she describes her pioneering efforts to create a functional and relevant learning environment for her students. She models ways to create contexts for integrated language learning within administrative and economic restraints and is a source of inspiration for those who work in similar, challenging situations.

Build a Literate Classroom (op. cit.) by Donald Graves is part of a series of handbooks for teachers entitled *The Reading/Writing Teacher's Companion*. Other titles in the series include: *Investigate Nonfiction, Experiment with Fiction, Discover Your Own Literacy* and *Explore Poetry*. Each book encourages the teacher to experiment with reading and writing in the classroom. From the ideas presented, the reader is encouraged to try an "action," which includes suggestions for implementing the idea. For example, to help students understand the durable power of writing, Graves suggests keeping folders of children's work to help them discover a sense of history about their writing. Students can examine their work to observe progress. He also suggests discussing with students what writing can do that speaking or reading cannot.

WHAT DO YOU THINK? What minority cultures have been represented in the populations of the schools you have attended? How might you begin to learn more about the cultures in your community? How will your knowledge of and respect for the cultures of your students affect the way you support their writing efforts? If you were to begin building your own portfolio today, what things might you put in it that represent the areas outlined by Donald Graves?

XI. Exploring Professional Literature

Book Links: Connecting Books, Libraries, and Classrooms is a booklist publication of the American Library Association. Designed for teachers and parents as well as librarians, it provides a wealth of information for educators who use the integrated approach to language learning. "Classroom Connections," a regular feature, provides multigrade bibliographies related to broad themes, such as dinosaurs, wetlands or World War II. Background information is provided for each theme, and boxed ideas describe techniques to use in theme teaching. Annotations describe the content of each book, and information is provided about the publisher, cost, number of pages and appropriate grade levels.

"The Inside Story" features interviews with authors, illustrators and others associated with the publication of books, which can be used as background information to enhance appreciation of books and the craft involved in producing them. "Visual Links" explores the techniques of illustration and provides ideas for helping students appreciate these techniques and incorporate them into their own artistic expressions. Suggestions for using a specific book are included in "Book Strategies." In addition to the extensive description of a book's contents, there are suggestions for discussion, activities and research and an annotated list of fiction and nonfiction related to the same theme. Quality paperback books are featured in "Paperback Plums," which also list books printed in Spanish.

WHAT DO YOU THINK? This is a resource that has to be experienced to fully appreciate. Choose an issue and explore one of the themes. How do you think this publication might be useful to you as a teacher?

XII. Resources for Teaching

The following books include a wide range of ideas for introducing writing activities to students at every instructional level.

The Writing Process in Action: A Handbook for Teachers[21] This handbook describes an array of prewriting activities designed to help students generate and organize their ideas, make relationships among these ideas, and create fluency. Other chapters discuss decision making in writing, organizational patterns, linguistic structure, revision, proofreading and evaluation. The authors discuss ways to use writing as means of discovery and learning in the content areas. They include a resource chapter that features ideas for composition, journal starters and sample editing and response forms.

Children's Writer's & Illustrator's Market[22] Most libraries will have the latest edition of this helpful handbook. It lists magazine and book publishers that are interested in material written by children. Most provide copies of the published work for young authors and a few involve payment. Some editors will include helpful comments about work that is returned.

Answering Students' Questions About Words[23] This little handbook provides answers to questions students ask about language, such as why the same words have different meanings and why different words can have the same meaning. It traces the origins of words in English from different cultures and provides meanings for common root words, prefixes and suffixes. This is excellent background material for teachers at all levels and a good source for mini-lessons and classroom teaching charts. It would be a helpful reference book to have on hand for readers and writers at the intermediate level.

Writing Is Reading: 26 Ways to Connect[24] This little book contains twenty-six basic ideas (one for each letter of the alphabet) for connecting reading and writing. Each entry describes an activity tied to literature and provides a list of books to support the particular activity. Examples are: Alphabet books, Bookmaking, Character development, Dreams, Endings and Fairy tales. The book also gives theoretical background for making literature connections and cites research that supports this approach. References include lists of twenty-six books for making reading–writing connections at both the primary and intermediate levels.

Getting the Knack: 20 Poetry Writing Exercises[25] This book is intended for anyone who would like to write poetry. Full of wonderful ideas to use with students of all ages, it includes step-by-step instructions for creating poems from a variety of experiences, in many different and imaginative forms. The authors show how to find inspiration for poetry in headlines, letters, recipes and lists and how to respond to this inspiration in a similar format. Each exercise builds confidence in the writer to find patterns, beauty and ideas in the most common of sources.

Context-Responsive Approaches to Assessing Children's Language[26] This is a series of essays by educators that provides many ideas for evaluating student writing (reading, speaking, listening) in the context of language use. Alternate approaches to assessment, methods of student self-evaluation and interactive assessment are discussed.

Portfolio Assessment: Getting Started[27] This is a helpful "how-to-do-it" book that includes start-up suggestions and ideas for assessing and managing portfolios. There is a discussion on the benefits of portfolio use and a trouble-shooting guide for possible problems. There is also a bibliography.

Writing Workshop Survival Kit[28] Good ideas to begin using writing workshops in the classroom are provided. It contains mini-lessons, exercises and checklists for a broad range of writing activities. Topics cover the creation and management of writing workshops, prewriting strategies, drafting, revision, editing and publishing. Mini-lessons cover all genres, including news articles, plays, letters and poetry. Lessons cover writing techniques and mechanics, and bibliographies include books and resources for the teaching of writing.

The Reading–Writing Workshop: Getting Started[29] The authors feature a more structured and teacher-centered approach to writing workshops, but there are enough helpful tips included to make it useful as a reference. Management ideas, checklists, evaluation forms, and ways to use peer conferencing and student editing are provided.

In the Middle: Writing, Reading, and Learning with Adolescents (op. cit.) Although this classic work chronicles the experiences of a middle school teacher, many of the activities described can be used in the upper-intermediate grades. In anecdotal fashion, the author tells how to set up and use writing workshops. She discusses reading–writing connections, mini-lessons, group share sessions, editing conferences and evaluation. The appendices include reading and writing surveys, lists of favorite fiction, and examples of dialogue journals.

Literacy Through Literature[30] This book was included in the bibliography in Chapter 4, but its rich store of writing activities warrants its inclusion in this chapter also. These interesting exercises include using the plots, settings and characters of favorite literature to create story maps, literary report cards, passports, posters, letters, journals, book awards, sociograms, news reports, plot profiles, interviews and patterned writing. Imagine interviewing the Big Bad Wolf, issuing a report card to Templeton the rat, or creating a sociogram for the characters of Rabbit Hill. Students enjoy making "Wanted" posters for story villains and writing letters to the editor on behalf of Wilbur the pig.

Living between the Lines (op. cit.) This is a handbook of ideas for introducing writing into the classroom. The book is full of anecdotes and examples of children's writing that illustrate the authors' basic principles for meaning-centered writing instruction. Particularly helpful are the insights the authors share about helping children realize their potential as writers. Ms. Calkins has also written *The Art of Teaching Writing* and *Lessons from a Child*.

Lasting Impressions: Weaving Literature into the Writing Workshop[31] Better writing results when students are immersed in good literature, according to the author of this book of anecdotes and observations of New York City elementary schools. In the first part of the book, the author explores the relationship between literature and writing at several grade levels and shows how to help students value good literature. She also makes suggestions for reading aloud, sharing books, talking about literature and keeping a writer's notebook. Mini-lessons, conferencing, author studies and reading-response groups are discussed in the second part of the book, in the context of using literature to improve writing.

Which of the books described above draw your interest? Do they have common features? Which content do you know something about? Which seem to address concerns you have?

XIII.   Reflections

From a Teacher's Journal—Jackie Hogue, Fifth Grade

I've been experimenting with spelling. My students are making their own dictionaries, using a spiral notebook with one letter of the alphabet on each page. They enter words they don't know how to spell as they are writing. To find the correct spelling, they look up the word. If they can't find it, they can ask their partner for help or they can ask me. I've noticed several commonly misspelled words in their writings, such as: before, because, when and where. I put these words up on a chart as I notice them, so they can refer to them as needed for their writing.

I let the kids choose spelling words from their current area of study. They study four words a night and write sentences using these words. The next day, the people in their group check each other's sentences and help to revise and edit them. After a quiz on the words, the children pass their sentences and words to another group for grading. The work is in pretty good shape because it has already been checked by the child and the group. I also give them four words a week that are commonly misspelled. These words and the ones they've chosen are on the weekly test.

I keep an English chart on display and we write rules as we discover mistakes in sentences. The children also have an English notebook in which they record these rules. We use the English grammar textbook as a reference. I use their spelling sentences and sentences from other writing projects to teach grammar and parts of speech. Only the sentences with "good mistakes" are chosen. Sometimes a student will proclaim proudly, "That's my sentence!"

I tried the author's chair. The kids love it. They all want to share their journal writings. I walk around the room and talk to two or three of them about their books while others are writing. Sometimes two or three read to me from their journals during writing time. Sometimes I write while they write. I always read while they read. Since school began, I've read *Shiloh* and *Maniac Magee*. It's a good time for me to read children's literature.

I made a chart entitled "Writing Conferences," with questions students can ask each other, such as "How's it going?" "How does it sound when you read it out loud?" "What is the most important thing you are trying to say?" "How do you want the reader to feel?" "What do you want me to listen for?" For self-evaluation, the kids answer to: "What did you do that you really liked?" "What would you change?" "How can someone else help you?"

I'm working on portfolios and writing folders. I haven't figured out what works best for us, but it's getting better. The kids are keeping their pieces in the writing folder. I want them to keep working on the pieces, put the ones of their choice in the portfolio and tell why they chose it. That's the plan.

Sometimes it's really hard to integrate the language arts, because I'm bound by the state assessments developed by the district. For instance, I had to give a geography test and prepare the students for a test required for plants and environment. I just try to be as creative as I can within these parameters.

I went through the process of writing a paragraph, using information they already knew and they chose fossil fuels. I wrote whatever they told me to write. We talked about topic sentences and supporting details. Then we put the sentences in order and changed words or crossed out words that didn't fit in the paragraph. Next, the kids played COPS. One group checked the paragraph for capital letters (C), one for omissions, such as indentation (O), one for punctuation (P) and one for spelling (S). Finally, we rewrote the paragraph together. The kids used this model to write a paragraph in groups, telling something they learned about plants. It took a long time, longer than I thought it would.

We wrote our legends, a local district assessment for language arts. I read a legend to the class, and they read several themselves. We talked about the dynamics of a legend and recorded them on a chart. The kids did not want to write a legend, but after they got started they were fine. I've already recorded them for state purposes. The legends were put into their writing folders so the children can refine them even further. The most valuable assessments came from the kids themselves. They expressed what they liked and what improvements might be made. Each student took notes for further refinements.

I noticed that at the beginning of the year, much time, effort, instruction and peer support were involved in each individual writing assignment. Sometimes it took three or four days for a student to go through the writing process to produce a paper. Now, even though I don't see a big improvement in their finished products, I notice that it takes much less time and support for them to write. For example, at the beginning of the year, I observed that Edie had great ideas, but her language and spelling skills were lacking. She had a lot of peer help in class, and Mom supported her greatly at home. The last paper she wrote was a five-paragraph persuasive paper. Edie wrote, revised and edited the paper, without a partner. She rewrote the paper in one afternoon, and it was the best in the class!

I need to keep my journal from last year handy, so I can skim through it and add new ideas for future use. I noticed that some techniques I used last year, I forgot to use this year. In some cases, I haven't had time to use certain activities because my class is larger and it takes longer to accomplish the goals. Sometimes I forget the value of writing for myself!

WHAT DO YOU THINK? The teacher above mentions using the English grammar textbook as a reference. On what occasions might this text be helpful? Although she faces many challenges as she tries to integrate language learning into the curriculum, this teacher provides a helpful model for teachers in similar situations. What do you see in her practice that is hopeful and encouraging?

TRYING OUT THE CHAPTER IDEAS

1. What do you think about the use of developmental spelling? What are its advantages to young writers? What concerns might parents have with this approach to spelling? How might you address these concerns?
2. Examine the handwriting of other people in your class or members of your own family. What makes their writing easy to read? Do any

of the samples you observed look like the models from handwriting programs? How do you account for this?

3. As you complete a writing exercise, monitor your behavior. When you have written a few sentences, what do you do? If you reread what you have written, what effect does this have on the next thing you write?

4. **If you can:** Practice taking key words and creating captions with kindergarten children.

5. Sit in on a writer's workshop at the primary and intermediate levels. What kinds of interactions do you notice? What differences in interaction do you notice between the two levels?

Notes

1. Donald Graves, *Build a Literate Classroom* (Portsmouth, N.H.: Heinemann, 1991).

2. Lucy McCormick Calkins with Shelley Harwayne, *Living between the Lines* (Portsmouth, N.H.: Heinemann, 1991).

3. Marilyn A. Boutwell, "Reading and Writing Process: A Reciprocal Agreement," *Language Arts* 60 (September 1983): 723–730.

4. Lucy McCormick Calkins, *Lessons from a Child: On the Teaching and Learning of Writing* (Portsmouth, N.H.: Heinemann Educational Books, 1983).

5. Robert J. Tierney and P. David Pearson, "Toward a Composing Model of Reading," *Language Arts* 60 (May 1983): 568–580.

6. Kenneth Goodman, E. Brooks Smith, Robert Meredith, and Yetta M. Goodman, *Language and Thinking in School: A Whole Language Curriculum*, 3d ed. (New York: Richard C. Owen Publishers, 1986).

7. Sandra Stotsky, "Research on Reading/Writing Relationships: A Synthesis and Suggested Directions," *Language Arts* 60 (May 1983): 627–642.

8. A. A. McClure, "Children's Responses to Poetry in a Supportive Literacy Context," unpublished doctoral dissertation, Ohio State University, *Dissertation Abstracts International*, 46/09-A (UMI No. DA85-26218).

9. Nancie Atwell, *In the Middle: Writing, Reading, and Learning with Adolescents* (Portsmouth, N.H.: Heinemann, 1986).

10. Ellen Levin, *I Hate English!* (New York: Scholastic, 1989).

11. Yoshiko Uchida, *Journey Home* (New York: Macmillan, 1978).

12. Lawrence Yep, *Dragonwings* (New York: Harper & Row, 1975).

13. Lawrence Yep, *Dragon's Gate* (New York: Scholastic, 1993).

14. Fran Leeper Buss with Daisy Cubias, *Journey of the Sparrows* (New York: Dell, 1991).

15. Nicolasa Mohr, *Felita* (New York: Dial, 1987).

16. Muriel Stanek, *I Speak English for My Mom* (New York: Whitman, 1989).

17. Donald Graves, *Portfolio Portraits* (New York: Macmillan, 1994).

18. Sylvia Ashton-Warner, *Teacher* (New York: Simon and Schuster, 1963).

19. Jeanette Veatch, *Reading in the Elementary School*, 2d ed. (New York: Richard C. Owen Publishers, 1978), pp. 11–13.

20. Donald Graves, "Building Portfolios," presentation at TAWL, Southern Illinois University Conference, Belleville, Illinois, October 22, 1994.

21. Jackie Proett and Kent Gill, *The Writing Process in Action: A Handbook for Teachers* (Urbana, Ill.: NCTE, 1986).

22. Lisa Carpenter, ed., *Children's Writer's & Illustrator's Market* (Cincinnati, Ohio: Writer's Digest Books, 1993).

23. Gail E. Tompkins and David B. Yaden, Jr., *Answering Students' Questions About Words* (Urbana, Ill.: ERIC Clearinghouse on Reading and Communication Skills and the National Council of Teachers of English, 1986).

24. Eileen Tway, *Writing Is Reading: 26 Ways to Connect* (Urbana, Ill.: ERIC Clearinghouse on Reading and Communication Skills and the National Council of Teachers of English, 1985).

25. Stephen Dunning and William Stafford, *Getting the Knack: 20 Poetry Writing Exercises* (Urbana, Ill.: NCTE, 1992).

26. Jessie A. Roderick, ed., *Context-Responsive Approaches to Assessing Children's Language* (Urbana, Ill.: National Conference on Research on English, 1992).

27. Allan A. DeFina, *Portfolio Assessment: Getting Started* (New York: Scholastic Professional Books, 1992).

28. Gary R. Muschla, *Writing Workshop Survival Kit* (New York: The Center for Applied Research in Education, 1993).

29. Norma R. Jackson with Paula L. Pillow, *The Reading–Writing Workshop: Getting Started* (New York: Scholastic Professional Books, 1992).

30. Terry D. Johnson and Daphne R. Louis, *Literacy Through Literature* (Portsmouth, N.H.: Heinemann Educational Books, 1987).

31. Shelley Harwayne, *Lasting Impressions: Weaving Literature into the Writing Workshop* (Portsmouth, N.H.: Heinemann, 1992).

CHAPTER NINE

Mini-Lessons

Students complete research projects following a mini-lesson for a small group. The teacher provides immediate opportunities for students to practice and apply the new skill, which was taught in the context of a popular dinosaur study. How will you discover the skills your students need to learn?

The important thing is not so much that every child should be taught, as that every child should be given the wish to learn.

—John Lubbock

LOOKING AHEAD   1. What is a mini-lesson?
2. How do mini-lessons differ from traditional lessons?
3. What is the purpose of a mini-lesson?
4. What are the benefits of mini-lessons?
5. Where do teachers get ideas for mini-lessons?
6. What do mini-lessons look like in the classroom?
7. How do you plan for and present mini-lessons?

IN 25 WORDS   Mini-lessons involve the direct teaching of a concept, skill or strategy
OR LESS   in response to students' need to know.

I. Focus: The Mini-Lesson

Mini-lessons are brief presentations of less than five minutes that introduce a single concept or demonstrate a skill. The content of these lessons is determined by the learning needs of a particular group of students, which teachers discover as they observe their students during guided reading, writer's workshop, content area study and individual conferences. For example, several students or the entire class may not understand how to use an index or the table of contents. Others may need help with paragraphing, reading aloud with expression or organizing a research report. Mini-lessons are presented to one or several students or the entire class, depending on how many persons require the instruction.

In contrast, lesson topics in traditional classrooms are presented in an established sequence, often determined by the order of their presentation in a text. When teachers present these lessons, they frequently discuss multiple concepts, and the lesson may last from ten to twenty minutes. Instruction in traditional classrooms is presented to the entire class or to small ability groups, but each grouping receives essentially the same instruction.

To understand the difference between a mini-lesson and a traditional lesson, it might be helpful to observe how a topic would be presented using each of these lesson forms. You will notice in the following descriptions that each lesson involves a presentation by the teacher that is intended to help students develop a skill. Each involves the students in the lesson and both forms include student practice exercises. The differences between the two are in the origin of content, the types of practice exercises and the uses of this practice for future learning.

In the traditional classroom, a teacher begins a lesson on synonyms and antonyms by asking all students in the class to read two pages in their English textbooks. When students have finished reading, she asks them to define synonyms and antonyms and to identify the difference between them. She writes a list of words on the board and asks students to volunteer examples of synonyms and antonyms for each one. Students are asked to rewrite ten sentences from the book and substitute synonyms for the underlined words in each sentence. They are also asked to identify pairs of words as either synonyms or antonyms. The teacher's presentation lasts fifteen minutes, and students are given an additional twenty minutes to complete the practice exercise. They hand in their papers, which the teacher grades and returns to them the next day. They review the correct answers in class, and students take their papers home or throw them away.

In the classroom that integrates language learning, the teacher notices that students frequently overuse certain words in their compositions and believes that their writing skills could improve if they were more aware of synonyms. She asks each student to bring a book they are reading and some writing they want to improve with more interesting words. She begins the mini-lesson by asking students to analyze their writing to find words they use frequently and to think of one or two other words they could use instead. Students take turns sharing the words they substituted, and the teacher records them on a chart. She tells the class that the words they have generated are synonyms, or words that mean the same, and she writes this word at the top of the chart. In their writing notebooks, students write "Synonyms" at the top of a page, followed by the definition. They search their favorite books for synonyms that could be used in their own writing and record these in their notebooks. During the independent writing period that follows, students analyze their writing for repeated use of the same words and substitute synonyms. On the following day, the teacher will introduce the use of the thesaurus, which will provide students with an additional resource for their writing. Throughout the year, students will continue to record examples of synonyms in their notebooks and will refer to this page and the thesaurus for ideas when they want to make their writing more interesting.

Table 9.1 compares traditional lessons and mini-lessons.

TABLE 9.1
Comparison of Traditional Lessons and Mini-Lessons

Traditional Lesson	Mini-Lesson
Several concepts or skills presented	Single concept or skill presented
Presentations are sequenced	Presentations are responsive to need
Presentation lasts 10–20 minutes	Lessons last less than 5 minutes
Everyone receives the same instruction	Instruction meets individual needs
Practice is predetermined	Practice uses student experience
Practice exercises are discarded	Exercises become learning resources

WHAT DO YOU
THINK? Were you grouped for reading instruction in elementary school? If so, what do you remember about this experience? Did you enjoy reading aloud? Do you remember working in a workbook? If you were assigned to an ability group, did you agree with your placement? Can you think of other uses for mini-lessons in the classroom?

II. The Importance of Mini-Lessons

Lev Vygotsky believes that students learn most successfully in what he terms the **zone of proximal development**.[1] This term refers to a range of tasks that students can accomplish with the help of a more skilled person. Mini-lessons are designed to work within this developmental zone of individuals, with demonstrations and explanations that build on students' current levels of understanding. Both teachers and classmates can help individuals develop their skills by sharing ideas, strategies and techniques for learning. The mini-lesson format also encourages language development. As students work together with teachers or peers to find examples and practice applying skills, they talk about what they are doing. This dialogue helps them organize their efforts and internalize the language they are learning as they complete a task.[2]

Vygotsky sees language as the medium of social experience and as the chief tool for thought. He believes that thinking is an activity that is created through dialogue in social interactions, developing best in classroom environments that provide opportunities for problem solving and discussion. When teachers use mini-lessons effectively, there are frequent opportunities for students to talk and solve problems as they work together to explore new ideas and practice new skills.

Jerome Bruner[3] refers to activities like the mini-lesson as **scaffolding**, in which teachers provide students with temporary support for their learning and language use. The goal of scaffolding is the student's ability to use skills and strategies independently, so the support is gradually withdrawn as students increase their proficiency. When teachers present mini-lessons, they begin with students' current levels of understanding or skill and use the support of student experience and familiar materials to introduce new skills or concepts. Practice activities are related to an immediate task, but as students gain proficiency, teachers provide opportunities for them to apply these skills in new situations, as they gradually withdraw the more familiar supports.

Bruner also believes that children have a natural will to learn, as evidenced by their behavior in situations outside of school. In the most ordinary of circumstances, children are characterized by their curiosity, their desire to work together to solve problems of mutual interest and their striving for competence. Mini-lessons capitalize on these naturally occurring characteristics by creating classroom situations in which children can satisfy their curiosity and help each other gain competence with a task.

WHAT DO YOU
THINK? Can you think of an experience where someone gave you the kind of assistance with a difficult learning task that enabled you to complete the task on your own? How do you feel when you can achieve a task independently?

III. Looking into Classrooms

A brief, single-topic presentation, student-generated examples and immediate practice are characteristic of mini-lessons at all levels of instruction. The frequency of mini-lessons, types of groupings, presentation format and practice applications will vary from classroom to classroom. In each case, however, the experience and skills of the individual students in a class will determine the variations that occur. You have already observed how teachers conduct mini-lessons during reading and writing conferences. The following observations demonstrate the use of mini-lessons with small groups of students and with the entire class.

Kindergarten Level

During playtime, Mrs. Jamison meets with three children who are confusing the sounds for *d* and *b*.

"Did everyone bring a book with words?" she asks. Each boy holds up a picture book and shows her the words inside.

"Good," she says. "We're going to be detectives today."

The three boys lean forward on their chairs.

"And the first thing we need to do is find some letters. Who thinks he can find a *d* in a story?" she asks, and they dive into their books.

"Here's one," Matthew says, pointing to a *d* in dinosaur.

"Here's one, here's one," Joshua says, as he finds a *d* in dash.

"I got one," Brady adds, locating a *d* in drink.

"Good, good," Mrs. Jamison says. She says each of the words they have indicated. "Matthew, how does your mouth go when you start to say 'dinosaur'?"

Matthew opens his mouth.

"Say 'dinosaur,' " the teacher asks, and he complies.

"Where is your tongue when you start to say that word?" she asks.

He points behind his teeth.

"Good," she says. "When you are ready to make the *d* sound, your tongue is right here against the roof of your mouth, right above your front teeth. What about Joshua's word, 'dash'? Where is your tongue when you start to say that word?"

They all experiment, suddenly conscious of their mouths and the sounds. "Where you said. Right up here," Joshua says, with his finger inside his mouth, against his front teeth.

"And how about your word, Brady?" the teacher asks.

He has already experimented. "It's there," he says, pointing in his mouth.

"Okay, you've found where *d* starts. Where did you tell me again?" she asks.

They all point and show her.

"All right, you're about halfway through the case," she says. The boys grin and look at each other. "Someone else has been using *d*'s sound and he wants it back. It's his sound and no one else's. Who do you suppose might want to use *d*'s sound?"

The boys shrug their shoulders.

"Let's find out," the teacher says. She turns around to a Big Book resting on the easel behind her and begins to read the familiar *Chicka Chicka Boom Boom*,[4] a story they have practiced in guided reading.

"Chicka Chicka **Doom Doom**," she reads.

The boys look at each other, and Mrs. Jamison continues to read, substituting the sound of *d* each time she reads a word that begins with *b*.

"Mrs. Jamison," Joshua interrupts, "you're reading it silly!"

"Oh!" she says. "What's wrong?"

"You're saying the words wrong," Matthew exclaims. "It's 'boom boom,' not 'doom doom'!"

"Oh!" the teacher exclaims. "So are you telling me that this *b* is saying *d*'s sound? I must have put my mouth in the wrong place."

The boys look at each other.

"What does your mouth do when you start to say 'boom boom'?" she asks.

They put their lips together.

"Where's your tongue?" the teacher asks.

They think for a minute.

"Just in there loose," Matthew says.

"Not on the roof of your mouth, behind your teeth?"

They shake their heads.

"Feel the shape of your lips," she directs and demonstrates by tracing her lips from under her nose to her chin. "It makes the *b* shape," she says and shows them again. They imitate her. "You make *b* lips to say the *b* sound," she adds.

"Let's see how good a detective you are," and she opens the Big Book to the beginning. "I'm going to start reading this story. But I'll leave out some words and you use your detective skills to show me how your mouth should be to say the word."

She begins to read "I'll beat you to the top of the coconut tree" and stops at the word "beat."

The boys watch each other and purse their lips.

"Excellent!" the teacher says. "Keep watching," and she continues reading until she reaches the words "boom boom!" Again they purse their lips. She continues reading. "Skit skat skoodle doot."

"Mrs. Jamison, a *d* word!" Brady exclaims, trying to show her his tongue on the roof of his mouth.

"Good for you, Brady. Let's see everyone ready to say 'doot.'"

She continues reading and stops at the words "dears" and "dust," then "breath" and "down," each time observing how they place their mouths to form the first sound of the words.

"How many *d* words are in your head?" she asks.

Matthew lists dinosaur, dungeon, Dad, Davey, do and dumb. Joshua thinks up dum-dum, dodo, dude, dummy, dust, duck and dare. Brady thinks longer, rolling up his eyes with the effort. "Dastardly," he says finally. "Dastardly Dan, the villainous man," he quotes from a TV program.

"What great words!" the teacher exclaims. "What about some *b* words now?"

They list four or five words each.

"How will you remember about *b* and *d* words?" Mrs. Jamison asks them.

"I'll do this," Matthew says, tracing his mouth, "and this." He grimaces and shows his tongue.

"I'll copy some words out of my book and practice," Joshua answers.

"I know 'em," Brady replies. "I know 'em, I know I know 'em," he adds with confidence.

"Good for you," the teacher says. "Maybe you'll show me an example when you come for your conference tomorrow."

WHAT HAPPENED HERE? ONE PERSPECTIVE

Mrs. Jamison uses the boys' experience with favorite books and a story from guided reading to explore the differences in the two sounds. They can already recognize letters; she is trying to help them associate the letters with the correct sound (sound–symbol association). By drawing attention to the position of their lips, tongue and teeth as they pronounce the two sounds, she provides them with a temporary tool to associate sound and symbol.

The teacher begins this practice with words they identify from their own reading. She also refers to words found in a book used in a shared reading experience and those that are generated from the boys' own experience. When she substitutes "doom doom" for "boom boom" in one of their favorite stories, the boys immediately see the importance of associating the correct sound with its symbol.

The boys generate, identify, describe and analyze letter sounds and think of ways to practice them before they leave the mini-lesson. Mrs. Jamison will check this skill when the boys request their key words, when they volunteer in guided reading and while they are doing independent reading or writing.

Primary Level

Mrs. Scott asks the table helpers to distribute the Skills Notebooks from the baskets in the writing center. This year she budgeted the cost of the notebooks from the workbook fund, because they replaced workbooks in her second-grade classroom.

"Does everyone have two books to use for the mini-lesson?" Mrs. Scott inquires. Student nod their heads and hold up their books. Most have picture books, but a few students have chapter books. "Here are some secret words from our read-aloud story, *Rabbit Hill*,[5]" she says and writes two sentences on the board, underlining several words.

Why—why <u>it's</u> Uncle Analdas.

Last autumn even they had gone, leaving the empty house with <u>its</u> desolate black windows and <u>its</u> shutters flapping through the winter storms.

"Let's read these sentences together," she says. When they finish, she asks them what they notice about the three underlined words.

"They're the same," Jacob says.

Angela raises her hand. "The first one has an apostrophe."

"They sound the same," Jacob says.

"They do sound the same," Mrs. Scott responds. "And Angela used the correct term for the marking on the first one. Is there anything else different about them?"

The children study the words. Daren raises his hand. "The second one tells the windows and shutters belong."

"That's correct. The windows and shutters belong to the house. How about this one?" she asks, pointing to "it's."

"It means 'it is,' " Keesha volunteers.

"You're exactly right," the teacher says. "It's a contraction, and the apostrophe shows that a letter is left out." She adds apostrophes to the "its" in the second sentence. "If you were to write this in a story, what might your readers think?"

The children giggle.

"Who wants to read it aloud?" the teacher asks.

Megan volunteers. "Last autumn even they had gone, leaving the empty house with <u>its</u> desolate black windows and <u>its</u> shutters flapping through the winter storms."

"That **sounds** all right," the teacher says. "Who can read what it means?"

"Last autumn even they had gone, leaving the empty house with <u>it is</u> desolate black windows and <u>it is</u> shutters flapping through the winter storms," Jacob reads. The class giggles again. "It doesn't make sense," he comments.

"That's a good observation," the teacher agrees. "That little apostrophe doesn't look like much, but it makes a completely different word. Now that you know the secret about these words, who thinks they can find some examples in their books?"

There is a flurry of paging through books to find the secret words. Students know from past experience with secret words that they must write down the words "its" and "it's" and one or two words immediately following each one. Those who find their examples immediately look for more. Mark is looking at the book *Dinosaurs*[6] by Gail Gibbons and finds "its tail" and "its back." He cannot find an example of "it's," so he moves to his second book, *Dinosaur for a Day*[7] by Jim Murphy. He finds "Still, the Hypsilophondon raises its head slowly to peer over the bushes." Later in the book he finds "Its children follow" and "Its children try to keep up." There are no "it's" in the book, and he notices that the author uses "it is" throughout the book, instead of the contraction. I wonder why? he says to himself.

There is still time to look for more examples, so Mark opens *Ginger Pye*[8] by Eleanor Estes, a book he is currently reading. He begins reading and notices that, just like in the other books, there are more "its" than "it's" in the story. Then he notices that "it's" is at the beginning of sentences more often than "its" and wonders why. After he finds five examples of both, he tallies the locations of the words in the sentence under two headings: Beginning of the Sentence and Inside the Sentence. When everyone is ready to continue the mini-lesson, Mark has tallied two chapters and discovers that "it's" is at the beginning of sentences almost ten times more often than "its."

"What did you find for the first word?" Mrs. Scott asks, nodding to a group of students in the back of the room. One by one, they respond: its bill, its helmet, its feet, its roots. "Great!" she says as she records their responses on the board under "its."

"Look at all your examples," she says. "The bill, the helmet, the feet and the roots all belong to something or someone. Does anyone remember what we call words that show belonging?"

"Possessives," several children respond.

"Good," Mrs. Scott comments. "Let's play the possessive game for a minute. Whose book is that?" she asks, pointing to Zachary's book.

"Zach's," his tablemates respond.

"Use a pronoun," she asks. "Now whose book is it?"

"His!" they reply.

"This is the book's cover," she says, pointing to the front of the book. "What are these?"

"Pages," they respond.

"Whose pages?" she asks.

"The book's pages."

"If this is its cover, then these are . . ." she ripples the pages.

"Its pages," they say.

"Then this 'its' is . . . ?"

"A possessive pronoun," they respond.

"Great!" the teacher says. "Now show me some 'its' in this classroom."

"Its legs," someone says, pointing to the desk. Others contribute its stand, its chalk, its shelves, its eraser.

The teacher asks another table of students for their list of examples for "it's" and records their findings on the board: It's dark outside, It's the same thing, It's a duck, It's going to be fun.

"Make a page for these two words," Mrs. Scott says, and students write "its" and "it's" at the top of a page in their Skills Notebooks. She writes the two words on the board and next to the words writes "belongs to" and "it is." The children copy the words and the definitions.

"You did a good job unlocking the secret words today," she says. "Now they're not a mystery to you anymore and it's time to write examples."

Students begin to enter the examples from their papers or the board into their Skills Notebooks. Mark raises his hand and the teacher moves over to his table. He shows her his discovery and she is delighted.

"Why do you think this is true?" she asks.

"I don't know. I didn't think about it yet."

"How will you start thinking about it?" she asks.

He looks at the words for a minute. "Well, maybe I could look at the sentences . . . maybe there are more times we use one because it's a certain kind of word."

"You've made a good start on your thinking," the teacher observes. "Keep gathering your evidence and see what you notice."

"I could call up Dr. Blake at the college," he suggests. "He said I could call him if I had some questions." Dr. Blake is a parent volunteer who works with gifted students at the school.

"Another good idea," the teacher replies. "I know he'll be interested in your discovery, and so might Mr. Wright. Why don't you see if he's in his office?" Mark leaves with his data to share with the principal, who is also the fifth-grade English teacher. When Mark has completed his inquiry, Mrs. Scott encourages him to make a graph to explain what he has found to the class.

WHAT HAPPENED HERE? ONE PERSPECTIVE

This lesson was derived from writing conferences where Mrs. Scott noticed repeated instances of misuse of the contraction "it's" and possessive "its" in student writing. She sets up the lesson as a mystery to be solved, drawing the initial examples from a favorite read-aloud book and continuing with examples generated by her students from books they are reading.

As students examine the differences between the two words and search for examples, they are developing a clear idea of the correct use of each one. This activity will make them more alert to the correct use of these words in their writing. If they forget which is which, they can refer to the definitions and examples in their Skills Notebooks.

Students like Mark are able to locate and record examples for the mini-lesson very quickly. Most students use picture storybooks for this exercise because examples can be found easily by readers of all proficiency levels. But Mrs. Scott encourages students who complete their searches to continue looking in chapter books, where they often discover patterns or more complex examples. This is what happens in Mark's case. He is challenged by the assignment and is not forced to wait for everyone to finish, as a penalty for the rapid way he processes information. Mark has the time and opportunity to notice the relative frequencies of the two words and begins to analyze the reasons for this. He saves his discovery to show the teacher, and she helps him think of a way to share his information with the rest of the class. She also encourages him to share his ideas with the principal and the parent volunteer, who will respond with enthusiasm to his discovery. This kind of support validates Mark's highly developed analytical thinking and helps him communicate his ideas more effectively to his classmates.

Intermediate Level

"Many of you have the same question when you come to your writing conferences," Mr. Yamaguchi begins. " 'How can I make the beginning of my story more interesting?' That's what we're going to talk about today. Did everyone bring a copy of the book you're using for literature study?"

The sixth-grade students, sitting in their literature groups, pull out copies of the book their group has chosen to explore Native American culture. Four different books are represented in the six groups of students: *Sing Down the Moon*,[9] *Ishi, Last of his Tribe*,[10] *Bearstone*[11] and *Sweetgrass*.[12]

"It's always helpful to look at the ways good writers begin their books," the teacher says. "Everyone read the first page or two of your book. For many of you, this might have been the way you decided which book you wanted to read for literature study. Try to identify what it is about these first pages that got you interested."

Students begin to read. Some jot down a few notes. After a few minutes, Mr. Yamaguchi says, "Well, what do you think? Why did you choose your book?"

Janyce raises her hand. "I chose the book about Ishi because I found out it was a true story, and then when I read the first page it was so full of details about Indian life, I felt like I was almost there."

Mr. Yamaguchi writes the word "details" on the board. "Good," he says. "Anyone else?"

Willis says that he chose *Bearstone* because it is a contemporary story and he wanted to know more about how Native Americans live today. "And I liked the way it started out," he says. "The main character, Cloyd, he's in this hospital and all, trying to find his father. And the way he gets in is really cool, 'cause he says he's delivering some flowers, 'cause maybe they won't let him in otherwise."

"Something is happening right away?" the teacher asks.

"Yeah," Willis replies. "I like that."

The teacher writes "action" on the board.

Tracy says, "In the beginning of my book [*Sing Down the Moon*], Bright Morning is really happy, but she reminds herself not to show it, because when her brother was happy once he got struck by lightening and was killed. After that I sort of knew that something bad was going to happen to her."

"What's the word for that?" Mr. Yamaguchi asks.

He waits, while Tracy refers to her Word Book. "Foreshadowing?" she asks.

The teacher writes the word on the board.

"How about this group?" The teacher indicates four girls who read the book *Sweetwater*. They look at each other and giggle.

"Well?" the teacher asks.

"It's a little embarrassing," Sonja says. "Oh, well," she hesitates, "we might as well be honest." She takes a deep breath. "It looked romantic."

The class laughs and Mr. Yamaguchi smiles. "Nothing wrong with that," he says. "Did it turn out to be romantic?"

The girls look at each other. "Sort of," Kayla answers for the group. "After the first part it tells how she lived and about a smallpox epidemic. She was really brave. It was a good story."

"But the author got you interested in reading the story by emphasizing something else at the beginning?"

The girls nod their heads, and the teacher writes the word "audience" on the board.

"What purpose do you think the author had in writing your book?" the teacher asks.

The girls look at each other. Ariel says, "She wanted to tell the story of Sweetgrass, because it's a really good story."

The teacher nods for her to continue.

"So . . . maybe she started out the way she did, so we'd keep reading."

"Do you think she had a sense of her audience?" the teacher asks.

"Yeah," Kayla replies. "She really did. We couldn't stop reading it."

"You've identified a number of ways that authors try to draw you into their stories," Mr. Yamaguchi says, reading the list from the board. "Details, action, foreshadowing and a sense of audience. Now think for a minute about your most current writing project. You're writing historical fiction, where each of these things is an important element of the story. What kinds of details do you want to read about in books?"

"Where they lived, how they dressed, what they ate," Samantha says.

"And what they look like," Kayla adds.

"I like to know about what their houses were like and how they cooked and got their food," Janyce says.

"I like it when they tell about hunting or battles," Blake offers. "All the details about what happens. I like that."

"Gory stuff, you mean," Tyler says.

"That too," Blake replies. "But mostly just details, so you know what it's like to be there."

"I like it when they tell something about the main character so you want to know more about them," Cordell adds.

"Yeah, like Maniac Magee," Brian says.

"While you're full of these ideas, jot down a few details you could use to begin your own stories," the teacher suggests, and he waits while students make entries in their writing journals.

"I'll give you about ten more minutes to think about ways you could introduce some of the other literary devices you've identified into the introduction of your stories," the teacher says. "Then go on with your independent writing for the rest of the hour. I'll see Tyler, Kayla and Zach for conferences during that time."

WHAT HAPPENED HERE? ONE PERSPECTIVE

Mr. Yamaguchi gets his students involved in solving a writing problem by encouraging them to use the work of other authors as a model. They examine books they are currently reading to identify the methods writers use to draw readers into their stories. In the course of the discussion, the teacher helps them identify several literary devices frequently used by writers to develop reader interest. He then moves directly to their own writing and asks them to think how they might respond as writers in light of what they like as readers. He also provides sufficient time for them to apply what they have learned by scheduling independent writing time immediately after the mini-lesson.

Mr. Yamaguchi treats the comments of his students with dignity and models a thoughtful response to the girls who chose a book for its romantic qualities. This sets the tone for a focused discussion that demonstrates the value of a sense of audience.

WHAT DO YOU THINK?

You probably noticed that each of the teachers portrayed above drew from his or her own personality and teaching style to present the mini-lessons described here. Which teacher's style seems most compatible to your own? When you observe other teachers in the classroom, do you ever think: "I could do that," or "I don't think I'd be comfortable doing that"?

IV. Preparing for Mini-Lessons

You can begin to prepare to use mini-lessons in your classroom immediately by reviewing the content of what you may be expected to teach, observing a class to practice assessing learning needs, and thinking about the kinds of information and skills that can be presented in this format. When you have your own classroom, you can prepare more specifically, but the process will already be familiar to you.

Content

One of the best ways to prepare to use mini-lessons is to examine the curriculum objectives for the grade level you are preparing to teach. What language concepts, strategies or skills will students be expected to learn at this level? What literature will they read and what literary devices will they examine? Exploring these requirements will give you practice in examining similar objectives at any level of instruction. You might also review standard English grammar textbooks to reexamine your own understanding of key ideas and constructions. For example, can you easily identify parts of speech or instances of figurative language? Your own understanding of these concepts is key to your ability to help your students understand them.

You might also want to review the professional books described in the Resources for Teaching section of this chapter and seek out others in your school library or local teacher's store. Teaching journals and magazines contain many good ideas for introducing and practicing language skills, and you might want to keep a file on these. You will also want to collect and record good ideas from your methods classes, teacher workshops and classroom observations.

Personal Preparation

When you have decided on a specific topic for presentation, you will want to consider your own preparation for presenting a mini-lesson. What do you already know about this skill or concept? What do you need to research or review? The following steps can be used as a guide to help develop your lesson:

1. Consult resources relevant to what you will be teaching, such as curriculum guides, grammar books, English textbooks and content area texts or trade books.
2. Create an outline for the mini-lesson. Limit the presentation to a single idea or skill.

3. Look for examples of the mini-lesson topic that will be familiar to your students. Note these on your outline.
4. Anticipate questions your students might ask.
5. Practice presenting the mini-lesson, either to someone else or on tape for self-review.
6. Check the time. If your presentation exceeds five minutes, you might want to consider dividing your material into two or more sessions.

When you have decided on a topic and prepared the ideas for the mini-lesson, you will want to consider some or all of the following questions:

1. What do I want students to know or be able to do as a result of this lesson?
2. How will they demonstrate this skill, strategy or knowing? When and how will it be evaluated?
3. What will I need to write on the board? (before, during or after the lesson)
4. What will students need to bring with them?
5. How will I begin?
6. How will I involve their experience?
7. How will I involve literature they are reading?
8. How will this skill, strategy or knowledge be practiced or used?

You might want to begin assembling a file of ideas for good writing. Collect real-life models for students to use as guides for their writing, such as examples of letters, playscripts, informational articles, brochures, pamphlets and newsletters. Look for interviews with favorite children's authors and save their comments on writing. School book clubs frequently include these kinds of articles in the teacher's packet, so you may be able to get copies from cooperating teachers in the schools where you observe or student teach. You will also encounter good ideas about mini-lessons from reading in teacher's journals or magazines. Record any that sound interesting and include them in your file of ideas.

Analyzing Learning Needs

Individual reading or writing conferences When you observe that students demonstrate a lack of knowledge or skill that would help them understand or communicate more effectively, you can: teach it immediately, if time permits; make a note to teach it later; or record the problem on a checklist and look for other students who may need similar instruction.

Guided reading or FAST presentations When you observe students experiencing difficulties with language, make notes or record the event on your skills checklist. Often, your awareness of a problem will begin with the difficulties of a single student, but it will also focus your observations on similar problems experienced by others.

Writer's workshop This is an excellent time to observe and record what students perceive as their difficulties with expression and communication. Note these problems and record them on a checklist to see if they warrant presentation to the entire class or if they can be addressed during individual conferences.

Daily classroom observations   As you watch students write and listen to them read and talk to each other, monitor their performance: What do they need to know or what skills do they need to develop to become more successful and independent learners? It is helpful to keep a small notebook to enter topics for mini-lessons, recording any skills or strategies needed and any ideas you might have about how to present them.

From your notes and checklists, review the possibilities for mini-lessons. List the topics and the numbers of students involved. Decide when to address individual problems and when a small task group should meet. What skill, strategy or information would assist language development for the entire class? When would be the most effective time to introduce and practice a particular skill or concept? It is important to schedule mini-lessons immediately before an opportunity to practice them.

Types of Mini-Lessons

In addition to learning a concept or skill needed to improve their reading and writing, students benefit from other kinds of instruction that can be presented effectively in the mini-lesson format:

Informational mini-lessons can introduce and provide practice for room routines, individual conferences, guided reading, independent reading, FAST and the use of centers. They can demonstrate art projects and illustrate elements of music, art, dance and other physical performances. Mini-lessons can show students how to use notebooks, construct a portfolio, write in a particular genre and demonstrate effective group interaction.

Prewriting and postwriting exercises help students develop ideas and explore possibilities for writing. Word banks, Venn diagrams, and reading or writing logs can be introduced with mini-lessons. They are also a good format for demonstrating brainstorming, clustering, webbing and timed writing. Postwriting activities, such as revising, editing, proofreading and publishing, can be presented effectively in a mini-lesson format, as can peer-editing, which helps students identify writing problems from the viewpoint of an audience. The elements of proofreading can be addressed in mini-lessons, with students working in small groups to assess final drafts for spelling, punctuation and grammatical problems. Mini-lessons to share the final products of writing might demonstrate ways to participate in the FAST presentations or describe the elements of publishing, such as bookbinding and illustration techniques.

If you plan to introduce methods of **classroom book publishing** to your students, you will want to have a variety of materials on hand. It is helpful to have a writing or publishing center, where students can secure materials and bind their own projects. After each element of the center is demonstrated in a mini-lesson, you might want to display posters with directions for creating books and other materials. It is also helpful to display examples of published material—greeting cards, magazines, newspapers, books, calendars and posters—to provide ideas.

Materials and equipment for constructing and binding books, such as colored construction paper, lined and unlined paper, crayons, markers, pens, pencils, and scissors, will be needed. For book covers, include lightweight cardboard, laminated construction paper, cloth and wallpaper samples. You will also need a large stapler and staples, binding that can be machine or hand-stitched, a punch or hammer and nails to create binding holes, tape for binding edges of covers, rubber cement glue, rulers, rings, yarn and brass brads. Some schools have a binding machine and plastic binders available for teacher use. Research reports can be bound in ready-made binders obtained from office supply stores.

Mini-lessons that should precede publishing include introduction to or review of the parts of a book, including cover, title page, author page, dedication, body (the text and pictures), and check-out pockets (if you plan to circulate student books). You can explore other features of publishing by encouraging students to examine favorite books as models for: placing illustrations and borders; determining size and style of type; creating headlines, subheads, captions and initial letters. You will also want to help students examine the wide range of graphic materials that can be used, including original drawings, traced and clip art, photocopied photos, original photos, charts, graphs, maps and computer art. You might want to examine issues of *Book Links* (reviewed in Exploring Professional Literature, Chapter 8), which contain articles about elements of publishing that are of interest to students.

Mini-lessons can include instructions on making any kind of book, from a simple folded book to more complex chapter books bound for permanent use in the classroom or school library. Resource books listed at the end of the chapter have ideas for many different kinds of books, such as ABC, dictionaries, riddle books, autobiographies, almanacs, cookbooks, atlases, books of advice and pop-up toy books. Enlist your students' sense of audience as they prepare class project books, helping them consider whom the books might be shared with. Possible audiences could be the classroom, the principal, other teachers and students, parents, siblings and other family members, local librarians, senior-citizen centers, day-care centers, doctors' and dentists' offices.

WHAT DO YOU THINK?   Are you aware of the structural elements of literature? What will you need to know yourself before you can help students develop language skills and strategies? Have you explored the typical content of language learning at the grade level you plan to teach?

V. Including Everyone

Mini-lessons provide an excellent format for meeting the special needs of many students. Because learning groups are task oriented, students focus on developing the particular skills they need to read what they want to read and write what they want to share and communicate. Group membership is based on an individual's need to know, not on generalized ability or a labeled deficiency.

What kinds of difficulties can you expect your students to have with reading and writing? Beginning readers and writers may reverse letters (confuse *b*, *d* or *g*), lack a system of sound–symbol associations (be unable to match sounds with letters) or have inaccurate sound–symbol associations (mispronounce words). Students at all levels may have difficulty with letter formation, handwriting, spelling, standard grammar use and comprehension problems. Many problems are developmental and will correct themselves with time and experience in classrooms where there are opportunities to participate in a wide range of language activities. But as you observe your students, you will begin to notice that some will experience more difficulty developing skills than others. How can you assist the learning of these students with mini-lessons?

In addition to regular observations to determine the need for certain kinds of mini-lessons, you may want to learn how to use the Reading Miscue Inventory, a survey that helps teachers identify reading strengths and difficulties in their students. Kenneth Goodman[13] describes **miscues** as "deviations from expected responses to the print in oral reading." Miscues involve inaccurate identification of words or the insertion of words or meanings not contained in the text.

Research in reading indicates that readers notice only enough of individual words to confirm their expectations in reading. These miscues reflect their attempt to make sense of what they are reading, in terms of their own understanding and experience. Readers typically predict what is coming next from what they already know. They make inferences and merge them with what is already known, until what is gained from the text is a combination of what the reader brings to the text and the intention of the writer. Miscue analysis helps teachers identify the successful and unsuccessful strategies children are using to understand printed text.

It takes time and practice to develop skill in using the Reading Miscue Inventory,[14] but most teachers believe it is worth the effort. As you gain experience analyzing the oral reading of your students, you will develop increased skill in spotting the strengths and problems of individual readers. Using the inventory has the additional benefit of monitoring your own behavior as you listen to children read and attempt to guide this process. You become increasingly aware of the value of not interrupting students as they read, so that you can identify the particular strategies students are using to bring meaning to print.

Students can also learn to identify their own miscues through mini-lessons, and this monitoring can be practiced in small groups. This kind of self-analysis redirects attention from letter-by-letter and word-by-word reading and helps students learn to appreciate their own efforts to make sense of what they read. Children who experience difficulties with reading often have misconceptions about the abilities of skilled readers. They may also regard their own strategies as ineffective or as a form of cheating. Mini-lessons and group sharing of strategies can help these students revalue themselves as readers.

Miscue analysis should be used with materials that an individual child finds interesting or appealing. You will want to see how a child interacts with print that contains a story or information he or she really wants to know. Informal miscue analysis can be used in any situation where a student is reading aloud, either individually to you or in a small group. Students are never interrupted in their reading, but are asked to describe what they have read when they are finished. When there are omissions or additions to the text, students are asked to reflect on these and to talk about their strategies for figuring out the meaning of what was read. As students discuss their strategies, you will want to make brief notes. For a more permanent record, plan to tape record the reading to produce a typescript for marking and analysis.

The information gained from miscue analysis provides additional ideas for mini-lessons. In the beginning you may want to use this inventory with children who are experiencing the most difficulty with reading. But as you gain skill with the instrument, you will find yourself picking up ideas for mini-lessons from informal observations of reading-aloud behavior in other students.

Books to Create Understanding

Each of the following books features a main character who is a writer.

Dear Mr. Henshaw[15] This Newbery Award winner features a young boy who writes to his favorite author, trying to resolve his feelings about his parents' divorce. Although the author writes back only once, the boy's own writing brings him insight into his problems and a sense of control over them.

Harriet the Spy[16] Precocious eleven-year-old Harriet pretends to be a spy and records her observations of people all around her Manhattan neighborhood. Many of her notes are uncomplimentary, and when her friends find the notebook, she is forced to look at life in a different way.

Where the Lilies Bloom[17] Readers rarely forget Mary Call Luther, the heroine of this story about an Appalachian family. When her father dies, Mary Call and her family hide the fact of his death and work to support themselves by gathering and selling herbs. A caring teacher notices the quality and sensitivity of her writing and hopes to save her from the usual fate of most young mountain girls. The responsibility of trying to save the family farm, protecting her older sister from an unsuitable suitor, and feeding and clothing her younger siblings is finally too much for her. The resolution is surprising and provides insight into the gifted mind of a young girl.

WHAT DO YOU THINK?   Which of the books above most draws your interest? Do any of them touch on your own experience or of students you plan to teach?

VI. Step-by-Step: Presenting a Mini-Lesson

In your preparation for the mini-lesson, you have chosen a concept, skill or strategy to introduce or review with your students. The following steps are a suggested format for the presentation of a lesson:

1. **Preparation** Before you begin a mini-lesson, make a quick check to see that everyone has all the required materials: pencils, paper, books, notebooks or examples of writing. If you are working with a small task group, review the possibilities for independent work with the rest of the class, such as centers or individual reading and writing projects.

2. **Groups** Ask students to form the appropriate groups. If you will be meeting with a small task group, try to find a quiet corner of the room and make certain everyone else has plans for an independent work period. If the mini-lesson will involve the participation of the entire class, you may want to allow students to sit in small study groups, depending on the application of the skill or concept that will follow. Writing workshops may involve small groups or the entire class sitting in a large circle.

3. **Purpose** Whether you are teaching one student, a small group or the entire class, introduce the topic and explain why this particular topic or skill was selected for a mini-lesson. Will it give students new ideas for creating characters in their stories, help them figure out words when they are reading independently or show them how to use the new computer center? The following are some possible introductions:

> Many of you want to write historical fiction. Today we're going to study the elements of historical fiction by examining one of your favorite books.

> Most of the class is still having difficulty with paragraphing. If you're interested in a review, please bring something you're working on and join us at the front of the room.

> I've brought the three of you together for a mini-lesson because you all wanted to learn how to use the thesaurus.

> Today we're going to create some guidelines for our trip to the zoo.

> Most of you are ready to assemble your ABC books. Mrs. Skingley will show you how to use the punch and the binder.

4. **Presentation** Make a brief presentation—no longer than five minutes—that defines or describes a concept, demonstrates a skill or strategy or involves the group in developing guidelines.

5. **Examples** As you present the idea or demonstrate the skill, give frequent examples that are familiar to students. For instance, you might illustrate effective story settings by reading one by their favorite author. Ask students to find examples of a concept by drawing from their own experience or by examining familiar books or their own writing, research, or projects in progress.

6. **Practice** When the topic has been introduced, described and illustrated with examples, move students immediately into some form of practice. Depending on the topic of the mini-lesson, students might role-play, generate examples from their own experience, list guidelines, look for examples in books they are reading or divide into groups to practice interactive skills. You will want to walk around the room to observe the practice, providing assistance where needed and encouraging students to help each other. After five or ten minutes, ask your students to share examples or describe their practice experience.

7. **Recording** When you are satisfied that students understand the idea or have learned the skill, ask them to record their understanding of the lesson

in the appropriate notebook or journal for future reference. Their notes might include drawings, charts, definitions, descriptions, outlines, guidelines, or procedural steps, depending on the topic of the mini-lesson. In small task groups, you may want to assign additional practice for students to continue on their own, such as searching favorite books or their own experience for more examples.

8. **Application** When appropriate, you will want to provide an opportunity for students to continue working with a concept or skill on their own in an independent work period, such as those associated with literature groups or writer's workshop. Students might also: begin research journals in math, science or the social studies, using reference materials for a project; read aloud into a tape recorder; or write in a particular genre.

Informational Mini-Lessons

The following ideas have been successfully introduced in the mini-lesson format. As you can see, the possibilities are endless.

1. What to do when you come into the room in the morning (at recess, in the cafeteria, after lunch, when visitors come)
2. How to read together (with a partner, in small groups, with a Book Buddy, at the computer, into a tape recorder)
3. What to do at the chalkboard (in the art or science center, library, computer lab, writing or listening areas, housekeeping centers)
4. How to take care of the plants in the room (animals, displays, chalkboard, furniture)
5. How to use and take care of books (the computer, science displays, art and writing materials, blocks, toys, housekeeping items)
6. How to make books (all different shapes and kinds, puppets, charts, art projects)
7. How to create art projects (science demonstrations, oral biographies)
8. How to create and conduct an activity such as an interview, panel discussion, TV show, radio program
9. The important elements of poetry (other genres)
10. How to write a biography (other genres)
11. How to create and use a portfolio (research notebook, literature journal, diary, personal dictionary, reading or writing log)
12. How to conduct an author study (research a topic in science, math or social studies)
13. How to jump rope (hit the ball, tag a runner, climb a pole, swing safely)
14. Guidelines for reading to a partner (working in groups, preparing for conferences, reading aloud, reading independently, settling differences)

Mini-Lessons for Writer's Workshop: Prewriting Activities

Word Banks Students list all the words they can think of that are related to the topic they want to write about; then they group the words into categories. This can be an individual activity or one that involves the entire class; primary and intermediate students can also work in small groups of three or four. For example, if a student is writing about a grandparent, she might list all the words she associates with her own grandfather, such as: kind, generous, patient, funny, white hair, fun, glasses, brightly colored neckties, playing the piano, playing monopoly, making swings, playing ball, baking brownies, blue eyes, summer vacations, working in the garden, running a bank, playing in the band, joining the circus band, teasing. These items can then be grouped into categories, such as: appearance, personal qualities, work activities, recreational activities and family anecdotes. These categories, in turn, can be arranged into a sequence of topic sentences to generate a story or profile about the grandparent.

Venn Diagrams This is an excellent way to help students visualize contrasts and comparisons. Draw two large overlapping circles on the board or on a chart. Using a favorite story of your students, choose two characters, settings or events and ask them to list some characteristics that are the same and some that are different. Perhaps you might choose Arthur Denizen and his son, Will, from *Dinotopia*.[18] On the left side of the diagram you will write "Arthur" and on the right side "Will." If one of the elements of contrast is cautious and daring, you will write "cautious" under Arthur's name and "daring" under Will's. Other comparisons might include: middle-aged and teenager, anxious and confident, realistic and romantic. Then ask students to think of characteristics they have in common. Possible answers here would be: both are men, curious, explorers, hardworking and ethical. If students can think of episodes in the story that illustrate these characteristics, they are prepared to write about one or both characters in an interesting way.

Brainstorming Demonstrate to students how to generate ideas about a topic by writing down anything that comes to mind. After ideas are exhausted, review each one, organize them into categories and rate them for usefulness. This activity has the advantage of placing creativity before editing and is often the source of imaginative approaches to a topic.

Clustering/webbing Demonstrate this writing technique with a topic familiar to your students, such as ideas from a theme or content area study. Write the topic in the middle of a page. Around the topic, record any subtopics you can think of. For example, you might write "World War I" in the middle. Around this word you might write: participants, civilian involvement, time period, economic background, political context, causes, weapons, battles, political leaders, military leaders. Each of these subtopics would in turn create a cluster of concepts. Ask students how these concepts might relate to each other and draw lines to indicate connections. This helps organize ideas and shows how they relate to each other. You may want to draw a line around each topic and subtopic for better visualization.

Timed Writing This is a good exercise to help students develop fluency in writing. Ask students to help generate a list of open-ended topics, or let them write on any topic they choose during a five-minute period. The goal is to generate as many sentences about the topic as possible in a short period of time. Students can also begin with the same word and write a chain of associations, such as PEACE, quiet, river, stream, fishing, bite, dog, fur. . . . The idea is for students to experience an easy flow of words to create confidence in their ability to produce writing.

Elements of Good Writing

Demonstrate the importance of writing about things that one knows well or feels strongly about by asking students to write about something they know little about for five minutes; then ask them to write about something they know a lot about for the same time period. Contrast the two pieces and discuss what they observe about their writing. Demonstrate how to provide information with details and how to create logical organization with a beginning, middle and end. Review concise writing in the literature they are reading and explain how to avoid unnecessary words and repetitions. Show students how to replace passive sentence constructions with action words and how to use dialogue to describe a character or setting. Review appropriate uses of writing conventions such as spelling, punctuation, capitalization and paragraph indentation as they are needed.

Mini-lessons that help students write more complex sentences are helpful. Ask students to write any sentence that gives a statement of fact, such as "The dog chased the cat." Help them expand the idea by adding modifiers and then other parts of speech and phrases to extend it into a compound, complex or cumulative sentence: "The little brown dog barked and chased the frightened cat under the lilac bush" or "When the terrified tabby caught sight of the barking Doberman, she slid quickly under the porch."

Another popular mini-lesson for all ages can be conducted as either a group or individual activity. Ask students to choose a sentence from a favorite book, add their own experience and write a sentence like it. They might also imitate the format of the book, create new characters or describe a different setting.

Elements of Successful Reading

Demonstrate techniques and strategies that are characteristic of effective reading. Possible presentations include: decoding and comprehension strategies; book self-selection techniques; predicting the content of reading material; confirming predictions; scanning for important words; noticing topic sentences; rereading favorite parts of a book or parts that were confusing; making connections between the book and self; comparing the book with ones previously read; reflecting on what was learned through reading; reflecting on how the book may have changed one's ideas; comparing the ideas of the book with one's own values.

Rhetorical Stance

Help students read and write more effectively by helping them identify the elements of rhetorical stance in the books they are reading. Show how rhetorical stance can be used to guide their reading and how each element is related to and determined by each of the others.

Purpose   What is their reason for writing? Do they want to explain something, express their feelings, entertain, persuade someone to do something, or record ideas, facts or events? One of the best ways to contrast the results of different purposes in writing is to ask students to choose an advertisement of a favorite item, such as video games, soft drinks, music, or food. Tape a copy of the ad at the top of a piece of paper and then write a review of the item or service as a consumer advocate. How does this purpose for writing change the content and style of the writing?

Voice

This is the point of view of the book. Is the story told in first person ("*I* never intended to stay on the island that long."), second person ("To create a terrarium, *you* will first have to find a container large enough to hold small plants and animals."), or third person ("He raced down to the shore, afraid of what he would find."), where the story is told by a narrator or an unidentified storyteller who knows the thoughts and feelings of the characters? Proett and Gill[19] suggest the following exercises to help students discover how voice influences the content, language, emphasis and tone of writing. They also help students identify who is speaking, describing events or explaining the action.

1. Ask students to select an issue with two sides (bedtime, junk food, curfews, appropriate school clothes) and write two paragraphs, one from each side of the issue (parent, student, teacher). What differences can be observed in vocabulary and the tone of the writing?
2. Let students create a conversation about an issue (sharing treats, toys, play equipment, money, friends, parental attention) between the good and selfish sides of their consciences.
3. Have students create a conversation between themselves and characters in a story about story events. Write a sympathetic or critical interview of the character's behavior.

Form

When students have identified their reasons for writing and their intended audience, they must then decide what form the writing will take. Mini-lessons can review the possibilities, such as a letter, article, journal or diary entry, essay, poem, drama, story, interview, newspaper, literature review, TV or radio program, biographical sketch, picture book, historical fiction, fantasy, folktale, tall tale, or informational nonfiction.

Audience

Help students evaluate both their reading and writing by identifying the persons for whom a piece is intended. What might they already know about this topic? What might they need to know in the way of background? What opinions are readers likely to have about this topic? Are they likely to be sympathetic with or critical of the characters in the story or the theme of nonfiction? To help students develop a sense of audience in their own writing, ask them to describe a current local fad in clothes, music or toys to a friend who lives far away and then describe the same thing to a grandparent. This demonstrates how writers adjust the telling of a story to accommodate age and experience. You might also ask students to explain something they have just learned (subtraction, dinosaurs, space, alliteration) to a much younger child. This will help them be more alert to terms and ideas that might be misunderstood.

Content

How do authors use descriptions and dialogue in their writing? Provide the opportunity for students to try these techniques in their own writing. Read the descriptions of Wanda and the other girls in *The Hundred Dresses*[20] to show how characters can be created by describing their clothes. Read a passage from *Slake's Limbo*[21] to illustrate how the character of Slake is created by depicting the harshness of the subway station where he lives.

You can help students apply this technique to their own writing by comparing a generalization to an idea enhanced by description and dialogue. An example might be: "My grandma is the best!" Compare this statement with the following:

> When my grandmother came to the door, she was wearing her favorite blue and white apron. It was the one that covered her up from her neck to her knees, so I knew what we would be doing all morning. "Grandma," I said. "I hope you didn't start baking bread without me."

Ask students to create some generalizations; then ask them to **show** rather than **tell** about a character, event or setting. In a fifth-grade class, one student first described a baseball game by writing: "It was a neat ball game." Then he turned the generalization into the following by describing the action:

> When he hit the ball it went up and up and up until it was almost out of sight. "It's a home run!" the announcer said. We barely heard him because we were jumping up and down on the bleachers and cheering. I didn't think the ball would ever land. There were two runners on base and now we were ahead, three to one!

Another student described an unusual store at the mall:

> I leaned down to see what was attracting all the attention in the glass case. Suddenly I was face to face with a tarantula. "Wow, sharks!" someone cried, from across the aisle. What kind of pet store was this anyway?

Another way to add interest to the content of writing is to compare and contrast ideas. Ask students to compare days of the week, grade levels, birthday celebrations, or favorite books, movies, or TV programs. How is each one different from the other? How is each the same? An interesting exercise that explores self-concept and practices imagination involves responses to the following, which can be arranged in prose or poetry: What day of the week are you? What holiday, sound, food, clothing, time of year, place, sport?

Mini-Lessons for Writer's Workshop: Postwriting Activities

Postwriting includes revising, editing, proofreading and publishing. Editing begins with reading the first draft aloud to catch awkward constructions, repeated words or unclear ideas. Revision may involve changing words, ideas or basic organization. The piece may then be read aloud to a small peer-editing group to identify writing problems from the viewpoint of an audience. Proofreading in these groups assesses the final draft for spelling, punctuation and grammatical problems. Students may share the final product with others by reading it aloud to the entire class during Friday Afternoon Sharing Time or by publishing it in book format.

When students help develop criteria for evaluating writing, they look more closely at their own and others' work. They also become more aware of the skill involved in good writing. You can help students develop skills of evaluation by creating an example of poor writing, one that has problems with organization, vocabulary and coherency. Use little dialogue or details and omit punctuation that would help establish clear meaning. Project the paper from an overhead and ask your students to help analyze the writing. What makes it difficult to understand? How could it be improved?

Ask students to generate a set of questions that could be used to analyze their own and others' writing. One group of intermediate students created the following guidelines to help them edit each other's work:

What details were effective?
What was the best sentence on the paper? Why did you like it?
Was the piece well organized?
If a part was unclear, what might help?
Was there something you wish the author had included?
Would dialogue make it more interesting?
Should there be more specific details to assist understanding?

Encourage students to practice editing their own writing in a variety of groupings: on their own, in pairs, in small groups and as an entire class. Assign a focus derived from the particular mini-lessons and provide time to revise in light of what has been learned. Never force students to share writing they feel is private, but encourage them to record ideas they do not want to share in their journals or diaries.

To introduce classroom book publishing, you might want to invite a local publisher or writer to talk to the class. *How a Book Is Made*[22] by Aliki also provides a good introduction for publishing and is available in picture book and videotape formats. As each element of book publishing is introduced in mini-lessons, enlist the help of aides, older students or parents to help with publishing. This is an excellent activity for cross-grade Book Buddies. They can take dictation, type or enter text into the word processor; they can also laminate covers and help with assembly. Be sure to provide a mini-lesson for any helpers to explain how you want them to assist your students.

WHAT DO YOU THINK? Which of the ideas for mini-lessons are especially appealing to you? Have you had experience with any of the prewriting or postwriting techniques described above? Which will you want to observe in the classroom before you try them yourself?

VII. If This Is Your Situation

If you must use a basal reader system or are required to follow a certain sequence in language arts teaching to accommodate a team-teaching situation, you can still use the concept of mini-lessons to help your students develop language skills and strategies. Let students use their favorite books to find examples for required lessons. As examples are generated, they can be recorded in writing notebooks and used as references for student writing.

If composition topics are assigned by district or state mandates, use the mini-lesson to talk about the criteria that will be used to evaluate student writing. In most cases, you can allow students to choose their own topics of writing for practice. In some schools there will be separate spelling and handwriting programs. Encourage children to find words from spelling lists in their favorite books and to practice handwriting skills as they create compositions to share with others. Students can also expand their spelling lists by adding words they especially want to know how to spell. Many students enjoy creating outlandish sentences that use words they must learn how to spell. A fourth grader produced this one: "When the lion learned there would be big chunks of meat for breakfast, he was very *punctual* about getting up." Another student wrote: "I guess I'm not very *punctual*, because I was tardy twice this week." This exercise helps children play with the words and tie them to their own experience.

WHAT DO YOU THINK?   Can you think of other ways to use mini-lessons within highly structured situations? How do the teachers you observe adapt their instruction to meet the purpose of state or district mandates?

VIII.   Evaluating Mini-Lessons

Mini-lessons begin and end with the evaluation process. As you observe your students in language learning activities throughout the day, you will be taking notes on skills, strategies and knowledge that might assist their development. From these observations you will create mini-lessons on a wide range of topics. How will you know if these presentations are effective? Continue to observe your students to see if they apply the strategies and use the skills. Do they show progress in developing these skills, or will it be necessary to review material with a certain individual or a small group of students?

Remember that you will be watching for progress, not perfection. Peter Winograd[23] suggests that teachers think of the levels of student progress in the following terms:

Beginning   This term describes students who need lots of guidance during language learning activities.

Developing   These students are more involved in all activities of the classroom; they respond to reading and produce writing, with teacher modeling and support.

Independent   At this level, students are autonomous in their learning behavior and are highly involved in reading, writing and responding.

These same categories can be used to assess the use of skills, strategies or information presented in mini-lessons. At the beginning level, students will make a few attempts to apply a skill or strategy, but will need frequent review and teacher support; developing students will show progress in their applications of the mini-lessons to language learning situations; and those who have achieved the independent level will use the skills and strategies appropriately and consistently.

The same observation checklist used to develop mini-lessons can be used to evaluate their effectiveness. When you notice students using reading, writing, listening or speaking strategies that have been reviewed during mini-lessons, record their use with a check in the appropriate column. Some teachers like to keep anecdotal records of these events, such as: Troy brought the discussion group back on track today by saying, "We need to listen to each other more carefully."

WHAT DO YOU THINK? If you had to evaluate your teaching skills according to the performance levels above, in what areas would you be a beginner, developing or independent? Why do you think these might be good categories for evaluating performance?

IX. Creating Partners

Many parents become concerned if their children do not receive phonics instruction as part of their primary school experience. Their concern is that their children may not be able to read as effectively or be able to spell unless they learn the individual sounds that comprise words. They may not understand the idea of learning sound/symbol relationships in the context of unlocking words a child wants to know. If phonics is not systematically taught in the school, they may purchase drill cards and use them with their children at home.

You already know that it is helpful to inform parents about the skills and strategies that are introduced to students during individual reading conferences. It is easy to add the skills or strategies introduced in mini-lessons to the individual take-home cards described in Creating Partners in Chapter 6. Parents will already be expecting these cards and usually will be eager to help support the development of these skills at home. At the kindergarten level, you will need some assistance from an aide to add this information to children's cards, or you can type the information into a computer label maker and let the children attach them to their own cards. At the primary and intermediate levels, this information can be copied from a chart or chalkboard by the children themselves.

Many teachers send these cards home in a small plastic bag that is numbered with a key. (Remember that you will not want to put children's names on take-home items, for safety reasons.) Inside each bag is a folded set of activities parents can do at home, such as listening to children read aloud, providing time for independent reading and encouraging practical writing. There should also be a set of guidelines to help parents assist their children effectively, such as providing a special time and place for this work at home, joining them for these activities and encouraging students to be as self-directed as possible in completing the exercises.

WHAT DO YOU THINK?   Did your parents ever help you with your homework? What kind of experience was this for you? For your parents? What kinds of language learning do you think children can successfully practice at home?

X. Perspectives: Phonics

Kenneth Goodman[24] describes phonics as the system that relates speaking and spelling. Traditionally, phonics has referred to a way of teaching children by isolating the sounds that make up words and teaching these as preparation for learning to read. There is great variation, however, in how similar sound symbols are pronounced and experienced by children, due to differences in regional dialects and intonation. Consider, for example, the associations made between the letters in the word *help*. Students might hear the same word pronounced *hep*, *help* or *hay-up*, depending on the region where they live. To prevent confusion in written communication, we agree on a single spelling, even if we disagree on how this spelling relates to certain sounds. Goodman describes phonics as both a personal and social system, which enables us to make connections between our personal speech—including the dialect of culture or community—and the social conventions of writing.

Goodman points out that the most effective use of phonics instruction is to support readers in their efforts to make sense of print as they read and write. He believes that the system of phonics is best learned in the context of learning to read and write, not as a prerequisite for these activities. When children are initially forced to use only phonic information to make sense of what they are reading, they may lose track of the meaning. The most effective readers combine meaning and grammar cues with phonic information.

It is helpful to remember that **traditional school grammar** developed from Latin grammar. School grammar follows a fixed set of rules that were derived from the application of Latin grammar to English language study. Latin is an inflected language; that is, the function of a word in a Latin sentence is indicated by its ending. For example, if you write the sentence "The squirrel climbed the tree," in Latin you would add a certain ending to each noun to show its function in the sentence. With this ending in place, the position of the nouns would not be important. You would know by the ending on each word which one was to be the subject or object. When English language study was introduced into the school curriculum in England, it was considered a lesser language that must be fitted into the mold of the more sophisticated Greek and Latin models. Unfortunately, Modern English is not an inflected language; the meaning of words is determined by their position in a sentence rather than their ending.

WHAT DO YOU THINK? Was phonics taught as part of your learning-to-read program in elementary school? Did you have systematic grammar instruction? What do you remember about any direct reading instruction you received? Did you wonder why there were so many exceptions to spelling rules?

XI. Exploring Professional Literature

In addition to the professional journals reviewed in this section in previous chapters, many teachers also read and use materials from magazines such as *Learning*[25] and *Instructor*.[26] These commercially prepared magazines differ in appearance, content and purpose from professional journals. **Professional educational journals** are published by associations of educators who provide a forum for members to share ideas with each other. They generally publish articles that deal with a single curriculum area, like the language arts, mathematics or science. These articles address both the theoretical and practical interests of their membership and promote professional values. Publication of journals is usually supported by membership dues.

Teacher's magazines, on the other hand, feature colorful presentations, provide ideas for many curriculum areas and generally address the practical concerns of their readers. Because they are a commercial venture, you will find many more advertisements in these magazines. You have observed in previous chapters how journal membership can be helpful to you as a professional educator. Commercial magazines can also be valuable, when you are aware of their particular strengths and limitations. Many teachers read these magazines to get ideas for art projects, theme teaching, discipline, making use of scarce resources and communicating with parents. These articles deal with the nuts-and-bolts management of the classroom and include personal accounts of how teachers solve everyday problems. Most also feature reviews of children's books and popular literature.

Both journals and magazines can contribute to your effectiveness as a teacher. You might choose to use these two resources in much the same way that you select who informs you about the news. Most people tune in to network news shows to catch up quickly on what is happening in the world. When they want a clearer or more thorough understanding of the causes and consequences of these events, they choose the longer, news analysis programs. These feature in-depth interviews with persons connected with the news, more lengthy discussions and debates from both sides of the issue, and attempts to place the news in a historical perspective.

In a similar manner, commercial teacher's magazines provide a quick review of current trends in instruction. Teachers use them to get acquainted with these trends and to get an idea of how other teachers are applying new methods. When they want to understand more about a current trend in instruction, they read the more in-depth articles in a journal, which will place the information within a theoretical framework, debate the issue from several points of view, refer to previous writing about an issue and present research evidence to support any claims for instructional effectiveness.

WHAT DO YOU Why do you think that teachers might read magazines more frequently
THINK? than journals? From your own experience with these periodicals, what
values do you see for each in your own teaching?

XII. Resources for Teaching

The Reading Teacher's Book of Lists, 3d edition[27] This desktop reference
contains examples and definitions of many different kinds of words. A helpful
resource for teachers, it can also be used by students as a reference for foreign
phrases, proofreading, lists of books and literature activities. A user's guide
suggests the most helpful sections to review at various grade levels and for
ESL students. Readers can find lists of homophones, homographs, and
heronyms and their meanings. Also included are daily living words, work
words, picture words, collective nouns and lists of vocabulary for all grade
levels in mathematics, science and the social studies. The Greek and Latin
roots of words are included, along with words that have been shortened,
blended or put together to form new words. Synonyms, antonyms, analogies,
similes, metaphors, idioms, proverbs and euphemisms are described, and there
is an entire chapter on phonics. The book also provides learning and study
skills, writing strategies and enrichment activities. There is a helpful section
on signs, symbols and abbreviations, including state abbreviations and capitals, Roman numerals, the manual and braille alphabets, and the Morse code
and Native American symbols. A reference section at the end of the book
provides nondiscriminatory language guidelines, handwriting charts, literary
and computer terms and the names of reading organizations and publishers.

Writing Workshop Survival Kit[28] Part 1 of this excellent handbook has many
helpful hints about setting up, conducting and evaluating a writing workshop
for intermediate-level students. Part 2 contains 100 sample mini-lessons on
types of writing, the art of writing and the mechanics of writing, including
such topics as personal narratives, essays, fiction, screenplays, imagery, active
and passive constructions, strong verbs, and sentence combinations for point
of view.

Grammar for Teachers: Perspectives and Definitions[29] This handbook, published by the National Council of Teachers of English, has an excellent
discussion of the theories of grammar, but it also contains discussions and
definitions that provide a helpful reference to teachers who must teach the
specifics of grammar at the intermediate levels.

Book Factory[30] This is an inexpensive guide for creating all kinds of books.
It provides bookbinding and illustration tips and decoration ideas for borders
and bookmarks. Each kind of book is described and illustrated, with directions
and lists of materials required. The materials in these books can be duplicated
for classroom use in centers or writing workshops. Some of the more interesting ideas include books of homonym riddles, specialized dictionaries, animal
readers (writing a book that would interest an animal), accordion books,
choose-the-ending books and autobiographies.

More Book Factory[31] Another in the *Book Factory* series, this book offers
additional ideas for all kinds of book projects, including ABC books, books
of advice, almanacs, manners manuals, rebuses, riddles, atlases, cookbooks,

novels, folklore, plays, Who's Who and word histories. Also included are step-by-step directions for creating a classroom publishing company and ways to use desktop publishing. Also available in this series are: *Picture Book Factory*, which has directions for creating picture books at all instructional levels; *Writing Hangups*, which features ideas for posters, banners, bulletin boards, mobiles, borders, calendars and other displays; *Greeting Cards*, which provides ideas for making cards for all occasions; and *Report Factory*, which describes multimedia projects for the content areas. All of these books are distributed by Good Apple, Inc., Box 299, Carthage, IL 62321-0299 and are available in most teacher's stores.

WHAT DO YOU THINK? Have you ever explored a teacher's store? What kinds of things do you enjoy looking at? How important do you think it is to have a clearly defined approach to instruction when you are considering the purchase of commercially prepared materials?

XIII. Reflections

From a Teacher's Journal—Jackie Hogue, Fifth-Grade

I let Ryan facilitate a class discussion with *Island of the Blue Dolphins*. Lauren wanted to read her paragraph written from the point of view of Rontu because she had included a simile. We had discussed different forms of figurative language previously, and when students found them in books, they wrote the examples on chart paper.

Jozie wanted to read a simile from the book, but it turned out not to be one. Ryan faltered as the facilitator. Kristen didn't know if it was a simile; Jackie wasn't sure and said we should look at examples on the chart. I hadn't said a word until that point, but agreed that they might look at the definition written on the chart. In a short period of time, they could say with confidence that the example was not a simile and they knew why. They worked it out by themselves.

Jozie was not embarrassed, because the environment of the class encourages risk-taking, and all questions and mistakes are used as learning experiences. I try to say to the kids, "That's a good question," or "What a great mistake!"

I just read where kids write like the stories they read. That seems to make a good case for reading the best literature.

TRYING OUT THE CHAPTER IDEAS
1. The next time you observe in a classroom, note any difficulties students are experiencing that could be addressed with a mini-lesson. What kinds of information, strategies or skills would help them read, write or discuss better?
2. The distinct value of journals and magazines is something best experienced firsthand. When you have examined a copy of a teacher's magazine of your choice, you might want to read one of the articles that deals with some aspect of teaching that interests

you. Using the periodical guide, find the same topic in *Language Arts* or *The Reading Teacher* and read an article on the same topic that draws your interest. What do you notice about each?

3. With your cooperating teacher's permission, plan and present a mini-lesson to a small group of students that will help increase their skill in reading or writing.

4. If you are student teaching, assess a skill or strategy that would be helpful for all students in the classroom to know and present a mini-lesson. This might be in the context of a guided reading session, a writer's workshop or a topic that addresses an informational issue, such as a research technique.

Notes

1. Lev Vygotsky, *Mind in Society* (Cambridge, Mass.: Harvard University Press, 1978).
2. Laura E. Berk, "Vygotsky's Theory: The Importance of Make-Believe Play," *Young Children* (November 1994): 30–39.
3. Jerome Bruner, "Vygotsky: A Historical and Conceptual Perspective," in *Culture, Communication and Cognition*, edited by J. V. Wertsch (Cambridge, Mass.: Cambridge University Press, 1985).
4. Bill Martin, Jr. and John Archambault, *Chicka Chicka Boom Boom* (New York: Scholastic, 1989).
5. Robert Lawson, *Rabbit Hill* (New York: Viking, 1945).
6. Gail Gibbons, *Dinosaurs* (New York: Holiday House, 1987).
7. Jim Murphy, *Dinosaur for a Day* (New York: Scholastic, 1992).
8. Eleanor Estes, *Ginger Pye* (New York: Scholastic, 1951).
9. Scott O'Dell, *Sing Down the Moon* (New York: Dell Yearling, 1992).
10. Theodora Kroeber, *Ishi, Last of His Tribe* (New York: Bantam, 1989).
11. Will Hobbs, *Bearstone* (New York: Avon, 1989).
12. Jan Hudson, *Sweetgrass* (New York: Scholastic, 1984).
13. Kenneth Goodman, ed., *Miscue Analysis: Applications to Reading Instruction* (Urbana, Ill.: National Council of Teachers of English, 1973).
14. Yetta M. Goodman, Dorothy Wilson, and Carolyn Burke, *Reading Miscue Inventory: Alternative Procedures* (Katonah, N.Y.: Richard C. Owen, 1987).
15. Beverly Cleary, *Dear Mr. Henshaw* (New York: William Morrow, 1983).
16. Louise Fitzhugh, *Harriet the Spy* (New York: Harper & Row, 1964).
17. Vera and Bill Cleaver, *Where the Lilies Bloom* (New York: Harper & Row, 1969).
18. James Gurney, *Dinotopia: A Land Apart from Time* (Atlanta: Turner Publishing, 1992).
19. Jackie Proett and Kent Gill, *The Writing Process in Action: A Handbook for Teachers* (Urbana, Ill.: NCTE, 1986).
20. Eleanor Estes, *The Hundred Dresses* (New York: Scholastic, 1973).
21. Felice Holman, *Slake's Limbo* (New York: Scholastic, 1974).
22. Aliki, *How a Book Is Made* (New York: Crowell, 1986).
23. Peter Winograd, "Developing Alternative Assessments: Six Problems Worth Solving," *The Reading Teacher* 47, no. 5 (February 1994): pp. 420–423.
24. Kenneth Goodman, *Phonics Pfacts* (New York: Scholastic, 1993).

25. *Learning*, published by the Education Center, Inc. For subscription information, write Learning, P.O. Box 54293, Boulder, CO 80322-4293 or call 1-800-753-1843.

26. *Instructor*, published by Scholastic, Inc. For subscription information, call 1-800-544-2917.

27. Edward Fry, Jacqueline Kress, and Dona Lee Fountoukidis, *The Reading Teacher's Book of Lists*, 3d ed. (Englewood Cliffs, N.J.: Prentice Hall, 1993).

28. Gary R. Muschla, *Writing Workshop Survival Kit* (West Nyack, N.Y.: The Center for Applied Research in Education, 1993).

29. Constance Weaver, *Grammar for Teachers: Perspectives and Definitions* (Urbana, Ill.: National Council of Teachers of English, 1979).

30. Murray Suid and Wanda Lincoln, *Book Factory* (Palo Alto, Calif.: Monday Morning Books, Inc., 1988).

31. Murray Suid and Wanda Lincoln, *More Book Factory* (Palo Alto, Calif.: Monday Morning Books, Inc., 1991).

CHAPTER TEN

Using Media and Technology to Support Language Learning

*Does improved technology mean progress? Yes, it certainly could
mean just that. But only if we are willing and able to answer the next
question: progress toward what?*

—Leo Marx, in **Technology and the Future**[1]

LOOKING AHEAD

1. In what ways can technology be used to support language learning?
2. How do good films and videotapes enhance the understanding and appreciation of literature?
3. How can film and interactive programming enhance conceptual learning in the sciences and social sciences?
4. How might technology affect the way students think?
5. How does technology help support full participation by all students?
6. What kinds of interactive programs are available for classroom use?
7. How can teachers gain technological support for their classrooms?
8. How might class discussions influence television viewing habits?

IN 25 WORDS OR LESS

The selective use of technology and high-quality programs in the classroom provides shared experiences, stimulates language response, and expands understanding of complex ideas.

I. Focus: How Does Technology Affect Language Learning?

Children are directly influenced in their everyday language learning by many forms of technology. Depending on the circumstances of individual families, students are variously exposed to television, films, video and audio presentations, computer programs, the Internet and interactive video. From these sources children develop new vocabulary, expand their knowledge of people, places and things, and form opinions and attitudes. It is no longer a matter of **whether** technology will influence children's learning, but rather **how** it will be utilized for learning by informed educators. The purpose of this chapter is to suggest ways that you can positively support children's language learning through the use of technology.

You can help students make intelligent and analytical responses to the technology in their lives when you encourage them to read, write, listen and talk about the ideas delivered or mediated by technology. You can also provide opportunities for students to actively use technology, such as the computer word processor, to express ideas and feelings and enhance their communication with others. From these experiences, students learn how to use technology as a tool to share ideas, solve problems and seek answers to things they want to know.

Schools vary in the amount and sophistication of technological equipment they are able to provide for their students, but it is helpful for all teachers to be aware of what is available:

Interactive video (students select audio and video presentations from laser-disc storage) and **multimedia programs** (film and sound presentations that can be randomly accessed through a menu of choices) provide information and create new questions about what is seen and heard. As students use this equipment to follow their interests and solve problems important to them, they come in contact with new ideas that continue and refine their original inquiry. For example, they can learn to consider the entire earth as a system with programs such as the Geosphere Visual Library, which graphically demonstrates the interrelationship of all the earth's systems and shows how changes in one system, such as wildlife habitats, affects all others.

Many schools have access to the **Internet** (a worldwide electronic bulletin board and user service), which permits the interaction of teachers, students, libraries and experts in all fields. With this technology, students can exchange information and ideas with their peers throughout the United States and the world or participate in the world's largest concert via satellite hookup with schools around the world. They can tour distant historical sites with expert guides and visit the bottom of the sea with camera and crew.

Computer programs make it possible for students to safely witness events that would be too dangerous to observe personally, such as simulations of the splitting of the atom, a volcanic eruption or battle engagements filmed by war photographers. It also allows students to observe filmed events as remote in time as the Great Depression or the first flight of the Wright brothers. Through high-quality video film, students can go places where only a few with specialized expertise are privileged to visit, such as the surface of the moon or the bottom of the ocean. They can obtain a true bird's-eye view when cameras are attached to the wings of migrating geese or look at the underside of a glacier through recording equipment carried by a walrus. Cameras speed up time to show how a cactus blooms and slow it down to track the movements of a hummingbird in flight. Audiotapes permit children to listen to a book read aloud by its author, and public television brings them previews of books presented by children their own age.

Classroom discussion is stimulated, rather than supplanted, when students share a common experience with film or computer programs like the ones described above. Students are motivated to seek more information about topics that interest them in these presentations, and each of these experiences can serve as an impetus for a variety of responses in writing. The descriptions in the following sections suggest ways that technology might be used to support learning in the classroom. Other ideas are limited only by your own imagination.

WHAT DO YOU   Can you think of other examples of the ways technology expands
THINK?   opportunities for learning? What kinds of technologies do children now
take for granted that have been developed in your lifetime? What
technologies are comfortable for you to use?

II. The Importance of Technology to Language Learning

Technology is changing the way we get information and transform it into
knowledge. From word processors to the Internet, technology affects the
processing and sharing of information and the ways we are able to relate to
persons at a distance. In the classroom, technology increasingly is affecting
the way children learn language and use it to inquire, respond and share
information and knowledge. It is important to realize that if we want to
prepare children to be lifelong learners, that preparation will have to include
learning new ways to use language to communicate within a world society.

With the advent of the computer, teachers have the opportunity to help
children develop new ways of thinking about the world. During the decade
of the 1980s, computer literacy for students was generally regarded as a
necessity in a world that increasingly used computers for communication and
problem solving. Others saw the computer as the perfect teacher, able to
process information quickly and interact with students patiently. Still others,
such as Seymour Papert, believed that interaction with the computer could
actually change the way students think. Papert developed the Logo programming language, which encourages children to solve problems in a variety of
ways by constructing their own knowledge and building on their everyday
experience.

High-quality technological programs encourage responses in students
that provide practice in critical thinking, reading, writing, listening and
speaking. Like good books, quality programs increase a child's vocabulary
and improve comprehension of concepts. Working with programs as a class
provides a common experience to be talked about and initiates responses
that can be shared as a group. Books recorded on audiotapes allow children
to enjoy stories they cannot yet read independently and provide the opportunity for individual practice of reading skills. Good literature portrayed on
videotapes or filmstrips offers large pictures on a screen for easy group
viewing. The best examples of dramatic film contain excellent charac-
terizations, good music and authentic settings, which provide students with
an enriched experience of the story.

In terms of language learning, Bertram Bruce[2] found that the best and
most productive use of computers in the classroom is for creating, storing
and editing student writing. Students learn to be better readers and writers[3]
when it is easier for them to enter and revise text. They also learn new words
more quickly when they are assisted in their computer text reading by audio
prompts (via speech synthesizer).[4] When students participate in "invisible
writing" exercises (entering text with the monitor screen turned off), they

Draft 1 (handwritten)

<u>Helen Keller</u>

Helen Keller was born on a hot day on June 27, 1880 in Tuscumbia, Alabama. Her middle name was Adams. Her parents names were Kate and Captain. She had a younger sister named Mildred.

Helen was very ill when she was 19 months old. Everybody thought she would die. The illness left her blind, deaf and dumb. When Helen was blind she would know when somebody would cross her.

One hot summer day in August Helen's mother was cooking in the kitchen

Draft 2

Helen Keller
by

Helen Keller was born on a hot day on June 27, 1880 in Tuscumbia, Alabama. Her middle name was Adams. Her parent's names were Kate and Captain. She had a younger sister named Mildred.

Helen was very ill when she was 19 months old. Everybody thought she would die. The illness left her blind, deaf and dumb. When Helen was blind she would know when somebody would cross her.

One hot summer day in August Helen's mother was cooking in the kitchen and Helen was playing on the floor. Helen's mother had to get something in the pantry and Helen had the key to lock the door. So she shut the door and locked it. Her mother was yelling and pounding on the door. She thought it was a game. The maid heard all the yelling and pounding on the door. But Helen had fallen asleep. The maid came in and unlocked the door.

When Helen got in trouble she did not get a punishment, like when Helen locked her mother in the pantry. She even got dirty quickly but she never got in trouble for it.

Helen liked candy a lot. Sometimes her mother would drop pieces of candy in her mouth, but other times she would grab for it.

When Helen was six she and her family went north to see a special doctor. They went home disappointed because the doctor couldn't help Helen. But a lady called Miss Annie Macy Sullivan came to help Helen from Perkins School on March 3, 1887. Annie helped her on a special typewriter and taught her

Draft 3

Helen Keller
by
Bethany Strom

Helen Keller was born on a hot day on June 27, 1880 in Tuscumbia, Alabama. Her middle name was Adams. Her parent's names were Kate and Captain. She had a younger sister named Mildred.

Helen was very ill when she was 19 months old. Everybody thought she would die. The illness left her blind, deaf and dumb. When Helen was blind she would know when somebody would cross her.

One hot summer day in August Helen's mother was cooking in the kitchen and Helen was playing on the floor. Helen's mother had to get something in the pantry and Helen had the key to lock the door. So she shut the door and locked it. Her mother was yelling and pounding on the door. She thought it was a game. The maid heard all the yelling and pounding on the door. But Helen had fallen asleep. The maid came in and unlocked the door.

When Helen got in trouble she did not get a punishment, like when Helen locked her mother in the pantry. She even got dirty quickly but she never got in trouble for it.

Helen liked candy a lot. Sometimes her mother would drop pieces of candy in her mouth, but other times she would grab for it.

When Helen was six she and her family went north to see a

Draft 4

Helen Keller
by
Bethany Strom

Helen Keller was born on a hot day on June 27, 1880 in Tuscumbia, Alabama. Her middle name was Adams. Her parent's names were Kate and Captain. She had a younger sister named Mildred.

Helen was very ill when she was 19 months old. Everybody thought she would die. The illness left her blind, deaf and dumb. When Helen was blind she would know when somebody would cross her.

One hot summer day in August Helen's mother was cooking in the kitchen and Helen was playing on the floor. Helen's mother had to get something in the pantry and Helen had the key to lock the door. So she shut the door and locked it. Her mother was yelling and pounding on the door. She thought it was a game. The maid heard all the yelling and pounding on the door. But Helen had fallen asleep. The maid came in and unlocked the door.

When Helen got in trouble she did not get a punishment, like when Helen locked her mother in the pantry. She even got dirty quickly but she never got in trouble for it.

FIGURE 10.1

A student's use of technology as part of expression is illustrated on the first pages of successive drafts of a biography. Computer word processing and a picture scanner allow this third-grade student to move from a handwritten first draft of a biography to a professional-looking final copy. Notice the influence of peer-editing on the first draft. Notice also how she experiments with typefaces and rearranges the text to accommodate pictures.

are often able to create ideas more freely, without being distracted by text or wanting to edit their work during the creation process.[5]

Can you imagine what classrooms will look like at the end of your teaching career? Do you think there will be schools or classrooms as we know them now?

III. Looking into Classrooms

Kindergarten Level

"Mrs. Jamison," Benny shouts, as he enters the classroom, "look what I got for my birthday!" He hands the teacher a videotape of *The Tale of Peter Rabbit*.[6]

"Wonderful!" she says, with appreciation. "Can you share it with the rest of the class?"

"That's why I brought it," he says. "My mom says I can keep it at school while you show it to everybody."

Mrs. Jamison is delighted. At the beginning of the year, she sent home a list of videotapes and books that would add to several themes throughout the year. *The Tale of Peter Rabbit* arrived at a good time for their study of animal stories. She will take the film home tonight to review it before showing it tomorrow. She knows that the video version differs slightly from the book, but still retains the essential ideas and appealing art of the original story.

Mrs. Jamison included *The Tale of Peter Rabbit* in her video wish list because it is not available in Big Book form. Showing the tape will allow everyone to see the pictures as they listen to the story. This is especially important for Amy, who is partially sighted and would have difficulty with the small book of the original tale.

At the beginning of the film, an actress portrays Beatrix Potter, who is writing *The Tale of Peter Rabbit* to entertain a nephew who is ill. A live rabbit sits beside her at the desk, munching a lettuce leaf. In this introduction, students are introduced to the author's purpose for writing the story, her model for the main character, and the clothing, hairstyles and living conditions of the time period. Mrs. Jamison knows there will be questions about many elements of the film, including the fact that the film is a story about how a story was written. The class has already seen several films about how stories are animated and will have some background to appreciate the artistic effort of *The Tale of Peter Rabbit*.

Mrs. Jamison plans to watch the film with pen and paper in hand, making notes in her teaching journal about places to pause. When her students have watched the entire film through once, she will begin it again and ask questions to begin their discussion, such as:

1. What do you like about this story?
2. What do you think this story is about?

3. What character did you like best?
4. Who would you like to be in this story?

She will also ask other questions to help children analyze the content of the story and look more closely for details:

1. What does the animator tell us about the characters by the way he makes them move?
2. What do you notice about the colors the filmmaker uses?
3. What happened first in the story? Next? Next?
4. What part of the story is the most exciting to you?
5. What part of the story do you like best?
6. What do you think Peter might do tomorrow?
7. Do you think he might ever go back to the garden?
8. Does this story remind you of any other story you have heard or read?
9. Could this story really happen?
10. Have you ever had an experience like Peter's?

When they have talked about the film, Mrs. Jamison will create a story chart with her students, outlining the major scenes of the story. They will read the story chart together and take turns acting out each scene for each other. From this activity, they will learn how scenes are created in a film story and how action occurs within a scene. They will practice identifying the sequence of action in a story plot and analyze characters who make the action happen.

Analyzing video versions of stories has made Mrs. Jamison's students more critical as viewers. There were mixed reviews for animated videotapes of *Madeline*,[7] books that relate the adventures of a little girl in a French boarding school. "It takes a whole half hour to tell the story," Jessica says. "There are all kinds of songs and it makes the story go too slow."

Kevin agrees. "I like the book better," he says. "It tells the story just right."

"You like the pacing of the book better than the movie," Mrs. Jamison says, introducing a term that can be used again.

"Yeah, that's right," Kevin says. "The pacing. I like the book pacing better."

"I **liked** the tape," Maggie protests. "The story is just the same, but there's singing too, and I like it."

"Me, too," Amy agrees. "It's more fun, 'cause you get the story **and** some extra parts. It doesn't change the story."

"I'm glad you're thinking about what you like about tapes and books," Mrs. Jamison says. "Everyone has reasons for making certain choices, and I'm always glad to see you talking about your reasons."

Other uses of technology in this classroom are apparent. Near the library corner, there are three microcomputers, where Mrs. Jamison, her classroom aide, the student teacher, parent volunteers and Book Buddies from the sixth grade enter stories dictated by the kindergarten students. There are also programs that feature a review of letters and words for those who enjoy practicing them in this way. Three times a week, Book Buddies from the sixth grade spend their noon hour reading together with kindergarten students. They also write stories together and enter them on the word processor. Other popular activities include using the graphic program to draw pictures for books they are writing together, watching literature videos, listening to books on audiotapes and practicing the alphabet with a *Sesame Street* program.

One morning a week, the school's CD-ROM interactive video system is located for the day in the kindergarten room. This week students will watch animals move and listen to their sounds on National Geographic's *Mammals: A Multimedia Encyclopedia*. The class has used the program several times to study animals, and Mrs. Jamison will encourage students to tell her how to use the program to access pictures of rabbits, guinea pigs, squirrels and hamsters. Together they have read portions of the program on mammals and have looked up a great number of animals alphabetically.

WHAT HAPPENED HERE? ONE PERSPECTIVE

Mrs. Jamison uses videotaped literature to extend the experience of a story with her students. Following the same procedures used in guided reading, she helps students identify details and analyze the components of the story. The computers in her classroom are available as tools for students to express their ideas, to share with others or to respond artistically to literature and their own experience. She models the use of multimedia technology as a tool for exploring new and interesting things and encourages her students to develop confidence and competence in using these tools.

By encouraging a buddy system with older students, Mrs. Jamison helps build bridges of communication and support between grade levels. Older students who work regularly with the younger ones are protective of them on the playground and interested in their academic progress. This relationship builds the self-esteem of both students in the relationship and creates bonds that continue on through the school experience. Each is proud of the other's accomplishments, encouraging both to work hard and achieve. They plan projects together and stay alert for books, tapes and programs the other might enjoy.

Primary Level

"What did you think of this version of *The Secret Garden*?"[8] Mrs. Ingram asks her third-grade class. They have just finished viewing the 1948 version. The previous week they saw a more recent adaptation produced by the BBC.

"It was better than the first film," Julie answers. "I liked how they made the whole movie in black and white until they went into the garden. Then it was in color."

"It was more like the book," Will volunteers. "And everybody looked more like I imagined them."

"Me, too!" several children chorus.

"I didn't like the black and white at first," Maria admits. "But then when the garden was all in color, it made it even more beautiful."

"It was like *The Wizard of Oz*," Julie says. "It was black and white until after the tornado and Dorothy got to Oz." The others nod in agreement.

"This is called contrast," Mrs. Ingram adds. "Filmmakers add interest to their stories by using contrast, just like authors who write books. What do you think the filmmaker was trying to say by making part of the movie in black and white and part in color?"

"That the garden was beautiful?" Maria suggests.

Mrs. Ingram waits for Maria to finish her idea.

"I mean, it was really different than when it was all full of weeds," she adds.

"I think it was to show there was hope," Seeja says.

"Can you add more to that?" Mrs. Ingram asks.

"Well, . . . in the story, nobody had much hope about things. Colin didn't think he'd ever get well and Mary didn't like it much in that big old house. The black and white part was like that."

"So you're saying that the garden . . . ," Mrs. Ingram prompts and pauses.

"The garden is in color, 'cause it's more hopeful . . . happier."

Others join in. "They plant flowers." "And birds come back to it." "And Colin learns to walk there to surprise his dad."

"They create the garden . . . ," she begins.

"They make it pretty again, the way it was before," Maria says.

"When the mother was still alive," Julie adds.

"Did anything else change, besides the garden?" Mrs. Ingram asks.

There is a pause.

"Colin changed. He learned to walk and he didn't have temper tantrums anymore," Julie says.

"And Mary changed, too," Will adds. "She wasn't cross or angry like she used to be."

"Everybody changes, even the dad . . . Mr. Craven. He's happy that Colin isn't crippled," Daren says.

"So the children changed the garden and the garden changed them?" Mrs. Ingram asks.

"Yeah," they agree.

"How do you think that happened . . . that the garden changed them?" she asks.

"Maybe they were happy because it was so nice," Maria suggests.

"Colin was probably just glad to be outdoors," Daren says. "I hate it when I have to be inside when I'm sick."

"Yeah, and you see other kids playing, like your friends, and they're having fun and you're not," Will adds.

"What about Mary?" the teacher asks. "Why did the garden change her?"

Another pause, while the students think.

"I think maybe it was because she was taking care of something," Seeja suggests. "Remember in *The Bear's House*, Fran Ellen felt good when she took care of her baby sister?"

"Go on, Seeja," the teacher encourages.

"Well, Mary started taking care of the garden and she liked it when things grew. She took care of it and she felt important."

As the conversation continues, the class contrasts the previous film interpretations with the one shown today. They make a graph on the computer and print it out to indicate class members' favorite version of the story (book, first movie, second movie). Individually they will write their responses to the movie in their personal journals.

WHAT HAPPENED HERE? ONE PERSPECTIVE

The filmmaker's interpretative use of color in the film leads students to discover and discuss metaphors in the story that had not been apparent to them when they originally listened to it. Seeing the garden come alive in technicolor impresses them with its symbolism and leads to a more sophisticated analysis of the story than might otherwise have been possible. Viewing two versions of the story enables the students to see how filmmakers interpret ideas about a story in different ways. The previous week, the class read *Lon Po Po: A Red Riding Hood Story from China*[9] and talked about the similarities and differences between the Chinese and Western versions. The discussion about the two film versions of *The Secret Garden* emerges from this previous conversation and helps students begin to develop the idea of storyteller perspective.

Mrs. Ingram asks open-ended questions that prompt creative and thoughtful responses. When students respond, she encourages them to expand their ideas and gives them sufficient time to think about what they want to say. When her students describe an element of the film, she names it for them, adding a term to their vocabulary that will permit them to think about the idea of "contrast" in future discussions.

The reactions from her students are thoughtful and indicate a serious processing of the story elements. Some students respond by identifying with various characters, while others make connections with other books they have read. Several draw upon the class's community memory to make relationships between story themes. Technology has made it possible for students to discover new layers of meaning in this classic story and has heightened their awareness of the elements of storytelling as they are used in filmmaking.

A word processor is available for use at the three computers in the writing corner. Students are given time each day to enter their own stories and save them on individual discs for printing out when they are finished. Once a week, the computer with laser-disc technology is located in the third-grade classroom. As a group, they explore information related to current theme studies in science or social studies. Individual students take turns researching their own questions on the CD-ROM encyclopedia or viewing programs of special interest.

Intermediate Level

"Man, they didn't even show why the 54th Massachusetts was called the Glory regiment," Marcos complains. "I thought that was one of the most important parts of the story. They even called the movie *Glory* and then they didn't show why. The stuff in the movie doesn't mean as much without knowing that."

"Well, you knew it, didn't you?" Anwar responds.

"Only because I'd already read a book about the Glory regiment," Marcos says.

"Well, what's the problem then?" Anwar asks.

"What about everybody who doesn't know anything about the Civil War or the African American regiments? Most people are only going to see the movie, so it should be accurate."

Mr. Williams's sixth-grade class has just finished watching the movie *Glory* on videotape. It traces the formation of the African American regiment from Massachusetts (the 54th) during the Civil War and chronicles the heroism of its men and their commander, Colonel Robert Gould Shaw, in their gallant and tragic assault of Fort Wagner near Charleston, South Carolina.

"What do some of the rest of you think?" Mr. Williams asks.

"I liked the movie because it made everything seem real," Becca says.

The teacher waits for her to explain.

"You could really see what it was like, to be a soldier . . . to be an African American soldier. It was a terrible life, but they kept going. It made me tired just to watch them march through all the rain and the swamps."

"See," says Anwar, gesturing to Marcos, "the movie makes things real."

"Big deal," Marcos replies. "What's the point if it leaves out important things?"

"What specifically did they leave out that you feel is important to know?" Mr. Williams asks.

"All right," Marcos begins. "For example, the movie leaves out the part where the governor of Massachusetts gives this big speech to the regiment before they leave for war. That's an important part of the story. Remember, he tells them . . ." Marcos picks up his copy of *Undying Glory*[10] and reads a short passage.

> "Wherever its folds shall be unfurled, it will mark the path of glory," the governor said to Shaw as he handed him the American flag . . . "You will never part with that flag so long as a splinter of the staff or a thread of its web remains within your grasp." (p. 34)

"That speech is important to the whole story," Marcos continues. "The colors went forward even when the flag bearer was shot down. And listen to this part that Governor Andrew says about the regiment."

> Then, looking out over the long lines of armed black men in the shape of a huge square, Andrew declared: "I know not, Mr. Commander, when, in all human history, to any given thousand men in arms there has been committed a work at once so proud, so precious, so full of hope and glory as the work committed to you." (p. 34)

"What do you think?" the teacher asks the class again. "Does Marcos have a point?"

"Well, that does sort of make it different to know that," Becca says.

"Maybe different things about stories are important to different people," Will says.

"What do you mean?" Mr. Williams asks.

"Well, maybe the movie writers were trying to tell something different about the regiment, like from the point of view of the soldier, not really the history stuff."

"If they tell a story that really happened, what is their responsibility for historical accuracy?" Mr. Williams asks.

There is a buzz of responses. Everyone is trying to talk at once.

"Whoa, wait a minute," the teacher interrupts. "This looks like a good question for discussion. Let's look at this question," he says, turning to the blackboard, "and two others that are related." He writes all three questions on the board, which everyone copies before they divide into small discussion groups.

1. What story was the movie trying to tell?
2. What story was the book trying to tell?
3. What is the responsibility of both for historical accuracy?

The groups interact with each other for thirty minutes, examining the book, recalling the movie and debating the questions. At the end of the period, Mr. Williams asks each group to report its discussion. One group has decided to write to the author of the book and the producer of the movie, asking them about their purposes in telling the story of the 54th Massachusetts. Marcos's group plans to write to two Civil War historians they have seen on *Civil War Journal*, a documentary program that airs on a cable channel. Another group points out that both the movie and the book credit historical sources to document authenticity. Almost everyone thinks that the purposes for writing the book were different from the purposes for making the movie.

"A movie has to entertain," Anwar says. "And this one might have invented some parts of the story to be more entertaining. That's what movies do. This one is historical fiction."

"Well, the book was more of a biography of Colonel Shaw," Marcos admits. "It probably wasn't trying to do the same thing as the movie. A biography has to be historically accurate as much as possible. There are all kinds of quotes from original documents, like letters and journals and newspapers. Stuff that was really written when it happened."

"That's just it," Jennifer adds. "I think the movie was trying to show what life in the army was like, day to day. The book looked at things more from a historical point of view and was more objective. But the movie still should have told about Colonel Shaw's wife and showed how he changed his mind about his regiment. That was one good thing about the book. It showed parts of his letters to his wife and his father, so you knew more how he felt. The movie didn't do that."

"Do books ever get the facts wrong?" Mr. Williams asks.

There is a pause in the discussion.

"Let me read you something from a mystery story I ran across the other day," the teacher says, and he picks up a book from his desk. "This is a story about a valuable letter that is stolen from a key character in the book. In this passage he's telling the main character why the letter is valuable. Listen to his description and tell me what you think."

Mr. Williams reads a passage that tells of a letter supposedly written by Abraham Lincoln to comfort a widow who had lost her husband in battle.

He says that he understands this loss, since he has recently lost his own son, Todd. When he finishes reading, he looks up at the class.

"Does he mean Tad Lincoln?" Jennifer asks.

"I'm not sure who he means," Mr. Williams replies. "What do you know about this from other things we've studied?"

"Lincoln's oldest son's name was Robert Todd," Marcos says. "But he lived until the 1920s. He's the only son who lived to grow up."

"Yeah," Anwar agrees. "Tad's real name was Thomas."

"Do you remember the names of the sons who died while Lincoln was still alive?" the teacher asks.

"Just a minute," Claire says. "Our group studied Lincoln's family and we have some notes about his children." She looks in her notes. "Here it is . . . one son, Eddie, died when they still lived in Springfield. And Willie was the one who died in the White House. Tad was the youngest and he died seven years after the war was over."

"That can't be right then, what it says in the story," Will says. "Tad was still alive after President Lincoln was killed."

"This book is realistic fiction," Mr. Williams says. "Does it have to be accurate?"

"If it's not accurate, it's not realistic," Jennifer declares.

"Are there some things you can change in a story that you can't change in a biography?" the teacher asks.

"You can't change facts," Marcos says.

"How does this letter compare with the one President Lincoln wrote to Jethro in *Across Five Aprils*[11]?" the teacher asks.

"That was a real letter," Marcos says, "or at least very like one that was really written by President Lincoln."

"So you're saying that Lincoln could have written the letter in *Across Five Aprils*, but not the one in this book?"

"Right. It can be a made-up story, but it has to show people saying and doing things they really would or it doesn't make sense."

"You can't change what a famous person would really do," Anwar says. "I think we should write to that author, too."

"One last question," Mr. Williams says. "What's the difference between what a book or film should do with a biography and what can be portrayed as historical fiction?"

There is a pause while students consider the question. Marcos ventures an answer. "With biography, you have to use things that the person said or wrote, or what reliable people said or wrote about them. It has to be the real thing. You can't make stuff up about a person and call it a biography."

"And how is that different from books like *Across Five Aprils* or the one I just read the excerpt from?" Mr. Williams asks.

"*Across Five Aprils* is true to the people in it and what was happening. Part of it actually happened and the rest is what could have happened," Jennifer says.

"So . . . what about the movie?" the teacher asks.

"It's more like historical fiction," Marcos ventures. "It's based on true stuff, but not every word or event is exactly how it happened."

"And the other book about the Lincoln letter," Will says. "It's supposed to be realistic fiction, but it's not. The author could make up other stuff that happened in the story, even the letter from Lincoln, but she can't change the facts, like which son died in the White House."

WHAT HAPPENED HERE? ONE PERSPECTIVE

Watching a videotaped movie production that uses history as its setting challenges these students to analyze what they see and hear. High-quality film productions help give students a sense of being there, but this experience is enhanced when they have opportunities to interact with books and each other to compare their responses. Mr. Williams encourages students to respond to the movie within the whole-class grouping and moves them into smaller groups when everyone shows interest in getting into the discussion. He challenges them to search their own experience as individuals and to consult their collective memory for shared experiences that will advance the discussion.

You probably noticed how the teacher encouraged students to analyze their ideas about the movie and related books by asking: What do you think? What do you mean? Do books have to be accurate? What do you know about this from other things we've studied? You probably also observed how eager his students were to contact persons who had made story decisions about historical events. Mr. Williams modeled this response early in the year when he encouraged students to write to their favorite authors and to contact professors at the local university for information on a science project. Throughout the year, they have learned to consult primary sources for information and to evaluate carefully what they see and hear for authenticity.

Mr. Williams observes his students' reactions to television programs and is pleased to notice an increased selectivity in viewing habits. As students learn criteria for evaluating books and stories, he asks them to analyze their favorite programs, using the same criteria. Once a week they talk about their responses to TV programs, using the following questions:

1. What do you like about this program?
2. In what ways can you identify with the characters or situation?
3. What do you like about the main character(s)?
4. What is the program basically about?
5. What values do you think the program is trying to promote?
6. How "real" is the story?
7. What makes the show funny? (powerful? real?)
8. Are the characters consistent from week to week (day to day)?

Encouraging students to analyze what they watch helps them begin to notice elements of programs beyond the obvious and moves them from being passive receptors to critical participants. They learn to value and defend their own opinions at an age when the pressure to conform is beginning to encroach on their individuality.

WHAT DO YOU THINK?

How do you evaluate the accuracy of television drama that is derived from recent events in the news? How might you help children evaluate these stories when they watch them at home?

IV. Preparing to Use Technology in the Classroom

Preparation for using technology for student learning will include provisions for hardware, software and interaction. **Hardware** is a term used to describe the instruments of instructional technology: television sets, computers, monitors, modems, fax machines, tape recorders, videotape recorders and players, audiotape recorders and players, and CD-ROM interactive video players. **Software** is material used to record and play back information, such as videotapes, computer discs, audiotapes and compact discs (CDs). Word processors, spreadsheets, data banks and programs for accessing the Internet are also software. **Interaction** refers to the environment you create for students to respond to movies, television and computer presentations and includes the preparation of dialogue questions and opportunities for discussion, writing, or artistic response.

Hardware

Perhaps it seems obvious, but **always** check out any equipment you plan to use in advance. You may have memories of teachers struggling with movie projectors and filmstrip machines that failed to operate correctly. It is better to wait until you feel comfortable and competent using the equipment than to create distraction in the classroom with technology that does not work easily. If the equipment in your school does not operate dependably, it is better not to use it at all because it tends to rule instructional time rather than support it.

The best policy is to experiment with hardware in your classroom at a time when you can read instructions and try out the software you want to use. If you feel uncomfortable around machines, it may be because you lack experience operating them. Give yourself a chance to learn and practice before you call in someone else to operate the equipment in your classroom. Consider asking a fellow teacher, a parent volunteer, a friend or a student to help you learn about the equipment. If you still feel uncomfortable with the technology but want to provide your students with the experience, enlist the help of a parent, teacher's aide or student volunteers to operate the equipment on a regularly scheduled basis. In some schools, there are media specialists who can assist you on a daily or weekly basis.

Whether you operate the equipment or someone else does, it is a good idea to consider in advance what will happen if the equipment does not operate correctly, if it does not arrive on time (this happens with shared-use technology) or the person responsible for operating the equipment is late or does not arrive at all. Your goal in using technology is to provide students with an experience that will enhance their learning. If the technology is not available, plan to extend their understanding in other ways. You might:

1. Choose an additional book or magazine article to read aloud.
2. Provide additional opportunities for students to read supplementary material on their own.

3. Conduct a guided reading session on the book or topic they are studying.
4. Use the time to promote additional responses to the book or topic through writing or artistic expression.

If students are to use audio book tapes or computer programs on their own, you will want to instruct everyone on the proper use of equipment. Enlist student ideas for necessary guidelines and help them simplify their ideas (see Chapter 3 for ways to brainstorm guidelines with a class). As mentioned in Chapter 3, students usually think of guidelines in terms of what they are *not* supposed to do; help them state their ideas in positive terms. Guidelines seem to work the best when they are simple, practical, visible and student generated. When you and your class have decided on the guidelines, post them somewhere close to where the equipment will be used, so they can be referred to easily.

One of the biggest problems with student use of equipment is rough handling. Buttons or keys are punched too hard in repeated use, resulting in broken keyboards and tape recorders. It is in everyone's best interests to protect the equipment. Be sure to demonstrate to students **exactly** how you want them to use the machines. Ask your students to show you that they understand this instruction by demonstrating how **they** will use the equipment.

Software

Just as you would read any book before using it in class, you will want to preview any television programs, videotapes, audiotapes or computer programs before using them in the classroom. When you want students to watch a program that cannot be previewed, consult your professional journals or the television station that is broadcasting it to find out as much as you can ahead of time. Often, schools will be alerted by public television stations or cable companies when special programs in science, the social sciences or the arts are being broadcast.

If software is to be used by individual students working on their own or in small groups, your review of audiotapes and computer programs will alert you ahead of time to any difficulties students might have. Take notes in your teaching journal that will help you prepare students for these independent experiences. If the programs will require a teacher or helper to be available, consider using these programs during Book Buddies time or when an aide can be present. Avoid using software that cannot be managed easily by students working independently or with a partner.

When you plan to use a tape, film, television program or interactive video to create a common experience for your class, you will need to prepare for the interaction that accompanies this presentation in the same way that you prepare for a guided reading session. Guided watching helps students develop skills of analysis, as they learn to observe details and make connections between their own experience and the media presentation. Ask questions similar to those used in guided reading and encourage students to respond to the presentation in writing, discussion or artistic expression.

What kinds of questions will help students develop analytical skills? What questions will encourage them to interact with each other, sharing ideas and enlarging their view of the world? Here are some suggestions:

1. How does the film establish a point of view? If this story were written in a book, who would be the narrator? The main character? An objective third person?
2. How does the film emphasize the importance of certain characters, by placing the camera view from their perspective or by focusing on their reactions in key scenes?
3. How does sound or the intensity of background music indicate the occurrence of important events? How does music and the use of light help establish the mood of a setting? Compare these techniques with the way writers emphasize the importance of characters or events and the way they create the mood for a story.
4. What do you think the filmmaker is trying to say in this film? or What do you think this movie or program is about?
5. How does the director use scenes and sounds to interpret the story or make a statement? Compare this to the way a book author or illustrator creates story with words or drawings.
6. How are characters made important visually, by filming from below to make them look bigger or from above to make them look smaller? This technique is well demonstrated in the movie depiction of *The Borrowers*,[12] but students can also observe this camera angle in cartoons.
7. What are some camera techniques for establishing a setting in just a few seconds? An example is showing the outside of a building where the characters are located to indicate where the action is. Ask students to compare this way of establishing setting with the way it is done in the first few paragraphs of a book.
8. At the beginning of the film or program, what makes you want to see more of it?

Many teachers are intimidated by computers or programs that their students seem to understand better than they do. Some resolve this by not bringing the new technology into the classroom. Others discover distinct benefits in this kind of situation, like the fifth-grade teacher quoted in Seymour Papert's book, *The Children's Machine: Rethinking School in the Age of the Computer*:[13]

The first few times I noticed that the students had problems I couldn't even understand, let alone solve, I struggled to avoid facing the fact that I could not keep up my stance of knowing more than they did. I was afraid that giving it up would undermine my authority as a teacher. But the situation became worse. Eventually I broke down and said I didn't understand the problem—go discuss it with some of the others in the class who might be able to help. Which they did. And it turned out that together the kids could figure out a solution. Now the amazing thing is that what I was afraid of turned out to be a liberation. I no longer had to fear being exposed. I was. I no longer had to pretend. And the wonderful thing was that I realized that my bluff was called for more than computers. I felt I could no longer pretend to know everything in other subjects as well. What a relief! It has changed my relationship with children and with myself. My class has become much more of a collaborative community where we are all learning together. (pp. 65–66)

As this teacher allowed his students to explore beyond his own level of knowledge and expertise, he gained a new perception of himself as a colearner in the classroom.

WHAT DO YOU   What kinds of experiences have you had with computers and video
THINK?   recording? Do you feel comfortable operating this kind of equipment? In what areas will you want more experience?

V. Including Everyone

Technology offers many possibilities for extending and enriching the experiences of all students, especially those just beginning to learn English, those who have learning difficulties or those who are physically or mentally challenged. Listening stations that feature headphones and tape recorders provide the opportunity for students to practice reading books with the **impress method** at any time. When they listen to a story and follow the words in the accompanying book, they are using both sight and sound to impress the reading experience on their memories. Monitor displays in large print are available for students who have vision problems, and they can conserve reading time by listening to books read aloud on tape. Special earphones are available for students with hearing problems that allow them to listen to books at a level that is comfortable and not harmful to their hearing.

If you have students who are challenged physically by muscular dystrophy or cerebral palsy, you may be provided with a computer and other video equipment that provides them with assisted reading and writing support. A rod attached to a headstrap allows these children to touch a large keypad to enter data, which is then read aloud through the sound system on the computer.

Students who have attention difficulties respond particularly well to earphones and taped books, which shut out other distractions to their learning. The best rule of thumb is to maximize the use of any media that will enhance participation by all students. Be alert to any use of equipment that might impede student interaction with presentations or interaction with the rest of the group. This includes attention to students who may want to involve themselves in computer activity to the exclusion of reading and interacting with other students.

For children who face the challenge of English as a second language, computer programs provide the benefit of individual tutoring. Multimedia programs provide instant response, offer the child multiple ways of learning and accommodate individual proficiency levels. Students can draw freehand on computers, label pictures, make sentences and record ideas about pictures using a microphone. Programs such as Mercer Mayer's *My Grandma and I* read a story aloud while the action is played out on the screen. The program will pause under student control and allow the student to read the words. If a word is not familiar, the child can touch the screen and the computer will pronounce the word or give its meaning.

Technology provides excellent support for the visual, auditory and physical challenges some students face and offers extended opportunities for individualized practice and instruction. For all children in the classroom, technology offers visual and auditory experiences that extend and enhance language learning and that encourage student responses in reading, writing, research and problem solving.

Books to Increase Understanding

The following books enable the reader to enter the lives of children who face daily challenges of disability. Their stories provide insight and understanding into experiences most of us do not have to face.

Tuck Triumphant[14] A family adopts a Korean orphan and discovers that he is deaf. The story describes how the family deals with a challenge it believes to be insurmountable. This book is a sequel to *The Trouble with Tuck*, which dealt with the blindness of Tuck, a pet Labrador retriever. The resolution of both stories is highly creative and inspirational.

My Buddy[15] This is a touching story of a young boy with muscular dystrophy, who is assisted by a golden retriever named Buddy. Based on a real boy and his dog, the book describes the challenges the boy faces daily and the help he receives from his companion dog.

Helen Keller's Teacher[16] As a little girl, Helen Keller lost her sight and hearing as the result of illness. A teacher who was partially sighted herself reached out to Helen and helped her learn how to meet the severe challenges of her disability. This inspiring story champions the brave and determined Helen and her equally courageous teacher, Annie Sullivan.

WHAT DO YOU THINK? In what ways has the use of technology enhanced your own learning? Have you examined the equipment available for special-needs students? Did you attend school with children who faced physical challenges? How were they included in the regular program of the classroom?

VI. Step-by-Step: Using Technology in the Classroom

In the classrooms described above, teachers used videotapes to provide additional language and learning experiences for third-grade students who had read *The Secret Garden* and sixth-grade students who were studying the Civil War. They also used audiotapes in listening centers and provided opportunities for students to use the word-processing capabilities of the computer. One of the teachers incorporated interactive video-disc technology into a theme study to extend her students' understanding of animals. These individual or shared sight/sound experiences created new responses to the books from which the films were adapted and helped students discover new layers of meaning in the topics under discussion. In the sections below, suggestions are given for possible uses of technology in the classroom—ideas to help you start thinking about how you might use programs and equipment in your own classroom.

Educational Television

Excellent programs to support learning can be found on the public broadcasting stations. Supported by corporate and individual charitable donations, they are broadcast without commercial interruption. The best of these programs feature in-depth treatment of topics in the sciences (polar bears, undersea exploration, weather), social sciences (Civil War, civil rights, biographies) and the arts (classic and contemporary children's literature, ballet, opera, painting, sculpture, architecture). Most schools will have yearly schedules of PBS programs that will help you identify material that can be used to extend or enrich literature and theme studies in your classroom. Local television guides will confirm the broadcast of particular programs in your area.

In most cases, you will have to tape these programs when they are broadcast and use them at a time that is convenient for you. Many teachers record programs at home, but some schools will provide this service for you. School or district media centers often have permanent copies of programs that can be checked out for use in the classroom. Many of these are also available from your public library.

Although there are regular daily programs on public broadcasting that feature elements of reading instruction, most of these are aimed at supporting basal reading programs, with an emphasis on letter identification. You might want to watch for programs that model a more integrated approach, such as those that feature reading aloud or review books in an appealing way. *Reading Rainbow* is a program that explores a single book or topic in a half-hour format. Children from ages five to ten review books they enjoy and tell why they like them. Many teachers use this peer-review technique in their own classrooms and tape reviews of books to be used in other classes. Some schools sponsor a regular exchange of taped student book reviews with pen pal schools in the United States or in other countries. Teachers also tape student reviews for exchange at grade level in their own school or districtwide and encourage older students to create interesting reviews of books to promote reading in younger readers.

Cable television provides exceptional programming to support and extend literature and theme studies. Most schools can access special student news programs and presentations on literature, science, social studies and the arts through arrangements with local cable companies. *The Discovery Channel, The History Channel, The Arts and Entertainment Network* and *The Learning Channel* are just a few examples of cable networks that design programs specifically for instructional use. Information about the specific support they offer teachers is available from each of these sources or your cable company.

Videotaped Programs These are generally available in your school or district media centers and can also be borrowed from your local, regional and state library systems. You can examine video programs with students, using questions similar to those used for evaluating illustrations in books. For example:

1. How did the producers of the movie, TV program or documentary create this effect?
2. Did it look the way you imagined? How would you have done it differently?
3. Did they stick to the story? The facts?
4. Why do you think they might have changed the story or facts?
5. Were the characters accurate? The setting?

Before class, you will want to practice using the pause or review buttons so you can emphasize and repeat portions of the tape or draw attention to features you want students to notice.

Audio- and videotapes can enhance students' experience of literature in valuable ways. Treat your students to the voice of Dylan Thomas reading his autobiographical sketch, "A Child's Christmas in Wales," as film portrays the Christmas he remembers from his boyhood. Add the sight and sound of the perpetual Narnian winter with a film version of *The Lion, the Witch and the Wardrobe*. Let students hear Robert Frost or Maya Angelou recite their gifts of poetry to newly elected American presidents with interactive video. Allow them to hear the charming children's voices of the Beatrix Potter films to help them identify even more closely with their animal counterparts.

Tape Recorder Creative teachers have been making good use of the tape recorder for years. This technology is usually standard equipment in most schools and can be used in the following ways:

Oral biographies Students interview family members or friends about their early lives.

Special effects Students create sound accompaniments to writing projects that are to be shared in class or sound tracks to accompany student plays and puppet shows.

Story extenders Prerecorded sounds enhance the experience of a story: geese honking, waves dashing against the shore, the thud-thud of cannon in battle, the rat-a-ta-ratta of air hammers or the blare of taxi horns in the city.

Read-aloud practice Students can record their reading for self-evaluation purposes. They can also work in pairs to evaluate each other's reading.

Listening stations These are places in the classroom where students can listen to books as they follow along or look at the pictures. A listening center can be as modest as a single tape recorder with a set of earphones. It may involve multiple earphones for a group of children who want to listen to the same book or recording equipment that will allow a number of students to listen to different books. Sets of books and tapes are available from commercial sources, such as school book clubs, or you can create them yourself with the help of teachers, parent volunteers or students.

Interactive Video   These systems use a special type of compact disc player, television equipment or a computer and sound system to create a multimedia experience for the viewer. Encyclopedias and entire libraries are stored for easy access on laser video discs. Special programs in the content areas allow students to read about colonial times, see reenactments from Williamsburg, listen to period music and research special interests associated with the founding of the country. Other discs feature moving pictures and sounds of domestic and wild animals. Still others chronicle the African American experience with visual and audio profiles of famous scientists, politicians and artists.

Computers   This technology can assist language learning in several ways, but perhaps its most important function is as a word processor, to facilitate the creating, editing and storing of student writing. While word processing is the most commonly used computer tool, there are also programs with speech synthesizers to help students learn unfamiliar words and ones that include an on-line dictionary and thesaurus, text commentaries, spelling and grammar checkers and writing tutorials. Databases on floppy and compact discs provide entire libraries of information for students to browse for ideas or explore for research. Other programs allow student writers to examine their writing line by line or assist them as they write or analyze poetry.

The best computer programs are those that are the most basic and allow for flexible and creative use by students. These include simple word processing packages, graphics packages that feature freehand illustration of stories and a variety of print fonts to publish books, and Logo programming, where children write about their experiences and keep journals of their exploration and experimentation.

Word Processing   Most primary classes use some version of the Bank Street Writer,[17] a simple word processing package that allows students to write, revise their work, store it on a disc and retrieve it with easy-to-use menu commands. Intermediate students may use AppleWriter or WordPerfect in a Windows format, which allows students to enter and manipulate text in more complex ways.

Graphics   Using these programs, teachers and students can create their own books, complete with illustrations and different typefonts. Students can also use these packages to create original artwork as a response to literature.

Internet   Schools that participate in this access ramp to the information highway allow students to experience real-time interaction with other users via the computer and a modem (computer phone). Students can talk to experts and other students across the United States and the world using a variety of user services and e-mail (electronic messages). This system provides limitless opportunities for students to explore ideas and access information they want to know.

LogoWriter   This program includes both word processing and graphics production as part of its highly interactive programming. It encourages students to practice language and thinking skills, using models from one subject area to explain or understand ideas in another. By using what the authors refer to as "macrocontexts," students learn to relate learning tasks to their everyday experience by asking: Have I seen a problem like this before? What do I already know that might help me with this problem? Obviously these kinds of questions are useful thinking tools in any area of the curriculum.

The goal of Logo programming is to help children see themselves as designers of knowledge. This metaphor is similar to the one used by constructivists when they say that students are "meaning-makers." Designers of Logo programming believe that with this computer language, children can program to learn rather than learn to program. As children design programs to play with words or move the turtle (a triangle-shaped cursor) around the screen, they are asked to predict, guess, explain and reflect on what happens. A record of this thinking is kept in student journals. The ideas of younger children are recorded by the teacher during whole-class explorations or by an aide or Turtle Buddy for individual interaction with the programs.

Observe how this first-grade teacher uses the techniques of guided reading to talk about Logo:

"What do you think this command is called?" Mrs. Terry asks, as she types in a command and the cursor disappears.

"Ghost!" Jeffrey guesses.

"A good guess!" Mrs. Terry replies. "Why did you guess that?"

"Because it disappears and comes back just like a ghost," Jeffrey says.

"That would be a good name for the command," Mrs. Terry agrees. "Let's enter the first letter of ghost and see what happens." She enters G. An error message appears. "We'll have to keep trying," the teacher says. "Who remembers what the cursor is called?"

"Turtle!" Ben says. "Disappearing turtle. Try *DT*."

"Good idea," the teacher agrees and enters *DT*. Again, there is an error message. "Watch as I enter the command again and see if that gives you a clue." She enters *HT* and the cursor disappears.

"Do it again," someone asks, and all watch the screen carefully.

"*HT*," Debbie says. "That's the command. *HT*."

"What do you think it stands for?" Mrs. Terry asks.

There is silence while everyone thinks.

"Help turtle?" Kevin guesses. The teacher types in the command. There is an error message.

"Heavenly turtle? Like when he disappears, he goes to heaven?" Meg adds. The command is typed and an error message occurs.

"Good guesses," Mrs. Terry says. "Very creative. Think about what the command helps the turtle do."

"Hide!" Debbie says. "It hides the turtle. *HT* is hide turtle."

The teacher types in Hide Turtle and the cursor disappears. The children clap their hands and someone pounds Debbie on the back to congratulate her.

This session was a cooperative exploration, one that focused on thinking and problem solving. Finding and using just the right words in an understandable order are basic principles of communication, and the experience above creates a model that the teacher can refer to later when there are problems to solve in writing. This experience also helps the rules of grammar make sense, as tools of clear communication.

In addition to its use for word processing, LogoWriter can also teach the elements of summarizing to help students better understand and remember what they read or hear. This special program lists members of a category that students can summarize in a word or sentence. Children can also create categories of their own. For example, they may be given the following list: tomato, chicken noodle, vegetable, mushroom, cream of chicken. The category, of course, is soup. One student created the following list: ball, spoon, bottle, toys, hat. It mystified his classmates until an older brother recognized the list as "things a baby throws on the floor"!

Students can also use LogoWriter to compose summaries of paragraphs, writing the basic idea of what the paragraph is about without repeating features or including features that are unimportant. From Logo programming, students also learn the idea of a variable and how syntax works. If they do not write the command correctly, the computer cannot execute the command. It emphasizes the importance of good communication to understanding.

Additional features of LogoWriter include the idea of geometry microworlds, where students can experiment with line, shape and space. It is possible to create a cursor that acts as an object would in a vacuum, allowing students to explore the principles of Newtonian physics. Students can create graphs and charts, make maps, explore the mechanics of simple machines, such as gears and levers, and experiment with ideas such as work, force and ratio. At all levels of instruction, students write about their explorations in Logo journals, recording their questions and discoveries each time they interact with the program. Journal entries stimulate new ideas about things to try and provide a resource for individual and group problem solving. These activities help students develop skills of **metacognition**, the ability to analyze and reflect on one's own thinking.

WHAT DO YOU THINK? Have you ever explored Logo? Does it sound interesting or appealing to you? Where might you get some experience working with this program?

VII. If This Is Your Situation

If you have had little experience using computers or audio-visual equipment, you will want to begin gaining this experience as soon as possible. Many universities have computer or curriculum labs where students can build their skills in this area. If these facilities are not available, you can gain experience by volunteering to help with computers or audio-visual equipment at the school where you observe or student teach. Experienced teachers are usually happy to help you learn and appreciate any assistance you can provide for them in the classroom.

Even if you are computer literate, you may be thwarted in your opportunities to use this knowledge if your school has limited facilities available. Many older school buildings are prohibited by wiring codes from installing computers and restricted from repairing their wiring by shrinking budgets. You can help the decision makers in your districts by sharing your expertise and researching how other districts solve similar problems. Grants are available from corporations that help fund these projects for schools. Some schools set up a separate computer lab, which allows special wiring to be brought in for just one room. While it is preferable to have this equipment available in each classroom, this situation will still allow your students to become familiar with the equipment, develop word-processing skills and explore quality programs.

WHAT DO YOU THINK? How do you assess your own information and skill with computers and other supportive technology? Would you feel comfortable in a situation where your students understood computers better than you?

VIII. Evaluating Progress

The most basic questions to ask about the use of technology in the classroom are these: Does it support or enhance instruction in a way that is obviously helpful and valuable? Or does the use of technology get in the way of instruction and waste time? The following questions are designed to help you evaluate the positive and negative aspects of media use.

Positive signs

1. Does it generate excitement in a topic or a story?
2. Do students seek out more information in books or reference materials?
3. Do they report watching educational stations?
4. Do parents comment on a change in TV viewing or requests for computer programs?
5. Does it increase the quality and quantity of discussion, writing, and reading?
6. Does it increase the level of participation and response?
7. Does it provide an experience students otherwise could not have? (It is better to go to the zoo to see live animals than to watch live animals on tape, but if a zoo trip is not possible, provide the tape.)
8. Does it stimulate imagination rather than reduce the need to create one's own images?
9. Does it increase the desire to read or the necessity to read?
10. Is the response active?

Negative signs

1. Are students bored with films, tapes, or TV?

2. Are they absorbed exclusively in technology to the exclusion of reading and other activities?
3. Does technology interrupt or get in the way of a learning experience?
4. Do students become less active participants in their learning?
5. Does it use time that could be better used for other activities?
6. Is it used to fill time or to cover lack of preparation? It is better to have students take out a book and read it than to waste time watching a film that has no purpose.
7. Does it reduce the need for imagination?
8. Is the response passive?
9. Does it reduce the need for reading to find information?
10. Does it reduce the desire to read for information, problem solving or pleasure?

Any use of technology that reduces student participation or response should be looked at closely. Books with computer sound chips that actually read a story can be used to generate interest in reading or encourage participation by students who have learning disabilities. But these are transition or novelty features for most students and should be used with discretion. The best rule of thumb is to look at the consequences of this interaction. If students read more as a result or seem to show better understanding, then using media readers can be helpful. If students consistently choose this type of assisted reading, you may want to explore other ways to help them interact with books.

WHAT DO YOU THINK? Can you think of examples in your own experience where the use of technology helped you learn something that could not have been gained in any other way? Do you remember any instances where the use of technology interfered with your learning?

IX. Creating Partners

If your school has computer facilities, you may want to team your class with one that is older or younger in a Tech Buddies program. Children at different grade levels usually work very productively at the computer—exploring the Internet, creating e-mail, developing skill at word processing, exploring Logo worlds, creating stories or making books, or using desktop publishing and a printer. Students who are computer literate also enjoy helping teachers master the fundamentals of computing and are usually very patient and creative mentors.

You may want to invite parents, other teachers and business/professional people from the community to demonstrate the different ways computers are used for work and learning. Visits to the local newspaper or printshop can provide an interesting look at the ways technology supports the work of people who write or publish for a living.

WHAT DO YOU THINK? When you imagine the work the children in your classroom will do when they are grown, what do you see them doing? What kinds of language and learning skills will they need?

X. Perspectives

Seymour Papert, who pioneered the programming language called Logo, believes that computers can influence the way students learn. While it is true that computers are excellent information processors, Papert does not see this function as being the most important to education. He believes the most important role for the computer is to help students learn how to think about the world. Papert observes that computers in many schools have limited use and that their real impact will not be realized until all children have their own computer to explore ideas and create their own knowledge. He believes that the computer can actually influence the way students learn, as they are challenged to think about their own thought processes and problem solving. This use of the computer will eventually make teaching more interesting and challenging, if not easier. Papert writes in *Mindstorms*:[18]

> The revolution I envision is of ideas, not technology. It consists of new understandings of specific subject domains and in new understandings of the process of learning itself. . . . In my vision, technology has two roles. One is heuristic: The computer presence has catalyzed the emergence of ideas. The other is instrumental: The computer will carry ideas into a world larger than the research centers where they have incubated up to now. (p. 186)

When computers are used effectively, they can help students explore the world in ways previously undreamed of. Through the Internet, CD-ROM and Logo programming, students can search out ideas and alternative solutions for the questions they ask. Like a good teacher, a high-quality computer program can activate student curiosity, provide support or a safe environment to investigate an idea and supply a framework that will help students develop the knowledge and skills they seek.

WHAT DO YOU THINK? What kinds of things make you curious? Do you closely observe nature or life around you? What kinds of things do you notice? In what ways can you see yourself encouraging curiosity in your classroom?

XI. Exploring Professional Literature

Science and Children is a journal of the National Science Teachers Association (NSTA). Designed for elementary teachers, it features articles describing science activities for the classroom. Classroom activities integrate language learning with scientific inquiry and feature many opportunities for children to discuss, read and write about topics in science. Whether you teach science in your own classroom or in a departmentalized situation at the intermediate level, this journal provides helpful professional assistance.

The journal also contains reviews of research related to science education and helpful tips from practicing educators. Software programs are reviewed as a regular feature, with information on cost, hardware requirements and operation. Each program is classroom tested by the reviewers, with both positive and negative results noted. Reviews also recommend grade levels where the programs might be most appropriate and provide suggestions for using the software in the context of a classroom science program. *NSTA Reports!*, a newspaper with current information on science teaching, reviews pertinent equipment, books and tapes and provides readers with lists of materials that can be ordered inexpensively or free.

Each issue of the journal contains games and posters or charts for classroom use. Members of NSTA receive *Science and Children* (or its instructional-level equivalent), *NSTA Reports!* and special mailings of interest to elementary science teachers. Student memberships are less than half the cost of memberships for practicing teachers. Information on membership in NSTA is available from Member Services Department, National Science Teachers Association, 1840 Wilson Blvd., Arlington, VA 22201-3000, or you can contact them at (703) 243-7100.

WHAT DO YOU THINK? Do you enjoy reading about science and exploring scientific ideas? What science programs do you watch on television? What is appealing to you about these programs? How might you use children's literature and language activities to explore ideas in science?

XII. Resources for Teaching

The following resources will assist you in developing technological and media support for your classroom program.

Welcome to . . . CD-ROM[19] This book provides helpful reviews of 100 of the best programs available on CD-ROM software. Reviews include the formats in which the program is available, the publisher, appropriate age-level use and list price. The content of the program is described, along with any special sound or interactive features. This is an excellent book to use as a reference when you want to know the important learning features of a program for your students.

Welcome to . . . Internet: From Mystery to Mastery[20] This is an easy-to-understand guide to the Internet. Chapter 6 is especially helpful for teachers, as it describes the educational resources available. Distance learning provides television classes, and the National Education BBS (bulletin board service) provides resources for students in grades K through 12. You can access listings for educational software and obtain literature reviews. Card catalogs in libraries all over the world can be accessed through the Internet, as can the

ERIC (Educational Resources Information Center). Big Sky Telegraph is a consortium of educators interested in sharing resources and information about computers and on-line education. Kidsphere Educational Network is an international network for students and teachers. Bookstores and sources for art and music are available, as are weather maps, data from the U.S. Naval Observatory, the NASA Lunar and Planetary Institute, and the Extragalactic database. You can also find Hubble telescope information, shuttle and satellite images and earthquake information.

The Discovery Channel This channel provides teacher's guides with suggestions for using programs in the curriculum areas of literature, science, social studies and humanities. Programming features regular presentations or uninterrupted video with study questions and answers. You can find out more about these programs through your school or local cable company or by writing or calling directly.

The Arts and Entertainment Network Drama, literature, history, biography and the arts are featured in an appealing format. Programs can be taped and used in the classroom for one-time use if your school does not have cable facilities.

National Public Radio Programs feature literature, arts, science, technology and current events. Daily in-depth interviews and essays deal with current events, environmental issues, politics, the arts, history and literature.

Public Broadcasting System Excellent presentations are given in drama, literature, history, biography, current events, social issues, politics, science, and the arts. Many programs are available in school media centers or the public library.

Shelly Duvall's Fairy Tale Theatre Well-drawn adaptations of classic folktales and fairy tales, which appeal to all ages, are featured.

Reading Rainbow Various themes related to a well-written book are explored by the show's host. Topics are as varied as scuba diving, spelunking and square dancing. Children reviewers promote other books related to the theme by telling what the book is about and why they enjoyed the book. Watching the program can provide both teachers and students with good ideas about new books to explore.

Seeding Mindstorms with LogoWriter: Using Logo in the Elementary Classroom.[21] This manual features forty-three lessons with LogoWriter, described by the authors as classroom environments that are learner directed and teacher guided.

STEP is a NASA-sponsored program for children in K–12 classrooms. It brings images from the United States, Russian, Chinese and Japanese weather satellites into classrooms via an inexpensive antenna and receiver linked to a personal computer with display software. These images promote class discussions and relate to studies in physical science, math, geography and the social sciences. STEP offers training and implementation for teachers, ongoing support, a newsletter and an electronic bulletin board. More information is available from STEP@ERIM, P.O. Box 143001, Ann Arbor, MI 48113.

WHAT DO YOU THINK? Are you familiar with any of the resources described above? What has been your experience with them? How will this experience affect the types of resources you help make available to your students?

XIII. Reflections

From a Teacher's Journal—The Author

Does previous knowledge influence the way a person experiences an event? If I did not already believe this, my experience with Eric Carle's book *The Very Quiet Cricket* confirmed it. Gail Nave, the kindergarten teacher at Summerfield, handed me the book to look at one morning, while she took her class to P.E. I sat in the empty kindergarten room and enjoyed the charming story, which was made even more delightful by the coincidental (I thought) chirping of a cricket in the cloakroom as I turned the last page. When Gail returned, I told her about my experience. She laughed as she showed me that it was a computer chip in the book that produced the chirp.

Later in the day, I observed the book being read aloud to a small group of primary children. When the last page was turned and the book chirped, I expected them to be surprised, but one boy said immediately, "Neat-O! A computer chip!"

In class, I recommended the book to my students, and about a year later one of them called me with this story. She had finished reading the book aloud to a group of children who had few experiences with any books, much less one with a computer chip in it. She opened and closed the book several times to show them that something in the book was creating the sound.

"Why do you suppose the chirping stops when I close the book?" she asked them.

"Because you're squashing the cricket, teacher!" one boy exclaimed.

TRYING OUT THE CHAPTER IDEAS

1. Have you ever read a book and then seen the movie made from it? Or have you ever seen a movie and then read the book it was based on? What was your experience? Which did you enjoy the most? Why do you think this happened?

2. What do you remember about the technology used in your own schooling? Describe any event you can recall and evaluate it, using the criteria from Section 6.

3. What value do you see in helping students become critical observers of what they read, watch on TV or listen to on the radio?

4. Do you think that books (and reading) will become obsolete in the next century? Imagine the conditions that might bring this about.

5. Visit a school that uses multimedia technology and ask to see how CD-ROM applications are used in the classroom.

6. Visit an electronics store and request demonstrations of multimedia encyclopedias and other available educational programs.

7. Tape an oral biography from someone in your family. Share your project with other class members.

8. Conduct taped interviews, asking older friends or family members about their favorite radio programs when they were children. Compare your findings with other class members.

9. Watch a television program that could be used for classroom instruction. Write down any ideas that occur to you as you watch it.

10. Locate someone who uses the Internet. Sit in on a session and observe the kinds of information that can be accessed through this system.

Notes

1. Leo Marx, "Does Improved Technology Mean Progress?" in *Technology and the Future*, 6th ed., edited by Albert H. Teich (New York: St. Martin's Press, 1993).
2. Bertram Bruce, "Roles For Computers in Teaching the English Language Arts," in *Handbook of Research on Teaching the English Language Arts*, edited by James Flood et al. (New York: Macmillan, 1991).
3. B. Bruce and S. Michaels, "Classroom Contexts and Literacy Development: How Writing Systems Shape the Teaching and Learning of Composition," technical report (Urbana, Ill.: Center for the Study of Reading, University of Illinois at Urbana-Champaign, 1989).
4. G. W. McConkie and D. Zola, "Computer Aided Reading: An Environment for Development Research," paper presented at the Society for Research on Child Development, Toronto, Canada, 1985.
5. S. Marcus and S. Blau, "Not Seeing Is Relieving: Invisible Writing with Computers," *Educational Technology* 11(1983): 12–15.
6. Family-authorized version of Beatrix Potter's *The Tale of Peter Rabbit* (Bergenfield, N.J.: Viking, 1987).
7. Ludwig Bemelmans, *Madeline* (New York: Viking, 1987).
8. Francis Hodgson Burnett, *The Secret Garden* (Scranton, Pa.: Harper & Row, 1962).
9. Ed Young, trans., *Lon Po Po: A Red Riding Hood Story from China* (New York: Philomel, 1989). A 1000-year-old tale, colorfully illustrated with impressionistic paintings.
10. Clinton Cox, *Undying Glory: The Story of the Massachusetts 54th Regiment* (New York: Scholastic, 1991).
11. Irene Hunt, *Across Five Aprils* (River Grove, Ill.: Follett, 1964).
12. Mary Norton, *The Borrowers* (New York: Harcourt, 1953). The adventures of little people who live unseen by their human companions. They "borrow" the things they need for food, clothing and shelter from humans. Now you know what happened to the socks that never come out of the dryer!
13. Seymour Papert, *The Children's Machine: Rethinking School in the Age of the Computer* (New York: Basic Books, 1993).
14. Theodore Taylor, *Tuck Triumphant* (New York: Doubleday, 1991).
15. Audrey Osofsky, *My Buddy* (Salt Lake City, Utah: Henry Holt, 1992).
16. Margaret Davidson, *Helen Keller's Teacher* (New York: Scholastic, 1965).
17. Bank Street College of Education, The Bank Street Writer. Available at computer software stores or from Scholastic Inc., P.O. Box 7502, Jefferson City, MO 65102-9968.
18. Seymour Papert, *Mindstorms: Children, Computers and Powerful Ideas* (New York: Basic Books, 1980).
19. Tom Benford, *Welcome to . . . CD-ROM* (New York: MIS:Press/Henry Holt, 1993).
20. Tom Badgett and Corey Sandler, *Welcome to . . . Internet: From Mystery to Mastery* (New York: MIS:Press/Henry Holt, 1993).
21. Richard Lehrer, Joan Littlefield, Betty Wottreng, and Nan Youngerman, *Seeding Mindstorms with LogoWriter: Using Logo in the Elementary Classroom*, rev. 2d ed. (Fontana, Wisc.: Interactive Education Technologies, 1993).

CHAPTER ELEVEN

Exploring the Curriculum with Language, Literature and Themes

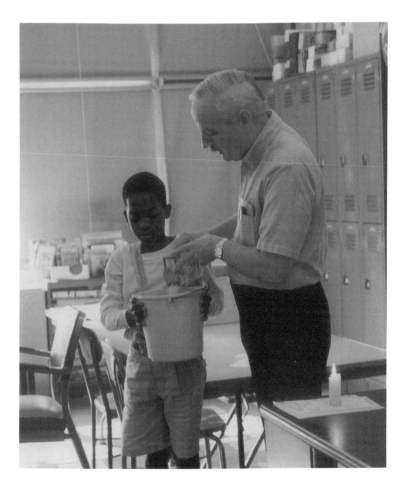

WHAT'S HAPPENING HERE? This teacher supports his students' natural interest in science with hands-on experiences in the classroom. Students talk together to predict and explain scientific phenomena and read to find out more about what they have experienced. It is important to provide a variety of opportunities for students to explore ideas in the content areas, including reading, writing and drawing their understanding of what they observe.

Knowledge is of two kinds. We know a subject ourselves, or we know where we can find information upon it.

—Samuel Johnson

We cannot create observers by saying "observe," but by giving them the power and means for this observation . . .

—Maria Montessori

You don't want to cover a subject; you want to uncover it.

—David Hawkins

LOOKING AHEAD

1. What is exploratory language and why is it important to learning?
2. How can children's trade-book literature assist content area learning?
3. How are themes used to organize classroom learning?
4. What is a theme cycle and how does it differ from a theme unit?
5. What are the alternative languages of learning?
6. How can drawing or drama help students learn?
7. What information does artistic response provide to the teacher?
8. What is information literacy?
9. How does resource-based learning help students develop literacy?

IN 25 WORDS OR LESS   Integrating language learning into content area studies allows students to develop language skills as they explore ideas in mathematics, science and the social studies.

I. Focus: Using Language, Literature and Themes to Explore the Curriculum

Each of the previous chapters in this text examined an activity of literacy learning in the classroom: reading aloud, independent reading, literature selection, exploration of literature in groups, individual conferences, writing, listening, speaking, mini-lessons and learning with technology. This chapter focuses more specifically on the ways language and literature can be used as tools to understand concepts in the content areas and to make connections among many kinds of knowledge.

Traditional schooling methods often assume that students are empty containers to be filled up with knowledge. Teachers who help students use language and literature to explore the world see children as persons who already possess experience and knowledge relevant to the concepts and ideas of content learning. They know that students have intimate contact with people, places and things that are the same object of study by mathematicians, scientists and social scientists. They also know that many of their questions are of the same kind, such as: How does the world work? and Why do people behave the way they do? When language is used to promote an integrated view of the curriculum, students learn that their thoughts and questions about the world encompass all disciplines of knowledge and that there are many ways to respond to and communicate these ideas. They begin to see school as a place that will help them find answers to the very real questions they have about the world.

It is important for students to have the time and materials necessary to explore ideas and communicate what they are learning in a variety of ways. In addition to reading, writing, listening and speaking, children need opportunities to expand their understanding of literature, mathematics, science and the social studies through the expressive arts of music, drawing, painting, sculpting, model-making, drama and movement. According to Karen Gallas,[1] these expressive arts are powerful **alternative languages of learning**, which allow students to think about ideas and share what they have learned in more complex and personally meaningful ways. The arts allow children to speak creatively about what they understand, what they are thinking and what they want to know. They help make children's thinking visible, to themselves, their peers and the teacher. These responses permit a more accurate assessment of children's understanding and often generate new kinds of conversations among students and between students and teachers.

As students observe and talk about mathematical and scientific concepts in their experience, they learn how to translate their questions about the world into these special languages. In the process, they discover the power of these languages to explore ideas and events. When students write about an object or event in the classroom and compare their observations with those of other students, they learn that others may see things differently than they do. Others may see things they missed or from a different perspective. When they think, write and talk about future events or the causes of natural phenomena, they learn to speculate, predict and hypothesize. They begin to see that when persons talk about ideas, the conversation flows outward to encompass all kinds of knowledge. As they observe, discuss, research, organize and share what they discover in the content areas, they also come to know and appreciate the language tools that mathematicians, scientists and social scientists use for inquiry and communication.

One of the most widely used methods of relating learning across subject matter disciplines is the **theme**, which is a broad idea or concept around which learning can be organized. There are several approaches to theme learning, including the **theme unit**, **theme topic** and **theme cycle**. These approaches vary in terms of their comprehensiveness, the level of teacher organization required and the amount of student participation encouraged in the planning and development of the theme.

In the traditional classroom, themes usually refer to **units of study**. These units may be developed by individual teachers, curriculum committees or commercial publishers. Although most involve active student participation, the teacher (school district, teaching team, state, publisher) selects the theme to be studied and plans the activities. Typically, the content areas of social studies or science provide the unifying theme, with all areas of the curriculum drawn upon to study a particular topic, such as Animals or China. Books may be read aloud to introduce theme studies, and trade books related to the theme are usually made available to students. Teachers who use theme units believe that organizing the curriculum in this manner provides many opportunities for students to practice language skills and helps them begin to see how different areas of knowledge are related.

When teachers first begin to work with themes in the classroom, they may capitalize on strong or immediate interests of children, such as dinosaurs, insects or some aspect of the popular culture, such as music or film. They use these themes as organizing tools for some or all areas of the curriculum and often repeat the themes from year to year because they are successful with a succession of classes. Others may use the same themes but adjust the literature base and content to accommodate the special needs or abilities of individual classes. A social studies unit on Australia might center on the history, geography and sociology of the continent, but also reach into science with a study of its plant and animal life. Mathematics could be involved if students analyze the population statistics with graphs, fractions, ratios and percentages. They might also investigate the music, dance, literature and art of the country and respond to their study with various kinds of writing and artistic expression. Evaluation of student learning in theme units usually involves individual or group projects and a written exam over the content.

Another way themes are used as organizing devices for instruction is the **topic** approach. Themes in literature, such as Survival or Courage, or broad themes drawn from the content areas, such as The Environment, Communities, or The West, create a framework to relate together required topics of study in various subject areas. In contrast to the theme unit, which draws from other curriculum areas to enhance a study, the topic approach creates an umbrella under which all areas of the curriculum can be explored. For example, the broad theme of The West might relate the study of Laura Ingalls Wilder's *Little House* books in literature to a historical study of Western expansion in the nineteenth century. Theme topics often involve students in researching the people, geography, history, science, mathematics, art and music of the time period. Students may create newspapers, conduct interviews, work together on research teams, construct team projects and write stories, poems and plays to respond to the study. Expert visitors might demonstrate pioneer crafts, or a Native American speaker might be invited to describe the impact of western expansion on the indigenous populations.

The most highly integrated organization of the curriculum is found in the **theme cycle**, where teachers enlist the active participation of students in choosing and developing themes to explore throughout the year, based on what they want to know about the world. As Altwerger and Flores[2] point out, the term "theme cycle" is used because topics of study are never exhausted.

As new ideas are introduced, related and explored, they create additional interest in the topics and provide direction for further study.

Teachers using theme cycles begin by asking students what they would like to study during the year, drawing from the specific interests, needs and abilities of their classes to create and explore a succession of themes. As questions and ideas are listed, the teacher adds concepts or topics that are grade-level or district requirements and relates them to the interests students have expressed. Students help group the suggestions into broader topics and select from the list those in which they have the greatest interest. Students vote on nine themes for the year and one is assigned for each month. When it has been decided which theme will begin the year, each student lists five things (or anything) he or she already knows about the topic and five things each would like to know. Teachers often refer to this activity as KWL, KWLC or KWLCQ, depending on the level of integration of the theme. These letters refer to these questions:

What do you **know**?
What do you **want** to know?
What did you **learn**?
What **connections** can you make with other knowledge or your own experience?
What new **questions** did this study create in your mind?

Theme units usually feature KWL, theme topics include connections, and theme cycles utilize all five questions. When teachers help students create a theme cycle, the lists of things they know and the list of things they want to know can be generated in class or deliberated more intensely as a homework assignment. This preparation allows everyone to participate in the discussion that follows and acknowledges the value of student knowledge and experience.

As students share their ideas, the teacher records the discussion on two charts, one that lists what students already know and another that lists the questions they have. All contributions are accepted, and if the accuracy of any information is challenged, it is marked with an asterisk for further research. Information and questions are placed in categories that can be suggested by the teacher or the students. Student decide on the ideas in the theme that particularly interest them and explore the various ways these ideas might be studied. They discuss available resources, both human and material, and talk about ways their learning can be shared with other class members or a broader audience.

When theme cycles are used at the kindergarten/primary levels, students often create talking murals to express what they know and want to know about a topic. They draw a picture and write (or dictate) something they know about the topic in a cartoon balloon. This mural can be added to as students learn more about the topic under study, or a new mural can be created to display the new knowledge. At the primary and intermediate levels, students often write what they know and what they want to know about a topic in a research or learning journal. Answers to their questions are recorded in the journal as their research proceeds. Students also record their sources of information in a bibliography, with brief annotations of the books they have read or consulted. The role of the teacher at this point is to organize learning experiences to help students discover what they want to know. This is accomplished by encouraging the formation of flexible groups and by creating workshops and learning stations to explore the major ideas of the theme.

Theme cycles are more comprehensive than either the unit or topic approaches in their potential to allow students to see how all forms of knowledge are interrelated. Because theme cycles encourage students to create categories of investigation from their own questions and to organize their inquiry, students more effectively discover how knowledge is connected by large ideas. Unlike the theme unit or topic, theme cycles are unique to individual classrooms, with their particular stores of knowledge, interests and available resources.

The chapter on mini-lessons (Chapter 9) illustrated how focused periods of direct instruction can help students learn concepts and practice skills in a meaningful context. This chapter will describe strategies that can help students organize and develop their inquiry in the content areas. These can each be introduced and explored in the mini-lesson format for individual or group use. While it is helpful to give students experience with a number of inquiry strategies, it is important not to dictate the use of any particular ones. Students should have opportunities to experiment with a wide range of strategies and then be allowed to choose those that are the most effective for them personally.

WHAT DO YOU THINK? Do you use any of the alternative "languages of learning" described above in your own learning? Do you ever diagram your ideas, make charts, draw pictures, sing or create stories to help make ideas more clear to you?

II. The Importance of Language Learning across the Curriculum

In addition to the literacy skills of reading, writing, speaking and listening, students will increasingly need to develop **information literacy**. The National Forum on Information Literacy (NFIL) defines information-literate students as those who can

> successfully complete a complex problem-solving process that requires them to define the need for information, determine a search strategy, locate the needed resources, assess and understand the information they find, interpret the information, communicate the information, and, finally, evaluate their conclusions in view of the original problem.[3]

Patricia Breivik, coauthor of *Information Literacy: Educating Children for the 21st Century*, believes that resource-based learning helps students develop this literacy because it encourages students to be active learners. In classrooms that provide a wide range of informational resources and opportunities to pursue information of interest, students become informationally literate.

They learn how to create their own questions, locate information to solve them, share their discoveries and evaluate the effectiveness of their inquiry. When classroom learning is organized around literature, language and themes, students increase their perception of the interrelatedness of knowledge. When these elements are used as ways to learn about the world, they provide students with tools for organizing and understanding complex concepts and relating them to their personal experience.

Literature   Increasingly, children's trade books in mathematics, science and the social studies are replacing the traditional textbook in the content areas. Barbara Moss[4] points out that trade books have the following advantages:

1. They permit individualized reading, according to interest and ability.
2. They provide students with a wide range of materials at a variety of reading levels.
3. Trade books encourage students to read more challenging material to find out what they want to know.
4. They allow students to explore topics in greater depth and offer creative and comprehensive explanations of concepts.
5. In the better examples of these books, complex terminology and abstract concepts are clearly explained.
6. Information is more current.
7. Attractively illustrated trade books provide visual appeal and draw student interest.
8. Trade books are more apt to be written and organized in a style that is reader considerate (helpful organization and clear writing style that students can readily understand).
9. Most can be used flexibly to introduce, expand, or enrich an endless variety of themes.

Language   In addition to high-quality trade literature, it is important for students to have many opportunities throughout the day to talk and write about what they are learning and thinking. Douglas Barnes[5] believes that talking and writing are tools of thought, as well as means of communication. He encourages teachers to help students interpret what they see and hear in terms of their own experience and understanding, by providing many opportunities for students to discuss what they are reading and writing. Carol Gilles and Kathryn Pierce[6] describe these discussions as exploratory talk—dialogue that relates to, and emerges from, life experiences. They believe that literature is a powerful tool for encouraging exploratory talk because it provides valuable information, new perspectives about a topic and ideas that draw students' interest for further inquiry.

James Britton et al.[7] and Peter Medway[8] refer to children's exploratory talk and writing as **expressive language** and believe, as do Piaget and Vygotsky, that children's thinking develops as they talk. It is equally important for children to have opportunities to record what they are learning about in writing.[9] Exploratory writing in science, social studies and math journals helps children sort out what they are learning, connect it with their experience and record their responses to content and processes.

Themes Integrating language learning with learning in the content areas encourages students to see language as a tool for discovering information that is helpful and interesting to them. As they inquire about topics of genuine interest, they learn how to use human, technological and informational resources. Working together to share the efforts of inquiry, they develop or improve their communication skills. Organizing learning around themes helps children develop strong interests and provides opportunities for them to study areas in depth. According to Hughes,[10] an integrated curriculum is authentic to the extent that it resembles the way people really learn, as they work to solve problems or follow compelling interests. When themes are used effectively, they feature the transfer of concepts across disciplines and involve the active participation of students to construct meaning, gain insights and use the knowledge obtained.

WHAT DO YOU THINK? From your own experience, what kind of literature helps you learn about a topic? Which do you prefer? Have you ever been a student in a classroom where learning was organized around a theme? What did you like or dislike about this approach to learning? Does it help you organize your thoughts to write or talk about something you want to learn?

III. Looking into Classrooms

Kindergarten Level—Exploring Mathematics with Language

"Mrs. Jamison, look!" Brian says, as the teacher moves into the corner area where he is working. "I made a train story."

"Tell me about it," she says, as she kneels down to get a closer look at his work.

"See these trains here?" he asks, and the teacher nods her head.

"There's ten of 'em, and they're going up this steep mountain." He illustrates his story by moving the small models up an incline he has made from some blocks. "Only these get loose and roll back down the mountain." He separates three of the trains and slides them back down the incline. "That's ten minus three."

"A great story," Mrs. Jamison agrees. "Did you make a picture story about it?"

"Yep," he says, showing her a page in his math journal, where he has drawn the three trains rolling down a mountain.

"Can you make a symbol story to go with that?" she asks, and Brian writes $10 - 3 =$ in his book.

"How will you solve it?" she asks.

"By counting," he replies.

"Show me," the teacher asks.

"These trains up on the mountain . . . I counted them to see how many were left," he replies.

"So your story is . . . ?"

"Ten minus three is seven," he says.

"Are you going to make other math stories with the train?" she asks.

"Yep, there's lots I can make," he replies, already turning his attention away from the teacher as he configures another train disaster.

Mrs. Jamison stops next to observe three girls who are sorting keys.

"Look at this one, Mrs. Jamison," Claire says, holding up an ornate skeleton key. "I never saw one like this before."

"That's an old key," Mrs. Jamison comments. "My grandfather had several of those."

"We're sorting out first and then we'll make the story," Claire explains. She and two other girls have made piles of keys on the rug.

"How are you sorting?" the teacher asks.

"Well, we put square tops here and rounds here and these are sort of curvy," Amy explains.

"And then we put all the ones that have bumps on one side here," Beth says, "and all the ones with bumps on two sides over here," she gestures.

"Then what?" the teacher asks.

"Then we get the story," Claire responds.

"This pile with the bumps on both sides has nine keys in it. And some are round heads and some are square heads and some are just curvy."

The teacher waits.

"So we can say three bumpy round head keys plus five bumpy square head keys plus one bumpy curve head key are . . . ta da! Nine bumpy-side keys!" The girls spontaneously clap.

"How will you write your story?" the teacher asks.

"Symbol stories," they say in unison, picking up their notebooks to record $3 + 5 + 1 = 9$. They will also experiment with writing the story in a variety of ways, such as $5 + 3 + 1 = 9$ and $1 + 3 + 5 = 9$ and will test these stories with their keys to see if they get the same totals when the symbols are rearranged.

Mrs. Jamison moves over to the classroom aquarium, where Noah is attempting to draw a picture of what he sees in his math journal. "Minus, plus . . . plus, minus . . . minus. There . . . no, plus again," he mutters to himself.

"How's it going?" Mrs. Jamison inquires, looking over his shoulder at a picture of seven goldfish.

"I can't get the story to stop," he says. "They keep plussing and minusing."

"You wish they'd all stop moving?" the teacher asks.

"Yeah . . . no . . . they gotta move. They're hard to draw though."

"What can you do?"

"Well, I know there's seven fish in there. So . . ."

Mrs. Jamison waits.

"I could make up one of the stories I saw."

"Like what?" she asks.

"Well, there were three that swam around the back of the castle and I could draw them that way and tell a story about that."

"How would it go?"

"These seven fish were swimming along . . . and then they heard 'Help! Help!' 'What's that?' one fish said. 'I don't know,' a second one said. 'Let's go find out,' the third one said, and they swam around the back of the castle."

"Sounds exciting," the teacher says.

"Yeah," Noah agrees. "And then it gets better. Only one fish swims back."

"This sounds like several math stories," Mrs. Jamison observes.

"Yeah, and there's going to be even more," he announces. "I forgot I can make imagination stories."

"So what is the first story you will draw?" she asks.

"Just four fish here," he gestures. "Then . . ." he pauses and thinks. "I want to show all the story's parts, so I'll make this castle so you can see through it . . . you can see the fish behind it . . . or . . ." He studies his picture and then crawls around on the floor to the side of the aquarium. "I could draw it from the side, then you could see the fish at the front and back . . . yeah, that's it." He turns the page of his notebook and starts to draw. Mrs. Jamison will return later to hear the stories he creates from his observations. He will tell her four stories about the first episode, including symbolic representations for three plus four, four plus three, seven minus three and seven minus four. He will also create a longer story about the single fish that returned from a fierce battle behind the castle, with seven minus three, plus one.

WHAT HAPPENED HERE?

Mrs. Jamison uses a program called *Mathematics Their Way*[11] as the basis for math instruction in her classroom. It stresses individual development of math concepts and the use of real things and situations to talk about mathematics. Within this program, children begin talking about numbers at the **concept level**, with objects they can touch and manipulate. As they gain experience, they move into the **connecting level**, representing their exploration with pictures and experimenting with the language of mathematics. At the **symbolic level**, students write mathematical symbol stories to represent the events or objects they are exploring.

The assignment for this independent math period was to find something in the room to write a math story about. Children in this class are emerging as math learners and are at various stages of development in their ability to find or create problems and represent them with pictures or symbols. As the teacher circulates through the room, she asks students to tell her about the stories they are creating. Some are imaginative, many are action-filled and others reflect a complexity of developing thought. Noah's reference to imagination stories comes from the daily student talk sessions, where Mrs. Jamison encourages children to talk about anything that interests them. This language activity replaces the traditional show-and-tell and features a speaker's chair where each child sits to share his or her thoughts. Eager to create an impression, some of the children invented stories about trips and possessions. Because she wanted to encourage children to talk, but wanted to avoid the inevitable arguments that ensue about what is true or untrue, they agreed that stories could be real or pretend, but the storyteller had to tell which it was. This allowed the use of imagination without a penalty.

Karen Gallas (op. cit.) describes a similar approach and refers to these imaginative creations as fake stories.

Creating math stories throughout the room allows children like Brian the opportunity to be physically active in his exploration of math concepts, while he is learning to use the language of mathematics to describe his play activity. The group of girls sorting keys are seeking more challenging aspects to their math stories and enjoy moving directly into symbolic representation. Both Brian and Noah are working alone today to follow individual interests, but on other days, they join other students to follow similar interests. In each case, children are gaining experience with the relationships of numbers in a concrete way and are learning to use the language of mathematics to talk about and solve problems in their environment.

The guidelines for these sessions were established early in the year by the students, in response to Mrs. Jamison's modeling and questions like: What rules do we need so that everyone can do math play? They role-played various situations in response to her question: What kinds of problems might happen? The final guidelines, worked out over a period of several weeks, are: Work together with no fights or work alone; stay in your own area; think math while you play.

Students ask math questions throughout the day, such as: What time is it? How long do we have to wait? How many cookies can I have? Do we have enough money to buy this? How big is that giraffe? Who gets the most? Is that fire engine bigger than the one downtown? Why are there 29 days in February this year? Mrs. Jamison points out to the children that they are asking mathematical questions, to help them become aware of the uses of this special language. She also calls attention to math events by asking questions like: How many crackers will we need today? How many cartons of milk are left? Can someone count out enough papers for this group? What math story could you tell about the birds in that tree? What math story does this book tell? Although a specific time is set aside for students to find math stories as they play, they frequently make observations throughout the day, such as: "Two chicks are hatching out! That's twelve minus two!" and "I read a book this morning and another one this afternoon; that's one plus one."

As Mrs. Jamison interacts with individuals and groups of students, she makes brief notes about their progress. For example, she makes a note to ask Brian if he can make the same math story about anything else in the room, helping him begin to develop the idea that this kind of language can be transferred to other objects and events. She notes that both Bobby and the three girls are adding and subtracting a sequence of numbers and plans to introduce the idea of grouping to them sometime during the week. As she talks to her students about their stories, Mrs. Jamison explores their conceptual development with invitations such as: Tell me about it. Show me. How will you show that in your picture? What will the symbol story look like? In this session and others throughout the day, she activates students' own problem-solving skills by asking questions like: How could you solve that problem? What else could you do? What else could you make out of this material? Where else could you find the answer to that?

Mrs. Jamison reads aloud from books that feature math concepts and uses Big Book versions of books such as Eric Carle's *The Very Hungry Caterpillar*,[12] *Rooster's Off to See the World*[13] and *1,2,3 to the Zoo: A Counting Book*.[14] She has a large selection of books that feature counting, addition and subtraction, time, measurement, sizes and comparisons, including such titles as: *Hippos Go Berserk*,[15] a counting book in rhyme; *Ten Bears in My Bed*,[16] the familiar "roll over, roll over" rhyme; *If You Take a Pencil*,[17] a cumulative story; *Mouse Count*,[18] which portrays the arithmetic of ten mice and a hungry snake; and *Moja Means One: Swahili Counting Book*,[19] which depicts the sounds and sights of East Africa.

Children sing and dance to mathematically themed music, such as *Ten Little Monkeys* and *Over in the Meadow*. They march to the music of John Philip Sousa, singing "One, two, three four, one, two, three four," and waltz as they hum "one, two, three" along with the music. Students also listen to Prokofiev's *Peter and the Wolf* and talk about the story and the instruments used to tell the story. They listen to *Carnival of the Animals* and move around the room, portraying each one.

WHAT DO YOU THINK?　Think about some questions you have asked recently. How many of them involved a mathematical concept? How have you used mathematics in an ordinary living task today? Look around the room where you are and think of some ways you express what you see and experience in mathematical language.

Primary Level—Exploring Science with Language and Literature

"I want to make a circle graph to show how many kinds of bats there are compared to other mammals," John Stephen announces to the rest of Mrs. Taylor's third-grade class. Students are seated in a circle on a rug in the back of the room, sharing problems and questions about their research. At the beginning of the year they chose the theme Scary Animals to study in October. A wide range of animals has been selected for study by individual students, including crocodiles, bats, sharks, snakes, spiders, wasps, tigers, wolves and bears.

"I can show you," Caleb offers. "I made one when I asked everybody which animals they were most scared of."

"Thanks, Caleb," Mrs. Taylor says. "There's a handout on graphs at the math center you can check with, too."

Several students write down the information on graphs in their science notebooks.

"Anyone else have a question?"

"I don't have a question," Blaine says, "but I brought my animal to show."

Several girls move back from the circle. Blaine's animal is a scorpion. He takes a book out of a sack and opens it to a pop-up version of a scorpion. The girls act relieved and move closer to see the three-dimensional picture in *Nature's Deadly Creatures: A Pop-up Exploration.*[20] He shows a king cobra, a black widow spider, a Gila monster, a blowfish and a blue-ringed octopus, demonstrating how to lift flaps to see photographs and illustrations of each animal.

"Anyone else?" the teacher asks, as Blaine puts the book back in his sack.

"Me," Alexandra volunteers. "Has anybody seen anything about wolves? I can't find too many books just about wolves."

"Did you find the Explorer Book on wolves?" John Stephan asks Alexandra.

"No, I didn't know there was one," she answers.

"I don't know if we have it, but it's listed in the back of my book on bats." Alexandra makes a note about the book.

"I know a book about wolves," Caleb offers. "It's a little hard to read, but I've got it at home. You can borrow it for a while."

"What is it?" Alexandra asks.

"*The Call of the Wolves,*"[21] Caleb answers. "It tells about how a wolf gets shot and tries to get home through a blizzard. There's stuff at the back that tells about wolves and I think there's a list of books, too."

"Can I borrow it?" Alexandra asks, as she writes down the title.

"Sure," he replies.

"Did you do a computer search in the library?" Emily asks.

"Not yet. I've been trying to read the books we have in the room first," Alexandra replies.

"You better do it right away," Jamal says. "I found lots about alligators when I did one yesterday."

"Can somebody show me how to do one?" Morgan asks. "I forget how."

"Are there other people who want a review of the search?" the teacher asks.

A few hands go up.

"You can go down to the library after discussion," Mrs. Taylor says. "Anyone who remembers how to search can help the others."

"This isn't a question," Adrienne says, "but my notes about bats keep getting mixed up. I've written down a lot of things, but I don't know how to start writing."

"What have you tried?" Mrs. Taylor asks.

"Well, I just start at the beginning, but then I find something that should go in before, and it's a mess," she admits.

"You know what I do?" Terisha asks. "My sister showed me how to write down just one fact on one index card. Then you can put the cards together that go together. It really works."

"Could you show me how you do it?" Adrienne asks.

"Sure, but then I've got to do my own stuff."

"Thanks," Adrienne says.

There are a few more questions and then a number of students leave for the library, where several are coached on using the computer search. In the room, Terisha shows Adrienne her stack of index cards and how she sorts them to organize her writing. Several other students also observe this organizational technique and ask the teacher for index cards. Other students look for pictures of their animals so they can draw them, and some take notes from special reference books on animals. All work from lists of questions they developed as a class or added on their own as their study progressed. These include: Where does this animal live? What does it look like? Is it endangered? Why do people think it is scary? Are there any myths or legends about this animal? Do different cultures have different ideas about this animal? How should you act around this animal to be safe? What does it eat? How many babies does it have? How does it take care of its babies? Are they born alive or do they hatch from eggs?

Several decide to model their animals in clay for the class exhibit, and two girls work on a puppet show that involves a discussion between their two animals. One boy is creating a newspaper, the Swamp Times, edited by Anthony Alligator. Jamal and Morgan are coordinating the construction of an alphabet book for the kindergarten and ask students to sign up to write and illustrate an alliterative sentence about their animal. Jamal begins the book with "A asked the alligator annoying questions" and Morgan adds "C cracked the crocodile's crazy coconuts." They will read the book aloud to the kindergartners during a Book Buddies session and leave it in the classroom for them to enjoy at other times.

When the research session is over, students take a few minutes to look at their notes and write down something they learned about their animal that was especially interesting. They also write a note to the teacher, ranking their work for the morning on a scale from 1 to 5, and tell why they think this is an accurate self-evaluation. In small groups, students share their day's discoveries with each other, and there is a great deal of support and encouragement for each speaker. The discovery notes are handed in to the teacher, along with their self-evaluations. Notes are handed back at the end of the day to take home and share with parents.

Later in the day, students will take turns observing the large tarantula Mark has brought to school. They will practice drawing the spider and dance to a recording of *The Tarantella*. The class also will begin planning ways to share its study with other classes. With the help of the art teacher, students will create masks to use with a drama they are writing about endangered animals. They will also begin writing their own animal creation myths, based on those read aloud from cultures around the world. A collection of their drawings and reports will be bound into a classroom book, and children will take turns sharing the book at home with their families.

WHAT HAPPENED HERE?   The scary-animal study was chosen by children at the beginning of the year and planned for October, to coincide with Halloween. From an initial interest in animals that are frightening to many people, students gained new respect for the particular characteristics of each animal studied and learned valuable information about the contributions each makes to the environment. They discovered that ancient peoples often deified animals that were dangerous to humans and that animals are a part of the creation myths of many cultures. They talked about the fact that what frightens one person may not frighten another. With a wildlife

Learning Log

CELLS
BY TY

9/93

Learning Log

Gr. 3

9/13/94

Cells   Bethany

There   are   many   different   kinds   of   cells   in   your
body. Some   of   them   are   called
bone cells, white   blood   cells, fat
cells, muscle cells, nerve   cells, skin   cells
and   red   blood   cells. They   come   in
many   different   sizes, shapes   and   colors.
There   is a circle   in   the   middle   of
your   cell. It.   is   called   the   nucleus.
It   is   the   control   center. Then   there
is   a   bigger   thing   around   it. It   is
called   the   cytoplasm. It   stores   food.
Then   there   is a   ring   around   the
cytoplasm. It   is   called   the   cell
membrane. It _ protects _ the   food.

Excellent

You learned a lot!

Sp. = 100%

There are millions of cells in your
body. Here are some of their names:
muscle cells, brain cells, skin cells,
blood cells, lung cells, liver cells,
bone cells and fat cells. Cells have
three different parts called the
cytoplasm, the cell membrain and the
nucleus. The nucleus is the control
center. The cytoplasm stores food. The
cell membrain is like a filtering
system. It lets the good stuff in and
keeps the bad stuff out. Red blood
cells carry oxygent through your body.
When they are bright red, they are full
of oxygen and when they are dull red,
they need oxygent. When they don't have
oxygent they are going back to the
heart. Then the heart pumps the blood
to the lungs where they get oxygent.

MUSCLE
CELLS

FAT
CELLS

RED BLOOD
CELLS

NERVE
CELLS

FIGURE 11.1
(1) A page from a science learning log. This third-grade student took notes as she researched the topic and incorporated information she learned from group discussions.
(2) A page from a learning log kept on a word processor. The student has added drawings from his research.

biologist, they explored ideas about healthy fear and the necessary precautions to take with animals that sting, bite or scratch.

As students drew their animals, they became familiar with their anatomy and began to analyze why certain physical aspects are frightening to humans, such as disproportionately large teeth, rough-looking skin or small eyes. From a CD-ROM program, they discovered that several of the animals they researched are endangered and that some have not changed in appearance for millions of years. They also learned that the most ferocious of today's animals are tame by the standards of land and sea animals that lived long ago.

A large matrix drawn on butcher paper is fastened to the chalkboard, where students record data about their animals: size, color, species, outstanding features, habitat, food requirements and environmental contribution. On a bulletin board under the headings of "I used to think . . ." and "Now I know . . . ," students have fastened index cards with ideas they had about their animals before and after their study. One boy wrote, "I used to think that all bats were vampires that sucked out your blood" and "But now I know that most bats eat insects and fruit."

The sharing sessions before and after their research sessions allow students to draw on each other's expertise and permit the teacher to identify strategies or content that might be helpful to student inquiry. Most take notes about the issues raised in the problem-solving session because they realize they might need this information at a later time. Students who received a review of the computer search were prompted by their tutors to take notes for future reference. As students pursue individual interests, they add to the knowledge of the entire class through sharing sessions. They can also choose to respond to what they are learning in a multitude of ways that maximize their learning strengths and help develop those that are emerging.

WHAT DO YOU THINK?   If your class chose this same theme to study, what special interests and knowledge would you have to share? Would you like to be a student in this class? What animal would you choose to study? How would you choose to share what you learned?

Intermediate Level—The Theme Cycle

At the beginning of the school year, Mr. Hahn encourages his fifth-grade students to contribute ideas about what should be studied in the next nine months. After much deliberation, they agree on the following themes for the year:

> Why are military bases being closed?
> Why are so many area farmers going out of business?
> What is the information superhighway?
> What makes movies and TV shows popular?
> What would it be like to live on the space station?
> How will genetic engineering change the future?
> How does global warming affect us?
> What makes people around the world look different?
> What makes a person a hero?

The topics chosen reflect their own personal concerns: The nearby military base employs or supports the employment of many of their parents, and local small farmers must work at other occupations to support their families. Their choices also reflect a desire to know more about their environment: the positive and negative effects of the increased uses of technology, scientific research, life in space, and the influence of the media.

Students chose the military base closing to study first, since that directly affects nearly every person in the class. Many have parents who are enlisted personnel or civilian staff, while others are concerned that the base closing will affect their parent's jobs, even though they are not employed by the base. Area farmers are aware that the possible joint use of the base as a commercial airport will affect the value of their land.

Students begin their research by leaving a message on an Internet bulletin board, hoping to hear from persons who have survived a similar experience in another area. They receive a number of supportive letters, including one from a congressman and several from classes in areas where bases had been closed. From a pamphlet sent from another area of the country, the teacher makes enough copies for students to study in small groups. He asks them to read and analyze the pamphlet for its effectiveness in communicating convincing arguments for keeping a base open. Students examine the materials using two criteria: Would this material help someone make up his or her mind about this issue? If not, what information is missing?

"Well, what do you think?" Mr. Hahn asks, when the groups have completed their review of the pamphlet.

"This thing has real problems," Darren begins.

"How so?" the teacher responds.

"Well, to start with, there's nothing to it, just a whole list of statements. I don't think anybody would read it."

Mr. Hahn puts the brochure on the overhead for the discussion. "What would make it better?" he asks.

Darren looks at Paula, who refers to some notes she took during their group's discussion. "If *we* were doing it . . . ," she pauses for effect and looks around the room, "we'd do it right, of course." She waits for the rest of the class to respond, and they do, in various ways. Other members of her group flash a victory sign.

"First, we wouldn't put all this junk on the front cover. No one's going to read all that to start with. We'd get their attention with a photograph of a base family, you know, with the dad all dressed up in his uniform and a family with a whole bunch of kids. Then we'd print the words 'Unemployed' over the top of the picture, and at the bottom, 'Don't let it happen.' "

"So you want to personalize the closing, and you want that to be the first thing the reader sees?" Mr. Hahn asks.

"Right," Paula agrees. "Then we can go on to some of the stuff they put on the first page, about how it will make other people lose their jobs, like fast-food places and people who work in all the stores where base people buy stuff."

"Yeah, and look at all the ways they said the same thing," Jordan adds. "Our group combined a lot of the things, so it doesn't look like so much to read."

"You want to send the message in fewer words," the teacher observes.

"Yeah," Kyle responds from his group, "and we think they could say it plainer . . . what they said . . . it should use words that everybody understands."

"So you're saying that it should aim toward a broader audience?" the teacher asks.

"Yeah, that's right," Kyle agrees. "In plain language everyone can understand."

"More like a commercial," Brian adds. "Short and to the point. You want to get their attention, not bore 'em to death."

"You're trying to persuade the reader, but is there a difference between what you want to have happen here and a commercial?" Mr. Hahn asks.

"Well, the goal's the same," Brian finally says. "We want to sell the reader something . . . get 'em to write to their congressmen and the president and anybody else who will decide what happens."

Mr. Hahn waits for the idea to develop.

"But on TV or whatever, they sometimes lie . . . or they don't really tell you everything," Kate replies. "Like when you were a little kid, you'd see really good stuff on the cartoon shows, that makes you want to buy it, or like cereal or whatever and it never was as good as it looked."

"So the difference is . . . ?" Mr. Hahn asks.

"We're trying to get the facts out to everybody, so they know what's happening and can help do something," Lori concludes.

As they talk about the defects of the pamphlet, Mr. Hahn writes their criticisms on the board under the heading "What's Wrong." When the discussion concludes, he writes another heading entitled "How to Fix It," and the group reviews the suggestions made during the discussion. From these suggestions the students create five criteria for effective persuasive writing. In small groups they begin to construct their own informational pamphlets, which they will present to the local base/civilian committee.

WHAT HAPPENED HERE?

This study was generated by students who wanted to contribute in some way to support an issue in the community that would affect their lives. In the process, they explored issues of accuracy and honesty in pamphleteering and ways to persuade an audience. They reached out to other communities experiencing similar distress and received a number of helpful suggestions. From a poorly designed pamphlet, they developed criteria to evaluate informational/persuasive messages, which they then applied to their own writing of similar material. Reading, writing, talking and thinking about this problem made them feel more involved in helping to solve a problem of mutual concern.

In a previous year, Mr. Hahn's students generated other themes that related to their proximity to the military base. Because the military engagement of Desert Storm had touched their lives personally, they wanted to research the reasons for war. Students generated questions such as: Why did we fight in Desert Storm? If wars are so bad, why do we keep having them? Why do people join the military? What is the special role of our base? What do our parents do at the base? What other wars did our families fight in? What do the reserves do? What does the National Guard do? Will there always be wars?

Themes differ each year to accommodate the interests and concerns of each particular group of students. When students have identified their concerns, Mr. Hahn helps them develop questions that will assist their research and suggests sources of information. He knows that nearly any topic of interest to his students will involve the development of required skills and investigation of the content that is required at his grade level. For example, in fifth grade, students are required to study American history, the body systems, historical novels, persuasive speaking, maps, ratios and graphs. The year Mr. Hahn's class researched the base closings, students traced their local base back through the history of

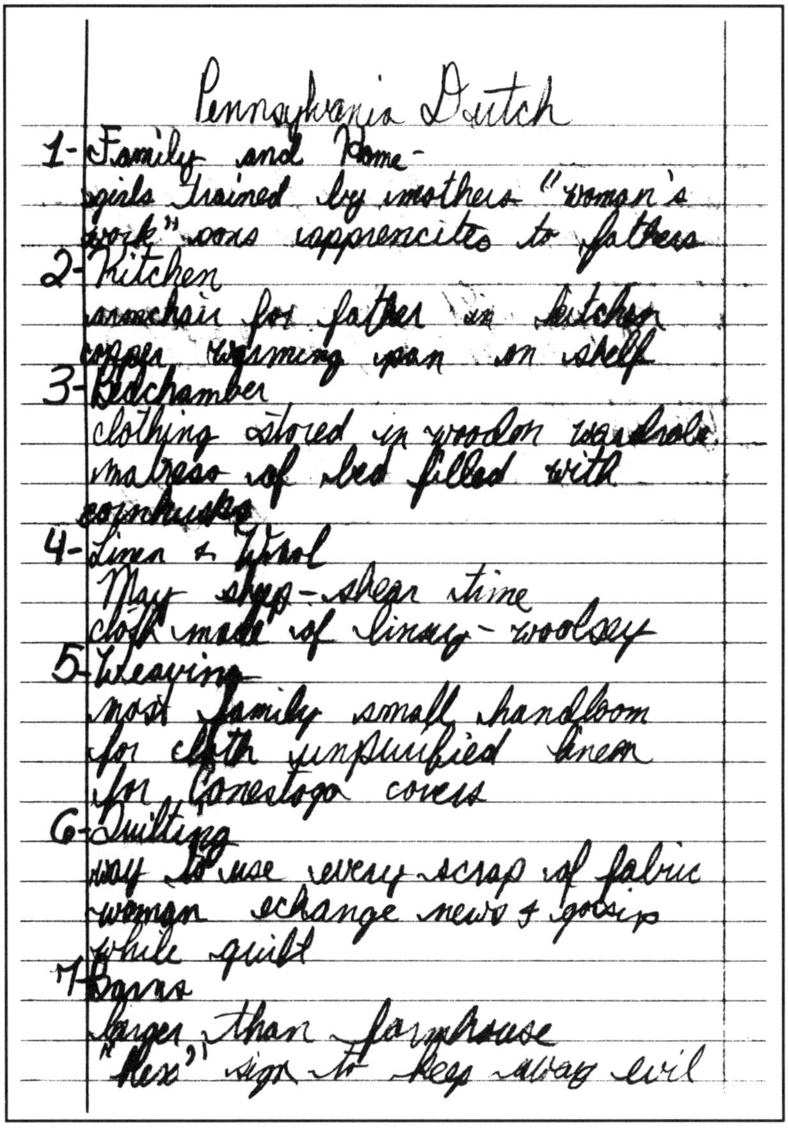
Pennsylvania Dutch
1- Family and Home-
girls trained by mothers "woman's work" sons apprencites to fathers
2- Kitchen
armchair for father in kitchen
copper warming pan on shelf
3- Bedchamber
clothing stored in wooden wardrobe.
matress of bed filled with cornhusks
4- Linen & Wool
May sheep-shear time
cloth made of linsey-woolsey
5- Weaving
most family small handloom
for cloth unpurified linen
for Conestoga covers
6- Quilting
way to use every scrap of fabric
woman echange news & gossip
while quilt
7- Barns
larger than farmhouse
"Hex" sign to keep away evil

FIGURE 11.2
Research notes from a student's social studies learning notebook. Note that she has created categories to explore as part of her research about the Pennsylvania Dutch settlers.

American wars in this century, then continued their research back into the forts of the eighteenth and nineteenth centuries. Historical novels, such as *Calico Captive*[22] and *Tree of Freedom*,[23] helped them gain a perspective on the involvement of forts in American history. They examined famous speeches in American history that were concerned with ideals and defense, such as Patrick Henry's speech, the Gettysburg Address and Roosevelt's address following Pearl Harbor. As students researched the base closings in other areas, they learned to use a variety of maps and invited one of the student's fathers to describe the use of maps in military planning. To conduct surveys connected with their study, they had to learn how to use graphs to record and share their information.

When the year's study involved the causes of war, paramedics and doctors who served in Desert Storm introduced the function and care of the body systems in the context of maintaining the health of troops. Mr. Hahn provided historical novels that portrayed America's experience with war, such as *My Brother Sam Is Dead*,[24] *Johnny Tremain*,[25] *Fallen Angels*,[26] *Sarah Bishop*[27] and *Undying Glory: The Story of the Massachusetts 54th Regiment*.[28] They examined the metaphors and similes in these novels and used figurative language to express their own ideas about war.

Students developed criteria for persuasive speaking and writing and explored issues of war and peace in shared-pair discussions. They traced their own families' experiences in previous wars and collected oral biographies from parents and grandparents. They investigated the various branches of the government involved in the declaration of war and the management of armed forces, and they examined relevant historical documents, such as the Declaration of Independence, the Federalist Papers, the U.S. Constitution, the United Nations Charter and the Gettysburg Address. They studied the effects of westward expansion on the indigenous peoples and the consequences of the introduction of slavery to support the development of eastern and southern economies in colonial America. They used the language of mathematics to examine and manipulate data from their research and to record the results of their interviews and surveys. Graphing skills were developed to share the information gained from these computations.

Students examined war as a topic for artistic expression, including such classic expressions as Tchaikovsky's *1812 Overture*, Sibelius' *New World Symphony* and the paintings of Picasso. The class listened to recordings of songs from U.S. wars, such as "Yankee Doodle," "Dixie," "You're in the Army Now," "Anchors Away," "Wild Blue Yonder," and the patriotic band music of John Philip Sousa. They examined the role of patriotic music of all kinds with visits by military musicians from the base. They researched the role of drummer boys and buglers in military units and created dramas about Johnny Shiloh and Orion P. Howe (Civil War drummer boys) from historical documents. They also examined and compared the influence of musicians and entertainers during contemporary wars.

This study reached out into the community, as students interviewed members of the armed forces who had fought in both world wars and the Korean and Vietnam conflicts. The genealogical librarian at the public library gave them tips for tracing ancestors who fought in U.S. wars. She also helped them locate community members who had been displaced by wars in other countries and one who had lived in a concentration camp during the Holocaust. A local doctor's parents had been interned in a camp for Japanese Americans during World War II, and he spoke to the class about his family's loss of home and business. Parents of several students had family members from countries that were involved in wars against the United States, including Japan, Korea, Germany, and North Vietnam. Others had suffered as civilians in those countries. Several students had grandparents who survived the bombings in London during World War II. One student's great-great-grandfather had been a buffalo soldier in the West.

Because so many of the students' parents were involved in the military base, additional issues were brought up for discussion, such as the difficulties faced by families who must say goodbye to parents sent on duty, getting adjusted to new communities when a parent is transferred, and the role of ritual and ceremony in dealing with loss. The class visited local cemeteries to locate graves of soldiers from each of the U.S. wars and helped the local scout troop place flags on the graves of persons who had served in the military. With letters to the editor and in cooperation with local veteran's groups, they helped revive the local Memorial Day celebration to honor local veterans.

Mr. Hahn adds his expertise and special interest in living history. On weekends he performs with an area Civil War reenactment group. Each year several reenactors talk to the class about the experiences of volunteer soldiers during the Civil War. He also brings the movie *Gettysburg* and videotapes of the Lincoln–Douglas debates to class to share with his students. He has Native American friends who visit the class to share a historical perspective on the frontier conflicts of several centuries.

WHAT DO YOU THINK?   How might the questions generated by students be different at other grade levels? in a school not located near a military base? in different areas of the United States? If you were the teacher in this classroom, what special knowledge, interests or abilities would you be able to share?

IV. Preparing to Use Language, Literature and Themes in the Content Areas

Content   As you prepare for students to use language and literature to learn in all areas of the curriculum, you will want to begin by reviewing the content of what you will be teaching. Make a list of specific concepts and skills your students will be expected to learn or develop. Begin to assemble children's books that relate to these areas by reviewing the holdings of your school and public libraries. What books will you read aloud to create interest in a topic? What reading levels must you accommodate for independent reading? Will it be possible to borrow additional sets of reference books for student research? You will also want to check these sources for video- and audiotapes and computer programs that relate to the areas of study at your grade level.

Materials   What things will you need to conduct science demonstrations and experiments? What kinds of manipulatives are available for learning in math? Are there dramas, simulations or kits available for use in social studies?

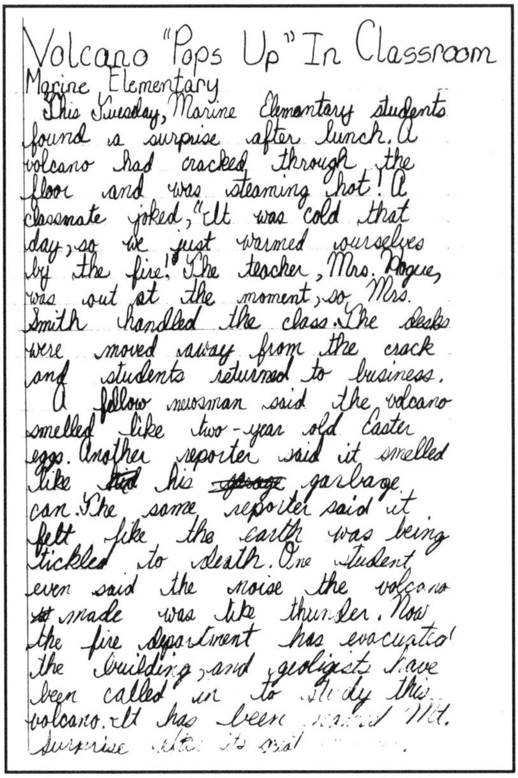

Volcano "Pops Up" In Classroom

Marine Elementary

This Tuesday, Marine Elementary students found a surprise after lunch. A volcano had cracked through the floor and was steaming hot! A classmate joked, "It was cold that day, so we just warmed ourselves by the fire." The teacher, Mrs. Pogue, was out at the moment, so Mrs. Smith handled the class. The desks were moved away from the crack and students returned to business.

A fellow newsman said the volcano smelled like two-year old Easter eggs. Another reporter said it smelled like his garbage can. The same reporter said it felt like the earth was being tickled to death. One student even said the noise the volcano made was like thunder. Now the fire department has evacuated the building, and geologists have been called in to study this volcano. It has been named Mt. Surprise after it's real

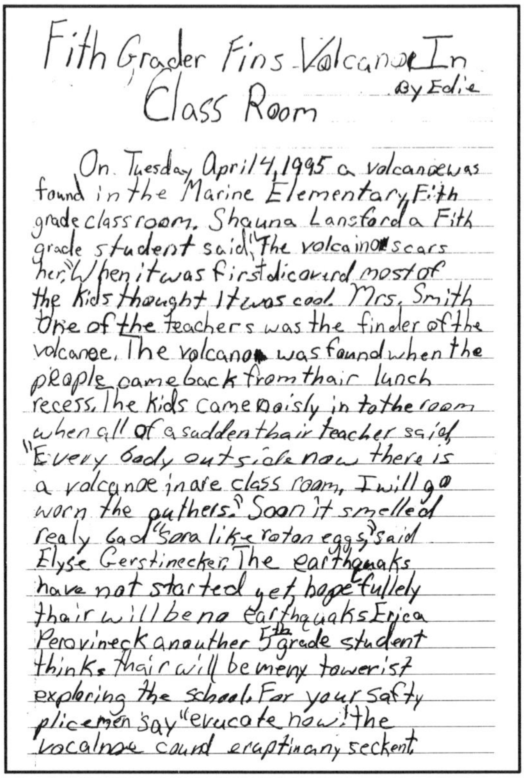

Fith Grader Fins Volcanoe In Class Room

By Edie

On Tuesday April 4, 1995 a volcanoe was found in the Marine Elementary Fith grade class room. Shauna Lansford a Fith grade student said, "The volcaino scars her." When it was first dicovred most of the kids thought It was cool. Mrs. Smith One of the teachers was the finder of the volcanoe. The volcanoe was found when the people came back from thair lunch recess. The kids came noisly into the room when all of a sudden thair teacher said "Everybody outside now there is a volcanoe in are class room, I will go worn the outhers." Soon it smelled realy bad "Sora like rotan eggs," said Elyse Gerstinecker. The earthquaks have not started yet hopefullely thair will be no earthquaks Erica Perovineck anouther 5th grade student thinks thair will be meny towerist exploring the school. For your safty plicemen say "evucate now! the vacalnoe cound eraptin any seckent"

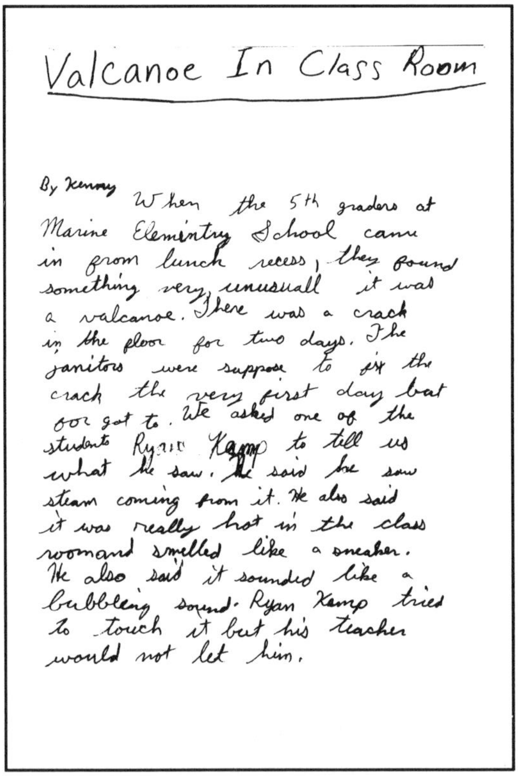

Valcanoe In Class Room

By Kenny

When the 5th graders at Marine Elemintry School came in from lunch recess, they found something very unusuall it was a valcanoe. There was a crack in the floor for two days. The janitors were suppose to fix the crack the very first day bat oor got to. We asked one of the students Ryan Kamp to tell us what he saw. He said he saw steam coming from it. He also said it was really hot in the class room and smelled like a sneaker. He also said it sounded like a bubbleing sound. Ryan Kamp tried to touch it but his teacher would not let him.

FIGURE 11.3

These articles are part of an assessment of student knowledge about volcanoes. What would happen if a volcano suddenly began to erupt in the classroom? Students responded to this hypothetical situation with news stories. Notice how the writers incorporate information they have learned about volcanoes into their article.

What materials will you need to have in the classroom for students to use for artistic responses to their learning?

Opportunities   Plan how you will provide opportunities for students to use exploratory talk and writing as they encounter ideas in the content areas. Add individual notebooks or a three-ring binder with partitions to the list of required student supplies if you plan for students to create learning journals in the content areas. What genres of literature and other types of writing will you want to have on hand or displayed to provide models for students' reporting of their research?

Contexts   Each of the language activities described in previous chapters can be used to help students explore concepts in mathematics, science and the social studies. You may want to review the preparation and presentation sections of these chapters as you prepare to use these activities in the context of content area learning. You will also need to consider the school and community contexts in which these activities are planned. What ethnic and racial groups are represented in the school's population? Is this composition changing? What challenges do the children in your school face in their community? Is there homelessness? Is the economy changing? Are many people out of jobs? How might the concerns your students bring to school be addressed in the curriculum?

Resources   You will also want to explore the resources of your school and community. What services are available from your school's media center, the public library, local businesses and civic organizations? What museums, wildlife sanctuaries, historical locations or natural landmarks are located in your area? From what sources can you obtain books and other reading material to support your classroom program? Are there parent or civic groups that might provide financial support to purchase instructional materials? If you know that you plan to invite a paramedic, a lawyer or a wildlife biologist to your classroom, talk to them in advance about a possible presentation. Are they easy to talk to? Do they enjoy working with children who are the age of your students? Have other teachers found them to be effective presenters?

Practice   Any learning activities you plan to use with your students must be practiced so that you will feel comfortable and familiar with them. Most of the activities described below can be adapted to any elementary instructional level.

***Learning Logs
(notebooks,
journals)***

This activity can be used in any of the content areas. Students use math journals to record their experiences as they explore mathematical concepts and work with computation. How did they solve a problem? What did they have trouble with? What did they learn that will help them apply the concept in another situation? In social studies or science, these notebooks are a good place to document research, keep track of references and record questions, opinions and accounts of learning. When a study is completed, students can use these journals to evaluate their learning by comparing their original knowledge of a topic to their new learning. Emerging writers can use these books to draw pictures of what they observe and what they are learning. They can also cut out pictures from magazines and paste or tape them into their learning journals.

Cluster Webs   Students begin by writing the name of the topic in the middle of a piece of paper and drawing a circle around it. They create three to five ways the topic can be described and place these words in circles around the page, connecting them by lines to the central topic. From each of these clusters, more subtopics can be created and connected as they relate to other clusters. For example, if the topic is Oceans, you might generate: Major, Flora, Fauna, Geography and Geology. Each of the oceans derived from the Major category will further subdivide, according to the distinct characteristics of ocean. But each ocean will also have elements in common, and these relationships can be indicated by connecting lines. This activity helps students organize ideas and consider how these ideas relate to each other. It can be used successfully by individuals or small groups in the late primary and intermediate grades and with the entire class and teacher assistance at the kindergarten and early primary levels.

Word Bank   This is another strategy for individual or group use, depending on the maturity of the class. Students list words they think of in response to a topic. For example, when asked to generate any words that they associate with insects, they might produce: bugs, bees, spiders, creepy-crawly, fly, ant, butterfly, moth, fly, buzz, crawl, legs, antenna, feelers, ant hill, hive, nest. They then decide categories that these words might fit in, such as Homes, Food, Movement and Characteristics. It is a good idea to keep a list of these words available on a classroom chart to assist student writing.

Venn Diagrams   These visual aids help students compare and contrast elements of a topic. They place distinct elements in the far sides of two large overlapping circles and place elements in common where the circles overlap. For example, if students compare Venus and Earth, surface temperatures and distance from the sun would differ and be placed separately. Similarities, such as the presence of an atmosphere and certain atmospheric gases, would be placed in the overlap. Older primary and intermediate students can generate these individually or in small groups. Teachers can use pictures on charts or felt boards when they use this activity with kindergarten children.

Outlining   This activity can follow one of the activities described above in order to create a framework for writing. Some students find this helpful because outlining moves ideas from a graphic form into an intermediate stage that allows them to evaluate content before it is written into a final report. Outlining helps some students visualize the major ideas of a topic and establish the proper sequencing of a presentation. Others may feel limited by the structure of an outline, but may refer to one after they have written, as a way of editing for content.

Data Chart   Students gather the same data on different subjects within a topic and organize it into a chart. For example, they may record the ages, national origins, educational levels, and professional careers of the signers of the Declaration of Independence. This type of recording makes comparisons and contrasts apparent, indicates areas to analyze further, suggests possibilities for interpretation and reveals connections between subjects that were not previously noticed.

Study Mural This activity is especially suited for kindergarteners, primary students and students whose writing skills are still developing. Students draw pictures directly on large sheets of mural paper or draw individual pictures to tape onto a bulletin board to illustrate their answers to two questions: What do I already know? What do I want to know? As the study progresses, students can add pictures to illustrate their answers to the question: What am I learning?

WHAT DO YOU THINK? Which of the research strategies are most appealing to you? As you try them out, note which ones seem comfortable and helpful and any that seem to be awkward and nonproductive for you personally. Why might students favor some activities over others?

V. Including Everyone

An often overlooked special population in the classroom are children sometimes referred to as gifted. It has been traditionally assumed by many teachers that children who learn quickly, exhibit precocious skill or demonstrate great creativity in their approach to learning do not need any special attention. It also is often assumed that these children can take care of themselves in the classroom program or can be adequately challenged by take-out programs of one to two hours per week. Some schools group these children in their own classes and keep them in these ability tracks throughout the elementary grades. These practices, and the assumptions on which they are based, may deprive both the gifted students and their classmates of productive interactions.

When students excel in *one* area, such as math or reading, teachers may assume that they have similar ability in *all* areas; consequently the help necessary to support their learning is not provided. Gifted students often hesitate to ask for help or are turned away by teachers who tell them they should know how to perform a task. At the other extreme, teachers frequently do not help students perform at their best level when a small effort produces work that is substantially better than their peers. Highly creative children sometimes arrest at the level of idea production and do not complete projects, even when self-selected. To develop their abilities, they need help from their peers and the teacher in the form of encouragement to translate their ideas into a form that can be shared and responded to by others.

Take-out programs encourage children to think of their gifts as something they share only with others of similar intellect or ability. They may withdraw from their classmates when their ideas or interests are not understood. Others hide their abilities and even intentionally produce failing work in order to be accepted. When children's talents are utilized within the classroom, they learn how to communicate effectively with peers of differing interests and abilities. They see themselves as contributors to a community that requires the best efforts of all its members.

Classrooms that integrate literature and language throughout the curriculum provide a distinct learning advantage to these children and their classmates. They have increased opportunities to make decisions about their learning and to develop their autonomy as learners, as they select books at their individual reading level and pursue special interests in depth. There are also increased opportunities for these students to interact with others who have similar interests and share their special talents with the entire class. In groups, they learn to better organize and clarify their ideas for speaking and writing. They learn how to explain ideas so that they can be understood by an audience and are drawn into the community of the classroom.

You will want to provide a wide variety of reading materials for these students, with content that challenges and interests them. Encourage students to share their hobbies, interests and writing with the rest of the class. Special interests draw students of varying abilities together, an interaction you will want to foster. You may also want to establish a mentor program for students who show strong interest and ability in a particular subject area. High school teachers and university professors are often willing to meet with students with highly developed special interests in their areas. You may also suggest that their parents apply for a library card at a local college or university to provide access to more challenging reading materials. Depending on the particular talents of your students, you may want to encourage them to enter school, district, state and national competitions in writing, speaking, science, math, art, music or sports. Check the current edition of *Children's Writer's & Illustrator's Market*[29] for information on markets for children's writing and art.

Books to Increase Understanding

The following books include selections from both fantasy and realistic fiction. Each book is a Newbery medal winner and all portray characters who display unusual giftedness as children. As you read, consider how you might relate to the main character(s) as a teacher.

> *A Wrinkle in Time*[30] by Madeleine L'Engle describes a fantastic journey through time and an epic battle against an evil force threatening the universe. Meg Murry's father is a physicist who tesseracts (goes through a wrinkle in time) to research the force and disappears. Meg and her little brother, Charles Wallace, go in search of their father with the assistance of supernatural helpers. Meg's reflections about her experiences at school and those of her brother, who is a genius, provide a look inside the minds of gifted children. This book is the first in the Time trilogy, which includes *A Wind in the Door*[31] and *A Swiftly Tilting Planet*.[32]

> *The Giver*[33] by Lois Lowry is a science-fiction novel that describes a utopian community where there is no hunger, disease, pollution or fear. At the ceremony of Twelve, when each child is assigned a lifelong profession, Jonas is chosen to be the Receiver of Memories, the most highly respected position among the Elders. The old receiver, whom Jonas calls The Giver, passes on

to him all the terrible memories from which the community is spared: neglect, starvation, misery and despair. He also discovers other experiences that no one shares, such as color, music and love. As Jonas's knowledge and insight increase, he is estranged from his friends and family because they cannot understand his new experience of reality. He learns some terrible truths about the community and is finally forced to leave in order to protect the life of a young child.

Dicey's Song[34] by Cynthia Rylant is the second book in the Tillerman family series. The story begins in *The Homecoming*,[35] which describes the journey of four young Tillerman children who set out on foot to find their grandmother, who lives in another state. Abandoned by both parents, they are led on their search by Dicey, who is the oldest. This story very sensitively portrays the variety of giftedness among four siblings: James in science, Dicey in writing, Sammy in athletics and Maybeth in music. Each must struggle with special challenges in the schooling process because of their talents.

The Planet of Junior Brown[36] by Virginia Hamilton is a haunting book whose characters and events are not soon forgotten. This is the story of two eighth-grade boys who face challenges that might destroy them. Buddy is homeless, but provides for himself and a group of young homeless boys by working all night at odd jobs. He also protects his friend Junior Brown, a musical prodigy who struggles with mental illness. Both are befriended by the school janitor, a former teacher, who tries to make a difference in the lives of both boys.

WHAT DO YOU THINK? What has been your own experience with gifted students? If you displayed academic giftedness as a child, were these talents encouraged, supported or developed in elementary school? Did you ever have a friend who was exceptionally gifted? What did you like about being friends with this person? Did you ever feel resentful toward students who learned quickly and easily?

VI. Step-by-Step: Creating a Theme Cycle

Your own teaching situation will determine the extent to which you can integrate the content areas in your curriculum. This section describes how to begin a theme cycle and how to organize activities that support learning in this manner. Begin with whatever is comfortable for you and expand the thematic concept as you gain experience with your students and resources. Most of these activities can be used, with minor adaptations, at any level of elementary instruction.

Experienced teachers[37] suggest the following steps for setting up a theme cycle:

1. Ask students what they would like to learn about during the year.
2. Add any topics required by your district or state.
3. Help students group the suggestions into broad categories of study.
4. Ask students to vote for nine themes, each one lasting a month.

When the list is established, each student should have his or her own copy and a copy should go home to parents. Explain that this is a list of topics that will be studied during the year and describe the skills and content that will be included as part of these studies. Enlist parents' help by asking if they have expertise, information or materials that they would be willing to share with the class. Copy the list to your principal and post it on the teacher's bulletin board to see if colleagues might direct you to resources that would be helpful in pursuing these themes. Take the list to your school or district media specialist and the public librarian. They will be able to direct you to relevant resources and may even be willing to plan special programs to assist the studies.

Begin with the most popular theme and ask students to list five things they already know about the topic and five things they would like to know. Be sure to allow enough time for students to think about this question, even a day or two. This allows everyone the opportunity to think about the topic and make a contribution to the class discussion. Use a chart or the blackboard to list students' ideas in both categories. If you use the blackboard, you can copy your final list onto a chart for later reference. When all contributions are acknowledged, ask students to suggest ways they could group their questions. For example, if students want to know what kinds of foods astronauts eat in space, if eating in space is different than on earth and if they have a special diet, these questions might be grouped together under Nutrition in Space. You are now ready for your first research session.

Research Sessions

Whether students are following individual research interests or participating as a group, the research period generally includes: (1) a time to consult other students and the teacher about individual research problems: (2) an independent, paired or group study period; (3) time to respond to what they are learning in writing and other means of expression, such as drawing, painting, making models or creating drama; (4) time to share the day's discoveries in small groups or as a class; (5) student self-evaluation of the day's work.

Consultation

You might want to begin the research sessions with the opportunity for students to share problems they are experiencing with their research. This allows other students to share strategies that have been successful for them. It also permits you to make suggestions that might be helpful. If a number of students are experiencing a particular difficulty, you can offer a mini-lesson to demonstrate a special skill or strategy to those who are interested. For example, if many students express frustration with the mechanics of computer searches or are having difficulty finding information using an index, you can review the basic skills with them before they begin their day's research. When only one or two students are experiencing difficulty, other students often volunteer to help.

Writing

Some teachers encourage students to keep a record of all their learning in a journal to help them relate the different areas of knowledge. Others ask students to keep separate journals for math, science and social studies.

Whatever you decide for your class, you will want to introduce students to the concept of a learning journal by modeling one you make yourself. Typical entries will include the date and one or more of the following: books or other resources consulted, interviews, observations of events, and reflections on these events. It is also appropriate for students to draw or sketch in these journals and paste or tape in pictures, newspaper articles or other relevant materials. These records of their thinking and research encourage children to consider the world and their experience in mathematical, scientific and historical/ geographical/sociological terms. In these notebooks, they wonder about things that draw their interest and find ways of answering the questions they have.

Science journals will include observations and drawings of natural phenomena and descriptions of classroom experiments or demonstrations. Many teachers ask students to respond to: Where do you see science happening? and What do you wonder about? It is appropriate to include science-related poetry, jokes, riddles, cartoons, news articles and magazine pictures in these journals. Students may want to include current events related to science and questions they have about these events. Some create their own glossaries of scientific terms. Others create a KWLCQ (see Section 1) for objects and events that draw their interest, recording what they know about something, what they want to know, what they learn, connections they make with their own experience and questions they still have. Encourage students to list and briefly annotate books they read that are science related. If they are researching a topic, this bibliography will be helpful to them when they want to review an idea for their writing.

You will also want to encourage students to create their own stories to explain questions they have, such as: What makes the stars twinkle? or Why do animals have fur? When these narratives are shared in class or in small groups, they begin discussions that help students think through their ideas about scientific phenomena.

Teachers often ask students to record where they see math, both in class and outside of school, in a **math journal**. At the kindergarten and early primary levels, students draw pictures of math problems and record math sentences they have created with manipulatives. At the late primary and intermediate levels, math journals are used for individual reflection and as part of small-group interaction to record how problems are solved. One teacher[38] encourages students to share problem-solving strategies as they work together and to reflect on their experience after the work period. If they helped someone with a problem, they respond to:

1. I helped _____ with problem # _____.
2. The difficulty seemed to be _____.
3. This was my helping strategy _____.
4. In the end, he or she seemed _____ and I felt
   _____.

If they received help, they respond to:

1. I got help with problem # _____ from _____.
2. I was having trouble _____.
3. He/She helped me by _____.
4. Now I feel _____ about this kind of problem.

She also provides creative ways for students to reflect on their experiences with math by posing questions such as, "If math were an animal, it would be . . . ," prompting students to explore both their ideas about mathematics and their own feelings of mathematical proficiency.

Other questions often posed for consideration in journals are: What resources did you use? What did you have trouble with? What did you learn? Students may also enter their own questions about math, for discussion with the teacher or in small groups, and list books they have read that have math-related themes. Math journals may also include math-related poetry, riddles, jokes, news articles, pictures and current events.

Students can record a wide variety of information in **social studies journals**, including a record of their research, questions they are seeking answers to and lists of references for their inquiry. They may also relate the subject matter to their own experience, with sections such as: people and places I wonder about; geography I notice; history that is happening; and current events that interest me. Students can include articles related to a theme or anything that particularly interests them, along with jokes, cartoons, and riddles that are related to geography, history, political science, anthropology or sociology.

Independent Study

During the period of independent study, students need to be free to walk around the room, to consult with each other and the teacher, and to refer to books and other materials. Although they will be working from the lists of questions they have generated as individuals and/or as a group, encourage students to write down any new questions that occur to them as they pursue their research. Depending on the grade and maturity level of your students, this independent work period can last from one-half hour to two hours.

Many teachers encourage students to adopt a research project that reflects a strong individual interest, unrelated to any theme study in the classroom. Lois Bridges Bird distinguishes between traditional school-assigned research and what she calls real research:[39] "Real researchers are driven by a passionate desire to learn; they've stumbled across a puzzle, and they can hardly sleep until they've solved it (whereas students struggling with the traditional research paper often have trouble staying awake)" (p. 296).

She suggests that students be given the opportunity to research individual interests and share them with the rest of the class. As they find out everything they want to know about a self-chosen topic, students begin to feel like experts. They practice the skills of a researcher and in the process become more proficient problem-solvers.

Creative Responses

Provide a variety of materials for students to respond to the ideas they discover in their research, such as:

1. Paper for writing, drawing and painting: lined, plain, and construction paper; tag and poster board.
2. Paints, crayons, clay, paper-mache, markers, paste, glue, tape, paper punches, brads, staplers and staples.
3. Fabric and items for construction, such as cans, bottles, pipe cleaners, boxes, cartons and popsicle sticks.

4. Woodworking tools and materials: hammers, screwdrivers, wood, nails and screws.

Your students' artistic expression will help you evaluate more accurately what they understand. At the kindergarten level, pictures are the beginning of writing and provide a starting place for literacy discussions: "Tell me about your picture," or "What would you like to say or write about your picture?" As the conversation continues, you can begin to identify what students know and help them expand their understanding. Students who are extremely articulate or who think in more abstract terms can often share their understanding of concepts through drawing. You may recall how the second grader in the Chapter 5 narrative was encouraged to make a graph of his discovery. This suggestion helped him organize what he knew and communicate it to the class. It also became a topic of discussion because other students were visually attracted to his data. Children with language, learning or social interaction problems can often express themselves in an artistic medium, frequently drawing the admiration of other children and allowing the teacher to determine the depth of their understanding.

Students need a variety of ways to represent what they have learned. As they choose a presentational format, they develop skill in transferring information from one form to another and learn which forms are most effective or appropriate for particular data. The following suggestions are ways for students to share what they have learned. Other ideas can be found in the Step-by-Step section of Chapter 7, which describes presentations for Friday Afternoon Sharing Time:

Pictures of observations or events
Photographic displays or albums
Video or slide presentations
Posters or charts
Maps and models
Diagrams, tables, graphs, flow charts, time lines
Informational bulletin boards
Surveys, interviews, questionnaires
Newspapers, letters to the editor, editorial cartoons

Taped or written oral histories and interviews
Debates or panel discussions
Mock TV or radio shows
Reenactments of historical events
Role-playing, puppet shows
Music, art and dance of other cultures
Costumes and food from different cultures
Realia kits of three-dimensional objects

Drawing is an excellent way for students to build specialized speaking, reading and writing vocabularies. Representing an object or animal from firsthand observation or pictures expands a student's basic knowledge of an organism and the ability to represent it in form and thought. For some children, it is a both a way of examining a phenomenon to learn about it and a method of externalizing this learning to share with others. For example, students might decide to draw pictures or create a dance in response to an exhibit of the life cycle of a frog. When they have observed the process, they will return to examine the frog more closely for details of appearance and movement—seeing how its legs or eyes move—and will modify or expand their artistic interpretation. From these observations, new questions arise,

FIGURE 11.4

(1) This fifth-grade student designed a poster to try to persuade colonists in the 1700s to move to the Middle Colonies.

(2) First draft of an informational pamphlet to persuade colonists to move to Philadelphia.

such as: Where were the frog's legs when it was a tadpole? Why does it have such a long tongue? What are these little knobs on its fingers? These kinds of questions and interactions help teachers become aware of how well students understand what they are observing.

Just as children come to a new appreciation and understanding of literary genres by writing in them, they also gain increased knowledge of and appreciation for persons of all cultures throughout history, as they work to express their ideas in the forms of folktales, poetry and other artistic media. Native American tales, Rudyard Kipling's *Just-So Stories* and the origin tales of cultures around the world take on new meaning when students wonder about and try to express their understanding of natural phenomena in these forms.

Sharing and Evaluation

Each research session should conclude with the opportunity for students to share what they have studied in small groups. These meetings encourage students to organize their thinking about what they have learned and share the excitement of their discovery. When all students have had an opportunity to talk briefly about their work, they complete a self-evaluation of the day's session. Students rate themselves on a scale they have developed as a class and write the reasons they believe this is an accurate assessment of their performance.

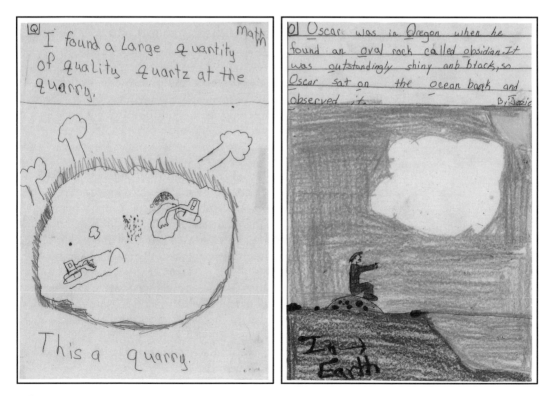

FIGURE 11.5
Fifth-grade students created an alphabet book of alliterative sentences to demonstrate what they learned in geology.

Ideas for Assisting Inquiry

The following are activities used by teachers to help students organize, interpret and decode the information they find in their research. Remember that you will be modeling ways for children to create questions, discuss ideas, interact with their peers and modify conclusions from their reading and research. Help your students sort out what they are discovering by asking, "Is this a fact?" "How do you know this?" "Where else could you look?" "Have you tried the strategy we talked about yesterday?"

Specialized Terminology

One of the characteristics of content area learning is specialized terminology, such as divisor, probability, osmosis, force, latitude or population density. Traditionally, these terms have been defined and illustrated with a few examples from a text. Children's trade literature often provides the necessary bridge between complex symbols or concepts and familiar experience. Teachers can assist this process by using the mini-lesson to provide demonstrations and opportunities for students to talk, write and draw their way to an understanding of these concepts.

Class Matrix

This is a visual summary of the types of information students are seeking about a topic. Create a chart with descriptors, such as the parts of insects or immigrant cultures in the United States, and keep it on display as students add relevant information. Blank matrices can be also be duplicated for student use in recording independent research. Both types of matrices allow students to compare and contrast data in a study. For example, they might record the size, color, food and habitat of a variety of insects. This information allows them to rank insects by size and compare their other characteristics and habits. A matrix of immigrant cultures might enable students to compare climates and geography in countries of origin and areas of settlement in the United States.

Talking Murals

Before you begin a theme study, attach a long piece of mural or inexpensive butcher paper to the chalkboard (remember to use fasteners that will not leave marks on the chalkboard). When students have discussed what they already know about a topic or theme, allow them to draw pictures that represent their understanding. If they can write, they can describe their pictures in cartoon balloon fashion over what they have drawn. The teacher or an aide can write what the children say about their pictures for those who are still developing writing skill. As the study progresses, students can add to the mural as they add to their own understanding. Some teachers vary this activity by having children draw individual pictures, which are then attached to the mural or posted on a large bulletin board. Teachers also encourage students to talk and write about their pictures: "Tell me about your picture." "How does it show what you know about frogs?" "How does your picture show what you've learned?"

Literature

You might want to review the criteria for good informational trade literature in Chapter 4 as you collect resource materials for your class. Be sure to select attractive, well-written books. Science and math materials should explain

A Secret Discussion By Elyse Gerstenecker

"Mama, we gonna steal away tonight, right?" Bethlem asked.

"No, child, not tonight," answered Mama. "Tomorrow night we'll follow the drinking gourd, and Old Tom will save us!"

"Mama, what is Canada?" Bethlehem questioned.

"Canada is a place where freedom grows," the old woman answered. "Now git in bed, ya' hear?"

THE NEXT NIGHT

Old Tom crept into the cabin. "All clear," he said.

"Mama, where we goin'?" Bethlehem sleepily asked.

"We goin' to the place where freedom grows," whispered Mama. "Now hush, girl!"

"Here it is!" Old Tom said. "Come on, git in the wagon!"

"Mama, we goin' to Canada, right?" Bethlehem whimpered.

"Yeah," Old Tom broke in, "we gonna go to Canada and the Promised Land!"

FIGURE 11.6
How might it feel to run away to freedom? This fifth grader uses writing to think about this question from the viewpoint of the participants.

concepts clearly and make connections with students' experience. If you use historical fiction, it should be a good story and accurately portray persons and events. Because most fiction is written from a single perspective, you will want to encourage your students to reflect on other points of view by asking, "What are other ways of looking at this?" or "How might another character have interpreted these events?" These questions help students become aware of the interpretative nature of history. The use of multiple books about people and events will help students develop more complex concepts, answer questions they have and add additional perspectives. Encourage students to review the authors' credentials and resources and to consult the encyclopedia or experts for confirming or disproving evidence.

Biographies of famous artists, dancers, actors and poets take students into the minds of creative persons and locate their artistry in a particular historical time and culture. Books such as *Black Pilgrimage*,[40] *Grandma Moses: Painter of Rural America*,[41] *Isamu Noguchi: The Life of a Sculptor*[42] and *A Young Painter: The Life and Paintings of Wang Yani—China's Extraordinary Young Artist*[43] provide primary and early intermediate students with representations of the work of a wide range of artists of varying cultural backgrounds and ages. Books such as *Leonardo da Vinci*,[44] *Marc Chagall: Painter of Dreams*[45] and *Pablo Picasso: The Man and the Image*,[46] which are suitable for use at the intermediate levels, demonstrate the interaction between artistic genius and the politics and cultures of particular times and places in history. As students examine the representations of artists' work, you will want to encourage them to experiment with the techniques of individual artists to express their own ideas.

Personal/Historical Time Lines

This activity helps children make personal associations with events happening in the world. Ask children to identify one event in their lives per year and match this event with an event that happened nationally or internationally. If children choose the day they were born and successive birthdays, they can add any event that happened during a particular year. Older children may want to add other important events, such as moving to a new city, a vacation trip, a new pet, the birth of a sibling or a first bicycle. They might also want to find several events within a year or match personal/historical events to particular days or months. This can also be a class project, with everyone contributing both personal and historical events to the project.

Observation

It is important to provide many opportunities for students to observe natural processes, such as the hatching of eggs or the metamorphoses of frogs or butterflies. As students talk about what they observe, you will want to encourage them to call on their own experiences to create narratives for these events. These narratives can serve as hypotheses that can be tested with reading or further observation. As students use stories to think about scientific events, they gain experience with one of the most powerful of scientific tools—analogical thinking (comparing an unfamiliar event with one that is familiar, to better understand it).

Manipulatives

The National Council of Teachers of Mathematics and the National Science Teachers Association both recommend that students experience the concepts of these disciplines through firsthand experience, with manipulatives and demonstrations. Learning proceeds from concrete experiences to the more symbolic, and to leave out this critical foundation often delays students' understanding of mathematical or scientific concepts. Many school districts provide manipulative materials for classrooms, but it is possible to enlist the aid of parents to develop good collections of interesting items to use for measuring, counting, computing and other mathematical functions. Many basic scientific concepts can also be demonstrated with ordinary materials available in most homes.[47] Science educators at universities and educational service centers often have kits of experiments and demonstrations they will loan to teachers.

When children arrive in your classroom from schools in other countries, they may speak little or no English, but most will speak the language of mathematics, so this is a good place to begin a productive dialogue. Using manipulatives, you can discover what students know about one-to-one correspondence, counting, matching, sorting and categories. Number problems allow you to talk with a student in a language you both understand. When students work together in small groups to create and solve their own problems, they adopt newcomers and work tirelessly to help them develop the English skills they need. In these groups, children will hear the names of numbers and kinds of computation repeated frequently. It is possible for them to communicate with their peers and the teacher by drawing pictures to represent story problems and for others to draw pictures of theirs to supplement language limitations.

WHAT DO YOU THINK? Did you experience any of the learning activities described above as part of your own elementary school education? Which of the activities seem like ones you would enjoy? What do you remember about science and the social studies during your elementary school years?

VII. If This Is Your Situation

Many schools must meet state-mandated requirements in content area subject matter and writing instruction. They may require that specific topics in science, history and health be taught or that certain books be read. Others require writing samples from each student and may stipulate topics and form. The best way to meet these mandates is to involve your students in the process, creating as many opportunities for their decision making as possible.

When state achievement tests in the content areas are mandated, explain to your class that administrators in the district or state want to make sure that everyone learns specific things and that they have created tests to measure what students know. Create a mini-lesson to demonstrate the forms these tests might take, such as multiple choice (students choose the correct answer from several choices) and constructed answer (students create their own response to a question), and talk about how to answer questions in these formats most effectively. Discuss the content of the test and ask students to create some possible questions. Create some questions of your own and go through them step by step with the class. Give them some sample multiple-choice questions dealing with the content area and let them work in groups to practice their test-taking strategies. Discuss with the entire class how the answers were attained.

When the state requires students to produce a certain type of writing, such as comparing and contrasting, persuasive or expository, you can tell your students about this requirement at the beginning of the semester. In mini-lessons you can demonstrate how to respond to content area research in each of the forms and allow them to choose one of the required forms when they write about what they are learning. Tell them that the only requirement is that you must have a sample of each type of writing by the end of the semester. If your state or district requires samples of specific types of writing more often, or if they require responses to a specific topic, you can simply tell your students about the requirement, demonstrate the form in a mini-lesson and help them practice their responses.

Many states or districts administer achievement tests that evaluate spelling proficiency. Generally, these tests present the student with four choices for the correct spelling. You can make a running class list of words most often misspelled and add those that are most frequently misspelled by children at your grade level. Let groups create multiple-choice tests of these words for other groups. Students can also practice tests for math by writing story problems and posing four solutions from which to choose. Involving students in dealing with a testing situation not only helps them practice the format and content of tests, but it also models a way for them to gain control over a difficult situation.

WHAT DO YOU THINK?   What experiences have you had as a student with standardized testing? How do you respond to testing situations? Have you ever taken a test that did not measure what you knew about a subject? What do you believe is the best way to discover what a student knows?

VIII. Evaluating Progress

It is important to involve students in the evaluation of their own performance in the content areas. At the beginning of a study, ask them what elements should be considered in evaluating their work. Add any that are not suggested and explain why these are important to include. From the assembled list, group those that belong together and decide as a class which ones are most important. Students can write these criteria for evaluation in their content area logs and use them for guidelines as they begin their research. These guidelines may include the number and kinds of books or resources used for research, their correct citation for reference and the form of reporting. Be sure to indicate all areas in which students have a choice, such as which books and other resources to use, persons to interview, organizations to contact and possible ways to respond to and share their information through art, dramatic presentations, simulations, prose, poetry or dance.

What kinds of ideas will you be looking for as you brainstorm evaluation criteria with your students? Emphasize techniques that will help students self-evaluate as much as possible. Encourage them to review their writing by asking themselves questions like: Is this report clear and understandable? Is this information correct and current? What did I learn that I did not know before? How can I demonstrate what I have learned?

It is helpful to allow time at the end of each research period for students to share briefly what they have discovered, with a small group or the entire class, and to evaluate themselves in their learning logs. Some teachers provide students with guidelines to help them evaluate their work. These sheets may ask students to assign themselves a grade and to justify it, both in terms of the effort they made to learn and the quality of the learning itself. Additional questions may ask students to make connections between their learning in a content area, other areas of the curriculum and their personal experience. Some teachers ask students to reflect on questions like: How might what you have learned make a difference in your life? The following form is an example of a student self-evaluation sheet. It can be adapted easily for use in the classroom at higher and lower instructional levels.

What do I know a lot about?
Where did I look? (number and kinds of references)
Who did I talk to?
What problems did I face and how did I solve them?
What questions do I have now that I did not have before?
Is the information I want to share presented in an understandable way?
What is something that shows I learned?
What do I know now that I did not know before?

You will want to observe students as they seek and share information in a research study. Examine what they produce for evidence of progress in finding information, organizing their thinking and sharing their responses to learning. Content area journals and logs allow you to follow children's thinking and learning as they explore a topic. You will also want to carefully examine artistic expression of any kind to evaluate levels of understanding that might not be as apparent in other language responses.

WHAT DO YOU THINK? Choose a class you are presently taking or have taken in the past. If you could choose any way for your learning to be evaluated in this class, what would it be? Why do you think you chose this method of evaluation?

IX. Creating Partners

Most communities have a wealth of resources to expand and enrich your students' content area learning. Local historical societies frequently staff the genealogy room in the public library to help young researchers. They may also have a local museum or welcome visitors to local historical landmarks, such as old schools and farmhouses. Many will come to your classroom and bring items of interest to share with the class, such as toys, clothes and utensils from other time periods. Some will set up displays and demonstrate crafts or everyday activities from times past, such as churning butter, quilting, cider making and spinning. A list of historical societies in your area can be found in your public library's copy of the *Directory of Historical Organizations in the United States and Canada*, published by the American Association for State and Local History, 172 Second Ave N., Suite 202, Nashville, TN 37201.

You may also want to explore partnerships between the schools and the business community in your area. Many businesses will help students organize small-business enterprises to help them learn concepts of the marketplace. If this idea sounds interesting, you can obtain information on setting up a partnership with a business in your community by contacting the National Association of Partners in Education, 209 Madison St., Suite 401, Alexandria, VA 22314. Your local Chamber of Commerce will know of businesses and organizations in the community that might be willing to serve as classroom resources. What professionals in your community use mathematics as integral parts of their jobs? You might want to consider sponsoring a math day for your class and invite architects, engineers, computer specialists or accountants to demonstrate how they use mathematics to perform their work.

Be sure to investigate any children's museums in your area. There are four hundred museums in the United States that feature science, history and the arts in special museums designed for children to explore. To find out about any museums in your area, contact the president of the Association for Youth Museums at the Children's Museum of Memphis, 2525 Central Avenue, Memphis, TN 38104, or call (901) 458-2678.

Other community resources you will want to explore include such organizations as the YMCA, which often sponsors special programs in health, physical fitness or safety for children. Local health-care professionals, such as doctors, dentists, nurses and hospital staffs, are usually willing to participate in school-sponsored wellness days. Contact your local or area newspaper to see if they sponsor a program called *Newspapers in Education (NIE)*. Class sets of newspapers are delivered to schools on a weekly basis, accompanied by helpful ideas for relating the content of the newspaper to all areas of the curriculum. Parent groups and community members frequently volunteer to help pay the subscription costs when they know that teachers want to use these resources in their classrooms. Another program you might want to explore is *Wee Deliver*, sponsored by the United States Post Office. It involves students in setting up and running a mail delivery system in their schools.

You can help your students and your presenters have a successful experience with a little advance preparation. Before a visit, help your students generate a list of questions to ask their visitors and review the guidelines for good audience participation. Provide your presenters with some background on what your students are currently studying and the list of questions your students have about their topic. You will also want to inform visitors about the approximate attention span of your class and their level of understanding of the subject matter.

Be sure to notify the special teachers (art, music, physical education) in your building when you begin a theme study in any area. These persons can enhance and enrich any content area study with recordings, dances, songs, craft projects, artistic techniques and biographies of famous artists and musicians. If you do not have specialists in your school, you can find many resources in your school or public libraries to help you make connections with art and music. Consider using some of the following[48] to enhance content area studies:

Recordings to complement studies in geography, weather, science and history include: *Grand Canyon Suite* by Ferde Grofe, *The Four Seasons* by Antonio Vivaldi, *The Flight of the Bumblebee* by Rimsky Korsakov, *El Salon de Mexico*, *Billy the Kid*, and *Rodeo* by Aaron Copeland, *Three Places in New England* by C. Ives, *Pines of Rome* (fourth movement) by Respighi, and the *1812 Overture* by Tchaikovsky.

Videotaped movies that deal with social issues include: *Oklahoma!*, *The King and I*, *South Pacific*, *West Side Story*, and *Romeo and Juliet*. Help students explore architecture with books like: *A Roman Town*, *An Ancient Greek Town*, *A Castle*, *An Egyptian Town*, *A Galleon*, and *An Ancient Chinese Town*, which are part of a series edited by R. J. Unstead, and *City*, *Cathedral* and *Pyramid* by David Macaulay. Historic lifestyles are portrayed in Aliki's *The King's Day* and *A Medieval Feast.*

WHAT DO YOU THINK? Do you remember any visitors to your class in elementary school? Who was your favorite? Most people can recall at least one of these events. Why do you suppose they are memorable?

X. Perspectives: The Narrative

Learning in science and the social studies is enhanced by the use of narratives, both those of published literature and those produced by children themselves. Egan[49] suggests that narratives, with their emphasis on human response to historical events, can be the beginning of historical understanding for students. With narratives, students can imagine themselves in a historical situation because there is a personal connection to these events. Historical fiction provides details that associate events and persons with aspects of living that are familiar to students and introduces experiences that are interesting and novel, such as what people wore, what they looked like, what they ate and drank, what they did in their leisure time, what their homes looked like, their likes and dislikes, their friends and enemies.

When Levstik[50] studied the impact of literature on historical interest and understanding, she found that students strongly associate themselves with the characters in historical fiction and biography, express the desire to be like these persons and think about what they might have done in similar circumstances. Teachers can assist this identification for younger children by encouraging them to reflect on ways they are like historical figures and by providing opportunities for them to role-play parts of the stories that reflect positive traits. Levstik believes that historical stories reflect the values of a culture and are part of the way we come to understand ourselves and the world.

Gallas (op. cit.) believes that children's own narratives help make their thinking visible, so they can reflect upon it, extend and modify it in light of the responses from others. When students are encouraged to create stories to explain what they observe in natural events, they engage in hypothetical thinking. When they try to explain what they see happening in terms of other things that are familiar to them, they are thinking analogically, a process that is helpful to scientists as they reach out to the unknown. Students use their own and others' narratives as a way to make sense of the world. As they tell stories about what they are trying to understand, their explanations are challenged and become more refined. They modify their ideas to make their explanations more plausible and examine their past experiences to support or refute the explanations of other students. Through narrative interaction they begin to see learning as an integrated process and relate what they are learning throughout the curriculum. As they share narratives with each other, they learn that there are many ways to understand the world and to communicate what they are thinking.

XI. Exploring Professional Literature

Teachers examine a wide variety and a great quantity of instructional materials during the year. Commercial publishers have displays at every conference they attend, materials are advertised in teacher's magazines and teacher's stores have stocks of every teaching aid imaginable. How will you know what to select from this great array of offerings? Your task will be simplified if you know what you want to accomplish in your classroom and how you will use activities to support your program. If you want your students to read the highest-quality literature and to write about literature, experiences in their lives and ideas in the content areas, you will probably focus primarily on providing them with good books to read and plenty of opportunities to write. You will be less likely to purchase prepared activities that involve students in filling in the blanks, doing word finds or puzzles. You will search for books of every kind to integrate language learning into the entire curriculum, including picture books, poetry, topical fiction and informational literature.

When you review materials that might be helpful to your classroom program, you will want to be alert to terms such as "reproducibles," which are duplicatable materials that may not match the needs and interests of your classrooms. Students are more interested in games they or other students have created. They can draw their own masks and puppets and enjoy creating puzzles and quizzes for each other. Duplicated materials tend to reduce creativity, individual involvement and choice, occupying student time with busy work rather than meaningful reading and writing experiences.

Commercial materials that can be helpful are usually those that are the most basic. They allow you to use them in many ways and easily adapt to the program needs of individual classrooms. Examples of these kinds of books are how-to-do-it manuals that provide ideas for puppets, dramas, craft projects and generic classroom activities of all levels. A good way to tell if the material will be helpful is to assess your response when you review it. If you think, "That's a good idea. I could use it *this* way in *my* class," then you are using the materials to support your own particular program and not allowing them to direct your program.

Commercial materials can also provide ideas for activities and materials you can construct yourself or adapt to your own program. Many items like games, posters and banners can be inexpensively produced from ideas you glean from these sources. Consider using an overhead projector to make your own poster-size enlargements of objects or bulletin board materials. If you trace around the picture with pencil and then a heavy marker, you can produce interesting and innovative materials on your own. If you have created a framework of ideas for content area learning, it is easy and rewarding to add activities that support your program.

WHAT DO YOU THINK? What resources for teaching especially appeal to you? Why do you think teachers often resort to commercially prepared material for their students? Do you see any comparisons with home-prepared and fast food?

XII. Resources for Teaching

The following are resources for using language and literature to explore concepts in the content areas.

The Astonishing Curriculum: Integrating Science and Humanities through Language[51] If you are interested in reading more about how to integrate the curriculum using language and literature, this collection of essays by practicing teachers provides both information and inspiration. Writers describe ways they use group discussions, journals, hands-on activities and research to identify and support students' questions about the world. Articles are richly anecdotal and contain many examples of student dialogue and written work.

Scholastic News This weekly periodical for students is available for every elementary instructional level, including *Let's Find Out* for kindergarten and *Scholastic News*: Grades 1–2, 2–3, and 4–6. These full-color newspapers feature national and international news, stories about science and technology, human-interest stories and contests. Teachers receive posters and ideas for activities in the classroom. For grades 3–6, there is an accompanying *Scholastic News* video, produced in conjunction with NBC News. Information is available by calling 1-800-631-1586.[52]

Using Nonfiction Trade Books in the Elementary Classroom: From Ants to Zeppelins[53] is a collection of articles by authors and educators. Articles discuss a variety of issues related to the use of nonfiction literature for content area learning and provide helpful ideas for integrating this genre into the entire curriculum. Especially interesting are articles by authors of informational literature, such as Russell Freedman and Patricia Lauber. Other articles provide criteria to evaluate nonfiction, list ways to use informational books to develop reference skills, and present ideas for using nonfiction literature in theme teaching.

The Multicultural Game Book[54] provides instructions for 70 games from 30 countries representing every continent in the world. Designed for elementary students ages 5 to 11, each game description includes information on the skills required, appropriate age level, number of players and the materials required. The games include those that require both physical and mental effort and settings appropriate for classrooms and outdoor playgrounds. Sample gameboards and other drawings help create clear and simple directions for each game. Large maps, suitable for posting on a bulletin board, identify the places of origin for the games, which are grouped together by continent. A brief historical background is provided, which can serve as a springboard to learning more about the children who play these games in other countries. Many games are similar to those played by American children, and they will enjoy making comparisons.

Multicultural Math: Hands-on Activities from Around the World[55] is a collection of math activities from every continent. Topics include: names and symbols for numbers in different cultures, the abacus, money, mental arithmetic, linear measurement, cooking, calendars, magic squares, architecture, quilts, tessellations in Islamic culture, and Native American beadwork. All activities conform to the NCTM standards in multiculturalism. Each lesson includes a presentation of the concept, practice using the concept and questions to explore the concept further. Also included are extension ideas and ways to tie the discussion to other areas of the curriculum. For each presentation, there is a bibliography of books appropriate for students who want to explore a concept further.

Read Any Good Math Lately? Children's Books for Mathematical Learning K–6[56] is full of good suggestions for using literature to introduce, expand or enrich the study of mathematics. The authors believe that fiction and nonfiction literature that includes mathematical concepts helps children appreciate the authentic contexts in which mathematics naturally occurs. In the context of a narrative, mathematics is no longer a set of facts and computations, but a tool for describing and understanding the world.

Anno's Math Games III[57] is the third volume in a series of books that illustrate math concepts in intriguing ways. This book explores the concepts of topology, triangles, mazes and positional relations. Each book features mathematic notes in an afterword to help teachers adapt the material for all grade levels, K–6. Topological ideas are introduced by the series' characters, Kriss and Kross, and a magic liquid that causes shapes to shrink or expand. The section on triangles features quilts, kaleidoscopes, baskets and paperfolding. The well-known seven-bridge puzzle of Konigsberg, one- and two-line mazes, and circuit theory are featured in the mazes exploration. The concept of left and right is explored through gears and directions along a series of roadways. Maps encourage readers to discuss positional relations and can be used to introduce x and y coordinates.

From Sea to Shining Sea: A Treasury of American Folklore and Folk Songs[58] is an illustrated anthology of 140 songs, stories, poems and essays introduced in historical context, from pre-Columbian time to today. The book is beautifully illustrated by Caldecott Award winners, which adds greatly to the quality of the reading experience. End-of-the-book references help teachers locate topics by categories such as chronology, geographical region, story type, ethnic/religious group, song type and author. The songs and stories of the major cultural groups in the United States are included.

The Story of Ourselves: Teaching History through Children's Literature[59] In this collection of articles, well-known writers share their ideas on writing and illustrating nonfiction books. There is an annotated bibliography, including both fiction and nonfiction, that focuses on various aspects of American history.

Themes: Animals[60] is one of the best in a series of thematic presentations, which also include books on celebrations, seasons, water and fantasy. If you are wondering how experienced teachers integrate language learning throughout the curriculum and how all areas of the curriculum are related, this is a good model to review. The authors present activities that help students develop language skills as they learn scientific concepts and vocabulary, write stories, and participate in poetry, origin stories, songs and chants.

The Children's Book Store This is an excellent source of materials to integrate history, science and the social studies with music and art. You can obtain a list of its resources by writing to: 67 Wall Street, Suite 2411, New York, NY 10006 or calling 1-800-668-0242.

WHAT DO YOU THINK? Which of the resources annotated above most draws your interest as a teacher? Which do you think might be most helpful to you personally? Do you have any special interests or talents in art or music? How might special interests of any kind contribute to your teaching?

XIII. Reflections

From a Teacher's Journal—Jackie Hogue, Fifth Grade

I love the idea of reading and writing about a topic of interest. I must follow a district-directed curriculum, but my kids are able to research areas of a required topic. Since I don't have workbooks, my school allows me to buy books for topics of study. I also request books two to three weeks in advance from the public library. The children are eager to learn because they have so many wonderful books of many reading levels to choose from. I have found that no two years of a study are the same. Each group of kids has different interests.

I also demonstrate all kinds of writing to my students and encourage them to try out the different forms. For example, when we study ancient Indians, I introduce contrast and comparison writing. They choose two groups, such as the Mayan and Aztec, to compare and contrast. We also contrast prejudice and tolerance during the colonial period. I want my students to be able to write in many forms, including expository, persuasive and poetic.

. . . My plan to teach contrast and comparison with Native Americans has been foiled. The kids asked if they could write historical fiction like *The Island of the Blue Dolphins*, using the information they'd learned. I had no choice but to say yes! Maybe we can compare and contrast their stories to the *Island* book!

Aaron, who needs lots of support, told me the ancient Indian study was the "funnest" research he'd ever done. Because his family farms, he chose to learn about Inca farming. He's armed with information to give to the class! "Is it okay if our team meets on the bus going home tonight, so we can share information?" he asked. Wow!

We read legends for an hour today, and then I asked students what they noticed about all these stories. Immediately, they could tell me the elements of a legend, which I listed on a chart. My students are required to write a legend for a state assessment. I'm curious to see how well they will write. . . . Everyone read their legends aloud, while I wrestled with three checklists for state assessments. In my mind, the most valuable assessment took place when the children read their legends to the class. Everyone clapped for the readers, told them what was good and what might make their stories better. Each made notes and put the legends into writing folders to polish and improve as they have time.

WHAT DO YOU THINK? This journal was written by an experienced teacher who was moving toward an integrated curriculum. If you have a colleague like this when you begin teaching, what might you learn from her?

TRYING OUT THE CHAPTER IDEAS

1. What do you think children are curious about? Ask several elementary students: "What's something you'd like to learn more about, if you had the chance?" Record their responses in your journal.
2. What mathematics programs have you observed at the elementary level? In what ways do they incorporate language and literature?
3. Have you observed an elementary science class? Were there opportunities for students to talk about what they observed or read about? In what ways was writing involved? Were there attractive science trade books available in the classroom?
4. What kinds of inquiry have you observed in the social studies? Do you know teachers who involve community members in their social studies programs?
5. What opportunities for artistic expression have you observed in elementary classrooms? Are you making notes of ones that look especially interesting?
6. Interview three different teachers about the way they teach concepts in the content areas. Compare the levels at which they integrate language learning and literature into these studies. Which approach seems most manageable to you?

Notes

1. Karen Gallas, *The Languages of Learning: How Children Talk, Write, Dance, Draw, and Sing Their Understanding of the World* (New York: Teachers College Press, 1994).

2. Bess Altwerger and Barbara Flores, "Theme Cycles: Creating Communities of Learners," *Primary Voices K–6* 2, no. 1 (1994): 2–6.
3. Philip Cohen, "Developing Information Literacy," *Education Update* 37, no. 2 (1995): 1.
4. Barbara Moss, "Children's Nonfiction Trade Books: A Complement to Content Area Texts," *The Reading Teacher* 45, no. 1 (September 1991): 26–31.
5. Douglas Barnes, *From Communication to Curriculum*, 2d ed. (Portsmouth, N.H.: Heinemann, 1992).
6. Kathryn M. Pierce and Carol Gilles, eds., *Cycles of Meaning: Exploring the Potential of Talk in Learning Communities* (Portsmouth, N.H.: Heinemann, 1993).
7. J. Britton, T. Burgess, N. Martin, A. McLeod, and H. Rosen, *The Development of Writing Abilities (11–18)* (Portsmouth, N.H.: Boynton/Cook, 1975).
8. Peter Medway, *Language in Science* (Hatfield, England: Language in Science Working Party, The Association for Science Education, 1980).
9. Pat D'Arcy, *Writing Across the Curriculum: Language for Learning* (Exeter, England: Exeter University School of Education, 1977).
10. M. Hughes, *Curriculum Integration in the Primary Grades: A Framework for Excellence* (Alexandria, Va.: Association of Supervision and Curriculum Development, 1991).
11. Mary Baratta-Lorton, *Mathematics Their Way: An Activity-Centered Mathematics Program for Early Childhood Education* (Reading, Mass.: Addison Wesley, 1976).
12. Eric Carle, *The Very Hungry Caterpillar* (East Rutherford, N.J.: Putnam, 1969).
13. Eric Carle, *Rooster's Off to See the World* (East Rutherford, N.J.: Putnam, 1987).
14. Eric Carle, *1,2,3 to the Zoo: A Counting Book* (East Rutherford, N.J.: Putnam, 1987).
15. Sandra Boynton, *Hippos Go Berserk* (Waltham, Mass.: Little, Brown, 1979).
16. Stan Mack, *Ten Bears in My Bed: A Goodnight Countdown* (New York: Pantheon, 1974).
17. Fulvio Testa, *If You Take a Pencil* (Bergenfield, N.J.: Dial/Penguin, 1982).
18. Ellen Stoll Walsh, *Mouse Count* (New York: Trumpet Club, 1994).
19. Muriel Feelings, *Moja Means One: Swahili Counting Book* (New York: Dial, 1971).
20. Frances Jones, *Nature's Deadly Creatures: A Pop-up Exploration* (Bergenfield, N.J.: Dial/Penguin, 1992).
21. Jim Murphy, *The Call of the Wolves* (New York: Scholastic, 1989).
22. Elizabeth George Speare, *Calico Captive* (New York: Dell, 1957).
23. Rebecca Caudill, *Tree of Freedom* (New York: Viking, 1949).
24. James Lincoln Collier and Christopher Collier, *My Brother Sam Is Dead* (New York: Macmillan, 1974).
25. Esther Forbes, *Johnny Tremain* (New York: Dell, 1971).
26. Walter Dean Myers, *Fallen Angels* (New York: Scholastic, 1988).
27. Scott O'Dell, *Sarah Bishop* (New York: Scholastic, 1980).
28. Clinton Cox, *Undying Glory: The Story of the Massachusetts 54th Regiment* (New York: Scholastic, 1991).
29. Alice P. Buening and Christine Martin, eds., *Children's Writer's & Illustrator's Market* (Cincinnati, Ohio: Writer's Digest Books, 1995).
30. Madeleine L'Engle, *A Wrinkle in Time* (New York: Dell, 1962).
31. Madeleine L'Engle, *A Wind in the Door* (New York: Dell, 1973).
32. Madeleine L'Engle, *A Swiftly Tilting Planet* (New York: Dell, 1978).
33. Lois Lowry, *The Giver* (Burlington, Mass.: Houghton Mifflin, 1993).
34. Cynthia Rylant, *Dicey's Song* (New York: Random House, 1982).
35. Cynthia Rylant, *The Homecoming* (New York: Random House, 1981).
36. Virginia Hamilton, *The Planet of Junior Brown* (New York: Macmillan, 1971).

37. See, for example, the accounts of Elena Castro, "Implementing Theme Cycles: One Teacher's Way," and Marty Andrews-Sullivan and Esther Orono Negrete, "Our Struggles with Theme Cycles," *Primary Voices K–6* 2, no. 1 (1994): 7–14, 15–19.

38. Martha Eggers, Assistant Professor of Education at McKendree College, Lebanon, Illinois.

39. Lois Bridges Bird, "Supporting Real Research," in *The Whole Language Catalog* (Santa Rosa, Calif.: American School Publishers, 1991).

40. Tom Feelings, *Black Pilgrimage* (Fairfield, N.J.: Lothrop, 1972).

41. Zibby O'Neal, *Grandma Moses: Painter of Rural America* (Bergenfield, N.J.: Viking/Penguin, 1986).

42. Tobi Tobias, *Isamu Noguchi: The Life of a Sculptor* (Scranton, Penn.: Crowell/HarperCollins, 1974).

43. Zheng Zhensun and Alice Low, *A Young Painter: The Life and Paintings of Wang Yani—China's Extraordinary Young Artist* (New York: Scholastic, 1991).

44. Richard McLanathan, *Leonardo da Vinci* (New York: Abrams, 1990).

45. Natalie S. Bober, *Marc Chagall: Painter of Dreams* (New York: Jewish Publication Society, 1991).

46. Richard B. Lyttle, *Pablo Picasso: The Man and the Image* (Riverside, N.J.: Atheneum/Macmillan, 1989).

47. Don Herbert and Hy Ruchlis, *Mr. Wizard's 400 Experiments in Science* (North Bergen, N.J.: Book Lab, 1968).

48. This list was compiled by Dr. Nancy Ypma, Associate Professor of Music at McKendree College, Lebanon, Illinois.

49. K. Egan, "Accumulating History," in *History and Theory: Studies in the Philosophy of History #22* (Hanover, N.H.: University Press of England, 1983), pp. 66–80.

50. L. S. Levstik, "The Relationship between Historical Response and Narrative in a Sixth-Grade Classroom," *Theory and Research in Social Education* 14 (1986): 1–15.

51. Stephen Tchudi, ed., *The Astonishing Curriculum: Integrating Science and Humanities through Language* (Urbana, Ill.: National Council of Teachers of English, 1993).

52. Scholastic Book Clubs, Inc., P.O. Box 7503, Jefferson City, MO 65102-9966.

53. Evelyn B. Freeman and Diane Goetz Person, eds., *Using Nonfiction Trade Books in the Elementary Classroom: From Ants to Zeppelins* (Urbana, Ill.: National Council of Teachers of English, 1992).

54. Louise Orlando, *The Multicultural Game Book: More Than 70 Traditional Games from 30 Countries* (New York: Scholastic, 1993).

55. Claudia Zaslavsky, *Multicultural Math: Hands-on Activities from Around the World* (New York: Scholastic, 1994).

56. David Whitin and Sandra Wilde, *Read Any Good Math Lately? Children's Books for Mathematical Learning K–6* (Portsmouth, N.H.: Heinemann, 1992).

57. Mitsumasa Anno, *Anno's Math Games III* (New York: Philomel, 1991).

58. Amy Cohn, comp., *From Sea to Shining Sea: A Treasury of American Folklore and Folksongs* (New York: Scholastic, 1993).

59. Michael O. Tunnell and Richard Ammon, *The Story of Ourselves: Teaching History through Children's Literature* (Portsmouth, N.H.: Heinemann, 1993).

60. Marlene McCracken and Robert McCracken, *Themes: Animals* (Winnipeg, Manitoba: Penguin, 1988).

CHAPTER TWELVE

Language and Literature in Three Classrooms

WHAT'S HAPPENING HERE? Enthusiasm for learning is characteristic of the teachers portrayed in this chapter and throughout the book. These teachers read constantly and are excited about sharing new books and ideas with their students and colleagues. In their classrooms, students are active participants in their own learning and are encouraged to respond to what they learn in creative ways.

It is the supreme art of the teacher to awaken joy in creative expression and knowledge.

—Albert Einstein

A teacher affects eternity; he can never tell where his influence stops.

—Henry Adams

LOOKING AHEAD   1. How do experienced teachers begin the school year?
2. What schedules do they follow?
3. What resources do they use for instruction?
4. How are themes, language and literature used across the curriculum?
5. How do experienced teachers address special learning needs?
6. What professional and children's books do experienced teachers use and recommend?

IN 25 WORDS   Teachers who use language and literature successfully throughout the
OR LESS   curriculum share a common belief that children learn best through active participation.

I. Focus: Three Views of Language and Literature in the Classroom

In this chapter, you are invited to spend the day in three classrooms where language and literature are integral to learning in all areas of the curriculum. In previous chapters, you looked closely at individual activities that promote language and content area learning. Now you can observe how these activities function as integral parts of a daily schedule and are incorporated into planning for the entire school year.

In the sections that follow the classroom observations, teachers talk about their classroom programs and respond to the concerns they most frequently hear expressed from beginning teachers, such as: How do you start the school year? How do you introduce the different activities? and What kind of schedule do you follow? They also address such questions as: How do you provide for the needs of special learners? and How do you involve parents and the community in your program?

The teachers portrayed in this chapter are lifelong learners, who are continually growing in their understanding of how children learn. They all read extensively, attend conferences to improve their professional knowledge, have a long history of sharing ideas with others and support the efforts of their colleagues to introduce new ways of teaching into their classrooms. Visitors are always welcome in their classrooms, and because they see themselves as learners, they openly discuss the ways they want to change and improve. Over a period of years, they have interacted with college and university students as instructors and mentors for student teaching, and each has been widely recognized by students, colleagues and administrators for professional excellence.

As you enter the classrooms in these narratives, you will notice that each teacher exhibits a particular style as he or she interacts with the students. One or more of these persons may provide you with an additional teaching model to complement those you will have from firsthand observations of practicing teachers. Although the grade levels and teaching contexts of these teachers differ, they share common beliefs about teaching and learning. Whether they teach in rural or urban situations, to students of economic privilege or deprivation, all believe that learners should be active inquirers in the classroom. They create a print-rich environment for their students and provide many opportunities for students to develop and practice skills in reading, writing, listening, speaking and thinking. All have created a community of learners in an environment that encourages sharing and risk taking.

Visits to each of these classrooms begin with a day-long observation and conclude with the teacher's description of his or her practice. As you join these teachers and their students for the day, notice your own reaction to their approach to teaching. Does it feel comfortable to you? Can you see yourself teaching in this manner? Do you begin to see how the activities of language learning fit into a day's classroom program?

II. A Day's Visit in Kindergarten

Gail Nave, Summerfield Grade School, Summerfield, Illinois

"Mrs. Nave, what do those words say?" Aaron asks, pointing to a new poem written on the story chart.

"Just a minute, Aaron. I need to finish here first," she replies. School has not begun yet, and Mrs. Nave is providing background for the day's activities to a classroom visitor.

"Now! Mrs. Nave, I need to know now!" he insists. "I need to know what those words say!"

Mrs. Nave excuses herself to read the new poem aloud to Aaron, who then rushes over to anther boy to share the news. "Guess what the new poem says?" he asks, and the two of them continue to puzzle out the words on the chart.

When Aaron first began school in the fall, he did not notice the words on the chart or pay any attention to the many books displayed around the room. They were not a part of his experience, previous to attending school. But as he listened to books read aloud and shared the foot-tapping, finger-snapping shared reading sessions, he began to observe that printed words were associated with exciting and rewarding experiences. He discovered that books had pictures of things he was interested in, like animals, trucks and cars. He was encouraged to write his own ideas about what he heard, saw and thought about, and soon he encountered new print with the intensity recorded above.

In this classroom, kindergarten children arrive at school over a twenty-minute period of time in the morning. Some walk, while others arrive in buses on a staggered schedule. When they come into the room, they sign in, fasten a clip clothespin with their name on it beside a picture of a lunch tray or a lunch box to indicate their lunch choice and deposit any notes, book club orders or lunch money envelopes in a basket. They move on to free-choice activities at various centers around the room: housekeeping; blocks (tinkertoys and legos); "The Write Place," which features paper and writing utensils; computers, with programs such as Math Rabbit and Alpha-bears; The Library Corner, with class-made books and multiple copies of regular-sized versions of the Big Books from shared reading; puzzles and learning games; a listening station with books and tapes; and a painting center.

Most children do not have many toys in their homes so at first they are attracted to areas that feature these things. By February, however, Mrs. Nave notices that most of the children cluster in small groups during this free-choice time, reading, singing and chanting to each other from books or from the songs, poems and stories on charts around the room. Students especially enjoy reading the books they have written and published themselves. Each book is a collection of their memories and common experiences: field trips, visitors, theme studies and favorite books. Many of these class books begin as displays on bulletin boards. "Look Who Goes to Kindergarten" at the beginning of the year features children's self-portraits and conversation bubbles. Inside the bubble, the teacher or an aide writes whatever the child wants the class to know about them, such as "Hi! My name is Lisa. I love pepperoni pizza."

After free-choice time, students move to writer's workshop, which features the word of the day. This word, written prominently on the blackboard, is associated with the current theme, such as "butterfly" from a study of insects or "spider" from their current read-aloud book, Charlotte's Web.[1] Students draw a picture to illustrate the word or create their own words and pictures. Today the word is "leprechaun," which they have heard in read-aloud books and in discussions about St. Patrick's Day. To assist their writing, students consult other words on their discussion chart and books about leprechauns that are displayed in the room. Some label their pictures with words, such as "shamrock," "rainbow," "pot of gold," or "green hat." All use developmental spelling to tell their stories. Above the chalkboard, Mrs. Nave has placed the manuscript alphabet for children to use as a model for their writing. She makes her own alphabet cards, writing the letters on an enlarged version of the blue and red dotted-line primary paper available to students.

When everyone has drawn and written, it is time for Morning Meeting. Students retrieve clipboards from a large plastic tub in the front of the room and gather on the rug in front of a large calendar. Also posted here are the Poem of the Month and an enlarged copy of the Letter of the Month, written to the students from the teacher. On the clipboards are copies of the calendar, poem and letter. At the end of the month, Mrs. Nave will send these materials home, where parents will help children continue their reading practice. There are usually no books in her students' homes, and she is eager for children to have printed matter in their hands that they can read.

Each morning, students interact with the calendar, adding on the numbers of successive days, the month's name and the days of the week. They talk about what happened yesterday, what will happen today and what they will do tomorrow. They count the number of months in the school year before February and say the names of the months that will follow. They create questions for each other, such as: How many days have there been since the beginning of the year? How many days have there been since the beginning of the month? How many days until the end of the month? They talk about the birthdays that occur during the month and count the number of days left until these special days. In the beginning, Mrs. Nave writes in the numbers on the individual student calendars before they are duplicated, and children draw Xs through each day as it occurs. By the third month, however, children are writing in their own numbers.

Students draw pictures on their calendars to note birthdays, holidays and special events like field trips, visitors, the first snowfall, early dismissal and days off. The teacher writes the day's number on an appropriate seasonal shape (sun, leaf, snowflake, flower) and fastens it to the register tape that makes a border around the room. This is part of the 100 days counting project, and at the end of 100 days, there will be a celebration. Children make frequent estimates about how far the tape will go around the room before the end of 100 days.

There is also a Lost Tooth of the Month activity, and for every lost tooth the children chant, "I lost a tooth, but I don't care; another one is growing there!" Each month has a tooth on it, with the names of children who lost teeth that month. The group talks about tooth statistics and makes comparisons, such as the fact that more people lost a tooth in September. They also examine their calendars to find the month when the fewest children lost teeth.

On their copies of the teacher's letter, students find the word "love" and draw a heart around it. They also draw pictures to illustrate other words in the poem or the letter and draw blocks or circles around the letter of the day. Poems of the month are repetitive and rhythmic, allowing children to join in immediately. At Christmas, Mrs. Nave uses "I wish you a Merry Christmas," and in late spring, Robert Louis Stevenson's verse: "The world is so full of a number of things, I'm sure we should all be as happy as kings." The large chart letters and poems are saved and hung up on nails above the blackboard, so children can refer to them during the year.

During each Morning Meeting a child reads or tells about Griswold's visit to his or her home the night before. Griswold, you will remember from Chapter 1, is the stuffed bear that goes home with a different child each night

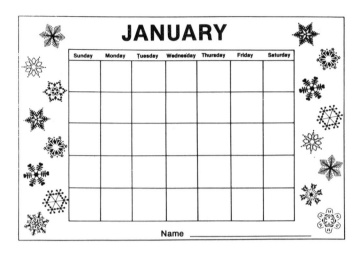

January

Dear Boys and Girls,

January is the winter month.
Don't forget your hat and mittens.
Let it snow! Let it snow! Let it snow!

Love,
Mrs. Nave

Five little snowmen standing in a row.

Each has a hat and a big red bow.

Out came the sun and it shown all day.

One little snowman melted away.

FIGURE 12.1
These are the materials students have on their clipboard during the month. Each day they add a number to the calendar and draw pictures of important events, such as birthdays and holidays. They read the letter and poem together and interact with the words and letters to practice their reading skills.

and returns with a story of the visit written in his journal. Children may also choose to draw a picture about the visit and talk about the visit firsthand. By the end of the year, many are writing sentences and brief stories in the journal themselves and sit in the author's chair to read. Griswold travels to various homes in a book bag, along with his journal, which is enclosed in a ziplock bag. The journal is a spiral notebook that has hard plastic covers to withstand repeated use. As the smaller spiral notebooks are filled, they go into a three-ring binder and are placed in the library center for student reading and review.

Morning Meeting is followed by a read-aloud session, to which the students respond enthusiastically. P.E. is out-of-doors today, followed by a snack and restroom break. After this, the children settle down with favorite books for silent, sustained reading. Each chooses a favorite spot for reading: some sit at tables, while others stretch out on the rug or tuck themselves away under tables and behind shelves. Mrs. Skingley, the music teacher, joined the class before SSR and participates by reading her own book. When the independent reading period is finished, she works with the students on a song she is teaching them to sing and perform in sign language. On other days of the week, this may be a time for a shared reading experience, using Big Books or other predictable stories, poems and songs written on a chart tablet. The morning closes with math activities and another story. In the afternoon, the teacher will read aloud from a chapter book and they will explore their current study theme. During the last half hour of the day, students will look at books with their Book Buddies from second grade or listen to a book read aloud by a guest storyteller.

In Her Own Words—Gail Nave

Because most of my children have never been in an educational setting prior to enrollment in kindergarten, I need to "ease" into my program. However, on Day One, I begin establishing the program, and throughout the year it remains pretty well intact. Children respond very well to this predictable schedule. On the first day of school my students are reading, writing, and immersed in quality literature. From the first day, my students "Sign In," even if they are unable to write the "kindergarten way." This daily exercise establishes the need to write and demonstrates the power of writing. Through careful prodding I am able to get them to take risks and show them they are valued as learners. We also begin writing workshop on the first day, with modeling for the children about what I would like to see on their papers: words, a picture about the words, their name and the date, stamped with the library stamp. I will continue modeling for the first week or so and periodically through the year as the need arises. Within days, the students are able to independently file their writing efforts in hanging files.

The types of activities in the daily schedule remain the same from day to day, but there is flexibility in how long each activity lasts. I like to allow more time for activities when children are really involved and move on if their attention wavers.

Our Daily Schedule

Morning

Free choice of activities in centers: art, blocks, writing, reading, science
Writing workshop: individual writing and drawing projects
Morning Meeting: discussing ideas together
Mini-lesson: reading and writing strategies
P.E.: outdoors or in the gym, according to the weather
Music: experiences to enrich the theme study
Shared reading: predictable books, nursery rhymes, chants, poetry
Math: manipulative experiences

Afternoon

Storytime: reading aloud from a chapter book
Afternoon theme study: reading, writing, talking and thinking about
concepts in science and the social studies.

I begin planning for the year with a broad overview of where I want
students to be by the end of the year; then I am able to better pace activities,
based on the abilities of my students. I do not use workbooks or rely heavily
on ditto sheets, but I must meet the objectives established by the district. I
identify the skills my students will be expected to know by the end of the
year and incorporate these objectives into mini-lessons throughout the year,
as they are needed. I also identify a sequence for reviewing letters and sounds
in shared reading. I have discovered, however, that my students always learn
far more than I set out to teach them! The children are in charge of their
learning, and I am quick to point out that this year belongs to *them*. I had
my year in kindergarten a long time ago.

Most of our themes begin with the KWL approach: Children contribute
ideas about what they already know about a topic and we list things they
would like to know; at the end of each session, we review what we have
learned. I also like to introduce the theme with an especially appealing book,
to get them "hooked." When the children walk into the classroom on the
day a new theme is being introduced, they will see new books displayed that
deal with that topic along with pictures or a chart on the easel.

Although I must use some of the materials adopted by the district, I
supplement from many other sources. In many respects my program seems
to be driven by the introduction of new books. Given the fact that many of
my children are environmentally disadvantaged, a good number are not
familiar with the language of print. If I expect them to read print, they must
first hear the language of print and hold books in their own hands. While
students in my class are basically practicing how to read, they surprise
themselves by becoming quite accomplished readers by the end of the year.
I believe that children first **act** as readers and then they **become** readers.

Any book I share with my class is one I am genuinely excited about. There
are far too many good books to read to waste time on ones that are so-so. I
now always identify the author and illustrator of the book, a practice I did

not always do. I continue to be amazed at how adept my class is at identifying authors and illustrators. I might ask the children what they think a certain book might be about, based on the title and cover illustration. Then I read the book in its entirety, trying to avoid interruptions, as the first reading should be for sheer pleasure. Usually I hear whispered requests to read it again, just as I am closing the book. And YES, I do read it again that day and many other days as well. During later readings I will certainly pause for discussion or bring attention to some particular part. At the end of the school year, children vote on their favorite chapter book, and we read it again.

I delight in the first day of SSR. I place a tub of wordless books in the center of the floor, and we sit on the floor in a circle. I pick up a book and start looking at it silently. Sometimes others join me by selecting a book. Other times they just stare. When I have finished the book, I share what a wonderful story it was. This creates a model and everyone soon joins me. I have discovered that at this age, independent reading time will not be silent. I soon discovered that vocalizing is part of developmental reading and that if I occasionally walked around the room and *listened* while children were reading to themselves, I had a wonderful opportunity to see how well their reading strategies were developing.

I use many resources for my students' learning. Visitors are always a welcome addition to the classroom, and I invite a different storyteller each Friday. That person might be the principal, other school personnel, a family member or family friend. They are asked to share several of their favorite children's books with the class. I try to take the class on as many field trips as the district will allow, to help broaden my students' knowledge of the world around them. We go to the apple orchard, visit the dairy farm, go to the post office to mail valentines to our Book Buddies, attend a performance at the St. Louis Symphony, and attend the all-school Outdoor Education Day. Most years, we are able to squeeze in a trip to the St. Louis Zoo, Grant's Farm, or the Continental Bakery.

I try to increase my professional knowledge and skill by attending meetings of our local TAWL group, which provides excellent monthly programs. They also bring in outstanding speakers several times a year for Saturday conferences. My all-time favorite conference is the Illinois Kindergarten Conference, held in Chicago in late winter. Not only do I hear wonderful keynote speakers, but the presentations by fellow teachers provide me with many ideas to bring back to the classroom. I also regularly read *The Reading Teacher*[2] for ideas to use in my teaching.

If I were a beginning teacher, I would purchase for my library the four professional books that have had the most influence on my teaching: *What's Whole in Whole Language*[3] by Kenneth Goodman, because it gives an overview of this kind of teaching in clear terms; *Joyful Learning*[4] by Bobbi Fisher, because it is written by a former kindergarten teacher *for* kindergarten teachers and has applications for both half-day and full-day programs; and *Transitions: From Literature to Literacy*[5] and *Invitations*[6] by Regie Routman, because I have found many useful ideas for my own teaching in both of these books. If I had to recommend the best books to read aloud, they would include: *Chicka Chicka Boom Boom*[7] by Bill Martin, Jr.; *How Many Bugs in a Box?*[8] by David Carter; *The Very Quiet Cricket*[9] by Eric Carle; and *Griswold's Journal*, a continuing account of our room mascot's visits to student homes.

My student teachers regularly ask me: Do you teach phonics? Can I really do all this when I'm a teacher? and Where do I start? This is how I answer them: I do teach the sounds of letters, but in the context of helping students figure out how to spell a word for their writing or to read a word in a book they are interested in. Sometimes at the beginning, teaching can seem overwhelming, but you *can* do it! You must be patient with yourself and your students. Teachers who expect miracles or try to do too much at one time will soon burn out. This is an evolving process that takes years to develop, but what fun we have along the way!

Begin with an area that interests you most, and the area in which you are most comfortable. Visit other teachers and observe the way they present and manage activities in their classrooms. Then choose the best of what you see and mold it to fit your own situation. While you are in the classrooms, ask the teachers why they do certain things. Ask lots of questions.

The first year I introduced daily writing, I eventually discovered that children only become writers when they have the time and opportunity to improve their skills. I learned to be patient, waiting for results. One day, I apologized to the class because I had forgotten to pick up balloons for our calendar. Without a blink of an eye, Travis, who was helper of the day, told me he would write me a note to help me remember. Much to my amazement, he did just that and slipped it on my desk. From then on, children were quick to write notes for me to remind me of things I should know. I had convinced the children that they were writers with a real audience.

I believe in whole-group instruction for the most part, with limited grouping by common needs in the form of mini-lessons. Children learn so much from each other and I learn from them, too. Immersed in a print-rich environment and provided with many opportunities to practice reading, they come to see the joy of reading and believe that they can learn to read as well. They are actively involved in learning throughout the day. My children know up front that the word "can't" does not exist in our room. I expect all students to succeed in my program, and I try to create an environment in which all can meet with some measure of success. Patience goes a long way, and if we provide enough opportunities to practice literacy skills they will suddenly bloom when we least expect it.

Each time I learn that I am getting a child with special needs, I tend to be a bit apprehensive. As soon as he/she arrives, however, those fears vanish and we all seem to adapt very easily. Children fought over the opportunity to join Charley in a quiet game when the weather did not allow him to be as active as he would like (he was born without sweat glands and could not perspire to cool his body). Kate participated in all aspects of physical education and was cheered on by her teammates, even though she was slowed down by braces because of cerebral palsy. Thomas's frequent epileptic seizures did not alarm his classmates. Another student was quick to get a resting mat for Thomas because she knew that Thomas would need to rest afterwards from seizures that physically drained him. Added to these special needs were those of foster children, who were emotionally drained. To each child, my classes have responded in an accepting and caring way. This may be partly due to the fact that limitations and differences are not pointed out or emphasized and partly a result of the bonding we enjoy as a community of learners. Without exception, all of my students make great strides.

My classroom library has books of every kind and description. I also have class books the children have made throughout the year. These books will later find new homes with class members who take them home in May. Many show the wear and tear of daily handling since they are always favorites, given the fact that their own efforts are between the covers. In addition to the class books, there are also multiple copies of regular-sized versions of the Big Books we use in shared reading. Children are already familiar with the text and can use these books to practice their reading skills during free-choice time or SSR. Before children begin handling the books, we read *Benjamin's Book*[10] by Alan Baker, the story of a hamster who spoils a page in a book and tries to clean it up. This book sets the tone for handling books with care.

I have all kinds of trade books in my classroom, not only in the library, but around the room, on chalkboard ledges, the piano, the window ledges and any other available space where children might be drawn. During our study of spiders at Halloween, I might read aloud from a factual book about spiders, help students examine a Big Book version of *The Very Busy Spider*[11] by Eric Carle, and share with them some of the Anansi tales.

I make a real effort to introduce my children to many different kinds of literature. A fun activity that required little effort on my part and thoroughly held my students' attention was gathering different versions of a folktale. Each day I read a different version, while the children develop their listening skills to fill in a chart of common elements. For example, at Thanksgiving, when we are getting ready for our feast with our Book Buddies, I share a different version of *Stone Soup*[12] each day. The children listen for the main characters in the story and try to remember the different ingredients that go in the soup. We then record this information on a chart. Once the chart is completed, we are able to develop many math concepts: "There were more _____ than any other ingredient."

We vote on our favorite version and dramatize the one that is chosen. As a culminating activity, we make stone soup as our contribution to the Thanksgiving feast. We also use this activity with different versions of *Little Red Hen* and *The Mitten*, identifying the animals involved in the stories.

Look! Different authors retold <u>Stone Soup</u> using different foods.

Food / Author	Water	Stone	Barley	Beans	Beef	Butter	Carrots	....
Ann McGovern	X	X					X	
Marcia Brown								
Diane Peterson								
John Warren Stewig								
Tony Ross								
TOTALS								

FIGURE 12.2
Sample chart for the ingredients in stone soup.

1

2

3

444

4

5

FIGURE 12.3

Writing and picture responses to the stone soup activity:
(1) Notice the detail of steam coming from the pot and bowl of soup.
(2) This child lists the important ingredients for the soup.
(3) The vegetables in this picture are brightly colored, as is the roaring fire.
(4) This picture is rich in detail and contains many story elements.
(5) All the ingredients are creating soup over a roaring fire in this picture.

Students are able to familiarize themselves with story elements and learn that although the characters and settings varied, the problem is generally the same, as is the resolution of the problem.

I also used the stone soup activity with environmentally deprived first graders, who were equally receptive. I brought in a number of the ingredients that I knew they were not familiar with and passed the food around so children could examine it. They were then given a small piece of plain paper to draw, color and cut out their own pictures of the food. Children experimented with spelling the names of the food on a chart. Then we looked up the standard spellings and wrote them in a different color. The students were amazed at how close their approximations were to the correct spelling, a point which I also emphasized. The children then shared words that described the food, which I recorded on the chart. Then they pasted their pictures of food around the words.

One of my favorite topics to study is St. Patrick's Day. Although this study only lasts for two days, the children really enjoy it. We begin with a brief overview of Ireland and the historical meaning of St. Patrick's Day. They love it when I pull down the map, whispering to each other, "She's pulling it down again!" There are some wonderful books about this holiday, which I read and make available to them. The first day children decorate styrofoam cups. I tell them that they will be used for our party, but that night I put them in the oven for a short time and they shrink, taking on a strong resemblance to a leprechaun's hat.

When the children arrive the next day, they see that the room is not orderly. The leprechaun has even left his green footprints on the "Sign In" sheet. Needless to say, the children are high all day. We make green glasses to read with—oak tag with green cellophane for the lenses. For math, we cover black construction paper with different-colored shamrocks; then we count and graph the number for each color.

Probably the highlight of the day is when Mr. Kamm, the principal, comes into the room wearing a sparkly green tie and reads the story of *Jeremy Bean's St. Patrick's Day*.[13] Jeremy fails to wear anything green to school, and after the offer of many green articles, he finally decides that the principal's tie will do. It is a beautifully written book and very heart-warming. We do the traditional potato prints, wear green shamrock name tags, and I'm Mrs. O'Nave for the day. Although many teachers distance themselves from holiday themes, I feel it is important to tell about these holidays, so that children understand why they are celebrated. However, I do not concentrate on subjects like ghosts and goblins at Halloween, but rather have areas of concentration on owls and spiders. My holiday themes are generally light on holiday, but heavy on literature.

Given the nature of five- and six-year-olds, most of my evaluation is done through "kid-watching." I can generally be seen with a clipboard, circulating around the room. On the clipboard is a checklist of one or two items of reading or writing student behavior to observe. Within their language development portfolio, you might find writing samples and informal reading inventories, as well as emergent reading and writing checklists. Self-stick notes are a "must" because they can be quickly added to the child's individual folder, along with other anecdotal notes. I do occasionally use formal assessment because it is required for report cards and often demanded by parents, who want to see documented proof of their child's progress. However, from my own notes and checklists, I know much more about each child's strengths and weaknesses than any paper-and-pencil test can show.

WHAT DO YOU THINK? How does Mrs. Nave integrate literature and language learning throughout the curriculum? How important to her students' learning is her belief that everyone can succeed? How do the day's activities in Mrs. Nave's classroom compare with your own experience in kindergarten? Would you like to have been a student in this kindergarten? If you do not plan to teach kindergarten, what elements of her teaching practice might apply to the grade level you plan to teach? What do you see as the greatest challenge that this teacher faces? What do you think are this teacher's greatest strengths?

III. A Day's Visit in the Third Grade

Dr. Dick Koblitz, Captain School, Clayton, Missouri

When students enter their area of the third-grade pod, they focus on the warm-up exercise on the blackboard at the front of the room:

> **i gots a knu book calld the 5 little girbels askt Amy.**
> **dr amery tooked a plain to hawai on thersday.**

The two sentences contain types of misspelled words, grammatical errors and punctuation problems that students frequently make in their writing.

"Look at that," Shannon whispers to Bethany. "I'm getting the dictionary," she adds, as the girls settle down at one of six round tables situated around their open-area classroom.

"You have to try it on your own first," Bethany whispers back.

"I know," Shannon says. "But we're going to need the dictionary before we're through."

When students finish their editing, they begin reading books of their own selection. Some read individually and others look at books in pairs, talking about the pictures or content. Books and print surround the students. There are two baskets of theme-related books (Argentina) and shelves of picture books and chapter books on every subject, in every genre, at a variety of reading levels. Beyond the pod is a computer area that stocks additional class sets of books and manipulative materials. Another adjoining area provides sinks, water and surfaces for science demonstrations and experiments. On the wall, charts developed by the students display concepts from all the content areas. Twelve charts grouped together list multiples of familiar objects, from one through twelve. Another group of charts lists common objects that are solid geometrical shapes. A prominently displayed theme cycle web groups the students' interests in learning for the year, and another web displays facts about spiders from *Charlotte's Web* (op. cit.), which students have just finished reading. A student-made chart portrays concepts related to vertebrates, while another lists synonyms for the commonly used word "said." Other displays include a learning web for Argentina and a list of questions students have about the pampa.

"Mark your places, please," Mr. Koblitz says. Students put bookmarks in the books they are reading and the class moves into a discussion of the editing exercise.

"The *i* needs to be capitalized, and you need to take the *s* off of 'gots,' " Charles begins, and Mr. Koblitz makes the corrections.

"That still sounds wrong," someone remarks.

"Is the grammar correct?" Mr. Koblitz asks.

"I think it would be better to say 'have' instead of 'got,' " Shannon adds.

"What if someone asked you what you got for your birthday?" Bryce asks. "Then you might say, 'I got a book.' " Shannon agrees, but sticks by her first suggestion because she does not know the context of the sentence.

Colton says that "knu" should be spelled "knew," and Mr. Koblitz changes the spelling. Immediately, several students object. "That's not the right word. It should be 'new.' "

"It's not the wrong spelling," Bryce says. "It's the wrong word. 'Knu' is an animal."

"That's not how you spell 'gnu,' " Michael says. "I looked it up in the dictionary last night for something I was reading. It's *g-n-u*, not *k-n-u*."

Bryce agrees, "Oh, yeah . . ."

Someone adds the *e* in "called," and then there is a discussion about how to correctly indicate a title in writing. A student says that titles are not underlined in books, and another student remarks that book titles are italicized in print. The teacher says that underlining is a convention to indicate italics in writing. There is a discussion about the spelling of "gerbils." Several attempts are made to spell it correctly, but they all look wrong to the students.

"I've got a dictionary," Shannon announces. "Shall I look?"

"Please," says the teacher.

She provides the correct spelling, and several children murmur, "Oh, yeah . . ."

"Read us the definition, too," the teacher suggests, and she does.

"What else?" the teacher asks.

"That word 'askt' is misspelled," Colton says, "but it should be changed to something else."

"Why?" the teacher asks.

"Because it doesn't make any sense. They're telling something, not asking something."

"What would you replace it with?" Mr. Koblitz asks.

"It should be 'said,' " Amy offers.

"Could it be something else?" the teacher asks.

"Exclaimed," Shannon suggests.

"No," several others protest. "That doesn't make sense."

"What if . . . what if someone asked you, 'Why are you so excited?' and you answered, 'I got a new book!' " Bryce asks. "Then it would make sense." He again defends a response on the basis of a possible context.

They continue editing, noticing the need for capitals and periods to indicate abbreviations. For each instance of editing, the teacher asks students to explain the error and the correction: "Why do we need a capital here?" "A period?" "A new word?" They come to the word "hawai" and Charles says it should have another *i* and a capital letter. "Why?" asks the teacher.

"Because it's a place," Charles says.

"What kind?" the teacher asks.

"A state," he replies.

"Which one?" he asks.

The class replies, "Fiftieth."

"Where is it?" he asks.

"In the Pacific Ocean," they say, and he adds that it is the only state that is a group of islands.

When the class edit is complete, students check their own papers, then turn them over. Mr. Koblitz draws a vertical line on the board. On one side he writes the letters *gn* and on the other he writes "soft *g*." This exercise also draws on information the teacher has gained from observing spelling errors in student writing. He draws a circle around the *gn* and asks students what words they know that start with these letters. As they say words, he records them: gnarled, gnome, gnu and gnaw. Someone suggests "newt," but other children remind him that there is no *g*. He looks it up in the dictionary to be sure.

After each contribution, the teacher asks students to tell what the word means and to use it in a sentence. When a student says "gnashed," he asks if they know a famous children's book that has that word in it. Immediately, someone says, "They gnashed their terrible teeth . . . ," and another student says, *"Where the Wild Things Are."*[14]

"By whom?" the teacher asks.

"Maurice Sendak," they reply. The students make remarks to each other about the book, telling when they read it and how much they liked it.

"Can you guess what *gn* word means a small biting insect with two wings?" the teacher asks.

There is a short pause, and then the class responds, "Gnat!"

They move on to soft *g*, and the class generates gel, gelatin, George, Georgia, gin and gerbil.

"What's unusual about the word 'George'?" Mr. Koblitz asks.

Students study the word. "It's got *two* soft *g*'s," someone says. The teacher encourages them to look for soft *g* at the ending and middle of words also, and they produce sage, edge, sedge, ledge and merge.

The teacher asks them what merge means, and they are uncertain.

"Like you merge from the ground . . . you come up out of it," Bryce tries.

"No, that's e-merge," Michael says.

"I had to merge this morning when I was coming to work in my car," Mr. Koblitz says.

"Rush? Does it mean rush?" Scott asks.

"I had to wait for other cars before I merged," the teacher says.

"Move in slowly?" Shannon asks.

"You're on the right track," he agrees.

The teacher asks the students to notice what they see after all the soft *g*'s, and they reply *e*. "What might you say about *g* when it's followed by *e*?" the teacher asks.

"It sounds like *j*," Bethany answers.

"Can you think of any other letter that makes a *g* soft?" the teacher asks.

Students think for a minute and come up with *y*, producing gym and gypsy as their evidence. Mr. Koblitz says they will study something in fourth grade that begins with soft *g*, and they think of geometry, geography and Egypt.

Throughout this session, Mr. Koblitz draws from his students' experiences with writing to help them practice editing skills. As students interact to correct the errors together, they add to their vocabularies, make connections with other knowledge they have and discuss the value of writing conventions. When the session ends, one person at each table collects the editing papers and hands them in. The class then moves to a carpeted area near a discussion chart.

Mr. Koblitz asks the students if they know anything special about the day, and they respond with "The first full day of spring!" They talk about the vernal equinox and the Latin meaning of the terms, which describe days and nights of equal length and the greening of the earth in the Northern Hemisphere.

Evan tells the group about an experiment he and his family did on the vernal equinox the evening before. "We set an egg on end and it was supposed to balance."

"How could it do that?" Colton asks.

"Gravity," Michael answers.

"Can't be gravity," he argues. "There's always gravity."

The discussion continues with Evan saying that the egg failed to balance. Mr. Koblitz asks where he heard about the experiment and suggests they find out more about it—why the egg was supposed to balance and why it might not have in Evan's case. Evan promises to bring information to school the next day.

Mr. Koblitz was absent the previous school day to attend a state conference, so he begins the discussion on the Argentine pampa by asking students to tell him about a book read aloud to them the previous day.

"It's about a girl in the city who goes to visit her grandfather on the pampa, and she becomes a gaucho," Emily begins. The discussion continues, as others add to the story and contribute details.

"From reading this story, what did you learn that was new?" the teacher asks.

"There's a kind of ostrich that lives in South America," Colton begins.

"A rhea," Shannon injects.

"Yeah, a rhea, and the father bird takes care of the eggs," Scott adds.

Mr. Koblitz adds "rhea" to a chart they have constructed, under the heading of "What kinds of animals live on the pampa?" Michael adds the fact that silver mined in Argentina is used to make silver coins throughout the world.

"Was this fiction or nonfiction literature?" the teacher asks. The students debate this question and finally decide that the story is fiction, but is full of interesting facts.

"Let's review your questions about Argentina and see if you've found any more answers in your research," the teacher says. He opens a chart that lists questions the children developed at the beginning of the study. Each day the teacher records new information the students discover about these questions.

"What sports do people play?" the teacher reads from the chart. There are several answers and some speculations. In the trade books they have read and in several reference books, they have discovered that Argentineans play soccer and ride horses. From a newspaper, they discover that the Argentineans competed for a world medal in baseball. But they also discover a comment in the same article that says that the sport is almost nonexistent in Argentina.

"What does 'nonexistent' mean?" the teacher asks.

"It means most people don't play it," Bryce responds. "They don't have any big teams."

They move on to other questions. "How many people live on the pampa?" the teacher reads. "Did anyone find out?"

"Yeah, we did," Bryce says, and he gets up to find his research papers. While he looks, Colton consults the encyclopedia and comes back with a figure of approximately 28 million people.

"Is that for just the pampa or all of Argentina?" Mr. Koblitz asks.

"It's for all of Argentina," Colton replies. "It doesn't tell how many live on the pampa."

"In the back of this book it says that approximately two-thirds of the people in Argentina live on the pampa," the teacher says, showing students the figure in the book.

"Two-thirds," Bryce mumbles, looking up from his notes. "Two-thirds . . ."

"If you know that, could you figure out how many people that would be?" the teacher asks.

"How would you do it?" Charles asks.

"Well, you could start by estimating," the teacher says. "If you round twenty-eight off to the nearest number, what would that be?" he asks.

"Thirty," comes the reply.

"If you divide thirty into three parts, you would have *one* third. How much would that be?"

"Ten," they reply.

"How many thirds do you want to find?"

"Two," the class responds.

"Two tens are . . . ?"

"Twenty," comes the answer.

"Twenty million people live on the pampa," Charles says.

"Wait . . . hold on," Bryce says. "I found our notes and we got a different number. It said about *thirty-two* million in the place we looked before."

"Why might the two figures be different?" the teacher asks.

"Maybe the encyclopedia is old," Shannon suggests. Evan looks at the copyright date, which is 1988. The source for thirty-two million is a later statistic.

"We can enter this figure for now and update it if we find a more recent source," the teacher suggests. "If this is the more recent population, and two-thirds still live on the pampa, how many people would that be?"

"Maybe about two thousand more than before," Michael says.

"Two thousand! Out of four more million? No way!" Colton exclaims.

"I meant two million," Michael says. "Two *million!*"

"How could you figure it out?" Mr. Koblitz asks.

"Same as before," Shannon responds. "Find one-third and then make two-thirds."

"What if you wanted to find out more exactly?" the teacher asks.

"Use the calculator," Bryce says, and he goes to get his.

"Tell us what you're doing," Mr. Koblitz says.

"We're putting in the exact figure, then we're dividing it by three." The teacher nods. "Now we get 10.66666 million. So then we multiply by two," Bryce says, and he completes the computations. "It's about twenty-eight million," he says.

"Nooooo," comes the response from the class. "Couldn't be," Michael says. "That's too much. That's what the first figure was for the whole country."

"Wait," Bryce says. "Oops, sorry. . . . I must have pushed the wrong number. Wait . . . okay . . . it's about 21 million."

"More like it," Michael comments.

The boys then use the calculator to figure two-thirds of the first figure and discover that it is 19.32 million.

When students have reviewed all their previous day's research, Mr. Koblitz asks what they know about cowboys in the United States. As they contribute their ideas, he lists them on the chart. Charles says that cowboys ride horses and wear hats. Scott says that cowboys wear boots and get dirty. Someone says that cowboys carry guns, but Emily modifies this by saying that cowboys may wear guns, but they don't use them often. John says that they have spurs on their boots and have special packs to hold tobacco. Someone says that cowboys brand cattle, but Nora declares that they use earmarkers nowadays instead.

"Those are the old western things," Bryce protests. "My dad was a cowboy, and he didn't wear spurs or chew tobacco."

"Are you saying that some of these things might be stereotypes?" Mr. Koblitz asks.

"Yeah, like from the movies and TV," Shannon offers.

"Maybe he wasn't a regular cowboy," Charles suggests.

"What kinds of things did your father do?" the teacher asks.

"He took care of cows . . . and sheep," he responds.

"You mean cattle, not cows," Michael corrects.

"Okay, yeah . . . cattle," Bryce says.

"How did your father dress?" Mr. Koblitz asks.

"Jeans," Bryce responds. "And a hat and boots . . . he wore those."

"Where did he work?" Michael asks.

"In southwest Missouri, on the Arkansas border," Bryce replies.

"Neat-o," someone remarks.

"Did he work for someone on a ranch?" Colton asks.

"It was his own ranch," Bryce says.

"Who's running it now that you live up here?" Michael asks.

"He's paying someone else to take care of it for him," Bryce responds.

"Let's read about real cowboys and see if we can find some of the answers to these questions," Mr. Koblitz says. They review note-taking strategies, and while Mr. Koblitz reads aloud from a book about contemporary U.S. cowboys, students practice taking notes on facts about cowboys. The book is full of pictures and information. Cowboys are shown roping cattle, shoeing horses, repairing machinery, tending sick animals, transporting horses to the range and feeding and caring for animals. When he is finished, the teacher asks, "Who has some good notes?" Students review their notes and compare the information with their original questions. Then the teacher tells them they will read more about South American gauchos the next day and compare them with U.S. cowboys.

After returning from P.E., students begin a literature discussion of *Tuck Triumphant*,[15] the book they are currently studying together. Conversation is lively, as students talk about the meaning of words and events in the story and give their interpretations of the feelings and actions of the main characters. They find similes in the writing and define the terms "tantrum" and "earth tremors" in terms of their own experiences. When literature study concludes, Mr. Koblitz asks the group about an event in the news involving a famous basketball player. This leads to talk about how games are scored.

"How many different ways could Michael Jordan score 10 points?" he asks, and the group brainstorms a number of possibilities. He shows them how to write their suggestions, using parentheses, and models the language used to express these groupings. "So if Michael scores 2 three-pointers, 1 two-pointer and makes 2 free throws for 1 point each, how would you write this?"

Charles says, "You'd multiply 3 times 2, 1 times 2 and 2 times 1."

"What else would you need to do?" the teacher asks.

"Put each thing in parentheses," Michael answers, directing the teacher to put in the necessary marks. "And add them up . . . put in plus signs and an equals after."

"How would you read this, then?" Mr. Koblitz asks.

Emily volunteers. "The quantity 3 times 2, plus the quantity 2 times 1, plus the quantity 2 times 1 equals 10."

They practice creating, writing and reading other combinations. Then the teacher asks, "How many different ways could Michael score 10 points?"

"Millions!" Michael declares.

"Hundreds!" someone else says, moving the number down.

"I say nine," Emily says, finally.

"Why do you say nine?" Mr. Koblitz asks.

"Because 3 times 3 is 9," she answers.

"Let's test your hypothesis," the teacher says. He gets out a bag filled with the students' names on cards. He draws the cards out in groups of three, and the corresponding persons group together to make a chart that will explore the possible scoring combinations. Across the top of the chart are the numbers 3, 2 and 1, representing the individual scoring possibilities. In each column under these numbers, students write the number of each of these kinds of points and create a number sentence. Students group together around the room, figuring out ways to make the greatest number of combinations.

In Emily's group, the students quickly create a combination and Emily is eager for them all to practice, using the correct mathematical language to read what they create. "Now let's read it," she says, and they read together, "The quantity 3 times 0, plus the quantity 5 times 2, plus the quantity 1 times 0 equals 10."

Another combination is generated. "Now read the problem," Emily coaches, and another student begins reading. "Quantity!" she says. "Use the word 'quantity' to read it!" she reminds him.

Writer's workshop begins the afternoon session. LaTrice reads a biography of Thurgood Marshall that she has written and discusses several pictures of her subject from an accompanying book. Students like the pictures she chose to have scanned onto her final copy because they portray Justice Marshall as a child and as an adult. Emily reads a lengthy account of the life of Abraham Lincoln. Already published as a poet in a national children's magazine at the age of eight, Emily is an accomplished writer who enjoys sharing her work with the class. Other students enjoy her work, giving her their concentrated attention through four pages of reading. She asks for comments when she has finished.

"You know what I like?" Evan says. "I liked that you put in things that kids would be interested in, like that story about Lincoln making those footprints on the ceiling."

"Yeah," Kaitlin agrees, "I liked all the funny things you told about him."

"How do you think those stories helped this biography?" Mr. Koblitz asks.

"You'd want to read it because it had funny stories in it," Charles suggests.

"It made him seem more like a person," Shannon says.

"Emily, what do you think?" the teacher asks.

"It was those things and also to show his character," she concludes. "To show what kind of person he was."

Before the group enters the independent writing phase of writer's workshop, Mr. Koblitz asks each student what he or she plans to work on for the next hour. Some will continue writing on first handwritten drafts of their biographies, while others will edit into their second, third and fourth drafts. Several children check out laptop computers from the computer technologist, and others go to the computer center to scan photographs and pictures into their final copies. Several students work on projects together, each contributing research for the biography and sharing responsibility for illustrations. Writer's workshop is followed by an hour of art (alternated with music on other days), and the day concludes with the teacher reading aloud from *The Cricket in Times Square*.[16]

Throughout the day, students work on their own, in pairs, in flexible small groups and within the grouping of the entire class. These arrangements allow students to follow individual interests and create a sense of community from their shared experiences. In discussions with the whole group, the teacher encourages students to use exploratory talk, figure out problems, make relationships among kinds of knowledge and relate ideas to their own experience. He models the strategies of researchers when he asks students to ask questions, compare accounts of events and provide documentation for the facts they present.

Mr. Koblitz follows the guidelines for the district curriculum and utilizes the many resources they provide, and it is evident from his instruction that students are learning in all the content areas throughout the day. Math, science, literature and social studies are not restricted to set periods. The special languages and thinking of these disciplines are used to help students learn about the world within any context. He maximizes the resources available to these students by creating conditions in the classroom that activate students' natural curiosity, maintain their interest and direct their inquiry into productive and rewarding experiences.

Mr. Koblitz models the values of a lifelong learner in his own professional life. He reads widely in the professional literature, is active in professional groups at the local, state and regional levels, and is the cofounder of the local TAWL group. He also travels extensively to visit innovative schools in the United States, England, Australia and New Zealand and to attend classes and conferences throughout the world.

In His Own Words—Dr. Dick Koblitz

When I first began to experiment with classroom organization, I read a lot of professional literature—Kenneth Goodman's[17] research on miscue analysis, Frank Smith's[18] theories on the reading and writing processes and Don Holdaway's[19] developmental model—and it all made a great deal of sense to me. I began trying to implement some of this new research and thinking in my classroom. Reading aloud took a more prominent place in the daily schedule, and I began to allow the children time to read for pleasure each day. I brought more and more books into the classroom and started reading a lot of children's literature myself. I had the children write every day, instead of just once a week. It was all very successful, and the children's progress in learning written language was outstanding.

Our daily schedule is very flexible, with large blocks of time devoted to shared language experience and workshops in reading, writing and math every day. The teaching and learning of written language are totally integrated, and language is taught across the curriculum. In my classroom today, children are learning written language by *using* language for a variety of meaningful and personal reasons. My overall goal for all my students goes far beyond my old goals of just getting through the curriculum and having acceptable test scores. Today I want all my children to develop positive self-esteem and become independent learners, so they will be able to and want to learn outside the classroom away from me. Today I teach from a whole-to-part instructional mode rather than the traditional part-to-whole. I try to integrate the curriculum rather than fragment it. And I teach from a model based on children's strengths rather than their weaknesses.

Now when I begin a new year with a class, we make a big chart of the topics we want to study and learn more about. This is when I find out what the kids know, what they are interested in and what they want to learn about. Many of their interests will include concepts we have to study in science or the social studies. Those that cannot be included this way can be explored in a literature study. For instance, some of the kids are really interested in dinosaurs and so am I. That is not part of the required curriculum, but after the Easter break, we will do a literature study group, reading lots of different books about dinosaurs, so they can pursue that interest. Other interests are very individual. For example, Evan is really interested in World War I and the aircraft involved, but he is the only one in the class. When students in my class have these individual passions for a topic, I encourage them to read and write about it, do all kinds of research, complete a project and share what they learn.

The more you help students make relationships between their experience and the content areas, and among the subject areas, the better you get at it and the more natural it becomes to teach in this manner. When you are just beginning to teach this way, it is difficult to see all these relationships. Just like the thing that came up with the map this morning, when we were talking about the population of the Argentine pampa. I did not anticipate it, but it came up naturally and we worked with it.

There are basic units of study in literature, health, social studies and science that we cover in the third grade, and there are target outcomes in terms of general content and ideas for each of these. For each required area, there are all kinds of lesson suggestions for classroom activities. The district also supplies the literature and all necessary materials and equipment to support these studies. We can choose to do the same thing in our own way or in another way, as long as we meet the district objectives.

There is a core curriculum in literature for each grade level that includes three books selected for intensive study. In third grade, we study *Charlotte's Web* (op. cit.), *The Hundred Dresses*[20] and *Stone Fox*.[21] Beyond that we can select anything we want to. Before *Tuck Triumphant* (op. cit.), one literature group read a biography of Harriet Tubman and another read a biography of Mahatma Gandhi. Before that, two different groups read *Sadako and the Thousand Paper Cranes*[22] and *Faithful Elephants: A True Story of Animals, People and War*.[23] We met together to discuss similarities in the two books. The kids are writing their own biographies now and have chosen subjects such as Abraham Lincoln, Thurgood Marshall, Jackie Robinson, Helen Keller and Albert Einstein.

I have a special interest in developmental spelling and try to integrate the teaching of spelling into a total literacy curriculum rather than teaching it as a separate subject. I feel that I am actually *teaching* spelling, rather than just *testing* it, when spelling is learned in the context of stories, reports and poems written by the children themselves. This allows me to help students move from one developmental stage to the next and really gets them to focus on patterns, rules and word structure in their own writing and in all subject areas. My students also learn to be careful spellers by using dictionaries and computer spell-checks as they write their first drafts and published pieces. When we look at the large number of words most children are spelling conventionally and begin to examine the wide repertoire of strategies they are using in their invented spellings, we can begin to appreciate the sophisticated knowledge children are developing as they investigate and learn how our very complex alphabetic system of written language works.

When children have the opportunity to use developmental spelling in their writing, they develop a fluency of expression that otherwise might not be encouraged. When Adam began second grade, his first journal entry was "My dump [truk] is big." He had little to say in writing. Observe how much he has to say in an entry written several months later:

> Snow is white. Snow is very cold. It is [beutiful]. Snow is fun. sometimes snow gets so deep it is unbelievable. Some people hate snow [becase] snow is so slick. Some people get drunk and they do donuts. Some times it gets to eight

feet. Today the weather man said it is going to be two feet. Snow is terrific. Some kids love [makeing] snowmen. Sometimes snow [terns] into slush. And sometimes there are icicles. Snow covers the [hole] [u]nited [stats] of [ameraca].

When Ty entered second grade he often wanted to use words in his writing that he could not yet spell. Over a period of two months, his spelling developed in the following ways:

September	October	November
Favrite	favirite	favorite
Babys	babies	babies
sailler	sillyer	sillier
geting	getting	getting
multply	multaply	multeply
brout	boghut	brought
butiful	beautyfull	beautifull
dauter	daghter	daughter
nawe	naw	gnaw
anwser	anwser	anwser
caracter	charectr	character

By the end of the school year, standard spelling had developed for these and many other words. In words like "daughter" and "brought," notice how contact with these words in reading leads him to use certain unsounded letters in these words, as he moves toward the correct spelling.

Beginning teachers usually have many questions about using themes in the classroom. One of the best books I have read about themes is Jerry Harste and Kathy Short's book *Creating Classrooms for Authors: The Reading–Writing Connection*.[24] Another good collection of ideas for theme teaching are the Scholastic source books,[25] which can give you a model to get started. The focus of these materials, which are available for both primary and intermediate grades, is on integrating different types of literature into the curriculum. Using the activities they suggest as a model, you can begin with your own students' interests and also incorporate the curriculum required in your own district. The themes they use are typical for most grade levels and coordinate well with the requirements of most districts. The binders provide ideas about materials and how to use them, kinds of learning activities that appeal to students and ways to make relationships among all kinds of literature and the content areas.

There is no one right way to do a theme cycle because each class and teacher is different. We usually begin with a KWL chart, beginning with the questions: What do you know? and What do you want to know? Their responses give me information that will help direct the activities we do. If students know a lot about the particular topic, then we do not have to do a lot of background building. If they do not have a lot of information, then I might spend time reading aloud or showing videos to help build prior knowledge for their independent research. These kinds of experiences help students generate questions about the topic and also help guide their individual research. Each day I ask, "What have you learned?" and they share the results of their research with the entire group and record any information that answers their original questions.

When you first begin teaching, I think it really helps if you have a colleague, mentor or someone else to work with and use as a model. If you have a good relationship with this person, you don't feel like you're being evaluated, that you're doing things wrong or making a mistake. In this district, there is a mentor teacher for every beginning or new teacher. These teachers are usually selected from the same grade level or specialty area, and they help guide the new teacher through the first year. When you begin to interview for a position in a school, you might look to see if the curriculum is textbook driven. Although it might be a challenge at first, I think it is really helpful if you're not bound to a textbook, because it forces you to create your own reading and writing activities and create the curriculum with your students.

It also helps to be around people who share a common philosophy. If you have a choice, and really want to teach with an integrated approach, try to find a school where this kind of teaching is done. This will provide you the necessary support to introduce your own ideas in a context where there is respect for what teachers know and do. When my students begin third grade, they are already familiar with reader's workshop, writer's workshop, KWL, and independent inquiry from their previous three years in school. So on the first day of school, we just begin with finding out what they are interested in. When I get kids that do not have that background, I spend some time with them, talking about the activities and modeling them. Fortunately, this is the kind of program new students can drop into and function fairly well, because students are encouraged to talk to each other and help each other with ideas and problem solving. Also, every child who moves into the district is assigned a mentor. I just got a new little boy, Dimitriy, from Siberia. He reads fairly well, but speaks little English. His mentor stays close beside him in the classroom to explain things and help him become familiar with school routines.

We have a number of hearing-impaired children because our school is one of the central locations for these children within the Special School District. Last year, two children with hearing difficulties were part of the classroom activities in the morning and then spent the afternoons with the hearing-impaired specialist. When they came in the classroom, they wore special hearing aids and I used a microphone and wore a monitor on my belt, so they could hear me. I received a lot of help from the specialist in the hearing-impaired lab, who gave me suggestions about how to work with the children. This teacher was also available for consultation any time I had any problems and would come into the classroom to work with the children.

There is a lot of parent involvement in our school program. At the beginning of the year I conduct an extensive parent survey to discover any interests, hobbies and expertise that parents might want to share with the class. When we studied the animals of the Serengeti, visitors came to class to show a video and tell about a safari experience. The class also visited the St. Louis Zoo to attend a special program devoted to animals of the Serengeti Plain. When we studied the pioneers, students went to the Museum of Western Expansion at the Gateway Arch and to Shaw's Arboretum, where they could see examples of prairie grasses. When we began our study of biographies, a storyteller come to class to talk about Harriet Tubman.

In addition to the regular school program, the school also sponsors clubs that meet for thirty to forty-five minutes before and after school, where students can explore foreign languages, literature, drama, poetry, science, and technology. Once a week, I meet with a multiage Reading Club that discusses books that students are reading.

WHAT DO YOU THINK?   How does Dr. Koblitz integrate literature and language learning throughout the curriculum? In what ways does he help students use the specialized languages of the content areas to interpret their experience? How do you think this classroom accommodates individual learning needs and abilities? In what ways do you think students learn from each other in this classroom? Did you notice how the teacher uses questions to help students explore ideas? If you do not plan to teach at the primary level, what ideas from this classroom would still be useful? What do you see as the particular strengths of this teacher? What similarities did you notice between Dr. Koblitz's classroom program and Mrs. Nave's?

IV. A Day's Visit in the Fifth Grade

Jackie Hogue, Marine School, Marine, Illinois

Visitors to Mrs. Hogue's fifth-grade classroom always find students productively engaged in learning activities. They read and talk together in small groups and as an entire class. They explore and respond to ideas across the curriculum in writing and with artistic creations. If you walk through the room during literature study, you will find students intent on their discussions and eager to share their ideas with each other. On one particular day, a group of four boys sat together, discussing Laura Ingalls Wilder's *Farmer Boy*.[26] Students could choose to read any Wilder book and then meet with others who chose the same book. Three of the four boys in the *Farmer Boy* group live on farms themselves.

"How would you feel if you were Almanzo on Christmas Day?" David asks the rest of his group.

"That's a good question," Aaron replies. "I'd feel really good."

"Yeah, me too. That's a good question," Scott comments.

"He got a jackknife and them boots," Jerry adds.

"What would you have done about Frank when he tried to scare the colt?" David asks.

"Man, I'd beat him up," Scott says.

One boy tells about an uncle who beats horses and the boys respond with outrage. After a brief discussion about beating animals, the boy serving as secretary returns the group to the original discussion. "What would you have done about Frank?" he asks Jerry.

"I'd grab him by the leg and pull him off the stall, like Almanzo," Jerry replies. "I don't know why Royal got so mad at Almanzo. He was just trying to keep Frank away from the colt."

"He didn't see it," Aaron says. "He thought they were both messin' around in the stall."

"Why do you think he [Frank] was doin' all that stuff anyway?" Jerry asks. The boys think about the question for a minute, and no one says anything.

"Maybe . . . ," Scott begins.

"He was dumb!" Aaron says.

"No, he wasn't dumb, but he showed off a lot," David suggests

"Maybe he wanted to show Almanzo he knew about horses," Scott says.

"That's a dumb way to do it," Aaron says.

"He was a town boy," David responds.

"I don't remember that," Aaron says.

"Yeah, I know he was . . . there was somethin' in one of the chapters. Was it Fourth of July? No . . . wait, I'll find it . . . it was at church. I know it was at the church 'cause Frank had on the store-bought cap . . . yeah, here . . . listen: 'Frank's father was Uncle Wesley; he owned the potato-starch mill and lived in town. He did not have a farm. So Frank was only a town boy and he played with town boys.' He didn't know about horses or anything. Maybe he wanted to prove something," David concludes.

"Maybe," Aaron agrees.

During the discussion the teacher has joined the group and listens for a while. When they finish talking, she asks, "Do you know what I like about the way you answered these questions? Your reasons came from something you read. You're using inferences, something you understand from what's going on in the story. The author doesn't say it exactly, but you have to figure it out, by trying to think about how this character feels . . . how you would feel if you were this character. You also tried to justify your answers. It's fine to have an opinion, but you want your opinion to be more than 'That's just the way I feel about it.' You used what you read to give reasons."

The secretary for the group gives the teacher a copy of their discussion questions. The previous day Mrs. Hogue talked with the group about what constitutes a discussion question and she reviews this first. "Did you ask good questions today?" she asks. They look at each other, and then one boy responds that they could have done better, but they're improving. Another boy mentions that they wander off the topic sometimes when they're discussing connections.

"What could you do to help this?" the teacher asks.

"Just remind each other, I guess," Aaron says.

"It worked today," David remarks.

"Now that you're aware of what happens, you can make a choice," the teacher observes, and the boys nod their heads.

"Do you know what I like about many of these questions?" she asks. She has quickly observed the list made by the secretary. "You have to be a good reader to ask these kinds of questions. You have to think about what you're reading and use your own experience." The boys seem pleased with her observations. The teacher stays a brief time with each discussion group, commenting on what she sees to be the strengths of their interactions. She asks them to reflect on any problems in discussion and encourages them to think of solutions.

All students in the classroom have a folder where they keep notes from their reading. They take turns being secretary and recording the questions and interactions of the group. These notes, including the vocabulary words discussed by the group, are handed in to the teacher at the completion of a book study.

A group of students (three girls and one boy) who are reading *On the Banks of Plum Creek*[27] invite a visitor into their group to talk about their literature circle. In the following interview, the visitor's questions are designated with a **V** and the student responses are numbered, according to the person responding. Student #1 is a boy.

V: What kinds of things do you write in your folder notes?

S1: We keep our questions in here.

V: What kinds of questions?

S2: Questions that we think of when we read. And we write down the page number, so we can talk about it in our group.

V: Anything else?

S3: The page numbers of our favorite parts of what we read, and our connections and any hard words. We make a bookmark for each book and write the hard words on them. Then we talk about them in our group and figure them out.

V: What if you can't figure them out?

S2: We read the story around the word, you know, before and after, to figure them out.

V: What if you still don't know the word?

S1: Then we ask Mrs. Hogue and she gives hints, but she doesn't tell us.

V: What kinds of hints?

S1: Well, . . . she'll say, "Do you know any other word that looks like it?" or "Look at this part. What does it mean?" or we'll look in the dictionary.

V: What do you do with these words?

S4: We choose our twelve spelling words from the list. Our own list. Then we write sentences that tell something about the word, then we study and give each other tests until we learn them.

V: What does "connections" mean?

S2: That's how the book connects with us. Some experience we have that's like the people in the book.

V: How do you decide what to read?

S3: We decide together. Mrs. Hogue might say for us to choose a Laura Ingalls Wilder book when we're studying something from that time. Then a bunch of us look at the books and decide.

V: What gets you interested in a book?

S1: Well, sometimes the title is interesting or we read about it on the back cover. Sometimes Mrs. Hogue tells us a little about it.

S2: And sometimes our friends will tell us about a book and we get interested that way.

V: Do you read in class at other times?

S4: We read what we want during silent reading and other times, and most of us take our books home to read.

V: How do you decide how many chapters you'll read?

S3: We decide together and the secretary writes it down. Yesterday we read ten chapters, mostly at home. Sometimes we read to ourselves or to our family. The day before we only read five chapters. Most of us wanted to read seven, but one of our group had to do work on his farm that night.

Later in the session, several groups complete their reading and discussion and begin to work on response projects. Some write in journals, and others plan drawings or models for the bulletin board that will represent the book they have just read. Several students create a scene from the story, while others make models of period houses and furnishings. One group has finished all its work and decides to choose another book. Sean, who is the only boy in the group, is not happy with the book the girls want to read for their second selection. He wants to read *Farmer Boy*, but no copies are available. The teacher encourages him to use his own social skills to solve the problem. He drifts around the room after half-hearted attempts to join another group.

"What I'm concerned about is that you're wasting time that you could be using to enjoy reading," the teacher tells him. "Take five minutes and try to decide on something you'd like."

Sean goes to the library center and picks up a copy of the book his original group has decided to read. He begins to look through it, sitting apart from his group.

"Can I read alone?" Sean asks.

"That won't work, Sean," the teacher answers. "You need someone else to discuss your reading with."

Sean's group makes a reading assignment and then they all sit apart to read. Sean reads in the new book for a while and then tells the teacher he doesn't like it. Mrs. Hogue suggests that he might want to look for another one and also that he might want to invite someone else to join him. Sean thinks about a boy who has been out of the room for special classes and decides to ask him to share a book. Mrs. Hogue agrees to this arrangement. If the other boy agrees, they can study the book together as partners. The second boy is willing, and the two boys look at several books, finally choosing *Long Winter*.[28] As they look through the book, they begin to get interested and stay involved until time for lunch. Students are so wrapped up in their reading that it is with some reluctance that they mark their places and put away their books.

Students in Mrs. Hogue's fifth grade begin the day with a discussion of current events, which they prepare for by reading the newspaper or watching the news on television. Following this discussion, the teacher reads poetry aloud to the class, which students monitor for examples of figurative language. In the context of books and poetry read aloud, Mrs. Hogue introduces personification, alliteration, hyperbole, idioms, similes and metaphors. Students look for examples of figurative language in their reading and are encouraged to use them in their writing. When they find an example, they add it to the list on a prominently displayed chart at the front of the room. "This can be a problem sometimes," Mrs. Hogue observes. "I will be reading aloud to them and hear them saying 'simile' or 'metaphor' under their breath!"

Poetry reading is followed by math, which involves students immediately in writing. Mrs. Hogue writes a problem on the board and asks students to solve it by using fraction blocks. "What is the rule for adding factions?" she asks. "Can you write the rule?" Writing the rule enables all students to work on the problem at their own pace. The teacher is able to evaluate the level of individual student understanding by reading what they have written, and students get a better idea of what they know or need to know about a concept by exploring the idea with language. When the class works with a story problem, Mrs. Hogue posts key words from the problem on the board, so students can refer to them as they work. Students work together in pairs, analyzing problems for relevant and irrelevant words and numbers.

At the beginning of the day, Mrs. Hogue posts the work for the morning on the board, and after math, students move from activity to activity at their own pace. They meet together in small groups to review their spelling sentences and then move into the literature groups described above. On other days, they might use this time to read short stories, study a class novel or examine copies of *Weekly Reader*.

When students return to the classroom in the afternoon, they resume their reading from the morning or select new books to read during silent, independent reading time. The balance of the day, students read, conduct research, write and work on displays related to their study of the Middle Colonies. At other times in the semester, afternoon research might be organized around a topic in science, such as the environment or geology. Mrs. Hogue is required to teach specific subject matter and must use the text adopted by the district for content area learning. She tries to involve her students in using texts and exploring knowledge in ways that stimulate their own curiosity about a topic and utilize the resources of the textbook. When she introduces a study of the Southern Colonies, for example, she gives students a list of ten true-or-false questions about the colonies and lets them work in small groups to complete the answers from their own information. When they complete the test, they use their texts to confirm their answers.

Students might also use their textbooks as a springboard for reviewing a topic in a content area. They begin by examining the headings in the chapter to help them decide what is important and then develop a list of research topics, which are posted on the board. Next they read the material in the text to get an overview of the topic and choose an area that most interests them. They form interest groups to research an individual area in more depth, using trade books, documents, maps and reference books. When students encounter reading that is too difficult for them, Mrs. Hogue offers groups the option of being read to. Others may read the material in small groups, in pairs or by themselves. When the teacher presents information about a reference, she always asks the class how they plan to find the information in that source. This provides an opportunity to review the use of indexes, glossaries and other special locator helps.

All during the year, Mrs. Hogue looks for articles related to the theme studies. Someone brought in an old letter, which she photocopies and places in a file folder for students to read. She saves old *Weekly Readers* and copies interesting facts and articles from old textbooks. For example, she found a copy of slave rules in the colonies in an old social studies text, which she places in a folder called "Life of Slaves," to help students compare slave life and the life of the average colonial citizen.

Students often create a book to demonstrate what they have learned during a theme study. After these projects have been available for the class to examine or displayed in the hall for other classes to enjoy, students sign up to take these books home for parents to review. There is a special sheet in the back of each book where parents can write messages back to the students who created the project. Projects constructed by the entire class include a *Vertebrate Encyclopedia*, a *Big Book of Body Systems* and *An Almanac* from the Colonial America study. A weekly newspaper is produced by the class, with each student writing a column about events and learning that occurred during the week. Students also write poetry books, and several poems they entered in a national contest were published.

When she reviews a student's writing, Mrs. Hogue selects strengths to praise, such as the use of vivid adjectives or effective dialogue and then asks questions that will help students enlarge or improve on expression. She believes that writing about what has been read improves comprehension because students must understand what they have read in order to write about it. She sees errors in reading and writing as providing direction for instruction. In her classroom, errors are not penalized, but are regarded as steps in development. Direct teaching, when it occurs, is in the form of mini-lessons—demonstrations that model effective strategies for reading and writing. In mini-lessons, the teacher might introduce a concept from the content areas, explain a literary device or demonstrate ways to use resources effectively.

For individual reading conferences, the teacher asks students to complete a form like the following and bring it to the conference to guide their discussion:

Individual Reading Conference

Student: _____

1. What book did you choose to read?
2. Who is the author of your book?
3. What character in this book was like a character from another book?
4. Is there a lesson to be learned from this book? What is it?
5. If you could, would you change the ending of the story?
6. Can you find a compound word in the book?
7. Would you read a favorite page for me?

Questions on other forms include those suitable for the genre being read and ones that review the mastery of grammatical forms expected of students by the district. For these forms, Mrs. Hogue includes questions like:

1. If you could, would you like to be a character in this story? Why?
2. What do you think the author is trying to tell people in this story?
3. What experience did a character in this book have that you would like to have?
4. Would you like to be like any character in the story? Why?
5. Was there a lot of exaggeration in the story?

6. Is the story real or make-believe?
7. What do you think was the best part of the story?
8. What other books have you read by this author?
9. Did the illustrations help you understand this book?
10. Tell me the setting of this story.
11. Can you find a one-syllable word in the book? a two-syllable word? Can you find a contraction in the book? What two words make this contraction? Can you find a noun? Can you find a verb?
12. Show me a word that was not familiar to you. How did you figure it out?
13. Is there anyone else in the class who might enjoy reading this book?

When the class studied geology, they were identifying examples of figurative language in the books they were reading in literature circles. Students asked to make a book that would describe what they had learned in geology using alliteration. They decided to make an alphabet book, with each student contributing a page. Each page included a letter of the alphabet, an object, event or idea that began with that letter and a sentence that described the concept and used alliteration. Drawings on the page explained or illustrated the sentences. The pages were laminated and bound together with a laminated cover and a plastic spiral. This book, like all others made in class, was sent home on a rotating basis to share with students' families. Here is an example:

M—Mark, Mike and Martha made up their minds that marble is metamorphic rock because the minerals in the marble were changed by heat and pressure. (The illustration shows the mineral and color changing in the rock.)

To gain practice using the thesaurus, students were asked to bring their favorite nursery rhyme books to school to read aloud in groups. As a class, they used the thesaurus to rework a rhyme and then were eager to try one on their own or with a partner. When the rhymes were completed they were read aloud in a sharing session, then printed with colored markers on large sheets of paper to display in the hallway. Kindergarten and first-grade teachers brought their classes to look at the rhymes and try to guess the originals. The display drew interest from every grade level in the building, and other classes asked to create their own. The following is an example:

Hey diddle, diddle
The kitten and the stringed instrument,
The calf leaped over the heavenly body.
The small puppy chortled
To observe such a game
And the china jogged away
With the dining utensil!

In addition to samples of students' creative work around the room, there are signs and charts everywhere—pinned to cork stripboard, fastened with E-Z clips and hanging from wire with clip clothespins. Rules for the room were created by students at the beginning of the year and are posted in front of the room, with examples of appropriate and inappropriate behavior. This room is rich in student-generated print.

In Her Own Words—Jackie Hogue

I believe that it is important to help my students build on what they know and for them to have high expectations for their learning. I also believe it is important for students to have as many choices as possible about the ways they will learn and to be actively engaged throughout the school day. I have been influenced in my own thinking about teaching by Nancie Atwell's *In the Middle: Writing, Reading, and Learning with Adolescents*,[29] Regie Routman's *Transitions* (op. cit.) and articles in *The Reading Teacher* (op. cit.). I also take many classes at the university, read constantly and attend the TAWL meetings when this is possible.

Early in the year, I begin a theme study on ancient Indians by reading *Motel Mysteries*,[30] an entertaining book that speculates what archaeologists might find if they would unearth the remains of a typical motel and how they would interpret these discoveries. The children make a display that would be uncovered in the year 2492 by archaeologists of the future. Each child brings an item for the display and writes a paragraph explaining how scientists might interpret the use of the item.

After a brief overview of the ancient Indians (Incas, Mayas, Aztecs, Anasazis, Hohokams and Cahokians), the children read the general information in the textbook. They discuss what they already know about these peoples and what they would like to learn. I write their questions on chart paper, leaving space for them to record answers as they find them: How did the Indians get food? In what kinds of homes did they live? Where did they live? When did they live? Why did they live a particular kind of life? Students can also add their own questions to the chart, as their research progresses. They research two or more of the Indian groups, using trade books, encyclopedias, children's magazines and books made by previous students. They also use the resources of the city library and take notes in a "Fun Facts" notebook.

At the end of each day, the children share one piece of information they learned in a whip format, which takes only a few minutes to complete. After several days of research, students gather around the chart to share answers they have found to their original questions. I write the facts on chart paper so the information is available to them at all times. Students locate the Indian groups on a map and label a time line to show when each group lived. Each student chooses two Indian groups to compare and contrast. I model the assignment in a mini-lesson before students begin their work. When they finish writing, they meet in groups to revise and edit their papers.

Because Cahokia is located nearby, the class spends more time studying this group. They read brochures from Cahokia and study information provided by the Cahokia Mounds Museum. One time the children found a game in a trade book that the Cahokians played, explained it to their physical education teacher, and then played it in P.E. The students also find information about the arts and crafts of the Native Americans and make many of these craft items in their art class. I try to keep the art teacher informed about what we will be studying and pass on any art or craft ideas that I find that will relate to our studies.

The culminating activity for the study of ancient Indians is a field trip to Cahokia to visit the museum area and see the movie *City of the Sun*. I also take students on a walking tour of the plaza and the smaller mounds, giving them additional information at the different stops along the way. To prepare for the educational classes on Indian diversity, students learn about and debate the repatriation issue, which helps them ask more knowledgeable questions. When they return to school, students write stories from the viewpoint of the Cahokian child, adult or chief and share these in groups.

I like to bring parents and other members of the community into the classroom to share ideas, experiences, skills and artifacts with the students. From a questionnaire sent home at the beginning of the year, I choose parents who are interested in the study of Indians and invite them to share their expertise with the class. Parents with Native American heritage tell legends and teach songs, games, dances and even some of their language. They show students papoose carriers and Indian craft items, such as blankets, beaded work, dolls, looms, basketry, and feathered headpieces. Presenters allow children to examine and wear clothing and provide samples of food, such as frybread and jerky.

Students read *Sign of the Beaver*[31] and *Island of the Blue Dolphins*[32] as class novels. They keep notes in a reading folder, listing vocabulary words to discuss and questions or comments about their reading. They also respond to general questions suitable for the discussion of any book. Soon the children are asking each other the same types of questions:

Discussion Questions

Author

What do you know about the author?

What is the author trying to tell you in this story?

What did the author have to know about to write this story?

Characters

Who are the most important characters?

Do you know anyone like these characters?

Choose one character. Why is this character important?

Do any characters do things you think are good?

Do any characters do things you think are wrong?

Did any character change in the story?

Plot

What was the problem/goal in this story?

What important things happened because of the problem?

What was the solution? How did the story end?

Were you able to predict the ending?

What other way might the story have ended?

What do you think was the best part of the story?

The Story—Setting

Where does the story take place?

When does the story take place?

What words or what part of the story helped tell about the setting?

Mood

How did you feel while reading this story? Why?

What was the funniest/saddest/most exciting/strangest part of this story?

What do you remember most about the story?

Style

What do you like about the way the author has written the story?

Were there any unusual or neat ways of saying things?

How does the author keep you interested in the story?

List important words under these headings: people, animals, places, things.

During this study, I read to the children from *Sing Down the Moon*[33] at the end of the day. Other literature books related to the theme were also available for them to read during silent reading time. After their daily reading, students record their responses in their journals for ten minutes. Three students volunteer each day to share their entries with the class. The rest of the children respond to these comments.

We also enjoy a game day. The children create board games in any format, using the information they have learned in their research. They write clear directions, provide or create all pieces to play and sit in groups to play their games. It is a wonderful way for me to evaluate their knowledge. I only give tests when I am required; otherwise, I evaluate research, reading folders and projects, using rubrics to help me focus on the concepts and skills that are to be evaluated.

In the spring, one of our first theme studies is Colonial America. I begin the study of New England by reading aloud to the class from *The Witch of Blackbird Pond*,[34] chosen for its description of New England life and the Puritan church. Some students wish to read the book silently, so I give them that option. The vocabulary is quite difficult, and I notice that students will shift back and forth between reading alone and joining the group on a daily basis.

Students respond to the reading by making daily entries in their journal, following entry guidelines. When they write, I encourage students to invent spelling for words they are not sure of and to demonstrate skills they already know. They learn to spell words they are using and to write ideas that are important to them. They also learn to spell as they proofread their writing, in an effort to be understood by others. Later, we list some of these words on charts and discuss spelling rules.

Students also make a diorama or mobile of a scene from the book and write a paper describing the scene. Each group generates a list of words from its research and creates sentences to indicate understanding. As groups complete these sentences, I walk around the room and note sentences that might be used to discuss grammatical constructions or sentence formation. Only one or two concepts are discussed each day, such as run-on sentences, compound sentences, or parts of speech. Students find applicable grammar rules in their English books and I record them on chart paper, which is hung on the wall for future reference. They also write these rules in their own personal English notebooks.

Students also read about New England villages and learn about craftsmen, such as the tanner, cooper, chandler and blacksmith. I always model how to take notes, which students keep in their social studies notebooks. They read about the schools of that time and the Puritan church. I have two sets of books for the children to investigate: *The Historic Communities*[35] and the *Early Settler Life Series*,[36] along with other articles I have found for them to read. We also use the textbook, encyclopedias and library books. Students draw a New England village on mural paper that includes the church, school and village green. They label the pictures with keys to explain tools and other items in each craftsman's shop and prepare a paper that describes the particular job that was researched.

The Middle Colonies are introduced with KWLC. I am required to use texts for all instruction, so students begin by reviewing the text material on the Middle Colonies. Then we discuss what they **know** and what they still **want** to know about the topic. Each day, we review together what we've **learned** and the **connections** we've found with other areas and our own experience. I provide students with books, articles and other resources on Ben Franklin, William Penn, Middle Colony farms, the Quakers and other related topics. Because our resources are limited, students must take turns using reference materials. I list the projects I want the children to complete on a chart, and they rotate assignments as materials become available.

One project asks them to read a book (several are available) about Ben Franklin and to write predictions as they read. When they finish reading, they indicate which of their predictions were correct or incorrect. They take notes on interesting facts and record the main character, the setting and major events in the plot. To supplement their information, they also use the encyclopedia and take notes on facts they did not learn in the book.

For another project, they use three different sources of information to learn about the Quakers. Because religion determined different colonial lifestyles, we talk about the differences between the Quakers and the Puritans, and students compare and contrast them in writing. Students draw maps of the colonies and key the information. They also produce an almanac as a class project. Students are always interested in learning more about the topics they study, so I post extra-credit projects, which may involve research or reading literature related to the topic.

When we study the Southern Colonies, kids look through the textbook at the bold print to help them decide which topics to research. I read excerpts from *To Be a Slave*[37] by Julius Lester using guided imagery. The students write their feelings as they listen to these first-person accounts and later write a dialogue between two characters from the Southern Colonies, using the information they have learned. Many of the papers express strong emotions. They read *The House of Dies Drear*[38] by Virginia Hamilton, which describes the Underground Railroad, and I read *Runaway to Freedom*[39] by Barbara Smucker to them each day. They also read related books as part of their research. After studying all the colonies, the kids decide which colony they would like to move to and make advertisements to persuade others to join them. They also write persuasive papers, using the advertisements as their outlines.

In the past, students have organized an Early American Day. They brainstormed activities for the day and decided who would take certain responsibilities. They dressed as Early American children, brought their lunches in buckets and used dippers to drink from kettles. They also brought old books to study, used slates for ciphering, conducted a spell-down, and insisted there be no electricity for the day. One year another teacher and a friend, who are both colonial dance buffs, dressed in costume and taught the children to dance. Our art teacher helped the students make simple costumes for the dance event.

EXPLORER'S BOOK REPORT

by

Elyse Gerstenecker

I was determined at first to get the Muscovy Company to provide a ship for my voyage. I was looking for a northern way to get to Asia. When I went for my interview, I fooled the men by saying it was warm at the North Pole. I was planning to sail around it. In May of 1608, my ship set sail. I must say, I had a worthless crew! At least I had a good cabin boy - my own son. I sailed up the English Channel towards Greenland. When I got there, I had to wait a while to get through an ice fringe. Finally, I got to Spitzbergen. I could not get through. My crew and I headed home.

When I got home, I told the Company about my trip. When I mentioned the whales there, they decided to send a boat out for whaling. I refused to go, but they gave me a ship for a second expedition. This time, I sailed around Spitzbergen to Novaya Zembya. I looked all about for a strait, or some way to get through, but couldn't find any. I went back to England.

This time, when I asked for a ship, the Moscovy Company turned me down. They did not want to hear anything more about me. But my friend, Dr. Placius, a Dutchman, suggested going to the Dutch East India Company. They accepted me, and I sailed under the Dutch flag. I sailed **north**, then my men grumbled of the cold. I started southwest. I came to a large land and traded with the natives there and sent an exploration team up a river. One of my friends, John Colman, was shot with an arrow. Since the river became shallower, we turned home.

When I got back, the English demanded I sail for them. I was sent by Sir Dudley Digges. I sailed west to the New World, through a strait, and into an ocean. It was there that my crew turned on me because they were convinced they could be better off without me, a crazy coot! I was thrown into a small rowboat with my son, the ship's carpenter, and a few sick men. I was shocked to find out my mate, Robert Juet, was in charge of the mutiny! I was left in the bay (as I had found it to be) to die! Who am I?

I think this book is very well-written because of all the details. I also like it because of all the adventures. I recommend this book for people who like to know every piece of information in a story.

FIGURE 12.4

Who is the explorer? The student provides a first-person narrative that incorporates all the information she has found in her research about the explorer.

As we study other subjects throughout the year, the children choose class, group and individual projects to display the knowledge and skills that they have learned. When the students research explorers, they read books about early explorers and write first-person reports. Students listen carefully and attentively to try to identify the explorer from the clues given.

Using pizza boxes as a stage, students create scenes of their explorers. The lids contain illustrative maps of the explorer's routes and a time line of important events in the explorer's life. We also draw the Santa Maria in chalk on the playground surface, using the actual dimensions of the ship. When students study the Revolutionary War, they make a time-line mural of cause-and-effect events leading to the war. They also create individual newspapers about famous people and the battles of the Revolutionary War.

I like to use games and simulations to help students learn concepts. In the fall, students study how animals survive by playing "How Many Bears Can Live in This Forest?" They also play "Web of Life" to learn how animals depend on each other; the "Musk Ox Game" to learn the concept of predator/prey; and "Turtle Hurtles" to learn the life cycle of a sea turtle. These games come from *Project Wild*[40] and *Project Aquatic*.[41] The class also takes a field trip to the "Treehouse," an animal sanctuary for predatory birds, where injured owls, falcons, eagles and other birds and mammals are brought for rehabilitation and eventual release into the wild.

During our study of the environment, a group decided to draw a six-foot tree, with suggestions on each leaf about ways to save the earth. Others wrote a play and raps about the rain forest, complete with student-made props and music. This was presented to the younger children and parents at school and videotaped to show at a parent–teacher meeting.

As previously mentioned, I send home a questionnaire (Figure 12.5) at the beginning of the year for parents to fill out and return. Their replies provide many resources for our studies. I also ask each child and parent to complete a survey (Figures 12.6 and 12.7) at the completion of the Indian unit. The end-of-the-year survey for students (Figure 12.8) asks essentially the same questions as those asked on surveys completed after each theme study with some additions. The end-of-the-year survey for parents (Figure 12.9) asks for a response to the year's curriculum.

I noticed that as the year progressed, students increasingly favored learning skills in the context of reading children's literature and content area trade books. They also preferred learning how to spell in the context of their writing. The great majority believed that they were better readers, writers and spellers at the end of fifth grade. Responses from the parent surveys indicated that students were more enthusiastic about school, and most parents believed that their children had learned more than in previous school years. They gave a variety of reasons, including: school was more interesting and fun because children enjoyed the research, writing and other projects; children felt they had more control over their learning because they could make choices; they wanted to know more; they remembered more by learning this way; and the children had to think more.

In response to the question about study habits, parents noticed that students were more willing to study, write and work on self-initiated projects. The most frequently observed behavior was that their children read more for

Dear Parents,

As we study our science and social studies units, there are occasions when we need your expertise. If you would be willing to share that knowledge with our class, we would appreciate it.

My career _____

Spouse's career _____

Special interests _____

Examples:
  identify leaves
  geology
  Revolutionary War buff
  Indians
  colonial era

☐ Yes, I could come to class and share with the kids.

_____   _____
Name   *Telephone number, home or work*

☐ No, I am sorry I cannot help at this time.

If there are any grandparents who would like to share, please have them send me information.

Thank you!
Mrs. Hogue

FIGURE 12.5
Sample questionnaire sent to parents at the beginning of the school year.

1. Would you rather use spelling words from the spelling book or choose your own?
2. Would you rather do English worksheets or learn through your own writing?
3. Would you rather read from the basal reader and work skill sheets or read a novel and do activities?
4. Would you rather read the social studies book or library books to study Indians?
5. Would you be more likely to read a book about Indians in the future?
6. Do you feel that you are a better reader than you were at the beginning of fifth grade?
7. Do you feel that you are a better speller than you were at the beginning of fifth grade?
8. Do you feel that you are a better writer than you were at the beginning of fifth grade?
9. Is school more fun now that you are learning a different way?

FIGURE 12.6
Child's survey after completion of a theme study on Indians.

1. Have you had more discussions with your child about schoolwork while he/she was studying Indians?
2. Has your child seemed more interested, the same, or less interested in schoolwork while he/she was studying Indians?
3. Has your child read more at home during this time?
4. Comments?

FIGURE 12.7
Parent's survey after class completion of a theme study on Indians.

1. Do you feel that you learned a lot, some, or very little this year?
2. Do you feel that you are a better reader (writer, speller), the same, or a worse reader (writer, speller) than you were at the beginning of fifth grade?
3. What did you like best about fifth grade?
4. What would you change?

FIGURE 12.8
Child's end-of-the-year survey.

Dear Parents,

Once again I need your input so that I might adjust the curriculum to better fit the needs of our children in the future. As you may know, the children have been exposed to a more child-based, research, hands-on, whole learning approach rather than to a total textbook and worksheet learning approach. Many of the other teachers at our school are also striving toward a child-based approach to learning. Please return this survey to me as soon as possible. I have really enjoyed working and sharing with your child this year.

1. Have you noticed a change in your child's attitude toward school? Is he/she more enthusiastic, about the same, less enthusiastic?

2. Do you feel your child has learned more, the same or less in terms of knowledge and skills than in previous school years?

3. Have you noticed any changes in your child's study habits this year? If so, what are they? *Examples:* reads more, reads more difficult books, reads more fact-based books, more willing to study, better writing skills, improved grades, works on self-initiated projects such as story writing, play writing, poetry writing, artwork.

Thank you!
Mrs. Hogue

FIGURE 12.9
Parent's end-of-the-year survey.

enjoyment and to find information. Some parents were amazed at the creative skills of their children and their willingness to present projects and speak in front of their classmates. They also felt that the children communicated more easily and understood better what was expected of them. In the first survey, a few parents felt that basic spelling and English were not being emphasized enough, and several were concerned because students were not using textbooks and workbooks in the traditional way. In response to the surveys, I added an emphasis on phonetic, spelling and grammar rules. As the year progressed, these concerns diminished.

WHAT DO YOU THINK? How does Mrs. Hogue integrate literature and language throughout the curriculum? What kinds of things does she do to help parents feel included in the classroom program? Would you enjoy being a student in her classroom? Which of your own interests and abilities would have been more developed if you had attended this fifth grade? How are the activities and Mrs. Hogue's approach to student learning similar to Mrs. Nave's and Dr. Koblitz's? How does this teacher work productively with limited resources? What do you see as her greatest strengths?

Notes

1. E. B. White, *Charlotte's Web* (Scranton, Penn.: Harper & Row, 1952).
2. *The Reading Teacher*, a journal of the International Reading Association. Reviewed in **Exploring Professional Literature** in Chapter 1 of this text.
3. Kenneth Goodman, *What's Whole in Whole Language* (Portsmouth, N.H.: Heinemann, 1986).
4. Bobbi Fisher, *Joyful Learning* (Portsmouth, N.H.: Heinemann, 1991).
5. Regie Routman, *Transitions: From Literature to Literacy* (Portsmouth, N.H.: Heinemann, 1988).
6. Regie Routman, *Invitations* (Chicago, Ill.: Rigby, 1992).
7. Bill Martin, Jr., *Chicka Chicka Boom Boom* (New York: Scholastic, 1989).
8. David Carter, *How Many Bugs in a Box?* (New York: Simon and Schuster, 1988).
9. Eric Carle, *The Very Quiet Cricket* (New York: Philomel, 1990).
10. Alan Baker, *Benjamin's Book* (New York: Lothrop, 1987).
11. Eric Carle, *The Very Busy Spider* (East Rutherford, N.J.: Putnam, 1985).
12. Ann McGovern, *Stone Soup* (New York: Scholastic, 1986). Marcia Brown, *Stone Soup* (New York: Macmillan, 1982).
13. Alice Schertle, *Jeremy Bean's St. Patrick's Day* (Fairfield, N.J.: Lothrop, 1987).
14. Maurice Sendak, *Where the Wild Things Are* (Scranton, Penn.: Harper, 1963).
15. Theodore Taylor, *Tuck Triumphant* (New York: Doubleday, 1991).
16. George Selden, *The Cricket in Times Square* (East Rutherford, N.J.: Farrar, 1960).
17. Kenneth Goodman, ed., *Miscue Analysis: Applications to Reading Instruction* (Urbana, Ill.: National Council of Teachers of English, 1973).
18. Frank Smith, *Understanding Reading: A Psycholinguistic Analysis of Reading and Learning to Read*, 3d ed. (New York: Lawrence Erlbaum Associates, 1986).
19. Don Holdaway, *The Foundations of Literacy* (Portsmouth, N.H.: Heinemann, 1979).

20. Eleanor Estes, *The Hundred Dresses* (Orlando, Fla.: Harcourt, 1944).

21. John Reynolds Gardiner, *Stone Fox* (Scranton, Penn.: Harper, 1980).

22. Eleanor Coerr, *Sadako and the Thousand Paper Cranes* (East Rutherford, N.J.: Putnam, 1977).

23. Yukio Tsuchiya, *Faithful Elephants: A True Story of Animals, People and War* (Boston: Houghton Mifflin, 1988).

24. Jerome C. Harste and Kathy G. Short, with Carolyn Burke, *Creating Classrooms for Authors: The Reading–Writing Connection* (Portsmouth, N.H.: Heinemann, 1988).

25. Jane Boskwill and Paulette Whitman, *Whole Language Sourcebook* and *Moving On—Whole Language Sourcebook for Grades 3–4* (Canada: Scholastic-TAB Publications Ltd., 1986, 1988).

26. Laura Ingalls Wilder, *Farmer Boy* (Scranton, Penn.: Harper, 1953).

27. Laura Ingalls Wilder, *On the Banks of Plum Creek* (Scranton, Penn.: Harper, 1953).

28. Laura Ingalls Wilder, *Long Winter* (Scranton, Penn.: Harper, 1953).

29. Nancie Atwell, *In the Middle: Writing, Reading, and Learning with Adolescents* (Portsmouth, N.H.: Boynton/Cook, 1987).

30. David Macaulay, *Motel Mysteries* (Burlington, Mass.: Houghton Mifflin, 1991).

31. Elizabeth George Speare, *Sign of the Beaver* (New York: Dell, 1983).

32. Scott O'Dell, *Island of the Blue Dolphins* (Burlington, Mass.: Houghton Mifflin, 1960).

33. Scott O'Dell, *Sing Down the Moon* (Boston: Houghton Mifflin, 1970).

34. Elizabeth George Speare, *The Witch of Blackbird Pond* (Boston: Houghton Mifflin, 1986).

35. Bobbie Kalman, *The Historic Communities* (New York: Crabtree Publishing Company, 1992).

36. Bobbie Kalman, *Early Settler Life Series* (New York: Crabtree Publishing Company, 1992).

37. Julius Lester, *To Be a Slave* (New York: Scholastic, 1968).

38. Virginia Hamilton, *The House of Dies Drear* (New York: Macmillan, 1968).

39. Barbara Smucker, *Runaway to Freedom* (Scranton, Penn.: Harper, 1978).

40. Western Regional Environmental Education Council, *Project Wild* (Boulder, Colo.: Johnson Publishing, 1992).

41. Western Regional Environmental Education Council, *Project Aquatic* (Boulder, Colo.: Johnson Publishing, 1987).

Index